ANNALS
OF THE
ROYAL BOTANIC GARDEN, CALCUTTA

ANNALS

OF THE

ROYAL BOTANIC GARDEN, CALCUTTA

VOL. X

1. THE SPECIES OF DALBERGIA OF SOUTH-EASTERN ASIA.

BY D. PRAIN.

2. THE ACONITES OF INDIA: A MONOGRAPH,

BY OTTO STAPF, Ph.D., F.L.S.
TO WHICH IS PREFIXED

A SKETCH OF THE LIFE OF FRANCIS HAMILTON (ONCE BUCHANANAN). SOMETIME SUPERINTENDENT OF THE HONOURABLE COMPANY'S BOTANIC GARDEN, CALCUTTA,

By D. PRAIN.

GYAN

Published by

Gyan Publishing House
5, Ansari Road
Daryaganj, New Delhi-110002
Phone: 011-47034999, 9811692060
E-mail: books@gyanbooks.com

Distribution Network
gyanbooks.com
India, USA, Canada, UK, Australia, France

ISBN : 978-81-212-2237-2 (HB)
First Published, 1905

2nd Impression 2021

Printed at: Gyan Press, Delhi.

Annals of the Royal Botanic Garden, Calcutta
Author: D. Prain

ANNALS

OF THE

ROYAL BOTANIC GARDEN, CALCUTTA.

Vol. X.

1. THE SPECIES OF DALBERGIA OF SOUTH-EASTERN ASIA,

By D. PRAIN.

2. THE ACONITES OF INDIA: A MONOGRAPH,

By OTTO STAPF, Ph.D., F.L.S.

TO WHICH IS PREFIXED

A SKETCH OF THE LIFE OF FRANCIS HAMILTON (ONCE BUCHANAN), SOMETIME SUPERINTENDENT OF THE HONOURABLE COMPANY'S BOTANIC GARDEN, CALCUTTA,

By D. PRAIN.

CALCUTTA:
Printed at the Bengal Secretariat Press.
1905.

ANNALS

OF THE

ROYAL BOTANIC GARDEN, CALCUTTA.

Vol. X, Part I.

ANNALS

OF THE

ROYAL BOTANIC GARDEN, CALCUTTA.

Vol. X.

PART I.

THE SPECIES OF DALBERGIA OF SOUTH-EASTERN ASIA.

By

D. PRAIN,

Superintendent of the Royal Botanic Garden, Calcutta.

CALCUTTA:

Bengal Secretariat Press.

1904.

PREFACE.

THIS paper provides descriptions and figures of the Asiatic *Dalbergias*. The genus *Dalbergia* is economically important: it includes not a few trees which yield esteemed timbers. It is also taxonomically difficult; generally, since it does not lend itself readily to natural subdivision, and in detail, because its species are hard to delimit. Some of the difficulties are accidental, occasionally perhaps subjective; many, however, are real.

In works published between 1781, when the genus was proposed by the younger Linnæus, and 1851, when Bentham first methodically subdivided it, misconceptions as to its natural limits so vitiate the accounts of *Dalbergia* as to make it uncertain whether individual species really belong. Since 1851, thanks entirely to Bentham's satisfactory characterisation, the number of species referred to the genus that are not *Dalbergias* has been small. Difficulties as to species have not, however, diminished in the same way. Partly from the recognition as distinct of forms that prove on examination to belong to already established species, partly because *Dalbergias* from China, Indo-China, Malaya, and Papuasia have in local treatises been referred too hastily to recognised Indian ones, it is uncertain, in any work published between 1851 and 1901, that particular species, reported from regions other than their *loci classici*, are entitled to the specific epithets applied.

This state of affairs was first appreciated by the writer when, in 1896, at the request of SIR GEORGE KING, he undertook to arrange the Malayan material of the genus preserved in the Calcutta Herbarium. Two articles in the *Journal of the Asiatic Society of Bengal* for 1897, which were the outcome of this study, invite comparison with similar articles by Miquel in 1855, by Kurz in 1876, and by Baker in the same year. The account of the Indian species by Baker, in the *Flora of British India*, was written with all the benefit of reference to the writings of Miquel, of Bentham, and of Kurz, and all the advantage of access to fuller suites of material than were at their disposal: it therefore throws much light on points that to Miquel and to Kurz were obscure. It is to be hoped that the writer's articles, prepared with corresponding advantages, throw some light on points that were obscure to Baker. But it is not unusual, in studies of the kind, to find that as one doubt disappears another arises: the results of 1897 were therefore published with the feeling that they leave as much to be desired as do the contributions of Miquel, of Kurz, and of Baker.

The two pitfalls of taxonomy have been incidentally mentioned. The multiplication of forms among the Asiatic *Dalbergias*—some 140 names have been employed for 86 actual species—has in many cases been due to original definitions that are inadequate, or at any rate imperfect. This undue recognition of species, though unfortunate, has thus been largely accidental. But excessive differentiation, though troublesome to the general systematist and, from its tendency to exaggerate his inferences, vexatious to the student of distribution, is a fault that, in spite of the strictures to which it is subjected, causes comparatively little inconvenience. If error be, as in human affairs it often is, unavoidable, it is in this direction that, in regional treatises, it is safer to err. For purely local needs it is indeed at times advisable, in the interests of lucidity, to treat as a species a form that the monographer can only admit as a variety. Even when, in more general treatises, two really conspecific forms are kept apart, the intelligent layman is willing to believe that some distinction exists which is not apparent to the untrained eye. The harm done by excessive integration, which some authors consider a virtue, though oftener overlooked, is so much greater that it can hardly be overstated. Here the laity criticise less leniently, and when two forms that, to the observer in the field, are obviously distinct have been authoritatively united in the herbarium, the damage done to the science which field- and cabinet-worker alike desire to advance is incalculable. The subjective effect of the habit is equally detrimental; habit becomes second nature, and at times the reducer hides, under the cloak of a specious erudition, work that is unsound. The indirect results of unbalanced reduction, even when applied in good faith, are more damaging still. The maker of invalid species as a rule only exaggerates actual facts; the geographical botanist is usually able to discount this exaggeration by a simple arithmetical process. Unconsidered identification, on the other hand, obscures the facts of distribution and evades computation; it is, besides, too often a cause of offence on the part of those weaker brethren who prefer the statement of a text to the harvest of the eye. But it is in the domain of applied science, whereof taxonomy is at once the mistress and the handmaid, that the evils of undue integration are most patent; only those whose duty it is to deal with economic problems can fully appreciate the confusion that may result when the same name is applied to two, or three, or more distinct forms, or adequately realise the reproach to taxonomy that the custom involves.

The economic importance of the genus *Dalbergia* rendering it desirable to put an end to the doubts that prevailed as to the identity and distribution of its Asiatic species, a study has been undertaken of the material preserved in a number of important collections. The herbaria consulted have been—in Asia, those of Calcutta, Buitenzorg, Hong-Kong, Saharanpur, Peradeniya: in England, those of Kew, the British Museum, and the Linnean Society: in France, those of the Jardin des Plantes, of Mm. Drake del Castillo and L. Pierre: in Germany, that of the Royal Herbarium, Berlin: in Switzerland, those of Mm. de Candolle and Barbey-Boissier: in Holland, that of Leiden: in Italy, that of Signor Beccari. For the kindness with which they have afforded the writer opportunities of increasing his knowledge of this difficult genus, he is under deep obligations to Dr. Treub, Mr. Ford, Mr. Duthie,

Mr. Willis; to Sir W. T. Thiselton-Dyer, Mr. Murray, and the staffs of Kew and the British Museum; to M. Bureau, M. Drake del Castillo, M. Pierre, and the late M. Franchet; to M. C. de Candolle and Mr. Barbey; to Professor Engler; to the late Professor Suringar, and to Signor Beccari. Mr. Bailey has kindly contributed specimens of the only *Dalbergia* in the Brisbane Herbarium; Dr. van Romburgh and Dr. Koorders have equally kindly helped in clearing up difficulties connected with the species of Celebes; Dr. J. V. Suringar of Leiden, Messrs. W. B. Hemsley and E. G. Baker of London, and Dr. Harms of Berlin have given kind and ready help in clearing up difficulties of a bibliographical nature. To all these friends the writer wishes to tender his warm thanks.

The descriptions now given are as full and the figures are as complete as the material available has made it possible to provide. The general system of arrangement adopted is one that the writer finds to be more convenient and believes to be less unnatural than any system hitherto proposed. A conspectus of the system precedes the descriptive section, and is itself preceded by a review of its evolution and by a sketch of the distribution of the Asiatic species. The main object, however, is the delimitation of the species, and an attempt has been made, doubtless with incomplete success, to steer a middle course between the shoal-waters of over-differentiation and the whirlpools of excessive integration. In not a few instances, as will be seen, complete material of certain forms is wanting: while the defects, in several cases, leave us still in doubt as to the natural position, it is hoped that they do not leave us in doubt as to the validity of the species concerned. An ideal, because complete, knowledge of our Asiatic *Dalbergias* is still a long way off, but the best means of attaining this knowledge is to provoke further research by indicating the points that are still in debate. To this end it seems therefore advisable to make available, here and now, all the information regarding this genus that the writer, during seven years of enquiry, has been able to collect.

Calcutta;

5th April 1903.

CONTENTS.

PART I.—INTRODUCTION.

PART II.—CONSPECTUS SYSTEMATICUS.

PART III.—DESCRIPTIONS OF THE ASIATIC SPECIES OF DALBERGIA.

LIST OF PLATES.

[PLATES 5—91 to follow letter-press.]

THE

SPECIES OF DALBERGIA

OF

SOUTH-EASTERN ASIA.

I.—INTRODUCTION.

§ 1. *Historical Review of the Delimitation of the genus Dalbergia.*

THE name *Dalbergia* was proposed in 1781 by the younger Linnæus,* in memory of Charles Gustavus and of Nicholas Dalberg, two Swedish botanists connected with Surinam, in order to accommodate two species, one a tree from Ceylon which he named *D. lanceolaria*, the other a shrub from Surinam, which he termed *D. Monetaria*. Lamarck in 1790† dealt with the same two species, taking however the opportunity of invalidating the genus by adding, as a variety of *D. lanceolaria*, a plant figured by Rheede in 1686,‡ for which in 1763 Adanson§ had proposed the generic name *Solori*. The effects of this error have been far-reaching, and have been perpetuated in works so authoritative and so recent as the *Index Kewensis* of Hooker and Jackson, and as the *Revisio* of Dr. O. Kuntze.

To the genus in 1798 Roxburgh|| added three new species, *D. latifolia*, *D. paniculata*, and *D. rubiginosa*; all Indian, and all species that have stood the test of further examination, whether as regards their generic position or their specific rank. Willdenow, who in 1800¶ again took the genus in hand, added two more species to those of Linnæus and Roxburgh. His two additions were, however, somewhat unfortunate; one of them, *D. heterophylla*, is in reality *Derris uliginosa*; the other, *D. arborea*, is the tree on which Adanson in 1763** had based his genus *Pongam*, a name modified by Lamarck in 1797†† to *Pungamia* and by Ventenat in 1803‡‡ to *Pongamia*; the last-mentioned name is that now generally employed to designate it. When in 1806 Persoon§§ collated the species known to him, he corrected the latter error; the former, however, escaped his notice, and it happens that he deals with the same species in two different places, naming it in one *Dalbergia heterophylla*, in the other *Derris triphylla*. Two more species were added in the *Synopsis*; these are quite as unfortunate as the additions made by Willdenow; one of them, *D. domingensis*, is really a *Lonchocarpus*; the other, *D. Diphaca*, is an *Ormocarpum*. The most important feature of Persoon's digest is the transfer there, by Richard, of *D. Monetaria* to the genus *Ecastaphyllum*. Poiret, dealing with the genus in 1811, speaks of the

* *Supplementum Plantarum* 52, 316.

† *Dict. Encyc. Meth.* ii. 255.

‡ *Hort. Malabar.* vi. t. 22.

§ *Fam. Pl.* vi. 327.

|| *Coromand. Pl.* ii. 7, 8, 9, tt. 113, 114, 115.

¶ *Species Plantarum* iii. 2, 900.

** *Fam. Pl.* ii. 322.

†† *Illustr.* t. 603.

‡‡ *Jard. Malmais.* t. 28.

§§ *Synops.* ii. 276.

genus *Ecastaphyllum* as having been 'established' by Richard: it had, however, been already proposed in 1756* by P. Browne for a species from Jamaica. The bearing of this proposal will be dealt with in a subsequent paragraph; it is enough to remark that Poiret accepts the transfer of *D. Monetaria*, but does not correct the error of Lamarck as regards var. *β.* of *D. lanceolaria.*† Of the eight additional species which Poiret adds to the two mentioned by Lamarck, only the three cited from Roxburgh really belong to the genus; the others are species of *Lonchocarpus* or of *Sesbania*. He only doubtfully admits Persoon's *D. Diphaca*, which is an *Ormocarpum;* he similarly treats Desfontaine's *D. latisiliqua*, an American species that still remains doubtful because, though admitted into the list of *Dalbergias* given in the *Index Kewensis*, it is not dealt with by Bentham in his revision of the group *Dalbergieae.*‡ Three years later an exceedingly important reference to *Dalbergia* was made by Roxburgh, in the form of a list of the species of this genus under cultivation in the Honourable Company's Botanic Garden at Calcutta§ in the year 1814, with a supplementary list of those species of which he had only seen Herbarium specimens and had prepared botanical descriptions for the manuscript of his *Flora Indica*. The latter work was not published till 1832, but the list, supported as the proposed species are by contemporary descriptions and drawings, thoroughly deserves full acceptance. For the benefit of those who may wish to consult this list, which was repeated in De Candolle's *Prodromus*, it seems advisable to give it once more in full with the names duly noted by which the various species are now known—

Dalbergia ougeinensis *Roxb.*	= Ougeinia dalbergioides *Benth.*
latifolia *Roxb.*	= Dalbergia latifolia.
Sissoo *Roxb.*	= Dalbergia Sissoo.
emarginata *Roxb.*	= Dalbergia latifolia.
frondosa *Roxb.*	= Dalbergia lanceolaria *Linn. f.*
paniculata *Roxb.*	= Dalbergia paniculata.
zeylanica *Roxb.*	= Dalbergia lanceolaria *Linn. f.*
robusta *Roxb.*	= Derris robusta *Benth.*
marginata *Roxb.*	= Derris marginata *Benth.*
scandens *Roxb.*	= Derris scandens *Benth.*
tamarindifolia *Roxb.*	= Dalbergia tamarindifolia.
stipulacea *Roxb.*	= Dalbergia stipulacea.
rimosa *Roxb.*	= Dalbergia rimosa.
reniformis *Roxb.*	= Dalbergia reniformis.
alata *Roxb.*	= Derris thyrsiflora *Benth.*
parviflora *Roxb.*	= Dalbergia parviflora.
ferruginea *Roxb.*	= Dalbergia ferruginea.
Crowey *Roxb.*	= Derris robusta *Benth.*
rubiginosa *Roxb.*	= Dalbergia rubiginosa.
volubilis *Roxb.*	= Dalbergia volubilis.
spinosa *Roxb.*	= Dalbergia spinosa.

* *Nat. Hist. Jamaica* 299.

† Poiret does not appear to have formed any definite opinion with regard to *Ecastaphyllum*, or indeed with regard to the group of artificial 'genera' that go to form the natural genus *Dalbergia*, for in 1804 we find him referring *Dalbergia Amerimnon* to *Pterocarpus* (*Encyc. Meth.* v. 729); even after Richard had in 1806 'established' both *Amerimnon* and *Ecastaphyllum*, we find Poiret referring *D. Monetaria* in 1811 to *Pterocarpus* also (*Encyc. Meth. Suppl.* iv. 610). Loureiro [*Flor. Cochin-Chin.* 431 (1790)] has also a *Pterocarpus*, which is not the *Pterocarpus* of Linnæus of 1747, nor that of 1763; neither is it the *Pterocarpus* of Bergius of 1763. It is the tree now known as *Pongamia glabra*.

‡ *Journ. Linn. Soc.* iv. *Suppl.* (1860).

§ *Hortus Bengalensis*, p. 53, p. 98.

Though it is clear from this list that the characters which separate *Derris* from *Dalbergia* had not been fully realised, and that Roxburgh had been unable from its original description to recognise *D. lanceolaria*, it will be observed that the *Hortus Bengalensis* adds no fewer than ten distinct species to *Dalbergia*, a very substantial addition to our knowledge of the genus.

Dennstedt, who in 1818 published a Key to the *Hortus Malabaricus*,* by name refers to three *Dalbergias*; as it so happens, not one of them is a member of the genus. The three are *Dalbergia arborea* and *D. heterophylla*, exactly as limited by Willdenow; with *D. lanceolaria*, in the sense, however, of Lamarck and not of Linnæus. The first, as already explained, is the *Pongam* of Adanson; the third is that author's *Solori*. The second, which is in reality *Derris uliginosa*, is the *Salken* of Adanson;† it is somewhat remarkable that, though the plant on which this genus was founded is nowadays correctly referred to *Derris*, the 'genus' itself is, by the authors of the *Index Kewensis* and by Dr. Kuntze, by oversight referred to *Dalbergia*. There are, however, two *Dalbergias* figured in the *Hortus Malabaricus*; one of them, *D. torta* (Rheede's *Karin-tagera*‡), is referred by Dennstedt to *Cassia*; the other, which is Rheede's *Ana-mullu*,§ Dennstedt has named *Amerimnum horridum*. The genus *Amerimnon* was originally 'proposed' for a West Indian shrub by P. Browne in 1756,‖ it was established in Persoon's Synopsis in 1806¶, and accepted by De Candolle in 1825;** by most subsequent authors it has been merged in *Dalbergia*. There is no doubt that *Amerimnon* and *Dalbergia* are congeneric, and recently certain writers, notably Dr. Kuntze and Mr. Hiern, would insist on the substitution of the name *Amerimnon* for the name *Dalbergia* throughout. The objections to this proposal will be dealt with in a subsequent paragraph; in the meantime, however, it may be noted in passing that Dr. Kuntze, usually so accurate, has overlooked the fact that Dennstedt and Blanco had already anticipated his views and his action, with the result that Kuntze uses the name *Amerimnon sympatheticum* for a species that nearly three quarters of a century earlier had been duly named *A. horridum* by Dennstedt. In 1821 Roth†† published as a new species *D. arborea*, Heyne (not of Willdenow), which he considered to be very closely related to *D. lanceolaria*, but to be nevertheless distinct. In the writer's opinion, however, the differences, though marked, are not so great as to be specific, for *D. lanceolaria* is a somewhat variable plant. In the same place Roth published a description of the fruits of *D. rubiginosa*, which had previously been unknown. In 1823 Blume founded, on what was really one of Roxburgh's species of *Dalbergia*, *D. tamarindifolia*, a new genus—*Endespermum*.‡‡

In 1825 the condition of the genus was reviewed by De Candolle.§§ Only one new species was proposed, but this species (*D. timorensis*) was not really new: it is simply the *Dalbergia lanceolaria* β of Lamarck, not of Linnæus, and the *Dalbergia scandens* of Roxburgh; it is not a *Dalbergia*, but a *Derris*. Sprengel in 1826‖‖ issued another and less exhaustive review, for he only gave 14 species. He readmitted *D. Monetaria*, which

---

* *Schluessel zum Hortus Indicus Malabaricus* 20.
† *Fam. Pl.* ii. 322 (1763).
‡ *Hort. Malabar.* vi. 25.
§ *Hort. Malabar.* viii. 40.
‖ *Nat. Hist. Jamaica* 288 t. 31, f. 8.
¶ Persoon, *Synops.* ii. 278 (Amerimnum).
** *Prodromus* ii. 421 (Amerimnum).
†† *Nov. Plant. Species*, 330.
‡‡ *Cat. Gew. Buitenzorg*, 92.
§§ *Prodromus* ii. 416.
‖‖ *Syst. Veg.* iii. 193.

Richard had removed to *Ecastaphyllum*; included Willdenow's *D. arborea*, which is a *Pongamia*; Poiret's *D. pentaphylla* and *D. heptaphylla*, which are *Lonchocarpi*; and added for the first time a species—*D. sericea* (Spreng., not of G. Don), which is a *Millettia*. He thus intensified the pre-existing confusion, but added nothing to our knowledge of the genus. The review of the genus presented by G. Don in 1832* is not really greatly in advance of those that had preceded it, for the same old confusion recurs, with indeed the addition of still another genus (*Mundelea*) to the list of those mistaken for *Dalbergia*; Don's *D. Barclayii* is a *Mundelea*. He has, however, described as new several species that are truly *Dalbergias*, the only one that interests us being *D. sericea* from Nepal, a quite distinct species, confused by Wallich with *D. hircina*, which is a name that had been proposed by Hamilton for *D. lanceolaria*.

The next considerable addition to the genus *Dalbergia* was made by Wallich when the distribution of the Honourable East India Company's Herbarium took place.† Graham, then Professor of Botany in the University of Edinburgh, seems to have been mainly responsible for the identification of the various species. With a genus so difficult as *Dalbergia*, and where so great a mass of material had to be dealt with, it is not surprising that a few errors should have crept into the list. The species for the first time named in this list are:—*D. ovata* Grah.; *D. foliacea* Wall.; *D. cana* Grah.; (*D. tingens* Ham. = *D. stipulacea*); *D. cultrata* Grah.; (*D. glauca* Wall. = *D. ovata*); (*D. cassioides* Wall. = *D. stipulacea*); (*D. rufa* Grah. = *D. tamarindifolia*); (*D. multijuga* Grah. = *D. tamarindifolia*); (*D. livida* Grah. = *D. stipulacea* in part and *D. tamarindifolia* in part); *D. rostrata* Grah.; *D. stipulata* Wall. (the name of this species had to be altered subsequently to *D. velutina* Benth.); (*D. purpurea* Wall. = *D. cana* Grah.); (*D. hircina* Ham. = *D. lanceolaria*, but part of the issue, though not Hamilton's part, is = *D. sericea*); *D. torta* Grah.; (*D. flexuosa* Grah. = *D. reniformis*); (*D. horrida* Grah. = *D. spinosa*); *D. sissoides* Grah. The names within brackets prove on examination to belong to species already supplied with names, so that Wallich's list differentiates only eight previously unknown *Dalbergias*. Under *D. paniculata*, however, was issued *D. multiflora* Heyne, which is not *D. paniculata*, as Wallich and Graham supposed, but is the species previously designated by Dennstedt *Amerimnum horridum*, and subsequently named by Nimmo‡ *Dalbergia sympathetica*; while under *D. hircina* was included not only Hamilton's plant of this name, which is *D. lanceolaria*, but another which, just about the time the list was issued, was differentiated by G. Don as *D. sericea*. The Wallichian collection therefore contains in all nine species not formerly known. The Wallichian list includes *Dalbergia ougeinensis*, which is an *Ougeinia*, also *D. robusta* and *D. scandens*, which are species of *Derris*, sect. *Brachypterum*. In 1834 Wight and Walker-Arnott, in their account of *Dalbergia* § still retained *Derris* (*Brachypterum*) *scandens* in *Dalbergia*, but from this time onward the limits of *Dalbergia* have been, in all important works on Indian botany, carefully observed, and the additions to the genus that have from time to time been made do not require to be recorded, since they appear from the citations given under the individual species dealt with in this work.

---

* *Gen. Syst. Gard.* ii. 374.

† *Lith. Cat.*, 5847—5877 (1832).

‡ Grah. *Cat. Bomb. Pl.* 55 (1839).

§ *Prodr. Penins. Ind.* i. 264.

§ 2. *Sketch of the attempts to classify the species of Dalbergia.*

The year 1834* is marked by the first real step in advance as regards the internal classification of the species of *Dalbergia*. To have thrown out of *Dalbergia* all foreign elements save the *Brachyptera* was to have done much; and if it may be said that we owe this to Graham's assortment of the Wallichian *Dalbergias* in 1832, we have to recognise that Wight and Arnott went still further when, while retaining *Derris scandens* in *Dalbergia*, on account of its pod, they treated it, because of its opposite leaflets and its versatile anthers, as the type of a distinct subgenus. More important, however, was their proposal to subdivide the true *Dalbergias* into two distinct groups according to the monadelphous or isodiadelphous arrangement of the stamens, because this proposal became the basis of the first attempt made by Bentham in 1851† to divide the genus into natural sections. Bentham at the same time reduced to *Dalbergia* the Malayan *Endespermum* proposed by Blume, the African *Podiopetalum* proposed by Hochstetter, and the American *Triptolemea* proposed by Martius, subdividing the whole into three sections:—(1) *Sissoa*, with the stamens monadelphous and the pod long and straight; (2) *Selenolobium*, with the stamens of *Sissoa*, but the pod short and lunate; and (3) *Dalbergaria*, with the pod of *Sissoa*, but the stamens isodiadelphous. The subdivision was convenient, and at the time it was proposed appeared to be natural. There were, however, only 29 species then known, and of these only two—*D. spinosa* and *D. torta*—were known to have the pods of *Selenolobium*, though, as a matter of fact, two other species, whose fruits were then unknown to Bentham—*D. parviflora* and *D. reniformis*—have *Selenoloboid* pods. Miquel, when in 1855 he described the Malayan species of *Dalbergia*,‡ adopted Bentham's three sections and observed, what Bentham had overlooked, that *D. parviflora* must be a *Selenolobium*. He did not, however, suggest any alteration in the principle of classification. In 1860 Bentham returned to this subject in the course of his classical essay on the *Dalbergieae*,§ a model of lucidity and method. The pod, as he there explains, which had formerly been chiefly relied on in separating *Dalbergia* from other Leguminosae, must now be abandoned as a primary guide. A limitation based entirely on the pod involves, as we have seen in the historical review of the genus prior to 1834, the inclusion of many species with different foliage and inflorescence and, above all, with very different stamens—species that are much better referred to *Derris* and to *Lonchocarpus*. If insisted upon, it would logically involve the suppression of various distinct and apparently quite natural genera like *Platymiscium* and *Leptolobium*. On the other hand, if rigidly applied, the character afforded by the pod would involve the exclusion from *Dalbergia* of the species for whose accommodation Bentham has proposed the section *Selenolobium*, and would further emphasise the exclusion of the quite artificial genus *Ecastaphyllum*. Restricting in this fashion the generic importance attached to modifications of the pod, Mr. Bentham explains that, had he for the first time been grouping the species of this genus, he would have divided it into three artificial sections—(*a*) *Dalbergia*, with a long straight pod; (*b*) *Selenolobium*, with the pod thicker and lunate or reniform; and (*c*) *Ecastophyllum*, with the pod orbicular or nearly so. The actual delimitation adopted was a modification of this design.

* Wight & Walker-Arnott, *Prodr. Penins. Ind.* i. 264.

† *Plantæ Junghuhnianæ* i. 254.

‡ *Flor. Ind. Bat.* i. 1, 126.

§ *Journ. Linn. Soc.* iv. *Suppl.*

Ecastaphyllum, though so very artificially distinguished, had become so well known under this name that it appeared to Bentham convenient to retain it as a genus; *Selenolobium* is, as in the *Plantae Junghuhnianae*, treated as a section of *Dalbergia; Dalbergia* proper is further subdivided into *Triptolemea*, *Sissoa*, and *Dalbergaria*. *Dalbergaria* is precisely the section of this name proposed nine years earlier. *Sissoa*, however, is somewhat curtailed owing to the separation of *Triptolemea*, within which are placed all the species, previously referred to *Sissoa*, that have very small flowers disposed in 2—3-chotomous cymes. For the species, as known to Bentham, the system thus provided was at least quite convenient; so satisfactory, indeed, did it prove that when, in 1865, Bentham had occasion to again review the *Dalbergieae*,* he adopted the same four sections; and when, in 1869, Baillon independently reviewed the Leguminosae that author also found it unnecessary to modify Bentham's arrangement of 1860. It is, of course, easy now, when the details of structure and the limits of species are better known than they were in 1860, to point out certain objections to a system which, as Bentham has expressly warned us, provides us with sections that are defined by rather uncertain characters; indeed, he has himself indicated in the *Genera Plantarum* the feature which chiefly invalidates it, since he has pointed out that *D. reniformis*, which in 1860 he had referred to *Dalbergaria*, might be referred to *Selenolobium* equally with the species he had already placed in that section. Now these other species, but for their semilunar pods, would have been species of *Sissoa;* so that within *Selenolobium* there is the same cleavage as there is within *Dalbergia* proper, since we have *D. parviflora*, by flowers a *Triptolemea*, in which Bentham has placed it, and by fruit a *Selenolobium* as Miquel has pointed out ; *D. torta*, by flowers a *Sissoa*, and *D. reniformis*, by flowers a *Dalbergaria*, are, by pods, equally *Selenolobia*. Any system of delimitation that is to be logically exact must, in view of these facts, either further subdivide *Selenolobium* exactly as *Dalbergia* proper is subdivided or must accept Bentham's verdict as to the unimportance of modifications of the pod not only so far as the limitation of genera, but so far as the limitation of sections is concerned. There is, however, a further and, the writer believes, valid objection, not to the results, which are really good, but to the presentation of the four sections admitted by Bentham. They cannot be stated serially without remark because, besides being of unequal rank, they are the outcome of a successive dichotomy as follows :—

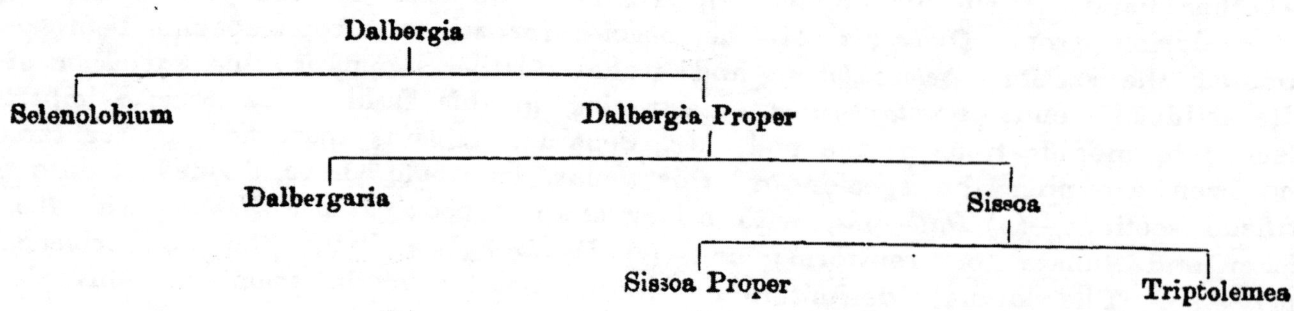

* *Genera Plantarum* i. 544.

† *Histoire des Plantes* ii. 312

The year 1876 was marked by the appearance of two very important papers on Asiatic *Dalbergias*,—one by Kurz* on the species of Burma, the other by Baker on the whole of the species of India.† Both authors modify Bentham's system: Baker does so only to the extent of suppressing the concluding dichtomy of the preceding paragraph, reverting to the system proposed by Bentham in 1851 and followed by Miquel in 1855, with the result that the section *Triptolemea* disappears. For Baker's action there is much to be said; it is not altogether convenient to unduly multiply groups that are separated by characters of unequal value. It is not, however, possible to endorse Baker's view that groups which, as Bentham truly says, cannot be considered to be well-defined or natural sections, constitute subgenera. Kurz, who independently does the same thing as Baker with reference to *Dalbergia* proper, which he divides into the subgenera *Dalbergaria* and *Sissoa*, has, with reference to *Selenolobium*, adopted a view that probably no one will accept—certainly hitherto no one has endorsed. The chief objection that can be taken to Baker's treatment of the genus is that he should have raised the section *Selenolobium* of Bentham to the rank of a subgenus instead of acting upon Bentham's hint and formally distributing its species among *Sissoa* and *Dalbergaria*. Kurz, however, has done more than treat Bentham's section *Selenolobium* as a subgenus of *Dalbergia*—he has removed it from *Dalbergia* entirely, and, in spite of its very different anthers, has merged *Selenolobium* in *Drepanocarpus*. Taubert, in his useful revision of the Leguminosae in 1894,‡ has taken what the writer believes to be a step in advance by reducing the genus *Ecastaphyllum* to *Dalbergia*. In the suggestion there is nothing original: as long ago as 1860 Bentham pointed out that, if naturally treated, *Ecastaphyllum* is a section of *Dalbergia*, and even then only an artificial section. From considerations of convenience alone, Bentham consented to recognise the group *Ecastaphyllum* as a genus; Taubert's action in merging it in *Dalbergia*, as Bentham in 1860 might have done, is rather a proof of the extent to which our views as to convenience have changed than a mark of advance in our knowledge. The most noteworthy feature of Taubert's action lies in his having merged *Ecastaphyllum* in the section *Selenolobium* instead of recognising in it a distinct section, as Bentham was inclined to do. That Taubert is right in what he has done is certain: *Ecastaphyllum* is in no way to be distinguished from *Selenolobium*. The defect of Taubert's system lies in its not going sufficiently far; in its not recognising that the cleavage-plane which permits us to separate *Selenolobium* is not parallel to, but intersects the cleavage-planes between the remaining sections; and in its failing to take this opportunity of suppressing entirely the quite artificial and, in the light of our later knowledge, impracticable and contradictory section *Selenolobium*. Except for the real merit of having incorporated *Ecastaphyllum* definitely in *Dalbergia*, Taubert's system makes no advance on Bentham's system. He has not accepted Baker's union of *Triptolemea* and *Sissoa;* still less has he countenanced Kurz's transfer of *Selenolobium* to *Drepanocarpus*.

It is with some reluctance that the writer now offers a further criticism of the system thus universally adopted. As regards the section *Selenolobium*, it is

---

* *Journ. As. Soc. Beng.* xlv. 2, 278; also *For. Flor. Brit. Burm.* i. 336, 341 (one year later).

† *Hook. f., Flor. Brit. Ind.* ii.

‡ Engler & Prantl, *Natürlich. Pflanzenfam.* iii. 3, 335.

improbable that any one who makes a serious and prolonged study of the genus will fail to agree with the statement that this section is not real, but imaginary. The pods of species of the postulated section by no means agree with each other: their only common feature is a negative one; they are not samaroid pods, as is the case with the bulk of the *Dalbergias*. Their nearest allies are not *Sissoae* or *Dalbergarieae* or *Triptolemeae* in particular, but are to be found scattered throughout the genus. Some have pods with a thick corky mesocarp, others have little or none of this suberous thickening; still other species, *e.g.*, *D. stipulacea*, combine a local suberous thickening of the mesocarp opposite the seed with a samaroid structure elsewhere. Finally, and perhaps most important consideration of all, the structure of the pod in all the species of *Selenolobium* or *Ecastaphyllum* is such as to adapt the organ for dispersal by water or for the protection of the contained seed in swampy forests, and just in so far as it is possibly the result of environment does this structure fail to afford a character that is taxonomically useful. However, even after the species of *Selenolobium* are relegated to their natural positions within the genus, matters do not appear to be entirely satisfactory. Bentham's section *Triptolemea* is a useful and a fairly natural section; his section *Dalbergaria* is even more natural and quite as useful. But Bentham's *Sissoa* is residual rather than natural, since it includes many species that are precisely *Dalbergarias* except that they have monadelphous instead of isodiadelphous stamens; many species that are practically *Triptolemeas* except that they have larger flowers and usually longer styles; and finally, many species that, agreeing in the main with the monadelphous species which in other respects are exactly like *Dalbergaria*, differ from these as regards vexillum as much as these differ from *Dalbergaria* as regards stamens. If, then, the species of *Dalbergia* must be divided into sections at all, and when the crowd of species to be dealt with is considered, such a subdivision seems very desirable, these sections ought clearly to be groups of as nearly as possible equal natural rank. When such a subdivision is made, five sections must be recognised. These sections aggregate themselves naturally in two larger groups that may be treated as subgenera. The characters on which this classification depends are detailed in the systematic part of this review; it is sufficient for the moment to say what they are and to explain what relationship they bear to the groups proposed by previous writers. All the *Ecastaphylla* of America and Africa appear to be *Dalbergarieae* as to flowers. One of the Asiatic *Ecastaphylla* (*D. Beccarii*), however, is certainly and the other (*D. Albertisii*) is probably a *Triptolemea*. Three of the *Selenolobia* are undoubtedly *Dalbergarieas*, and there is possibly a fourth belonging to the same section. Two of them are, however, *Triptolemeae*, and in all probability a third belongs to the same section. The remainder belong to that section of the old and undifferentiated *Sissoa*, where the flowers are neither like the flowers of *Triptolemea* nor like the flowers of *Dalbergaria*. These species thus disposed of, the genus *Dalbergia* is easily divisible into two subgenera: (*a*) SISSOA, of which the well-known species, *D. Sissoo*, exhibits in a well-marked fashion most of the characteristics; and (*b*) AMERIMNON, of which *D. Amerimnum* may be taken as the type. This SISSOA does not correspond exactly with the section of that name proposed by Bentham in 1851 or with the corresponding subgenus recognised by Baker and Kurz in 1876, since it eliminates all those species that have monadelphous stamens, but have at the same time hastate wing-petals. AMERIMNON, on the other hand, does not (apart altogether from the inclusion of certain *Selenolobia*) correspond with the *Dalbergaria* of these authors, since it includes the monadelphous species that have wing-petals like those of the isodiadelphous ones. Within SISSOA we find two sections—(1) *Triptolemea*, which is practically identical with the *Triptolemea* of Bentham, Baillon and Taubert, deviating only in the inclusion of a group of species with small flowers and short styles that are by these authors relegated to their *Sissoa*; and (2) *Podiopetalum*, of which *D. armata* from Africa may be taken as typical, but which also includes *D. Sissoo* itself. Under AMERIMNON again we find three sections—(3) *Endespermum*, of which *D. tamarindifolia* may be considered typical, and which as a genus was well characterised by Blume; (4) *Miscolobium*, of which the American *D. foliolosa* and the Asiatic *D. velutina* may be considered good representatives; lastly, (5) *Dalbergaria*, which, save for the inclusion of a few *Selonolobii*, is exactly the section of this name as characterised by Bentham.

The arrangement now adopted the writer believes to be more natural, and finds to be certainly more convenient than any system hitherto suggested. It has been arrived at, not by the method of adopting arbitrary characters and subdividing the genus according to these, but by the opposite method of first throwing the different species into small groups of closely allied forms, and subsequently bringing together the more closely allied of these apparently natural groups. The method is only an amplification, in the light of the evidence afforded by fuller and more complete suites of specimens, of the Benthamian method; the underlying motive is the same—to facilitate the identification of the species. An examination of the often complex synonymy will show how necessary some such modification is: whether the system now proposed will stand the test of further discovery and investigation is a point that can only be tested by experience. In the accompanying sheet (PLATE 1) is exhibited a schematic view of the disposition of these natural groups with reference to each other and to the subgenera and sections to which they severally belong. The unbroken lines mark the sectional limits; the dotted lines show the cleavage that artificially separates the *Selenolobia* and *Ecastaphylla*. The relative position of the sections is shown with approximate accuracy in the subjoined diagram:—

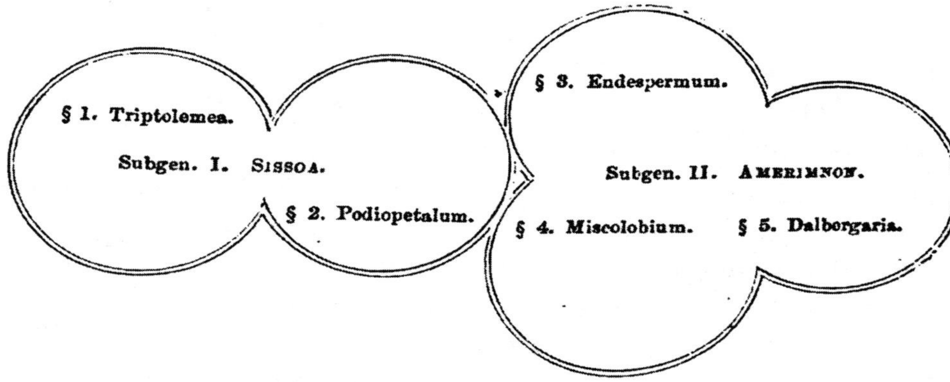

§ 3. *The validity of the generic name Dalbergia.*

Before proceeding to give a formal definition of the genus, it is necessary to bestow a little consideration on the name that it ought to bear. Leaving out of account the names *Endespermum* Bl. (1823),* *Semeionotis* Schott (1829),† *Miscolobium* Vog. (1837),‡ *Triptolemea* Mart. (1837),§ *Leiolobium* Benth. (1838),‖ and *Podiopetalum* Hochst. (1841),¶ which have been applied to species of *Dalbergia*, and neglecting the terms *Drakensteinia* Neck. (1790)** and *Hecastophyllum* H. B. & K. (1834),†† proposed for *Ecastaphyllum*, since the *Supplementum Plantarum* was issued in 1781, we have several other names with priority as to *date* over the name *Dalbergia* that call for consideration. In the *Index Kewensis* and in the *Revisio Generum Plantarum* of Kuntze—works that have been prepared with very great care—two such names, both dating from 1763, are by some oversight cited under *Dalbergia*. These are *Salken* Adans. and *Solori* Adans.;‡‡ the plants on which these genera are founded being respectively *Derris scandens* and *Derris uliginosa*, the names do not further trouble us. There are, however, several others that must be considered. Taken in inverse chronological sequence, we find *Acouroa* Aubl. (1775);§§ *Pterocarpus* Berg. (1769)‖‖ and *Ecastaphyllum* P. Br. (1756) ¶¶ applied to species with nummular pods, and *Amerimnon* P. Br. (1756)*** applied to species with samaroid pods.

As regards the name *Acouroa*, the fact that it applies only to a species with nummular pods appears to the writer to exclude it from further consideration. If the species characterised by pods of this kind are to be artificially separated as constituting a distinct genus, the earlier name *Ecastaphyllum* would be with propriety adopted to designate them. With the name *Pterocarpus* matters are different, since we have seen that though Bergius appears to have confined its incidence to species with nummular pods, Poiret at least employed it to designate both species with nummular and species with samaroid pods. However, the name is not available for the genus *Dalbergia* because in 1747 it was used by Linnæus to designate a species of *Derris*, and in 1763 it was again used to designate a species of the genus usually recognised as *Pterocarpus*. Kuntze, insisting on absolute priority, uses the name for the genus here spoken of as *Derris*; others, with whom the writer agrees, prefer to employ the name *Pterocarpus*, as Linnæus did in 1763, when he had perfected his system of nomenclature, rather than to use it as Linnæus did in 1747, when that system had not yet been matured. In any case we are left free to consider, without reference to Bergius' name, the remaining two names proposed by P. Browne in 1756.

The point that has first to be clearly appreciated is that there was no confusion of ideas on the part of P. Browne: he used the name *Ecastaphyllum* for a species with nummular pods, the name *Amerimnon* for a species with samaroid pods. So long as the two groups of species thus indicated were kept apart, it is clear that for the genus with nummular fruits the proper name was *Ecastaphyllum*; for the genus with

* *Cat. Gew. Buitenzorg*, 23.
† *Wiener Zeitschr.* iii. 804.
‡ *Linnæa* xi. 200.
§ *Flora* xx. *Beibl.* 122.
‖ *Ann. Wiener Mus.* ii. 94.
¶ *Flora* xxiv 657.
** *Elem.* iii. 33.
†† *Nov. Gen. & Spec.* vi. 387.
‡‡ *Fam. Pl.* ii. 322, 327.
§§ *Pl. Guian.* 753, t. 301.
‖‖ *Vet. Acad. Handl. Stockh.* 116.
¶¶ *Hist. Jamaic.* 299.
*** *Hist. Jamaic.* 288.

samaroid fruits the true name was *Amerimnon*. However inconvenient their action may be, there is therefore no doubt that Kuntze and Hiern are logically justified in proposing to suppress the name *Dalbergia* and replace it by the name *Amerimnon*. Indeed, from a strictly logical standpoint, the name *Dalbergia* was at all times indefensible if the separation of the species with nummular and with samaroid fruits be justified, because the genus *Dalbergia* was expressly devised to include species with fruits of both types. From the moment, however, when Bentham showed that the group *Ecastaphyllum* is not a natural genus, and particularly from the moment that Taubert carried Bentham's conclusion into actual practice, the names *Amerimnon* and *Ecastaphyllum*, being partial, were rendered alike incorrect and inappropriate, and the name *Dalbergia* became the only name that can with any propriety be applied to the whole genus.*

§ 4. *Distribution of the Asiatic species of Dalbergia.*

The genus *Dalbergia* is widely distributed throughout South-Eastern Asia, and extends from Beluchistan, the Concan and Ceylon to Kiangsu in China, the Philippines and New Guinea. Two species extend eastward from the Philippines and north of New Guinea to the Caroline Archipelago; two species cross from New Guinea into North Australia. One of these latter species extends eastward to New Caledonia, Fiji and Vavau. This Melanesian species is *D. torta*, a member of the section *Endespermum*, with pods so modified as to adapt them for dispersal by ocean currents; its wide distribution shows that it is a typical member of the Indo-Malayan Strand-flora. The presence of *D. torta* in islands so remote as Fiji and Vavau is thus readily accounted for, and Melanesia, so far as *Dalbergia* is concerned, possesses only a species that occurs in every other natural area in South-Eastern Asia that has a sea-coast. The two species that occur in the Carolines are again *D. torta* and with it a species whose pods are similarly, though less obviously, adapted for dispersal by water. This is *D. ferruginea*, which occurs everywhere throughout Papuasia and Eastern Malaya, but does not appear to cross the Wallace line to the west. The two that occur in Australia are once more *D. torta* and another species, *D. densa*, characteristic of New Guinea, the Moluccas and the Key and Aru Archipelagos; in Australia it is confined to the coast of Queensland and certain islands in Torres Strait. So far as *Dalbergia* is concerned, then, both Micronesia and Australia are mere prolongations of Eastern Malaya and Papuasia.

Ceylon, the south-western extreme of our area, is in like case. Here there are only three species, one of these being again the littoral *D. torta*; the others are *D. rostrata*, a species that extends from Celebes to South India, and *D. lanceolaria*, a species that extends throughout the Indian Peninsula as far as the North-Western Himalaya. Ceylon is thus a meeting ground of Malayan and Indian influences, and, so far as *Dalbergia* is concerned, has no distinguishing features. Since, however, all three Ceylon species occur in Malabaria, while only two occur in Malaya, we conclude that, so far as *Dalbergia* is concerned, Ceylon is a mere annex of Malabaria.

* An exactly converse instance has been already fully explained by the writer (*Journ. As. Soc. Beng.* lxvi. 2, 404). The genus *Mucuna*, as founded by Adanson in 1763 and as accepted by all subsequent authors, in reality is a complex of two extremely distinct and natural genera founded by P. Browne, viz., *Stizolobium* and *Zoopthalmum*. So long as we are content to accept Adanson's erroneous complex as a genus, we are logically bound to accept and use Adanson's name *Mucuna*; so soon as it is realised that in reality two genera are confused under this name, Browne's two names, *Stizolobium* and *Zoopthalmum*, will come into use and Adanson's name must be abandoned.

A region similarly outlying and similarly destitute of distinctive features is the North-west Frontier or Indian Desert region. Here, again, there are three species. Two of these—*D. lanceolaria* and *D. latifolia*—are very characteristic of India generally, though both cross the Gangetic plain to the Himalaya; the third is *D. Sissoo*, a species very characteristic of the sub-Himalayan forests from Assam to the Panjab and Beluchistan, but rarely, if ever, met with wild to the south of the Gangetic plain and Rajputana. As the desert region has thus two species that are characteristic of the Indian Peninsula as against one that is characteristically sub-Himalayan, we may treat the area as an annex of India Proper, though, just as Ceylon is a meeting place of Indian and Malayan influences, India Deserta is a meeting place of Indian and Himalayan influences.

Existing political boundaries and ethnological considerations render it not inexpedient to divide South-Eastern Asia into five fairly equal botanical provinces: India; Indo-China; China; Malaya; Papuasia. India may be further fairly naturally subdivided into four sub-areas: (1) Malabaria, including Ceylon, Malabar, and the Concan with the hinterlands of the two latter as far eastward as the influence of the south-west monsoon is directly felt; (2) Coromandelia; Coromandel, the Dekkan, Central India, or the whole Indian Peninsula to the east of Malabaria and south of the Gangetic plain; (3) India Deserta; the area of scanty rainfall in Scinde, Rajputana, the Panjab, and along the trans-Indus frontier; (4) the Himalayan ranges, from the Indus to the Brahmakund, through which the waters of the Sanpo reach the Brahmaputra. Indo-China seems to lend itself to further subdivision into the following subareas: (1) Assam-Arracan; a block of hill-ranges lying between the Brahmaputra and the Irrawaday rivers, and extending from the Mishmi-Kachin countries, which are of Himalayan character and which border on Tibet and China, as far as the Andaman islands, which are a southward prolongation of the Yomah of Arracan and have a mixed Burma-Malay vegetation; (2) Shan; another region of hills and plateaux lying east of the Irrawaday, bounded on the west by the Mekong as far south as 20° N. lat., afterwards by the Meinam; this subarea includes to the south Tenasserim, where, again, there is a marked Malayan element in the vegetation; (3) Siam-Anam; a region of plains and lower hills extending southward from 20° N. lat. and east of 100° E. long., including Siam, Laos, Cochin-China generally. In the extreme north-east of Indo-China lies the province of Tongking, too small to be considered a subarea apart, yet, so far as the genus *Dalbergia* is concerned, calling for special treatment. Hitherto only four *Dalbergias* have been definitely recorded from Tongking—none of them endemic; if we except *D. torta*, which occurs on nearly every coast throughout South-Eastern Asia, and is not therefore characteristic of Indo-China in particular, none of the four occur either in the Anam-Siam or in the Shan subareas. One of the Tongking species—*D. rimosa*—is characteristic of the Himalayan area, where it extends from Sikkim to Upper Assam; of the northern portion of Western Indo-China, where it extends from Sylhet and Cachar to Kachin; and of South-Western China (Yunnan). The other two species—*D. Balansae* and *D. tonkinensis*—extend to Tongking from South-Eastern China. There is a fifth species, the identity of which is doubtful, in the same area. This is *D. pinnata* (Derris pinnata *Lour.*), usually identified with *D. tamarindifolia*, which, if Loureiro's description be exact, cannot well be the case. The diagnosis given by Loureiro agrees best with the description of *D. Millettii*: should the two prove to be the same, then Tongking has three species that extend from South-Eastern China. Tongking has been only inadequately explored botanically, and the absence of forms peculiar to the province or common to Tongking and Central Indo-China, or to Tongking and the rest of Eastern Indo-China may be but an index of this imperfect investigation; as matters stand, however, it seems necessary to separate Tongking from the rest of Indo-China and treat it as an annex of China.

An examination of the list of species in which the distribution is tabulated will show that, so far, 23 species have been collected within Chinese territory. One of these species—*D. obtusifolia*—has, however, to be eliminated; it is Chinese only in name, and can be included in a Chinese list only because it occurs in the Taping Valley in South-Western Yunnan. Physiographically, for the valley forms part of the catchment area of the Irrawaday, this Taping Valley is a portion of Central Indo-China; of the two *Dalbergias* reported from the valley, one occurs nowhere in China outside its limits; no exclusively Chinese *Dalbergia* enters the valley. The reasons that call for the annexation of Tongking to China equally demand the recession of the Cis-Salwin part of Yunnan, drained into the Irrawaday, to Central Indo-China.

China then, modified by the inclusion of Tongking and the separation of the Taping Valley, has 22 species of *Dalbergia*. If we exclude the littoral species, *D. torta*, which extends throughout South-Eastern Asia, we have then 21 species of *Dalbergia*, of which two—*D. fusca* and *D. stipulacea*—extend to Eastern Indo-China; four—*D. fusca*, *D. stipulacea*, *D. burmanica*, and *D. tamarindifolia*—extend to Central Indo-China; and seven—*D. stipulacea*, *D. burmanica*, *D. tamarindifolia*, *D. rimosa*, *D. assamica*, *D. Kingiana*, and *D. mimosoides*—extend to Western Indo-China.

When the occurrence of these species within the Chinese Empire is examined more in detail, useful subdivision of the region into three subareas is possible. These are: (1) South-Western China; comprising Yunnan and Western Szechuen to the west of long. 105° E.; (2) Central China; Eastern Szechuen, Kweichou, Hunan, Hupeh, Kiangsi; (3) Eastern China; Chekiang, Fokien, Kwang-tung, Kwangsi, and Tongking. Central China has only four species—*D. stenophylla*, *D. Dyeriana*, *D. hupeana*, and *D. Balansae*. Only one of these, *D. stenophylla*, is confined to the region, and it affords little direct proof of isolation because it is closely allied to *D. Millettii* of Eastern China, and equally closely allied to *D. mimosoides*, which occurs throughout South-Western China and extends thence to Assam and Sikkim. *D. Dyeriana* occurs both in Central and in South-Western China, but it is more distinctive of the central region and seems only to cross into Yunnan, but not to be widespread in that province. Similarly, *D. hupeana* occurs both in Central and in Eastern China; in this case, however, the species is clearly distinctive of Central China, and its occurrence in Kwangtung among the eastern provinces may be due to its being there a planted species. On the other hand, *D. Balansae*, which merely overflows into Central China (Kiangsi) from Eastern China, and is in no sense distinctive of Central China, may be in Kiangsi only planted. The endemic factor ¼, or 25, is low, and the subarea is not at all an isolated one. South-Western China has fourteen species. These are—*D. obtusifolia*, *D. tamarindifolia*, *D. mimosoides*, *D. Dyeriana*, *D. fusca*, *D. Kingiana*, *D. Henryana*, *D. burmanica*, *D. assamica*, *D. stipulacea*, *D. polyadelpha*, *D. szemaoënsis*, *D. rimosa*, and *D. yunnanensis*. But, as has been explained, the first species—*D. obtusifolia*—is only Chinese because the Taping Valley, which is a portion of the catchment area of the Irrawaday Valley, forms part of the political system of China; it has therefore to be excluded when, as here, only natural facts are under consideration. *D. fusca*, *D. burmanica*, *D. tamarindifolia*, *D. stipulacea*, *D. assamica*, *D. rimosa*, *D. Kingiana* are Indo-Chinese or Himalayan species that cross the frontier into South-Western China, the only one going on into Eastern China being *D. rimosa*. Of the remaining species, *D. mimosoides* does not afford evidence of isolation; it extends to Assam and Sikkim, has a related species (*D. stenophylla*) in Central China and another allied form (*D. Millettii*) in Eastern China. *D. Dyeriana* is even less distinctive, since it appears to be a mere overflow from Central China: *D. Henryana* is hardly more distinctive than *D. mimosoides* because, though itself undistributed, a very close ally (*D. Kingiana*) extends to the adjacent Kachin country in Western Indo-China, and another ally (*D. Benthami*), not quite so intimate, but still near, occurs in Eastern China. *D. yunnanensis* has a close ally (*D. Collettii*) on the Shan Plateau in Central Indo-China; *D. szemaoënsis* belongs to a group of species most strongly represented in Indo-China: the most distinctive species of Western Indo-China is *D. polyadelpha*. By the most liberal computation, then, the endemic factor for South-Western China is only $\frac{3}{13}$, or 23. Eastern China, as defined above, though with fewer species, shows a higher degree of isolation. Here there are nine *Dalbergias*: *D. Millettii*, *D. Hancei*, *D. Benthami*, *D. tonkinensis*, *D. sacerdotum*, *D. rimosa*, *D. hupeana*, *D. Balansae*, *D. torta*. Of these, the first five are endemic, though, for reasons already made clear, the evidence of *D. Millettii* as to isolation is not conclusive, while that of *D. Benthami* is not great. On the other hand, the evidence of *D. Balansae* is greater than would at first sight appear, since it is widespread in Eastern China, but only overflows, and then perhaps only as a planted species, into Kiangsi in Central China; and *D. hupeana*, which only occurs, and again perhaps only as a planted tree, in Kwang-tung, gives nearly as strong negative evidence in favour of the isolation of Eastern China as the positive evidence of *D. Balansae*, *D. Hancei*, *D. tonkinensis*, and *D. sacerdotum*, which are all distinctively Eastern Chinese species. The two that remain are *D. rimosa*, a species widespread in South-Western China, Western Indo-China, and the Eastern Himalaya, which extends to Tongking without having so far been met with in Central Indo-China; finally, *D. torta*, which occurs on the coasts of South-Eastern China and of Tongking, and has been reported from every coast throughout our Asiatic region except those of the Sunda islands and of Coromandel. The endemic factor for Eastern China is therefore $\frac{5}{9}$, or 55·5.

Excluding, then, the Central Indo-Chinese species that is Chinese only because it occurs in the Taping Valley, and including, as we must, within Chinese limits the province of Tongking, we have an area with 22 species, of which 13 are endemic, so that its endemic factor is $\frac{13}{22}$, or just under 60. The connection between China as a whole on the one hand and Indo-China or the Himalaya on the other is, however, almost entirely confined to South-Western China. If this district be excluded and the conjoined districts of Central and Eastern China be considered together, we have then an area with 11 species of *Dalbergia*, whereof 8 are endemic. The endemic factor for Central and Eastern China is thus $\frac{8}{11}$, or 72·7, indicating a degree of isolation higher than is to be met with in any similar area in South-Eastern Asia.

The Philippines, physiographically much isolated, with ten reported species of *Dalbergia*, have only three peculiar forms, *D. polyphylla*, *D. Mimosella*, and *D. Cumingiana*. One of the remaining species is the ubiquitous littoral *D. torta;* another reported sea-shore species—*D. spinosa*—occurs also on the coasts of Indo-China and Coromandel. The others are—(1) *D. tamarindifolia*, a species present both in Malaya and in Central Indo-China; (2) *D. parviflora*, widely spread in Malaya; (3) *D. ferruginea*, a species confined to Papuasia and the Caroline Archipelago; (4) *D. discolor*, a species common to the Philippines, Celebes, and Borneo; and (5) *D. Minahassae*, a species common to the Philippines and Celebes. The Philippine endemic factor is thus $\frac{3}{10}$, or 30, and is too small to admit of the treatment of the Archipelago as a distinct area. For our present purpose, and so far as the evidence from *Dalbergia* goes, it may conveniently be treated as a subarea of Papuasia, though, as a matter of fact, the Archipelago is more or less of a meeting ground of Papuasian, Malayan, and Indo-Chinese influences. The Papuan subareas proper have very few species of *Dalbergia*. New Guinea itself so far has only yielded four species; *D. Albertisii*, endemic; *D. densa*, extending throughout the Moluccas to the west and to Australia on the south, but not reaching Celebes or the Philippines; *D. ferruginea*, extending throughout the Moluccas and into Timor, Celebes, the Philippines, and the Carolines; finally, the widespread littoral species, *D. torta*. The endemic factor for New Guinea being ¼, or 25 only, the island cannot, so far as *Dalbergia* is concerned, be considered a natural area apart. In the Moluccas, the next subarea to the east, we find five species; again with only one—*D. Jahnii*, confined to the Key Archipelago,—endemic; the others are *D. densa* and *D. ferruginea*, mentioned in detail for New Guinea; the widespread *D. torta;* finally, *D. parviflora*, a species common throughout the Moluccas, but not impossibly only an introduction from Malaya, where it is widespread. The endemic factor for the Moluccas being ⅕, or 20 only, we cannot consider the Archipelago a distinct area. The last subarea to be considered in connection with Papuasia is Celebes. Here only six species have been collected so far, and of these none are endemic. The species are: as usual, the widespread *D. torta; D. Minahassae*, which is confined to Celebes and the Philippines; *D. ferruginea*, which does not extend to the west of the Wallace line; and three species which do extend to Malaya Proper. These are *D. discolor*, found also in Borneo and reported from the Philippines; *D. parviflora*, which extends from the Philippines and the Moluccas to the Malay Peninsula and Sumatra; and *D. rostrata*, which extends from Celebes to Ceylon and Southern India: there is thus no endemic factor. If all the Papuasian species are brought together, we find that, excluding the Philippines, we have nine species, of which four are endemic in the area: if the Philippines be added, we have 14 species, of which nine are endemic—a fairly definite indication of the advisability of treating all these south-eastern subareas, within which the genus is rather poorly represented, as portions of Papuasia. The endemic factor for Papuasia, of $\frac{9}{14}$, or 64·3, exceeds that for China as a whole, but is considerably lower than that for Central and Eastern China. It is noteworthy that, so far, the widespread *D. torta* has not been reported from any of the islands of the Sunda group to the east of the Wallace line; the only species so far reported from these islands is *D. ferruginea*, which occurs in Timor.

Malaya Proper, south of Indo-China and west of the Wallace line, is naturally divided into the four subareas of Borneo, the Malay Peninsula, Sumatra, and Java. In Borneo we find 13 species, of which five are endemic. These are *D. falcata, D. Beccarii, D. Havilandi, D. Hoseana*, and *D. borneënsis*, so that the endemic factor is $\frac{5}{13}$, or 38·4. Of the remaining eight, one is the widespread *D. torta;* the others, distributed beyond Malayan limits, are *D. discolor*, which goes to Celebes and the Philippines; *D. parviflora*, which is distributed throughout Malaya and passes east as far as the Moluccas and the Philippines; *D. rostrata*, which goes east to Celebes and west to Ceylon and Southern India; *D. tamarindifolia* and *D. velutina*, both occurring elsewhere in Malaya and extending to Indo-China, the former also reaching the Philippines, South-Western China and the Himalaya; the remaining two Bornean species—*D. phyllanthoides* and *D. Scortechinii*—are confined to Malaya. In the Malay Peninsula we find 13 species, of which three are endemic. These are *D. Hullettii, D. menoeides*, and *D. Kunstleri.* The endemic factor is here therefore $\frac{3}{13}$, or 23. Common to the Malay Peninsula and Sumatra, but not extending elsewhere, we have only two species—*D. Curtisii* and *D. stercoracea.* On the other hand, common to the Peninsula and to Borneo, but not in Sumatra, we have *D. phyllanthoides;* and common to the Malay Peninsula, Java, and Borneo, but not hitherto reported from Sumatra, we have *D. Scortechinii;* this species, though not yet collected in Sumatra, is present in Bangka. The rest of the Peninsular species are of wider distribution. They include *D. velutina,* which goes to Borneo on the one hand and extends to Indo-China on the other, existing not only in Tenasserim, but recurring in Sylhet; *D. tamarindifolia,* which is met with in every part of Malaya Proper, and occurs throughout Indo-China as well as in the Himalaya, South-Western China, and the Philippines; *D. rostrata,* which extends eastward to Celebes, and westward to Southern India; *D. parviflora,* which is everywhere in Malaya and goes east to the Philippines and the Moluccas; *D. latifolia,* Indian, but appearing in the Andamans; finally, the widespread *D. torta.* Sumatra has but six species of *Dalbergia,* and of these only one is subendemic; this is *D. Forbesii,* which, however, occurs also in Lingga. The remaining species are *D. Junghuhnii,* which recurs only in Java; *D. stereoracea* and *D. Curtisii,* which recur only in the Malay Peninsula; *D. parviflora,* which is widespread in Malaya, and extends to the Philippines and the Moluccas; *D. tamarindifolia,* throughout Malaya, Indo-China, the Himalayas, South-Western China, and the Philippines; lastly, the generally-distributed *D. torta.* It is to be observed that *D. rostrata,* which might be expected to occur in Sumatra, has not hitherto been reported from that island. Java, though as rich in species as Sumatra—it must be recollected, however, that Sumatra is not so well explored as Java—has no endemic species. The six Dalbergias present are: *D. Junghuhnii,* which goes to Sumatra only; *D. Scortechinii,* which goes to the Malay Peninsula and to Borneo; *D. parviflora,* which extends to the rest of Malaya and recurs in Celebes, the Philippines, and the Moluccas; *D. tamarindifolia,* which is found everywhere in Malaya, Indo-China, the Eastern Himalaya, South-Western China, and the Philippines; *D. rostrata,* which extends from Celebes to Southern India; and a species that is here referred to *D. sissoides,* but which may be a form of *D. latifolia:* in either case it extends to India. Here it is to be observed that *D. torta,* so widely spread throughout South-Eastern Asia, has not yet been recorded from the coasts of Java. The only other coasts of which the same is true are those of Coromandel and the Eastern Sunda Islands.

If the four Malayan subareas be treated conjointly, we find that there are 22 species, of which 14 are endemic. The endemic factor thus is $\frac{14}{22}$, or 63·6—a figure somewhat lower than the corresponding one for Papuasia, and not much higher than that for China as a whole.

Turning, again, to the divisions of India, we find that in Malabaria there are 14 species, four of which are endemic. These are *D. Gardneriana, D. rubiginosa, D. acaciaefolia, D. malabarica.* The endemic factor is thus $\frac{4}{14}$, or 28·5. Of the distributed species, one (*D. melanoxylon*) is a widely-spread African species, which is frequently planted in India, but appears to be wild in Canara and the Concan. Of the remaining nine, five occur in Coromandelia. Those that do not appear there are—*D. congesta,* which recurs in Western Indo-China; *D. sissoides,* which recurs in Java; *D. rostrata,* which is present in Ceylon and spreads from Java to Celebes; and *D. torta.* Of the five which Malabaria shares with Coromandelia, one species (*D. multiflora*) is peculiar to the conjoint area and another (*D. lanceolaria*) is nearly so, as it crosses the region of India Deserta to the lower Western Himalayan slopes only; it is also present in Ceylon. *D. latifolia* recurs in the Andamans and the Malay Peninsula, and is more widely distributed under the Himalaya than *D. lanceolaria*; it does not go to Ceylon. *D. paniculata* recurs in Central and Eastern Indo-China; *D. volubilis* occurs throughout the Himalaya, and is equally widespread in Indo-China.

In Coromandelia there is but one endemic species—*D. coromandeliana*, so that the endemic factor is $\frac{1}{6}$, or 16·6. Of the others, four have been mentioned in detail under Malabaria; the fifth (*D. spinosa*) is common in the Sundribuns at the head of the Bay of Bengal, occurs on Indo-Chinese coasts, and is reported from those of the Philippines. The degree of isolation for Malabaria is low, being little above that for the Malay Peninsula, which does not stand apart from the rest of Malaya; that for Coromandelia is still lower, and the two areas must therefore be taken conjointly. When thus united, the endemic factor for Peninsular India, including Ceylon and the Indian deserts, is only $\frac{6}{17}$, or 35·3—not much higher than the factors for the Philippines and rather lower than that for Borneo.

When the Himalayan and Sub-Himalayan area is considered, we find eleven species with only one (*D. sericea*) absolutely limited to the region. The existence of *D. sericea* is not, however, the full measure of evidence that this Himalayan tract is really a natural area, for *D. Sissoo* is almost as characteristic of the region as *D. sericea*, since it is even more widespread throughout the tract and only overflows westward into the Indian Desert region. However, it seems hardly worth while to recognise as a subarea apart, *for this genus*, a region with an endemic factor of $\frac{1}{11}$, or only 9; the question is, what is the most convenient and least unnatural measure to adopt? The distribution of the remaining species is: *D. lanceolaria*, to India and Ceylon only; *D. latifolia*, throughout India and to the Andamans and the Malay Peninsula; *D. volubilis*, to India and Indo-China equally; *D. rimosa*, to Western Indo-China, South-Western China, and Tongking; *D. confertiflora*, to Western and Central Indo-China; *D. stipulacea*, to Western, Central and Eastern Indo China, and to South-Western China; *D. assamica* and *D. mimosoides*, to Western Indo-China and South-Western China; *D. tamarindifolia*, to Western and Central Indo-China and South-West China, passing beyond this to Malaya and the Philippines. Now of those species distributed eastward across the Brahmaputra, all save *D. volubilis* are absent from India, and at the same time are confined to the Eastern Himalaya; while of those found both in the Himalaya and in India, one (*D. lanceolaria*) is confined to the Western Himalaya. The best solution of the difficulty seems to be, therefore, to annex the western half of the Himalaya to India and the eastern half to Western Indo-China. This renders our India practically co-extensive with the area occupied by *D. lanceolaria*, and gives it an endemic factor of $\frac{7}{17}$, or 41.

In Western Indo-China, between the Brahmaputra and the Irrawaday, there are 17 species, of which only two are endemic—*D. Wattii* and *D. Thomsoni*. The endemic factor, $\frac{2}{17}$, or 11·7, thus hardly exceeds that for the Himalaya. The distributed species are—*D. Kingiana*, to South-Western China only; *D. congesta*, to Malabaria only; *D. rimosa*, to the Eastern Himalaya, South-Western China, and Tongking; *D. spinosa*, to the coasts of Coromandel, Tenasserim, and the Philippines; *D. volubilis*, throughout India, the Himalaya, and Central Indo-China; *D. mimosoides* and *D. assamica*, to the Eastern Himalaya and South-Western China; *D. stipulacea*, *D. confertiflora*, and *D. tamarindifolia*, both to the Eastern Himalaya and to Central Indo-China, the first of these occurring also in South-Western China and Eastern Indo-China, the last of the three extending to South-Western China, the Philippines, and Malaya; *D. reniformis* and *D. velutina*, to Central Indo-China, the latter extending to Malaya; *D. latifolia* throughout India and in the Malay Peninsula; finally, *D. torta*, on almost every coast. If Western Indo-China and the Eastern Himalaya be treated conjointly, we have an area where 19 species, of which 4 are endemic, occur. The factor is thus $\frac{4}{19}$, or 21, indicating a degree of isolation smaller than that of Malabaria or of Borneo. It would appear as if in the conjoint area of Western Indo-China and the Eastern Himalaya we do not have a region that, as regards *Dalbergia*, is truly natural, but that we have rather a region of overflow, where Central Indo-Chinese, South-Western Chinese, and Indian influences meet. How far this is true will be more apparent when the remaining Indo-Chinese districts are considered.

Central Indo-China, the country between the Irrawaday and the Meinam rivers, is, so far as we know, the most important subarea in South-Eastern Asia as regards the number of species of *Dalbergia*. Here we have 21 species—almost as many as in the whole of Malaya, fully as many as in Western Indo-China and the Himalaya together. Only 6 of them, however, are endemic; these are *D. obtusifolia*, *D. cultrata*, *D. glomeriflora*, *D. cana*, *D. Kurzii*, and *D. Collettii*. The endemic factor is thus $\frac{6}{21}$, or 29—a factor much like that for Malabaria. Of the distributed species, *D. Oliveri*, *D. Hemsleyi*, *D. ovata*, *D. foliacea* go only to Eastern Indo-China; *D. fusca* to Eastern Indo China and South-Western China; *D. tamarindifolia* to the Philippines, Malaya, South-Western China, Western Indo-China, and the Himalaya; *D. velutina* to Malaya and to Western Indo-China; *D. parviflora* to Malaya, the Moluccas and the Philippines; *D. reniformis* only to Western Indo-China; *D. confertiflora* to Western Indo-China and the Eastern Himalaya; *D. stipulacea* to Eastern Indo-China, South-Western China, Western Indo-China and the Himalaya; *D. volubilis* to Western Indo-China, the Himalaya, and India; *D. paniculata* to India generally and to Eastern Indo-China; *D. spinosa* to the coasts of Chittagong, the Sundribuns, Coromandel, and the Philippines; *D. torta* nearly to every coast.

Eastern Indo-China, from the Meinam river to the Chinese Sea, but excluding Tongking, has yielded 16 species. No fewer than eight of these—*D. cochinchinensis*, *D. cambodiana*, *D. Pierreana*, *D. mammosa*, *D. Duperreana*, *D. bariensis*, *D. dongnaiensis*, and *D. Godefroyi*—are endemic, so that the endemic factor is $\frac{8}{16}$, or 50. Besides the almost ubiquitous *D. torta*, the distributed species are *D. ovata*, *D. foliacea*, *D. Hemsleyi*, and *D. Oliveri*, which go only to Central Indo-China; *D. fusca*, which goes only to Central Indo-China and to South-Western China; *D. paniculata*, which goes to Central Indo-China and recurs in India; finally *D. stipulacea*, which goes to Central and Western Indo-China, to South-Western China and to the Himalaya. The result of uniting Eastern and Central Indo-China is to give an area with 29 species, of which 18 are endemic, so that the endemic factor is $\frac{18}{29}$, or 62—a figure much like the factors for China as a whole, for Papuasia as a whole, and for Malaya as a whole.

If the conjoined area of the Eastern Himalaya and Western Indo-China be in turn added to the conjoined area of Central and Eastern Indo-China, we get a region where there are 40 species, of which 22 are endemic, so that the endemic factor is $\frac{22}{40}$, or 55. This gives an endemic factor for the whole of Indo-China, lower than the factor for Central and Eastern Indo-China taken conjointly; this suggests that the natural affinity of Western Indo-China is less with the country to the east of the Irrawaday than with the other adjacent regions.

In order to obtain an area with the highest possible endemic factor, it was necessary to separate South-Western China (Yunnan and Western Szechuen) from the rest of China. The result was the isolation of Eastern China, including Central China and Tongking, with an endemic factor of $\frac{8}{11}$, or 72·7. If South-Western China, with its endemic factor of $\frac{3}{13}$, or 23, be united to Indo-China east of the Irrawaday, we obtain a region with an endemic factor of $\frac{22}{38}$, or 57·8. As this is again a smaller factor than that for Central and Eastern Indo-China taken together, we have to recognise that the natural affinity of South-Western China with the region to the east of the Irrawaday is hardly so great as the affinity of South-Western China with the rest of China, the endemic factor for the whole Chinese Empire being nearly 60. If, however, the district of South-Western China, with its endemic factor of 23, be annexed to the area between the Irrawaday and the Ganges with its endemic factor of 21, we obtain a region where there are 26 species, of which 9 are endemic, and the endemic factor thus becomes 34·6. This union, giving an endemic percentage higher than that for either of the component parts, is at least justified by results. When in turn we add to the region between the Irrawaday and the Ganges, India to the south and west of the Gangetic plain, we obtain an area where the endemic factor is $\frac{19}{36}$, or 52·7. But this factor is still far below that for Eastern China, and it is only when the three regions—India proper; the Himalaya with Assam-Arracan and South-Western China; and Indo-China east of the Irrawaday—are taken conjointly that we obtain a region where the endemic factor of $\frac{41}{52}$, or 78·8, somewhat exceeds that for Eastern China.

Similarly, to attain a figure comparable with these factors, it is necessary to unite Malaya and Papuasia, when we get an endemic factor of $\frac{23}{30}$, or 76·6, which is more or less intermediate between the factor for India, the Himalaya, South-Western China and Indo-China taken together, and the factor for Eastern China.

Subjoined is given a conspectus of the facts presented in the foregoing paragraphs, in the form of tables showing (1) the distribution of the species of *Dalbergia* throughout South-Eastern Asia, and (2) the endemic percentages of the various subareas, provinces, and sub-subareas:—

TABLE I.—*Distribution of* Dalbergia *in South-Eastern Asia.*

Species.	I.—Northern.		II.—Central Subarea.										III.—Southern Subarea.											Remarks.
	(i) China.		(ii) Indo-Himalaya.								(iii) Indo-China.		(iv) Malaya.				(v) Papuasia.							
	E. China, including Tongking.	C. China.	S.-W. China.	E. Himalaya.	W. Himalaya.	India Deserta.	Malabaria.	Ceylon.	Coromandelia.	Assam-Arracan.	Shan-Tenasserim.	Siam-Cambodia.	Malay Peninsula.	Sumatra.	Java.	Borneo.	Celebes.	Philippines.	Moluccas.	Micronesia.	New Guinea.	Australia.	Melanasia.	
	I	I	II	II	II	II	II	II	II	II	II	II	III	II	III	III	III	III	III	III	III	III	III	Sub-areas.
	i	i	ii	ii	ii	ii	ii	ii	ii	ii	iii	iii	iv	iv	iv	iv	v	v	v	v	v	v	v	Provinces.
	1	2	3	4	5	6	7	8	9	10	11	12	13	14	15	16	17	18	19	20	21	22	23	Sub-subareas.
1. D. Albertisii ...	...	...	...	...	...	...	...	...	...	...	...	...	...	...	...	...	...	...	...	...	•	...	...	
2. D. Beccarii ...	...	...	...	...	...	...	...	...	...	...	...	...	...	...	...	•	...	...	...	...	...	...	...	
3. D. Cumingiana ...	...	...	...	...	...	...	...	...	...	...	...	...	...	...	...	...	...	•	...	...	...	...	...	
4. D. parviflora ...	...	...	...	...	...	...	...	...	...	...	[•]	...	•	•	•	•	•	•	•	...	...	...	...	4. Probably only planted in Tenasserim.
5. D. spinosa ...	...	...	...	...	...	...	...	...	•	•	•	...	...	...	...	...	...	•	...	...	...	...	...	5. Coasts only.
6. D. discolor ...	...	...	...	...	...	...	...	...	...	...	...	...	...	...	...	•	•	•	...	...	...	...	...	

Species.	I.—Northern.		II.—Central Subarea.										III.—Southern Subarea.											Remarks.
	(i) China.		*(ii) Indo-Himalaya.*								*(iii) Indo-China.*		*(iv) Malaya.*				*(v) Papuasia.*							
	E. China, including Tongking.	C. China.	S.W. China.	E. Himalaya.	W. Himalaya.	India Deserta.	Malabaria.	Ceylon.	Coromandelia.	Assam-Arracan.	Shan-Tenasserim.	Siam-Cambodia.	Malay Peninsula.	Sumatra.	Java.	Borneo.	Celebes.	Philippines.	Moluccas.	Micronesia.	New Guinea.	Australia.	Melanesia.	
	I	I	II	II	II	II	II	II	II	II	II	II	III	III	III	III	III	III	III	III	III	III	III	Subareas.
	i	i	ii	ii	ii	ii	ii	ii	ii	ii	ii	iii	iv	iv	iv	iv	v	v	v	v	v	v	v	Provinces.
	1	2	3	4	5	6	7	8	9	10	11	12	13	14	15	16	17	18	19	20	21	22	23	Sub-subareas.
7. D. rimosa	•	...	•	•	...	...	...	...	...	•	...	...	...	...	...	...	...	...	...	...	...	...	...	
8. D. Forbesii ...	...	...	...	...	...	...	...	...	...	...	...	...	...	•	...	...	...	...	...	...	...	...	...	
9. D. Thomsoni ...	...	...	...	...	...	...	...	...	...	•	...	...	...	...	...	...	...	...	...	...	...	...	...	
10. D. Junghuhnii ...	...	...	...	...	...	...	...	...	...	...	...	...	...	•	•	...	...	...	...	...	...	...	...	
11. D. Scortechinii ...	...	...	...	...	...	...	...	...	...	...	...	...	•	...	•	•	...	...	...	...	...	...	...	
12. D. Curtisii ...	...	...	...	...	...	...	...	...	...	...	...	...	•	•	...	...	...	...	...	...	...	...	...	
13. D. stercoracea ...	...	...	...	...	...	...	...	...	...	...	...	...	•	•	...	...	...	...	...	...	...	...	...	
14. D. Mimosella ...	...	...	...	...	...	...	...	...	...	...	...	...	...	...	...	...	...	•	...	...	...	...	...	
15. D. multiflora ...	...	...	...	...	...	...	•	...	•	...	...	...	...	...	...	...	...	...	...	...	...	...	...	
16. D. phyllanthoides	...	...	...	...	...	...	...	...	...	...	...	...	•	...	[•]	•	...	...	...	...	...	...	...	16. Doubtfully wild in Java.
17. D. coromandeliana	...	...	...	...	...	...	...	...	•	...	...	...	...	...	...	...	...	...	...	...	...	...	...	
18. D. melanoxylon ...	...	...	...	...	...	...	•	...	...	...	...	...	...	...	...	...	...	...	...	...	...	...	...	18. Widespread in Africa.
19. D. Millettii ...	•	...	...	...	...	...	...	...	...	...	...	...	...	...	...	...	...	...	...	...	...	...	...	
20. D. stenophylla ...	...	•	...	...	...	...	...	...	...	...	...	...	...	...	...	...	...	...	...	...	...	...	...	
21. D. mimosoides ...	...	...	•	•	...	...	...	...	...	•	...	...	...	...	...	...	...	...	...	...	...	...	...	
22. D. Hancei ...	•	...	...	...	...	...	...	...	...	...	...	...	...	...	...	...	...	...	...	...	...	...	...	
23. D. Dyeriana ...	...	•	•	...	...	...	...	...	...	...	...	...	...	...	...	...	...	...	...	...	...	...	...	
24. D. confertiflora ...	...	...	...	•	...	...	...	...	...	•	•	...	...	...	...	...	...	...	...	...	...	...	...	
25. D. yunnanensis ...	...	...	•	...	...	...	...	...	...	...	...	...	...	...	...	...	...	...	...	...	...	...	...	
26. D. Collettii ...	...	...	...	...	...	...	...	...	...	...	•	...	...	...	...	...	...	...	...	...	...	...	...	
27. D. foliacea ...	...	...	...	...	...	...	...	...	...	...	•	•	...	...	...	...	...	...	...	...	...	...	...	
28. D. cultrata ...	...	...	...	...	...	...	...	...	...	...	•	...	...	...	...	...	...	...	...	...	...	...	...	
29. D. fusca	...	...	•	...	...	...	...	...	...	...	•	•	...	...	...	...	...	...	...	...	...	...	...	
30. D. Sissoo	...	...	...	•	•	•	[•]	...	...	...	...	...	...	...	...	...	...	...	...	...	...	...	...	30. Doubtfully wild in Coorg.
31. D. Hullettii ...	...	...	...	...	...	...	...	...	...	...	...	...	•	...	...	...	...	...	...	...	...	...	...	
32. D. Havilandi ...	...	...	...	...	...	...	...	...	...	...	...	...	...	...	...	•	...	...	...	...	...	...	...	
33. D. rostrata ...	...	...	...	...	...	...	•	•	...	...	...	...	•	...	•	•	•	...	...	...	...	...	...	
34. D. Kingiana ...	...	...	•	...	...	...	...	...	...	•	...	...	...	...	...	...	...	...	...	...	...	...	...	
35. D. Henryana ...	...	...	•	...	...	...	...	...	...	...	...	...	...	...	...	...	...	...	...	...	...	...	...	
36. D. Benthami ...	•	...	...	...	...	...	...	...	...	...	...	...	...	...	...	...	...	...	...	...	...	...	...	
37. D. rubiginosa ...	...	...	...	...	...	...	•	...	...	...	...	...	...	...	...	...	...	...	...	...	...	...	...	
38. D. menoeides ...	...	...	...	...	...	...	...	...	...	...	...	...	•	...	...	...	...	...	...	...	...	...	...	
39. D. torta	•	...	...	...	...	...	•	•	...	•	•	•	•	•	...	•	•	•	•	•	•	•	•	39. Coasts only.
40. D. congesta ...	...	...	...	...	...	...	•	...	...	•	...	...	...	...	...	...	...	...	...	...	...	...	...	
41. D. Gardneriana ...	...	...	...	...	...	...	•	...	...	...	...	...	...	...	...	...	...	...	...	...	...	...	...	
42. D. Hoseana ...	...	...	...	...	...	...	...	...	...	...	...	...	...	...	...	•	...	...	...	...	...	...	...	
43. D. malabarica ...	...	...	...	...	...	...	•	...	...	...	...	...	...	...	...	...	...	...	...	...	...	...	...	
44. D. acaciaefolia ...	...	...	...	...	...	...	•	...	...	...	...	...	...	...	...	...	...	...	...	...	...	...	...	
45. D. tamarindifolia	...	...	•	•	...	...	...	...	...	•	•	...	•	•	•	•	...	•	...	...	...	...	...	
46. D. polyphylla ...	...	...	...	...	...	...	...	...	...	...	...	...	...	...	...	...	...	•	...	...	...	...	...	

Species.	I.—Northern. (i) China. E. China, including Tongking.	C. China.	II.—Central Subarea. (ii) Indo-Himalaya. S.-W. China.	E. Himalaya.	W. Himalaya.	India Deserta.	Malabaria.	Ceylon.	Coromandelia.	Assam-Arracan.	(iii) Indo-China. Shan-Tenasserim.	Siam-Cambodia.	III.—Southern Subarea. (iv) Malaya. Malaya Peninsula.	Sumatra.	Java.	Borneo.	(v) Papuasia. Celebes.	Philippines.	Moluccas.	Micronesia.	New Guinea.	Australia.	Melanesia.	Remarks.
	I	I	I	II	II	II	II	II	II	II	II	II	III	III	III	III	III	III	III	III	III	III	III	Subareas.
	i	i	ii	ii	ii	ii	ii	ii	ii	ii	iii	iii	iv	iv	iv	iv	v	v	v	v	v	v	v	Provinces.
	1	2	3	4	5	6	7	8	9	10	11	12	13	14	15	16	17	18	19	20	21	22	23	Sub-subareas.
47. D. Jaherii	...	...	...	...	...	...	...	...	...	...	...	...	...	...	...	...	...	...	•	...	...	...	...	
48. D. burmanica	...	...	•	...	...	...	...	...	...	•	•	...	...	...	...	...	...	...	...	...	...	...	...	
49. D. Pierreana ...	...	...	...	...	...	...	...	...	...	...	...	•	...	...	...	...	...	...	...	...	...	...	...	
50. D. densa	...	...	...	...	...	...	...	...	...	...	...	...	...	...	...	...	...	...	•	...	•	•	...	
51. D. velutina	...	...	...	...	...	...	...	...	...	•	•	...	•	...	...	•	...	...	...	...	...	...	...	
52. D. bornëensis ...	...	...	...	...	...	...	...	...	...	...	...	...	...	...	...	•	...	...	...	...	...	...	...	
53. D. obtusifolia ...	...	...	[*	...	...	...	...	...	...	...	•	...	...	...	...	...	...	...	...	...	...	...	...	53. China, only Taping Valley, S.-W. Yunnan.
54. D. ovata	...	...	...	...	...	...	...	...	...	...	•	•	...	...	...	...	...	...	...	...	...	...	...	
55. D. tonkinensis ...	•	...	...	...	...	...	...	...	...	...	...	...	...	...	...	...	...	...	...	...	...	...	...	
56. D. cambodiana ...	...	...	...	...	...	...	...	...	...	...	...	•	...	...	...	...	...	...	...	...	...	...	...	
57. D. glomeriflora ...	...	...	...	...	...	...	...	...	...	...	•	...	...	...	...	...	...	...	...	...	...	...	...	
58. D. latifolia	...	...	...	•	[*]	•	•	...	•	•	...	...	•	...	...	...	...	...	...	...	...	...	...	58. W. Himalaya planted only.
59. D. sissoides	...	...	...	...	...	...	•	...	...	...	...	...	...	...	•	...	...	...	...	...	...	...	...	
60. D. cochinchinensis ...	..	...	...	...	...	...	...	...	...	...	...	•	...	...	...	...	...	...	...	...	...	...	...	
61. D. polyadelpha ...	...	...	•	...	...	...	...	...	...	...	...	...	...	...	...	...	...	...	...	...	...	...	...	
62. D. sericea	...	...	...	•	•	...	...	...	...	...	...	...	...	...	...	...	...	...	...	...	...	...	...	
63. D. sacerdotum ...	•	...	...	...	...	...	...	...	...	...	...	...	...	...	...	...	...	...	...	...	...	...	...	
64. D. paniculata ...	...	...	...	...	...	...	•	...	•	...	•	•	...	...	...	...	...	...	...	...	...	...	...	
65. D. hupeana	•	•	...	...	...	...	...	...	...	...	...	...	...	...	...	...	...	...	...	...	...	...	...	
66. D. assamica	...	...	•	•	...	...	...	...	...	•	...	...	...	...	...	...	...	...	...	...	...	...	...	
67. D. Balansae	•	•	...	...	...	...	...	...	...	...	...	...	...	...	...	...	...	...	...	...	...	...	...	
68. D. Minahassae ...	...	...	...	...	...	...	...	...	...	...	...	...	...	...	...	...	•	•	...	...	...	...	...	
69. D. Oliveri	...	...	...	...	...	...	...	...	...	...	•	•	...	...	...	...	...	...	...	...	...	...	...	
70. D. lanceolaria ...	...	...	...	...	•	•	•	•	•	...	...	...	...	...	...	...	...	...	...	...	...	...	...	
71. D. Hemsleyi ...	...	...	...	...	...	...	...	...	...	...	•	•	...	...	...	...	...	...	...	...	...	...	...	
72. D. szemaoensis ...	...	...	•	...	...	...	...	...	...	...	...	...	...	...	...	...	...	...	...	...	...	...	...	
73. D. Wattii	...	...	...	...	...	...	...	...	...	•	...	...	...	...	...	...	...	...	...	...	...	...	...	
74. D. mammosa... ...	...	...	...	...	...	...	...	...	...	...	...	•	...	...	...	...	...	...	...	...	...	...	...	
75. D. Duperreana ...	...	...	...	...	...	...	...	...	...	...	...	•	...	...	...	...	...	...	...	...	...	...	...	
76. D. bariensis	...	...	...	...	...	...	...	...	...	...	...	•	...	...	...	...	...	...	...	...	...	...	...	
77. D. dongnaiensis ...	...	...	...	...	...	...	...	...	...	...	...	•	...	...	...	...	...	...	...	...	...	...	...	
78. D. Kurzii	...	...	...	...	...	...	...	...	...	...	•	...	...	...	...	...	...	...	...	...	...	...	...	
79. D. cana	...	...	...	...	...	...	...	...	...	...	•	...	...	...	...	...	...	...	...	...	...	...	...	
80. D. volubilis	...	...	...	•	•	...	•	...	•	•	•	...	...	...	...	...	...	...	...	...	...	...	...	
81. D. ferruginea ...	...	...	...	...	...	...	...	...	...	...	...	...	...	...	...	[*]	•	•	•	•	•	...	...	81. Borneo, only in Bangi Island.
82. D. stipulacea ...	...	...	•	•	...	...	...	...	...	•	•	•	...	...	...	...	...	...	...	...	...	...	...	
83. D. Godefroyi ...	...	...	...	...	...	...	...	...	...	...	...	•	...	...	...	...	...	...	...	...	...	...	...	
84. D. falcata	...	...	...	...	...	...	...	...	...	...	...	...	...	...	...	•	...	...	...	...	...	...	...	
85. D. Kunstleri ...	...	...	...	...	...	...	...	...	...	...	...	...	•	...	...	...	...	...	...	...	...	...	...	
86. D. reniformis ...	...	...	...	...	...	...	...	...	...	•	•	...	...	...	...	...	...	...	...	...	...	...	..	

Table II.—*Endemic factors for* Dalbergia *in the various subareas, provinces, and sub-subareas of South-Eastern Asia.*

Subareas.	Provinces.	Sub-subareas.			
I.—Northern ...	(i) E. China ...	E. China, including Tongking	0 sp.; F.=55·3	11 sp.; F.=72·7	11 sp.; F.=72·7
		C. China	4 sp.; F.=25		
I.—Central ...	(ii) Indo-Himalayan.	S.-W. China	13 sp.; F.=23	36 sp.; F.=52·7	
		E. Himalaya	10 sp; F.= 0		
		W. Himalaya	3 sp.; F.= 0		
		India Deserta	3 sp.; F.= 0		
		Malabaria	14 sp.; F.=28·5		
		Ceylon	3 sp.; F.= 0		
		Coromandelia	6 sp.; F.=16·6		52 sp.; F.=79·8
		W. Indo-China (Assam-Arracan)	17 sp.; F.=11·7		
	(iii) Indo-China.	C. Indo-China (Shan-Tenasserim).	21 sp.; F.=30	29 sp.; F.= 62	
		E. Indo-China (Siam-Anam)	16 sp.; F.=50		
III.—Southern	(iv) Malaya ...	Malay Peninsula	13 sp.; F.=23	22 sp.; F.=63·6	
		Sumatra	6 sp.; F.=16·6		
		Java	6 sp.; F.= 0		
		Borneo	13 sp.; F.=38·4		
	(v) Papuasia	Celebes	6 sp.; F.= 0	14 sp.; F.=64·3	
		Philippines	10 sp.; F.=30		
		Moluccas	5 sp.; F.=20		
		Micronesia	2 sp.; F.= 0		
		New Guinea	4 sp.; F.=25		
		Australia	2 sp.; F.= 0		
		Melanesia	1 sp.; F.= 0		

In Plate 2 and Plate 3, which illustrate this chapter, an attempt has been made to represent graphically the facts expressed in the preceding tables. In these plates the sub-subareas (Plate 2), provinces (Plate 3A), and subareas (Plate 3B) are indicated by circles the areas of which are in proportion to the number of species hitherto collected within each. Sub-subareas within which no endemic species has been found are enclosed in single, the others in double lines. The distribution of individual species is indicated in the series of small maps which occupy Plate 4.

When the distribution of *Dalbergia* by natural sections is examined, it is found that § *Triptolemea* is only represented in China by a single subendemic group of three species, the ¶ *Mimosoides*, and by *D. rimosa* of the ¶ *Rimosae*. India too has few species of this section; one of them a coast plant (*D. spinosa*), and three others—two of them, however, endemic,—all of them ¶ *Phyllanthoides*. Indo-China is still more poorly endowed; east of the Irrawaday we find only the same coast species (*D. spinosa*); west of that river occur *D. spinosa*, one of the Chinese group (¶ *Mimosoides*), and two other species, both of them ¶ *Rimosae*. Malaya has but one representative of the Indian group ¶ *Phyllanthoides;* the species is, however, an endemic one; there are, besides, five endemic ¶ *Rimosae*, of which group therefore Malaya is clearly the head-quarters. Two other species—*D. discolor* and *D. parviflora*—Malaya shares with Papuasia; another species (*D. Beccarii*) is endemic. Papuasia, besides the two species just mentioned, has three endemic ones—*D. Albertisii*, *D. Cumingiana* and *D. Mimosella*. Malaya has thus nearly twice as many *Triptolemeae* as any other province. When, however, we consider § *Podiopetalum*, we find that neither Malaya nor Papuasia possesses any species; that India has only one (*D. Sissoo*); that China has three; and Indo-China has four. In this section the species are in every case endemic.

The section § *Endespermum* is in every respect the most widely spread of all the sections, for it has one species (*D. torta*) which occurs in every province, and is present in all but two of the sub-subareas that have a sea-coast. Another species extends to four of the five provinces; this is *D. tamarindifolia*, universal in Indo-China and Malaya and extending to the Philippines, to South-West China, and as far as the Central Himalaya. A third extends to three of the five provinces; this is *D. rostrata*, almost universal in Malaya and extending to Ceylon and Southern India on the one side, to Celebes on the other. Examined by provinces, Eastern China has two, one of them endemic; Indo-China east of the Irrawaday has four, one of them endemic; India proper has seven, four of them endemic; South-Western China, Indo-China west of the Irrawaday and the Himalaya have between them six, two of these being endemic; Malaya has seven, four of them endemic; Papuasia has six, three of them endemic. The section § *Miscolobium* is chiefly Indo-Chinese—six species, with four of them endemic; Malaya has three, but only one endemic; Eastern China has one, which is endemic; South-Western China has also one, which is endemic; India has two, but neither of them are endemic; Papuasia has no *Miscolobium*. Of species of the section § *Dalbergaria*, however, Papuasia, though it has but two, has both endemic; Malaya is in the same position; China has six, four of them endemic; India has four, but only one of them is endemic; Indo-China west of the Irrawaday, with the Himalaya, has five, of which two are endemic. The focus of this section lies in Indo-China to the east of the Irrawaday, where thirteen *Dalbergariae* (nine of them endemic) are to be met with. The facts are shown more compactly in the subjoined table :—

TABLE III.—*Distribution of the various sections of* Dalbergia *in South-Eastern Asia.*

Subgenus.	Section.	Northern Area.		Central Area.						Southern Area.			
		E. China.		C. & E. Indo-China.		S.-W. China, W. Indo-China, E. Himalaya.		India.		Malaya.		Papuasia.	
		Number of species.	Endemic factor.	Number of species.	Endemic factor.	Number of species.	Endemic factor.	Number of species.	Endemic factor.	Number of species.	Endemic factor.	Number of species.	Endemic factor.
Sissoa ...	Triptolemea ...	3	66	1	0	4	50	4	50	9	77·7	5	60
	Podiopetalum	2	50	5	60	5	20	1	100	...	...	...	...
Amerimnon.	Endespermum	2	50	4	25	6	33	7	57·1	7	57	6	50
	Miscolobium	1	100	6	83	2	0	2	0	3	33·3	...	...
	Dalbergaria ...	3	100	13	69	6	50	4	25	2	100	2	100

When the distribution of individual species is considered, it will be seen, from the maps on PLATE 4, that they may be readily divided into a large class of localised species and a smaller class of comparatively widely distributed species. In § *Triptolemea*, as the small maps show, we have 14 of the former class as against 7 of the latter. These maps, moreover, show that if we except the littoral species, *D. spinosa*, which occurs on both sides and at the head of the Bay of Bengal and is again reported from the Philippines, all the *Triptolemeae* of Asia may be arranged in two groups—a northern, including *D. Thomsoni*, *D. rimosa*, *D. Cumingiana*, *D. Millettii*, *D. mimosoides*, and *D. stenophylla*, extending in a narrow belt from the Eastern Himalaya, across North-West Indo-China and Southern

China to the Philippines, with a southern group, which extends from Western and Southern India to Malaya and Papuasia, leaving a wide belt in Northern India and Central and Southern Indo-China without any representative of the section. The section § *Podiopetalum*, on the other hand, more or less occupies this intermediate space, overlapping, it is true, the area belonging to the northern group of *Triptolemeae*, but leaving the area occupied by the southern group quite free. The two most western *Podiopetala* (*D. Sissoo* and *D. confertiflora*) are rather widely spread; the remainder are mostly quite localised.

In the section § *Endespermum*, which is not quite so large as *Triptolemea* or as *Dalbergaria*, we have the same wide diffusion on the part of some of the species, notably on that of *D. torta*, which occurs on every shore except, apparently, those of Coromandel and of Java; of *D. rostrata*, which extends from Southern India throughout Malaya to Papuasia; of *D. densa*, which extends from the Moluccas to Australia; and of *D. tamarindifolia*, which is found throughout Malaya, Indo-China, and the Philippines, and extends to South-Western China and the Central Himalaya. Another species, *D. congesta*, has a remarkably dissociated distribution—not, however, a unique feature, since *D. paniculata* among the *Dalbergariae* exhibits the same peculiarity. The more localised species show the tendency to group themselves in a northern and a southern series of forms that we have already met with in *Triptolemea*; Northern India and, save for the presence of *D. tamarindifolia*, Central Indo-China being remarkably free from forms of this section.

The Asiatic *Miscolobia*, very like the Asiatic *Podiopetala*, occupy mainly the middle region which the *Triptolemeae* entirely and the *Endesperma* so largely avoid. With the exception of *D. borneënsis* and *D. polyadelpha*, the species of the section § *Miscolobium*, though rarely widely distributed, are not very narrowly circumscribed. None of the *Miscolobia* extend to Papuasia.

The section § *Dalbergaria*, which may also be divided into a class of localised and a class of widely-diffused species, shows no tendency to segregation into a northern and a southern group, but is fairly uniformly distributed throughout South-Eastern Asia. The widespread species are not, however, quite so numerous as compared with the localised ones, as was the case with *Endespermum* or *Triptolemea*; the most diffused being *D. ferruginea*, which fills Papuasia without, however, touching Australia or Melanesia; *D. lanceolaria*, which is spread throughout India; *D. stipulacea*, which is spread throughout Indo-China; and *D. volubilis*, which practically occupies the whole area filled by the two preceding species. *D. paniculata* has the same dissociated distribution as *D. congesta*. The localised species are chiefly Indo-Chinese and Chinese.

II.—CONSPECTUS SYSTEMATICUS.

DALBERGIA LINN. F.

Arbores fruticesve, erectae vel alte scandentes. *Folia* alterna, imparipinnata vel rarissime 1-foliolata, stipulis saepius caducis; foliolis alternis, stipellis 0. *Flores* parvi vel minimi, saepius numerosi, in cymas dichotomas vel in paniculas subcymosas axillares vel terminales dispositi, bracteis saepissime minimis subpersistentibus, bracteolis saepius minutis caducis rarius persistentibus. *Calyx* campanulatus, dentibus ad normam 5, 2 superioribus latioribus, infimo saepius ceteris longiore. *Corolla* purpurea, violacea, viridiflora, vel alba; vexillo ovato vel orbiculato, saepe emarginato, erecto vel reflexo vel refracto; alis oblongis basi cuneatis vel hastatis; carinae obtusae petalis dorso apice angulato vel rotundato connatis. *Stamina* in vaginam latere superiore fissam omnia connata vel vexillare rarissime soluto vel saepe omnino deficiente, vel vagina etiam latere inferiore fissa in phalanges 2 laterales disposita; antheribus parvis, erectis, didymis, loculis dorso appositis apice breviter vel rarius longitudinaliter dehiscentibus. *Ovarium* stipitatum, pauciovulatum; stylo incurvo brevi vel brevissimo crasso, vel tenui cylindrico vel subulato; stigmate parvo terminali. *Fructus* indehiscens, saepissime lomentum samaroideum praeter aream seminiferam tenue, oblongum ovatum vel lineare, nonnunquam omnino incrassatum orbiculare vel falcato-reniforme; saepius medio 1-spermum vel remote oligospermum et saepissime ad semina plus minus reticulatum. *Semina* plano-compressa, reniformia; radicula inflexa.

Species ad 100—120, in America, Africa et Asia tropica frequentes; species 2—3 in Australia et Polynesia.

SUBGENUS I. **SISSOA**.—*Vexilli lamina erecta; alae basi cuneatae rarius truncatae, rarissime subhastatae; carinae petalis cuneatis vel hastatis; stylo crasso, cylindrico, saepius brevissimo; staminibus ad normam monadelphis.*

§ 1. **Triptolemea.**—Flores minuti, saepius minutissimi; bracteolis infra calycem saepius persistentibus vel subpersistentibus; inflorescentia saepe dichotome cymosa; petalis omnibus ungue brevibus; stylo semper brevissimo.

§ 2. **Podiopetalum.**—Flores parvi, nonnunquam minuti, bracteolis infra calycem deciduis vel caducis; inflorescentia cymosim paniculata; petalis omnibus ungue longioribus; stylo crasso cylindrico, rarissime perbrevi.

SUBGENUS II. **AMERIMNON**.—*Vexilli lamina reflexa vel refracta; alae basi hastatae vel sagittatae; carinae petalis hastatis; stylo elongato tenui.*

§ 3. **Endespermum.**—Vexillum plus minus refractum; petalis omnibus ungue angustatis; staminibus ad normam monadelphis; stylo subulato.

§ 4. **Miscolobium.**—Vexillum reflexum vix tamen refractum; petalis ungue vexillo cuneato excepto angustatis; staminibus ad normam monadelphis; stylo subulato vel cylindrico.

§ 5. **Dalbergaria.**—Vexillum reflexum vix tamen refractum; petalis ungue vexillo cuneato excepto angustatis; staminibus ad normam isodiadelphis; stylo cylindrico vel subulato.

CONSPECTUS SPECIERUM ASIATICARUM.

§ 1. TRIPTOLEMEA.

¶ 1. **Nummularieae.**—*Legumen orbiculatum omnino incrassatum parum marginatum; frutices scandentes.*

Foliolis majusculis, acutis, 2-pollicaribus vel majoribus; floribus in paniculas terminales dichotome cymosas dispositis . . . . 1. *D. Albertisii.*
Foliolis parvis, obtusis, semipollicaribus vel minoribus; floribus in cymas parvas axillares dispositis . . . . 2. *D. Beccarii.*

¶ 2. **Parviflorae.**—*Legumen falcato-subreniforme omnino incrassatum; frutices scandentes.*

Floribus in paniculas terminales dichotome cymosas dispositis; foliolis versus apicem retusum angustatis:—
Foliolis subtus adpresse pubescentibus . . . . 3. *D. Cumingiana.*
Foliolis subtus glaberrimis . . . . 4. *D. parviflora.*
Floribus in racemos subcymosos axillares dispositis; foliolis apice late rotundatis . . . . 5. *D. spinosa.*

¶ 3. **Discolor.**—*Legumen samaroideum; floribus in paniculas terminales dichotome cymosas dispositis; arbor erecta.*

Foliolis majusculis, ultima ultra 2-pollicari, subtus pubescentibus . 6. *D. discolor.*

¶ 4. **Rimosae.**—*Legumen samaroideum; floribus in paniculas terminales vel etiam nonnunquam in axillis superioribus sitas dichotome cymosas dispositis, minutissimis; bracteolis infra calycem persistentibus vel subpersistentibus; frutices scandentes.*

Leguminibus plus minus oblongis, si subcultratis (*D. Thomsoni*), omnino subcoriaceis:—
Foliolis magnis, ultima ultra 2—3-pollicari:—
Foliolis obtusis vel acutis, subtus puberulis; legumine ad semina rugoso . . . . 7. *D. rimosa.*
Foliolis abrupte acuminatis, subtus glabris; legumine ad semina plano . . . . 8. *D. Forbesii.*
Foliolis minoribus vel parvis, nunquam ultra 2-pollicaribus:—
Foliolis subtus glabris:—
Foliolis 9—11, ovato-oblongis, ultima ceteris majore . . 9. *D. Thomsoni.*
Foliolis 11—15, elliptico-oblongis, omnibus subaequalibus 10. *D. Junghuhnii.*
Foliolis subtus plus minus puberulis vel pubescentibus:—
Foliolis 11—15; leguminibus anguste oblongis, rigidis . 11. *D. Scortechinii.*
Foliolis 7—9; leguminibus late oblongis, tenuiter coriaceis:—
Floribus blandis; foliolis fere 2-pollicaribus . . . 12. *D. Curtisii.*
Floribus stercoraceis; foliolis minoribus . . . . 13. *D. stercoracea.*
Leguminibus rotundatis, subcultratis, medio prominulis, margine submembranaceis; foliolis 7 vel pluribus: *species sede parum incerta* . . . . 14. *D. Mimosella.*

¶ 5. Phyllanthoides.—*Legumen samaroideum; floribus in paniculas axillares cymosas dispositis, minutis; bracteolis infra calycem deciduis; frutices scandentes.*

Leguminibus pubescentibus, late-ovatis; caule armato, ramulis inermibus . . . . 15. *D. multiflora.*

Leguminibus glabris:—

Ramulis inermibus; leguminibus late-ovatis . . . . 16. *D. phyllanthoides.*

Ramulis spinosis; leguminibus auguste-ovatis:—

Foliis fasciculatis cymisque secus ramulos spinescentes dispositis . . . . 17. *D. coromandeliana.*

Foliis sparsis cymisque axillaribus sæpius ramulis spinoscentibus distinctis . . . . 18. *D. melanoxylon.*

¶ 6. Mimosoides.—*Legumen samaroideum; floribus in racemos axillares dispositis, parvulis; bracteolis infra calycem deciduis; alis subhastatis; frutices scandentes.*

Foliolis subtus glabris; paniculis axillaribus congestis; leguminibus oblongis . . . . 19. *D. Millettii.*

Foliolis subtus pubescentibus; paniculis axillaribus evolutis:—

Leguminibus anguste oblongis; foliolis tandem, nervo mediano excepto, subtus glabris . . . . 20. *D. stenophylla.*

Leguminibus oblongis; foliolis subtus adpresse puberulis . . 21. *D. mimosoides.*

§ 2 PODIOPETALUM.

¶ 7. Foliaceae.—*Legumen samaroidum; foliolis obtusis; alis basi cuneatis; carinae petalis latere superiore basi hastatis; stylo cylindrico crassiore; bracteolis infra calycem obtusis brevibus; frutices scandentes.*

Floribus in paniculas axillares dispositis:—

Foliolis nunquam longitudine pollicaribus . . . . 22. *D. Hancei.*

Foliolis longitudine saltem pollicaribus . . . . 23. *D. Dyeriana.*

Floribus in paniculas terminales nonnunquam etiam in axillis superioribus dispositis:—

Leguminibus ad semina planis, ibique parum reticulatis . . 24. *D. confertiflora.*

Leguminibus ad semina rugosis, ibique magnopere reticulatis:—

Paniculis terminalibus atque simul ad axillas summas extensis; foliolis 13 vel pluribus, ultima ceteris haud majore:—

Calycis dentibus omnibus obtusis . . . . 25. *D. yunnanensis.*

Calycis dente inferiore ceteris longiore, acuto . . . 26. *D. Collettii.*

Paniculis omnibus terminalibus; foliolis sæpius 7, nunquam ultra 11, ultima manifeste ceteris majore . 27. *D. foliacea.*

¶ 8. Cultratae.—*Legumen samaroideum, oblongum; foliolis obtusis; floribus in paniculas axillares dispositis; alis basi cuneatis; carina petalis latere superiore basi hastatis; stylo cylindrico crassiore; bracteolis infra calycem subulatis brevibus; arbores elatae.*

Foliolis subtus glaberrimis . . . . 28. *D. cultrata.*

Foliolis subtus adpresse pubescentibus . . . . 29. *D. fusca.*

¶ 9. Sissoo.—*Legumen samaroideum, anguste ligulatum; foliolis acuminatis; alis carinaeque petalis cuneatis; stylo brevissimo, crasso; bracteolis infra calycem obtusis, majusculis, calycem aequantibus; arbor elata.*

Floribus in paniculas axillares dispositis . . . . 30. *D. Sissoo.*

§ 3. ENDESPERMUM.

¶ 10. **Rostratae.**—*Legumen samaroideum, latius ligulatum; foliolis paucis majusculis; bracteolis infra calycem subulatis, brevibus, caducissimis; frutices scandentes vel arbores parvae.*

Ovario stipite excepto glabro . . . . 31. *D. Hullettii.*
Ovario puberulo vel pubescente:—
  Foliolis pubescentibus, obtusis . . . . 32. *D. Havilandi.*
  Foliolis glabris, acuminatis . . . . 33. *D. rostrata.*

¶ 11. **Rubiginosae.**—*Legumen samaroideum, oblongum; foliolis majusculis vel mediocribus, paucis; bracteolis infra calycem obtusis; frutices scandentes vel arbores parvae.*

Foliolis acutis:—
  Foliolis 7—9, subtus tandem fere glabris; ovario glabro . . 34. *D. Kingiana.*
  Foliolis 4—5, subtus pubescentibus; ovario pubescente . . . 35. *D. Henryana.*
Foliolis obtusis:—
  Foliolis 5—7, versus apicem obtusum angustatis . . . 36. *D. Benthami.*
  Foliolis 3—5, apice lato obtusis . . . . 37. *D. rubiginosa.*

¶ 12. **Menoeides.**—*Legumen falcato-subreniforme, omnino incrassatum; foliolis paucis; bracteolis infra calycem obtusis; frutices scandentes.*

Foliolis 3, acutis, majusculis, 3-pollicaribus . . . . 38. *D. menoeides.*
Foliolis 5, rarissime 3 vel 7, obtusis, minoribus, vix 2-pollicaribus 39. *D. torta.*

¶ 13. **Congestae.**—*Legumen samaroideum, ovatum; foliolis mediocribus vel minoribus, paucis vel numerosis; frutices scandentes.*

Foliolis basi cuneatis, apice rotusis . . . . 40. *D. congesta.*
Foliolis basi apiceque rotundatis:—
  Foliolis 7—13:—
    Cymis congestis; foliolis 7—11 . . . . 41. *D. Gardneriana.*
    Cymis laxis; foliolis 9—13 . . . . 42. *D. Hoscana.*
  Foliolis 21—31 . . . . 43. *D. malabarica.*

¶ 14. **Polyphyllae.**—*Legumen samaroideum, angustius ligulatum; foliolis parvis rarius mediocribus, saepissime numerosis; frutices scandentes, rarius arbores parvae.*

Foliolis basi distincte obliquis, latere superiore rhombeis, inferiore cuneatis:—
  Foliolis subtus glaucescentibus; leguminibus rigide coriaceis . . . . 44. *D. acaciaefolia.*
  Foliolis subtus viridibus; leguminibus tenuiter coriaceis . 45. *D. tamarindifolia.*
Foliolis basi parum obliquis:—
  Foliolis vix semipollicaribus . . . . 46. *D. polyphylla.*
  Foliolis ultra semipollicaribus:—
    Vexilli lamina aequilonga ac lata; bracteis lanceolatis:—
      Foliolis glabris vel sparse puberulis:—
        Foliolis vix pollicaribus . . . . 47. *D. Jaherii.*
        Foliolis ultra pollicaribus . . . . 48. *D. burmanica.*
      Foliolis utrinque et praesertim subtus dense velutinis . . 49. *D. Pierreana.*
    Vexilli lamina quam lata longiore; bracteis bracteolisque obtusis; foliolis mediocribus vel majusculis . . 50. *D. densa.*

§ 4. MISCOLOBIUM.

¶ 15. Velutinae.—*Legumen samaroideum, oblongum; foliolis mediocribus vel parvis; bracteolis infra calycem obtusis, calyce brevioribus; stylo subulato; frutices scandentes.*

Foliolis 13—17 . . . . 51. *D. velutina.*
Foliolis 7—9 . . . . 52. *D. bornëensis.*

¶ 16. Ovatae.—*Legumen samaroideum, ovato-oblongum vel oblongum vel subligulatum; foliolis majusculis; bracteolis infra calycem obtusis, calyce brevioribus; stylo gracili cylindrico; arbores elatae.*

Foliolis obtusis; legumen oblongum . . . . 53. *D. obtusifolia.*
Foliolis acutis vel acuminatis:—
Paniculis dense congestis . . . . 54. *D. glomeriflora.*
Paniculis laxis:—
Foliolis 7 vel paucioribus:—
Legumen oblongum . . . . 55. *D. ovata.*
Legumen subligulatum . . . . 56. *D. cambodiana.*
Foliolis 8 vel pluribus; legumen ovato-oblongum . . . 57. *D. tonkinensis.*

¶ 17. Latifoliae.—*Legumen samaroideum, oblongum vel oblongo-lanceolatum vel subligulatum; foliolis majusculis; bracteolis infra calycem obtusis, calycem aequantibus vel subaequantibus; stylo gracili, cylindrico; arbores elatae.*

Floribus in paniculas laterales dispositis; foliolis obtusis vel retusis; legumine oblongo . . . . 58. *D. latifolia.*
Floribus in paniculas terminales dispositis; legumine oblongo-lanceolato vel subligulato:—
Foliolis acutis vel subacutis; legumine oblongo-lanceolato. 59. *D. sissoides.*
Foliolis acutis vel acuminatis; legumine subligulato . . 60. *D. cochinchinensis.*

¶ 18. Polyadelpha.—*Legumen samaroideum, oblongo-lanceolatum; foliolis mediocribus vel parvis; bracteolis infra calycem lanceolatis, calyce brevioribus; stylo subulato; arbor mediocris.*

Foliolis acutis, subtus glaucescentibus; staminibus polyadelphis 61. *D. polyadelpha.*

§ 5. DALBERGARIA.

¶ 19. Sericeae.—*Legumen samaroideum, anguste ligulatum; foliolis obtusis; stylo cylindrico; arbores elatae.*

Floribus in paniculas laterales dispositis; stipulis lanceolatis . . . . 62. *D. sericea.*
Floribus in paniculas terminales dispositis; stipulis spathulatis . . . . 63. *D. sacerdotum.*

¶ 20. Lanceolarieae.—*Legumen samaroideum, late ligulatum vel ovato-lanceolatum; foliolis obtusis; stylo gracili, cylindrico; arbores elatae.*

Floribus in paniculas vere terminales dispositis:—
Paniculis densioribus; calycis dente inferiore laterales vix excedente . . . . 64. *D. paniculata.*
Paniculis laxis; calycis dente inferiore lateralibus duplo longiore . . . . 65. *D. hupeana.*

Floribus in paniculas axillares vel infra-axillares dispositis :—
Floribus foliisque coetaneis :—
Calycis dentibus superioribus subreflexis . . . . 66. *D. assamica.*
Calycis dentibus superioribus erectis :—
Foliolis 13—15 . . . . 67. *D. Balansae.*
Foliolis 17—25 :—
Stipulis parvulis anguste lanceolatis; foliolis junioribus sparse puberulis . . . . 68. *D. Minahassae.*
Stipulis magnis foliaceis oblongis obtusis; foliolis junioribus dense sericeis . . . . 69. *D. szemaoensis.*
Floribus quam folia prius evolutis :—
Foliis ad apicem axis floriferi evolutis . . . . 70. *D. Oliveri.*
Foliis infra ramos axis floriferi evolutis :—
Vexillo supra basin calloso; foliolis subtus cito glabrescentibus . . . . 71. *D. lanceolaria.*
Vexillo haud calloso ; foliolis subtus pubescentibus . . . 72. *D. Hemsleyi.*

¶ 21. **Canae.** *Legumen samaroideum, late ligulatum; foliolis acutis vel subacutis; stylo subulato; arbores elatae.*

Foliolorum marginibus revolutis; leguminibus glabris . . . . 73. *D. Wattii.*
Foliolorum marginibus haud revolutis :—
Leguminibus glabris :—
Leguminibus ad semina umbonatis ; paniculis terminalibus . 74. *D. mammosa.*
Leguminibus haud umbonatis :—
Paniculis terminalibus :—
Foliolis vix 2-pollicaribus, ipso apice retusis . . . . 75. *D. bariensis.*
Foliolis 2-pollicaribus vel ultra 2-pollicaribus, apice acutis :—
Foliolis oblongis, basi rotundatis . . . . 76. *D. dongnaiensis.*
Foliolis angustis, basi cuneatis . . . . 77. *D. Duperreana.*
Paniculis axillaribus . . . . 78. *D. Kurzii.*
Leguminibus dense velutinis; paniculis axillaribus . . . . 79. *D. cana.*

¶ 22. **Volubilis.** *Legumen samaroideum, tenue, oblongum; foliolis obtusis; stylo breviore, crassiore, cylindrico; frutex scandens.*

Floribus in paniculas terminales dispositis; bracteis majusculis . . . . 80. *D. volubilis.*

¶ 23. **Stipulaceae.** *Legumen samaroideum, plus minus ad semina incrassatum; foliolis obtusis; stylo subulato; frutices scandentes vel erectae; bracteis majusculis obtusis.*

Leguminibus ad semina parum incrassatis; ovario hirsuto . . . 81. *D. ferruginea.*
Leguminibus ad semina magnopere incrassatis; ovario, stipite hirsuto excepto, glabro . . . . 82. *D. stipulacea.*

¶ 24. **Reniformes.** *Legumen falcato-subreniforme, omnino incrassatum; stylo subulato; arbores elatae, vel frutices erecti vel scandentes.*

Foliolis minoribus obtusis, rarius ultra pollicaribus; scandens . 83. *D. Godefroyi.*
Foliolis majoribus vel majusculis :—
Leguminibus planis; frutices scandentes :—
Mesocarpio leguminis tenuiter suberoso . . . . 84. *D. falcata.*
Mesocarpio leguminis crasse suberoso . . . . 85. *D. Kunstleri.*
Leguminibus verrucosis; mesocarpio crasse suberoso; arbor erecta . . . . 86. *D. reniformis.*

III.—DESCRIPTIONS OF THE ASIATIC SPECIES OF DALBERGIA.

DALBERGIA LINN. F.

AMERIMNON P. Br. Hist. Jamaic. 288 (1756).
ECASTAPHYLLUM P. Br. Hist. Jamaic. 299 (1756).
PTEROCARPUS Berg. Vet. Acad. Handl. Stockh. 116 (1769); Poiret Encyc. Meth. v. (1804) and Encyc. Meth. Suppl. iv. (1816) in part, not of Linn.
ACOUROA Aubl. Pl. Guian. 753 t. 301 (1775).
DALBERGIA Linn. f. Suppl. Pl. 52 (1781).
DRAKENSTEINIA Neck. Elem. iii. 33 (1790).
ENDESPERMUM Bl. Cat. Gew. Buitenz. 23 (1823).
SEMEIONOTIS Schott Wien. Zeitschr. iii. 804 (1829).
HECASTOPHYLLUM H. B. & K. Nov. Gen. et Sp. vi. 387 (1834).
MISCOLOBIUM Vog. Linnæa xi. 200 (1837).
TRIPTOLEMEA Mart. Flora xx. Beibl. 122 (1837).
LEIOLOBIUM Benth. Ann. Wien. Mus. ii. 94 (1838).
PODIOPETALUM Hochst. Flora xxiv. 657 (1841).
DREPANOCARPUS Kurz Pegu Rep. App. A. 49, B. 45 (1875); Journ. As. Soc. Beng. xlv. 281 (1876); For. Flor. Burm. i. 336 (1877), not of G. W. F. Mey.

Trees or large climbing shrubs. *Leaves* alternate, unequally pinnate, rarely 1-foliolate; stipules various, often small and usually deciduous; leaflets alternate, very rarely some of them subopposite; stipels 0. *Flowers* small or very small, usually numerous, white or rarely purple or violet, in dichotomous cymes or in subcymose axillary or terminal panicles; bracts very small, often persistent; bracteoles usually very small, generally deciduous. *Calyx* campanulate, 5-toothed; the lowest tooth usually the longest, the upper pair usually wider than the rest and often partially connate. *Corolla* papilionaceous; the standard ovate or oblong or orbicular, usually notched at the apex, its claw long or short; wings oblong, cuneate truncate or hastate at the base of the blade, claws usually long; keel-petals obtuse, always more or less connate at the apex behind, claws long, base of blade usually unilaterally hastate. *Stamens* 10 or 9, usually connate in a single sheath slit on upper side, occasionally in two lateral bundles of 5 each, sometimes with only 4 on each side, and the obvexillary stamen almost or quite free, very rarely 9 in a sheath below with a free vexillary filament; anthers small, erect, didymous, cells placed back to back; dehiscence by short apical, rarely by longitudinal chinks. *Ovary* stipitate; style slender or stout, long or short, usually incurved; stigma small terminal; ovules few. *Fruit* an indehiscent lomentum, usually oblong or linear, samaroid, slightly rarely greatly thickened and usually reticulated opposite the median solitary or the discrete 2 or more seeds, elsewhere flat and thin, but neither margined nor winged; rarely falcate and slightly or considerably thickened throughout, but not margined; very rarely orbicular or suborbicular and thickened throughout, slightly margined along the upper suture. *Seed* reniform, compressed; radicle inflexed.

SUBGEUNS I.—SISSOA.

Flowers with standard-blade erect; wings cuneate, rarely truncate, very rarely slightly hastate at junction of blade and claw; keel-petals cuneate or hastate; style cylindric, stout, often very short; stamens normally monadelphous.

The large primary group *Sissoa* is a fairly natural subdivision, and it can hardly be said that any of the groups that go to compose it, if we except the group *Sissoo* itself, bear a striking resemblance to any of the groups of *Amerimnon*. In the case of the exception mentioned, there is a curious similarity between *Sissoo* and the *Latifoliae*, since both have very large epicalycine bracteoles, quite covering the calyx till such time as they fall off. But except for this one character, and for the fact that, like *D. latifolia*, *D. Sissoo* is a *Dalbergia* and is a tree, the affinity between the two, so generally claimed in botanical treatises, is imaginary rather than real. The only group in which the best artificial character, that of cuneate wing-blades, breaks down is in the group *Mimosoides*, where the species in other respects are decisively *Triptolemeae* and have no great affinity with any species in *Amerimnon*. The pods of one of the groups, *Parviflorae*, are, it is true, very like the pods of the groups *Menocides* and *Reniformes*, but it is possible that similarity of pod throughout the genus is a feature more extrinsic than intrinsic; it is one that, to say the least, cannot be relied on as a taxonomic guide, and when the sum total of the characters exhibited by the various *Dalbergias* is considered, is one that it would be safer to neglect entirely than to treat as crucial. It is, however, one that it is convenient to use, with care, as a subordinate aid in classification. As an aid to specific identification, it is, perhaps because it is trivial, of considerable value.

§ 1. TRIPTOLEMEA.—Flowers usually minute, always very small; epicalycine bracteoles often persistent or subpersistent; inflorescence usually distinctly cymose; claws of all petals, especially of the standard, very short; style very short.

The section *Triptolemea* is a useful one to recognise within the wider group *Sissoa*, but it is not naturally separable from the section *Podiopetalum*, since the two pass into each other at various points; nor is it even easily artificially distinguished because every individual character breaks down. The best marks of a *Triptolemea* are the short style, the smaller flowers and persistent bracteoles, and the very short standard-claw. The flowers of some of the *Podiopetala*, however, are as small as those of some genuine *Triptolemeae*; most striking deviation of all, the style of *D. Sissoo*, the largest flowered of the *Podiopetala*, is short as in the *Triptolemeae*.

¶ 1. Nummularieae.—*Pod suborbicular, thickened throughout, and more or less distinctly margined; climbers.*

This is not quite a natural group, owing to the great difference in the foliage of the two members. Except as regards the pod, *D. Albertisii* seems very nearly related to *D. parviflora* of the *Parviflorae*, and to *D. rimosa* of the *Rimosae*; while, except as regards its pod, *D. Becoarii* is obviously very nearly related to the group *Phyllanthoides*. As regards pod, on the other hand, both species must be, to those who continue to recognise the artificial and unnecessary genus *Ecastaphyllum*, members of that genus.* The remaining *Ecastaphylla* are African and American, and are referable to *Amerimnon* § *Dalbergaria*, not to *Sissoa*; it is of course just possible, since the stamens of *D. Albertisii* are not yet known, that it too may have to be referred to that section; but it is unlikely, because the large terminal panicles of dichotomous cymes are so thoroughly in keeping with the characteristics of the remaining *Triptolemeae*. The *Ecastaphylla* of the section § *Dalbergaria* form a natural group to which the name *Monetarieae* may be applied.

* Spelling more properly *Ecastophyllum* or, with purists, *Hecastophyllum*.

1. Dalbergia Albertisii Prain Journ. As. Soc. Beng. lxx. 2, 62 (1901).

A climbing shrub, young branches terete. *Leaves* 9—10 in. long; leaflets 8—9, very dark-green, and quite glabrous above, paler and glabrous or minutely adpressed-puberulous beneath, firmly coriaceous; midrib impressed above, prominent beneath, secondary nerves rather numerous, ovate-acute with rounded base, terminal rather the largest, 2—2·25 in. long, 1·25 in. wide; rachis 5·5—6·5 in. long, and short petiolules glabrous. *Flowers* minute, secund, in ample terminal thyrsoid panicles with sparsely puberulous zigzag rachis 5 in. long, giving off at each angle stoutish horizontal branches 1 in. long, dividing at their apices into 2 or more reflexed cyme-branches; bracts and bracteoles deciduous; *calyx* campanulate, teeth short obtuse; *corolla* and *stamens* not seen. *Pod* indehiscent, thin, membranous, green, suborbicular, apiculate and 1-seeded, rarely oblong and 2-seeded, slightly cuneate at the base, 1—1·5 in. long, ·75 in. wide, distinctly stipitate, finely wide-reticulate throughout, with a firm narrow margin, finely lepidote-puberulous.

Papuasia: New Guinea; Fly River, *D'Alberits*!

This species, if the genus *Ecastaphyllum* be sustained, must be known as *Ecastaphyllum Albertisii*. As Bentham has, however, pointed out, *Ecastaphyllum* is a purely artificial group.

Plate 5. Dalbergia Albertisii *Prain.*—1, Fruiting specimen from Fly River, New Guinea, *n. s.;* 2, pod, opened, showing young seed *in situ*, *n. s.;* 3, young seed × 4; 4, young seed, in section × 4.

2. Dalbergia Beccarii Prain Journ. As. Soc. Beng. lxx. 2, 64 (1901).

Ormocarpum scandens Teysm. ex Prain Journ. As. Soc. Beng. lxx. 2, 64 (1901).

A climbing shrub, with slender, terete, densely finely pubescent branchlets. *Leaves* sub-bifarious, 1·5—1·75 in. long; leaflets 11—17, small, close-set, oblong, slightly retuse at apex, dark-green above, rather paler beneath, finely pubescent on both surfaces, ·4 in. long, ·2 in. wide; rachis 1—1·5 in. long and very short petiolules puberulous; stipules minute, lanceolate. *Flowers* very minute, secund, in small cymes in the lower leaf-axils, ·3 in. long, peduncles and short pedicels puberulous; bracts and bracteoles deciduous, very small, ovate; *calyx* campanulate, teeth small, two upper subconnate, obtuse, lateral acute, lowest lanceolate; *corolla* not seen; *stamens* 9, in one sheath split along upper side, the obvexillary filament more deeply separated than the lateral groups of 4 each, which are free in their upper third and alternately shorter and longer; *ovary* not seen. *Pod* small, irregularly ovate, apiculate, glabrous, coriaceous and firm, distinctly stipitate, pale-brown, 1-seeded, thickened and faintly reticulated opposite the seed, ·6 in. long, ·4 in. wide; *seed* reniform, ·3 in. long, ·2 in. wide, testa blackish, somewhat shining.

Malaya: Borneo; Kuching, *Beccari*! Kapuas, *Teysmann*!

This species is also an *Ecastaphyllum* (*E. Beccarii*) for those who prefer to retain that artificial genus.

Plate 6A. Dalbergia Beccarii *Prain.*—1, Branch of *Dalbergia Beccarii* from Kuching, Borneo, *n. s.;* 2, calyx, laid open and epicalycine bracteoles × 4; 3, basal bracteoles × 4; 4, stamens × 4; 5, seed, *n. s.*

¶ 2. **Parviflorae.**—*Pod falcate-subreniform, thickened throughout, not margined; climbers.*

Like the preceding, this is anything but a natural group. The first two species, which are abundantly distinct, were treated by Bentham as varieties of one. Bentham had no pods of either: he did not observe that the second species of the group is identical with *D. parviflora*, which he kept up tentatively as distinct; and still more remarkably, in spite of the fact that Roxburgh's description of *D. parviflora*, meagre though it be, indicates that *D. parviflora* cannot possibly be anything but a *Selenolobium*, Bentham has referred these to his § *Triptolemea*. That in this Bentham was right the writer is assured, but the action does not conform exactly with the scheme of classification that is being given effect to in *Journ. Linn. Soc.* iv. *Suppl.* Even yet the pod of *D. Cumingiana* is unknown, and it may well prove ultimately to be, as Bentham's note suggests, nearly related to *D. rimosa*, though it certainly is not a variety of that species. *D. parviflora* is, but for its pod, also one of the *Rimosae* group; *D. spinosa*, on the other hand, is, but for its pod, rather one of the *Phyllanthoides* group.

3. DALBERGIA CUMINGIANA Benth. Pl. Jungh. i. 255 (1851); Miq. Flor. Ind. Bat. i. 1, 129 (1855); Nav. & Fernand. Vill. Nov. App. Flor. Philip. 67 (1880); Vidal Phan. Cum. Philip. 42 (1885); Plant. Vasc. Filip. 111 (1886).

D. Cumingii Benth. Journ. Linn. Soc. iv. Suppl. 32 VAR. *typica* only (1860).

Dalbergia sp. Vidal Plant. Vasc. Filip. 112 in part (1886).

A woody climber with lenticelled branches and puberulous branchlets. *Leaves* 3·5—4 in. long; leaflets 7—9, ovate, apex obtuse emarginate, base cuneate or rounded, glabrous above, uniformly adpressed-pubescent beneath, finely reticulate-veined, ·75—1·75 in. long, ·4—1 in. wide; rachis 2—2·5 in. long, puberulous as are the short petiolules. *Flowers* minute, secund, in terminal thyrsoid panicles extending into the axils of the upper leaves, 6 in. long, 2 in. wide; rachis, branches and pedicels puberulous; bracteoles ovate, persistent; *calyx* campanulate, teeth obtuse or subacute, the lowest somewhat the longest; *corolla* white, petals short-clawed, standard wide-ovate, slightly emarginate; *stamens* 10, in one sheath split along upper side; *ovary* glabrous, style short; *ovules* usually 2. *Pod* not seen ripe, when young resembling that of *D. parviflora.*

PHILIPPINES: Luzon; Albay, *Cuming*! Iriga, *Vidal*! Pili, *Vidal*! Catarman; Samar, *Vidal*!

As ripe fruit of this is not yet known, it is uncertain whether it has a *Selenolobium* pod.

PLATE 7. Dalbergia Cumingiana *Benth.*—1, Flowering branch from Albay, Luzon (*Cuming* 1244), *n. s.*; 2, calyx, laid open × 4; 3, standard × 4; 4, wings × 4; 5, keel-petals × 4; 6, stamens × 4; 7, ovary, developing into fruit, *n. s.*; 8, the same opened, *n. s.*

4. DALBERGIA PARVIFLORA Roxb. Hort. Beng. 98 (1814); Flor. Ind. iii. 225 (1832); Miq. Flor. Ind. Bat. i. 1, 132 (1855); Benth. Journ. Linn. Soc. iv. Suppl. 33 (1860); Prain Journ. As. Soc. Beng. lxvi. 2, 121 in part (1897); lxx. 2, 63 (1901); Becc. Nelle Foreste di Borneo 358, 591, (1902).

D. parciflora Benth. Pl. Jungh. i. 255 (1851).

D. corymbifera Bl. ex Miq. Flor. Ind. Bat. i. 1, 130 (1855).

D. Zollingeriana Miq. Flor. Ind. Bat. i. 1, 130 (1855); Hassk. Neuer Schl. Rumph. 90 (1864); Nav. & Fernand. Vill. Nov. App. Flor. Philip. 67 (1880).

D. Cumingii VAR. *Zollingeriana* Benth. Journ. Linn. Soc. iv. Suppl. 32 (1860).

Drepanocarpus Cumingii Kurz Journ. As. Soc. Beng. xlv. 2, 282 (1876); For. Flor. Burm. i. 336 (1877).

Lacca lignum Rumph. Herb. Amboin. v. 17 t. 13 (1750).

A strong climber, 30—80 feet long, with lenticelled branches, the main stem armed with woody branching spines; branchlets quite glabrous. *Leaves* 6—8 in. long, leaflets 5—9, ovate-lanceolate, with narrowed but obtuse, slightly emarginate apex, base wide-cuneate or rounded; light-green, quite glabrous on both surfaces, finely reticulately veined, 2—3·5 in. long, ·75—1·5 in. wide; rachis 2—3 in. long and short petiolules glabrous. *Flowers* minute, secund, in terminal panicles extending into the axils of the uppermost leaves, 3—4 in. long, 3—5 in. wide; peduncles glabrous, branches and short pedicels puberulous; bracteoles ovate, ciliate, persistent, the epicalycine pair embracing lower third of calyx-tube; *calyx* campanulate, teeth obtuse, the upper two subconnate rather wide, the lower rather longer than the lateral pair; *corolla* white, petals short-clawed, standard rather narrowly obovate, emarginate; *stamens* 10, in one sheath split along upper side, the vexillary filament rather shorter than and more free than the others; *ovary* glabrous except for a few hairs on suture, stout; style short, stigma small; *ovules* usually three. *Pod* indehiscent, turgid, 1—3-seeded, when young falcate along upper, when ripe convex on both sutures; when more than one-seeded torulose; quite glabrous, ·75—2 in. long, ·6 in. wide; *seed* wide-reniform, ·5 in. long, ·35 in. wide.

INDO-CHINA: Tenasserim; in clearings in gardens, *Helfer*! MALAYA: Peninsula; Dindings, *Curtis*! Perak, *Wray*! *Kunstler*! Pahang, *Ridley*! Sumatra; *Zollinger*! *Teysmann*! Java; *Blume*! Borneo; Sarawak, at Bintulu, Sungei Mahan and Santubong, *Beccari*! Celebes; *Zollinger*! Moluccas; Halmaheira, *Teysmann*! Ambonia, *C. Smith*! PHILIPPINES: Luzon, *Naves & Fernandez Villar*.

This climbing species, known to the Malays as Acor Berangan, yields the *Kayoe Lakka* of commerce, which consists of the old dead heartwood from which the alburnum has been removed; it is used as incense, with other odoriferous woods, by the Chinese. The Philippine record for this species requires verification.

PLATE 8. Dalbergia parviflora *Roxb.*—1, Flowering branch from Perak, *n. s.*; 2, bud × 4; 3, calyx, laid open × 4; 4, standard × 4; 5, wings × 4; 6, keel-petals × 4; 7, stamens × 4; 8, ovary × 4; 9, ovary opened × 4; 10, ovule × 10; 11, young fruit, from Perak, *n. s.*; 12, the same opened, seeds hardly developed, *n. s.*; 13, twig with ripe fruits from Halmaheria, *n. s.*; 14, ripe fruit opened, showing seed *in situ*, *n. s.*; 15, seed, *n. s.*

5. DALBERGIA SPINOSA Roxb. Hort. Beng. 98 (1814); Flor. Ind. iii. 226 (1832); Voigt. Hort. Suburb. Calcutt. 241 (1845); Benth. Pl. Jungh i. 256 (1851); Journ. Linn. Soc. iv. Suppl. 49 partly (1860); Bak. in Hook. f. Flor. Brit. Ind. ii. 238 (1876); Nav. & Fernand. Vill. Nov. App. Flor. Philip. 67 (1880); Talbot Bomb. List 75 (1894); Prain Journ. As. Soc. Beng. lxx. 2, 64 (1901); Cooke Flor. Pres. Bomb. i. 400 (1902); Prain Bengal Plants 411 (1903).

D. horrida Grah. in Wall Cat. 5877 (1832), not *Ammerinnum horridum* Dennst. *Drepanocarpus spinosus* Kurz Journ. As. Soc. Beng. xlv. 2, 281 (1876); For. Flor. Burm. i. 37 (1877).

A large shrub, often climbing and generally with the smaller branches converted into straight pungent spines, sometimes with branches twisted and hooked; branchlets glabrous. *Leaves* 1·5—2·5 in. long, scattered or, on the spines, fascicled; leaflets 5—9, ovate, obtuse or retuse, base rounded, quite glabrous, ·4—·7 in. long, ·25—·5 in. wide; rachis ·6—1·5 in. long, and short petiolules glabrous. *Flowers* small, white, in axillary racemes, less often in few-branched panicles, 1—1·5 in. long; peduncles and long pedicels glabrous; bracteoles ovate, epicalycine pair embracing lower half of calyx-tube, very deciduous; *calyx* campanulate, glabrous, teeth ovate, obtuse except the longer lanceolate lowest; *corolla* white, petals shortly clawed, especially the wide-obovate retuse standard; *stamens* 10, either in 2 bundles of 5 each or less often in one sheath split on upper side; *ovary* stipitate, pilose; style short; *ovules* 1, rarely 2. *Pod* indehiscent, rigidly coriaceous, rather long-stipitate, glabrous, reniform, 1-, very rarely 2-seeded, 1—1·5 in. long, ·6 in. wide; *seed* reniform-falcate, ·65 in. long, ·3 in. wide.

INDIA: Coromandelia; S. Arcot, *Gamble*! Madras, *Heyne*! Sundribuns, *Griffith*! *Kurz*! *Clarke*! *Ball*! *Heinig*! *Lace*! *Prain*! Malabaria; Concan, *fide Talbot*. INDO-CHINA: Chittagong, *Roxburgh*! Burma; Rangoon, *Kurz*! Moulmein, *Wallich*! PHILIPPINES: Ilo-ilo; Panay, at Igbaras, *Naves & Fernandez-Villar*.

The wood-cutters of the Sundribuns know this species as *Amnta*. According to Kurz, the powdered roots "absorb alcohol, and a spoonful of the powder in a tumblerful of water is said to be sufficient to destroy in less than half an hour the effects of alcohol even in cases bordering on *delirium tremens*."

The record of this species from the Philippines requires verification; that from the Concan appears to be a mistake.

PLATE 9. Dalbergia spinosa *Roxb.*—1, Flowering branch from the Sundribuns, *n. s.*; 2, twig showing hooked branch, from the Sundribuns, *n. s.*; 3, bud × 4; 4, pedicel with bracteoles × 4; 5, calyx, laid open × 4; 6, standard × 4; 7, wings × 4; 8, keel-petals × 4; 9, stamens, usual arrangement × 4; 10, stamens, occasional arrangement × 4; 11, ovary × 4; 12, ovary, laid open × 4; 13, ovule × 12; 14, fruiting branch from S. Arcot, *n. s.*; 15, pod opened, showing seed *in situ*, *n. s.*; 16, seed, *n. s.*

¶ 3. Discolor.—*Pod samaroid; inflorescence a terminal panicle; a tree.*

The position of this group is somewhat doubtful. The species is no doubt a very distinct one; it was considered by Mr. Bentham, from Miquel's description, to be possibly closely allied to *D. foliacea*. The writer, after having seen the type material of the Leiden Herbarium, thinks that its alliance is rather with *D. rimosa*. The point must remain unsettled till flowers are obtained; there is, however, little doubt that it is, in the wide sense, a *Sissoa*, and it may be looked on as favouring Bentham's suggestion that this species is a tree. If it be a *Triptolemea*, it is the only tree in that section; whereas *Podiopetalum*, to which *D. foliacea* belongs, has at least three erect forms—*D. cultrata*, *D. fusca*, and *D. Sissoo*.

6. DALBERGIA DISCOLOR Bl. ex Miq. Flor. Ind. Bat. i. 1, 130 (1855); Benth. Journ. Linn. Soc. iv. Suppl. 41 (1860); Nav. & Fernand. Vill. Nov. App. Flor. Philip 67 (1880); Prain. Journ. As. Soc. Beng. lxx. 2, 61 (1901).

A tree? with glabrous lenticelled branches. *Leaves* 3—7 in. long; leaflets 5—9, the distal usually largest obovate, the lateral ovate or occasionally orbicular, rounded or narrowed at apex, emarginate, glabrous above, rusty adpressed-pubescent beneath, ·75—2·5 in. long, ·75—1·75 in. wide, chartaceous, finely reticulate; rachis 2·5—4·5 in. long and short petiolules pubescent. *Flowers* minute, subsecund, in dichotomously cymose terminal panicles, 2·5—4 in. long, 1·5—2 in. wide; bracteoles subpersistent; *calyx* campanulate, teeth all obtuse, subequal, short; *corolla* not seen; *stamens* 9, in one sheath split along upper side; *ovary* not seen young. *Pod* coriaceous, distinctly stipitate, oblong, subacute, glabrous, veined opposite the solitary or occasionally two seeds, 1·5—2·75 in. long, ·75 in. wide; *seed* reniform, compressed, ·4 in. long, ·2 in. wide, testa brown, shining.

MALAYA: Borneo; S. Coast, *Korthals*! Celebes; *Teysmann*! PHILIPPINES: Luzon, *Naves & Fernandez-Villar*.

This species is not very perfectly known, and only three specimens have been examined. Two of the specimens belong to the Leiden Herbarium. One of these, marked "Borneo, Korthals legit," has been written up by Miquel "*Dalbergia discolor* Bl. Miq."; it is the type of the species and from it fig. 1 of Plate 10 is taken. The other is written up "*Dalbergia discolor* Bl. VAR. *pallens* M."; it is marked simply "Borneo." Apparently Miquel never published this variety "pallens," and, as a matter of fact, it does not seem necessary to consider it varietally distinct. Its tomentum and venation are exactly as in Korthals' plant, and the different shape of the leaflets cannot be held of sufficient significance to justify its treatment as a variety. This Bornean plant without a record as to locality or collector is figured as fig. 2 of Plate 10. In Herb. Hort. Bogor. is a specimen from Celebes (*Teysmann* 12539), which appears to me to be precisely the same as the Bornean *D. discolor*. The species is also reported from Luzon in the Philippines by the Rev. Fathers Naves and Fernandez-Villar, a by no means improbable distribution, which it will, however, be well for subsequent workers to verify.

From the shrivelled remains of two flowers on the smaller figured specimen, it can be seen that the stamens are monadelphous and that the calyx is almost exactly like that of *D. rimosa*, near which species it seems best to place *D. discolor*.

PLATE 10. Dalbergia discolor *Bl.*—1, Branch in fruit from Borneo, *n. s.*; 2, branch in fruit of the form termed VAR. *pallens* by Miquel, from Borneo, *n. s.*; 3, two-seeded pod, opened to show one seed *in situ*, *n. s.*

¶ 4. **Rimosae**.—*Pod samaroid; inflorescence a terminal panicle, sometimes extending into the highest leaf-axils; flowers minute; epicalycine bracteoles persistent or subpersistent; climbers.*

A subnatural group. *D. rimosa* and *D. Forbesii*, though differing in pods, are very closely allied; *D. Thomsoni* stands somewhat apart, and in facies closely resembles *D. confertiflora* among the *Foliaceae*; *D. Junghuhnii*, *D. Scortechinii*, *D. Curtisii* and *D. stercoracea* are again closely allied to each other and are rather divergent alike from *D. Thomsoni* and *D. rimosa*. The four species mentioned approach pretty closely to the *Phyllanthoides*; and indeed with regard to the members of this subgroup and their relationship to *D. phyllanthoides*, the most extraordinary confusion has prevailed both in Herbaria and in literature. For this confusion it must be frankly admitted that Bentham, Miquel, Baker and the writer have been equally blameworthy; nor would the errors we have made been committed had we attended, as we ought, more carefully to Blume's judicious sorting and to Maingay's careful field-notes. The last species included in this group *Rimosae*, *D. Mimosella* from the Philippines, is one of which the writer has seen no specimen; while it is evident, from Blanco's on the whole clear description, that the species is a *Triptolemea*, and is either one of the *Rimosae* or one of the *Phyllanthoides*, it is not absolutely certain to which of the two groups it belongs.

7. DALBERGIA RIMOSA Roxb. Hort. Beng. 53 (1814); DC. Prodr. ii. 417 (1825); Roxb. Flor. Ind. iii. 233 (1832); Wall. Cat. 5853 (1832); Wight Ic. t. 262 (1840); Voigt Hort. Suburb. Calcutt. 241 (1845); Benth. Pl. Jungh. i. 255 (1851); Journ. Linn. Soc. iv. Suppl. 32 (1860); Brandis For. Flor. 148 (1874); Bak. in Hook. f. Flor. Brit. Ind. ii. 232 (1876); Prain Journ. As. Soc. Beng. lxx. 2, 61 (1901).

D. foliacea Wall. Cat. 5856 B in part (1832); Gamble Darjeel. List 29 (1896), not of Roxb.

Dalbergia sp. Drake del Castillo Journ. de Bot. v. 215 (1891).

A scandent or subscandent shrub, occasionally erect and 20—25 ft. high, with many spreading branches. *Leaves* 4—8 in. long; leaflets 5—9, usually 7, ovate or obovate, elliptic, subacute or obtuse, mucronate, firmly papery, rather closely veined, bright-green, glabrous above, paler and puberulous beneath, 2—3 in. long, 1—2 in. wide; rachis 2·5—5 in. long, puberulous as are the short petiolules. *Flowers* minute, in terminal corymbose panicles of dichotomous cymes, sometimes extending into the axils of the uppermost leaves, 8—10 in. long, 5—6 in. wide; bracteoles ovate-lanceolate, persistent, epicalycine pair hardly half as long as calyx-tube; *calyx* campanulate, 5-toothed, teeth obtuse except the rather longer lowest, the two upper subconnate; *corolla* white, petals short-clawed, especially the oblong emarginate standard; *stamens* 9, or sometimes 10, in a sheath split along the upper side; filaments free in their upper third, alternately shorter and longer; *ovary* shortly stipitate, puberulous; style short; *ovules* 1—2. *Pod* indehiscent, stipitate, oblong, glabrous, thickly coriaceous, veined everywhere, but very strongly so opposite the 1, rarely 2 seeds, 2—3 in. long, ·75—1·25 in. wide, brown; *seeds* much compressed, reniform, ·5 in. long, ·25 in. wide, testa brown, somewhat shining.

HIMALAYA: Sikkim; lower slopes and submontane forests of Terai and Duars, *Hooker*! *King*! *Gamble*! *Prain*! *Gammie*! *Haines*! INDO-CHINA: Assam; Brahmaputra Valley, *Jenkins*! *Simons*! *Mann*! *Masters*! *Peal*! Silhet, *Wallich*! *Clarke*! Cachar, *Prazer*! Khasia, *Hooker & Thomson*! *Griffith*! *Clarke*! *Mann*! *Gallatly*! Naga Hills, *Clarke*! *Watt*! Burma; Kachin Hills, Mogaya, *Shaik Muqim*! CHINA: Yunnan; Szemao, Western Mts., 5,000 ft., a large climber; South-Western Mts., 4,500 ft., a rambling shrub, 8 feet high, *Henry* 11887! 11952! TONGKING: Black river, edge of a lake near Rochers de Notre Dame, a climber, *Balansa*!

In Assam, according to Peal, this is known as *Elam Sali* or *Atam Sali*; the *sali* or bark is chewed.

PLATE 11. Dalbergia rimosa *Roxb.*—1, Flowering branch, from Sikkim, *n. s.*; 2, bud × 4; 3, pedicel with bracteoles × 4; 4, calyx, laid open × 4; 5, standard × 4; 6, wings × 4; 7, keel-petals × 4; 8, stamens × 4; 9, ovary × 4; 10, ovary, opened × 4; 11, ovule × 10; 12, fruits, from Assam, *n. s.*; 13, pod opened, showing seed *in situ*, *n. s.*; 14, seed, *n. s.*

8. DALBERGIA FORBESII Prain Journ. As. Soc. Beng. lxx. 2, 61 (1901).

D. parviflora Prain Journ. As. Soc. Beng. lxvi. 2, 121 partly (1897), not of Roxb.

A moderately large climbing shrub, with glabrous branches. *Leaves* 5—7 in. long; leaflets usually 5, ovate, acuminate, base rounded, the terminal slightly the largest, glabrous on both surfaces, closely finely reticulate, 1·5—3·25 in. long, ·75—1·6 in. wide;

rachis 2·5—3·5 in. long and short petiolules glabrous. *Flowers* many, small, secund, in dichotomous cymes, disposed in terminal wide panicles extending into the axils of the upper leaves, 5—6 in. long, 3—4 in. wide; bracteoles persistent, ovate-lanceolate; *calyx* campanulate, teeth obtuse except lowest subacute, subequal, short; *corolla* white, petals rather distinctly clawed, standard orbicular subauriculate, slightly emarginate; *stamens* 9, in one sheath split along upper side, occasionally in two lateral sheaths and sometimes with a tenth free vexillary stamen present; *ovary* glabrous, shortly stipitate, style short; *ovule* solitary. *Pod* indehiscent, distinctly stipitate, coriaceous, glabrous, oblong, rounded at apex, narrowed to the base, distinctly veined opposite the seed, 1·5—2·5 in. long, ·75 in. wide; *seed* reniform, compressed.

MALAYA: Sumatra; Bigni Telok, R. Rawas, 3,500 ft., *Forbes*! Lingga; *Teysmann*!

This is very nearly related to *D. parviflora*, and until an opportunity occurred of examining a fruiting specimen from Lingga was supposed to be a form of that species.

PLATE 12. Dalbergia Forbesii *Prain.*—1, Branch in young fruit from Bigni Telok, R. Rawas, Sumatra, *n. s*; 2, twig, showing leaf with break in sequence of size of leaflets, *n. s.*; 3, bud × 4; 4, pedicel with bracteoles × 4; 5, calyx, laid open × 4; 6, standard × 4; 7, wings × 4; 8, keel-petals × 4; 9, stamens × 4; 10, ovary × 4; 11, ovary, laid open × 4; 12, ovule × 10; 13 and 14, two pods, from the island of Lingga, *n. s.*

9. DALBERGIA THOMSONI Benth. Journ. Linn. Soc. iv. Suppl. 33 (1860); Bak. in Hook. f. Flor. Brit. Ind. ii, 236 (1876); Prain Journ. As. Soc. Beng. lxx. 2, 57 (1901).

A woody climber; branchlets sub-bifarious, glabrous. *Leaves* 3—4 in. long; leaflets 9—11, ovate-oblong, obtuse or retuse, base cuneate or rounded, the distal rather the largest, firmly chartaceous, closely finely reticulated, dark-green above, much paler beneath, quite glabrous on both surfaces, ·75—1·25 in. long, ·5—·8 in. wide; rachis 1·75—2·25 in. long and petiolules ·15 in. long, glabrous. *Flowers* minute, secund, in ample terminal panicles extending into the axils of the upper leaves, 8 in. long, 4 in. wide; peduncles quite glabrous, branches faintly puberulous, pedicels very short; bracteoles persistent, basal lanceolate, epicalycine pair ovate-lanceolate; *calyx* campanulate, glabrous, teeth very short, upper pair obtuse, lateral acute, lowest rather the longest, lanceolate; *corolla* greenish-white, petals all very short-clawed, standard orbicular emarginate; *stamens* 9, in one sheath or in two lateral bundles or with the obvexillary stamen also free; *ovary* minute, shortly stipitate, style rather distinct; *ovules* usually 2. *Pod* indehiscent, remaining green, rather thinly coriaceous, narrowed from below the middle to the very short stipe and also upwards, the subacute apex much rounded on the lower suture, finely reticulated throughout, quite glabrous, 2·5 in. long, ·85 in. wide; *seed* solitary.

INDO-CHINA: Assam; Patkoye, *Griffith*! Khasia Hills, *Hooker & Thomson*! *Clarke*!

PLATE 13. Dalbergia Thomsoni *Benth.*—1, Flowering branch from Khasia, *n. s.*; 2, bud × 4; 3, calyx, laid open × 4; 4, standard × 4; 5, wings × 4; 6, keel-petals × 4; 7, stamens × 4; 8, ovary × 4; 9, ovary, laid open × 4; 10, ovule × 12; 11, pod, from Patkoye, *n. s.*

10. Dalbergia Junghuhnii Benth. Pl. Jungh. i. 254 (1851); Miq. Flor. Ind. Bat. i. 1, 129 (1855); Benth. Journ. Linn. Soc. iv. Suppl. 33 partly (1860).

A woody climbing? shrub, with stoutish lenticelled branches. *Leaves* 3—4 in. long; leaflets 11—15, elliptic-oblong, obtuse, green and glabrous on both surfaces, ·75 in. long, ·4 in. wide; rachis puberulous, 2—3 in. long, petiolules very short, puberulous. *Flowers* minute, secund, in a condensed terminal thyrsoid panicle, 4—6 in. long, 2 in. wide; peduncles, branches and pedicels puberulous; bracteoles ovate, persistent, the basal acute, the epicalycine pair obtuse, embracing the lower third of the calyx-tube; *calyx* campanulate, teeth short, the two upper obtuse, wider than the acute lateral and the shortly lanceolate longer lowest; *corolla* white, petals shortly clawed, standard orbicular-oblong, emarginate; *stamens* 9, or sometimes 10, in a sheath split along upper side, filaments free in their upper third; *ovary* glabrous, style short; *ovules* 2—3.

Malaya: Sumatra; at 3,000 ft. elev., *Junghuhn*! Java; *de Vriese*!

The identity of this species has been confused in Herbaria and in systematic works owing to the fact that a second species, which occurs in Malacca and in Borneo, has been identified by Bentham partly with *D. polyphylla*, partly with this; and that by Baker and the writer two, if not three, other species have also been referred here. There is of course a good deal to be said for the view that all the forms in question represent only conditions of one protean species; but if this be the case, the treatment does not go quite far enough, since the Indian *D. multiflora* is another member of the same group, standing on the same footing, as regards *D. Junghuhnii*, that *D. stercoracea* Maing., *D. phyllanthoides* Bl., and *D. Curtisii* do. If this view be adopted, the name *D. multiflora* will apply to all the members of the group.

The only specimens absolutely in agreement with Junghuhn's original plant from Sumatra, here figured, are two examples—evidently of one gathering—now in the Leiden and in the Buitenzorg collections respectively. They are noted as having been obtained in Java by de Vriese.

It is probable that this species climbs, but it is not certain: the branches are much stouter than in the allied forms above enumerated, and the specimens available show no hooked branchlets. As yet fruits are unknown.

Plate 14. Dalbergia Junghuhnii *Benth.*—1, Flowering specimen from Sumatra (*Junghuhn* 233), *n. s.*; 2, bud × 4; 3, pedicel with bracteoles × 4; 4, calyx, laid open × 4; 5, standard × 4; 6, wings × 4; 7, keel-petals × 4; 8, stamens × 4; 9, ovary × 4; 10, ovary, laid open × 4; 11, ovule × 10.

11. Dalbergia Scortechinii Prain Journ. As. Soc. Beng. lxvi. 2, 444 (1897); lxx. 2, 57 (1901).

D. Junghuhnii Bak. in Hook. f. Flor. Brit. Ind. ii. 233 in part (1876), not of Benth.

D. Junghuhnii var. *Scortechinii* Prain Journ. As. Soc. Beng. lxvi. 2, 115 (1897).

A shrubby climber, 15—30 feet long, with twining glabrous branches, here and there twisted and thickened into spiral hooks. *Leaves* 6—8 in. long; leaflets 11—15, elliptic, closely puberulous beneath, glabrous except the midrib above, ·7—1·5 in., rarely in young shoots 2·5 in. long, ·35—·75 in., rarely 1 in. wide; *rachis* 3—4 in. long and petiolules ·15 in. long, densely puberulous. *Flowers* minute, secund, in an ample terminal and in smaller axillary panicles, 2—4 in. long, 1·5—3 in. wide; peduncles, branches and pedicels pubescent; bracts caducous; bracteoles persistent, basal very minute, lanceolate, acuminate, epicalycine pair ovate, obtuse, embracing lower third of calyx-tube; *calyx*-teeth short obtuse except the longer lanceolate lowest; *corolla* white, petals all very short-clawed; *stamens* 9, in two lateral bundles of 5 and 4 respectively, the sheath split both on upper and lower sides, or at times in two lateral bundles of 4 each, with the obvexillary filament free; *ovary* pubescent, shortly stipitate, style very short; *ovules* usually 3—4, rarely only 2, sometimes 5. *Pod* indehiscent, small, ovate-lanceolate, narrowed to both ends, glabrous, shortly stipitate, firmly coriaceous, 1·5—2 in. long, ·5 in. wide, 1—3-seeded; *seed* reniform, compressed, ·4 in. long, ·25 in. wide.

MALAYA: Penang; Ayer Etam, *Curtis*! Malacca; Bijong, *Scortechini*! *Maingay*! Singapore; Bukit Timah, *Ridley*! Bangka; *Teysmann*! Java; Djampong, *Teysmann*! Borneo; Sarawak, *Beccari*! *Haviland*!

Till an opportunity occurred of seeing fruits of this species, it did not seem advisable to separate it from *D. Junghuhnii* and the allied forms confused with that species.

PLATE 15. Dalbergia Scortechinii *Prain.*—1, Flowering branch from Malacca, *n. s.*; 2, bud × 4; 3, pedicel with bracteoles × 4; 4, calyx, laid open × 4; 5, standard × 4; 6, wings × 4; 7, keel-petals × 4; 8, stamens × 4; 9, ovary × 4; 10, ovary, laid open × 4; 11, ovule × 8; 12, twig in fruit, from Bangka, *n. s.*

12. DALBERGIA CURTISII Prain Journ. As. Soc. Beng. lxx. 2, 58 (1901).

D. discolor Miq. Flor. Ind. Bat. Suppl. 296 (1860), not of Bl.

D. Junghuhnii Bak. in Hook. f. Flor. Brit. Ind. ii. 233 in part (1876); Prain, Journ. As. Soc. Beng. lxvi. 2, 115 in part (1897), not of Benth.

A scandent shrub, with closely puberulous, sub-bifarious branchlets. *Leaves* 6—7 in. long; leaflets usually 7—9, oblong or elliptic, cuneate at base, rounded, obtuse, faintly emarginate at apex, glabrous and dark-green above, pale-green and rather closely puberulous except on the midrib beneath, 1·5—2 in. long, 1 in. wide; rachis 4·5 in. long and petiolules ·15 in. long, puberulous. *Flowers* minute, secund, in axillary and terminal panicles, 4—5 in. long, 3 in. wide; peduncles, branches and pedicels pubescent; bracts minute, caducous; bracteoles persistent, basal lanceolate, acuminate, minute, epicalycine pair ovate, obtuse, embracing lower third of calyx-tube; *calyx* campanulate, teeth all short, obtuse; *corolla* white, petals all short-clawed, especially the wide-oblong, emarginate standard; *stamens* 9, in one sheath split along upper side, filaments free in their upper fourth; *ovary* rather long-stipitate, closely pubescent except the stipe; style obsolete; *ovules* 2—3. *Pod*, only seen unripe, quite glabrous.

MALAYA: Sumatra; Lampongs, *Teysmann*! Malacca; *Maingay*! Penang; at 500 feet elevation, *Curtis*!

This is evidently very nearly related to *D. stercoracea*, but Maingay, who has collected both, notes that this has no stercoraceous odour and is probably distinct. The leaves of this, in the specimens of all three gatherings seen by me, are larger than is usual in *D. stercoracea*; their tomentum beneath is very different. It has besides a different calyx, different standard, and different ovary. The flowers too are quite half as large again as in *D. stercoracea*.

PLATE 16. Dalbergia Curtisii *Prain.*—1, Flowering branch from Penang, *n. s.*; 2, bud × 4; 3, pedicel with bracteoles × 4; 4, calyx, laid open × 4; 5, standard × 4;

6, wings × 4; 7, keel-petals × 4; 8, stamens × 4; 9, ovary × 4; 10, ovary, laid open × 11, ovule × 10; 12, immature pod, from Penang, *n. s.*

13. **Dalbergia stercoracea** Maing. ex Prain Journ. As. Soc. Beng. lxx. 2, 58 (1901).
D. Junghuhnii Bak. in Hook. f. Flor. Brit. Ind. ii. 233 in part (1876); Prain Journ. As. Soc. Beng. lxvi. 2. 115 var. *typica* in part (1897), not of Benth.
D. frondosa Miq. Flor. Ind. Bat. i. 133 var. *typica* only and excl. all syn. (1855), not of Roxb.

A shrubby climber, 15—30 feet long, with twining glabrous branches here and there twisted and thickened into spiral hooks. *Leaves* 3—4 in. long; leaflets 7—9, oblong or elliptic, cuneate at the base, rounded truncate or somewhat retuse at the apex, green and glabrous above, glaucescent and sparsely puberulous beneath, ·6—1·25 in. long; ·35—·75 in. wide, rachis 2·5—3·5 in. long, puberulous as are the petiolules ·15 in. long. *Flowers* intensely stercoraceous, minute, secund, in ample terminal and in smaller axillary paniculate cymes 3—4 in. long, 2 in. wide; peduncles, branches and pedicels pubescent; bracts minute caducous; bracteoles persistent, basal lanceolate, acuminate, very minute, epicalycine pair ovate, obtuse, embracing lower third of calyx-tube; *calyx* campanulate, teeth short obtuse except the longer lowest acute half as long as calyx-tube; *corolla* white, petals short-clawed, especially the oblong emarginate standard; *stamens* 9, in one sheath split on upper side, filaments free in their upper fourth; *ovary* shortly stipitate, pubescent towards apex; style short; *ovules* 2—3. *Pod* thin, membranous, greenish, glabrous, 2·5—3 in. long, 1—1·3 in. wide, 1-, rarely 2-seeded, slightly tapering to base, obtuse at apex; *seed* compressed, subreniform, ·5 in. long, ·3 in wide.

Malaya: Sumatra; *Korthals*! Malacca; *Maingay*! *Mueller*! *Derry*! Singapore; *Ridley*! *Hullett*!

Plate 17. Dalbergia stercoracea *Maing.*—1, Flowering branch from Malacca, *n. s.;* 2, leaf with larger leaflets, from Singapore, *n. s.;* 3, bud × 4; 4, pedicel with bracteoles × 4; 5, calyx, laid open × 4; 6, standard × 4; 7, wings × 4; 8, keel-petals × 4; 9, stamens × 4; 10, ovary × 4; 11, ovary, laid open × 4; 12, ovule × 10; 13, fruiting branch, from Malacca, *n. s.;* 14, unripe pod, with two seeds, from Singapore, *n. s.;* 15, unripe seed, *n. s.*

14. **Dalbergia Mimosella** Prain.
D. lanceolaria Nav. & Fernand. Vill. Nov. App. Flor. Philip. 67 (1880) not of Linn.
Amerimnon Mimosella Blanco Flor. Filip. Ed. i. 563 (1837); Ed. ii. 393 (1845); Ed. iii. ii. 357 (1878).

A shrub, about 6 ft. high. *Leaves* alternate, imparipinnate; leaflets 7—more-jugate, oval or linear, obtuse. *Flowers* very small, nodding, panicled; each floret with one wide bract and 2 linear epicalycine bracteoles; *calyx* hirsute, 2-labiate, 5-partite; upper lip 2-lobed, lower 3 teeth narrower; *corolla* 4-petalled, papilonaceous, smaller than the calyx; standard short, surrounding the receptacle; wings ovate-circinate, covered by the margins of the standard which they equal in length; keel rather shorter than the wings, slit below and emarginate above; *stamens* 10, in two lateral bundles of 5 each, the sheath split above and below; filaments free in their upper part, anthers purple, globose; *style* very short, hirsute, stigma globose. *Pod* stipitate, veined, indehiscent, round, subcultrate, very thin, projecting in the middle, the margin submembranous; *seed* usually solitary, occasionally a second rudimentary seed present, much compressed, reniform.

PHILIPPINES: Tala, *Blanco*; Luzon, at Mandeloyon, *Naves & Fernandez-Villar.*

This plant is known to the writer only from Blanco's description, which is here reproduced. That the species belongs to the section *Triptolemea* is evident from the fact that the flowers are very small and the further fact that the style is very short. The original description unfortunately does not say whether the panicles are terminal or only axillary; it is not therefore clear whether, among the *Triptolemeae*, its place be among the *Rimosae* or among the *Phyllanthoides.* The number of leaflets, however, indicates that probably it is a member of the former group rather than of the latter, for none of the members of the *Phyllanthoides* group have so few leaflets as 7. The erect habit, for Blanco describes it as a shrub as tall as a man, is unusual in the section, but too much stress should not be laid on this character, since other members of both groups may climb or be erect according to circumstances. The character of isodiadelphous stamens, on which the identification suggested by Naves and Fernandez Villars obviously depends, is not a reliable one; though characteristic, on the whole, of the section *Dalbergaria* to which *D. lanceolaria* belongs, it is not unknown in *Triptolemea* where *D. Scortechinii, D. phyllanthoides* var. *typica*, and *D. melanoxylon* casually if not constantly exhibit it. The other characters are quite antagonistic to the identification of the species with *D. lanceolaria.* It is of course not improbable that the editors of the third edition of Blanco had access to specimens of *D. frondosa* Miq. and had supposed that Miquel's plants so named, which are both obviously nearly related to Blanco's one, were really *D. frondosa* Roxb. The account that Blanco gives of the pod seems to show that the species forms a link between the *Nummularieae* and the rest of the *Triptolemeae.* Blanco gives the vernacular name as *Macápil.*

¶ 5. **Phyllanthoides.**—*Pod samaroid; inflorescence of axillary panicles rarely extending to the ends of the branches; flowers small; epicalycine bracteoles deciduous; climbers.*

This is apparently a quite natural group, and to the writer undoubtedly a group that should be referred to *Triptolemea.* It is, however, only right to point out that Bentham regarded two of the species of the group as *Sissoae*, not *Triptolemeae; D. multiflora* is his *D. sympathetica* and *D. melanoxylon* includes his *D. Stocksii.* The specific treatment accorded by Bentham to the forms of this group is, however, rather confusing, for *D. melanoxylon* he refers to § *Dalbergaria*, while *D. Stocksii*, which is the same plant, he refers to § *Sissoa. D. phyllanthoides*, when collected in Malacca, he has placed in *D. Junghuhnii;* when collected in Borneo he has referred it to *D. polyphylla. D. coromandeliana* he has, and in this he follows Wight and Arnott, placed in *Selenolobium* as a portion of *D. spinosa*, which it does not really greatly resemble. The most doubtful of the four as to sectional position is *D. melanoxylon*, which has a rather longer standard-claw and a rather longer style than are proper for a *Triptolemea*, so that it might almost equally well be relegated to *Podiopetalum.*

15. DALBERGIA MULTIFLORA Heyne ex Wall. in Cat. sub. n. 5848 (1832); Prain Journ. As. Soc. Beng. lxx. 2, 59 (1901).

D. sympathetica Nimmo in Grah. Cat. Bomb. Pl. 55 (1839); Voigt Hort. Suburb. Calcutt. 241 (1845); Benth. Pl. Jungh. i. 255 (1851); Journ. Linn. Soc. iv. Suppl. 42 (1860); Dalz. & Gibs. Bomb. Flor. 78 (1861); Bak. in Hook. f. Flor. Brit. Ind. ii. 234 (1876); Talbot Bomb. List, 75 (1894); Woodr. Journ. Nat. Hist. Soc. Bomb. xi. 426 (1897); Cooke Flor. Pres. Bomb. i. 398 (1902).

D. frondosa Wall. Cat. 5855 partly (1832), not of Roxb.

D. paniculata Wall. Cat. 5848 partly (1832), not of Roxb.

D. ferruginea Hohenack. ex Bak. in Hook. f. Flor. Brit. Ind. ii. 234 (1876), not of Roxb.

Amerimnum horridum Dennst. Schl. Hort. Malab. 34 (1818).
Ana-mullu Rheede Hort. Malabar. viii. t. 40 (1688).

A large climber, with sometimes thickened hooked branches, or casually erect and straggling; stems beset with strong spines; young branches sub-bifarious, pubescent. *Leaves* 2·5—3·5 in. long; leaflets 11—15, elliptic-oblong, apex obtuse, truncate or emarginate, base wide-cuneate or rounded, pale-green, pubescent above, densely pubescent beneath, but ultimately becoming glabrous above and occasionally only sparsely adpressed-pubescent beneath, ·25—·4 in. long, ·2—·3 in. wide; rachis 2—3 in. long, densely pubescent as are the short petiolules. *Flowers* minute, secund, in small axillary panicles, 1·5—2 in. long, ·75—1 in. wide; peduncles, branches and pedicels pubescent; bracteoles persistent, basal ovate-acute, epicalycine ovate-obtuse embracing lower third of calyx-tube; *calyx* campanulate, pubescent; teeth short, obtuse except the lowest longest; *corolla* white, claws of petals short, standard obovate, emarginate; *stamens* 9, in one sheath split along upper side; *ovary* densely pubescent, stipitate; *ovules* 2—4. *Pod* thin, bright-green, membranous, usually 1-seeded, occasionally 2—3-, rarely 4-seeded, 1·5—4 in. long, ·75—1 in. (occasionally 1·25 in.) wide, persistently velvety-pubescent, slightly reticulated opposite the seeds; *seed* reniform, compressed, ·4 in. long, ·25 in. wide.

VAR. *typica*: leaflets persistently pubescent beneath, rarely quite glabrous above.

INDIA: Malabaria; Concan, *Stocks*! *Kuntze*! Canara, *Hohenacker*! *Talbot*! Mysore, *Heyne*! *Wight*! Travancore, *Rheede* (Ic.)! *Lawson*!

VAR. *glabrescens*: leaflets glabrescent to glabrous beneath, quite glabrous above.

INDIA: Malabaria; Travancore, *Lawson*! *Bourdillon*! Coromandelia; Carnatic, *G. Thomson*! *Wight*!

This species is very nearly related to *D. phyllanthoides* from Malaya, and only differs in having a velvety-pubescent pod, that of *D. phyllanthoides* being quite glabrous. The two forms here separated as varieties hardly deserve varietal rank. Of Indian, as opposed to Malayan, species the nearest to this one is *D. coromandeliana*, which might be looked on as an extreme form were it not that its pods are quite glabrous.

PLATE 18. Dalbergia multiflora *Heyne*.—1, Flowering branch from Travancore, *n. s.*; 2, bud × 4; 3, calyx, laid open × 4; 4, standard × 4; 5, wings × 4; 6, keel-petals × 4; 7, stamens × 4; 8, ovary × 4; 9, ovary, laid open × 4; 10, ovule × 10; 11, flowering twig, from Canara, *n. s.*; 12, single pod of the broad type, *n. s.*; 13, seed, *n. s.*

16. DALBERGIA PHYLLANTHOIDES Bl. ex Miq. Flor. Ind. Bat. i. 1, 134 (1855); Prain Journ. As. Soc. Beng. lxx. 2, 60 (1901).
D. sennoides Bl. ex Miq. Flor. Ind. Bat. i. 1, 134 (1855).
D. frondosa VAR. *β*. Miq. Flor. Ind. Bat. i. 1, 134 (1855), not of Roxb.
D. Junghuhnii Benth. Journ. Linn. Soc. iv. Suppl. 33 partly (1860); Bak. in Hook. f. Flor. Brit. Ind. ii. 233 partly (1876), not of Benth. Pl. Jungh.
D. polyphylla Benth. Journ. Linn. Soc. iv. Suppl. 34 partly (1860), not of Pl. Jungh.
D. subsympathetica Prain Journ. As. Soc. Beng. lxvi. 2, 116 (1897).

D. littoralis Hassk. MSS. in Hort. Bogor.; Schimp. ex Schenk in Schimp. Bot. Mittheilung. aus den Tropen. iv. 1, 211 (1892); Taub. in Engl. Naturlich. Pflanzenfam. iii. 3, 336 (1894); Prain Journ. As. Soc. Beng. lxx. 2, 60 (1901).

A climbing shrub, 60—80 feet long, or casually a spreading shrub or small tree, 15—30 feet high, branches often thickened into curved or spiral hooks; branchlets puberulous or pubescent, surrounded at their point of origin by a cluster of scaly bracts. *Leaves* 1·5—3 in. long; leaflets 9—15, elliptic-oblong, rounded truncate or slightly retuse, base wide-cuneate or rounded, green and glabrous above, paler and pubescent with long adpressed hairs beneath, ·25—·4 in. long, ·2—·3 in. wide; rachis 1—2·5 in. long, densely pubescent as are the short petiolules. *Flowers* minute, secund, in small axillary panicles on the young branches, 1·5—2 in. long, ·75—1 in. wide; peduncles, branches and pedicels densely pubescent; bracteoles persistent, basal lanceolate, epicalycine pair ovate, embracing lower fourth of calyx-tube; *calyx* campanulate, teeth short, obtuse except the longer acute or lanceolate lowest; *corolla* white, petals all short-clawed, standard oblong to wide-obovate, emarginate; *stamens* 9, in one sheath split along upper side or at times in two lateral sheaths; *ovary* glabrous or slightly puberulous along one or rarely both sutures, shortly stipitate; style short; *ovules* 3. *Pod* indehiscent, thin, membranous, greenish, quite glabrous, 2·5 in. long, 1 in. wide, 1-seeded, very rarely 2-seeded, obtuse at apex, abruptly cuneate at base and shortly stipitate; *seed* reniform, compressed, not seen ripe.

VAR. *typica;* leaflets almost membranous. *D. phyllanthoides* Bl. loc. cit.

MALAYA: Java; *Blume*! *Nagel*! Borneo; *Barber*! *Motley*!

VAR. *sennoides;* leaflets firmer, usually larger. *D. sennoides* Bl. loc. cit.; *D. subsympathetica* Prain loc. cit.

MALAYA: Peninsula; Perak, *Scortechini*! *Wray*! *Kunstler*! Penang, *Curtis*! Malacca, *Griffith*! *Goodenough*! *Jagor*! *Maingay*! Java; cult.

This species, one of the group to which belong *D. Junghuhnii*, *D. stercoracea*, *D. Curtisii* and *D. Scortechinii*, is allied, most nearly of them all, to *D. multiflora*, the leading Indian member of the same group. It differs, however, very markedly in its glabrous instead of velvety pod; nor is it reported to have the spiny stem that characterises *D. multiflora.* From *D. Junghuhnii* it differs in the shape and texture of its leaflets and in the inflorescence not being a terminal leafless panicle. From *D. stercoracea*, so generally confused with *D. Junghuhnii*, it differs in having more numerous and differently-shaped leaflets and in apparently not having the stercoraceous odour. It is much less like *D. Curtisii* and *D. Scortechinii*, although, as will be seen from the synonymy, Miquel was inclined to treat this as a variety of *D. Curtisii.*

PLATE 19. Dalbergia phyllanthoides *Bl.*—1, Flowering branch, from Borneo, *n. s.;* 2, bud × 4; 3, pedicel with epicalycine bracteoles × 4; 4, calyx, laid open × 4; 5, standard × 4; 6, wings × 4; 7, keel-petals × 4; 8, stamens × 4; 9, ovary × 4; 10, ovary, laid open × 4; 11, ovule × 12.

PLATE 20. Dalbergia phyllanthoides *Bl.* VAR. sennoides *Prain.*—1, Flowering branch, from Perak, *n. s.;* 2, bud × 4; 3, pedicel with bracteoles × 4; 4, calyx, laid open × 4; 5, standard × 4; 6, wings × 4; 7, keel-petals × 4; 8, stamens × 4; 9, ovary × 4; 10, ovary, laid open × 4; 11, ovule × 10; 12, fruiting branch, from Perak, *n. s.;* 13, unripe seed, *n. s.*

17. **Dalbergia coromandeliana** Prain Journ. As. Soc. Beng. lxx. 2, 60 (1901).
D. spinosa W. & A. Prodr. i. 266 (1834), not of Roxb.

An erect glabrous shrub, the ultimate branches bifarious, horizontal, rigid, spinous. *Leaves* fasciculate on small tubercles, ·75—1·5 in. long; leaflets 7—9, rarely 11, elliptic or cuneate-oblong, obtuse or retuse, ·25—·35 in. long, ·12—·2 in. wide, glabrous on both surfaces, pale-green; rachis ·5—1·2 in. long, at first puberulous, but soon glabrous; petiolules very short, glabrous. *Flowers* minute, secund, in small recurved cymose panicles, fascicled on small tubercles, ·7 in. long, ·5 in. wide, peduncles puberulous, pedicels glabrous; bracteoles caducous, basal lanceolate, epicalycine ovate, subacute, embracing lower third of calyx-tube; *calyx* campanulate, teeth obtuse except lowest subacute, one-third as long as tube; *corolla* white, petals rather distinctly clawed; *stamens* 9, in one sheath split along upper side or in two lateral bundles or occasionally in two bundles with the obvexillary stamen also free; *ovary* glabrescent, distinctly stipitate, style short; *ovules* 2—4. *Pod* indehiscent, thinly coriaceous, ovate subacute, distinctly wide-reticulate throughout, base cuneate, rather long-stipitate, quite glabrous, 1-seeded, 1·75 in. long, ·6 in. wide; *seed* large, reniform, compressed, ·5 in. long, ·3 in. wide, brown, hardly shining.

India: Coromandelia; Shevagiri Hills, *Wight*!

This plant, which appears to be rare, for it has been only twice or thrice collected, and in each case by Wight, must be looked on as one of the doubtful species in this work. That it is not *D. spinosa* Roxb. an examination of the figure of that species will at once demonstrate. Wight and Arnott, following Wallich, were themselves uncertain as to the identity of the two, and the unqualified acceptance by subsequent writers of Wight's *D. spinosa* as identical with Roxburgh's, was not based on fuller knowledge. The affinity is with *D. multiflora*, and is so close that this may prove to be no more than an outlying form of that species, which, though it has no spines on the smaller branches, has a spinous main-stem. The size of the leaflets, much smaller in *D. coromandeliana* than in *D. multiflora*, is not a sufficiently differential feature, nor perhaps is the fact that the leaves are fascicled in the present plant, but not in *D. multiflora*. The pods differ in shape and size, but this again, having regard to the great variability within *D. multiflora*, is not an absolute character. The absence of all tomentum from the pods of *D. coromandeliana* must, however, be esteemed, at least for the present, as diagnostic, if for no other reason than because of its convenience. If, in spite of this difference, *D. coromandeliana* be reduced to *D. multiflora*, then *D. phyllanthoides*, which differs even less essentially than *D. coromandelia* does, must also be so reduced; while if *D. multiflora*, *D. phyllanthoides* and *D. coromandeliana* are treated as conspecific, it may be necessary to treat some of the other Malayan forms with which *D. phyllanthoides* has been so much confused as integral portions of the same protean plant.

Plate 21. Dalbergia coromandeliana *Prain.*—1, Flowering branch, Wight 798 (K. D. 821), *n. s.;* 2, bud × 4; 3, calyx, laid open × 4; 4, standard × 4; 5, wings × 4; 6, keel-petals × 4; 7, ovary × 4; 8, ovary, laid open × 4; 9, ovule × 10; 10, fruiting branch, from Shevagiri Hills, Wight (K. D. 822), *n. s.;* 11, seed *n. s.*

18. **Dalbergia melanoxylon** Guill. & Perr. Flor. Seneg. Tent. 227, t. 33 (1834); Benth. Journ. Linn. Soc. iv. Suppl. 47, (1860); Dalz. & Gibs. Bomb. Flor. Suppl. 24 (1861); Prain Journ. As. Soc. Beng. lxvi. 2, 446 (1897); lxx. 2, 59 (1901); Cooke, Flor. Pres. Bomb. i. 396 (1902).

D. Stocksii Benth. Journ. Linn. Soc. iv. Suppl. 42 (1860); Bak. in Hook. f. Flor. Brit. Ind. ii. 234 (1876); Talbot Bomb. List 75 (1894); Woodr. Journ. Bomb. Nat. Hist. Soc. xi. 426 (1897).

A shrub or a small tree with many wide-spreading drooping branches, or a climber; branches with occasional sharp spines; branchlets sub-bifarious, puberulous; bark white, sapwood yellow, heart-wood quite black, very hard. *Leaves* 4—8 in. long; leaflets 9—17, obovate or ovate-oblong, obtuse or retuse, sparsely adpressed-pubescent on both surfaces but especially beneath, ultimately nearly glabrous, finely reticulately veined, ·75 in. long, ·45 in. wide, in young shoots occasionally 1·5 in. long, 1 in. wide; rachis 3·5—7 in. long, and very short petiolules glabrous or faintly puberulous. *Flowers* small, subsecund, in terminal and axillary panicles, appearing rather before the leaves, 1·5—3 in. long, 1·5—2 in. wide; peduncles, branches and pedicels puberulous; bracteoles subpersistent, basal lanceolate, the epicalycine pair small, ovate, puberulous, embracing base of calyx-tube; *calyx* campanulate, teeth very short, obtuse except the lanceolate lowest equalling the tube; *corolla* white, petals short-clawed, standard oblong, slightly emarginate; *stamens* 9, in one sheath split along upper side or in two lateral bundles or occasionally in two bundles with the obvexillary stamen also free; *ovary* glabrous, distinctly stipitate; style short; *ovules* 1—2, rarely 3. *Pod* indehiscent, ovate or shortly oblong, glabrous, distinctly stipitate, uniformly wide-reticulate, 1-seeded, occasionally 2-seeded, rarely 3-seeded, 1—2·75 in. long, ·6 in. wide; *seed* reniform, much compressed, ·5 in. long, ·3 in. wide.

INDIA: Malabaria; Canara, *Talbot*! Concan, *Stocks*! Cultivated at Poona! Madras, Calcutta!—DISTRIB. Africa, from Senegal (*Lelievre*! *Heudelot*!) to Ethiopia (*Kotschy*!), Abyssinia (*Schimper*! *Plowden*!) and Mozambique (*Peters*!).

It is necessary to remark that, so far as it goes, the description given of *D. oblongifolia* G. Don [*Gen. Syst. Gard.* ii. 375 (1832)] is quite applicable to this species. If the two prove to be the same, the name *D. melanoxylon* must give place to Don's. Mr. E. G. Baker, who has kindly looked into this matter, however, informs the writer that there is no authentic example of *D. oblongifolia* Don, in the British Museum collection, where many of Don's types are preserved.

In India this is spoken of as "China Blackwood;" in Africa it is termed "Senaar Ebony."

PLATE 22. Dalbergia melanoxylon *Guill. & Perr.*—1, Young flowering twig, from the Concan, *n. s.*; 2, flowering specimen from a planted shrub, Poona, *n. s.*; 3, bud × 4; 4, calyx, laid open × 4; 5, pedicel with bracteoles × 4; 6, standard × 4; 7, wings × 4; 8, keel-petals × 4; 9, stamens × 4; 10, ovary × 4; 11, ovary, laid open × 4; 12, ovule × 10; 13, fruiting twig from a planted shrub, Calcutta, *n. s.*; 14, pod, laid open, showing seed *in situ*, *n. s.*; 15, seed, *n. s.*

¶ 6. **Mimosoides.**—*Pod samaroid; inflorescence axillary; flowers small; epicalycine bracteoles deciduous; wing-petals subhastate; climbers.*

That the three species in this group constitute a natural aggregation of forms is undoubted; the question indeed rather is whether they may not all be varieties of one species. Since, however, it seems on the whole better to hold with Franchet that two of the forms are distinct, it becomes necessary to separate the remaining form, which differs almost equally from the other two. Although in other respects *Triptolemeae*, and indeed *D. Millettii* has been by Bentham himself referred to that section, these three forms by the single character of wing-petals more closely approach the *Amerimna* than do any of the other *Sissoae*. Among the *Pediopetala* their nearest ally is *D. Hancei*, which but for its longer standard-claw might almost be placed in this group.

19. DALBERGIA MILLETTII Benth. Journ. Linn. Soc. iv. Suppl. 34 (1860); Flor. Hongkong. 92 (1862); Forbes & Hemsl. Journ. Linn. Soc. xxiii. 198 (1887); Prain Journ. As. Soc. Beng. lxx. 2, 57 (1901).

D. polyphylla Benth. Pl. Jungh. i. 256 partly (1851); Seem. Bot. Her. 375 (1855); not of Benth. in Journ. Linn. Soc. iv. Suppl.
Derris pinnata Lour. Flor. Cochin-Chin. 432 (1790) possibly.

A climber, with glabrous lenticelled branches, sometimes hooked; young branchlets glabrous or only very sparsely puberulous, surrounded at point of origin by scaly bracts. *Leaves* 1·5—2 in. long; leaflets 25—35, small, linear or narrowly oblong, obtuse or retuse, quite glabrous on both surfaces, close-set, ·4 in. long; ·2 in. wide; rachis 1·25—1·5 in. long, finely puberulous, petiolules glabrous; stipules ovate, deciduous. *Flowers* small, secund, in condensed axillary panicles, ·5 in. long, ·4 in. wide, along the young branchlets; peduncles, branches, and pedicels very sparsely pubescent; bracteoles glabrous, ovate, basal persistent, the epicalycine pair embracing lower third of calyx-tube, deciduous; *calyx* campanulate, nearly glabrous; teeth short, subequal, obtuse except the acute lowest, the two upper subconnate; *corolla* white, petals short-clawed, standard orbicular, emarginate; *stamens* 9, in one sheath split along upper side; *ovary* stipitate sparsely pilose; style short; *ovules* 2—3. *Pod* indehiscent, firmly coriaceous, reticulated, and somewhat indurated opposite the solitary, rarely 2 seeds, glabrous, ovate-obtuse, base rounded, stipitate, 2·25 in. long, ·75 in. wide; *seed* reniform, compressed, ·5 in. long, ·25 in. wide.

CHINA: Kwangtung; Hongkong, *Hance*! *Wilford*! *Ford*! *Champion*!

Except for its very short almost glabrous panicles, in which character it resembles *D. Hancei*, and for its quite glabrous leaves, there seems to be nothing to separate this species from *D. mimosoides* Franch., the pods of the two being practically identical. The leaflets vary a little in width just as do those of *D. mimosoides*, but they are smaller and narrower in *D. Millettii* than they usually are in *D. mimosoides*.

In a previous discussion of the species of *Dalbergia*, the writer attempted to identify with the Hongkong plant some Hupeh and Yunnan specimens. A closer study of these, and the supply of fuller material of the Hongkong plant kindly communicated by Mr. Ford, show that this treatment is not justified except in the wider sense in which *D. Millettii* is held to include both *D. mimosoides* and *D. stenophylla*. Their longer panicles show that neither the Hupeh nor the Yunnan plant agrees with *D. Millettii*; the former is *D. stenophylla*, the latter is *D. mimosoides*.

The fact that *D. Millettii* has glabrous leaflets renders it possible that in this species we have the plant described by Loureiro as *Derris pinnata* (Flor. Cochin-Chin. 432); the absence of any definite account of the root, however, leaves the point uncertain. Moreover, the species has not so far been collected outside Hongkong: even in the wider view that would accept both *D. stenophylla* and *D. mimosoides* as forms of *D. Millettii*, the species has not been collected in Cochin-China.

The most satisfactory treatment for the moment is to transcribe Loureiro's description of *Derris pinnata* and retain that Cochin-China plant as a species of *Dalbergia* of doubtful identity, in the hope that our colleagues, the French botanists in Eastern Indo-China, may take the matter up and settle the identity of Loureiro's species. The rhomboid base to the leaflets is the character that supports its identification with *D. tamarindifolia*; if, however, the leaflets be really glabrous that suggestion is hardly tenable.

DALBERGIA PINNATA sp. dub.

Derris pinnata Lour. Flor. Cochin-Chin. 432 (1790).

A climbing shrub, with long, unarmed, much-branched stem. *Leaves* pinnate; leaflets numerous, alternate, ovate-oblong with base rhomboid, small, glabrous, entire. *Flowers* on many-flowered lateral peduncles; *corolla* white. *Pod* 1-seeded.

COCHIN-CHINA: in forests.

The fleshy reddish root is used instead of, and for the same purposes as, the betel-nut (*Areca*), which is much chewed by the indigenous inhabitants along with the aromatic pan-leaf (*Piper Betle*).

PLATE 23. Dalbergia Millettii *Benth.*—1, Flowering branch, from Hongkong, *n. s.;* 2, twig showing spiral hook, from Hongkong, *n. s.;* 3, bud × 4; 4, pedicel with epicalycine bracteoles × 4; 5, calyx, laid open × 4; 6, standard × 4; 7, wing × 4; 8, keel-petals × 4; 9, stamens × 4; 10, ovary × 4; 11, ovary, laid open × 4; 12, ovule × 10; 13, twig in fruit, from Hongkong, *n. s.;* 14, twig with fruit of broader type, from same gathering as 13, *n. s.;* 15, pod opened, showing seed *in situ*, *n. s.;* 16, seed, *n. s.*

20. DALBERGIA STENOPHYLLA Prain Journ. As. Soc. Beng. lxx. 2, 56 (1901).

D. Millettii Harms in Engl. Bot. Jahrb. xxix. 415 (1900), hardly of Benth.

A climber, with lenticelled branches; branchlets sparsely puberulous or glabrous, surrounded at point of origin by scaly bracts. *Leaves* 2·5—4 in. long; leaflets 31—41, small, narrowly linear-oblong, obtuse, at first sparsely pubescent on both surfaces, soon glabrous except on midrib beneath, close-set, ·5 in. long, ·15 in. wide; rachis 2—3·5 in. long, finely adpressed-puberulous or glabrous, petiolules short, glabrous; stipules ovate, deciduous. *Flowers* small, secund, in axillary panicles along young branches, 2—2·5 in. long, 1·5 in. wide; peduncles, branches, and pedicels puberulous; bracteoles puberulous, basal persistent, the epicalycine pair embracing the lower third of calyx-tube, deciduous; *calyx* campanulate, finely puberulous; teeth short, the upper pair obtuse, subconnate, the lateral acute, the lowest longer, shortly lanceolate; *corolla* white, petals short-clawed, standard wide-ovate, obtuse; *stamens* 9, in one sheath split along upper side; *ovary* stipitate, sparsely pilose along sutures; style short; *ovules* 3. *Pod* indehiscent, thinly but firmly coriaceous, very faintly reticulated opposite the one or two seeds, glabrous, ligulate, subacute, base narrowed to the distinct stipe, 1·25—2 in. long, ·3 in. wide; *seed* reniform, compressed, ·35 in. long, ·2 in. wide.

CHINA: Hupeh; *Henry*! Szechuen; Kyminse, near Tchan-Keou, *Farges*!

This species is very nearly related to *D. Millettii* and to *D. mimosoides*, agreeing with latter in its elongated panicles, but more approaching the former in its comparative absence of pubescence. The leaflets, however, though as long as those of *D. mimosoides*, are as narrow as or narrower than those of *D. Millettii*, while the fruit is different from that of either of these species.

Kang-kin-ten is given by Farges as the Chinese name for the species.

PLATE 24. Dalbergia stenophylla *Prain.*—1, Flowering specimen, from Hupeh, *n. s.;* 2, bud × 4; 3, calyx, laid open × 4; 4, standard × 4; 5, wings × 4; 6, keel-petals × 4; 7, stamens × 4; 8, ovary × 4; 9, ovary, laid open × 4; 10, ovule × 12; 11, fruiting branch, from Hupeh, *n. s.;* 12, fruit, opened, showing seed *in situ*, *n. s.;* 13, seed, *n. s.*

21. DALBERGIA MIMOSOIDES Franch. Pl. Delavay. 187 (1890); Prain Journ. As. Soc. Beng. lxx. 2, 56 (1901).

D. tamarindifolia Roxb. Flor. Ind. iii. 233 partly (1832); Wight Ic. t. 242 (1840) as to the fruit.

D. Millettii Prain Journ. As. Soc. Beng. lxvi. 2, 446 (1897), hardly of Benth.

A climber, with glabrous lenticelled branches; young branchlets densely rusty-pubescent, surrounded at point of origin by scaly bracts. *Leaves* 2·5—4 in. long; leaflets

25—35, small, linear-oblong, obtuse or retuse, at first pubescent at length glabrous above, finely but sparsely adpressed-puberulous beneath, close-set, ·5 in. long, ·25 in. wide; rachis 2—3·5 in. long and very short petiolules at first densely pubescent, at length only puberulous; stipules membranous, ovate, deciduous. *Flowers* small, secund, in axillary panicles along the young branchlets; peduncles, branches and pedicels pubescent; bracteoles pubescent, ovate, basal persistent, the epicalycine pair embracing lower third of calyx-tube, deciduous; *calyx* campanulate, nearly glabrous; teeth short, obtuse except the rather longer lowest; *corolla* white, petals short-clawed, standard oblong-obovate, emarginate; *stamens* 9, or occasionally 10, in one sheath split along upper side; *ovary* stipitate, sparsely pilose along the sutures or glabrous, style short; *ovules* 3. *Pod* indehiscent, thickly coriaceous, somewhat indurated and reticulated opposite the solitary, rarely 2, seeds, glabrous, ovate-acute, base rounded, stipitate, 1·5—2·5 in. long, ·75 in. wide; *seed* reniform, compressed, ·4 in. long, ·25 in wide.

INDO-CHINA: Assam; Khasia Hills, *Mann*! *Collett*! *Gallally*! *Clarke*! CHINA: Yunnan; Tapintze, *Delavay*! Mengtze, *Henry*! Szechuen; Tatchienlu, *Pratt*! E. HIMALAYA: Sikkim; Tista Valley, below Choong-thang, 5,000 ft., *Prain*!

PLATE 25. Dalbergia mimosoides *Franch.*—1, Flowering branch, from Khasia Hills, *n. s.*; 2, bud × 4; 3, calyx, laid open × 4; 4, standard × 4; 5, wings × 4; 6, keel-petals × 4; 7, stamens × 4; 8, ovary × 4; 9, ovary, laid open × 4; 10, ovule × 10; 11, fruiting branch, from Khasia Hills, *n. s.*; 12, pod, laid open, showing seed *in situ*, *n. s.*; 13, seed, *n. s.*

§ 2. **PODIOPETALUM.**—Flowers small or medium; epicalycine bracteoles always deciduous; inflorescence not distinctly cymose; claws of all petals rather long, that of standard about as long as the rest; style usually stout, cylindric, rarely (*D. Sissoo*) short.

¶ 7. **Foliaceae.**—*Pod samaroid, oblong or ovate; leaflets obtuse; wings not hastate; style stout, cylindric; epicalycine bracteoles obtuse, shorter than calyx; climbers.*

This group, though perhaps only subnatural, nevertheless exhibits a fairly regular transition, among species that are clearly *Podiopetala* and that are all of scandent habit, from the small-leaved *D. Hancei* to the large-leaved *D. foliacea*. Perhaps it might be more convenient to treat the group as comprising two subgroups, distinguished by the axillary and the terminal inflorescences. *D. confertiflora* among those with a terminal inflorescence is very distinct from the remaining species in foliage and in fruit; *D. foliacea* is also very distinct; *D. yunnanensis* and *D. Collettii*, on the other hand, are in essentials remarkably alike, the chief difference being that the flowers of *D. Collettii* are considerably smaller than those of *D. yunnanensis*. But for its rather longer standard-claw and rather longer style than is usual in that section, and especially but for its remarkably close affinity to *D. yunnanensis*, one might with almost equal propriety refer *D. Collettii* to *Triptolemea*.

22. DALBERGIA HANCEI Benth. Journ. Linn. Soc. iv. Suppl. 33 (1860); Flor. Hongkong 93 (1861); Forbes & Hemsl. Journ. Linn. Soc. xxiii. 198 (1887); Prain Journ. As. Soc. Beng. lxx. 2, 57 (1901).

A woody climber, branches at times slightly hooked. *Leaves* 2—2·5 in. long; leaflets 9—11, narrow-oblong, obtuse truncate or retuse, base cuneate or rounded, dark-green and at first sparsely adpressed-pubescent but soon glabrous above, pale-green and persistently adpressed-pubescent beneath, ·6—·75 in. long, ·25—·35 in. wide; rachis 1·5—1·75 in. long, and petiolules ·15 in. long, quite glabrous; stipules membranous, lanceolate,

·3 in. long, very caducous, puberulous. *Flowers* small, secund, in dense axillary panicles, ·5—·75 in. long, ·3—·5 in. wide; peduncles and pedicels densely pubescent, bracts scaly, clustered, enclosing the young inflorescence, soon deciduous; bracteoles deciduous, the basal minute lanceolate, the epicalycine pair ovate, obtuse, enclosing base of calyx-tube, pubescent; *calyx* campanulate; teeth very short obtuse, pubescent externally; *corolla* greenish-white, petals all rather long-clawed, standard orbicular, emarginate, subreflexed, auriculate at base of blade; *stamens* 9, in a sheath split along upper side, inserted with petals one-third up calyx-tube, sometimes with a free vexillary stamen; *ovary* short-stipitate, pubescent; style rather long, stigma minute; *ovules* 3—4. *Pod* indehiscent, ovate lanceolate to ligulate, firmly coriaceous, glabrous, distinctly stipitate, 1—4 seeded, not very distinctly reticulated opposite the seeds, 1·5—3 in. long, ·4—·5 in. wide; *seed* reniform, compressed, ·3 in. long, ·2 in. wide.

CHINA: Kwang-tung; Hongkong, *Hance*! *Wilford*! *Weiss*! *Ford*! Macao, *Callery*! Canton, *Park*!

Park notes this as 'brought in wild from near Canton, a shrubby plant, rambling, *Robinia* in appearance.'

PLATE 26. Dalbergia Hancei *Benth.*—1, Flowering specimen, from Hongkong, *n. s.*; 2, bud × 4; 3, pedicel, with epicalycine bracteoles × 4; 4, calyx, laid open × 4; 5, standard × 4; 6, wings × 4; 7, keel-petals × 4; 8, stamens × 4; 9, ovary × 4; 10, ovary, laid open × 4; 11, ovule × 10; 12, fruiting branch, from Hongkong, *n. s.*; 13, pod, laid open, showing seed *in situ*, *n. s.*; 14, seed, *n. s.*

23. DALBERGIA DYERIANA Prain ex Harms in Engl. Bot. Jahrb. xxix. 416 (1900); Journ. As. Soc. Beng. lxx. 2, 44 (1901).

A large climber, with rather slender, blackish, glabrous, spreading, sub-bifarious branches, sometimes hooked. *Leaves* 3—5 in. long; leaflets 11—15, obovate-oblong, base cuneate, apex rounded retuse, thinly coriaceous, finely closely reticulate, sparsely adpressed-pubescent beneath, 1—1·2 in. long, ·3—·5 in. wide; rachis 2·5—3·5 in. long, and petiolules ·1 in. long, glabrous or sparsely pubescent. *Flowers* in lax rather few-flowered axillary panicles, 2 in. long, 1·25 in. wide, peduncles and pedicels, the latter ·1 in. long, puberulous; *calyx* puberulous, campanulate, with oblong to lanceolate basal bracteoles; teeth triangular obtuse, the two upper the widest, the lowest longer than the others, subacute; *corolla* yellowish-white, petals distinctly clawed, standard oblong, emarginate; *stamens* 9, connate in a sheath split on upper side, filaments free in their upper fourth, alternately shorter and longer; *ovary* stipitate, glabrous or puberulous; stipe always puberulous; style always glabrous, stigma small, capitate; *ovules* 2—3. *Pod* indehiscent, thinly coriaceous, distinctly stipitate, linear-oblong, 1—2-seeded, 2·5—3·5 in. long, ·5 in. wide, finely but distinctly reticulated opposite the seeds; *seed* oblong-reniform, ·5 in. long, ·2 in. wide, ·15 in. thick.

CHINA: Hupeh, *Henry* 3437! 4132! 4138! 4561! Szechuen; near Ky-min-se, *Farges* 1076! Yunnan; Mengtze, *Henry* 10503!

Farges gives the Chinese name in Szechuen as *Ta-kang-kin-ten.*

PLATE 27. Dalbergia Dyeriana *Prain.*—1, Flowering shoot from Mengtze, Yunnan, *n. s.*; 2, young calyx, with epicalycine bracteoles × 4; 3, calyx, laid open × 4;

4, epicalycine bracteoles × 4; 5, standard × 4; 6, wings × 4; 7, keel-petals × 4; 8, stamens × 4; 9, ovary, × 4; 10, ovary, laid open × 4; 11, ovule × 10; 12, fruiting branch, from Hupeh, *n. s.*; 13, pod, *n. s.*; 14, seed, *n. s.*

24. DALBERGIA CONFERTIFLORA Benth. Pl. Jungh. i. 255 (1851); Journ. Linn. Soc. iv. Suppl. 41 (1860); Bak. in Hook. f. Flor. Brit. Ind. ii. 233 (1876); Prain Journ. As. Soc. Beng. lxvi. 2, 114 (1897); lxx. 2, 56 (1901); Bengal Plants i. 411 (1903).

D. paniculata Wall. Cat. 5848 partly (1832), not of Roxb.

D. rubiginosa Kurz Journ. As. Soc. Beng. xlv. 2, 281 (1876); For. Flor. Burm. i. 347 (1877), not of Roxb.

D. Thomsoni Kurz For. Flor. Burm. i. 549 (1877), not of Benth.

A large climber, with lenticelled branches; branchlets sparsely puberulous, soon glabrescent. *Leaves* 4—6 in. long; leaflets 11—15, oblong, obtuse or retuse, base subcuneate, green and glabrous above, paler and sparsely puberulous beneath, firmly chartaceous, 1—1·5 in. long, ·5—·75 in. wide, the terminal rather the largest; rachis 3—4 in. long and petiolules glabrous. *Flowers* small, in ample terminal panicles extending into the axils of the uppermost leaves, 3—5 in. long, the panicle branches ending in corymbosely or subcapitately crowded cymes; peduncles, branches and pedicels rather densely rusty-pubescent; bracteoles ovate, densely pubescent, the basal deciduous, the epicalycine pair embracing lower fifth of calyx-tube; *calyx* narrowly campanulate, rusty-pubescent; teeth short obtuse except the lowest longer acute; *corolla* white, petals rather short-clawed, standard orbicular-oblong, emarginate; *stamens* 9, in one sheath split along upper side; *ovary* stipitate, pubescent along the sutures, elsewhere glabrous; style short; *ovules* 3—4. *Pod* indehiscent, thinly coriaceous, narrowly oblong, quite glabrous, apex subacute, base rounded, shortly stipitate, faintly veined opposite the 1—2, rarely 3 seeds, 2—3 in. long; ·75—1 in. wide; *seed* reniform, compressed, ·35 in. long, ·25 in. wide.

HIMALAYA: Daphla Hills; *Lister*! INDO-CHINA: Assam; Khasia Hills, *Simons*! Silhet, *Gomez & de Silva*! Chittagong; Kasalong, *Lister*! *Clarke*! Thandacheri, *Badal Khan*! Burma; Pegu, *Kurz*! Andamans; S. Andaman, *Man*! *Heinig*!

PLATE 28. Dalbergia confertiflora *Benth.*—1, Flowering branch, from Chittagong, *n. s.*; 2, bud × 4; 3, pedicel and bracteoles × 4; 4, calyx, laid open × 4; 5, standard × 4; 6, wings × 4; 7, keel-petals × 4; 8, stamens × 4; 9, ovary × 4; 10, ovary, opened × 4; 11, ovule × 12; 12, twig, in fruit, from the Andamans, *n. s.*; 13, pod, opened, showing seed *in situ*, *n. s.*; 14, seed, *n. s.*

25. DALBERGIA YUNNANENSIS Franch. Pl. Delavay. 187 (1890); Prain Journ. As. Soc. Beng. lxx. 2, 43 (1901).

A large climber, or a large shrub or small tree with subsarmentose trunk with numerous spreading branches, some of which are casually hooked. *Leaves* 8—12 in. long; leaflets usually 15, occasionally 13, often 17—19, rarely more, elliptic with rounded base and obtuse, occasionally emarginate apex, finely pubescent with adpressed hairs on both surfaces, more densely on the midrib beneath, the distal not exceeding the others, the lowest rather smaller than the rest, 1—2 in., rarely 3 in. long, ·5—·8 in., rarely 1—1·25 in. wide, rather dull-green above, paler beneath; rachis 6—9 in. long, puberulous; petiolules ·2 in. long, pubescent; stipules caducous. *Flowers* shortly pedicelled, in cymose terminal panicles extending into axils of upper leaves, with puberulous peduncle and branches, 6 in. long, 3 in. wide; *calyx* campanulate, sparsely pubescent externally, with 2 ovate, deciduous, membranous basal bracts, 5-toothed; teeth with ciliate margins, obtuse, the two upper subconnate, the lowest considerably longer than the lateral and as long as the tube; *corolla* white; petals all distinctly clawed, standard with oblong emarginate limb; *stamens* 9, connate in a sheath split along upper side, filaments free in their upper third, alternately shorter and longer; *ovary* glabrous or slightly puberulous along one suture and on the rather long stipe, style short, stigma small, capitate; *ovules* 2—3. *Pod* glabrous, indehiscent, distinctly stipitate, ovate or ovate-lanceolate, acute or obtuse, distinctly reticulated and somewhat thickened opposite the solitary seed, 2—2·5 in. long, ·8—1 in. wide; *seed* much compressed, orbicular-reniform, ·5 in. long, ·3 in. wide, ·15 in. thick; testa brown, smooth, not shining.

S. China: Yunnan; near Tapintze and at Yen-tzehay, *Delavay* 510! 654! 2050! Meng-tze, *Henry* 10205! Szemao Mts., 5000 ft., *Henry* 11898!

Very nearly related to *D. foliacea*, of which it exhibits the habit, but with larger flowers, more numerous and smaller leaflets, and smaller pods.

Plate 29. Dalbergia yunnanensis *Franch.*—1, Flowering branch from Yunnan, collected by Delavay, *n. s.;* 2, portion of branch with hooked branchlet, *n. s.;* 3, bracteoles × 4; 4, calyx, laid open × 4; 5, standard × 4; 6, wings × 4; 7, keel-petals × 4; 8, stamens × 4; 9, ovaries, one entire, one laid open × 4; 10, ovule, much enlarged; 11, fruiting spray, from a Yunnan specimen, *n. s.;* 12, fruit, laid open, showing seed *in situ*, *n. s.;* 13, seed, *n. s.*

26. Dalbergia Collettii Prain Journ. As. Soc. Beng. lxvi. 2, 445 (1897) in part, as to sp. Collett. only; lxx. 2, 445 (1901).
Dalbergia sp. Coll. & Hemsl. Journ. Linn. Soc. xxviii. 50 (1891).

A scandent shrub. *Leaves* 6 in. long; leaflets 13—15, narrowly elliptic, obtuse or subacute, membranous, dark-green, sparsely grey-pubescent above, rather densely pubescent, especially on the midrib beneath, 1·25 in. long, ·45 in. wide; rachis 4·25 in. long, grey-pubescent as are the pedicels, ·15 in. long; stipules caducous, membranous. *Flowers* in dense corymbose terminal panicles extending into the axils of the uppermost leaves, 4 in. long, 2 in. wide, peduncles and branches grey-pubescent; bracts ovate, bracteoles 2, large, ovate, membranous, caducous, embracing the lower half of the calyx-tube, grey-pubescent; *calyx* campanulate, ·1 in. long, upper teeth subconnate and lateral obtuse shorter than tube, lowest lanceolate nearly as long as tube; *corolla* white, ·2 long, petals short-clawed, standard oblong, slightly emarginate, not reflexed; *stamens* 9, in one sheath split along upper side; filaments free in their upper third, alternately shorter and longer; *ovary* very shortly stipitate, glabrous except on stipe and along lower suture, style short stout; *ovules* 2. *Fruit* not seen.

Burma: Shan Hills; at Kawlo, 5,000 ft., *Collett* 591! Ywangin, 4,000 ft., *Collett* 723!

The Lwekaw specimens associated with this by the writer in 1897 do not belong here, but are the same as *Dalbergia Hemsleyi*, which is a considerable tree, whereas this is noted by Collett on his

n. 591 as a scandent shrub. The pubescence in *D. Hemsleyi* is very like that in the present species, but the leaflets are fewer and larger and have a very different venation. The nearest ally of *D. Collettii* is not *D. velutina*, as suggested by Collett and Hemsley, *loc. cit.*; it differs by its smaller flowers in terminal panicles, by its differently-shaped and deciduous stipules, by its larger epicalycine bracteoles; also by the absence of auricles from the bases of the wing-blades. Its nearest ally is *D. yunnanensis* Franch., from which it mainly differs in the smaller size of its flowers and leaflets, and of which it may prove to be only a variety.

PLATE 30. Dalbergia Collettii *Prain.*—1, Flowering branch, from the Shan Hills, *n. s.*; 2, bud × 4; 3, pedicel and epicalycine bracteoles × 4; 4, calyx, laid open × 4; 5, standard × 4; 6, wings × 4; 7, keel-petals × 4; 8, stamens × 4; 9, ovary × 4; 10, ovary, laid open × 4; 11, ovule × 8.

27. DALBERGIA FOLIACEA Wall. Cat. 5856 (1832); Benth. Pl. Jungh. i. 255 (1851); Journ Linn. Soc. iv. Suppl. 41 (1860); Bak. in Hook. f. Flor. Brit. Ind. ii. 232 (1876); Kurz Journ. As. Soc. Beng. xlv. 2, 230 (1876); For. Flor. Burm. t. 247 (1877); Prain Journ. As. Soc. Beng. lxx. 2, 43 (1901). *D. cnudioides* Pierre MSS. in Herb. Pierre.

A large climber, with numerous spreading branches, some of which are casually hooked; occasionally erect, 20—25 feet high. *Leaves* 7—9 in. long; leaflets usually 7, occasionally 9—11, elliptic-oblong, obtuse or retuse, glabrous above, glabrous or finely puberulous beneath, the distal rather the largest, 1·5—4 in. long. ·75—2 in. wide, dull- or bright-green; rachis 4 in. long, petiolules ·2 in. long; stipules caducous. *Flowers* almost sessile, in wide cymose terminal panicles with puberulous branchlets, 4—9 in. long, 2—5 in. wide; *calyx* campanulate, glabrous or puberulous, with two ovate deciduous basal bracts, 5-toothed, teeth obtuse, the two upper subconnate, the lowest slightly longer than lateral and about as long as the tube; *corolla* white, petals all rather long-clawed; standard with oblong emarginate limb; *stamens* 10, less often 9, connate in a sheath split along upper side; filaments free in their upper third, alternately shorter and longer; *ovary* glabrous or slightly puberulous along one suture and on the rather long stipe; style short; stigma small capitate; *ovules* 2—3. *Pod* indehiscent, distinctly stipitate, subacute, reddish-brown, firmly coriaceous, glabrous, 1—2-seeded; very markedly reticulated opposite the seed, 3—4 in. long, 1—1·25 in. wide; *seed* much compressed, reniform, ·5 in. long, ·25 in. wide, ·15 in. thick; testa brown, smooth, hardly shining.

INDO-CHINA: Tenasserim; Amherst, *Wallich*! Panlong Creek, *Wallich*! Moulmein, *Wallich*! Kalian river, *Wallich*! Mergui, *Helfer* 1806! Pegu; Rangoon, *Cleghorn*! Pegu, *Kurz* 2602! Tharawadi, *Manson*! Shan Plateau; Fort Stedman, *Abdul Huq*! *Prazer*! Moné, *Abdul Khalil*! Siam; borders of the Great Lake, *Godefroy* 686! Cambodia; Pên Lovier, in the plains, *Pierre* 509!

Mr. Bentham and, following him, Mr. Baker state that this is a tree: Mr. Kurz, however, has noted that it is a climber, and specimens both from Burma and Siam have the branches not infrequently hooked. This is the case even with some examples which are noted by Prazer as being from a tree 20—25 feet high, which shows that, as is the case with a number of other species of *Dalbergia*, this is a climber when it has anything to rest on but can develop an erect habit and climb upon itself when no foreign support is available.

The specimens from Siam and Cambodia (*Godefroy* 686 and *Pierre* 509) agree absolutely; they differ from the majority of the Burmese specimens in having the leaflets beneath quite glabrous. Their fruit is as yet unknown; should it differ from that of *D foliacea*, they may have to be considered a distinct species and will then be known by the MSS. name *D. entadioides* which M. Pierre has proposed.

Wallich's n. 5856, on which the species is based, is much and differently mixed in various herbaria with *D. stipulacea*, *D. torta*, *D. volubilis*, and *D. rimosa*.

PLATE 31. Dalbergia foliacea *Wall.*—1, Flowering branch, from the Shan Plateau *n. s.*; 2, calyx with bracteoles × 4; 3, calyx, laid open × 4; 4, standard × 4; 5, wings × 4; 6, keel-petals × 4; 7, stamens × 4; 8, ovary × 4; 9, the same, laid open × 4; 10, ovule × 10; 11, fruiting branch, from Pegu, *n. s.*; 12, seed, *n. s.*

¶8. **Cultratae**.—*Pod samaroid, oblong; leaflets obtuse; wings not hastate; style stout cylindric; epicalycine bracteoles subulate, shorter than calyx; trees.*

The species of this group are clearly *Sissoae* of the section *Podiopetalum*, but stand well apart from all other groups in the genus except the *Rostratae*, which are clearly *Amerimna* of the section *Endespermum*, by the subulate epicalycine bracteoles. The triviality of the character adds to its value: in this case it is associated with a structure of the anthers that is not met with in any other Asiatic *Dalbergia*.

28. DALBERGIA CULTRATA Grah. in Wall. Cat. 5861 (1832); Benth. Pl. Jungh. i. 254 (1851); Journ. Linn. Soc. iv. Suppl. 39 (1860); Bak. in Hook. f. Flor. Brit. Ind. ii. 233 (1876); Kurz Journ. As. Soc. Beng. xlv. 2, 280; For. Flor. Burm. i. 342 (1877); Coll. & Hemsl. Journ. Linn. Soc. xxviii. 50 (1891); Prain Journ. As. Soc. Beng. lxx. 2, 45 (1901).

D. zeylanica Wall. Cat. 5847 B. (1832), not of Roxb.

A fine tree, 30—70 feet high, with glabrous lenticelled branches, branchlets subbifarious; trunk 2·5—3 feet thick, bark rather smooth, pale. *Leaves* 6—8 in. long; leaflets usually 7, occasionally 9, rarely 11, elliptic-obovate, when young subacute and covered beneath with fine deciduous hairs, when full-grown quite glabrous on both surfaces and obtuse almost always retuse at apex, finely reticulately veined, the distal rather the largest, 1—1·75 in. long, ·6—1·5 in. wide; rachis 5—6 in. long, glabrous, petiolules ·15 in. long; stipules minute, pubescent, very caducous. *Flowers* in short lateral, subfasciculate panicles 2 in. long; peduncles and slender pedicels, ·15 in. long, at first beset with scattered rusty hairs, soon glabrous; bracts lanceolate, caducous, bracteoles at base of pedicels and two, occasionally only one, at base of calyx, subulate, soon deciduous; *calyx* campanulate, ·15 in. long, at first with scattered deciduous hairs, soon glabrous, teeth subequal, ovate-acute, the two upper subconnate; *corolla* pale-rose with a yellow spot at base of standard, or white; petals all distinctly clawed, standard orbicular, emarginate; *stamens* 9, monadelphous, in a sheath split along upper side, filaments free in their anterior third, subequal, anthers with subapical slits soon coalescing to leave the anther, after pollen is shed, as a gaping 2-lipped cup; *ovary* quite glabrous, stipitate; style stout; stigma capitate; *ovules* almost always 3. *Pod* coriaceous, rigid, usually 1-seeded, 2 in. long, rarely 2—3-seeded, 3—4 in. long, ·6 in. wide, pale straw-coloured, faintly reticulated opposite the seed; *seed* compressed, reniform, brown, ·4 in. long ·25 in. wide.

INDO-CHINA: Burma; Pegu, *Kurz* 1787! 2609! *Wallich*! *McClelland*! *Brandis*! Shan Hills Terai, *Collett* 406! Taungyi, *King's Collector*! near Maymyo, *Prazer*! Tenasserim;

Paratola, 2,500 ft., Taepo, 5,000 ft., and Chuku Plains, *Gallatly*! Trogla, near the hills, *Wallich* 5847B! Tavoy, *Shaik Muquim*! Siam; Radboerie, *Teysmann* 6027!

Kurz gives the Burmese name as *Yendiké*.

PLATE 32. Dalbergia cultrata *Grah.*—1, Branch in flower and young leaf, from Pegu, *n. s.*; 2, pedicel with basal and epicalycine bracteoles × 4; 3, bud × 4; 4, calyx, laid open × 6; 5, standard × 6; 6, wings × 6; 7, keel-petals × 6; 8, stamens × 6; 9, ovary × 6; 10, ovary, laid open × 6; 11, ovule × 10; 12, fruiting branch, from Tenasserim, *n. s.*; 13, pod, one valve removed, showing seed *in situ*, *n. s.*; 14, seed, *n. s.*

29. DALBERGIA FUSCA Pierre MSS. in Herb. Pierre.

A tree; wood red. *Leaves* 4—6 in. long; leaflets 7—10, ovate, obtuse or retuse, base cuneate, dark-green glabrous above, finely adpressed-pubescent beneath, ·75—1·5 in. long, ·5—·75 in. wide; rachis 3·25—·45 in. long, sparsely pubescent as are the petiolules ·2 in. long; stipules caducous. *Flowers* in short axillary and infra-axillary panicles, 1·5 in. long, ·5 in. wide; pedicels ·2 in. long, slender; bracts and bracteoles not seen; *calyx* campanulate, 3 lower teeth wide-triangular, acute, the lowest one-half longer than the lateral, 2 upper rounded subconnate; *corolla* white, petals rather long-clawed, standard not seen; *stamens* in one sheath split above; anthers not seen. *Pod* stipitate, ligulate-lanceolate, firmly coriaceous, narrowed to both ends but more abruptly to the apex, 2·5—4 in. long, ·6 in. wide, 1-, rarely 2-seeded; *seed* reniform, compressed, ·4 in. long, ·25 in. wide.

INDO-CHINA: Cochin China; Bienhoa, near Baochung, *Pierre's collectors!* at Baochianh, *Pierre* 1706! Burma; Pinmona, *King's collector!* CHINA: Yunnan, Szemao Mts., 5,000 ft., *Henry* 11,667!

This is very near, perhaps too near, *D. cultrata* Grah; the calyx hardly differs, the wings and keel-petals are identical; the leaflets, however, are always distinctly smaller than in *D. cultrata* and differ markedly from those of that species in being persistently adpressed-pubescent beneath and in having a less prominent midrib. The Anamite name is *Câm-lai*. In Yunnan it is a small to medium tree.

PLATE 33. Dalbergia fusca *Pierre.*—1, Branch, with leaves and fruit, from Baochianh, *n.s*; 2, calyx, laid open × 4; 3, wing-petal × 4; 4, keel-petal × 4; 5, staminal sheath, anthers fallen × 4; 6, pod, laid open, showing young seed *in situ*, *n. s.*

¶ 9. **Sissoo.**—*Pod samaroid, narrow-ligulate; leaflets acuminate; neither wings nor keel-petals hastate; style very short, stout; epicalycine bracteoles obtuse, as long as calyx; a tree.*

This group, which contains but one species, is also a very distinct one. The characters of the main-group *Sissoa* are in the solitary member, *D. Sissoo*, shown in their most emphatic form since neither the wings nor the keel-petals are hastate and the standard, though quite large, is not thrown backward as in the *Amerimna*. But while the long standard-claw marks it as a typical *Podiopetalum* it shares with the *Triptolemeae* the short style, while it at the same time shares with the group *Latifoliae*—which in all other respects are very different and are quite typical members of the section *Miscolobium* among the *Amerimna*—the character of possessing very large caducous epicalycine bracteoles that, till they fall, quite envelope the calyx.

30. Dalbergia Sissoo Roxb. Hort. Beng. 53 (1814); DC. Prodr. ii. 416 (1825); Roxb. Flor. Ind. iii. 223 (1832); Wall. Cat. 5850 (1832); W. & A. Prodr. i. 264 (1834); Grah. Cat. Bomb. Pl. 55 (1839); Voigt Hort. Suburb. Calcutt. 241 (1845); Benth. Pl. Jungh. i. 254 (1851); Journ. Linn. Soc. iv. Suppl. 40 (1860); Dalz. & Gibs. Bomb. Flor. Suppl. 24 (1861); Bedd. Flor. Sylvat. t. 25 (1869); Stewart Panjab Pl. 65 (1869); Brand. For. Flor. 149 (1874); Bak. in Hook. f. Flor. Brit. Ind. ii. 231 (1876); Talbot Bomb. List 74 (1894); Gamble Darjeel. List 28 (1896); Woodr. Journ. Nat. Hist. Soc. Bomb. xi. 426 (1897); Prain Journ. As. Soc. Beng. lxx. 2, 40 (1901); Kanjilal Flor. Sch. Circ. 128 (1901); Cooke Flor. Pres. Bomb. i. 395 (1902); Prain Bengal Plants i. 411 (1903).

D. pendula Ten. Rend. Soc. Borb. Nap. i. 409 (1842).

A tree, 30—80 ft. high, with rough grey bark and usually a crooked stem that may be 4 ft. in diam. at 5 ft. from the ground, with numerous spreading branches; young shoots pendulous, sub-bifarious, pubescent. *Leaves* 6 in. long; leaflets usually 5, but often 3, occasionally 4, suborbicular, cuspidate, very rarely obtuse, occasionally, on young shoots after pollarding, ovate-lanceolate; pale-green, puberulous when young, smooth and shining when old, though sometimes more persistently puberulous in the drier western parts of its habitat; distal leaflets almost always the largest, 1—2·5 in. long and broad or in the adventitious narrower form, 1—2·5 in. long by ·5—1 in. broad; rachis 2·5—3·5 in. long, somewhat zigzag; petiolules ·2 in. long, at first puberulous, ultimately glabrous; stipules lanceolate, caducous. *Flowers* almost sessile, in short axillary subcymose puberulous panicles, 2·5 in. long; *calyx* campanulate, enclosed within 2 large, very caducous, membranous bracts, puberulous, 5-toothed, the two upper teeth rounded, the lateral pair subacute, shorter than the rather narrow acute lowest, all shorter than the tube; *corolla* yellowish-white, petals all rather long-clawed, standard with suborbicular, slightly emarginate limb; *stamens* 9, in one sheath split along upper side, filaments free in their upper fourth, alternately shorter and longer; *ovary* pubescent, rather long-stipitate, style very short, stigma capitate; *ovules* 4—6. *Pod* indehiscent, shortly stipitate, obtuse, strap-shaped, pale straw-coloured or ultimately brownish, firmly coriaceous, glabrous, 1—2 or rarely 3-seeded, distinctly but sparingly veined opposite the seeds, 2·5—3 in. long, ·5 in. wide; *seed* much compressed, reniform, ·3 in. long, ·2 in. wide, ·07 in. thick, testa brown, hardly shining.

N.-W. Frontier: Beluchistan; *Stocks* 718! *Lace* 3497! 3615! N.-W. Himalaya: Hazara, *Stewart* 32! Yunasar, *Schlich!* Below Komharsen, *Gamble* 6151! Chamba, *Clarke* 23723! Kangra, *Clarke* 23810! Dehra Dun, *King!* Rajputana: Ajmir, *Moir!* Makerji Hill, *Brandis!* Panjab: Campbellpur, occasional on river cliffs, *Stewart* 71! Sikkim: Terai, *Gamble!* Duars, *Prain!* Lower Hills, *Hooker!* Assam: Brahmaputra Valley, *Simons!* *Mann* 36!

Cultivated examples—Panjab: Lahore, *Brandis!* Delhi, *O. Kuntze!* Meerut, *Thomson!* *Clarke!* Chittagong: Sitapahar reserve, *Ellis!* Upper Gangetic Plain: Oude, *Wallich!* Saharanpur, *Royle!* Etawah, *Hume!* Lower Gangetic Plain: Bengal, *Wallich!* *Kurz!* *Prain!* Deccan: Poona, *Tilak!* *Cooke!* Gwalior, *Maries!* Saugor, *Jerdon!* S. India: Coorg, *Hohenacker!* Paulghat, *Wight!* *Naidoo!* Madras, *Heyne!*

It is not certain, though it is probable, that the species is nowhere truly wild save in the submontane forests, and then only in gravelly river beds, along the Himalaya from Upper Assam to the Panjab. It is given by Hooker as occurring up to 1,000 feet in Sikkim, and it occurs up to 3,000—4,000 feet in the North-West Himalaya and in Beluchistan. The only suggestion of its being possibly wild in S. India is a note by Hohenacker on a sheet in the Herb. De Candolle, where it is mentioned as occurring in the forests of Coorg, where the inhabitants know it as *Bihti Mara*.

Mr. Bentham states that the ovules may be 2—4, but the writer has never met with fewer than 4 ovules and 5—6 are quite common numbers. Roxburgh says the pod is 3-seeded, by which he must mean that pods occur which are 3-seeded, but not pods with more than 3 seeds.* Bentham also admits the existence of 3-seeded pods, but states that there may be only one seed. The writer has never met with a pod containing more than 2 seeds, and the proportion of 1-seeded to 2-seeded pods is in reality as 85 : 15. The leaves of this species in Rajputana and in Beluchistan remain long, sometimes apparently persistently, pubescent: those of the submontane forests and of trees planted in Eastern and Southern India early become glabrous.

The form of leaf with narrow leaflets is only known in cultivated trees, and has only been met with in the Panjab and in the Upper Gangetic plain; it appears to be strictly confined to the adventitious shoots that appear after pollarding. The terminal flower of a raceme often has three in place of the normal two basal bracts.

This species is often spoken of as nearly allied to *D. latifolia*. That both are *Dalbergias* and both are familiar timber-trees is true: beyond those fundamental characters there is, however, no obvious affinity between the two. The petals are very different, for in *D. Sissoo* neither the wings nor the keel-petals are auriculate, in *D. latifolia* both are; in *D. Sissoo* the style is very short and stout; in *D. latifolia* it is long and slender. In *D. Sissoo* the pod is narrow-ligulate, quite unlike that of *D. latifolia* and its allies, and most like that met with in the two otherwise very different species—*D. sericea* and *D. sacerdotum*.

Buchanan-Hamilton (*Martin's History*), writing of this species, says it is not indigenous in Purnea, away from the foothills, though it is extensively planted. He points out that it is a very different tree from the *Sisu* of South India, which is also a *Dalbergia*, and observes that the name *Sisu* in Purnea is likewise given to *Stillingia sebifera*.

PLATE 34. Dalbergia Sissoo *Roxb.*—1, Branch showing both flower and fruit (the latter a year old), from a tree cultivated in Bengal, *n. s.*; 2, leaf, full grown, from a Merwara specimen, *n. s.*; 3, leaf, young, of the narrow-leafed form, from the Panjab, *n. s.*; 4, calyx, laid open × 4; 5, standard × 4; 6, wings × 4; 7, keel-petals × 4; 8, staminal sheath × 4; 9, ovaries, one entire, one laid open × 4; 10, ovule, greatly enlarged; 11, seed, *n. s.*; 12, bud, showing enveloping bracteoles × 6.

---

* Mr. Baker describes the pod of *D. Sissoo* as having sometimes 4 seeds and as not being veined opposite the seed: possibly this description applies to the fruit of some other species.

SUBGENUS II.—AMERIMNON.

Flowers with the standard-blade reflexed or refracted; wings and keel-petals both hastate; style long, slender, usually subulate, rarely cylindric.

This is a very natural subgenus, the characters to be obtained from the petals being more uniform throughout its limits than they are in *Sissoa.* The reason for this is perhaps partly that there is much less variation in size of flowers here than in *Sissoa.* In character of pod there is much the same variety; all the types that prevail in *Sissoa* recur in *Amerimnon,* though the nummular type is in this subgenus absent from Asia.

§ 3. **ENDESPERMUM.**—Standard rather distinctly refracted at junction of rather small blade and narrow claw; stamens normally monadelphous; style subulate.

This section is, as regards the majority of its species, very distinct. A few, however, but for their monadelphous stamens, are very like climbing *Dalbergarias,* and a few, but for their refracted vexillum, are much like the *Velutinae* among the *Miscolobia.*

¶ 10. **Rostratae.**—*Pods wide-ligulate, samaroid; epicalycine bracteoles subulate; leaflets large, few; climbers or small trees.*

The epicalycine bracteoles, which are like those of the ¶ *Cultratae,* mark this group as very distinct not only from the rest of the *Endesperma* but from all the other Asiatic *Amerimna.*

31. DALBERGIA HULLETTII Prain Journ. As. Soc. Beng. lxvi. 2, 119 (1897); lxx. 2, 45 (1901).

A small tree with blackish, rugose, rusty-puberulous, thickish branchlets, leafless when in flower; stipules ovate-acute, ·25 in. long, rusty-pubescent. *Flowers* in short clustered racemes, 1—1·5 in. long, rising among tufts of triangular rusty-pubescent, small bracts in axils of fallen leaves; lowest pedicels longest, slender, ·3 in. long, rusty-pubescent as are the peduncles; bracteoles at base of pedicels ovate-lanceolate, long persistent, ·1 in. long; bracteoles below calyx small, subulate, deciduous; *calyx* campanulate, densely rusty-tomentose, ·15 in. long; teeth acute, half as long as tube; *corolla* white, petals long-clawed, standard orbicular, reflexed; *stamens* 9, rarely 10, in one sheath split along upper side; *ovary* glabrous, with long, densely pubescent stipe; *ovule* solitary.

MALAYA: Singapore, in swampy scrub jungle; *Hullett* 626!

This species is evidently very nearly related to the Bornean *D. Havilandi,* but differs in having a glabrous ovary, larger main-bracteoles and smaller stipules; leaves have not yet been seen. Mr. R. W. Hullett, who collected this plant in 1885, and who was asked in 1896 whether he had ever seen it again, has written (27th September 1896):—

"It was in a bit of swampy land covered with scrub, about five miles from Singapore. But now most of the scrub has been cleared away and I could find no signs. It was on 21st February 1885 that I collected it, and I shall look out about the same time next year and am not hopeless of success."

But unfortunately the search has so far *been* hopeless.

PLATE 35 A. Dalbergia Hullettii *Prain.*—1, Portion of flowering branch, *n. s.;* 2, young flower × 4; 3, pedicel with bracteoles × 4; 4, calyx, laid open × 4; 5, standard × 4; 6, 6′, wings × 4; 7, keel-petals × 4; 8, stamens × 4; 9, ovary × 4; 10, ovary, laid open × 4; 11, ovule × 4.

32. DALBERGIA HAVILANDI Prain Journ. As. Soc. Beng. lxx. 2, 45 (1901).

A small tree, with blackish, rugose, rusty-puberulous, thickish branchlets. *Leaves* 3—4 in. long; leaflets 1—3; when 3 the lateral ones subopposite, ovate obtuse or subacute, base truncate; pubescent, especially on the nerves above, densely velvety beneath, firmly coriaceous, 2—3 in. long, 1—1·5 in. wide; rachis ·5—1 in. long, densely velvety; petiolules velvety, ·15 in. long; stipules ovate, acute, ·3 in. long, densely velvety. *Flowers* in short clustered racemes, ·5—1 in. long, rising among tufts of triangular rusty-velvety bracts in axils of fallen leaves, lowest pedicels longest, slender, ·3 in. long, tawny-pubescent as are the peduncles; bracteoles at base of pedicels ovate-lanceolate, persistent, ·05 in. long; bracteoles below calyx small, subulate, deciduous; *calyx* campanulate, tawny-tomentose, ·15 in. long; teeth acute, half as long as tube; *corolla* white, petals long-clawed, standard orbicular, reflexed; *stamens* 9, in one sheath split along upper side or occasionally (*fide* Haviland *in filed-note*), also along lower side with then two bundles of 5 and 4 respectively; *ovary* densely pubescent with long pubescent stipe; *ovules* 2.

MALAYA: Borneo, near Kuching, *Haviland* 2894! 2895!

PLATE 35 B. Dalbergia Havilandi *Prain.*—12, Leafy twig, *n. s.*; 13, flowering twig, *n. s.;* 14, young flower × 4; 15, pedicel with bracteoles × 4; 16, calyx, laid open × 4; 17, stamens × 4; 18, wings × 4; 19, keel-petals × 4; 20, ovary × 4; 21, ovary, laid open × 4; 22, ovule × 10.

33. DALBERGIA ROSTRATA Grah. in Wall. Cat. 5867 (1832); Prain Journ. As. Soc. Beng. lxx. 2, 45 (1901).

D. Sissoo Miq. Flor. Ind. Bat. i. 128 (1855), not of Roxb.

D. pseudo-sissoo Miq. Flor. Ind. Bat. i. 128 (1855); Prain Journ. As. Soc. Beng. lxvi. 2, 118 (1897).

D. diversifolia Bl. ex Miq. Flor. Ind. Bat. i. 1, 128 (1855).

D. Championii Thw. Enum. Pl. Zeylan. 94 (1859); Benth. Journ. Linn. Soc. iv. Suppl. 39 (1860); Bak. in Hook. f. Flor. Brit. Ind. ii. 231 (1876); Trim. Ceyl. Flor. ii. 88 (1894).

D. nitida Zipp. ex Prain Journ. As. Soc. Beng. lxx. 2, 46 (1901).

Endespermum diversifolium Bl. ex Miq. Flor. Ind. Bat. i. 5, 128 (1855).

E. zeylanicum Champ. ex Thw. Enum. Pl. Zeylan. 94 (1859).

A shrubby climber, 15—25 feet long, with twining glabrous branches; occasionally erect, 15—20 feet high. *Leaves* glabrous, medium-green, 6 in. long; leaflets firm, usually 3—4, occasionally 5, rarely 2 or even solitary, oblong, slightly narrowed from beyond the middle to the cuneate or rounded base, widely rounded and abruptly cuspidate at apex, 2—4 in. long, 1—2 in. wide, the terminal usually distinctly the largest; rachis 2—3 in. long, petiolules 25 in. long, both glabrous; stipules caducous. *Flowers* in lax axillary panicles with subcorymbose branches, 2·5—3·5 in. long and nearly as wide; the peduncles and branches finely grey-downy; pedicels ·15 in. long, with small caducous ovate basal bracteoles and slender subulate bracteoles under the calyx; *calyx* campanulate, ·2 in. long, puberulous externally, teeth subequal in length, wide-triangular except the narrow lowest, the two upper subconnate; *corolla* creamy-white, the petal-tips flushed with pink; petals all long-clawed, standard irregularly orbicular-oblong, limb reflexed; *stamens* usually 9, in one sheath split along upper side, filaments free in their upper third, alternately shorter and longer, anthers ultimately gaping, cup-like; *ovary* long-stipitate, densely pubescent, usually 1-, but frequently 2-ovuled, style slender incurved, stigma minute. *Pod* indehiscent, brownish, ligulate, obtuse, firmly coriaceous, 3—4 in. long, ·5—·65 in. wide; *seed* solitary, oblong, ·75 in. long, ·25 in. wide, testa reddish-brown, smooth, shining.

MALAYA: Celebes; at Lepo-Lepo near Kandari, *Beccari!* Borneo; Kuching, *Haviland* 2111! Sungei Upanang, *Beccari* 3379! Gunong Woh, *Beccari* 2845! Igau, *Beccari* 3906! 3908! Singkawang, *Teysmann* 7875! Java; *Blume*! *Zippel*! *Hasskarl*! Malay Peninsula; Perak, *Kunstler*! *Scortechini*! *Wray*! Penang, *Curtis*! Singapore, *Wallich* 5867! *Hullett*! *Ridley*! CEYLON: moist regions from 2,000—4,000 feet, *Champion*! *Thwaites*! INDIA: Tinivelly; Tambraparni river, at foot of ghâts, *Beddome* 2424!

PLATE 36. Dalbergia rostrata *Grah.*—1, Flowering branch, from Perak, *n. s.*; 2, bud × 4; 3, pedicel with epicalycine bracteoles × 4; 4, calyx, laid open × 4; 5, standard × 4; 6, 6′, wings × 4; 7, keel-petals × 4; 8, stamens × 4; 9, ovary × 4; 10, ovary, laid open × 4; 11, ovule × 4; 12, fruiting branch, from Perak, *n. s.*; 13, seed, *n. s.*

¶ 11. **Rubiginosae.**—*Pod oblong, samaroid; epicalycine bracteoles obtuse; leaflets large to medium, few; climbers or small trees.*

A natural group, standing fairly intermediate between the *Rostratae*, which they resemble in foliage, and the *Congestae* and *Polyphyllae*, which they resemble as to epicalycine bracts.

34. DALBERGIA KINGIANA Prain Journ. As. Soc. Beng. lxvii. 2, 289 (1898); lxx. 2, 46 (1901).

A shrub, with lenticelled puberulous branches. *Leaves* 7—8 in. long; leaflets usually 7—9, ovate-lanceolate, acute, base cuneate, coriaceous, green and glabrous above, glaucescent and when young sparsely puberulous at length almost glabrous beneath, the distal leaflet hardly exceeding the rest, 3·5—4 in. long, 1·25—1·5 in. wide, rachis 3—4 in. long and petiolules ·2 in. long at first finely puberulous, ultimately quite glabrous. *Flowers* in short axillary panicles, 2·5—3 in. long, 2 in. wide; peduncles, branches and short pedicels rusty-tomentose; bracteoles at base ovate-lanceolate, obtuse, deciduous, epicalycine bracteoles deciduous, spathulate-lanceolate, embracing lower part of calyx-tube; *calyx* campanulate, extremely rusty-tomentose; teeth sub-equal in length, triangular, the two upper sub-connate; *corolla* white, petals all long-clawed, standard orbicular, faintly notched, reflexed; *stamens* 9, united in a sheath split along upper side, filaments free in their upper fourth and alternately shorter and longer; *ovary* long-stipitate, quite glabrous, style subulate, stigma minute; *ovules* 2.

INDO-CHINA: Burma; Kachin Hills, near Myitkyina, *Shaik Muzim*! CHINA: Yunnan; Szomao Mts., *Henry* 12848!

This species is very closely related to *D. Henryana* from Yunnan; it differs in having a perfectly glabrous ovary and ultimately glabrous leaf-rachis and leaflets which latter are distinctly glaucescent beneath. It is also nearly related to *D. Benthami* from Hongkong.

PLATE 37. Dalbergia Kingiana *Prain.*—1, Flowering branch from the Kachin Hills, *n. s.;* 2, bud × 4; 3, calyx, laid open × 4; 4, standard × 4; 5, wings × 4; 6, keel-petals × 4; 7, stamens × 4; 8, ovary × 4; 9, ovary, laid open × 4; 10, ovule × 10.

35. DALBERGIA HENRYANA Prain Journ. As. Soc. Beng. lxx. 2, 46 (1901).

A large woody climber, with closely rusty-pubescent young branches. *Leaves* 4·5—5 in. long; leaflets 4—5, ovate-acute, base cuneate or rounded, coriaceous, glabrous above, softly, rather densely pubescent beneath; the terminal leaflet rather the largest, 1·75—3 in. long, 1—1·5 in. wide; rachis 2—2·5 in. long and petiolules ·2 in. long, persistently rusty-puberulous. *Flowers* in short axillary panicles, 2·5—3 in. long, 2 in. wide; peduncles branches and pedicels rusty-tomentose; pedicels ·12 in. long with ovate, obtuse, deciduous basal and epicalycine bracteoles, the latter embracing the lower part of calyx tube; *calyx* campanulate, externally rusty-tomentose; teeth triangular, the lowest rather longest, the rest subequal, the two upper subconnate; *corolla* white, petals all long-clawed, standard orbicular, faintly notched, reflexed; *stamens* 9, united in a sheath split along upper side; filaments free in their upper fourth and alternately shorter and longer; *ovary* long-stipitate, pubescent as is the stipe; style subulate, stigma minute; *ovules* usually 2.

CHINA: Yunnan, at Mengtze, 5,000 feet, *Henry* 11,248!

Except in the longer lowest calyx-lobe and the pubescent ovary, this does not differ from *D. Kingiana* as regard flowers. The foliage, however, differs considerably, and it is not yet safe to suggest that the two are conspecific.

PLATE 38. Dalbergia Henryana *Prain.*—1, Flowering branch, from Mentgze, Yunnan, *n. s.;* 2, bud × 4; 3, pedicel with epicalycine bracteoles × 4; 4, calyx, laid open × 4; 5, standard × 4; 6, wings × 4; 7, keel-petals × 4; 8, stamens × 4; 9, ovary × 4; 10, ovary, laid open × 4; 11, ovule × 8.

36. DALBERGIA BENTHAMI Prain Journ. As. Soc. Beng. lxvii. 2, 289 (1898); lxx. 2 46 (1901).

D. rubiginosa Benth. Journ. Linn. Soc. iv. Suppl. 43 in part (1860); Flor. Hongkong 93 (1861); Forbes & Hemsl. Journ. Linn. Soc. xxiii. 198 (1887), not of Roxb.

A woody climber, or sometimes a shrub, with very long black glabrous branches. *Leaves* 4—6 in. long; leaflets 5—7, ovate, narrowed to the petiolule and to the obtuse, slightly retuse tip; coriaceous, glabrous above, minutely adpressed-puberulous beneath; the distal the largest, 1·25—2·5 in. long, ·75—1·5 in. wide; rachis 2—2·25 in. long and petiolules, ·2 in. long, finely adpressed-puberulous. *Flowers* in short axillary racemes or panicles, 1·5 in. long, 1 in. wide, peduncles and distinct slender pedicels, ·1 in. long, rusty-tomentose, basal bracteoles oblong, deciduous, epicalycine bracteoles short, lanceolate, obtuse, persisting; *calyx* campanulate, externally rusty-tomentose; teeth all sub-equal triangular obtuset; *corolla* white, petals all long-clawed; standard orbicular, emarginate, reflexed; *stamens* 9, in a sheath split along upper side, filaments free in their upper third, alternately shorter and longer; *ovary* long-stipitate, glabrous, style subulate; *ovules* 2, or often 3. *Pod* thinly coriaceous, glabrous, stipitate, ligulate, 1—2-seeded 2—3 in. long, ·6 in. wide, faintly reticulated opposite the seeds; *seed* reniform, compressed, ·45 in. long, ·2 in. wide.

CHINA: Hongkong, *Hance*! *Wilford*! *Wright*! *Ford*! *Seemann*! *Bodinier*! *Urquhart*! *Harland*!

The opportunity of seeing the fruits of this species, collected by Bodinier and communicated by Ford, finally settled the impossibility of following Bentham in his identification of it with *D. rubiginosa*.

PLATE 39. Dalbergia Benthami *Prain*.—1, Flowering branch, from Hongkong, *n. s.*; 2, bud × 4; 3, calyx, laid open × 4; 4, standard × 4; 5, wings × 4; 6, keel-petals × 4; 7, stamens × 4; 8, ovary × 4; 9, ovary, laid open × 4; 10, 11, pods, from Hongkong (*Bodinier*), *n. s.*; 12, seed, *n. s.*

37. DALBERGIA RUBIGINOSA Roxb. Corom. Pl. ii. 9, t. 115 (1798); Willd. Sp. Pl. iii. 2, 902 (1800); Roxb. Hort. Beng. 98 (1814); Roth Nov. Pl. Sp. 332 (1821); DC. Prodr. ii. 416 (1825); W. & A. Prodr. i. 265 (1834); Benth. Pl. Jungh. i. 255 (1851); Journ. Linn. Soc. iv. Suppl. 43 (ref. China excl.) (1860); Bak. in Hook. f. Flor. Brit. Ind. ii. 232 (1876); Prain. Journ. As. Soc. Beng. lxvi. 2, 443 (1897); lxx. 2, 47 (1901); Cooke Flor. Pres. Bomb. i. 397 (1902).

An extensive climber, with finely puberulous branches, often twisted into thickened hooks. *Leaves* 3—5 in. long; leaflets usually 5, but often 3, less often 7, ovate or elliptic-oblong, obtuse, thinly coriaceous, glabrous above, minutely puberulous beneath, the distal the largest, ·75—2·5 in. long, ·5—1·25 in. wide; rachis 1—2 in. long, ·5—1·25 in. wide, and petiolules, ·15 in. long, puberulous. *Flowers* in short axillary racemes or panicles, ·5—·75 in. long; peduncles and short pedicels, ·05 in. long, rusty-tomentose; basal bracteoles triangular-ovate, persistent, epicalycine bracteoles ovate, embracing lower fourth of calyx-tube; *calyx* campanulate, externally puberulous, slightly gibbous at base; teeth subequal, all obtuse, the two upper rather wider than the three lower; *corolla* white; petals all long-clawed, standard orbicular, emarginate, reflexed; *stamens* 9, in a sheath split along upper side, filaments free in their upper fourth, alternately shorter and longer; *ovary* glabrous, long-stipitate; style subulate, stigma minute; *ovules* 1—3. *Pod* indehiscent, thinly coriaceous, oblong, long-stipitate, 1·25 in. long, ·5 in. wide, reticulate opposite the seed; *seed* reniform, much compressed, ·5 in. long, ·25 in. wide.

INDIA: N. Canara; Ainslie Ghat, *Talbot*! Dodmune, *Talbot*! Nakund, *Talbot*! Concan; *Dalzell*! *Wight*! *Stocks*!

PLATE 40. Dalbergia rubiginosa *Roxb*.—1, Flowering specimen, from Concan coast, *n. s.*; 2, young flower × 4; 3, pedicel with epicalycine bracteoles × 4; 4, calyx, laid open × 4; 5, standard × 4; 6, keel-petals × 4; 7, wings × 4; 8, stamens × 4; 9, ovary × 4; 10, ovary, laid open × 4; 11, fruiting twig, from Canara, *n. s.*; 12, fruit opened, with seed *in situ*, *n. s.*; 13, seed, *n. s.*

¶ 12. **Menoeides**.—*Pod falcate-subreniform, thickened throughout; epicalycine bracteoles obtuse; leaflets few; climbers.*

A group that is only subnatural. The two Asiatic species it includes agree as to pods and as to flowers. If general appearance and habit be alone considered and the artificial character afforded by the fruit be neglected, *D. menoeides* might be treated as a member of the group *Rubiginosae*, *D. torta* as a member of the group *Congestae*.

38. DALBERGIA MENOEIDES Prain Journ. As. Soc. Beng. lxvi. 2, 120 (1897); lxvi. 2, 453 (1897); lxx. 2, 50 (1901).

An unarmed climber, with glabrous, twining, hooked branches. *Leaves* 5 in. long; leaflets 3, ovate-lanceolate, tapering to both ends, dark green glabrous above, paler sub-glaucescent, sparsely adpressed-puberulous beneath, 3—3·5 in. long, 1—1·5 in. wide; rachis 1·5 in. long, glabrous; petiolules very short, puberulous. *Flowers* very few, sessile, clustered at apices of short, puberulous, axillary peduncles, ·15—·25 in. long; epicalycine bracteoles ovate, embracing lower third of calyx-tube; *calyx* campanulate, sparingly puberulous externally; teeth short, obtuse, subequal, the two upper slightly connate; *corolla* white, petals all long-clawed, standard suborbicular, slightly emarginate, reflexed; *stamens* 10, in one sheath split along upper side, filaments free in their upper fourth; *ovary* stipitate, glabrous; style subulate, stigma minute; *ovule* solitary. *Pod* semilunar, greenish, flat, glabrous, firm, reticulated throughout, the upper suture recurved; 1·5 in. long, ·75 in. wide; apex acute; stipe rather short; *seed* solitary, reniform.

MALAYA: Perak; Krian, *Scortechini*!

PLATE 41. Dalbergia menoeides *Prain.*—1, Flowering branch, from Krian, Perak, *n. s.*; 2, young flower × 4; 3, pedicel with epicalycine bracteoles × 4; 4, calyx, laid open × 4; 5, standard × 4; 6, wings × 4; 7, keel-petals × 4; 8, stamens × 4; 9, ovary × 4; 10, ovary, laid open × 4; 11, ovule × 10; 12, portion of fruiting branch, from Krian, Perak, *n. s.*

39. DALBERGIA TORTA Grah. in Wall. Cat. 5873 (1832); A. Gray Bot. Wilkes Exped. i. 458 (1854); Prain Journ. As. Soc. Beng. lxvi. 2, 120 (1897); Volkens in Engl. Bot. Jahrb. xxxi. 464 (1901); Cooke Flor. Pres. Bomb. i. 397 (1902).

Karin-Tagera Rheede Hort. Malabar. vi. 25 (1686).

Cassia candenatensis Dennst. Schl. zum Hort. Malabar. 12 (1818).

Dalbergia monosperma Dalz. Hook. Journ. Bot. ii. 36 (1850); Benth. Pl. Jungh. i. 256 (1851); Miq. Flor. Ind. Bat. i. 1, 132 (1855); Thw. Enum. 94 (1859); Benth. Journ. Linn. Soc. iv. Suppl. 48 (1860); Flor. Hongkong. 93 (1861); Dalz. & Gibs. Bomb. Flor. 78 (1861); Seemann Flor. Vitens. 64 (1865); Bak. in Hook. f. Flor. Brit. Ind. ii. 337 (1876); Nav. & Fernand.-Vill. Nov. App. Flor. Philip. 67 (1880); Drake del Castillo Illust. Flor. Pacif. 156 (1886); Trim. Ceyl. Flor. ii. 89 (1894); Talbot Bomb. List 75 (1894); Woodr. Journ. Nat. Hist. Soc. Bomb. xi. 426 (1897).

Drepanocarpus monospermus Kurz Journ. As. Soc. Beng. xlv. 2, 281 (1876); For. Flor. Burm. i. 337 (1877).

Dalbergia candenatensis Prain Journ. As. Soc. Beng. lxx. 2, 49 (1901); Bengal Plants i. 411 (1903).

An unarmed littoral climber, with twining glabrescent branches, often twisted into spiral hooks. *Leaves* 3 in. long; leaflets 5, very rarely 3 or 7, obovate-oblong, obtuse, sometimes emarginate, dark-green glabrous above, paler, sparingly adpressed-pubescent beneath, ·6—·8 in. long, ·4—·6 in. wide; rachis 2 in. long, glabrous; petiolules ·1 in. long, glabrous. *Flowers* in sessile congested axillary panicles, 1—2 in. long, with very slightly puberulous branches; bracts small, ovate-lanceolate; bracteoles at base of pedicels ovate-lanceolate, the epicalycine pair larger ovate, embracing lower third of calyx-tube; *calyx* wide-campanulate, glabrescent; teeth short, wide-triangular, obtuse, the two upper subconnate; *corolla* white, petals all long-clawed, standard oblong, reflexed; *stamens* 9 or sometimes 10, in one sheath split along upper side, filaments free in their upper third; *ovary* stipitate, glabrous; style subulate, stigma minute; *ovules* usually solitary, sometimes 2. *Pod* indehiscent flat, brown, falcately recurved along upper suture, rather thick-walled throughout, usually 1-seeded, very rarely 2-seeded, shortly stipitate, ·9 in. long or, when 2-seeded, 1·5 in. long, ·5 in. wide; *seed* reniform, compressed, ·4 in. long, ·2 in. wide.

MICRONESIA: Carolines, *Volkens.* MELANESIA: Tonga; Vavau, *Crootz*! Fiji; Viti, *Seemann* 128! New Caledonia; *Pancher*! *Deplanche*! *Veillard*! NEW GUINEA: *Forbes*! AUSTRALIA: Queensland; Rockingham Bay, *Dallachy*! Cape York, *Daemel*! Northern Territory; Port Darwin, *Schultz* 744! PHILIPPINES; Luzon, Batangos, *Cuming*! *Vidal*! Manila, *Cuming*! Ilo-Ilo; Panay, at Igbaras, *Naves & Fernandez-Villar.* MALAYA: Moluccas; Amboina, *Forster*! Ceram Laut, *Forster*! *Warburg*! Celebes; Lepo-Lepo near Kandari, *Beccari*! Borneo; Sarawak, *Beccari*! Igau, *Beccari*! Bintulu, *Haviland*! Biliton; Blimbong, *Teysmann*! Sumatra; Indrapara, *Korthals*! *Miller*! Singapore; *Wallich*! *Kurz*! *Anderson*! *Ridley*! *Wichura*! Malacca; *Ridley*! Perak; *Scortechini*! *Wray*! Penang; *Wallich*! *Curtis*! Langkawi; *Curtis*! CHINA: Hongkong, *Hance*! Little Hongkong, *Ford*! INDO-CHINA: Tongking, *Balansa*! Annam; Haton, *Godefroy*! Cambodia; near Saigon, *Lefèvre*! Tenasserim; Mergui, *Griffith*! Amherst, *Falconer*! Martaban, *Wallich*! Andamans; Narcondam, *Prain*! S. Andaman, *Man*! *Heinig*! INDIA: Sundribuns, *Clarke*! *Heinig*! *Prain*! Ceylon; Pandure, Trincomali, and Kodiyar, *Thwaites*! *Trimen*! Malabar; Candenate, *Rheede*; Quilon, *Wight*! Concan; *Stocks*! *Law*!

This is known to the wood-cutters of the Sundribans as *Panchioli;* the Annamese name is *Cayme-mûk;* the Cambodian is *Bai-tuk.*

PLATE 42. **Dalbergia torta** *Grah.*—1, Flowering branch, from S. Andaman, *n. s.;* 2, flower × 4; 3, epicalycine bracteoles × 4; 4, calyx, laid open × 4; 5, standard × 4; 6, wings × 4; 7, keel-petals × 4; 8, stamens × 4; 9, ovary × 4; 10, ovary, laid open × 4; 11, ovule × 6; 12, twig, showing hooked branches, from Martaban, *n. s.;* 13, branch with fruit, from the Sundribuns, *n. s.;* 14, pod, laid open, showing seed, *in situ*, *n. s.;* 15, seed, *n. s.*

¶ 13. **Congestae.**—*Pod ovate, samaroid; epicalycine bracteoles obtuse; leaflets medium to small, few or many; climbers.*

A fairly natural group because, though their leaflets are of different shape and their pods are somewhat dissimilar, the general habit of *D. congesta* and *D. Gardneriana* is the same; indeed, the two species have so much in common that an author so careful as Mr. Baker has suggested their union. An examination of the figures of the two will, however, show that this is not a proposal which is convenient. On the other hand, though the number and size of the leaflets be different, *D. Gardneriana* and *D. malabarica* are very closely related in every essential character. It is to Beddome that the suggestion that *D. malabarica* is a distinct species is originally due, as a specimen in the Kew collection testifies; that specimen, however, has no fruits, so that Oliver and Baker, who have dealt with it, did not feel justified in giving it the specific rank proposed by Beddome. Fuller material now amply proves the justice of Beddome's original opinion, and demonstrates that while *D. malabarica* no doubt forms a connecting link between the *Congestae* and the *Polyphyllae*, it is to the former rather than to the latter group that it is most nearly allied. A recently discovered Bornean species, *D. Hoseana*, seems to serve as a further connecting link between the two groups.

40. Dalbergia congesta Grah. in Wall. Cat. 5872 (1832); W. & A. Prodr. i. 265 (1834); Benth. Pl. Jungh. i. 255 (1851); Journ. Linn. Soc. iv. Suppl. 43 (1860); Bak. in Hook. f. Flor. Brit Ind. ii. 232, syn. *D. Gardneriana* excl. (1876); Prain Journ. As. Soc. Beng. lxx. 2, 47 (1901).

A strong climber or an erect shrub with wide-spreading branches, sometimes a tree up to 30 feet high; young branches pubescent. *Leaves* 3—5 in. long; leaflets 5—11, cuneate-ovate, apex emarginate, thinly coriaceous, sparsely adpressed-pubescent on both surfaces, the distal rather the largest, ·75—1·75 in. long, ·4—1 in. wide; rachis 2—3 in. long, pubescent as are the short petiolules. *Flowers* in congested or open axillary panicles ·5—2 in. long, ·3—1·5 in. wide; branches and short pedicels rusty-pubescent; basal bracteoles ovate, epicalycine bracteoles ovate-acute, embracing lower third of calyx-tube,—all rusty-pubescent; *calyx* campanulate, glabrescent, slightly gibbous at base; teeth subobtuse subequal except the lowest longer and acute, the upper two subconnate; *corolla* white, petals long-clawed, standard orbicular, emarginate, reflexed; *stamens* 9, in a sheath split along upper side, filaments free in their upper fourth, alternately shorter and longer; *ovary* glabrous, stipitate; style subulate, stigma minute; *ovules* 2. *Pod* indehiscent, firmly coriaceous, ovate, shortly stipitate, glabrous, much reticulated opposite the solitary seed, 2 in. long, ·8 in. wide; *seed* reniform, compressed, not seen mature.

India: Nilgiris; Coonoor, *Noton*! *Gamble*! *Brandis*! *Prain*! Indo-China: Burma; Chin Hills, *Prazer*!

Plate 43. Dalbergia congesta *Grah.*—1, Flowering branch, from Coonoor, *n. s.*; 2, bud × 4; 3, pedicel with basal and epicalycine bracteoles × 6; 4, calyx, laid open × 4; 5, standard × 4; 6, wings × 4; 7, keel-petals × 4; 8, stamens × 4; 9, ovary × 4; 10, ovary, laid open × 4; 11, ovule × 10; 12, fruiting branch, from Chin Hills, *n. s.*; 13, pod, opened, showing young seed *in situ*, *n. s.*

41. Dalbergia Gardneriana Benth. Journ. Linn. Soc. iv. Suppl. 42 (1860); Prain Journ. As. Soc. Beng. lxvi. 2, 444 (1897); lxx. 2, 47 (1901).
D. congesta Bak. in Hook. f. Flor. Brit. Ind. ii. 232 in part (1876), not of Benth.

A climber, with densely rusty-tomentose branches. *Leaves* 2·75—3·5 in. long; leaflets 7—11, oblong-elliptic, obtuse or retuse, coriaceous, glabrous above, densely rusty-tomentose beneath,—all subequal, 1 in. long, ·6 in. wide; rachis 2—2·5 in. long, densely rusty-tomentose as are the short petiolules. *Flowers* in short, sessile, axillary cymes,

·5—·75 in. long, ·3—·4 in. wide; short pedicels densely rusty-tomentose; basal bracteoles ovate, epicalycine ovate-oblong, densely rusty-tomentose; *calyx* campanulate, slightly gibbous at base; teeth subequal, all subobtuse, the two upper subconnate, rather wider than the others; *corolla* white, petals all long-clawed, standard orbicular, emarginate, reflexed; *stamens* 9, in a sheath split along upper side; filaments free in their upper fourth; *ovary* villous, stipitate; style subulate, stigma small; *ovules* 1—2. *Pod* indehiscent, thinly coriaceous, narrow-oblong, long-stipitate, brown, shining, reticulated throughout, but especially opposite the seeds, 1·5 in. long, ·5 in. wide; *seed* solitary, compressed, ovate, ·4 in. long, ·2 in. wide.

INDIA: Nilgiris; *Gardner*! *Metz*! *Wight*! *G. Thomson*! *Clarke*! *Gamble*! *Perottet*!

It has been suggested by Mr. Baker that this is a variety of *D. congesta*. It is, however, more nearly related to *D. malabarica*, which is treated by Mr. Baker as a form of *D. tamarindifolia*.

PLATE 44. Dalbergia Gardneriana *Benth.*—1, Flowering branch, *n. s.;* 2, bud × 4; 3, pedicel and epicalycine bracteoles × 4; 4, calyx, laid open × 4; 5, standard × 4; 6, wings × 4; 7, keel-petals × 4; 8, stamens × 4; 9, ovary × 4; 10, ovary, laid open × 4; 11, ovule × 10; 12, fruiting branchlet, *n. s.;* 13, pod, laid open with seed *in situ, n. s.;* 14, seed, *n. s.*

42. DALBERGIA HOSEANA Prain sp. nov.

A shrubby climber, with rusty-velvety young branches. *Leaves* 2—3·5 in. long; leaflets 9—13, thinly pubescent above, more densely tomentose, especially on the rusty midrib beneath, crowded, elliptic to ovate-lanceolate, hardly or not oblique at the base, ·35—·6 in. long, ·25—·35 in. wide, membranous; rachis 1·5—3 in. long, densely rusty-pubescent, as are the very short petiolules; stipules lanceolate, rusty-pubescent. *Flowers* appearing with the leaves in small, lax, few-flowered, axillary corymbs, ·6 in. long, ·5 in. wide; peduncles ·2 in. long and very slender pedicels densely pubescent; basal bracteoles ovate-lanceolate, persistent, epicalycine bracteoles lanceolate, persistent, pubescent; *calyx* campanulate, glabrous except on margins of teeth, which are much shorter than the tube; all obtuse, the two upper teeth connate; *corolla* white, ·35 in. long, petals all long-clawed; standard narrowly ovate, entire, reflexed; *stamens* 9, in one sheath split along upper side, filaments free in their upper fourth; *ovary* long-stipitate, quite glabrous as in the stipe; style filiform, stigma minute; *ovule* solitary.

MALAYA: Borneo; Kuching, *Haviland & Hose* 3375!

A very distinct species, nearest to *D. malabarica* which it connects with the remaining *Congestae*, but easily recognized by its fewer thinner leaflets and its somewhat different calyx.

PLATE 45. Dalbergia Hoseana *Prain.*—1, Flowering branch from Kuching, Borneo, *n. s.;* 2, bud × 4; 3, flower × 4; 4, pedicel and bracteoles × 4; 5, calyx, laid open × 4; 6, standard × 4; 7, wings × 4; 8, keel-petals × 4; 9, stamens × 4; 10, ovary × 4; 11, ovary, laid open × 4; 12, ovule × 10.

43. DALBERGIA MALABARICA Prain Journ. As. Soc. Beng. lxx. 2, 48 (1901).
D. tamarindifolia VAR. *pubescens* Bak. in Hook. f. Flor. Brit. Ind. ii. 235 (1876); Cooke Flor. Pres. Bomb. i. 399 (1902).

A shrubby climber, with densely rusty-pubescent young branches. *Leaves* 3·5—4 in. long; leaflets 21—31, thinly pubescent above, densely tomentose beneath, crowded, elliptic-oblong, hardly or not oblique at the base, ·5 in. long, ·25 in. wide, moderately firm; rachis 3—3·5 in. long, densely pubescent, as are the very short petiolules; stipules lanceolate, rusty-pubescent. *Flowers* appearing with the leaves, in densely-congested sessile axillary corymbs, ·5 in. long, ·25 in. wide; peduncles densely pubescent, pedicels glabrous; basal bracteoles triangular-ovate, persistent, epicalycine bracteoles ovate-lanceolate, obtuse, persistent, pubescent; *calyx* campanulate, glabrous except on margins of teeth, which are nearly as long as tube, the 3 lower acute, the 2 upper connate, obtuse; *corolla* white, ·35 in. long, petals all long-clawed, standard ovate, entire, reflexed; *stamens* 9, in one sheath split along upper side, filaments free in their upper third; *ovary* glabrous except along upper suture; stipe long, pubescent; style filiform, stigma minute; *ovules* 2. *Pod* indehiscent, ovate-oblong, very thinly coriaceous, glabrous, long-stipitate, 1·25 in. long, ·6 in. wide, distinctly reticulately veined, especially opposite the seed.

INDIA: Concan; *Stocks*! Canara, *Talbot* 408! 3665! Quilon, *Wight*! S. Tinivelly, *Beddome*!

PLATE 46. Dalbergia malabarica *Prain.*—1, Flowering branch from Siddapore, N. Canara, *n. s.*; 2, epicalycine bracteoles × 4; 3, calyx, laid open × 4; 4, standard × 4; 5, wings × 4; 6, keel-petals × 4; 7, stamens × 4; 8, ovary × 4; 9, ovary, laid open × 4; 10, fruiting twig, from Halihal, N. Canara, *n. s.*; 11, young seed, *n. s.*

¶ 14. **Polyphyllae.**—*Pod ligulate, samaroid, with parallel sides; epicalycine bracteoles obtuse; leaflets small to medium, rarely large, usually many; climbers, rarely small trees.*

A very natural group forming the core, so to speak, of the section *Endespermum*, recognized by Blume, but by few subsequent authors, as a distinct genus. While fairly uniform in general habit, one of the species, *D. densa*, in certain localities developes larger and at the same time fewer leaflets than usual, and so brings the group into contact with the *Rubiginosae* and *Rostratae* at one extremity of the series of species it includes, much as *D. acaciaefolia* or *D. polyphylla* approach *D. malabarica* and the *Congestae* generally at the other extremity.

44. DALBERGIA ACACIÆFOLIA Dalz. in Kew Journ. ii. 37 (1850); Benth. Pl. Jungh. i. 256 (1851).

D. tamarindifolia Benth. Journ. Linn. Soc. iv. Suppl. 44 in part (1860), not of Roxburgh.

D. tamarindifolia VAR. *acaciaefolia* Bak. in Hook f. Flor. Brit. Ind. ii. 235 (1876); Cooke Flor. Bomb. Pres. i. 399 (1902).

A shrubby climber, or a tree with weak spreading branches; branchlets finely puberulous. *Leaves* 5—6 in. long; leaflets 41—51, quite glabrous, dark-green above, glaucescent, finely adpressed-pubescent beneath, crowded, linear-oblong, base and midrib oblique, apex retuse, firmly coriaceous, caducous, ·6 in. long, ·2 in. wide; rachis 4·5—5·5 in. long, puberulous; petiolules puberulous, very short. *Flowers* with the leaves, in rather lax axillary panicles with corymbose branches, 1—2 in. long, 1 in. wide, peduncles, branches and pedicels finely puberulous; epicalycine bracts rather large, ovate, embracing lower third of calyx-tube; *calyx* campanulate, slightly gibbous, rusty-pubescent externally; teeth shorter than tube, all obtuse, the two upper subconnate; *corolla* white, petals all long-clawed, standard orbicular-oblong, much reflexed and markedly auricu'ate at base of limb; *stamens* 10, in one sheath split above; *ovary* glabrous, distinctly stipitate; style filiform; *ovules* 2. *Pod* indehiscent, ligulate, obtuse, very firmly coriaceous, indurated and thickened opposite the seed, but not veined there or elsewhere, long-stipitate, 2·25 in. long, ·6 in. wide; *seed* solitary, compressed, reniform.

INDIA: Concan; *Law*! Canara; Dodmune, *Talbot*! Tinivelly Hills, *Naidoo*!

PLATE 47. Dalbergia acaciæfolia *Dalz.*—1, Flowering branch, from the Concan, *n. s.*; 2, bud × 4; 3, calyx, laid open × 4; 4, standard × 4; 5, wings × 4; 6, keel-petals × 4; 7, stamens × 4; 8, ovary × 4; 9, ovary, laid open × 4; 10, ovule × 10; 11, fruit, from the Concan, *n. s.*

45. DALBERGIA TAMARINDIFOLIA Roxb. Hort. Beng. 53 (1814); Flor. Ind. iii. 233 in part (1832); Wall. Cat. 5870 (1832); Wight Ic. t. 242 (excl. fruit) (1840); Voigt Hort. Suburb. Calcutt. 241 (1845); Benth. Pl. Jungh. i. 256 (1851); Miq. Flor. Ind. Bat. i. 1, 131 (1855); Benth. Journ. Linn. Soc. iv. Suppl. 44 (1860); Bak. in Hook. f. Flor. Brit. Ind. ii, 234 (1876); Kurz Journ. As. Soc. Beng. xlv. 2, 281 (1876); For. Flor. Burm. i. 348 (1877). Nav. & Fernand. Vill. Nov. App. Flor. Philip. 67 (1880); Vidal Plant Vasc. Filip. iii (1886); Woodr. Journ. Nat. Hist. Soc. Bomb. xi. 426 (1897); Prain Journ. As. Soc. Beng. lxvi. 2, 117 (1897); lxx. 2, 49 (1901); Cooke Flor. Pres. Bomb. i. 398 (1902); Prain Bengal Plants i. 411 (1903).

D. rufa Grah. in Wall. Cat. 5864 (1832).

D. multijuga Grah. in Wall. Cat. 5865 (1832); Zoll. & Mor. Syst. Verzeichn. 2 (1845).

D. livida Wall. Cat. 5866 in part (1832), not of Grah.

D. Blumei Hassk. Cat. Hort. Bog. 284 (1844); Pl. Jav. Rar. 400 (1848).

Endespermum scandens Bl. Cat. Gew. Buitenzorg 92 (1823); Flora viii. 1, 132 (1825).

E. retusum Bl. ex Miq. Flor. Ind. Bat. i. 1, 131 (1855).

An erect tree 15—40 feet high, with long flexuous sarmentose branches, or a shrubby climber, with densely pubescent young branches. *Leaves* 5—6 in. long; leaflets 25—41, thinly pubescent on both sides, rather paler beneath, crowded, trapezoid-oblong, ·6—·75 in. long, ·3 in. wide, moderately firm, caducous; rachis densely puberulous, 4·5—5·5 in. long; petiolules very short; stipules lanceolate, ·2 in. long, densely puberulous. *Flowers* appearing with the leaves, in congested sessile or shortly peduncled axillary panicles with corymbose branches, ·5—2 in. long, ·5—1 in. wide; peduncles, branches and pedicels densely puberulous; bracts and bracteoles at base of pedicel and under calyx ovate, puberulous, persistent; *calyx* campanulate, pubescent externally (in Himalayan) or glabrescent (in Indo-Chinese and Malayan specimens), pale greenish-yellow; teeth ovate, the two upper subconnate; *corolla* white, petals all long-clawed, standard ovate, reflexed; *stamens* 9—10, in one sheath split above; *ovary* glabrous, stipitate; style narrow; *ovules* 2—3. *Pod* indehiscent, thin, greenish, drying bright-brown, glabrous, long-stipitate, ligulate, subacute, 1—3-seeded; uniformly finely reticulate, 1·5—3 in. long, ·4—·5 in. wide; *seed* narrow, nearly straight, ·7 in. long, ·15 in. wide.

HIMALAYA: Nepal; *Wallich*! Sikkim; *Hooker*! *Lister*! *Prain*! CHINA: Yunnan; Szemao Mts. 4,500 feet elev., *Henry* 12147! INDO-CHINA: Assam; Sibsagor, Goalpara, Gauhati, *Simons*! *Peal*! *Jenkins*! *Mann*! *Clarke*! *Watt*! Silhet, *Gomez*! Naga Hills, *Abdul Huq*! *Watt*! Chittagong; Kodala, *Badul Khan*! Burma; Kachin Hills, Sadon, *Shaik Muqim*! Taping Valley (politically Chinese) between Poneshee and Tapen Khyong, *J. Anderson*! Tenasserim; Maulmein, Amherst, *Wallich*! *Griffith*! *Helfer*! *Falconer*! Andamans; S. Andaman, *Man*! *Kurz*! Barren Island, *Prain*! PHILIPPINES: Luzon; Morong, *Vidal*! San Mateo, *Naves & Fernandez Villar*. MALAYA: Langkawi, *Curtis*! Penang, *Wallich*! Perak, *Scortechini*! *Kunstler*! *Wray*! *Ridley*! Malacca, *Maingay*! *Derry*! Sumatra, *Korthals*! *Forbes*! Java, *Horsfield*! *Ploem*! *Zollinger*! Borneo, *Korthals*! *Motley*! *Creagh*! *Haviland*!

Derris pinnata Lour., Flor. Cochin-China, 432 (1790), is often referred to this species. From Loureiro's description his plant is clearly a *Dalbergia*, but that it is not *D. tamarindifolia* is almost certain, because Loureiro's plant has glabrous leaflets, which, even when they are mature, *D tamarindifolia* never has. Another, though perhaps less valid, objection to the identification is that *D. tamarindifolia* does not appear to have been collected in Cochin-China.

For some reason that is not quite clear *Endespermum scandens* Bl. has been considered a doubtful species, and in the *Index Kewensis* has been tentatively referred to *D. Championii*, *i.e.*, to *D. rostrata*. The description given by Blume is so very precise that no dubiety is possible; the numerous leaflets, pubescent on both sides, and the roundish epicalycine bracts are characters that alone suffice to make the suggestion alluded to impossible; the shape of the leaflets (oblique at the base, rounded on the upper, cuneiform on the lower side) indicates that Blume's plant can only be *D. tamarindifolia* among the Malayan *Dalbergias*.

PLATE 48. Dalbergia tamarindifolia *Roxb.*—1, Flowering branch, from Assam, *n. s.*; 2, bud × 4; 3, calyx, laid open × 4; 4, standard, from in front and from behind × 4; 5, wings × 4; 6, keel petals × 4; 7, stamens × 4; 8, ovary × 4; 9, ovary, laid open × 4; 10, ovule × 8; 11, fruiting twig, from Perak *n. s.*; 12, pod, laid open, showing seed *in situ*, *n. s.*; 13, seeds, *n. s.*

46. DALBERGIA POLYPHYLLA Benth. Pl. Jungh. i. 256 partly (1851); Journ. Linn. Soc. iv. Suppl. 44 partly (1860); Nav. & Fernand. Vill. Nov. App. Flor. Philip. 67 (1880); Vidal Phan. Cuming. Philipp. 38, 109 (1885); Rev. Plant. Vasc. Filip. 114 (1886); Prain Journ. As. Soc. Beng. lxx. 2, 48 (1901).

D. volubilis Llanos Mem. Acad. Cienc. Madr. (1858); App. Ad. Flor. Philip. Blanco Ed. iii. iv. 103 (1880) possibly.

A climbing shrub, with much lenticelled branches, puberulous when young. *Leaves* 3—4 in. long; leaflets 25—49, crowded, glabrous above, thinly pubescent beneath, linear-oblong or narrow-ovate, rounded equal or very slightly oblique at base, rounded or rarely sub-acute at apex, ·5 in. long, ·15—·2 in. wide, moderately firm, readily falling; rachis puberulous, 2·5—3 5 in. long, petiolules very short; stipules very narrowly lanceolate, rusty-pubescent, caducous. *Flowers* rather before the leaves, in congested sessile lateral panicles with corymbose branchlets, ·5—1·5 in. long, ·5—1 in. wide, peduncles and pedicels puberulous; basal and epicalycine bracteoles rather large, ovate, the latter embracing lower fourth of calyx-tube; *calyx* campanulate, glabrescent; teeth short triangular, obtuse, the two upper sub-connate; *corolla* white, petals all long-clawed; standard suborbicular, slightly emarginate, reflexed; *stamens* 9—10, in one sheath split along upper side; *ovary* glabrous, long-stipitate; style subulate, stigma minute; *ovules* 1—2. *Pod* indehiscent, coriaceous, distinctly stipitate, ligulate, rounded at both ends, 2 in. long, ·5 in. wide, usually 1-seeded, reddish-brown; *seed* narrow-oblong, ·5 in. long, ·15 in. wide, hardly reniform.

PHILIPPINES: Luzon; *Cuming* 1164! *Vidal* 2589! *Loher* 2232! 2240! Angat; *Llanos.*

Vidal gives the name in Luzon as *Payasi.* Llanos says that the pod of his *D. volubilis* is linear; *D. polyphylla* is the only Philippine *Dalbergia* so far known to the pods of which this epithet could be applied; the identification suggested is, however, merely tentative and the recognition of Llanos' plant must be left to botanists in the Philippines.

PLATE 49. Dalbergia polyphylla *Benth.*—1, Portion of flowering branch, from Luzon (*Cuming* 1164 in Herb. Berol.), *n. s.;* 2, portion of flowering branch, from Luzon (*Loher*), *n. s.;* 3, pedicel with epicalycine bracteoles × 4; 4, calyx, laid open × 4; 5, standard × 4; 6, wings × 4; 7, keel-petals × 4; 8, stamens × 4; 9, ovary × 4; 10, ovary, laid open × 4; 11, ovule × 10; 12, pod, from Luzon (*Loher*), *n. s.;* 13 pod, laid open, showing seed *in situ*, *n. s.;* 14, seed, *n. s.*

47. DALBERGIA JAHERII Buerck ex Prain Journ. As. Soc. Beng. lxx. 2, 47 (1901).

A large shrubby climber, with glabrous branches. *Leaves* 4—6 in. long; leaflets 15—23, ovate-oblong, base faintly obliquely cuneate, apex rounded or slightly emarginate, chartaceous, green above, slightly glaucescent beneath, finely sparsely adpressed-pubescent on both surfaces, ·75—1·5 in. long, ·3—·6 in. wide; rachis 3—5 in. long, and petiolules ·15 in. long, glabrous. *Flowers* in congested axillary panicles 1·25 in. long, 1 in. wide; peduncles, branches, and pedicels ·1 in. long, puberulous; bracteoles ovate, obtuse, puberulous; *calyx* campanulate, glabrescent; teeth small, triangular, obtuse or subacute; *corolla* white, petals all long-clawed, standard orbicular, emarginate, reflexed; *stamens* 10, in one sheath split along upper side; *ovary* glabrous, long-stipitate; style subulate, stigma minute; *ovules* 1—2. *Pod* indehiscent, narrow-oblong, rather firmly coriaceous, distinctly stipitate, 1·5—2·5 in. long, ·5 in. wide; *seed* reniform, narrow, solitary or often 2.

PAPUASIA: Key Archipelago, *Warburg* 20312! *Jaher!*

PLATE 50. Dalbergia Jaherii *Buerck.*—1, Flowering branch from Key archipelago, *n. s.;* 2, bud × 4; 3, pedicel with epicalycine bracteoles × 4; 4, calyx, laid open × 4; 5, standard × 4; 6, wings × 4; 7, keel-petals × 4; 8, stamens × 4; 9, ovary × 4; 10, ovary, laid open × 4; 11, ovule × 6; 12, fruiting twig, from Key archipelago, *n. s.*

48. DALBERGIA BURMANICA Prain Journ. As. Soc. Beng. lxvi. 2, 448 (1897); lxx. 2, 47 (1901).

A tree 20—25 feet high, with wide-spreading branches, or a climber; branchlets puberulous. *Leaves* 5—7 in. long; leaflets 9—13, when young narrowly ovate-acute, when full-grown oblong, obtuse or retuse, slightly unequal at the base, 1·5—2 in. long, ·6—·8 in. wide; dark-green, at first closely pubescent on both surfaces, ultimately quite glabrous above and very sparingly pubescent beneath; stipules small, lanceolate, very caducous; rachis 4—5 in. long and petiolules ·1 in. long, glabrous. *Flowers* in dense lateral panicles with corymbose branches, appearing shortly before the leaves,

1·25 in. long, 1 in. wide; peduncles, branches and pedicels rusty-pubescent; bracteoles at base of pedicels and under calyx lanceolate, acute; *calyx* campanulate somewhat gibbous at base, externally rusty-pubescent; teeth subequal, acute, the two upper rather wider than the three lower; *corolla* purple, ·25 in. long, petals long-clawed, standard orbicular, emarginate, reflexed; *stamens* 9, in one sheath split along upper side, filaments free in their upper fourth; *ovary* glabrous, stipitate; style slender, stigma small; *ovules* 1—3. *Pod* thin, glabrous, subligulate-oblong, stipitate, uniformly widely but very distinctly reticulate throughout, rather distinctly margined along two-thirds of upper suture, rounded at both ends; 1- or 2-seeded; 3—3·75 in. long, ·7 in. wide; *seed* compressed, narrowly oblong, ·5 in. long, ·25 in. wide; testa brown, dull.

INDO-CHINA: Burma, Ruby mines, *Abdul Huq*! Chin Hills, *Dun*! CHINA: Yunnan; Szemao Mts., 5,000 feet elev., *Henry* 11740!

The nearest ally of this species is *Dalbergia Jaherii* Buerck, from Papuasia, which is most easily distinguished by its smaller leaflets and its glabrescent calyx. The flowers are stated by the native collector to be purple; those of *D. Jaherii* are white.

PLATE 51. Dalbergia burmanica *Prain.*—1, Flowering branch, from Ruby mines district, Upper Burma, *n. s.;* 2, flowering branch, Chin Hills, *n. s.;* 3, bud × 4; 4, pedicel with bracteoles × 4; 5, calyx, laid open × 4; 6, standard × 4; 7, wings × 4; 8, keel-petals × 4; 9, stamens × 4; 10, ovary × 4; 11, ovary, laid open × 4; 12, ovule × 10; 13, twig with fruit, from Szemao Mts., Yunnan, *n. s.;* 14, seed, *n. s.*

49. DALBERGIA PIERREANA Prain, sp. nov.

A shrubby climber, with densely tawny-pubescent young branches. *Leaves* 6—7 in. long; leaflets 17—19, ovate-oblong, base faintly obliquely cuneate, apex rounded obtuse, chartaceous, densely velvety-pubescent beneath, more sparingly above, dark-green above, paler beneath, 1 in. long, ·75 in. wide, the terminal rather longer (1·3 in. long) and subacute with subequal narrowly cuneate base; rachis 5—5·5 in. long, and petiolules ·07 in. long, densely tawny pubescent; stipules small, lanceolate, caducous. *Flowers* in short axillary panicles 1·5 in. long, ·5 in. wide; rachis, branches and slender pedicels, ·1 in. long, densely tawny-pubescent; *calyx* campanulate, tomentose, ·15 in. long; teeth triangular, short, subequal; *corolla* white, standard not seen, claws of wings and keel-petals as long as the calyx-tube; *stamens* 10, in one bundle split along upper side; *ovary* (not seen young) glabrous except the long, sparingly pubescent stipe; style subulate, stigma minute; *ovules* 2. *Pod* rather narrow-oblong, distinctly stipitate, with rounded apiculate tip, quite glabrous, 2—2·75 in. long, ·5 in. wide, very thin; usually 1 seeded, occasionally 2 seeded; *seed* reniform, compressed.

INDO-CHINA: Cambodia; Samrong, on Mt. Gruavi, *Pierre* 1037!

A very distinct species, in general appearance remarkably like *D. velutina*, but differing in the small deciduous stipules, in the shape of the leaflets and in the flowers which are those of a genuine *Endospermum*. Its nearest allies are *D. burmanica* and *D. Jaherii*, but it is easily distinguished from both by its pubescence. *D. malabarica* and *D. Hoseana* are also fairly close allies, but from the first it is readily distinguished by its larger leaflets, open panicles, and different pods; from the second by its larger and more numerous leaflets, its larger panicles, and its smaller and less persistent stipules.

PLATE 52. Dalbergia Pierreana *Prain.*—1, Leafy twig, from Mt. Gruavi, prov. Samrong, Cambodia, *n. s.;* 2, fruiting twig, from same locality, *n. s.;* 3, calyx, laid open × 4;

4, stamens × 4; 5, keel-petals × 4; 6, fruit, laid open, showing seed *in situ. n. s.*; 7, seed, *n. s.*

50. DALBERGIA DENSA Benth. Lond. Journ. Bot. ii. 217 (1843); Pl. Jungh. i. 255 (1851); Miq. Flor. Ind. Bat. i. 1, 128 (1855); Benth. Journ. Linn. Soc. iv. Suppl. 43 (1860); Flor. Austral. ii. 271 (1864); F. von Muell. Pap. Pl. (1875); Schum. in Engl. Bot. Jahrb. ix. 202 (1888); Schum. Flor. Kais. Wilhelmsl. 202 (1889); Warb. in Engl. Bot. Jahrb. xiii. 329 (1891); Bailey, Queensland Flora, 443 (1900); Schum. & Laut. Flor. Deut. Schutzgeb. Sueds. 359 (1901); Prain Journ. As. Soc. Beng. lxx. 2, 47 (1901).

A climbing shrub, or a small tree with weak and climbing branches; branchlets closely lenticelled. *Leaves* 6—8 in. long; leaflets 3—15, broadly oblong or oval or elliptic, obtuse or retuse, glabrous above, minutely thinly pubescent beneath, papery, ·75—1·5 in., rarely 2—3 in. long, ·5—·75, rarely 1·5 in. wide; rachis about 3 in. long, petiolules ·15 in. long, glabrous or puberulous. *Flowers* secund or subsecund, in short axillary panicles 1·5—2 in. long; peduncles puberulous or pubescent; pedicels slender or stoutish, ·1—·2 in. long; basal and epicalycine bracteoles ovate, puberulous externally; *calyx* campanulate, slightly gibbous; teeth rounded except the narrowly triangular lowest, shorter than the tube; *corolla* white, petals all long-clawed, standard reflexed, narrowly cucullate, emarginate at the tip; *stamens* 9, in one sheath split along upper side, filaments free in their upper fourth; *ovary* sparsely strigose or glabrous; style subulate, stigma minute; *ovules* 2. *Pod* (only seen in VAR. *australis*) thin, glabrous, light-brown, long-stipitate, strap-shaped, obtuse, rather firmly coriaceous, very faintly reticulated opposite the 1—2 seeds; *seed* usually solitary, sometimes 2, narrowly reniform, much compressed, ·5 in. long, ·2 in. wide, pale-brown.

VAR. *typica*: *leaflets* usually 7—9, occasionally 11, rarely 3—5, slightly puberulous beneath; young branches and panicles slightly pubescent; *ovary* strigosely hairy.

PAPUASIA: Moluccas; Amboina, *Teysmann* 5120! Jobie Island, north of New Guinea, *Barclay*! Key archipelago; Keteil at Tual, *Beccari*! Aru Islands; *Warburg*! New Guinea; without exact locality, *Hinds*! Kaiser Wilhelmsland, *Hollrung* 84! 174! 477!

VAR. *australis*: *leaflets* usually 11—15, rarely 9—10, considerably smaller, more closely pubescent beneath; young branches and panicles densely pubescent; *ovary* glabrous.

AUSTRALIA: Possession Island, *R. Brown*! Prince of Wales Island, *R. Brown*! Albany Island, *Hill*! Torres Straits, *Moseley*! Stuart's River (*von Mueller*)! Queensland, without exact locality (*Bailey*)!

The Stuart's River specimens are named by Baron von Mueller, no collector's name is given; the specimens from Queensland were kindly presented by Mr. F. M. Bailey; they are the only ones with fruit in Herb. Calcutta. The fruit of VAR. *typica* the writer has not seen; its larger, fewer and less pubescent leaflets with its strigose ovary make it necessary for the present to consider it varietally distinct from the southern form. The specimens from German New Guinea are, however, very nearly intermediate between those from Australia and those from the Moluccas.

Plate 53. Dalbergia densa *Benth.* var. typica.—1, Flowering branch, from the Moluccas, *n. s.;* 2, flower with basal and epicalycine bracteoles × 4; 3, calyx, laid open × 4; 4, standard × 4; 5, a wing-petal × 4; 6, a keel-petal × 4; 7, stamens × 4; 8, ovary × 4; 9, ovary, laid open × 4.

Plate 54. Dalbergia densa *Benth.* var. australis *Prain.*—1, Flowering branch, from Queensland, *n. s.;* 2, pedicel with basal and epicalycine bracteoles × 4; 3, calyx, laid open × 4; 4, standard × 4; 5, wings × 6; 6, keel-petals × 4; 7, stamens × 4; 8, ovary × 4; 9, ovary, laid open × 4; 10, ovule × 10; 11, part of a fruiting branch from Queensland, *n. s.;* 12, single pod, laid open to show seed *in situ*, *n. s.;* 13, seed, *n. s.*

§ 4. **Miscolobium.**—Standard reflexed, but not distinctly refracted, the claw tapering gradually into the blade; stamens normally monadelphous; pod samaroid, rather narrow-oblong.

This section is not so well represented in Asia as it is in America. It stands practically intermediate between *Endespermum* and *Dalbergaria*, having the stamens of the former and the corolla of the latter.

¶ 15. **Velutinæ**.—*Epicalycine bracteoles obtuse or acute, shorter than the calyx; leaflets medium to small, not exceeuing 2 in. long; style subulate; climbers.*

A natural group apparently more nearly related to some American forms, especially perhaps to *D.* (*Miscolobium*) *foliolosa* of Brazil and Bolivia, than to any of the remaining Asiatic species. This group, agreeing as it does with the *Endesperma* as to style as well as in stamens, forms a closer link between *Endespermum* and *Miscolobium* generally than do the remaining groups. At the same time the fact that Haviland records the stamens of *D. bornëensis* as sometimes isodiadelphous helps to link the group, and therefore the section *Miscolobium* as a whole, with *Dalbergaria*.

51. Dalbergia velutina Benth. *var.* typica Prain Journ. As. Soc. Beng. lxvi. 2, 117 (1897); lxx. 2, 43 (1901).

D. velutina Benth. Pl. Jungh. i. 255 (1851); Journ. Linn. Soc. iv. Suppl. 43 (1860); Bak. in Hook. f. Flor. Brit. Ind. ii. 233 (1876); Kurz. Journ. As. Soc. Beng. xlv. 2, 281 (1876); For. Flor. Burm. i. 348 (1877).

D. stipulata Wall. Cat. 5868 (1832).

Cassia timorensis Hook. f. & Thoms. Herb. Ind. Or., in part.

A large climber, with densely rusty-pubescent branches. *Leaves* 6—8 in. long; leaflets 13—17, oblong, obtuse or subacute, membranous, dark-green, above puberulous to glabrescent, beneath pale rusty-velvety, distal not much if at all exceeding the others, 1·5—2 in. long, ·6—·8 in. wide; rachis 5—6 in. long, densely pale rusty-velvety as are the petiolules, ·1 in. long; stipules long-persistent, large obovate- or ovate- to linear-lanceolate, pale rusty-velvety, ·6 in. long, ·1—·25 in. wide. *Flowers* in rather dense axillary panicles with corymbose branches, 4 in. long, 2·5 in. wide, the peduncles, branches and short pedicels densely pale rusty-velvety, bracts at base of pedicels rather large, ovate, velvety; *calyx* campanulate, with two ovate-acute bracteoles embracing lower third of tube, densely pubescent, externally somewhat gibbous at base, upper teeth obtuse, subconnate, the others acute, the lateral rather shorter than the lanceolate lowest, which is as long as the tube; *corolla* white or with pinkish spots, petals all rather long-clawed, standard with orbicular, slightly emarginate, somewhat reflexed limb; *stamens* 9 or 10, in one sheath split along upper and sometimes partially separated along lower side, filaments free in their upper fourth, alternately shorter and longer; *ovary* glabrous except the rather long, sparsely pubescent stipe; style long, subulate, stigma minute; *ovules* 2—3. *Pod* indehiscent, shortly stipitate, thin, obtuse or subacute, brownish, 1—2-seeded, 2—3 in. long, ·6—·7 in. wide.

INDO-CHINA: Assam; Silhet, *de Silva* ! *Hooker & Thomson* ! Burma; Pegu, Bookee Hill, *Kurz* 1758 ! Rangoon, *Kurz* ! Tenasserim; Moulmein, *Wallich* ! *Falconer* ! Amherst, *Brandis* ! Tenasserim, *Helfer* ! MALAYA: Malacca, *Maingay*, 548 !

51/2. DALBERGIA VELUTINA Benth. *var.* MAINGAYI Prain Journ. As. Soc. Beng. lxvi. 2, 117 (1897); lxx. 2, 44 (1901).

A large climber or a rambling shrub with closely, shortly rusty-puberulous branches. *Leaves* as in the type, but glaucescent to glaucous, rusty-puberulous beneath, glabrous or very sparsely puberulous above; rachis dark rusty-puberulous as are the petiolules; stipules long, persistent, rather smaller than in type, and very closely, shortly dark-velvety. *Flowers* as in type, but *calyx* dark-rusty, very shortly and closely puberulous; *corolla* white.

INDO-CHINA: Tenasserim, *Helfer* ! Tavoy, *Shaik Muqim* ! Mergui, *Griffith*, 1798 ! MALAYA: Malacca, *Maingay*, 612! Singapore, *Ridley*, 5923! 6086! Borneo, *Haviland*, 1444!

Only unripe pods of the type have been seen by the writer; no fruits have been seen of VAR. *Maingayi*, which differs from the other chiefly in the character and amount of the pubescence, and which in Tenasserim appears to pass insensibly into the type.

PLATE 55. Dalbergia velutina *Benth.* VAR. typica.—1, Flowering branch, from a Rangoon specimen, *n. s.*; 2, flower × 2; 3, pedicel with basal and epicalycine bracteoles × 4; 4, calyx, laid open × 4; 5, standard × 4; 6, wings × 4; 7, keel-petals × 4; 8, stamens × 4; 9, ovary × 4; 10, ovary, laid open × 4; 11, ovule × 10; 12, pod from a Moulmein specimen, not quite ripe, *n. s.*

PLATE 56. Dalbergia velutina *Benth.* VAR. Maingayi *Prain.*—1, Flowering branch, from a Singapore specimen, *n. s.*; 2, single flower; 3, pedicel with basal and epicalycine bracteoles × 4; 4, calyx, laid open × 4; 5, standard × 4; 6, wings × 4; 7, keel-petals × 4; 8, stamens × 4; 9, ovary × 4; 10, ovary, laid open × 4; 11, ovule × 10.

52. DALBERGIA BORNEENSIS Prain Journ. As. Soc. Beng. lxx. 2, 44 (1901).

A large climber, with quite glabrous angular branches. *Leaves* 3—5 in. long; leaflets 7—9, oblong, obtuse, mucronulate, membranous, quite glabrous on both surfaces, somewhat glaucescent beneath, 1 in. long, ·5 in. wide, the terminal more cuneate at base and slightly larger than the rest; rachis 3 in. long and petiolules ·1 in. long, glabrous; stipules large, ovate or ovate-lanceolate, glabrous or sparingly puberulous, subpersistent, ·2 in. long. *Flowers* in lax lateral panicles with few corymbose branches, 2·5 in. long, 1·5 in. wide; the peduncles angled, glabrous, the branches and pedicels glabrous or very sparingly adpressed rusty-puberulous; bracts ovate with narrow bases, glabrous, bracteoles at base of pedicels and the pair under calyx narrowly subulate, adpressed rusty-puberulous; *calyx* campanulate, base slightly gibbous, externally adpressed rusty-puberulous; teeth acute, in length subequal, the upper pair wider than the three lanceolate lowest; *corolla* white, petals with claws all as long as calyx-tube, standard orbicular-oblong, emarginate, somewhat reflexed; *stamens* 10, rarely 9, in one bundle split along upper side; *ovary* long-stipitate, glabrous except the puberulous stipe; style subulate, stigma minute; *ovule* usually solitary. *Pod* thinly leathery, pale straw-coloured, finely uniformly reticulated throughout, 1-seeded, 2·25 in. long, ·75 in. wide; *seed* markedly reniform, ·5 in. long, ·2 in. wide.

MALAYA: Borneo; near Kuching, *Haviland* 2889! Kalong, *Haviland* 2890!

Very nearly allied to *D. velutina* VAR. *Maingayi*, but with a different calyx and standard and very different epicalycine bracteoles, and easily distinguished by its fewer, smaller, mucronulate, quite glabrous leaflets.

PLATE 57. Dalbergia borneënsis *Prain.*—1, Flowering branch, from near Kuching, *n. s.;* 2, bud × 4; 3, pedicel and epicalycine bracteoles × 4; 4, calyx, laid open × 4; 5, standard × 4; 6, wings × 4; 7, keel-petals × 4; 8, stamens × 4; 9, ovary × 4; 10, ovary, laid open × 4; 11, ovule × 10; 12, fruits, from a Kuching specimen, *n. s.;* 13, fruit, one valve removed, showing seed *in situ n. s.;* 14, seed, *n. s.*

¶ 16. **Ovatae.**—*Epicalycine bracteoles obtuse, shorter than calyx; leaflets large; style slender, cylindric; trees.*

A natural group, two of the members of which have been treated, though not perhaps very conveniently, as varieties of one species by Baker. The position of the two other species is not absolutely certain, but they are most probably members of this group.

53. DALBERGIA OBTUSIFOLIA Prain Journ. As. Soc. Beng. lxx. 2, 42 (1901).
D. ovata var. *obtusifolia* Bak. in Hook. f. Flor. Brit. Ind. ii. 231 (1876).
D. glauca Kurz Journ. As. Soc. Beng. xlv. 2, 280 (1876); For. Flor. Burm. i. 343 (1877) not of Wall.

A tree, 40—50 ft. high, with many spreading branches; young shoots pendulous, sub-bifarious, glabrous. *Leaves* 8—12 in. long; leaflets usually 5, occasionally 7, obovate or elliptic rarely the lowest orbicular, retuse or obtuse without or with a mucro, very rarely with a short cuspidate tip, subcoriaceous, bright green above, paler and often glaucescent beneath, the distal rather the largest, 2—5 in. long, 2—3 in. wide, rachis 4—5 in. long; petiolules ·2 in. long; stipules caducous. *Flowers* shortly pedicelled, in lax terminal and axillary panicles, 6—8 in. long, 5—6 in. wide; peduncles and pedicels at first sparsely pubescent; *calyx* campanulate, with 2 basal bracteoles less than half the length of the tube, 5-toothed, the teeth all obtuse and shorter than the tube; *corolla* yellowish-white, petals rather long-clawed except the oblong, shortly clawed, slightly emarginate standard; *stamens* 9, in one bundle, sheath split along the upper side, the filaments free in their upper third, alternately slightly shorter and longer; *ovary* glabrous, long-stipitate; style elongate, stigma small; *ovules* usually 3. *Pod* distinctly stipitate, 1—2-, very rarely 3-seeded, markedly veined opposite the seeds, firmly coriaceous, glabrous, 2—2·5 in. long, ·45 in. wide; *seed* much compressed, reniform, smooth but hardly shining, brown, ·4 in. long, ·25 in. wide, ·15 in. thick.

INDO-CHINA: Pegu; *Kurz* 1784! 2607 partly! Pak-choung, *Brandis*! Shan Plateau; Madoe, *Abdul Khalil*! near Fort Stedman, *Abdul Huq*! Taping Valley; near Momien, *J. Anderson*! Hukung Valley; *Griffith* 1809! Chindwin Valley; Katiah Hills, *Prazer*! Lower Chindwin, *Smythies*!

This species is nearly related to *D. ovata* Grah., but differs in having larger, obtuse leaflets with flowers not much more than half the size; the calyx-teeth too are all obtuse, and the basal bracteoles are much smaller: the fruits of the two are not distinguishable. Kurz gives the name *Madama* both for this and for *D. ovata*; for this Sir D. Brandis quotes the name *Madama bin*; Mr. Smythies, however, states that the name it bears in the Northern Burmese Forest Circle is *Padouk po*. Mr. Baker has treated this tree as only a variety of *D. ovata*; Mr. Kurz has, however, as the writer believes, rightly considered it a distinct species. The name used by Kurz is *D. glauca*, and he has employed that name under the impression that Wallich's *D. glauca* is this species. As a matter of fact, however, Wallich's *D. glauca* (Cat. n. 5862 from Moulmein) is identical with Wallich's own n. 5854 (from Martaban) which is the type of *D. ovata* Grah.; Mr. Baker's varietal name has therefore been adopted in a specific sense.

PLATE 58. Dalbergia obtusifolia *Prain*.—1, Branch with leaf and flowers, from the Shan Plateau, *n. s.*; 2, calyx with bracteoles × 4; 3, calyx, laid open × 4; 4, standard × 4; 5, wings × 4; 6, keel-petals × 4; 7, stamens × 4; 8, ovary × 4; 9, ovary, laid open × 4; 10, ovule × 8; 11, fruiting spray, *n. s.*; 12, pod, opened, showing seed *in situ*, *n. s.*; 13, seed, *n. s.*

54. DALBERGIA GLOMERIFLORA Kurz Journ. As. Soc. Beng. xlii. 2, 70 (1873); Bak. in Hook. f. Flor. Brit. Ind. ii. 236 (1876); Kurz For. Flor. Burm. i. 345 (1877); Prain Journ. As. Soc. Beng. lxx. 2, 50.

A tree, 30—40 feet high; young shoots densely tawny-tomentose. *Leaves* when young very densely tawny-tomentose; leaflets 7—9, ovate or obovate, acute, base rounded or cuneate, coriaceous, bright-green above, rather paler beneath, glabrous when old above, sparingly pubescent beneath, 2—2·5 in. long, 1·25—2 in. wide; petiolules short pubescent, stipules large, ovate-obtuse, herbaceous, glabrous. *Flowers* small, very shortly pedicelled or sessile, densely crowded in small congested panicles at the ends of young villous shoots in the axils of fallen leaves; *calyx* campanulate, partly enclosed in two deciduous herbaceous epicalycine bracteoles glabrous except their margins, one-third as long as calyx; teeth subequal subacute except the lowest, which is acute longer and narrower than the rest, all shorter than the tube; *corolla* white, petals rather long-clawed except the oblong shortly clawed slightly emarginate standard; *stamens* 10, in one bundle, the sheath split along the upper side, but the vexillary filament sometimes almost free from the rest, and partially divided along the lower side, the filaments all free in their upper third and alternately shorter and larger; *ovary* rather long-stipitate, glabrous except the stipe; style slender; *ovules* usually 4—5, occasionally fewer.

INDO-CHINA: Burma; Prome, *Kurz* 2611!

This species is only known from a single gathering by Kurz in the Prome district of Pegu, in 1871. It has been stated by its author to have the stamens united in two separate short sheaths; a careful examination of many flowers shows, however, that this is not always the case; indeed, it has not been met with by the writer in any instance. The character is, as a matter of fact, a very unreliable one in many species, and except for this character, which is not even usual in this tree, there is nothing to suggest its affinity with any other species of the *Dalbergaria* section. Its nearest ally is clearly *Dalbergia ovata,* of which it may even prove ultimately to be only a form. The differentiating characters are the smaller size of the flowers, the much more densely tomentose young shoots, and the greater number (7—9) of its leaflets. The structure of the flower is exactly that of *D. ovata,* except that the lowest calyx-lobe is here acute, in *D. ovata* it is obtuse.

PLATE 6B. Dalbergia glomeriflora *Kurz.*—1, Young shoot with young leaves and with fully developed flowers, *n. s.;* 2, loose leaflets gathered by Kurz under the same tree, *n. s.;* 3, pedicel with epicalycine bracteoles × 4; 4, calyx, laid open × 4; 5, standard × 4; 6, wings × 4; 7, keel-petals × 4; 8, stamens × 4; 9, ovary × 4; 10, ovary, laid open × 4; 11, ovule × 10.

55. DALBERGIA OVATA Grah. in Wall. Cat. 5854 (1832); Benth. Pl. Jungh. i. 254 (1851); Journ. Linn. Soc. iv. Suppl. 40 (1860); Bak. in Hook. f. Flor. Brit. ii. 231 (1876); Kurz Journ. As. Soc. Beng. xlv. 2, 280 (1876); For. Flor. Burm. i. 343 (1877) Prain Journ. As. Soc. Beng. lxx. 2, 43 (1901).

D. glauca Wall. Cat. 5862 (1832); Benth. Pl. Jungh i. 254 (1851).

A tree, 25—35 feet high, with many spreading branches; young shoots pendulous, glabrous. *Leaves* 6—9 in. long; leaflets usually 7, occasionally 5—6, rarely 4, ovate-acuminate, subcoriaceous, bright-green above, paler and at times glaucescent beneath, glabrous, the distal rather larger than the rest, 2—4 in. long, 1—1·5 in. wide, rachis 4—5 in. long; petiolules ·2 in. long; stipules caducous. *Flowers* shortly pedicelled, in lax terminal and axillary panicles 6—8 in. long, 5—6 in. wide, peduncles and pedicels at first puberulous; *calyx* campanulate, partly enclosed by two deciduous, puberulous, herbaceous bracteoles more than half as long as the calyx, 5-toothed, glabrous except on the margins of the teeth, the teeth subacute subequal except the lowest which is obtuse, longer and wider than the rest, all shorter than the tube; *corolla* yellowish-white, petals rather long-clawed except the oblong shortly clawed, slightly emarginate standard; *stamens* 9, in one bundle, the sheath split along upper side, the filaments free in their upper third, alternately slightly shorter and longer; *ovary* glabrous, rather long-stipitate; style elongate, slender, stigma small; *ovules* usually 3, sometimes 4—5, occasionally 1. *Pod* distinctly stipitate, 1—2-, very rarely 3-seeded, markedly veined opposite the seeds, firmly coriaceous, glabrous, 2—3 in. long, ·5 in. wide; *seed* much compressed, reniform, smooth but hardly shining, brown, ·4 in. long, ·25 in. wide, ·15 in. thick.

INDO-CHINA: Pegu; Rangoon, *Cleghorn*! Pegu, *Kurz* 1785! 2595! 2607 partly! 2610! Tenasserim; Moulmein, *Wallich* 5862! *Falconer* 566! *Parish* 240! *Beddome*! Martaban, *Wallich* 5854! Yainway, *Brandis* 1185! Thoungyne, 3,000 ft., *Lobb*! Tavoy, *Shaik Muqim*! Cambodia; between Saigon and Bienhoa, *Lefèvre* 320!

Though only doubtfully spoken of as a tree by Bentham, and though stated by Baker to be a climber, this is described by Beddome as a large tree, and by Parish as a middle-sized tree. Parish gives the name at Moulmein as *Thit-hsonk-yo* or 'Chisel-handle wood,' its timber 'being good for that purpose.' Kurz gives the name *Madama,* in Pegu, both for this and for *D. obtusifolia;* Shaik Muqim, who says it is a tree 30 feet high, gives the name as *Kan-ma* at Tavoy.

The bracteoles are like those of *D. latifolia* and *D. emarginata,* but are not so delicate in texture; they are moreover not quite so large and are less caducous. Kurz has proposed, without any particular necessity, a variety *β puberula.*

PLATE 59. Dalbergia ovata *Grah.*—1, Branch with leaves and flowers, from Pegu, *n. s.;* 2, calyx with bracteoles × 4; 3, standard × 4; 4, wings × 4; 5, keel-petals × 4; 6, stamens × 4; 7, ovaries, one entire, one laid open × 4; 8, ovule × 10; 9, fruiting spray, *n. s.;* 10, pod, opened to show seed *in situ*, *n. s.;* 11, seed, *n. s.*

56. DALBERGIA CAMBODIANA Pierre ex Brenier in Bull. Econ. Ind. Chin. v. 75; v. 404 (1902).

A fine tree, 120 feet high, stem 2·5—4 feet thick; wood red, hard, alternately banded with light and dark shades; young branches blackish or dark-brown, lenticelled. *Leaves* 5—7 in. long; leaflets usually 5, occasionally 4, rarely 3, subopposite, ovate, narrowed somewhat abruptly to a shortly widely acuminate obtuse and mucronate tip, base rounded, quite glabrous on both surfaces, closely finely reticulated, rather dark-green above, paler beneath, the terminal often much exceeding the others, 3·5—4 in. long, 2·5 in. wide, the others 2—2·5 in. long, 1·25—2 in. wide; rachis 1·75—2·5 in. long and petiolules ·15 in. long, glabrous; stipules deciduous. *Flowers* in lax subterminal panicles 3—5 in. long, 1·5—3 in. wide; peduncles surrounded at the base by a few ovate, subcoriaceous bud-scales; branches of panicle few, short, glabrous as are the very short pedicels ·06 in. long; bracts and bracteoles not seen; *calyx* campanulate; teeth all obtuse, the two upper subconnate; *corolla* and *stamens* not seen. *Pod* thinly coriaceous, subligulate, glabrous, long-stipitate, 2 in. long, ·35 in wide, 1—2-seeded, faintly reticulated opposite the seeds; *seed* rather narrowly ovate, compressed, ·25 in. long, ·15 in. wide, ·05 in. thick; testa black.

INDO-CHINA: Cambodia; Kamput prov., Camchay Mts., 1,600 feet, *Pierre* 1709!

This is an exceeding distinct species, but the material being incomplete its precise affinity cannot be positively stated. The facies of the specimens recalls *D. ovata*, though the leaflets are somewhat differently shaped and more resemble those of *D. glomeriflora*, a species of which so far only the flowers are known. The pods of *D. cambodiana* are very different from those of the other species here referred to the *Ovatae* whereof the fruits are known, and are more like those of *D. cochinchinensis* and *D. sissoides* which are typical members of the group *Latifoliae*, but the seeds differ very considerably. The *Ovatae* and the *Latifoliae* are, however, very closely related and might without much inconvenience be treated as constituting a single group; it is almost certain that *D. cambodiana*, when its flowers are known, will be found to belong to one or other of the groups; till the epicalycine bracteoles are seen it will not, however, be possible to say with certainty to which of the two it should be referred; the probabilities seem in favour of the *Ovatae*. The seeds are of a shape unusual in the genus *Dalbergia*.

The Kmer vernacular name is given as *Cra hnung* by Pierre; Breiner gives it as *Tra hnung*. The wood of this tree was formerly reserved in Cambodia for the needs of the king; it was at one time abundant in the western provinces of Cambodia, but is now rather scarce.

PLATE 60. Dalbergia cambodiana *Pierre.*—1, Branch in fruit from the Camchay Mts., Kamput, Cambodia, *n. s.;* 2, fruit, laid open, showing seed, *n. s.;* 3, seed, *n. s.*

57. DALBERGIA TONKINENSIS Prain Journ. As. Soc. Beng. lxx. 2, 42 (1901). *Dalbergia* sp. Drake del Castillo Journ. de Bot. v. 215 (1891).

A small or medium tree. *Leaves* 8—8·5 in. long; leaflets 9—11, ovate, base rounded, apex shortly abruptly acuminate, firmly subcoriaceous, sparsely puberulous when young, soon glabrous, 2·5—3·5 in. long, 1·5—2 in. wide; rachis 5—6 in. long, and petiolules 12 in. long, glabrous; stipules small, tawny-puberulous, deciduous. *Flowers* white, fragrant, in small corymbose axillary panicles 2 in. long, 1·5 in. wide. *Pod* firmly coriaceous, ovate or oblong, subacute, distinctly stipitate, 2 in. long when 1-seeded, 3 in. long when 2-seeded, ·75 in. wide, very distinctly reticulated opposite the seeds; *seed* reniform, compressed, ·35 in. long, ·2 in. wide.

CHINA: Hainan; *B. C. Henry*! TONGKING: Hanoi; *Balansa* 2184!

The material of this species available is insufficient for complete description, but is sufficient to show that we have here to do with a quite distinct form. Mr. Drake del Castillo has suggested that it is a *Sissoa*; the point can only be settled when flowers are available for examination.

PLATE 61. Dalbergia tonkinensis *Prain.*—1, Twig in young leaf, from Hainan, *n. s.*; 2, leaf from a Tongking specimen (*Balansa* 2184) in Herb. Berol. *n. s.*; 3, spray of pods, from a Tongking specimen (*Balansa* 2184) in Herb. DC., *n. s.*; 4, single pod, laid open to show seed *in situ*, *n. s.*; 5, seed, *n. s.*

¶ 17. **Latifoliae.**—*Epicalycine bracteoles obtuse, as long as the calyx; leaflets large; style slender, cylindric; trees.*

A very natural group of forms; indeed, it is doubtful whether the first two are more than varieties of one species. Most nearly related to the *Ovatae*, the *Latifoliae* deviate from these, and approach the group *Sissoo* among *Podiopetala*, in having very large epicalycine bracteoles.

58. DALBERGIA LATIFOLIA Roxb. Corom. Pl. ii. 7 t. 113 (1798); Hort. Beng. 53 (1814); DC. Prodr. ii. 416 (1825); Flor. Ind. iii. 221 (1832); Wall. Cat. 5852 (1832); W. & A. Prodr. i. 264 (1834); Grah. Cat. Bomb. Pl. 55 (1839); Voigt Hort. Suburb. Calcutt. 240 (1845); Wight. Ic. t. 1156 (1850); Benth. Pl. Jungh. i. 254 (1851); Journ. Linn. Soc. iv. Suppl. 38 (1860); Dalz. & Gibs. Bomb. Flor. 77 (1861); Bedd. Flor. Sylvat. t. 24, excl. main fig. (1869); Brand. For. Flor. 148 (1874); Bak. in Hook. f. Flor. Brit. Ind. ii. 231 (1876); Kurz. Journ. As. Soc. Beng. xlv. 2, 280 (1876); For. Flor. Burm. i. 342 (1877); Talbot Bomb. List 74 (1894); Gamble Darjeel. List 29 (1896); Woodr. Journ. Nat. Hist. Soc. Bomb. xi. 426 (1897); Prain Journ. As. Soc. Beng. lxx. 2, 41 (1901); Kanjilal Flor. Sch. Circ. 129 (1901); Cooke Flor. Pres. Bomb. i. 396 (1902); Prain Bengal Plants i. 411 (1903).

D. emarginata Roxb. Hort. Beng. 53 (1814); Flor. Ind. iii. 224 (1832); Wall. Cat. 5858 (1832); Voigt Hort. Suburb. Calcutt. 241 (1845).

D. Kydiana Roxb. MSS. ex Benth. in Miq. Pl. Jungh. i. 254 (1851).

A tree, 30—70 feet high, with rather smooth bark; stem fairly straight, reaching 4 feet in diam. at 5 feet from the ground, with numerous spreading branches; young shoots pendulous, sub-bifarious, glabrous. *Leaves* 6—9 in. long; leaflets 3—7, usually 5, but often 3—4, seldom 6—7, suborbicular, obtuse or emarginate very rarely subacute or acute, glabrous on both surfaces, green above, pale subglaucescent beneath, the distal usually rather the largest, 1·75—2·5 in. long, 1·25—2·5 in. wide; rachis 4—6 in. long, petiolules ·2 in. long. *Flowers* distinctly pedicelled, in lateral corymbose panicles, usually in the axils of fallen leaves, rarely one terminal; pedicels ·15—·2 in. long; *calyx* campanulate, slightly puberulous when young and enclosed by two large very caducous membranous bracteoles; 5-toothed, the two upper teeth subconnate, the lateral pair obtuse resembling the obtuse lower, all rather shorter than the tube; *corolla* white, petals all distinctly clawed, standard-limb suborbicular; *stamens* 9, in one sheath split along upper side, the filaments free in their upper third, indistinctly shorter and longer; *ovary* glabrous, rather long-stipitate; style slender, stigma small; *ovules* usually 5, sometimes as few as 3 or as many as 7. *Pod* indehiscent, distinctly stipitate, 1—3-seeded, sparingly but distinctly veined opposite the seed, 2—3·25 in. long, ·7 in. wide, firmly coriaceous, abruptly rounded to both style and stipe; *seed* much compressed, reniform, brown, smooth but hardly shining, ·4 in. long, ·25 in. wide, ·15 in. thick.

HIMALAYA: Submontane forests of Nepal, *Maries*! Sikkim Terai, *Hooker*! *Gamble*! RAJPUTANA: Abu, *King*! Merwara, *Brandis*! N. INDIA: Parasnath, *Anderson*! Tandi Forests, *Campbell*! Hundrugagh, *Prain*! Palamau, *Gamble* 8845! Singbhum, *Haines* 213! Orissa, *Lace*! C. INDIA: Chanda; *Burkill;* Chattisgarh; *Burkill.* S. INDIA: Ayamalais, near Coimbatur, *Wight*! Nilgiris, *Wight*! *Leschenault* 246! *Gamble* 14374! W. INDIA: Kala Nadi, *Ritchie* 230! Concan, *Stocks*! Mercara, *Metz*! Ahmadabad; Coa, *Burkill.* INDO-CHINA: Andamans, *Kyd.* MALAYA: Peninsula, Jurong, *Ridley*, 8444!

Cultivated examples: MADRAS: *Heyne*! LOWER BENGAL: *Wallich*! *Thomson*! *Kurz*!

The writer finds usually 5, rarely 4 ovules in ovaries of this species; Beddome, however, records 7; Bentham records 3: the flowers are faintly fragrant. Ritchie gives the vernacular name as *Shisham;* Kanjilal says *Wilayati Shisham,* in Dehra Dun, where it is only planted; Leschanault gives *Isoupou Putton.*

PLATE 62. Dalbergia latifolia *Roxb.*—1, Flowering branch, specimen from Mt. Abu, Rajputana, *n. s.;* 2, flower bud × 4; 3, the same, bracteoles removed × 4; 4, calyx, laid open × 4; 5, standard × 4; 6, wings × 4; 7, keel-petals × 4; 8, stamens × 4; 9, ovaries, one entire, one laid open × 4; 10, ovule, greatly enlarged; 11, twig with fruits, specimen from Nepal, *n. s.;* 12, seed, *n. s.*

59. DALBERGIA SISSOIDES Grah. in Wall. Cat. 5876 (1832); W. & A. Prodr. i. 265 (1834); Benth. Pl. Jungh. i. 254 (1851); Journ. Linn. Soc. iv. Suppl. 39 (1860); Bedd. Trans. Linn. Soc. xxv. 216 (1865).

D. javanica Miq. Flor. Ind. Bat. i. 1, 132 (1855); Benth. Journ. Linn. Soc. iv. Suppl. 38 (1860).

D. latifolia Koord. & Val. Bijdr. ii. 77 (1895), hardly of Roxb.

D. latifolia VAR. *sissoides* Bedd. Flor. Sylvat. sub t. 24 (1869); Bak. in Hook. f. Flor. Brit. Ind. ii. 231 (1876).

D. emarginata Prain Journ. As. Soc. Beng. lxx. 2, 41 (1901), hardly of Roxb.

An erect tree, 40—70 feet high, with rather smooth bark and straight stem with numerous spreading branches; young shoots pendulous, sub-bifarious, glabrous. *Leaves* 6—9 in. long; leaflets usually 7—8, rarely 5—6, obovate subacute, very rarely sub-orbicular obtuse, glabrous on both surfaces, green above, glaucescent beneath, the distal usually the largest, 1·25—2 in. long, 1—1·75 in. wide, rachis 4—6 in. long, petiolules

·25 in. long. *Flowers* distinctly pedicelled, in large terminal panicles with or without a few lateral in the axils of upper leaves of the same season; pedicels ·15—·2 in. long; *calyx* campanulate, when young slightly puberulous and enclosed in two large very caducous membranous bracteoles; 5-toothed, the two upper teeth subconnate, the three lower subequal, oblong, obtuse or subacute, as long as the tube; *corolla* white, petals all distinctly clawed, standard-limb entire with wavy margin; *stamens* 9 or less often 10, in one bundle split along upper side; filaments free in their upper third, alternately somewhat shorter and longer; *ovary* glabrous, rather long-stipitate; style slender, stigma small; *ovules* usually 4. *Pod* indehiscent, 1—3-, rarely 4-seeded, very distinctly veined opposite the seeds, 2—3·25 in. long, ·5 in. wide, firmly coriaceous, gradually cuneate towards both style and stipe; *seed* much compressed, reniform, pale-brown, smooth but hardly shining, ·35 in. long, ·2 in. wide.

MALABARIA: Travancore, 200 feet elev., *Bourdillon* 535! Nilgiris, at Segur, *Clarke* 11,?05! *Wight*: 931! Pulneys; at Kodaikanal Ghat, *Bourne* 139 R! MALAYA: Java; Madioen, Kediri, etc., *Heijer*! *Horsfield*! *Koorders*!

This species is very nearly related to *D. latifolia*, and may indeed be only a form of that tree; the distinctions, however, seem constant so far as India is concerned, and the woodcutters of Southern India are said to distinguish the two by their habit and their timber, and to give them different names. The two trees do not, as Gamble suggests (*Manual of Indian Timbers*, Ed. 2, 252), differ greatly as regards floral structure; the chief difference is as regards the position of the inflorescence. Both this and *D. latifolia* are reported from the Nilgiris, but these hills appear to be the northernmost limit of *D. sissoides*, and in the Pulneys, where Dr. A. G. Bourne has kindly looked into the matter at the writer's request, only one species or variety of Blackwood is to be found, for all Dr. Bourne's specimens are referable to *D. sissoides*, none to *D. latifolia*. From Travancore too only *D. sissoides* has been sent to Calcutta, though both trees are stated to occur there. The Java tree, which is certainly *D. javanica* Miq., has been referred by Koorders and Valeton, extremely careful observers who know the tree in the living state, to *D. latifolia*. The Java specimens, as a matter of fact, do not appear to the writer to agree exactly either with *D. latifolia* of Northern India or with *D. sissoides* of Southern India, but of the two they seem by their leaves and pods to agree better with *D. sissoides* than with the form to which Koorders and Valeton have referred it. Perhaps the Southern India and the Java trees are different geographical forms of the more widespread *D. latifolia*.

The Andaman form of *D. latifolia* by its inflorescence, and the Malay Peninsula form of the same trees by its leaves seem both to approach the Java form, though as regards its pods the Malay Peninsula tree is quite like the Northern Indian one and is unlike the Javanese tree. In consequence of this similarity on the part of the Andaman tree, as shown by a manuscript drawing by Roxburgh, and of the Java tree, the writer suggested two years ago that the name *D. emarginata* be adopted for the species. The fact was, however, overlooked that Bentham has recorded his having met with a *specimen* of Roxburgh's *D. emarginata*, named by Roxburgh himself *D. Kydiana*, from the Andamans, and that this specimen belongs to *D. latifolia*: this record is decisive, hence the present change. Bentham does not state in what Herbarium he saw this specimen; the writer has not succeeded in tracing it.

PLATE 63. Dalbergia sissoides *Grah.*—1, Flowering branch; specimen from Segur, Nilgiris, *n. s.*; 2, fruiting branch; specimen from Kodaikanal, Pulneys, *n. s.*; 3, bud, enclosed in bracteoles × 4; 4, calyx, laid open × 4; 5, standard × 4; 6, wings × 4; 7, keel petals × 4; 8, stamens × 4; 9, ovary × 4; 10, ovary, laid open × 4; 11, ovule × 8; 12, pod from Pulney specimen, *n. s.*; 13, immature seed from the same × 6; 14, pod, from Java specimen, *n. s.*; 15, ripe seed from the same, *n. s.*

60. DALBERGIA COCHINCHINENSIS Pierre ex Laness. Pl. Util. Col. Franç. 289 (1886); Brenier in Bull. Econ. Ind. Chin. v. 75; v. 402 (1902).

A tree, 80 feet high, stem 2—2·5 feet thick; wood dark-red taking on an ebony tint with age; bark grey, smooth, fibrous; young branches grey, much lenticelled. *Leaves* 6—8 in. long; leaflets 7—9, subopposite, ovate-acute, or shortly acuminate with an obtuse tip, base wide-cuneate, quite glabrous on both surfaces, pale-green above, glaucescent beneath, closely finely reticulated, 1·25—2·5 in. long, ·75—1 in. wide; rachis 4—7 in. long, and petiolules ·2 in. long quite glabrous; stipules ovate, very deciduous. *Flowers* in lax axillary panicles 3·5—6 in. long, 2—3 in. wide, the peduncles surrounded at the base by a few ovate membranous bud scales; branches few, very faintly puberulous as are the pedicels ·12 in. long; bracts and epicalycine bracteoles ovate, membranous, ·1 in. long, very caducous; *calyx* campanulate, thinly coriaceous, glabrous, ·15 in. long, the three lower teeth ovate-acute, the lowest rather longer than the lateral but hardly exceeding the two ovate-obtuse almost completely connate upper teeth; *corolla* white, standard ovate-oblong, slightly reflexed, with rounded slightly involute apex and wide-cuneate base tapering to the broad, short, stout claw; wings long-clawed with a large spongy thickened patch inside at upper edge of base of blade; keel-petals connate above, markedly auricled below, long-clawed; *stamens* 9, in one sheath split above, or 10, the tenth free on one side and nearly free on the other; filaments free in their upper third, alternately shorter and longer; *ovary* long-stipitate, quite glabrous; style very slender, stigma minute; *ovules* 3. *Pod* subligulate, thinly coriaceous, quite glabrous, 2—3 in. long, ·4—·5 in. wide, 1—2-seeded, hardly reticulated opposite the seeds; *seed* reniform, compressed, ·25 in. long, ·2 in. wide, ·07 in. thick; testa greyish-brown.

INDO-CHINA: Cochin-China; Bencat, on the Saigon river (fr.), *Pierre*! Baria, at the base of Mt. Dinh (fl.), *Pierre*! Phu-Quoc, Cam-Chay, also forests between the Dong-Naï and the Bin-Thuan, *Lanessan.*

This is Herb. Pierre 1710 and is a very fine and distinct species, nearest of the Asiatic *Dalbergias* to *D. latifolia* and *D. sissoides;* at one time plentiful it is now becoming rare owing to indiscriminate felling. The native names given in Herb. Pierre are Anam, *Trác;* Kmer, *Cra hauug;* the second name, it will be observed is also applied to *D. cambodiana.*

Both Lanessan and Brenier give the vernacular name as *Trác;* Brenier adds, however, that six trees are known by this vernacular term. These are *Trác den* (or Black Trác), *Trác vang* (or Yellow Trác), *Trác bong* (or Spotted Trác), *Trác trang* (or White Trác) and *Trác mát* (or Buff Trác). There is nothing in M. Brenier's remarks on these forms to indicate whether the names cited connote different species, or only different forms of one species, or in any way to assist in their botanical identification.

PLATE 64. Dalbergia cochinchinensis *Pierre.*—1, Twig, with leaves and flowers, specimens from base of Mt. Dinh, Baria, *n. s.;* 2, young bud × 8; 3, bud × 4; 4, calyx, laid open × 4; 5, standard × 4; 6, wing-petals × 4; 7, keel-petals × 4; 8, stamens × 4; 9, ovary × 4; 10, ovary, laid open × 4; 11, ovule × 8; 12, 13, pods from a specimen from Bencat, on the Saigon river, *n. s.;* 14, seed, *n. s.*

¶ 18. **Polyadelpha.**—*Pod oblong-lanceolate, samaroid; leaflets rather small; epicalycine bracteoles acute, shorter than the calyx; style slender, conical; a tree.*

This group seems best referred, on general grounds, to *Miscolobium;* the single species of which it is composed bears a considerable general resemblance to various American species of this section. The peculiar arrangement of the stamens, which recalls what is met with in the genus *Pterocarpus*, shows, however, that the group serves as a link between the sections *Miscolobium*, where the stamens are normally monadelphous, and *Dalbergaria*, where they are normally isodiadelphous.

61. Dalbergia polyadelpha Prain sp. nov.

A small to medium tree, 15—30 feet high. *Leaves* 4—8 in. long; leaflets usually 9, sometimes 7, occasionally 11—12, ovate-lanceolate, base cuneate or in the proximal sometimes rounded, apex gradually narrowed to the obtuse slightly mucronate tip, chartaceous, dark-green and glabrous except the puberulous midrib above, glaucescent and finely sparsely adpressed-puberulous beneath, the distal the largest, 1·5 in. long, ·65 in. wide, rarely 2·5 in. long, 1 in. wide, gradually diminishing to the proximal ·6 in. long ·35 in. wide; rachis 3—4 in. long, and petiolules ·12 in. long, finely puberulous; stipules ovate-lanceolate, pubescent, very caducous. *Flowers* in rather dense thyrsoid axillary or infra axillary panicles, 2·5 in. long, 2 in. wide; peduncle stout, glabrous; branches short, rusty-pubescent; slender pedicles ·2 in. long, very sparingly pubescent; bracts small, ovate, deciduous; epicalycine bracteoles deciduous, sparingly pubescent, ovate-lanceolate; *calyx* campanulate, tube externally glabrous below sparsely puberulous above, ·2 in. long; teeth unequal, lowest lanceolate as long as tube and longer than the subequal acute lateral and the ovate subconnate upper pairs; *corolla* distinctly lineate, standard wide-ovate, emarginate, the cuneate base passing into the short broad stout claw; wing-petals oblong, sagittate on upper side, long-clawed; keel-petals long-clawed united above, blades hastate on upper side below; *stamens* 10, connate at the base in a very short sheath, split on upper side, the filaments rather irregularly separated downwards from one-third to nine-tenths of their length so as to become irregularly and incompletely 3—5-adelphous; *ovary* glabrous except the long pubescent stipe; style subulate-conical, stigma minute; *ovules* 3—4. *Pod* oblong, coriaceous, glabrous except the short but distinct stipe, cuneate less often rounded at base, acute or acuminate at the apex, 2·5—3·5 in. long, 1 in. wide, strongly reticulated opposite the 1—2 seeds; *seed* subreniform-oblong, much compressed, ·35 in. long, ·25 in. wide, ·07 in. thick; testa black, shining.

China: Yunnan; Szemao, forests at 5,000 feet elev., *Henry* 11688! 12454! 12502!

A very distinct species, the precise localisation of which is rather difficult; the leaves and pods recall certain American *Miscolobia* more than they do any of our Asiatic *Dalbergias;* the calyx and corolla are however equally suitable for the sections *Miscolobium* and *Dalbergaria* and at first sight the fact that the staminal sheath is divided would suggest *Dalbergaria*, where the normal arrangement of stamens is an isodiadelphous one, as the most suitable place for this tree. The careful examination of many flowers shows, however, that no matter how deeply divided the stamens in *D. polyadelpha* may be, and no matter how many groups they are arranged in, the filaments are always monadelphous at the base, not quite divided into two bundles as in a normal *Dalbergaria*. This fact, combined with the likeness of the species to several undoubted *Miscolobia* from other regions, renders it advisable to treat *D. polyadelpha* also as a *Miscolobium*.

Plate 65. Dalbergia polyadelpha *Prain*.—1, Flowering branch from Szemao, S. W. Yunnan (*Henry* 11688), *n. s.;* 2, bud × 4; 3, pedicel with epicalycine bracteoles × 4;

calyx, laid open × 4; 5, standard × 4; 6, wings × 4; 7, keel-petals × 4; 8, stamens × 4; 9, ovary × 4; 10, ovary, laid open, × 4; 11, ovule × 12; 12, fruiting branch, from Szemao, S. W. Yunnan (*Henry* 12502), *n. s.;* 13, pod, opened, showing seed *in situ*, *n. s.*; 14, seed, *n. s.*

§ 5. **DALBERGARIA.**—Standard reflexed, but not distinctly refracted, the claw tapering gradually into the blade; stamens normally isodiadelphous.

This section includes the American and African *Ecastaphyllum*, which also have isodiadelphous stamens. It is most nearly related to the section *Miscolobium*, and only differs from that section as regards stamens. The character is not absolutely constant; in the group *Reniformes*, for example, the species *D. reniformis*, though usually isodiadelphous, is sometimes monadelphous—at all events in *young* flowers; in *D. Kunstleri* both arrangements seem about equally common. In the section *Sericeae*, while *D. sericea* seems always to have isodiadelphous stamens, *D. sacerdotum*, which in every other respect is clearly very closely related to *D. sericea*, has them monadelphous; in *D. sacerdotum*, however, the flowers examined were all very young, which possibly explains the condition observed.

¶ 18. **Sericeae**.—*Pod very narrow-ligulate, samaroid; style cylindric; leaflets obtuse; trees.*

Apparently a very natural group, including the two most exclusively northern Asiatic forms. Other species do occur where *D. sericea* grows, but except itself and *D. Sissoo* all of them naturally extend much further south, either to Indo-China, or to Peninsular India, or both.

62. Dalbergia sericea G. Don Gen. Syst. ii. 375 (1832); Prain Journ. As. Soc. Beng. lxx. 2, 51 (1901); Bengal Plants i. 410.

D. robusta Wall. Cat. 5849 A (1832), not of Roxb.

D. hircina Wall. Cat. 5871 B (1832); Benth. Pl. Jungh. i. 256 (1851); Journ. Linn. Soc. iv. Suppl. 46 (1860); Brandis For. Flor. 151 (1874); Bak. in Hook. f. Flor. Brit. Ind. ii. 236 (1876); Gamble Darjeel. List 29 (1896); Prain Journ. As. Soc. Beng. lxvi. 2, 449 (1897); Kanjilal Flor. Sch. Circ. 130 (1901), not of Ham.

D. assamica Benth. Journ. Linn. Soc. iv. Suppl. 45 partly—the Subsiwalik plant (1860); Bak. in Hook. f. Flor. Brit. Ind. ii. 235 partly (1876).

D. stenocarpa Kurz Journ. As. Soc. Beng. xliv. 2, 205 (1875); Bak. in Hook. F. Flor. Brit. Ind. ii. 238 (1876); Gamble Darjeel. List 29 (1878).

D. emarginata Royle ex Prain Journ. As. Soc. Beng. lxx. 2, 51 (1901), not of Roxb.

A considerable tree; young shoots sub-bifarious, silky-tomentose. *Leaves* 8—10 in. long; leaflets 13—19, sometimes 21, rarely 9—11, ovate slightly retuse, base rounded or cuneate, 1—1·75 in. long, ·75—1 in. wide, chartaceous, medium-green and very sparsely adpressed-pubescent above, glaucescent and rather closely pubescent beneath, distal leaflet hardly exceeding the rest; rachis 7—9·5 in. long, silky-pubescent as are the petiolules ·15 in. long; stipules subfalcate-lanceolate, silky-pubescent, caducous. *Flowers* in short rather dense axillary panicles, 1—2 in. long, ·5—·75 in. wide, the peduncles, branches and pedicels densely silky-pubescent; bracteoles lanceolate, obtuse, silky-pubescent; *caylx* campanulate, densely pubescent; teeth obtuse shorter than the except the lowest lanceolate as long as the tube; *corolla* white, petals all rather long-clawed, standard suborbicular, emarginate; *stamens* 10, in 2 lateral bundles of 5 each; *ovary* shortly stipitate, pubescent; style slender, stigma small capitate; *ovules* usually 4—5. *Pod* indehiscent, tapering below to the rather short stipe, apex acute, flat, brownish, coriaceous, narrowly ligulate, 1—5-seeded, glabrous, 1—2 in. long, ·25—·4 in. wide, reticulated opposite the seeds; *seed* reniform, compressed, ·2 in. long, ·1 in. wide, testa dull, brownish.

HIMALAYA: Dehra Dun; *Wallich*! *Royle*! Shimála, *Inayat*! *Mackinnon*! Garhwal, *King*! *Duthie*! Kamaon; *Strachey & Winterbottom*! *T. Thomson*! *King*! below Betwari, 5,000 ft.! *Duthie*! Ganges Valley, 3,000—4,000 ft., *Duthie*! Nepal, *Wallich*! Sikkim; Garidoora, *Clarke*! Choonbuttea, *Clarke*! Mungpoo, *Gammie*! Mahanadi, *Gamble*! Pankabari, *Gamble*! Ryang, *Lister*! *Prain*! Sivoke, *Gamble*! Tista Valley, 3,000—4,000 ft., *Prain*! Bootan; *Griffith*! Kalimpong, 4,000 ft., *Gamble*! Alipur Duars; Mahakalguri, *Heawood*!

PLATE 66. Dalbergia sericea *G. Don.*—1, Flowering branch, from Kumaon, *n. s.*; 2, bud × 4; 3, epicalycine bracteoles × 4; 4, calyx, laid open × 4; 5, standard × 4; 6, wings × 4; 7, keel-petals × 4; 8, stamens × 4; 9, ovary × 4; 10, ovary, laid open × 4; 11, ovule × 16; 12, twig with fruiting panicle, from Sikkim, *n. s.*; 13, pod, *n. s.*; 14, pod, opened, showing young seed, *n. s.*; 15, seed × 2.

63. DALBERGIA SACERDOTUM Prain Journ. As. Soc. Beng. lxx. 2, 42 (1901).

A tree; the young twigs soft, blackish, faintly puberulous. *Leaves* 8 in. long; leaflets 9—11, ovate, base cuneate, apex obtuse notched, membranous, finely reticulated, sparsely adpressed-puberulous on both surfaces, 2·5 in. long, 1·25 in. wide, the rachis 6 in. long, finely puberulous; petiolules ·15 in. long, puberulous; stipules spathulate-lanceolate, puberulous. *Flowers* in terminal thyrsoid panicles 3 in. long, 2·5 in. wide, the peduncle, branches and slender pedicels rusty-puberulous; bracteoles lanceolate obtuse, membranous, deciduous; *calyx* campanulate, 5-toothed; teeth all obtuse, the two upper somewhat connate, the lowest longer than the others; *petals* all short-clawed, standard orbicular faintly thickened at base; *stamens* 10, monadelphous, immature; *ovary* shortly stipitate, stipe hairy, elsewhere glabrous; *ovules* 4. *Pod* narrowly ligulate, thinly coriaceous, tapering to the stipitate base, apex acute; glabrous, 3-seeded, 3·5 in. long., ·35 in. wide.

CHINA: Shanghai, *Hélot & d'Argy* 75!

The flowers are young and the stamens are monadelphous; this, however, does not preclude the possibility of their being diadelphous at a later stage. Except for the monadelphous condition of the staminal sheath, all the characters of *D. sacerdotum* indicate a close affinity with *D. sericea* G. Don, next to which the writer would suggest that the species should stand. If the character of monadelphous stamens be held to outweigh every other consideration, then the species must be placed near *D. Sissoo.* The reverend Collectors give as its Chinese name *Te-Zu* or "Aloes-wood."

PLATE 67. Dalbergia sacerdotum *Prain.*—1, Branch from Shanghai, in Herb. Paris, *n. s.*; 2, calyx, laid open × 4; 3, standard × 4; 4, wings × 4; 5, keel-petals × 4; 6, stamens × 4; 7, ovary × 4; 8, the same, laid open × 4; 9, ovule × 10; 10, pod, *n. s.*

¶ 20. **Lanceolarieae.**—*Pod wide-ligulate to ovate-lanceolate, samaroid; style slender, cylindric; leaflets obtuse; trees.*

A very natural group. The species that deviates most from the others and stands apart as a subgroup by itself is *D. paniculata*, which has a different stem-structure, with alternating layers of wood and bast, and has the stamens differently inserted inside the calyx-tube. The remaining species exhibit a steady and gradual transition from one to the other.

64. DALBERGIA PANICULATA Roxb. Corom. Pl. ii. 8, t. 114 (1798); Hort. Beng. 53 (1814); DC. Prodr. ii. 417 (1825); Spreng. Syst. iii. 193 (1826); Roxb. Flor. Ind. iii. 227 (1832); Wall. Cat. 5848 partly (1832); W. & A. Prodr. i. 265 partly (1834); Grah. Cat. Bomb. Pl. 55 (1839); Benth. Pl. Jungh. i. 256 (1851); Journ. Linn. Soc. iv. Suppl. 45 (1860); Dalz. & Gibs. Bomb. Flor. 78 (1861); Bedd. Flor. Sylvat. t. 88 (1869); Brandis For. Flor. 151 (1874); Bak. in Hook. f. Flor. Brit. Ind. ii. 236 (1876); Talbot Bomb. List 75 (1894); Woodr. Journ. Nat. Hist. Soc. Bomb. xi. 426 (1897); Prain Journ. As. Soc. Beng. lxvi. 2, 449 (1897), lxx. 2, 51 (1901); Cooke Flor. Pres. Bomb. i. 399 (1902); Prain Bengal Plants ii. 1273 (1903).

D. nigrescens Kurz Pegu Rep. App. A. 48 and B. 45 (1875); Journ. As. Soc. Beng. xlv. 2, 279 (1876); For. Flor. Burm. i. 346 (1877).

D. anomala Pierre MSS. in Herb. Pierre.

A tree, 40—70 feet high; branchlets sub-bifarious, tawny-pubescent, turning black, as do the leaves, in drying. *Leaves* 4—6 in. long; leaflets 9—13, oblong or elliptic, base rounded or truncate, apex obtuse, notched, subcoriaceous, finely reticulated, at first sparsely pubescent, both surfaces soon glabrous above and nearly so beneath, ·8—1 in. long, ·6 in. wide, very rarely much larger (2 in. long and 1·5 in. wide); rachis 3·25—5 in. long, petiolules ·15 in. long, puberulous; stipules lanceolate, pubescent, caducous. *Flowers* in dense rusty- or tawny-tomentose terminal panicles extending into the axils of the uppermost leaves, 2—6 in. long, 1·5—3 in. wide; bracteoles ovate, pubescent, deciduous; *calyx* campanulate, purplish; teeth acute, subequal except the lowest slightly the longest, externally densely pubescent; *petals* white, rather long-clawed; standard oblong, subcuneate at base; *stamens* 10, in two lateral bundles of 5 each with occasionally only the upper side completely divided, inserted half way up the calyx-tube; *ovary* shortly stipitate, pubescent; style slender, stigma capitate; *ovules* usually 3. *Pod* narrow-oblong, rarely in Burmese examples ovate-oblong, tapering to both ends, very rigidly coriaceous, black, indurated and hardly reticulated opposite the seeds, 1—2-seeded, 2—2·5 in. long, ·75—1·25 in. wide; *seed* reniform, compressed, ·3 in. long, ·2 in. wide, testa brown, shining.

INDIA: Malabaria; Concan, *Gibson*! Travancore, *Lawson*! Coromandelia; Mysore, *Heyne*! *G. Thomson*! Cuddapah, *Naidoo*! *Gamble*! Circars, *Roxburgh*! Orissa, *Lace*! INDO-CHINA: Burma; Pegu, *Eyre*! *Kurz*! Upper Burma, at Ngah Kyoun, *J. Anderson*! Tobadowa, *Abdul Huq*! Kyaukse, *Abdul Huq*! Mandalay, *Abdul Huq*! Ava, *Griffith*! Kyoukmyoung, *Abdul Huq*! Shan Hills, *Abdul Huq*! Cambodia; Togninh, in Cay Cong, along the Saigon River, *Pierre* 136! Bienhoa, along the Cai River, also Pén Lovir, *Pierre* 1041!

In proposing the name *D. nigrescens* Kurz has noted that this tree also occurs in India, the Indian specimens to which he refers being named by himself and being *D. paniculata*. That he did not refer this tree to *D. paniculata* was because he followed Wight and Arnott in their identification, the greater part of their *D. paniculata*, as numerous specimens at Kew and at Calcutta show, being *D. lanceolaria*. As a consequence Kurz's *D. paniculata* from Burma is a tree which he supposed to be the same as Wight's *D. paniculata*, subsequently well characterised by Gamble as *D. Oliveri*, which is much more nearly related to *D. lanceolaria* than the present one. Gamble, however, states (*Manual of Indian Timbers*) that, as regards stem-structure, *D. paniculata* and *D. nigrescens* differ considerably, and it may ultimately prove necessary to distinguish the Indian from the Indo-Chinese tree included under the present species. If this be done, the Indo-Chinese one must be known as *D. nigrescens*. But if they do differ essentially in stem-structure, the fact remains that they are identical as regards leaves, flowers and fruits, and that both 'dry black'—a circumstance that does not occur in the case of any other Asiatic *Dalbergia* except the tree here described as *D. paniculata* var. *saigonensis*. In Orissa Lace finds that this species is known as *Babuklia*. The Cambodian tree for which Pierre has suggested the apposite name *D. anomala* is precisely Kurz's *D. nigrescens*; the Anamite vernacular name is *Xém quát*, the Kmer name is *Xnoul*.

VAR. *saigonensis* var. nov. (*D. saigonensis* Pierre MSS.) A tree, 50—70 feet high, stem nodose or verrucose, bark grey. *Leaves* 5 in. long; leaflets 8—11, all rather narrowly oblong, obtuse or retuse, 1·5 in. long, ·65 in. wide. *Pod* rather narrowly subligulate, 1·75—2·5 in. long, ·4 in. wide, 1—3-seeded; *seed* reniform, compressed, ·3 in. long, ·2 in. wide, testa quite black, shining.

INDO-CHINA: Cambodia; Saigon, at Thúdúc, *Pierre* 222!

Except in having usually rather fewer, and always decidedly narrower leaflets; in having always narrower pods; and in having black in place of brown seeds, this tree does not differ from *D. paniculata*: it 'dries black' in precisely the same fashion. In India, and especially in Central Indo-China, the pods of *D. paniculata* are often much broader than usual; not infrequently these broad pods occur on the same branch with pods of the usual size. The pods of VAR. *saigonensis* do not depart more from the normal in one direction than do the broad pods referred to in another. The combination, however, of an unusual shape of leaflet with a different colour of testa renders it advisable to distinguish the present tree at least as a variety: it may indeed ultimately prove necessary to recognise in *D. paniculata*, as here understood, three distinct species:—*D. paniculata* Roxb., Indian only; *D. nigrescens* Kurz, throughout Central and Eastern Indo-China; and *D. saigonensis* Pierre, in Eastern Indo-China only.

PLATE 68. Dalbergia paniculata *Roxb.*—1, Flowering branch from the Concan, *n. s.*; 2, bud × 4; 3, calyx, laid open × 4; 4, standard × 4; 5, wings × 4; 6, keel-petals × 4; 7, stamens, usual arrangement × 4; 8, stamens, occasional arrangement × 4; 9, ovary × 4; 10, ovary, laid open × 4; 11, ovule × 10; 12, fruiting twig from Cuddapah; 13, fruits of large-leafed form from Kyoukmyoung, *n. s.*; 14, seed, *n. s.*

PLATE 69. Dalbergia paniculata *Roxb.* VAR. saigonensis *Prain.*—1, Fruiting branch from Thúdúc, Saigon, *n. s.*; 2, pod, opened, showing seed *in situ*, *n. s.*; 3, another pod, with 3 seeds, seen from one edge, *n. s.*; 4, seed, *n. s.*

65. DALBERGIA HUPEANA Hance Journ. Bot. xx. 5 (1882); Forbes & Hemsl. Journ. Linn. Soc. xxiii. 198 (1887); Harms in Engl. Bot. Jahrb. xxix. 416 (1900); Prain Journ. As. Soc. Beng. lxx. 2, 53 (1901).

A tree, 20—30 feet high, with numerous spreading branches; branchlets sub-bifarious, glabrous. *Leaves* 8—10 in. long; leaflets 9—11, oblong-elliptic, obtuse or retuse, firmly chartaceous, closely reticulately veined, 1·75—2·5 in. long, 1—1·5 in. wide, glabrous above, puberulous but ultimating glabrescent beneath; rachis 6—7 in. long, and petiolules ·2 in. long, glabrous; stipules caducous. *Flowers* in lax terminal panicles often extending into the axils of the uppermost leaves, 3—8 in. long, 2·5—6 in. wide, peduncles and branches glabrous, pedicels sparsely rusty-pubescent; basal and epicalycine bracteoles ovate, pubescent, deciduous; *calyx* campanulate; lower tooth lanceolate, as long as tube and twice as long as lateral subacute; upper pair rather larger than lateral obtuse, subconnate; *corolla* white, petals all rather long-clawed, standard orbicular, emarginate; *stamens* 10, in two lateral bundles of 5 each, filaments free in their upper third; *ovary* shortly stipitate, glabrous except the stipe and base; style filiform, stigma capitate; *ovules* usually 2—3. *Pod* indehiscent, oblong or broadly ligulate, rather firmly coriaceous, apex acute, base tapering to the distinct stipe, 2—3 in. long, ·5 in. wide, faintly veined opposite the 1—2, rarely 3 seeds, glabrous; *seed* reniform, compressed, ·3 in. long, ·2 in. wide.

CHINA: Szechuen; *Farges*! Hupeh; Ichang, *Walters*! *Henry*! *Faber*! Chekiang; Ning-po, *Oldham*! *Cooper*! *Faber*! Kwangtung; *Sampson*! *Ford*! *Carles*! Nant'o, *Carles*!

Tan-mou-chou, the tree; *Tchan-keou*, the wood (*Farges*): *Paitan*, the local; white *Chandan*, the classical name (*Cooper*): the *Tán* tree (*Henry*). In Herb. Kew, Henry notes that the flowers of the *Tán* are white and yellow with some lilac markings inside one of the petals; they are slightly fragrant. The wood is used for the hammers of oil-presses and for the handles of tools such as planes and hammers; in this it resembles *D. ovata*, *D. Oliveri*, and *D. latifolia*.

PLATE 70. Dalbergia hupeana *Hance*.—1, Flowering branch from Hupeh, *n. s.*; 2, bud × 4; 3, pedicel with epicalycine bracteoles × 4; 4, calyx, laid open × 4; 5, standard × 4; 6, wings × 4; 7, keel-petals × 4; 8, stamens × 4; 9, ovary × 4; 10, ovary, laid open × 4; 11, ovule × 10; 12, branch in young fruit, from Hupeh, *n. s.*; 13, twig with ripe fruit, from Hupeh, *n. s.*; 14, pod opened, showing seed *in situ*, *n. s.*; 15, seed, *n. s.*

66. DALBERGIA ASSAMICA Benth. Pl. Jungh. i. 255 (1851); Journ. Linn. Soc. iv. Suppl. 45—Assam plant only (1860); Bak. in Hook. f. Flor. Brit. Ind. ii. 235—Assam plant only (1876); Prain Journ. As. Soc. Beng. lxvi. 2, 449 (1897); lxx. 2, 52 (1901).

D. lanceolaria Gamble Darjeel. List 29 (1896), not of Linn. f.

A tree, with numerous spreading branches; branchlets sub-bifarious, glabrous. *Leaves* 10—12 in. long; leaflets 13—21, oblong-elliptic, obtuse or retuse, chartaceous, 1·5—2 in. long, ·75—1·25 in. wide, sparsely adpressed-puberulous but soon glabrous above, subpersistently adpressed-pubescent beneath, closely finely reticulate-veined; rachis 8—10 in. long, and petiolules ·2 in. long, at first puberulous, soon glabrescent; stipules ovate-lanceolate, foliaceous, deciduous. *Flowers* in short lax axillary panicles, 4—6 in. long, 3 in. wide, peduncles glabrous, branches and pedicels finely sparsely puberulous; basal and epicalycine bracteoles ovate, deciduous; *calyx* campanulate, with a lanceolate lower tooth as long as tube and twice as long as the triangular acute others, the two upper subconnate and slightly reflexed; *corolla* white, petals all rather long-clawed, standard orbicular, emarginate; *stamens* 10, in two lateral bundles of 5 each, filaments all free in their upper third; *ovary* stipitate, sparingly hirsute; style slender, stigma small capitate; *ovules* usually 4. *Pod* indehiscent, oblong or broadly ligulate, thinly coriaceous, apex acute, base tapering to the distinct stipe, 2—3 in. long, ·5 in. broad, faintly veined opposite the 1—2, sometimes 3, very rarely 4 seeds, glabrous; *seed* reniform, compressed, ·25 in. long, ·2 in. wide.

HIMALAYA: Sikkim; submontane forests at Choklong, *Gamble*! Bootan; submontane forests in the Narchu Valley, *Prain*! INDO-CHINA: Assam; Brahmaputra Valley, at Sibsagar and elsewhere, *Griffith*! *Jenkins*! *Masters*! *Hooker & Thomson*! *Peal*! Mongsemdi, *Watt*! CHINA: Yunnan; Szemao Mts., 4,500 feet elev., *Henry* 12988!

In Assam this tree is known, according to Peal, as *Medeloa;* its timber is much esteemed.

PLATE 71. Dalbergia assamica *Benth.*—1, Flowering branch from Sibsagar, Assam, *n. s.;* 2, bud × 4; 3, pedicel with basal and epicalycine bracteoles × 4; 4, calyx, laid open × 4; 5, standard × 4; 6, wings × 4; 7, keel-petals × 4; 8, stamens × 4; 9, ovary × 4; 10, ovary, laid open × 4; 11, ovule × 10; 12, twig, in fruit, from Sibsagar, Assam, *n. s.;* 13, pod, opened to show young seed *in situ*, *n. s.;* 14, seed, *n. s.*

67. DALBERGIA BALANSAE Prain Journ. As. Soc. Beng. lxx. 2, 54 (1901).

D. lanceolaria Forbes & Hemsl. Journ. Linn. Soc. xxiii. 193 (1887); Drake del Castillo Journ. de Bot. v. 214 (1891), not of Linn. f.

A tree, 20—30 feet high; young branches sub-bifarious. *Leaves* 5—7 in. long; leaflets 13—15, ovate-oblong, obtuse or retuse, persistently puberulous beneath, chartaceous, finely reticulately veined, 1·25—1·5 in. long, ·75—·85 in. wide, rachis 4—6 in. and petiolules ·15 in. long, puberulous; stipules lanceolate. *Flowers* in lax axillary panicles 3—4 in. long, 2 in. wide, with glabrescent or puberulous peduncles and puberulous branches and slender pedicels; basal bracteoles ovate-lanceolate, epicalycine bracteoles lanceolate-obtuse, very caducous; *calyx* campanulate; the upper teeth subconnate subacute, lateral acute half as long as tube, lowest lanceolate as long as tube; *corolla* white, petals all rather long-clawed, standard orbicular 2-callose at base, slightly emarginate; *stamens* 10, in two lateral bundles of 5 each, filaments free in their upper fourth alternately shorter and longer; *ovary* stipitate, densely pubescent; style short conical, stigma minute; *ovules* 1—5, usually 3. *Pod* indehiscent, long-stipitate, tapering to both ends, usually 1-, rarely 2—3-seeded, firmly coriaceous, reticulated opposite the seeds, 3—5 in. long, 1 in. wide; *seed* subreniform, compressed; only seen immature.

CHINA: Kiangsi; Kiu-Kiang, *Shearer*! Kwangtung; *Sampson*! *Ford*! *Millett*! INDO-CHINA: Tongking; Mt. Bavi, *Balansa*!

Ford says this may be a small shrub or pass into a tree 20 feet high.

PLATE 72. Dalbergia Balansae *Prain.*—1, Flowering branch from Tongking, *n. s.;* 2, calyx, laid open × 4; 3, standard × 4; 4, wings × 4; 5, keel-petals × 4; 6, stamens × 4; 7, ovary × 4; 8, ovary, 1-ovuled, laid open × 4; 9, ovary, 5-ovuled, from the same specimen, laid open × 4; 10, ovules × 6; 11, ovule × 10; 12, fruiting twig from Kwangtung, *n. s.;* 13, fruit, opened to show young seeds *in situ*, *n. s.;* 14, young seed, *n. s.*

68. DALBERGIA MINAHASSAE Koord. Meded. 's lands Plantent. xix. 430, 630 (1898).

Dalbergia sp. Vidal Pl. Vasc. Filip. 112 in part (1886).

D. ferruginea Prain Journ. As. Soc. Beng. lxx. 2, 55 (as to Vidal 2598, 2606 only) (1901).

D. lanceolaria ? Llanos Mem. Acad. Cienc. Madr. (1858); App. ad Flor. Philip. Blanco Ed. iii. iv. 103 (1880) possibly.

A tree with spreading branches; branchlets puberulous, sub-bifarious. *Leaves* 8—11 in. long; leaflets 15—25, ovate-oblong, obtuse or emarginate, base cuneate and slightly unequal, 1·25—1·75. in. long, ·65—·75 in. wide, firmly papery, sparsely adpressed-strigose on both surfaces; rachis 6·5—9·5 in. long, minutely puberulous, as are the petiolules ·15 in. long; stipules lanceolate, subfalcate, deciduous. *Flowers* in axillary panicles 3—4 in. long, 1·5—2 in. wide, peduncles branches and pedicels puberulous; bracts minute, basal bracteoles ovate-acute small, epicalycine oblong-obtuse, all pubescent; *calyx* campanulate, externally pubescent; lowest tooth lanceolate about as long as the tube, the others subequal obtuse, the upper pair subconnate; *corolla* white, petals all distinctly clawed, standard orbicular, emarginate; *stamens* 10, in two lateral bundles of 5 each that are often not quite discrete, filaments free in their upper third, alternately shorter and longer; *ovary* densely pubescent, distinctly stipitate; style slender, stigma minute; *ovules* 4. *Pod* not seen.

PHILIPPINES: Morong, *Vidal*! Panay, *Vidal*! ? Angat, *Llanos*. EASTERN MALAYA: Celebes; Minahassa, *Koorders*!

In the Philippines this is known as *Halubanit;* in Celebes it is *Tapoelandang*. It is possible that this is *D. lanceolaria ?* Llanos, which is stated to have a linear silky pod, a character that effectually disposes of Llanos' own suggestion. The pod of *D. Minahassae* is as yet unknown, but the species has a densely velvety ovary and is thus *capable* of having a silky pod.

PLATE 73. Dalbergia Minahassae *Koord.*—1, Flowering twig from Minahassa, Celebes, *n. s.;* 2, end of a twig from Panay, Philippines, *n. s.;* 3, bud × 4; 4, pedicel with epicalycine bracteoles × 4; 5, calyx, laid open × 4; 6, standard × 4; 7, wings × 4; 8, keel-petals × 4; 9, stamens × 4; 10, free portion of filaments and anthers × 10; 11, ovary × 4; 12, ovary, laid open × 4; 13, ovule × 10.

69. DALBERGIA SZEMAOENSIS Prain sp. nov.

A tree, 20 feet high, with densely tawny-velvety young branches. *Leaves* with leaflets 19—21, when young densely velvety-pubescent on both surfaces; rachis and petiolules densely tawny-velvety; stipules large ovate-obtuse, ·6 in. long, ·25 in. wide. *Flowers* in lax panicles 6 in. long, 8 in. across, below the leaves on young branches that end in leafy shoots; peduncles, branches and pedicels all densely tawny-velvety; main panicle-branches 3 in. long, secondary 1—1·25 in. long, pedicels slender ·2 in. long, subsecund; bracts ovate, densely tawny, ·1 in. long, very deciduous; basal bracteoles wide-ovate and epicalycine pair ovate densely tawny, the latter embracing lower two-thirds of calyx-tube; *calyx* campanulate, tube glabrescent externally at base, pubescent above; teeth unequal, the lowest lanceolate twice as long as acute lateral and obtuse subconnate upper pairs, and rather longer than the tube; *corolla* purple, standard orbicular, reflexed, emarginate, somewhat thickened at the junction with the narrow distinct claw; wings wide-ovate, long-clawed, auriculate at base of blade on upper side; keel-petals long-clawed, connate above, auricled at base of blade; *stamens* 10, in two lateral bundles of 5 each; *ovary* stipitate, densely pubescent throughout; style slender conical, stigma small; *ovules* usually 3. *Pod* not seen mature; young pods oblong to suborbicular.

CHINA: Yunnan; Szemao Mts at 5,000 feet elev., *Henry* 11895!

A species nearly related to *D. lanceolaria*, *D. Oliveri*, *D. Hemsleyi* and their allies, but quite distinct by reason of the very large stipules. The young leaves are densely pubescent, but it does not therefore follow that they are so when adult; not being fully developed, measurements are not given for the leaflets or rachis.

PLATE 74. Dalbergia szemaoensis *Prain*—1, Flowering shoot from Szemao, *n. s.*; 2, bud with bracteoles × 4; 3, pedicels with bracteoles × 4; 4, calyx, laid open × 4; 5, standard × 4; 6, wings × 4; 7, keel-petals × 4; 8, stamens × 4; 9, ovary × 4; 10, ovary, laid open × 4; 11, ovule × 10; 12, immature fruit × 4.

70. DALBERGIA OLIVERI Gamble ex Prain in Journ. As. Soc. Beng. lxvi. 2, 451 (1897); lxx. 2, 53 (1901).

D. purpurea Bak. in Hook. f. Flor. Brit. Ind. ii. 235 partly (1876); Prain Journ. As. Soc. Beng. lxvi. 2, 449 (1897), not of Wall.

D. paniculata Kurz Journ. As. Soc. Beng. xlv. 2, 279 (1876); For. Flor. Burm. i, 345 (1877), not of Roxb.

D. Prazeri Prain Journ. As. Soc. Beng. lxvi. 2, 452 (1897); lxx. 2, 53 (1901).

D. laccifera Laness. Pl. Util. Col. Franç. 289 (1886) possibly.

D. aestivalis Pierre MSS. in Herb. Pierre, possibly.

A tree, 60—80 feet high, with pale flaky bark and a straight stem, 2—3 feet in diam. at 5 feet from the ground; young shoots spreading, sub-bifarious, slightly puberulous. *Leaves* 6—9 in. long, on young shoots sometimes 11 in. long; leaflets 13—17, rarely 9 or 11, on young shoots sometimes 19—21, ovate, subacute or obtuse emarginate, 1·5 in. long, ·85 in. wide, glabrous or finely sparsely adpressed-pubescent on both surfaces when young, soon quite glabrous, chartaceous, finely reticulately veined, distal leaflet hardly exceeding the others; rachis 5—7·5 in. long and petiolules ·2 in. long, glabrous; stipules lanceolate, glabrous or puberulous. *Flowers* in spurious lateral panicles with glabrous peduncles and sparsely puberulous branches and pedicels; each apparent panicle 3—6 in. long, 4—8 in. wide, terminating in a small leafy shoot, which develops before the fruits ripen; bracts at base of pedicels and bracteoles under calyx lanceolate, half as long as calyx-tube, puberulous; *calyx* puberulous or pubescent, campanulate, the two upper teeth subconnate obtuse, the lateral acute, shorter than tube, lowest lanceolate as long as tube; *corolla* white externally, lilac in bud, purple within, petals all long clawed, standard obovate or orbicular emarginate not thickened at base; *stamens* 10, in 2 lateral bundles of 5 each, all filaments free in their upper third, alternately shorter and longer; *ovary* glabrous except the stipe, or slightly pubescent in the lower half, rather long-stipitate; style slender, stigma capitate; *ovules* usually 3. *Pod* indehiscent, long-stipitate, tapering to the base, rounded or acute at apex, coriaceous, glabrous, usually 1-seeded, sometimes 2—3-seeded, reticulated throughout, but indurated and smooth opposite the seeds, 2·25—3·5 in. long, ·65 in. wide; *seed* reniform, somewhat compressed, ·45 in. long, ·25 in wide.

INDO-CHINA: Burma; Pegu, *Kurz*! Wuntho, *Oliver*! Bhamo, *Oliver*! Koni, *Prazer*! Chattiah, *Prazer*! Siam; *Teysmann*! Bienhoa, near Song-lu, *Pierre* 1704!

This Kurz terms *Ta-pouk-pen* or *Ta-bouk-ben;* in all Burmese recent collections, however, the name given is *Tamalan.* It has a fine hard red wood used for the handles of instruments in the same way as the woods of *D. ovata* and *D. latifolia* are used. The specimen of *D. aestivalis* Pierre examined has no flowers or fruits; as regards leaves it agrees very well with the present species: the native names are noted as *Chlieu-lai Bon-dam* (Moi) and *Cay cám lai* (Anam). The native name cited by Lanessan for his *D. laccifera* leads to a suspicion that it also is the same.

PLATE 75. Dalbergia Oliveri *Gamble.*—1, Flowering branch, pseudo-panicle, ending in a leafy branch, from Wuntho, *n. s.;* 2, leafy branch, fully developed, from Wuntho, *n. s.;* 3, bud, showing basal and one epicalycine bracteole × 4; 4, calyx, laid open × 4; 5, standard × 4; 6, wings × 4; 7, keel-petals × 4; 8, stamens × 4; 9, ovary × 4; 10, ovary, laid open × 4; 11, ovule × 8; 12, fruiting branch, from Chattiah, *n. s.;* 13, seed, *n. s.*

71. DALBERGIA LANCEOLARIA Linn. f. Suppl. Pl. 316 (1781); DC. Prodr. ii. 417 (1825); Benth. Journ. Linn. Soc. iv. Suppl. 45 (1860); Dalz. & Gibs. Bomb. Flor. 78 (1861); Brandis For. Flor. 151 (1874); Bak. in Hook. f. Flor. Brit. Ind. ii. 235 (1876); Trim. Ceyl. Flor. ii. 88 (1894); Talbot Bomb. List. 74 (1894); Woodr. Journ. Nat. Hist. Soc. Bomb. xi. 426 (1897); Prain Journ. As. Soc. Beng. lxx. 2, 52 (1901); Kanjilal Flor. Sch. Circ. 129 (1901); Cooke Flor. Pres. Bomb. 399 (1902); Prain Bengal Plants i. 411 (1903).

D. frondosa Roxb. Hort. Beng. 53 (1814); DC. Prodr. ii. 417 (1825); Roxb. Flor. Ind. iii. 226 (1832); Wall. Cat. 5855 (1832); W. & A. Prodr.; 266 partly (1834); Grah. Pl. Bomb. 55 (1839); Wight Ic. t. 266 (1850); Voigt. Hort. Suburb. Calcutt. 241 (1845); Benth. Pl. Jungh. i. 256 (1851); Thw. Enum. 94 (1859); Bedd. Flor. Sylvat. t. 88 (1869).

D. zeylanica Roxb. Hort. Beng. 53 (1814); Flor. Ind. iii. 228 (1832); Wall. Cat. 5847A (1832); Voigt Hort. Suburb. Calcutt. 241 (1845).

D. arborea Heyne in Roth. Nov. Sp. 330 (1821); DC. Prodr. ii. 417 (1825), not of Willd.

D. hircina Ham. in Wall. Cat. 5871A (1832).

D. paniculata W. & A. Prodr. i. 265 mainly (1834); Kanjilal Flor. Sch. Circ. 130 (1901), not of Roxb.

A tree, 50—60 feet high, with rather smooth grey bark and a straight stem, 2—3 feet in. diam. at 5 feet from the ground; young shoots spreading, sub-bifarious, rusty-puberulous or glabrous. *Leaves* 5—7 in. long; leaflets 7—11, less often 13 rarely 15, ovate-oblong, rarely suborbicular, obtuse or retuse, 1·25—1·75, rarely on young shoots 2·5 in. long, ·65—·8 in. wide, chartaceous, finely reticulately veined, when young usually densely finely rusty-pubescent, when mature glabrous or sparingly finely adpressed-pubescent on both surfaces or only beneath, distal leaflet hardly exceeding the others; rachis 3·5—5·5 in. long and petiolules ·15 in. long at first pubescent, soon glabrous; stipules subfalcate-lanceolate, on young shoots sometimes ·5—·75 in. long deciduous. *Flowers* in lax panicles, terminal and in the axils of young leaves on new shoots, 2—3 in. long, 2 in. wide, the peduncles, branches and pedicels at first rusty-pubescent; basal bracteoles lanceolate, epicalycine oblong very minute caducous; *calyx* campanulate, the upper teeth subconnate obtuse, the others acute, the lowest as long as the tube, externally pubescent; *corolla* blueish-white, petals all rather long-clawed; standard orbicular, emarginate, thickened at base; *stamens* 10, usually in 2 lateral bundles of 5 each, sometimes the vexillary stamen also free, all filaments free in their upper fourth and alternately shorter and longer; *ovary* pubescent, rather long-stipitate; style slender, stigma capitate; *ovules* usually 3. *Pod* indehiscent, long-stipitate, tapering to both ends, usually 1—3-seeded, rarely 4—5-seeded, coriaceous, reticulated opposite the seeds, 2·25—4 in. long, ·65 in. wide; *seed* reniform, somewhat compressed, ·45 in. long, ·25 in. wide.

INDIA: Sub-Himalayan Forests; Hardwar, *Hamilton*! Darhora, *Hamilton*! Sukhiya, *Hamilton*! Siwaliks, *Hearle*! Rajputana; Abu, *King*! Ajmir, *Jacquemont*! Coromandelia; C. India, *Jerdon*! Behar, *Hooker*! Chota Nagpur, *Gamble*! *Haines*! *Campbell*! *Clarke*! *Wood*! *Prain*! Orissa, *Lace*! Mysore, *G. Thomson*! Vellore, *Gamble*! Coromandel, *Heyne*! *Roxburgh*! Kurnool, *Gamble*! Tellicherry, *Metz*! *Wight*! Cottulam, *Leschenault*! Shevarois, *Perrottet*! Malabaria; Concan, *Stocks*! *Law*! Canara, *Talbot*! Belgaum, *Ritchie*! CEYLON: Central Province, *Thwaites*!

Leschenault gives as the vernacular name *Toda Cotty Morum;* Lace reports that in Orissa it is known as *Angaria.*

PLATE 76. Dalbergia lanceolaria *Linn. f.*—1, Flowering branch from S. India, *n. s.;* 2, twig with part of leaf and stipules, from a root-sucker from Chota Nagpur, *n. s.;* 3, young flower × 4; 4, epicalycine bracteoles × 4; 5, calyx, laid open × 4; 6, standard × 4; 7, wings × 4; 8, keel-petals × 4; 9, stamens × 4; 10, ovary × 4; 11, ovary, laid open × 4; 12, ovule × 10; 13, fruiting branch, from W. India, *n. s.;* 14, pod of unusual size, from a Parasnath specimen, *n. s.;* 15, pod, laid open, showing seed *in situ*, *n. s.;* 16, seed, *n. s.*

72. **DALBERGIA HEMSLEYI** Prain Journ. As. Soc. Beng. lxvi. 2, 450 (1897); lxx. 2, 54 (1901).

A tree, 20 feet high, with spreading branches; branchlets silky- to rusty-pubescent, sub-bifarious. *Leaves* 4—5 in. long; leaflets usually 5, sometimes 7, rarely 9, ovate-lanceolate or ovate or suborbicular, obtuse or narrow-truncate, emarginate, pubescent at length glabrescent above, densely rusty- or silky-pubescent beneath, dull-green on both sides, 1·5—2 in. long, ·75—1 in. wide, rather firm, finely reticulately veined; rachis 2·5—4 in. long, densely rusty or silky as are the petiolules ·15 in. long; stipules small, densely pubescent, deciduous. *Flowers* in axillary panicles 4 in. long, 1·5 in. wide, peduncles, branches and pedicels densely persistently rusty- or silky-tomentose; *calyx* campanulate, teeth acute, the lowest slightly exceeding the others, externally densely tomentose; *corolla* with petals rather long-clawed, standard orbicular emarginate, not thickened at the base; *stamens* 10, in two lateral bundles of 5 each, filaments free in their upper third; ovary not seen, stipe of young pods pubescent. *Pod* indehiscent, long-stipitate, tapering to both ends, 1—3-seeded, coriaceous, reticulate throughout, but especially opposite the seeds, 2·25—4 in. long, ·65 in. wide; *seed* reniform, compressed, ·45 in. long, ·25 in. wide.

INDO-CHINA: Burma; Shan Hills, at Fort Stedman, *Collett*! Indine, *Abdul Khalil*! Lwekaw, *Abdul Khalil*! Myingyin, *Prazer*! Cambodia; Xpong, on Mt. Pang-Chai, *Pierre* 1042!

PLATE 77. Dalbergia Hemsleyi *Prain.*—1, Specimen in young fruit, from Fort Stedman, *n. s.*; 2, calyx, laid open × 4; 3, standard × 4; 4, wings × 4; 5, keel-petals × 4; 6, stamens × 4; 7, fruiting branch from Myingyin, *n. s.*; 8, fruit from Indine, laid open, showing seed *in situ*, *n. s.*; 9, seed, *n. s.*

This species belongs to the same group as *D. lanceolaria*, *D. Oliveri* and *D. Balansae*, and is apparently the Shan and Cambodian representative of the group. It most resembles *D. lanceolaria*, though it has even fewer leaflets than that species usually has. Its agreement with *D. lanceolaria* is marked chiefly by the fact that the panicles are in the axils of leaves of the same season instead of issuing from below these. It has, moreover, the same dense pubescence that characterises *D. lanceolaria* when the leaves and shoots of that species are young. It differs, however, very markedly in having this pubescence persistent, whereas in *D. lanceolaria* the shoots and leaves beneath soon become nearly or quite glabrous. There is no marked thickening at the base of the standard-blade in this species; its flowers therefore become practically identical with those of *D. Oliveri*; nor are its pods and seeds very different from those of that species, which has sometimes pubescent branchlets and leaflets subpersistently pubescent (the form = *D. Prazeri*) beneath. The much more numerous leaflets of *D. Oliveri*, however, and the flowers springing not even from old leaf-axils, but in lateral pseudo-panicles, the main rachis of which ends in a leafy shoot and develops ultimately into a leafy branch, very amply distinguish that species from the present one.

No native name has been recorded from Burma for *D. Hemsleyi*, and it is not impossible that some of the remarks made regarding the wood of *D. Oliveri* are really applicable to this species. The Kmer name for this in Cambodia is *Xnoul*; this name is, however, also used for *D. paniculata*.

¶ 21. **Canae.**—*Pod wide-ligulate, samaroid; style subulate; leaflets acute or subacute; trees.*

A subnatural group. *D. Wattii* differs considerably in facies and in pod from the remaining species and, but for the inadvisability of unduly multiplying our groups, might be made to stand apart. It agrees with the other species as regards style, and it differs from the *Lanceolarieae*, with which it has much in common, both as to style and as to shape of leaflets. It thus forms a good connecting link between the *Lanceolarieae* and the *Canae* rather than a satisfactory member of either group. The remaining species, though sometimes very different in appearance and in size of leaflets and fruits, are in essential characters very closely allied.

73. DALBERGIA WATTII Clarke Journ. Linn. Soc. xxv. 17. t. 5 (1889); Prain Journ. As. Soc. Beng. lxvi. 2, 451 (1897); lxx. 2, 53 (1901).

A tree, 30 feet high, with spreading, sub-bifarious, glabrous branches. *Leaves* 6—8 in. long; leaflets 9—11, often subopposite, ovate-lanceolate acute with involute margins, dark-green glabrous above, glaucescent faintly hairy beneath, 2·5—3 in. long, 1 in. wide, membranous, finely reticulate; rachis 3·5—4 in. long, glabrous as are the very short petiolules; stipules ovate-lanceolate, foliaceous, deciduous. *Flowers* in axillary panicles 2 in. long 1·5 in. wide, peduncles, branches and pedicels sparsely pilose; basal and epicalycine bracteoles ovate-lanceolate, subpersistent, the latter half as long as calyx-tube; *calyx* campanulate, teeth acute, the two upper subconnate, all except the lanceolate lowest shorter than the tube; *corolla* white, petals all rather long-clawed, standard orbicular emarginate; *stamens* 10, in two lateral bundles of 5 each, filaments all free in their upper third; *ovary* with long pilose stipe, but itself glabrous except along one suture; style very slender, stigma minute; *ovule* usually solitary. *Pod* thinly coriaceous, glabrous, shortly stipitate, 2·25 in. long, ·75 in. wide, narrowed to the base, somewhat rounded at apex, veined opposite the solitary seed; *seed* reniform, compressed, ·45 in. long, ·25 in. wide.

INDO-CHINA: Manipur; Meitaphum, 5,000 ft. *Watt*! Mayung, 3,500 ft. *Clarke*!

PLATE 78. Dalbergia Wattii *Clarke*.—1, Flowering branch from Meitaphum, Manipur, *n. s.*; 2, pedicel with epicalycine bracteoles × 4; 3, calyx, laid open × 4; 4, standard × 4; 5, wings × 4; 6, keel-petals × 4; 7, stamens × 4; 8, ovary × 4; 9, ovary, laid open × 4; 10, ovule × 6; 11, twig in fruit, from Mayung, Manipur, *n. s.*; 12, pod, opened to show seed *in situ*, *n. s.*; 13, seed, *n. s.*

74. DALBERGIA MAMMOSA Pierre MSS. in Herb. Pierre.

A tree, 60 feet high; young branches blackish, glabrous. *Leaves* 6—8 in. long; leaflets 11—15, narrow-oblong, acute, base cuneate, quite glabrous on both sides, pale-green above, glaucescent beneath, rather thinly chartaceous, 1·5—1·75 in. long, ·5 in. wide; rachis 5—6 in. long and petiolules ·15 in. long glabrous. *Flowers* in axillary panicles 3 in. long, 2 in. wide; rachis and panicle branches very sparingly pubescent; bracts and bracteoles not seen; *calyx* narrowly campanulate; *corolla* and *stamens* not seen. *Pod* wide-ligulate, firmly coriaceous, glabrous, strongly reticulated except opposite the seeds, narrowed to the base, more or less rounded at the apex, 4—6 in. long, ·8 in. wide, considerably suberously thickened and umbonate opposite the solitary, rarely 2 seeds; *seed* reniform, compressed, ·35 in. long, ·25 in. wide, ·07 in. thick.

INDO-CHINA: Cochin-China; Baria, on Mt. Chóben, *Pierre* 1711 *bis*!

This tree, though not yet completely represented, since flowers are unknown, is undoubtedly a member of the group *Canae* in the section *Dalbergaria*. The leaves alone are sufficiently unlike those of the other allied species to warrant its recognition as distinct; the peculiarly umbonate suberous thickenings of the pod opposite the seeds supply a character that distinguishes it from every other known species of the genus. This species is very nearly related to the next species and bears the same Anamite name, *Cám lai*.

PLATE 79. Dalbergia mammosa *Pierre*.—1, Fruiting branch from Mt. Chóben in Baria, *n. s.*; 2, pod, opened, showing seed *in situ*, *n. s.*; 3, seed, *n. s.*

75. DALBERGIA BARIENSIS Pierre MSS. in Herb. Pierre.

A tree, 50—70 feet high; young branches brown, glabrous. *Leaves* 7—9 in. long; leaflets 13—15, ovate-oblong, abruptly narrowed to a retuse tip, medium-green above, pale-green beneath, firmly chartaceous, quite glabrous on both surfaces, 1·5—1·75 in. long, ·75 in. wide; rachis 5—7 in. long and petiolules ·2 in. long, glabrous; stipules not seen. *Flowers* in short axillary panicles 1·5 in. long; *calyx* narrowly campanulate; *corolla* not seen; *stamens* not seen. *Pod* wide-ligulate, firmly coriaceous, glabrous, faintly reticulated near the narrowly cuneate base, elsewhere smooth, 5 in. long, 1 in. wide, considerably thickened and suberous, but not umbonate, opposite the seeds; *seed* solitary, rarely two, reniform, compressed.

INDO-CHINA: Cochin-China; Bienhoa, Baria on Mt. Dinh, *Pierre* 137! near Chóben, *Pierre* 1711!

Very closely related to *D. mamnosa*, but with the pods not umbonate and with leaflets of very different texture and venation and somewhat different shape. As in the case of the preceding species, the Anamite name is *Cám lai*.

PLATE 80. Dalbergia bariensis *Pierre*.—1, Branch with leaves and fruit from Baria, Bienhoa, *n. s.*; 2, pod, laid open, showing seed *in situ*, *n. s.*; 3, seed, *n. s.*

76. DALBERGIA DONGNAIENSIS Pierre MSS. in Herb. Pierre.

D. purpurea? Laness. Pl. Util. Col. Franç. 289 (1886); Brenier in Bull. Econ. Ind. Chin. v. 404 (1902) possibly; not *D. purpurea* Wall.

A tree, 50—80 feet high; young branches blackish, glabrous. *Leaves* 6—8 in. long; leaflets 9—11, narrowly oblong, acute, base rounded or shortly cuneate, glabrous, even when young, on both surfaces, pale-green, chartaceous, 2 in. long, ·75 in. wide; rachis 4—6 in. long and petiolules ·2 in. long, glabrous; stipules small, ovate, deciduous. *Flowers* in axillary panicles 4 in. long, 3 in. wide; rachis and branches sparingly pubescent with tawny deciduous hairs; bracts small ovate, epicalycine bracteoles small, lanceolate; *calyx* narrowly campanulate, ·25 in. long; lower three teeth lanceolate, the lowest longer than the lateral pair and nearly as long as calyx-tube; upper pair ovate obtuse subconnate; *corolla* violet, standard orbicular reflexed, almost entire, rather short-clawed; wings wide-oblong, long-clawed, hastate at base of blade on upper side as are the long-clawed keel-petals; *stamens* 10, usually in two lateral bundles of 5 each, sometimes the lateral bundles more or less united below; *ovary* long-stipitate, glabrous except the long stoutish stipe; style slender, subconical, stigma capitate; *ovules* usually 2.

INDO-CHINA: Cochin-China; Bienhoa, between Pho-qua and the river Song-cai, *Pierre* 1705!

This species has the same vernacular name, *Cám lai*, Anam, as *D. bariensis* and *D. mammosa*. The differently shaped leaflets render it certain that this is not the flowering state of *D. mammosa*; it is not, however, so certain that we may not have in *D. dongnaiensis* the flowering state of *D. bariensis*, for the leaflets of the two are of somewhat similar shape; they are, however, so different in texture and venation that Mr. Pierre is probably right in treating these three forms, known to the people of Anam as *Cám lai*, as distinct species.

PLATE 81. Dalbergia dongnaiensis *Pierre*.—1, Flowering branch from Bienhoa, *n. s.*; 2, twig with full-grown leaf, from same locality, *n. s.*; 3, bud × 4; 4, pedicel with epicalycine bracteoles × 4; 5, calyx, laid open × 4; 6, standard × 4; 7, wings × 4; 8, keel-petals × 4; 9, stamens, usual condition × 4; 10, stamens, occasional arrangement × 4; 11, ovary × 4; 12, ovary, laid open × 4; 13, ovule × 8.

77. DALBERGIA DUPERREANA Pierre MSS. in Herb. Pierre.

A tree, 30—60 feet high; young branches blackish, glabrous. *Leaves* 6—10 in. long; leaflets 9—17, narrowly oblong, acute, base cuneate or rounded, medium-green above, paler beneath, firmly chartaceous, 2—2·25 in. long, ·65 in. wide; rachis 4—8 in. long and petiolules ·2 in. long, glabrous; stipules caducous. *Flowers* in terminal panicles 4 in. long, 3 in. wide, rachis and branches sparingly pubescent; bracts and bracteoles not seen; *calyx* narrowly campanulate, ·25 in. long, lower three teeth lanceolate the lowest the longest, upper two teeth ovate subconnate; *corolla* not seen; *stamens* 10, in two lateral bundles of 5 each; *ovary* not seen. *Pod* widely ovate-lanceolate, firmly coriaceous, glabrous, only faintly reticulated opposite the seeds, long-stipitate, rather abruptly narrowed to the acute apex and the cuneate base, neither umbonate nor suberously thickened, 5 in. long, 1·25 in. wide, 1-seeded; *seed* reniform, compressed, ·35 in. long, ·25 in. wide, ·07 in. thick; testa brown, shining.

INDO-CHINA: Cambodia; Samrong-tong, on Mt. Cherëer, *Pierre* 1039!

This species, though not completely represented, is quite clearly distinct from any hitherto described Asiatic *Dalbergia*. It is obviously another member of group *Canae*, which is so largely developed in Central and Eastern Indo-China; the present species, however, less resembles any of the other Cambodian members of the group than it does the two Burmese species *D. Kurzii* and *D. cana* itself. As regards foliage, *D. Duperreana* might almost be referred to *D. cana*, but the fruits are very different, being much larger and being, moreover, quite glabrous. The fruits are indeed much more like those of *D. Kurzii*, though they are not quite the same; the foliage is very different from that of *D. Kurzii*. No vernacular name is reported for this species.

PLATE 82. Dalbergia Duperreana *Pierre*.—1, Twig with leaves, from Samrongtong, Cambodia, *n. s.*; 2, part of a fruiting panicle, from same locality, *n. s.*; 3, pod, opened, showing seed *in situ*, *n. s.*; 4, seed, *n. s.*

78. DALBERGIA KURZII Prain Journ. As. Soc. Beng. lxvi. 2, 450 (1897); lxx. 2, 50 (1901).

D. purpurea Kurz Journ. As. Soc. Beng. xlv. 2, 279 (1875); For. Flor. Burm. i. 344 (1877), not of Wall.

A tree, 40—60 feet high; young branches glabrous. *Leaves* 8—18 in. long; leaflets 7—11, obovate-oblong or rarely oblong, base cuneate rarely slightly rounded, apex obtuse or rarely shortly acuminate, firmly chartaceous, glabrous above, sparingly puberulous when young, but soon glabrous beneath, 2—5 in. long, 1·25—2 in. wide; rachis 5—13 in. long, when young slightly puberulous; petiolules ·1 in. long, glabrescent; stipules small, obtuse or acute, deciduous. *Flowers* in lax corymbose axillary panicles 4—10 in. long, 3—6 in. wide, peduncles glabrous, branches and pedicels puberulous; bracteoles all lanceolate-acute, puberulous, the epicalycine pair half as long as calyx-tube; *calyx* campanulate, pale-purple, minutely puberulous; teeth triangular, the lowest longer than the rest, all acute, the two upper subconnate; *corolla* white or pale-rose, petals all rather long-clawed; standard orbicular, slightly emarginate; *stamens* 10, in two equal lateral sheaths and sometimes with one, sometimes with two lowest stamens free; filaments all free in their upper third, alternately shorter and longer; *ovary* stipitate, pubescent; *ovules* 1—3, often solitary. *Pod* indehiscent, flat, oblong-lanceolate, obtuse or acute, contracted rather abruptly to the stipe, firmly coriaceous, glabrous, indistinctly veined opposite the one or rarely two seeds, 4—6 in. long, 1—1·25 in. wide; *seed* shortly reniform, compressed, ·65 in. long, ·45 in. wide.

INDO-CHINA: Burma; Pegu and Prome, *M'Clelland*! *Brandis*! *Kurz*! *Forest Dept.*! Kalay Hills, *Prazer*! Ruby Mines Dist.; *Abdul Huq*! Shan Hills; *Alpin*!

A species known in Burma as *Thit-pot*, or *Thit-poh*, nearly related to *D. cana*, but readily distinguished by its leaves with fewer, much larger, and differently shaped leaflets and by its larger glabrous pods with larger seeds.

PLATE 83. Dalbergia Kurzii *Prain.*—1, Leaf from a Pegu specimen, *n. s.*; 2, flowering branch from a Pegu specimen, *n. s.*; 3, bud × 4; 4, calyx, laid open × 4; 5, standard × 4; 6, wings × 4; 7, keel-petals × 4; 8, stamens, usual arrangement × 4; 9, stamens, occasional arrangement × 4; 10, ovary × 4; 11, ovary laid open × 4; 12, ovule × 6; 13, fruiting twig, from a Pegu specimen, *n. s.*; 14, seed, *n. s.*

79. DALBERGIA CANA Grah. in Wall. Cat. 5859 (1832); Kurz Journ. As. Soc. Beng. xlii. 2, 70 (1873); Bak. in Hook. f. Flor. Brit. Ind. ii. 237 (1876); Kurz For. Flor. Burm. i. 344 (1877); Prain Journ. As. Soc. Beng. lxvi. 2, 450 (1897); lxx. 2, 50 (1901).

D. purpurea Wall. Cat. 5869 (1832); Benth. Journ. Linn. Soc. iv. Suppl. 46 in part (1860); Bak. in Hook. f. Flor. Brit. Ind. ii. 235 in part (1876).

A tree, 40—60 feet high; young branches at first puberulous, soon glabrescent. *Leaves* 10—24 in. long; leaflets 15—19, oblong to oblong-lanceolate, base cuneate, often slightly unequal, apex shortly and abruptly acuminate, firmly chartaceous, when young slightly pubescent on both surfaces, ultimately glabrous above and glabrous or sparingly puberulous beneath, 2—4·5 in. long, ·5—1 in. wide; rachis 6—20 in. long, glabrous; petiolules ·1 in. long, puberulous; stipules small, lanceolate, deciduous. *Flowers* in lax corymbose axillary panicles 3—3·5 in. long, 1·5—2 in. wide, the peduncles, branches and pedicels puberulous; bracteoles all lanceolate, acute, puberulous, the epicalycine pair half as long as calyx-tube; *calyx* campanulate, purple, faintly puberulous and soon glabrescent, teeth subequal triangular subacute, the two upper subconnate; *corolla* purple, petals all rather long-clawed; standard wide-oblong, slightly emarginate; *stamens* 10, in two equal lateral sheaths, filaments free in their upper third; ovary stipitate pubescent; *ovules* 1—3, often solitary. *Pod* indehiscent, flat, ligulate, obtuse, contracted rather abruptly to the stipe, firmly coriaceous, finely velvety throughout, indistinctly veined opposite the seeds, 3—4 in. long, ·5 in. wide; *seed* reniform, compressed, ·5 in. long, ·35 in. wide.

INDO-CHINA: Burma; Pegu, *Brandis*! *Kurz*! Tenasserim; Moulmein, *Wallich*! Tavoy, *Shaik Muqim*!

The Calcutta native collector gives the name of this as *Jaman-paté* at Tavoy.

PLATE 84. Dalbergia cana *Grah.*—1, Flowering specimen from Pegu, *n. s.*; 2, bud × 4; 3, pedicel and epicalycine bracteoles × 4; 4, calyx, laid open × 4; 5, standard × 4; 6, wings × 4; 7, keel-petals × 4; 8, stamens × 4; 9, ovary × 4; 10, ovary laid open × 4; 11, ovule × 10; 12, fruiting specimen from Pegu, *n. s.*; 13, pod, open and showing seed *in situ*, *n. s.*; 14, seed, *n. s.*

¶ 22. **Volubilis.** *Pod oblong, thin, samaroid; style rather short, cylindric; leaflets obtuse; a climber.*

A very distinct species which, owing to its style, it is impossible to associate with any of the other groups of *Dalbergaria*. Its general facies and its bracts show that it has considerable affinity with the *Stipulaceae*.

80. Dalbergia volubilis Roxb. Corom. Pl. ii. 48, t. 191 (1798); Hort. Beng. 53 (1814); DC. Prodr. ii. 417 (1825); Spreng. Syst. iii. 193 (1826); Roxb. Flor. Ind. iii. 231 (1832); Wall. Cat. 5874 (1832); W. & A. Prodr. i. 265 (1834); Grah. Cat. Bomb. 55 (1839); Benth. Journ. Linn. Soc. iv. Suppl. 46 (1860); Dalz. & Gibs. Bomb. Flor. 78 (1861); Brandis For. Flor. 152 (1874); Bak. in Hook. f. Flor. Brit. Ind. ii. 235 (1876); Kurz For. Flor. Burm. i. 346 (1877); Talb. Bomb. List 75 (1894); Woodr. Journ. Nat. Hist. Soc. Bomb. xi. 426 (1897); Prain Journ. As. Soc. Beng. lxvi. 2, 114 (1897); lxx. 2, 54 (1901); Cooke Flor. Pres. Bomb. i. 400 (1902); Prain Bengal Plants i. 410 (1903).

D. confertiflora Benth. Journ. Linn. Soc. iv. Suppl. 41 partly—Oudh and Concan plants (1860); Bak. in Hook. f. Flor. Brit. Ind. ii. 233 partly (1876); Talb. Bomb. List 75 (1894), not of Benth. in Pl. Jungh.

D. purpurea Benth. Journ. Linn. Soc. iv. Suppl. 46 partly (1860); Bak. in Hook. f. Flor. Brit. Ind. ii. 235 partly (1876), not of Wall.

D. stipulacea Gamble Darjeel. List 29 partly (1896), not of Roxb.

A large woody climber, 40—60 feet long, sometimes when deprived of foreign support a straggling bush, with twining glabrescent branches here and there thickened and twisted into spiral hooks; branchlets puberulous, sub-bifarious. *Leaves* 4—5 in. long; leaflets 11—13, obovate or ovate-oblong, when young often abruptly shortly acuminate, when full-grown obtuse or slightly retuse and faintly mucronulate, dark-green above, paler beneath, glabrous on both surfaces, ·75—1 in. long, ·5—·75 in. wide; rachis 3—4 in. long and petiolules ·15 in. long, glabrous; stipules rather large, ovate-lanceolate, wide-based, very caducous. *Flowers* in copious terminal panicles extending sometimes into the axils of the uppermost leaves, 8—12 in. long, 5—6 in. wide, with glabrous peduncles and numerous horizontal or decurved puberulous branches 1—3 in. long, the corymbs congested; bracts small, ovate, subpersistent, bracteoles at bases of pedicels lanceolate, persistent, epicalycine bracteoles ovate, persistent; *calyx* campanulate, densely puberulous, teeth lanceolate, the lowest longest, except the two upper obtuse subconnate; *corolla* pale-blue, petals all rather long-clawed, standard broadly orbicular, emarginate, reflexed at junction of blade and claw; *stamens* 10, usually in two lateral bundles of 5 each, occasionally the lower fissure incomplete, filaments free in their upper fourth; *ovary* pubescent, stipitate; style slender, short, stigma minute; *ovules* 1—2. *Pod* indehiscent, distinctly stipitate, linear-oblong, obtuse, rounded or slightly cuneate at base, distinctly reticulated throughout, especially opposite the 1 rarely 2 seeds, glabrous, 2—3 in. long, ·75—·85 in. wide; *seed* reniform, compressed, ·3 in. long, ·2 in. wide.

India: Malabaria; Travancore, *Lawson*! Malabar, *Stocks*! S. Kanara, *Metz*! N. Kanara, *Talbot*! Concan, *Stocks*! Coromandelia; Bolimpati, *Wight*! Kurnool, *Gamble*! Circars, *Roxburgh*! Ganjam, *Gamble*! Orissa, *Lace*! Chota Nagpur, *Anderson*! *Campbell*! *Wood*! *Gamble*! *Clarke*! *T. Thomson*! Behar; *Kurz*! *Ball*! *Campbell*! Central India; Sagor, *Jerdon*! Central Provinces, *Duthie*! Himalaya: Submontane forests; Kamaon Bhabar, *Strachey & Winterbottom*! Oudh, *Wallich*! *Duthie*! Gorakhpur, *Duthie*! Sikkim Terai, *Anderson*! *Gamble*! *Clarke*! Duars, *Gamble*! Indo-China: Assam; Goalpara, *Clarke*! Garo Hills, *Watt*! Chittagong; Thanacheri, *Hooker & Thomson*! *Gamble*! Demagri, *Lister*! Kodala, *Badalkhan*! Burma; Kachin Hills, *Shaik Muqim*! Chin Hills, *Prazer*! *Abdul Huq*! Bhamo, *J. Anderson*! Shway Yoe, *J. Anderson*! Pegu, *Brandis*! *Kurz*! Shan Hills, *Collett*!

Prazer! *Abdul Huq*! *Abdul Khalil*! Tenasserim; Moulmein, *Wallich*! *Cleghorn*! Endine Ghor, *Gallatly*! Mergui, *Helfer*! Andamans; S. Andaman, *Man*! *Heinig*!

PLATE 85. Dalbergia volubilis *Roxb.*—1, Flowering branch from Travancore, leaves young, *n. s.*; 2, leaf from Chota Nagpur, full grown, *n. s.*; 3, bud × 4; 4, pedicel with basal and epicalycine bracteoles × 4; 5, calyx, laid open × 4; 6, standard × 4; 7, wings × 4; 8, keel-petals × 4; 9, stamens, usual arrangement × 4; 10, stamens, occasional arrangement × 4; 11, ovary × 4; 12, ovary, laid open × 4; 13, ovule × 8; 14, twig in fruit from Tenasserim, *n. s.*; 15, pod opened, showing seed *in situ*, *n. s.*; 16, seed, *n. s.*

¶ 23. **Stipulaceae.** *Pod samaroid, but more or less thickened opposite the seeds; style subulate; leaflets obtuse; climbers or casually erect shrubs; bracts large, obtuse.*

A group composed of two very closely allied species which have, by Bentham and by Baker, in the absence of fruits, been considered forms of one. An examination of the figures will, however, show the impossibility of this reduction. The group is, in some respects, nearly allied to *D. volubilis*, but is nevertheless very distinct; its nearest ally is apparently *D. Godefroyi*, an Indo-Chinese species which, on account of its pod, it is necessary to refer to the *Reniformes*.

81. DALBERGIA FERRUGINEA Roxb. Hort. Beng. 98 (1814); Flor. Ind. iii. 228 (1832); Benth. Pl. Jungh. i. 256 (1851); Miq. Flor. Ind. Bat. i. 1, 133 (1855); Prain Journ. As. Soc. Beng. lxx. 2, 55 (1901); Volkens in Engl. Bot. Jahrb. xxxi. 464 (1901).

D. elliptica Span. Comp. Bot. Mag. i. 346 (1835); Linnaea xv. 197 (1841).

D. lanceolata Zipp. ex Span. Linnaea xv. 197 (1841).

D. lanceolaria Span. Linnaea xv. 197 (1841), not of Linn. f.

D. luzonensis Vog. Nov. Act. Nat. Cur. xix. Suppl. i. 133 (1843); Benth. Journ. Linn. Soc. iv. Suppl. 48 (1860).

D. limonensis Benth. Pl. Jungh. i. 256 (1851).

D. penduliflora Blume ex Miq. Flor. Ind. Bat. i. 1, 133 (1855).

D. stipulacea Benth. Journ. Linn. Soc. iv. Suppl. 48 partly (1860); Bak. in Hook. f. Flor. Brit. Ind. ii. 237 partly (1876); Nav. & Fernand. Vill. Nov. App. Flor. Philip. 67 (1880); Vidal Plant. Vasc. Filip. iii. (1886); Warb. in Engl. Bot. Jahrb. xiii. 329 (1891), not of Roxb.

D. Zollingeriana Koord. Meded. 's lands Plantent. xix. 431 (1898), not of Miq.

Endespermum penduliflorum Zipp. ex Miq. Flor. Ind. Bat. i. 1, 133 (1855).

A straggling shrub or a climber, branchlets rusty-pubescent, sub-bifarious, recurved, pendulous. *Leaves* 4—8 in. long; leaflets usually 15—21, rarely as many as 25 on young shoots, very rarely 13, ovate-oblong, obtuse or emarginate, base rounded and slightly unequal, ·75—1·25 in. long, ·45—·75 in. wide, firmly papery, sparsely adpressed-strigose on both surfaces, pubescence sometimes persistent, leaflets sometimes at length quite glabrous, rachis 3—6·5 in. long, persistently puberulous as are the very short petiolules; stipules wide-obovate, obtuse, membranous, pubescent, very caducous. *Flowers* in small axillary panicles or in large terminal pseudo-panicles extending or not into the axils of the upper leaves, the end of the flowering branch becoming leafy, occasionally the leafy terminal portion abortive or obsolete, 8—12 in. long, 4–6 in. wide, peduncles, branches and pedicels pubescent; main-bracts stipular, secondary similar but solitary, basal bracteoles cuneate or ovate-lanceolate, epicalycine ovate, all pubescent;

calyx campanulate, lowest tooth lanceolate longer than tube, lateral acute, upper pair rounded subconnate; *corolla* white, petals all distinctly clawed, standard orbicular, emarginate, often slightly cordate at base; *stamens* 10, in 2 lateral bundles of 5 each, filaments free in their upper third, alternately shorter and longer; *ovary* densely pubescent, distinctly stipitate; style slender, stigma minute; *ovules* 3—4. *Pod* indehiscent, glabrous except the stipe, with a thin but firm coriaceous margin, swollen but not corky, and reticulated opposite the seeds, narrowed abruptly below to a narrow flattened stipe, rounded at the apex with a slight apiculus, usually 1-seeded, but often 2- and sometimes 3-seeded and with a tendency to break off between the seeds, 1·25 in. long when 1-seeded, 2—2·5 in. long when 2—3-seeded, ·75 in. wide; *seed* orbicular-reniform, ·35 in. long, ·3 in. wide.

PHILIPPINES: Luzon; Manila, *Meyen*! *Vidal*! Panay, *Vidal*! Novaliches, *Loher*! Montalban, *Loher*! Samar; *F. Jagor*! *Vidal*! EASTERN MALAYA: Borneo; Bangi Island at Pankalan, *Fraser*! Celebes; Minahassa, *Koorders*! Moluccas; Tidore, *C. Smith*! *Teysmann*! Buru, *Buitenzorg Collectors*! Ceram, *Teysmann*! *Foerster*! Ceram Laut, *Warburg*! Timor, *Spanoghe*. PAPUASIA: New Guinea; Sigar, *Warburg*! Andai, *Beccari*! MICRONESIA: Carolines, *Voelkens*.

Koorders gives the name of this in Celebes as *Amoet-wosi*; Vidal gives it as *Balibagan* in Panay. The writer has seen two original specimens of this species, named by Roxburgh himself.

PLATE 86. Dalbergia ferruginea *Roxb.*—1, Specimen from Ceram, in flower, *n. s.*; 2, bud × 4; 3, pedicel with bracteoles × 4; 4, calyx × 4; 5, standard × 4; 6, wings × 4; 7, keel-petals × 4; 8, stamens × 4; 9, ovary × 4; 10, ovary, laid open × 4; 11, ovule × 10; 12, specimen in fruit, from Tidore, *n. s.*; 13, 1-seeded pod, laid open to show seed *in situ*, *n. s.*; 14, seed, *n. s.*

82. DALBERGIA STIPULACEA Roxb. Hort. Beng. 53 (1814); Flor. Ind. iii. 233 (1832); Wight Ic. t. 453 (1840); Voigt Hort. Suburb. Calcutt. 241 (1845); Benth. Pl. Jungh i. 256 (1851); Miq. Flor. Ind. Bat. i. 1, 133 (1855); Benth. Journ. Linn. Soc. iv. Suppl. 47 (1860); Bak. in Hook f. Flor. Brit. Ind. iv. 237 in part (1876); Kurz. For. Flor. Burm. i. 346 (1877); Gamble Darjeel. List 29 in part (1896); Prain Journ. As. Soc. Beng. lxvi. 2, 451 (1897); lxx. 2, 55 (1901); Bengal Plants i. 410 (1903).
D. tingens Ham. in Wall. Cat. 5860 (1832).
D. cassioides Wall. Cat. 5863 (1832).
D. livida Grah. in Wall. Cat. 5866 (1832).
D. cassinoides Miq. Flor. Ind. Bat. i. 1, 133 (1855).

A small straggling tree with spreading branches, or a climber; young branches sub-bifarious, glabrous or puberulous; bark brownish, fibrous. *Leaves* 6—8 in. long; leaflets 17—21, oblong to obovate-oblong, at first acute, ultimately obtuse or retuse at apex, cuneate or rounded at base, 1·25 in. long, ·5 in. wide, on young shoots sometimes as much as 2·25 in. long and ·85 in. wide, thinly papery, glabrous above dark-green, beneath sub-glaucescent and minutely adpressed-pubescent; rachis 5—6·5 in. long, puberulous as are the petiolules ·15 in. long; stipules membranous, ovate-lanceolate, obtuse, caducous. *Flowers* in pseudo-terminal panicles rising among a cluster of scaly more or less deciduous bracts and ending in a new leafy branch; peduncles pubescent, beset with many scattered empty ovate membranous bracts, branches similar, bracteoles like bracts but smaller, epicalycine pair enclosing two-thirds of calyx-tube; *calyx* campanulate, puberulous, teeth ovate, obtuse or subacute, shorter than tube except lowest lanceolate as long as tube; *corolla* pale-blue, petals all distinctly clawed, standard broad, orbicular, very slightly emarginate; *stamens* 10, in two lateral bundles of 5 each, filaments free in their upper fourth; *ovary* with long, pubescent stipe, elsewhere quite glabrous; style long slender, stigma minute; *ovule* solitary, very rarely ovules 2. *Pod* indehiscent, broad-ligulate to ovate-obtuse, base rounded above the distinct stipe, quite glabrous, firmly coriaceous, not veined except sometimes opposite the seed where the mesocarp is much suberously thickened, almost always 1-seeded, very rarely 2-seeded, 3·5—4·5 in. long, ·85—1·25 in. wide; *seed* reniform, ·6 in. long, ·35 in. wide.

HIMALAYA: Sikkim; Lower Hills and Terai, *Hooker*! *Anderson*! *Kurz*! *King*! *Clarke*! *Gamble*! *Prain*! Bootan; Lower Hills and Duars, *Gamble*! *Lister*! *Haines*! INDO-CHINA: Assam; Brahmaputra valley, *Hamilton*! *Jenkins*! *Simons*! *Clarke*! *Mann*! *Fisher*! *Peal*! Garo Hills, *Clarke*! Khasia Hills, *Hooker & Thomson*! *Clarke*! Manipur, *Watt*! Naga Hills, *Watt*! *Prazer*! *Abdul Huq*! Silhet, *de Silva*! *Clarke*! Chittagong; Kodala, *Badal Khan*! Burma; Kachin Hills, *Shaik Muqim*! Hukung, *Griffith*! Chin Hills, *Prazer*! Kalay Hills, *Prazer*! Shan Hills, *Abdul Khalil*! Pegu, *McClelland*! *Kurz*! *Brandis*! Tenasserim; Amherst, *Wallich*! Tavoy, *Gomez*! *Shaik Muqim*! Moulmein, *Wallich*! *Brandis*! *Cleghorn*! *Falconer*! Mergui, *Helfer*! Younzaleen, *Gallatly*! Cochin-China; Bienhoa, at Phoque, *Pierre*! CHINA: Yunnan, Szemao Mts., *Henry* 13429!

PLATE 87. Dalbergia stipulacea *Roxb.*—1, Branch in flower, from Sikkim, *n. s.*; 2, bud × 4; 3, pedicel with epicalycine bracteoles × 4; 4, calyx, laid open × 4; 5, standard × 4; 6, wings × 4; 7, keel-petals × 4; 8, ovary × 4; 9, ovary, laid open × 4; 10, twig, with fruit, from Garo Hills, *n. s.*; 11, pod from a Chittagong specimen, *n. s.*; 12, the same looked at from one edge, *n. s.*; 13, pod from another Chittagong specimen, collected in same locality as 11, *n. s.*; 14, seed, *n. s.*

¶ 24. **Reniformes**. *Pod falcate-subreniform, thickened throughout; style subulate; erect or climbing.*

A group that, it is to be feared, is only subnatural; *D. Godefroyi* departs widely in appearance from the remaining species and but for its thickened pods might have been more naturally placed in the *Stipulaceae*, which group it connects with this one. The others appear, however, to form a fairly natural group of allies.

83. DALBERGIA GODEFROYI Prain Journ. As. Soc. Beng. lxx. 2, 63 (1901).

A woody climber; branchlets sub-bifarious, recurved, puberulous. *Leaves* 3—3·5 in. long; leaflets 6—9, wide-ovate, firmly papery, finely puberulous on both surfaces, base rounded slightly unequal, apex obtuse or slightly emarginate, ·6—1·25 in. long, ·4—·7 in. wide; rachis 2—2·5 in. long and distinct petiolules puberulous; stipules not seen. *Flowers* in axillary subsimple racemes forming terminal leafy panicles; peduncle and branches puberulous; *calyx* campanulate, in fruit glabrescent or puberulous, teeth subequal obtuse shorter than the tube except the lowest lanceolate as long as tube; *petals* not seen; *stamens* in two lateral bundles, anthers not seen. *Pod* indehiscent, obliquely subreniform, thinly woody, finely closely velvety externally, not greatly margined around and not veined externally opposite the seed, narrowed below abruptly to a narrow flattened stipe, rounded at the apex with a slight apiculus, 1-seeded or rarely 2 seeded, with a tendency to break off between the seeds, the stipe also sometimes with an abortive seed in its upper part, 1·25 in. long, ·5 in. wide; *seed* orbicular, reniform; ·4 in. long, ·35 in. wide.

INDO-CHINA: Siam; borders of the Great Lake, *Godefroy-Leboeuf*!

The absence of flowers renders the position of this species somewhat doubtful. When first studied by him, the writer from the great general similarity of the fruit was inclined to place it in *Triptolemea*, next *D. parviflora*. The much larger calyx, however, which is hardly distinguishable from that of *D. ferruginea*, and the fact (though this last is not so valuable a character) that its stamens are isodiadelphous, coupled with its general similarity leads him now to think that the species is more satisfactorily placed in *Dalbergaria*. In any case its velvety pods indicate that it is abundantly distinct from either of the species mentioned.

PLATE 88. Dalbergia Godefroyi *Prain.*—1, Fruiting branch, from Siam, *n. s.*; 2, calyx × 4; 3, pod, laid open, showing seed *in situ*, *n. s.*; 4, seed, *n. s.*

The pod at *a* ⟶ has obviously been *at least* 2-seeded, the ultimate joint having snapped off, as happens sometimes in *D. ferruginea* and still more often in *D. parviflora*.

84. DALBERGIA FALCATA Prain Journ. As. Soc. Beng. lxx. 2, 65 (1901).

A climbing shrub; young branches angular, rusty-puberulous, their bases beset with ovate-acute subcoriaceous scaly bracts. *Leaves* 5—7 in. long; leaflets 5—9, the lateral sometimes subopposite, dark-green above, paler beneath, glabrous above, beneath finely adpressed-pubescent, ovate, shortly abruptly acuminate, the terminal rather the largest, 1·5—3 in. long, ·75—1·25 in. wide; rachis 4—5 in. long, and petiolules ·2 in. long, glabrous; stipules lanceolate, pubescent externally, deciduous. *Flowers* in axillary panicles, 2—3 in. long; peduncles, branches and pedicels rusty-puberulous; bracts deciduous; *calyx* campanulate, upper teeth obtuse subconnate, the others lanceolate the lowest the longest, rusty-puberulous externally; *corolla* not seen; *stamens* 10, in two lateral bundles of 5 each or in one sheath split along upper side; *ovary* stipitate, rusty-pubescent. *Pod* indehiscent, firm, falcate, finely puberulous but at length glabrescent, with a thin suberous mesocarp, 1-seeded or sometimes 2-seeded, 1·5—2·25 in. long, ·6 in. wide, ·25 in. thick, dark-brown externally with narrow grey lines along ventral suture; *seed* narrow-reniform, compressed, ·75 in. long, ·35 in. wide.

MALAYA: Borneo; Bintulu, *Beccari*! Sarawak, *Beccari*!

PLATE 89. Dalbergia falcata *Prain.*—1, Fruiting branch from Bintulu, Borneo, *n. s.*; 2, calyx, laid open × 4; 3, pod, laid open, showing seed *in situ*, *n. s.*; 4, seed, *n. s.*; 5, v. s. of seed, *n. s.*

85. DALBERGIA KUNSTLERI Prain Journ. As. Soc. Beng. lxvi. 2, 121, 453 (1897); lxx. 2, 65 (1901).

An extensive climber, 40—150 feet long, with stem 3—6 inches thick; young branches pubescent, beset at point of origin with scaly bracts. *Leaves* 10—12 in. long;

leaflets 7—9, the lateral subopposite, when mature dark-green glabrous above, sparsely pubescent beneath, when young densely tawny-pubescent on both sides, rigidly coriaceous, elliptic-acuminate, base rounded, 4—6 in. long, 2 in. wide; rachis 8 in. long, and petiolules ·3 in. long, at first densely pubescent at length glabrescent. *Flowers* in axillary panicles 4—6 in. long, 3—4 in. wide; peduncles, branches and pedicels densely rusty-puberulous; bracts ovate-lanceolate or lanceolate, pubescent, deciduous; *calyx* campanulate, teeth ovate-lanceolate, obtuse except the lanceolate lowest; *corolla* dark-blue, petals all long-clawed, standard orbicular, emarginate; *stamens* 10, usually in one sheath slit along upper side, only occasionally in two lateral bundles of 5 each, the lower side also being slit; *ovary* long-stipitate, pubescent especially on the stipe; style long slender, stigma small capitate; *ovules* 2—4. *Pod* indehiscent, finely persistently pubescent, not mamillate, mesocarp thick, corky, endocarp firm, usually 1-seeded sometimes 2-seeded, rigid, falcate or subfalcate, 1·5—2·5 in. long, ·9 in. wide, ·4 in. thick, with grey lines alongside the sutures when ripe, *seed* reniform, compressed, ·7 in. long, ·4 in. wide.

MALAYA: Perak; Goping, *Kunstler*! Kinta, *Kunstler*!

PLATE 90. Dalbergia Kunstleri *Prain.* 1, Flowering twig, from Kinta river, Perak, *n. s.*; 2, bud × 4; 3, pedicel with bracteoles × 4; 4, calyx, laid open × 4; 5, standard × 4; 6, wings × 4; 7, keel-petals × 4; 8, stamens, usual arrangement × 4; 9, stamens, occasional arrangement × 4; 10, fruiting branch from Goping, Perak, *n. s.*; 11, pod opened, showing seed *in situ*, *n. s.*; 12, cross section of pod, showing thickened mesocarp, *n. s.*; 13, seed, *n. s.*

86. DALBERGIA RENIFORMIS Roxb. Hort. Beng. 53 (1814); Flor. Ind. iii. 226 (1832); Wight Ic. t. 261 (1840); Bak. in Hook. f. Flor. Brit. Ind. ii. 238 (1876); Prain Journ. As. Soc. Beng. lxx. 2, 64.

D. stipulata Wall. Cat. 5868 partly (1832).

D. flexuosa Grah. in Wall. Cat. 5875 (1832); Benth. Pl. Jungh. i. 256 (1851); Journ. Linn. Soc. iv. Suppl. 48 (1860).

Drepanocarpus reniformis Kurz For. Flor. Burm. iv. 336 (1877).

A spreading bushy tree, 30—40 feet high; young branches rusty- or tawny-pubescent but soon glabrescent, with rusty-pubescent scaly bract at their bases. *Leaves* 7—12 in. long; leaflets 7—11, ovate or ovate-oblong, apex abruptly obtusely or retusely acuminate, base cuneate or rounded, when young very sparingly and fugaciously pilose, when mature quite glabrous, often subopposite, firmly chartaceous, 2—4 in. long, 1—2 in. wide; rachis 5—8 in. long, at first puberulous soon glabrous, petiolules ·25 in. long, persistently puberulous or pubescent; stipules ovate-lanceolate, rusty-pubescent, deciduous. *Flowers* in lateral panicles, 4 in. long, 2 in. wide, on the young branches; peduncles, branches and pedicels pubescent; bracteoles ovate, deciduous; *calyx* campanulate, rusty-pubescent, teeth ovate-obtuse except the rather longer acute lowest; *corolla* white, petals all long-clawed, standard orbicular, emarginate; *stamens* 10, in two lateral bundles of 5 each; *ovary* pubescent especially on the rather long stipe; style long slender, stigma small capitate; *ovules* 2—3. *Pod* indehiscent, when young rather closely pubescent but soon glabrescent, when mature uniformly lenticular-mamillate, often rather irregular, mesocarp thick corky, endocarp firm, usually 1-seeded, sometimes 2-seeded, rigid, falcate or subfalcate, 1·25—2 in. long, ·75 in. wide, ·4 in. thick; *seed* reniform, ·5 in. long, ·3 in. wide.

INDO-CHINA: Assam; Silhet, *Smith*! *de Silva*! *Clarke*! Cachar, *Prazer*! Burma; Pegu, *Kurz*! *Brandis*! Kareni, *Kurz*! Tenasserim; Martaban, *Kurz*! *Falconer*! *Cleghorn*! *Beddome*! Chuku Plains, *Gallatly*!

PLATE 91. Dalbergia reniformis *Roxb.*—1, Flowering branch from Silhet, *n. s.*; 2, bud × 4; 3, pedicel with bracteoles × 4; 4, calyx, laid open × 4; 5, standard × 4; 6, wings × 4; 7, keel-petals × 4; 8, stamens × 4; 9, ovary × 4; 10, ovary, laid open × 4; 11, ovule × 12; 12, twig with unripe fruit, from the Karen Hills, *n. s.*; 13, ripe fruits from Cachar, *n. s.*; 14, pod, laid open, showing seed *in situ*, *n. s.*; 15, cross-section of pod, showing thickened mesocarp, *n. s.*; 16, seed, *n. s.*

DOUBTFUL AND EXCLUDED SPECIES.

DOUBTFUL SPECIES.

Dalbergia aestivalis Pierre MSS.

Only a leaf-specimen of this proposed species has been available for study. It is certainly quite different from any of the other *Dalbergias* in Herb. Pierre, but it cannot as matters stand be distinguished from *D. Oliveri* Gamble and is almost certainly identical with Gamble's tree. The difficulty does not lie so much in any doubt on this point as in the possible identity of *D. aestivalis* with *D. laccifera* Laness. The note on the ticket reads:—"*Dalbergia aestivalis* Pierre. Crescit in vicinibus Song-lu in prov. Bienhoa. Arb. 20—30-metr. Moi. *Chlieu lai Bon dam* (*doûme*). Ann. *Cay cam lai*."

Dalbergia entadioides Pierre MSS.

This is known only in leaf and flower: it cannot be separated from *D. foliacea* Wall. by its flowers; the leaflets, however, though of exactly the same shape, are glabrous beneath. If when fruits are reported this is found to deserve specific rank, Pierre's name must be taken up for the species.

Dalbergia laccifera Laness. Pl. Util. Col. Franç, 289 (1886).

"(En Kmer. *Dom-chloeu-snuol.*) Arbre de 20 à 25 mètres sur 40 à 60 centimetres de diamètre. Bois gris brun, excellent pour le placage. Il sert à élever le *Coccus lacca* et les Cambodgiens prétendent qu'un arbre donne de 10 à 20 kilogrammes de laque par année." This note by Lanessan is an indifferent substitute for the description that is expected with a proposed new species. The name is not used by M. Pierre in his Herbarium; none of Pierre's specimens are noted as taken from a tree on which *Coccus lacca* is raised; we are therefore left with no guide except the vernacular name. "Snuol" does not assist greatly, since it is noted by Pierre as being applied both to *D. paniculata* and to *D. Hemsleyi*; the first species may be excluded since its timber is not suitable for veneering. We are therefore left to decide whether we have here to deal with *D. Hemsleyi*, or with *D. aestivalis*, to which latter the two names "dom" and "chlceu" are known from Pierre's notes to be applied, and are apparently restricted. The likelihood is therefore clearly greater that *D. laccifera* and *D. aestivalis* are the same tree; if this be so, then *D. Oliveri* and *D. laccifera* are almost certainly identical. The matter must be left to botanists in French Indo-China to settle; the important point is that, if the two be really the same, the name *D. laccifera* must replace the name *D. Oliveri*.

Dalbergia lanceolaria? Llanos Mem. Acad. Cienc. Madr. (1858), not of Linn. f.

This is said to have the "pod linear, silky," which effectively disposes of the identification proposed by Llanos. The ovary of *D. Minahassae*, a species allied to *D. lanceolaria* that does occur in the Philippines, is densely silky and it is possible that its pods, which are not yet reported, may also be silky. But this suggested identification is only tentative; besides it must not be forgotten that Lamarck disarranged the original *D. lanceolaria* by referring to that species *Derris* (*Brachypterum*) *scandens*. If Llanos relied on Lamarck's citations when he identified his Philippine plant, he may very well be referring to a species of *Derris*.

Dalbergia pinnata (*Derris pinnata* Lour. Flor. Cochin-Chin. 432).

Usually referred to *D. tamarindifolia.* There are, however (*vide ante* p. 49), certain features in Loureiro's description that are antagonistic to this identification and the species, which is obviously a *Dalbergia*, is more likely to be *D. Millettii* than to be *D. tamarindifolia.* The point can only be settled in the field by the botanists of Cochin-China and for the moment it is more advisable to treat this as a species of doubtful identity.

Dalbergia purpurea? Laness. Pl. Util. Col. Franç. 289 (1886), not of Wall.

To this species Lanessan gives no clue, the only certainty is that it is not Wallich's tree of the name; it would hardly matter if it were, since Wallich's name is a mere synonym. The probability is that this is one or other of group of four known as *Cám lai* in Kmer. It has been tentatively suggested that it is the same as *D. dongnaiensis,* which is the only one of the four where the flowers are known, and which happens to have them blue.

Dalbergia saigonensis Pierre MSS.

Referred in this paper (*vide ante* p. 89), as a variety, to *D. paniculata.* This tree may, however, when flowers are reported, prove to deserve the specific rank claimed for by M. Pierre, in which case Pierre's name will stand.

Dalbergia volubilis Llanos Mem. Acad. Cienc. Madr. (1858), not of Roxburgh.

All that Llanos says of this is:—"pod linear, subincurved," which is enough to prove that his plant is not Roxburgh's. The identification he suggests presupposes a climbing habit, and the only climbing *Dalbergia* in the Philippines of which it could possibly be said that the pods are "linear" is *D. polyphylla:* this identification (*vide ante,* p. 71) is, however, purely tentative and conjectural.

EXCLUDED SPECIES.

Dalbergia acuminata *Hassk.*	=	Derris uliginosa.
alata *Roxb.*	=	thyrsiflora.
angustifolia *Hassk.*	=	Millettia sericea.
arborea *Willd., not of Heyne*	=	Pongamia glabra.
argentea *Zoll.*	=	Derris thyrsiflora.
Crowey *Roxb.*	=	robusta.
Delavayi *Franch.*	=	Cladrastis Delavayi.
Diphaca *Pers.*	=	Ormocarpum sennoides.
glaucescens *Zipp., not of Benth.*	=	Derris elliptica.
heterophylla *Willd., not of Poir.*	=	uliginosa.
japonica *G. Don.*	=	Quid ? (see note below).
Krowee *Roxb.*	=	Derris robusta.
lanceolaria *Dennst., not of Linn. f.*	=	scandens.
lanceolaria var. β *Lamk*	=	scandens.
lanceolaria *Moon, not of Linn. f.*	=	Pericopsis Mooniana.
marginata *Roxb.*	=	Derris marginata.
Momsita *Ham.*	=	robusta.
Mooniana *Thw.*	=	Pericopsis Mooniana.
ougeinensis *Roxb.*	=	Ougeinia dalbergioides.
pubinervis *Span.*	=	Derris pubinervis.
pulchra *Voigt*	=	Millettia pulchra.
purpurea *Reinw., not of Wall.*	=	Derris elliptica.
radicans *Zipp.*	=	uliginosa.
repens *Span.*	=	uliginosa.
robusta *Miq.*	=	scandens.
robusta *Roxb.*	=	robusta.
rostrata *Hassk., not of Grah.*	=	malaccensis.
scandens *Roxb.*	=	scandens.
sericea *Spreng., not of G. Don*	=	Millettia sericea.
tephrosioides *W. & A.*	=	pulchra.
timorensis *DC.*	=	Derris scandens.
venusta *Zipp.*	=	scandens.

The only species of the list of which the identity is not clear is *Dalbergia japonica* G. Don. No *Dalbergia* reaches Japan; besides *D. japonica* has opposite leaflets. No *Derris* reaches Japan, nor does any *Millettia*. *Wistaria japonica* being a climber and having leaflets green beneath, with flowers that are not secund, should therefore also be excluded. *Sophora japonica* agrees with Don's description in being erect, in having secund flowers and leaves with opposite leaflets glaucous beneath; one is, however, unwilling to think that, with staminal features so divergent, G. Don had placed this species in *Dalbergia*. Perhaps some Japanese botanist will solve the problem.

INDEX.

B. S. Press—4639J—277—10-2-1904—W. M. D'C.

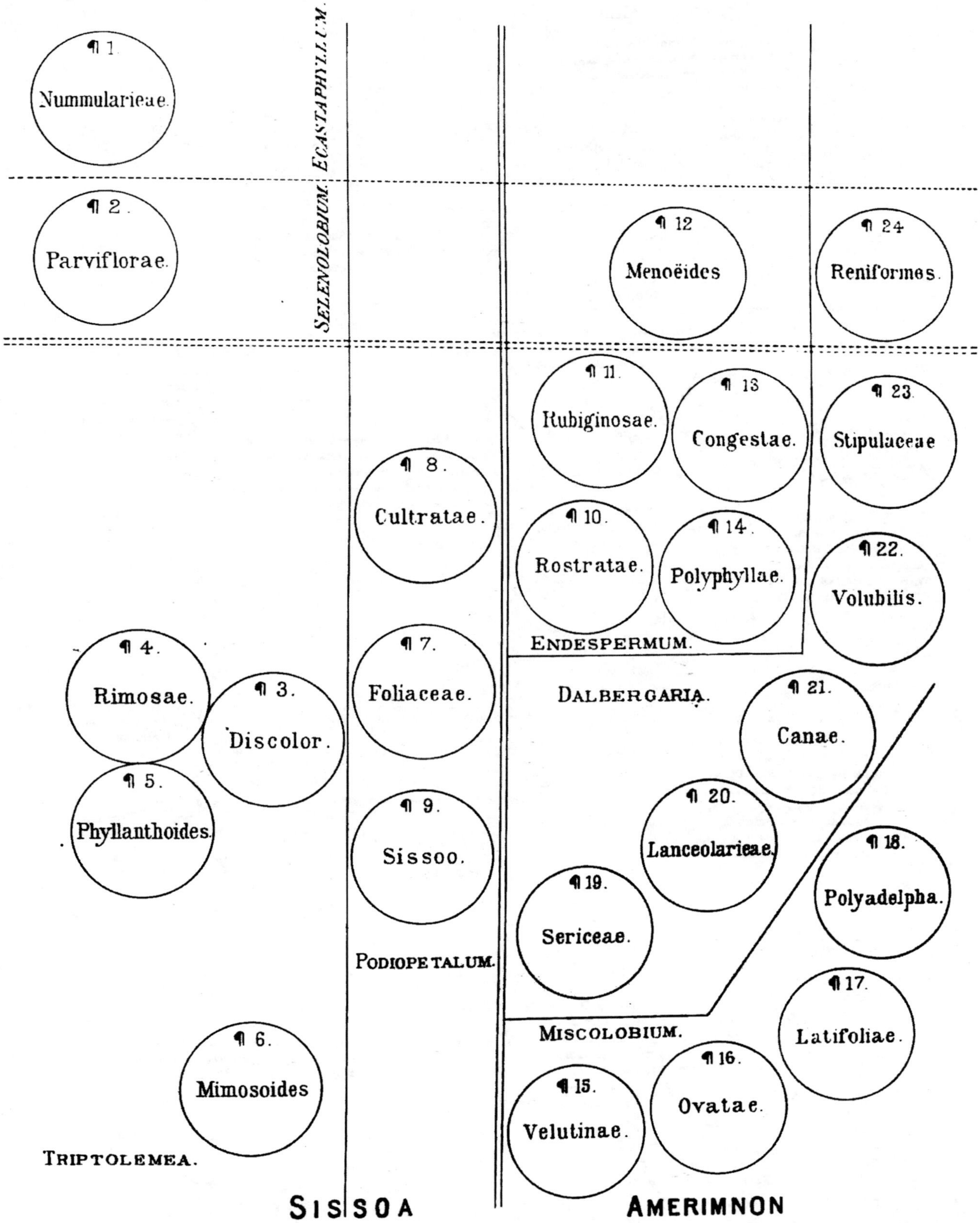

Lith by Chitra Silpi Co.

DISPOSITION OF ASIATIC GROUPS OF SPECIES OF DALBERGIA

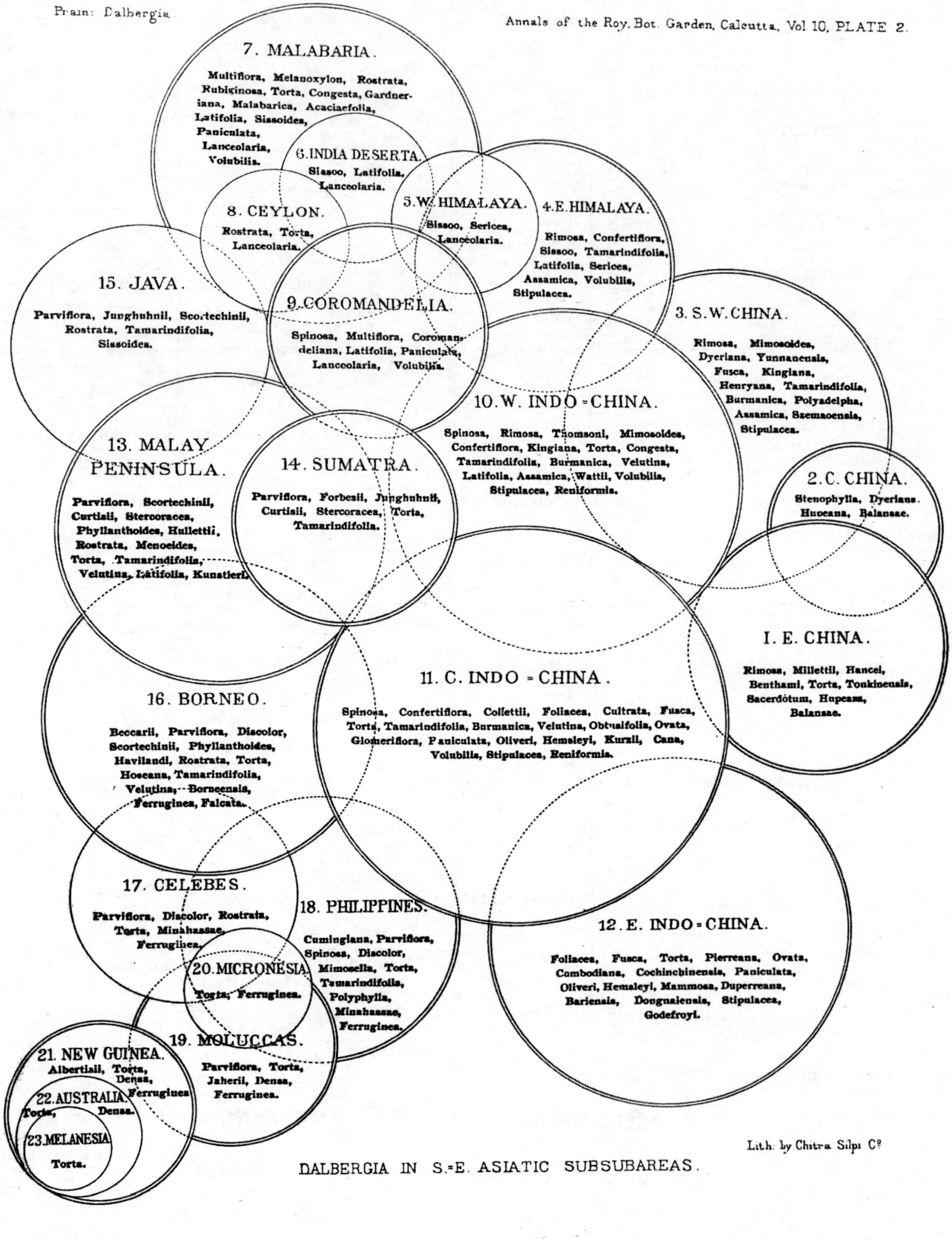

Lith. by Chitra Silpi C°

DALBERGIA IN S.-E. ASIATIC SUBSUBAREAS.

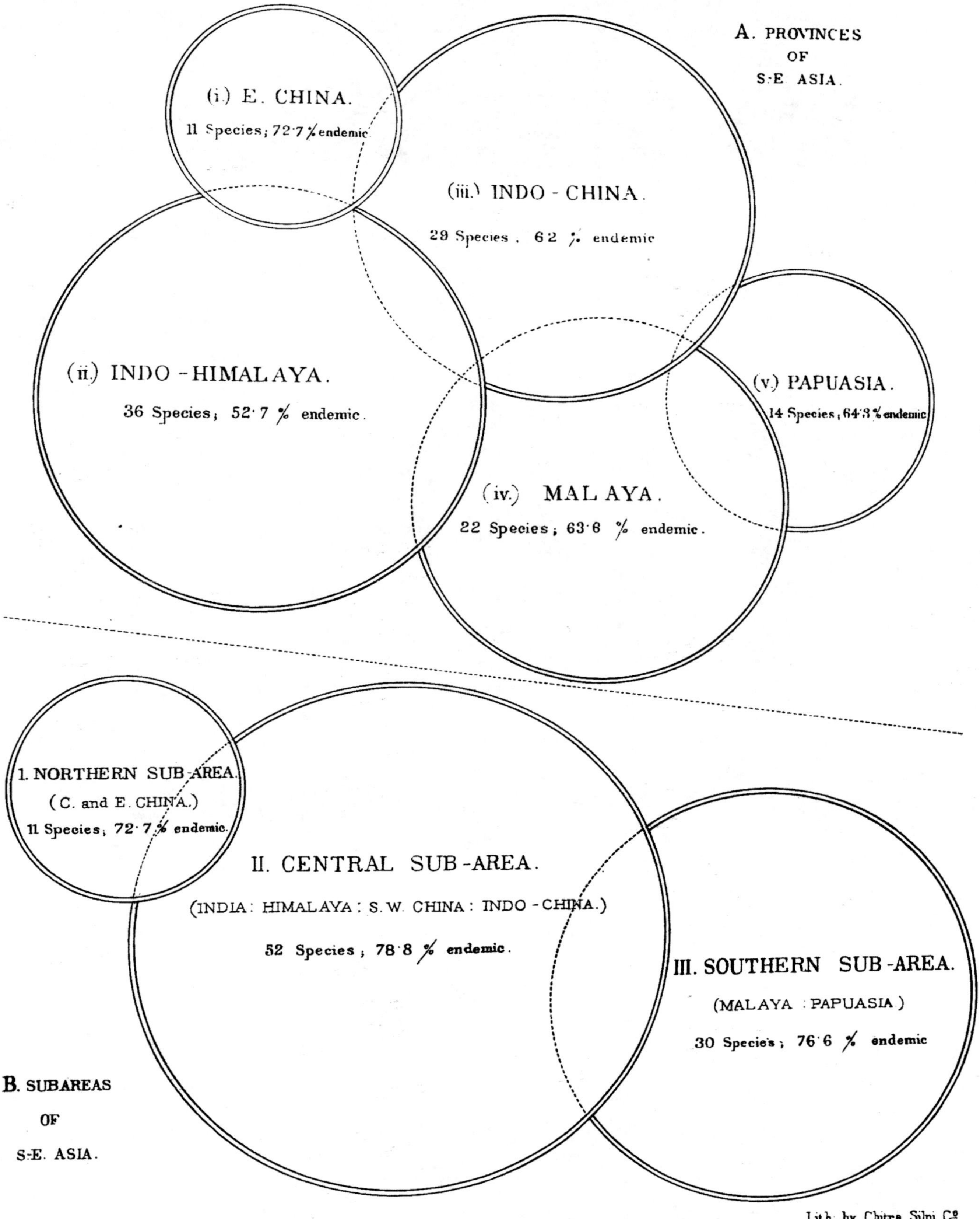

Lith by Chitra Silpi Co.

DALBERGIA IN S.-E. ASIATIC PROVINCES AND SUBAREAS.

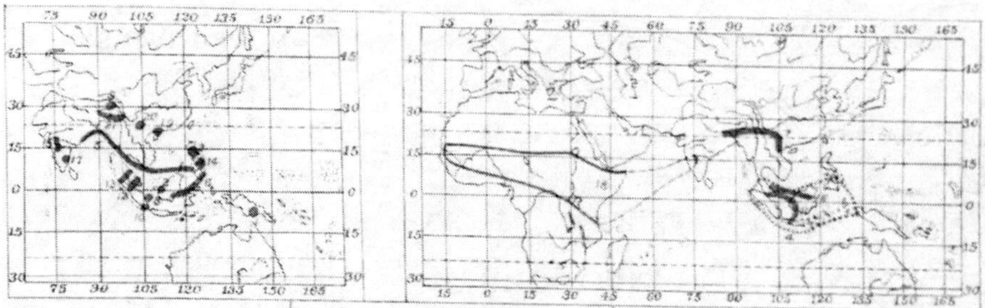

TRIPTOLEMEA.

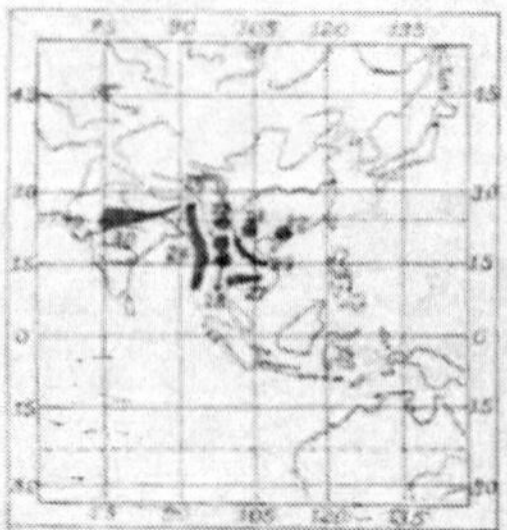

PODIOPETALUM.

1. Albertisii.
2. Beccarii.
3. Cumingiana.
4. Parviflora.
5. Spinosa.
6. Discolor.
7. Rimosa.
8. Forbesii.
9. Thomsoni.
10. Junghuhnii.
11. Scortechinii.
12. Curtisii.
13. Stercoracea.
14. Mimosella.
15. Multiflora.
16. Phyllanthoides.
17. Coromandeliana.
18. Melanoxylon.
19. Millettii.
20. Stenophylla.
21. Mimosoides.
22. Hancei.
23. Dyerana.
24. Confertiflora.
25. Yunnanensis.
26. Collettii.
27. Foliacea.
28. Cultrata.
29. Fusca.
30. Sissoo.

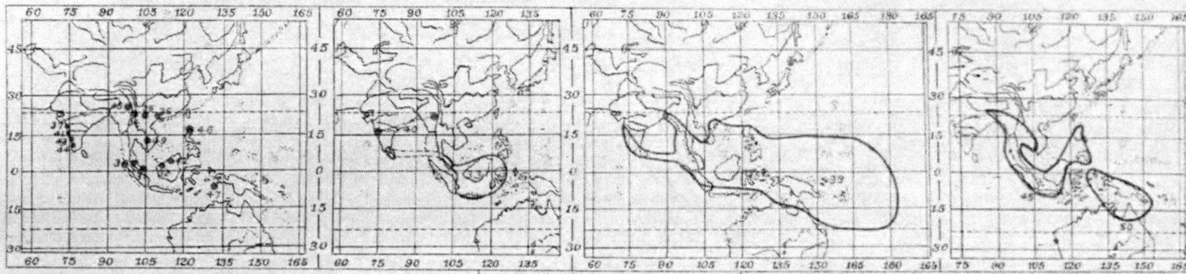

ENDESPERMUM.

31. Hullettii.
32. Havilandi.
33. Rostrata.
34. Kingiana.
35. Henryana.
36. Benthami.
37. Rubiginosa.
38. Menoeides.
39. Torta.
40. Congesta.
41. Gardneriana.
42. Hoseana.
43. Malabarica.
44. Acaciaefolia.
45. Tamarindifolia.
46. Polyphylla.
47. Jaherii.
48. Burmanica.
49. Pierreana.
50. Densa.

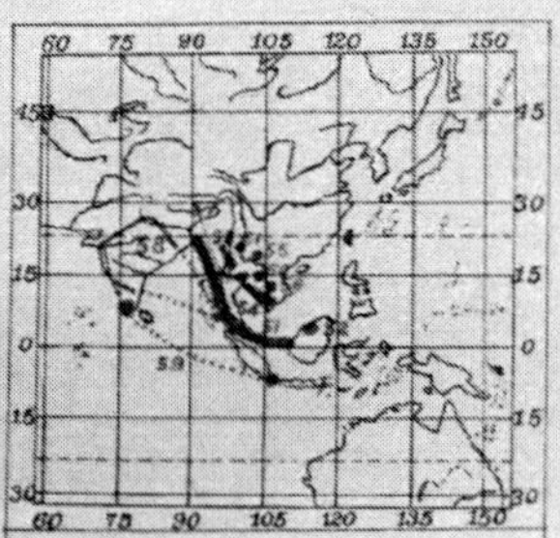

MISCOLOBIUM.

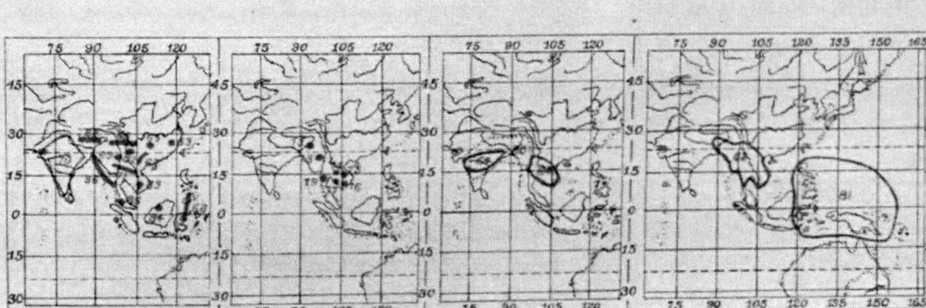

DALBERGARIA.

51. Velutina.
52. Borneensis.
53. Obtusifolia.
54. Ovata.
55. Tonkinensis.
56. Cambodiana.
57. Glomeriflora.
58. Latifolia.
59. Sissoides.
60. Cochinchinensis.
61. Polyadelpha.
62. Sericea.
63. Sacerdotum.
64. Paniculata.
65. Hupeana.
66. Assamica.
67. Balansae.
68. Minahassae.
69. Oliveri.
70. Lanceolaria.
71. Hemsleyi.
72. Szemaoensis.
73. Wattii.
74. Mammosa.
75. Duperreana.
76. Bariensis.
77. Dongnaiensis.
78. Kurzii.
79. Cana.
80. Volubilis.
81. Ferruginea.
82. Stipulacea.
83. Godefroyi.
84. Falcata.
85. Kunstleri.
86. Reniformis.

D. Prain del[t].

K. P. Dass lith.

DISTRIBUTION OF THE ASIATIC SPECIES OF DALBERGIA.

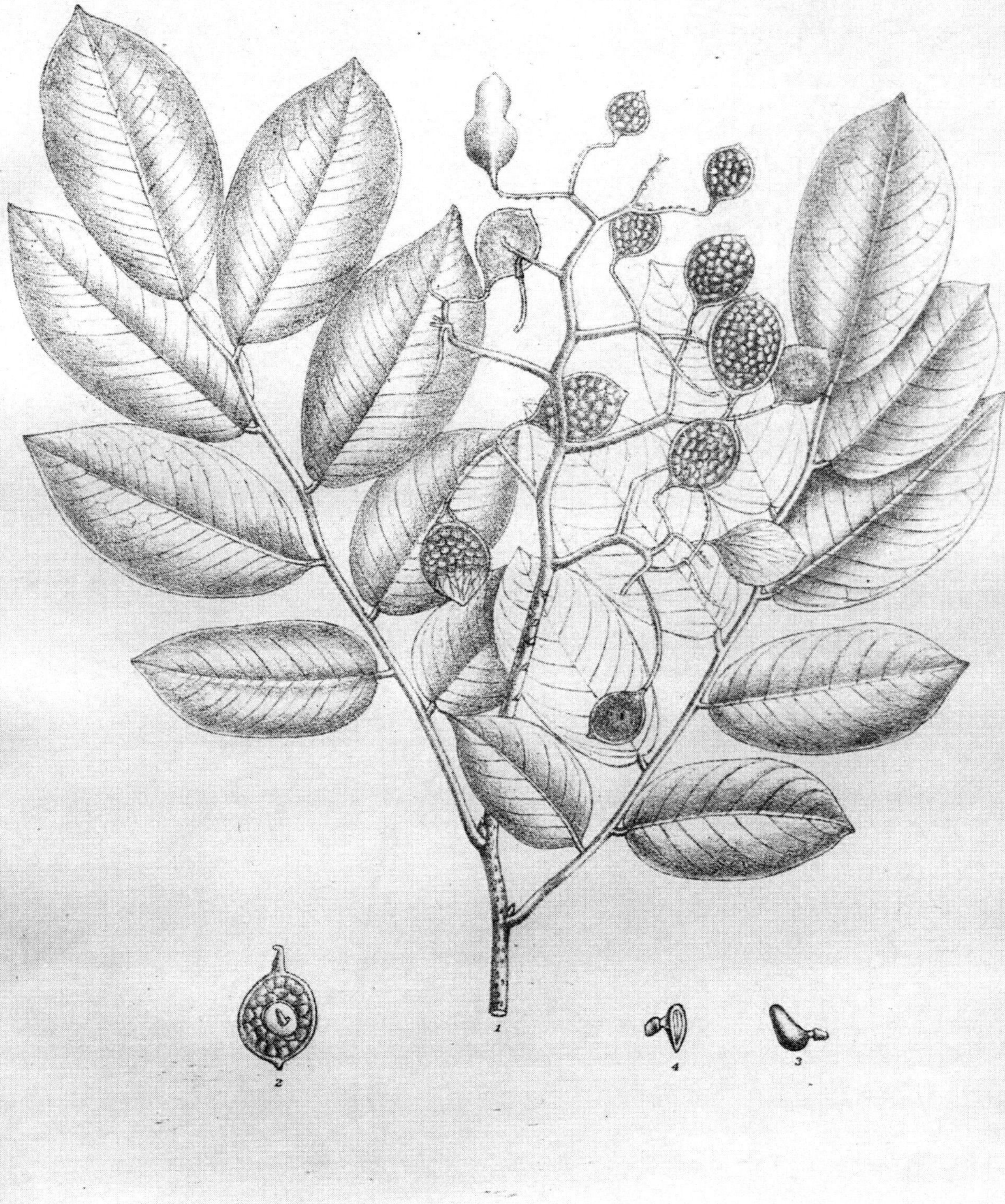

Drawn by K.P. Dass.

DALBERGIA ALBERTISII Prain.

Lith: by A.C. Singha.

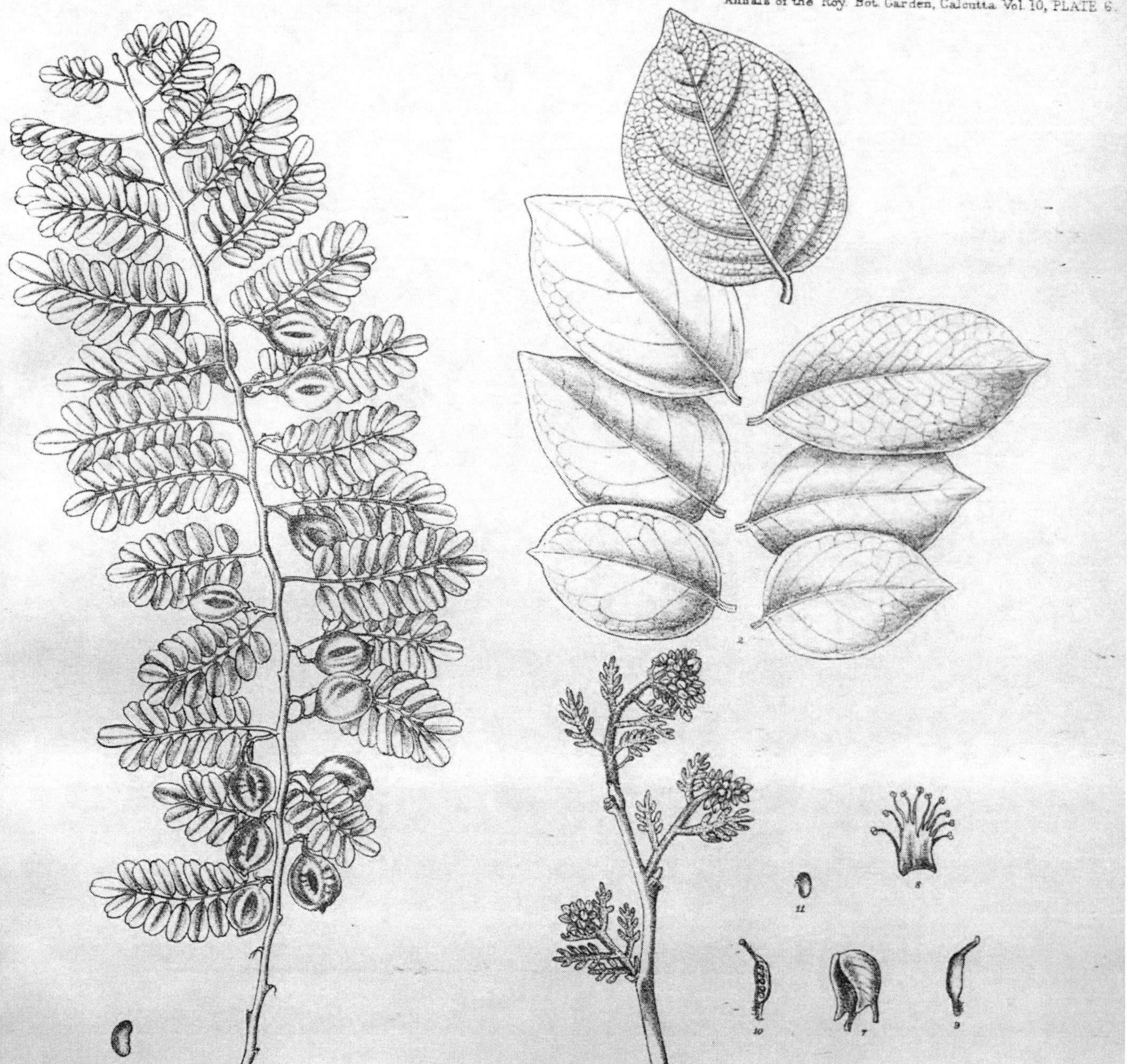

Drawn by A.L. Singh.

Lith: by A.C. Singha.

A. DALBERGIA BECCARII Prain.

B. DALBERGIA GLOMERIFLORA Kurz.

Drawn by K.P. Dass. Lith. by A. C. Singha.

DALBERGIA CUMINGIANA Benth.

Annals of the Roy. Bot. Garden, Calcutta, Vol. 10, PLATE 8.

Drawn by K. P. Dass.

DALBERGIA PARVIFLORA Roxb.

Lith. by K. P. Dass.

Drawn by K.P. Dass. | Lith. by K.P. Dass.

DALBERGIA SPINOSA, Roxb.

Ann. Roy. Bot. Garden, Calcutta, Vol. 10, PLATE 10

Drawn by D. N. Chowdhury.

Lith: by Chitra Silpi Co

DALBERGIA DISCOLOR Bl.

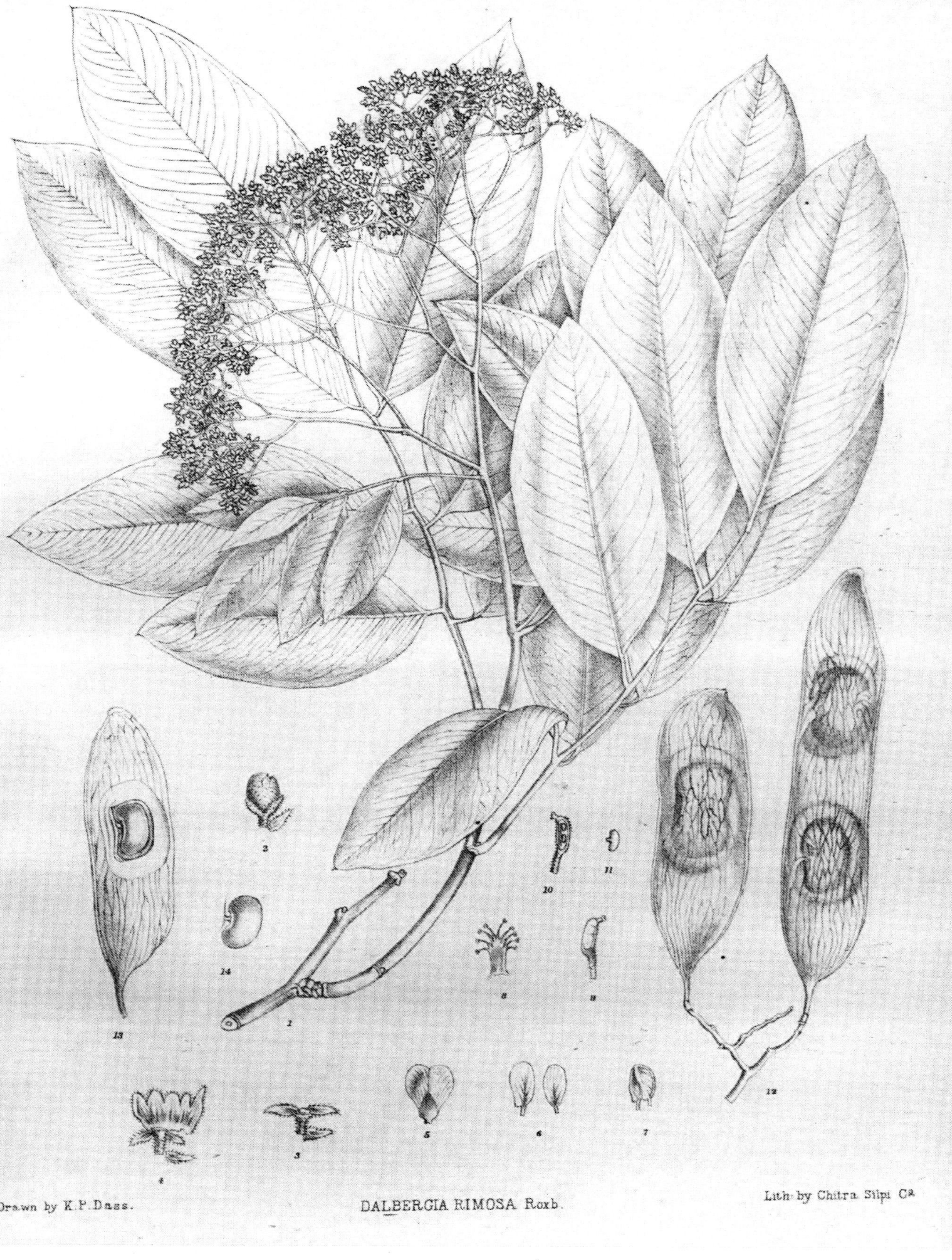

Drawn by K. P. Dass.

DALBERGIA RIMOSA Roxb.

Lith. by Chitra Silpi Co.

Ann. Roy. Bot. Garden, Calcutta, Vol 10. PLATE 12.

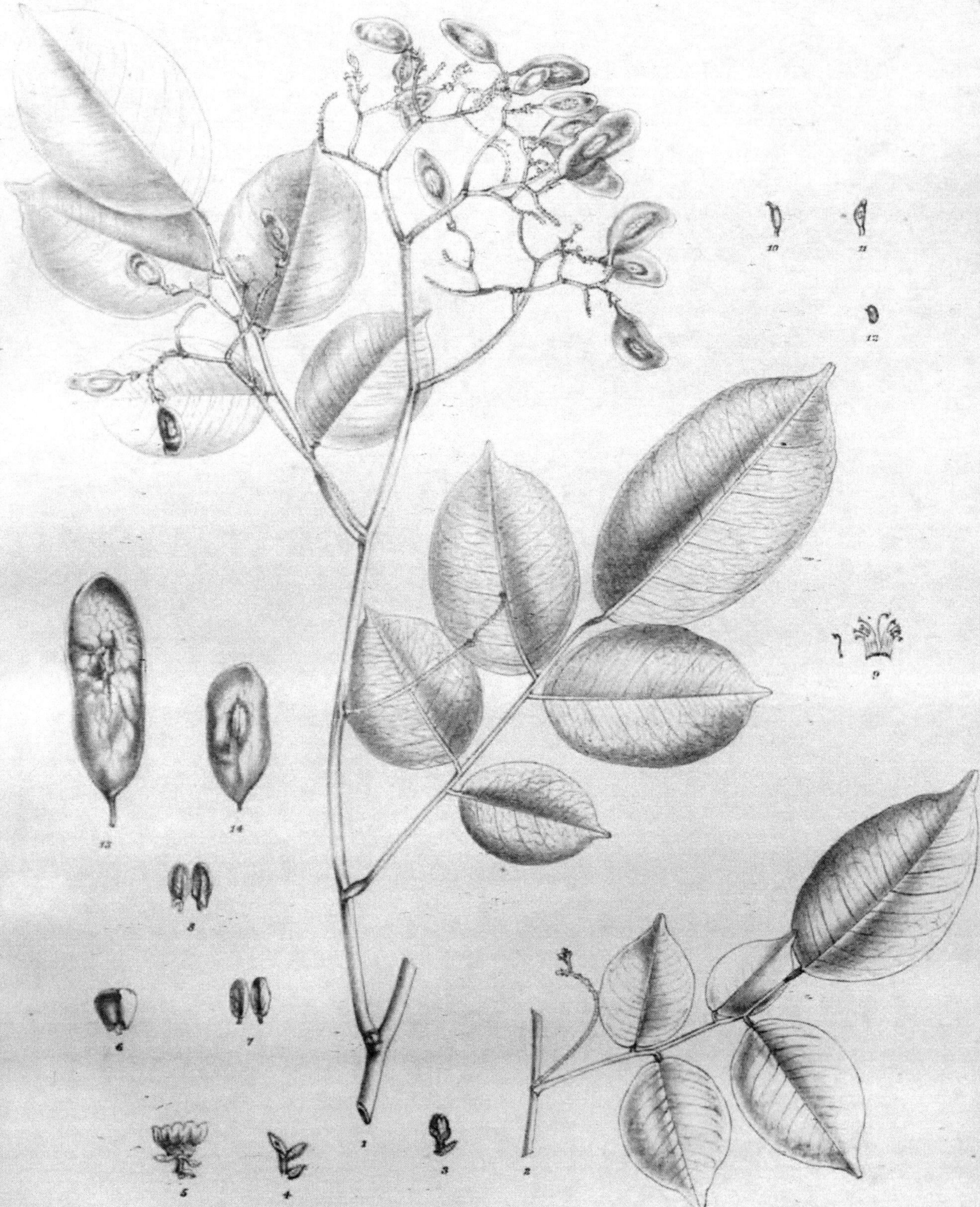

Drawn by K. P. Dass.

Lith: by Chitra Silpi Co

DALBERGIA FORBESII Prain.

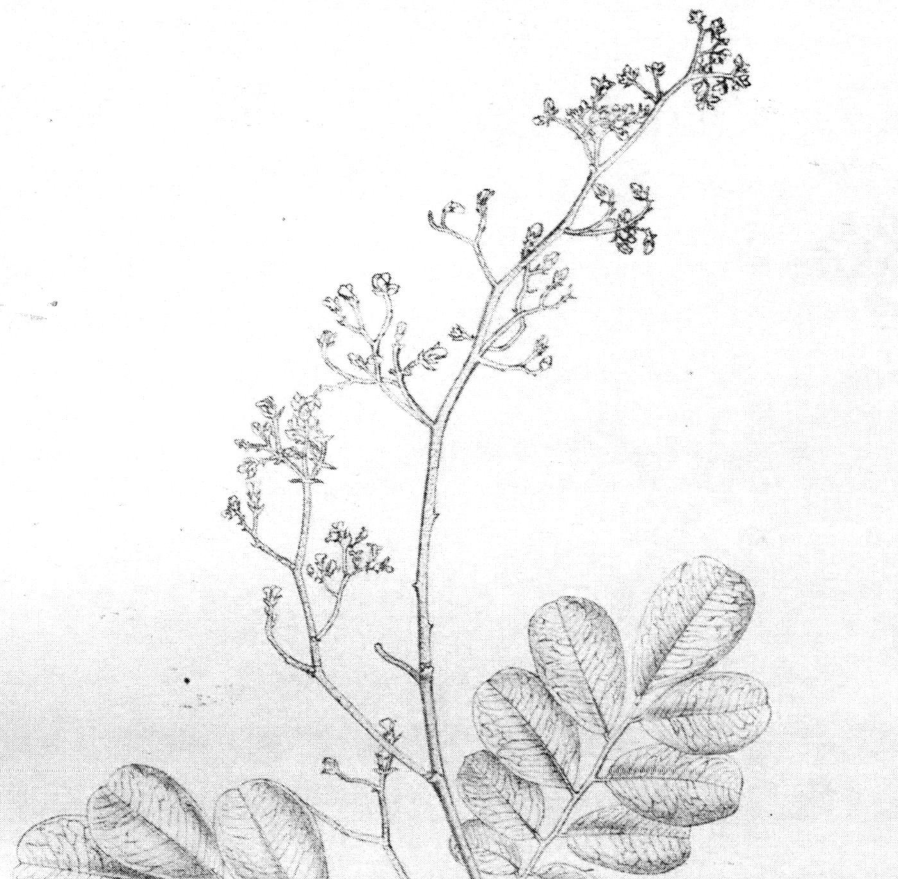

Drawn by K. P. Dass.

Lith: by Chitra Silpi C°

DALBERGIA THOMSONI Benth.

Ann. Roy. Bot. Garden, Calcutta, Vol. 10, PLATE 14.

Drawn by A. L. Singh.

Lith. by Chitra Silpi C°.

DALBERGIA JUNGHUHNII Benth.

Drawn by K.P. Dass.

Lith. by Chitra Silpi Co

DALBERGIA SCORTECHINII Prain.

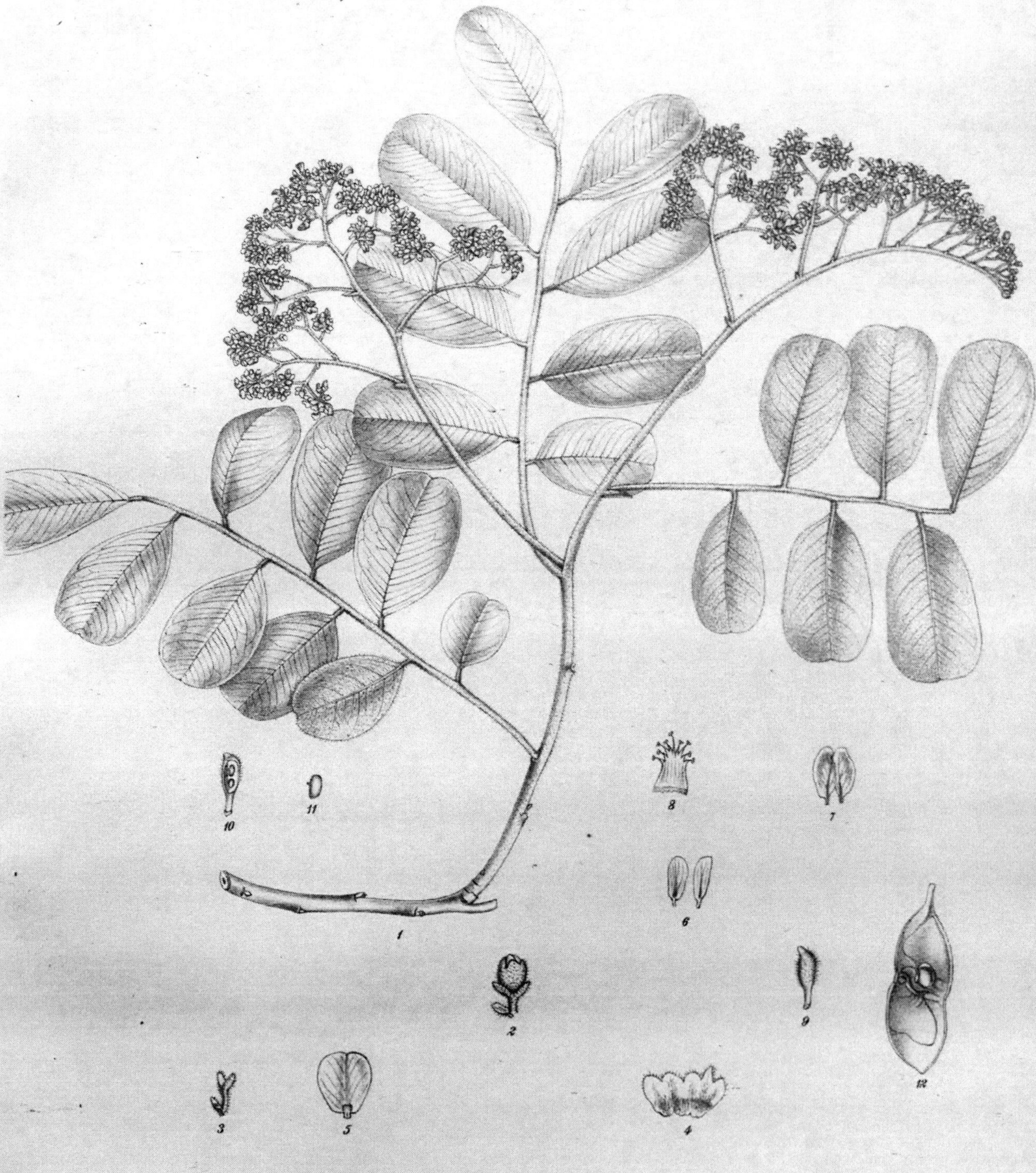

Drawn by K. P. Dass.

Lith. by S. C. Mondul.

DALBERGIA CURTISII, Prain.

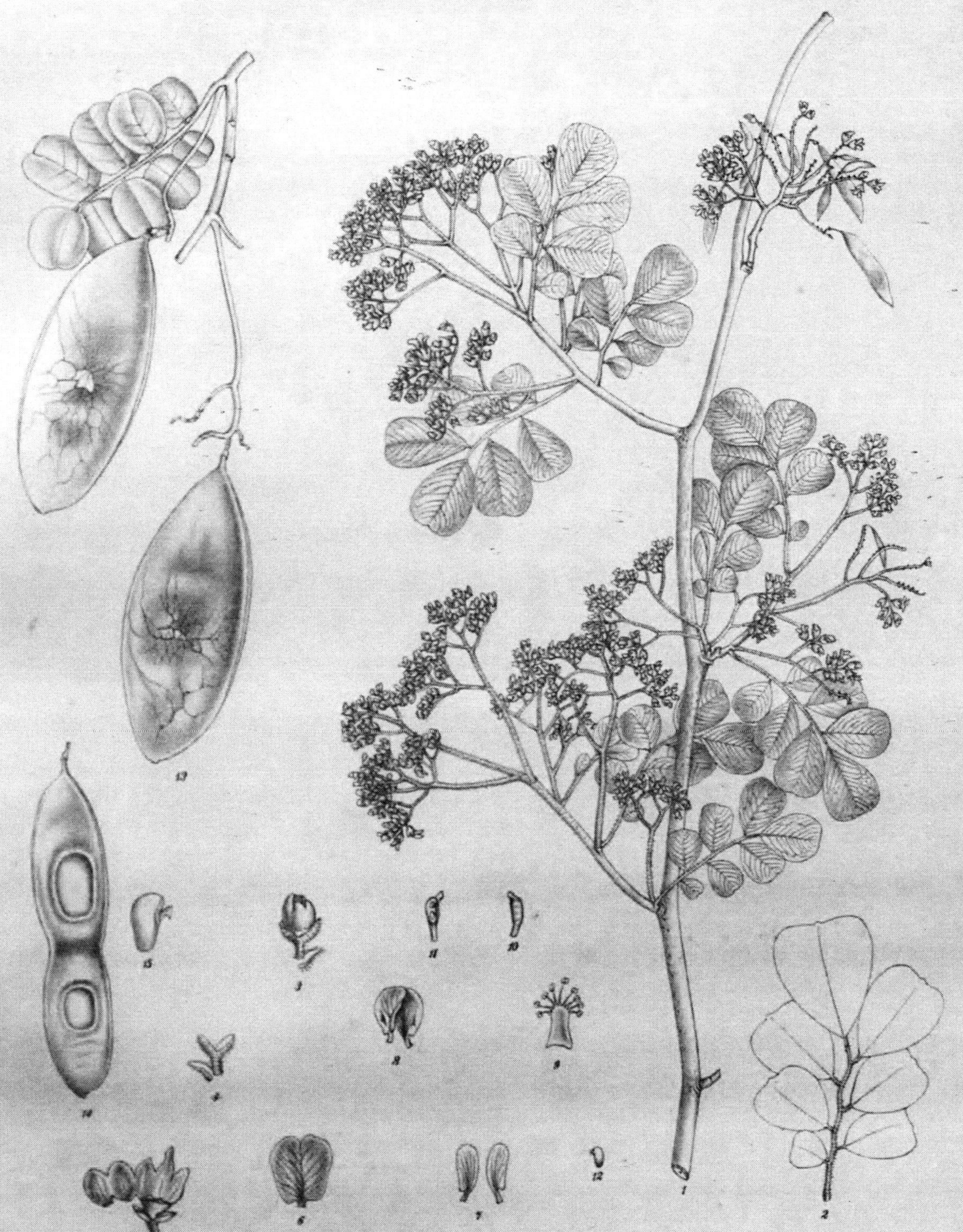

Drawn by K. P. Dass.

Lith. by S. C. Mondul.

DALBERGIA STERCORACEA Maing.

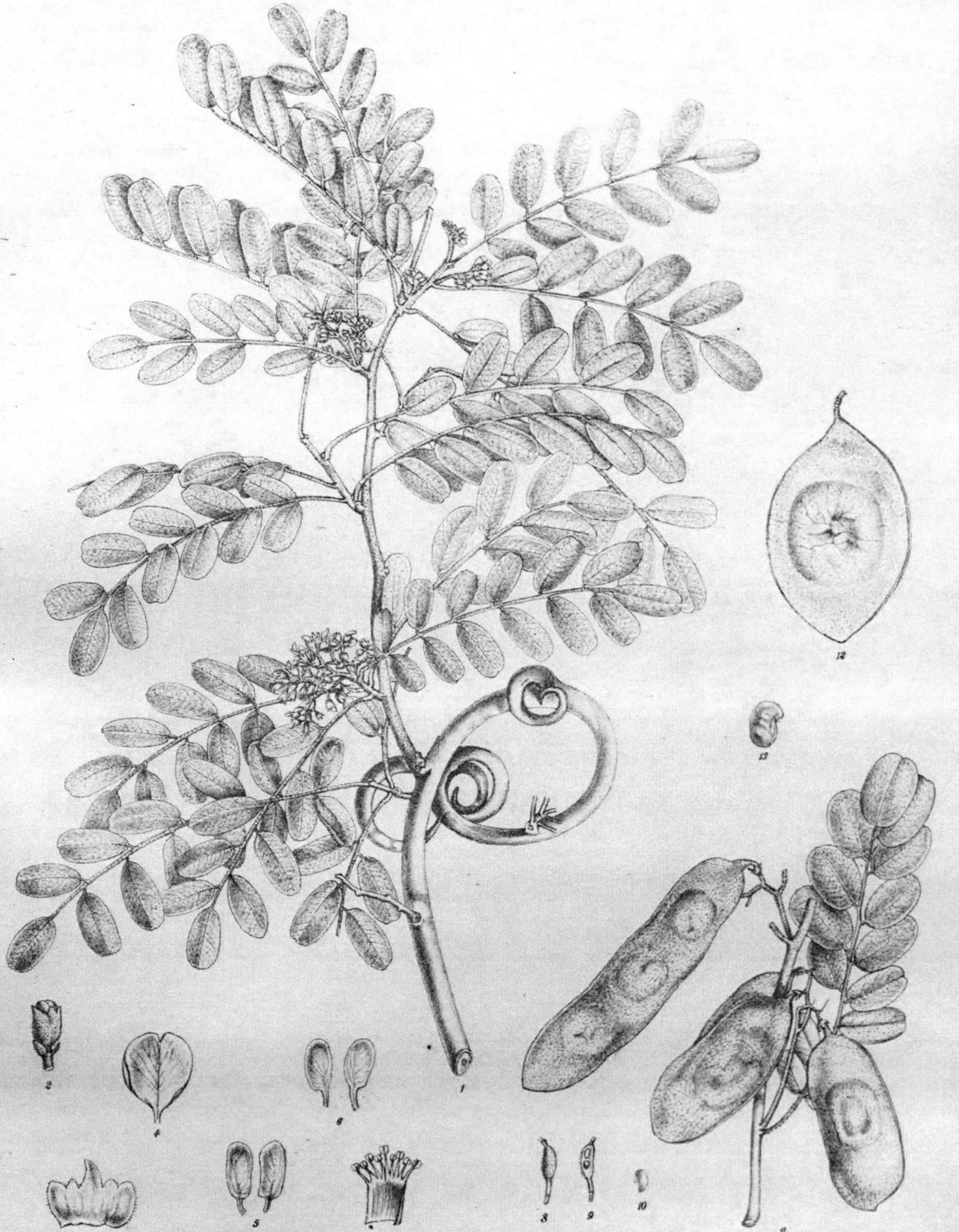

Drawn by K. P. Dass.

DALBERGIA MULTIFLORA Heyne.

Lith. by A. C. Chowdhary.

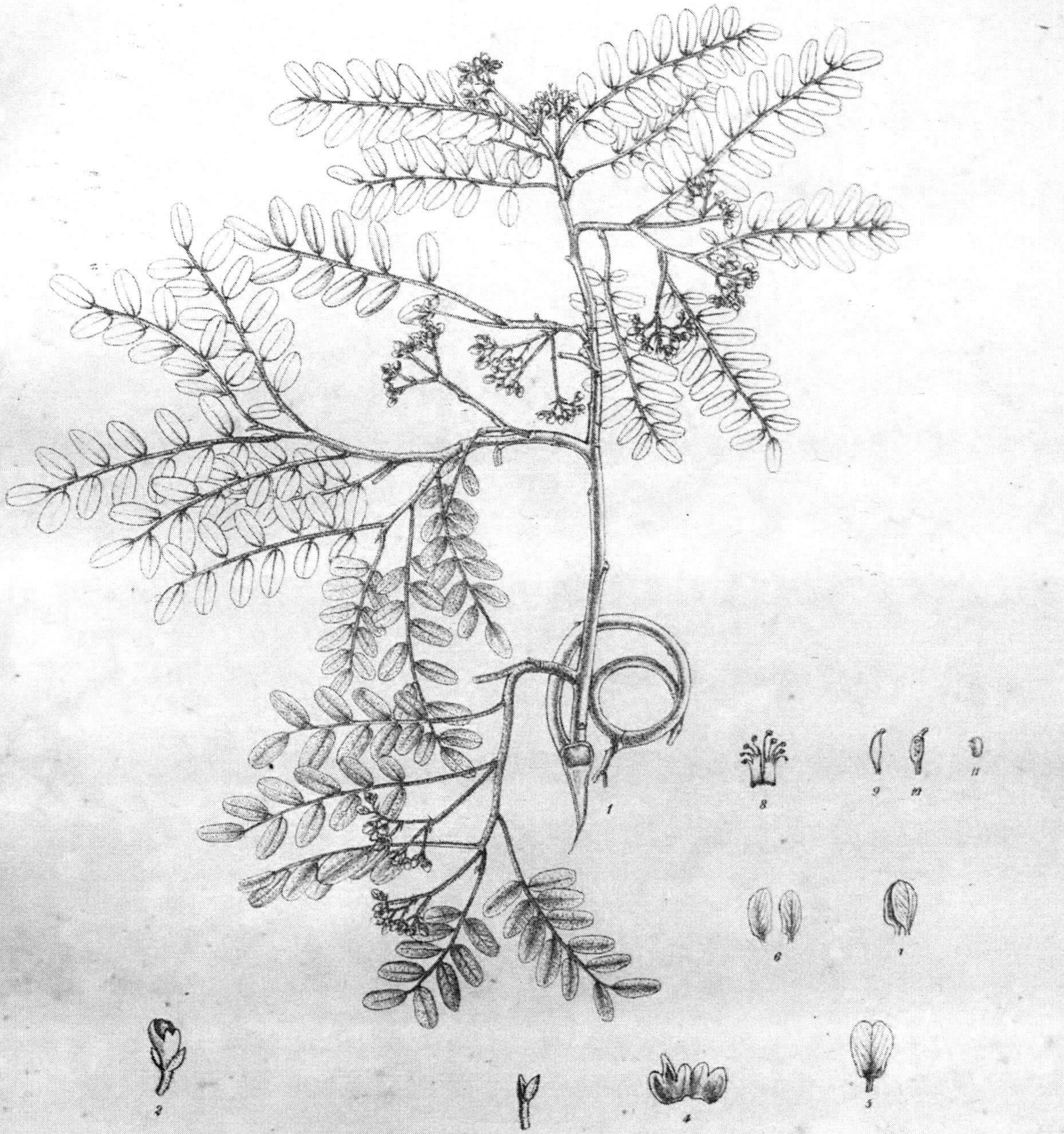

Drawn by D. N. Chaudhari.

Lith. by A. C. Chowdhary.

DALBERGIA PHYLLANTHOIDES Bl.

Annals of the Roy. Bot. Garden, Calcutta, Vol. 10, PLATE 20.

Drawn by A. D. Molla. Lith. by A. C. Chowdhary.

DALBERGIA PHYLLANTHOIDES Bl. var. SENNOIDES Prain.

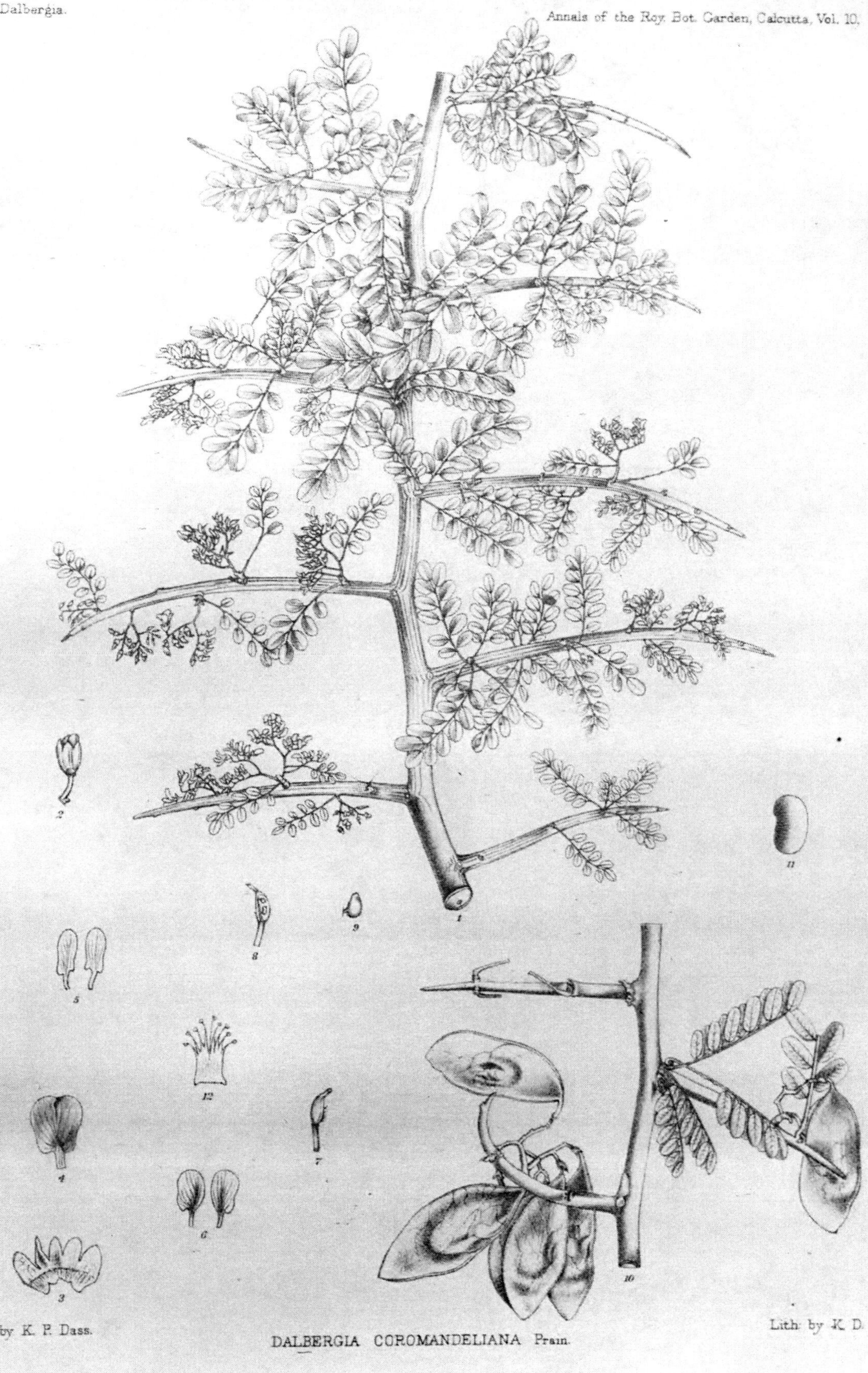

Drawn by K. P. Dass.

DALBERGIA COROMANDELIANA Prain.

Lith: by K. D. Chandra.

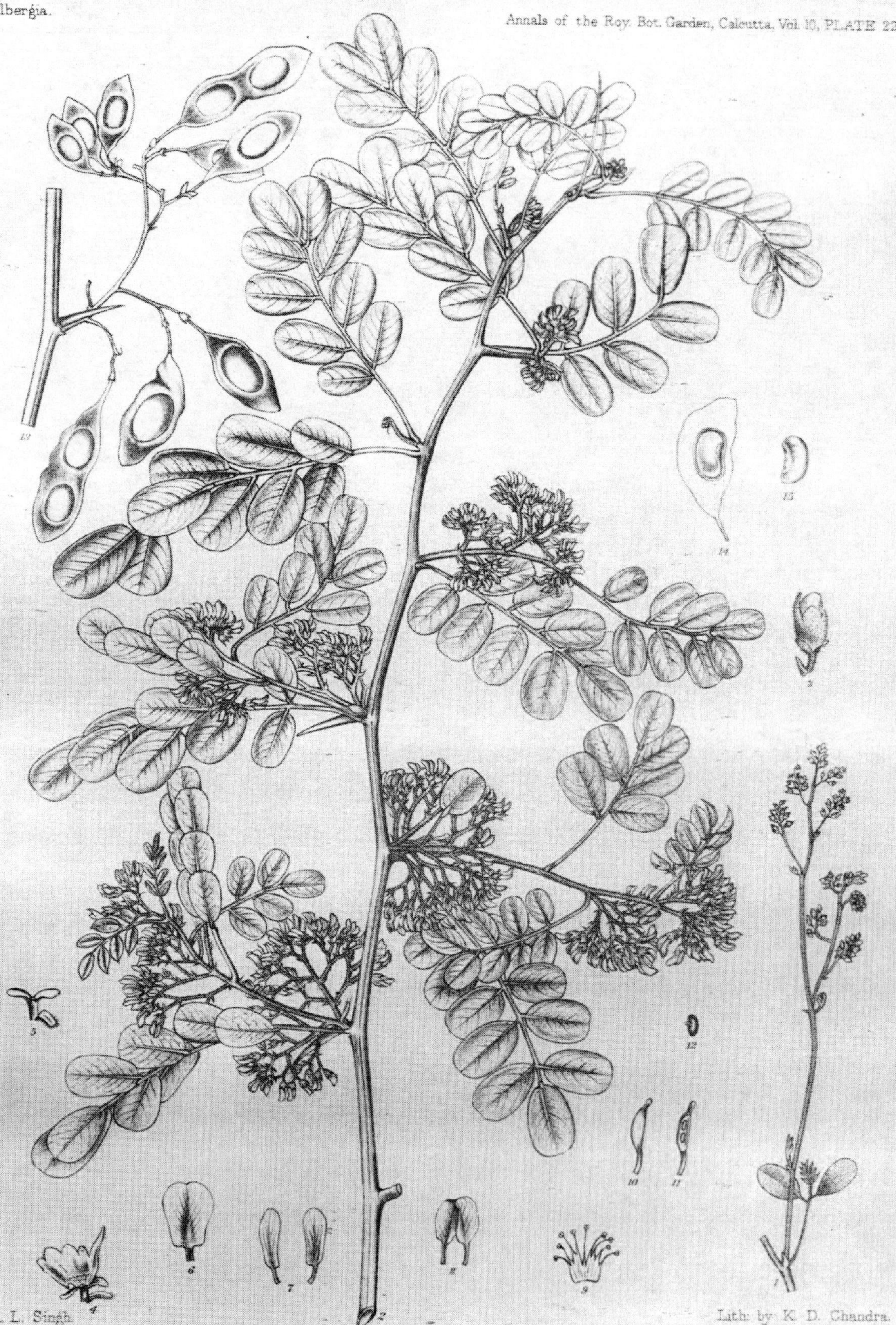

Drawn by A. L. Singh.

Lith: by K. D. Chandra.

DALBERGIA MELANOXYLON Guill. & Perr.

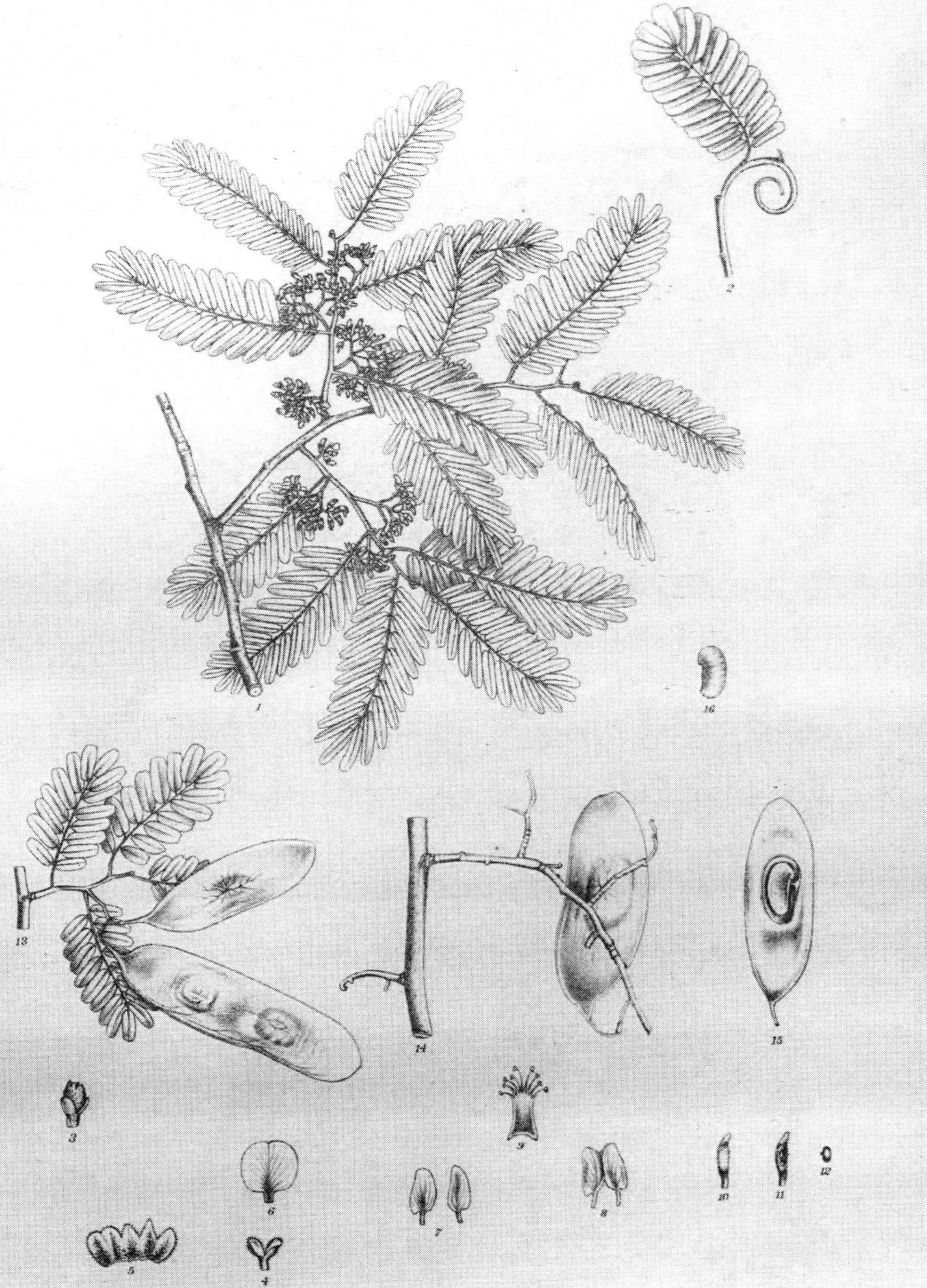

Drawn by K. P. Dass. Lith: by K. D. Chandra.

DALBERGIA MILLETTII Benth.

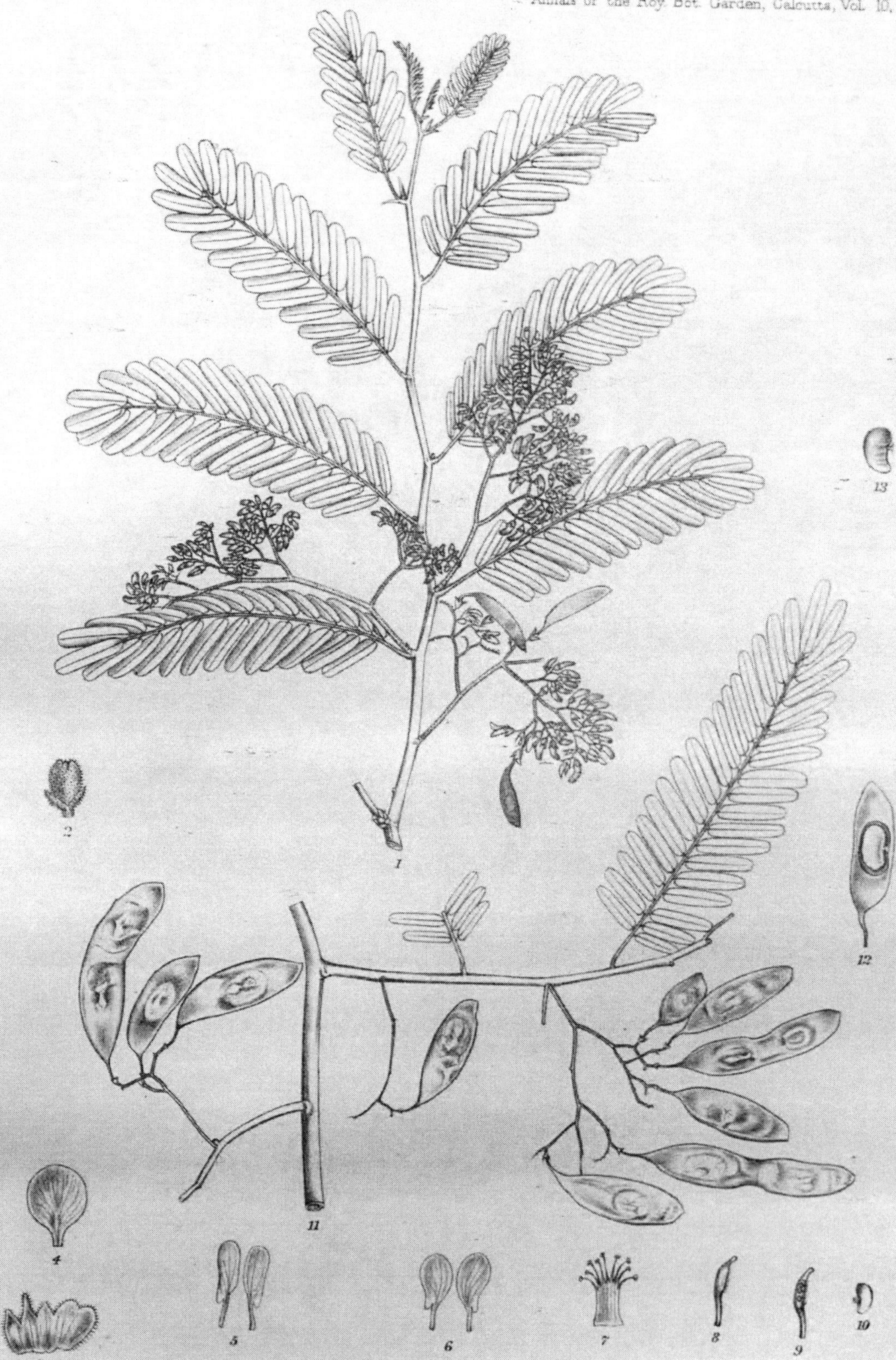

Drawn by K. P. Dass.

DALBERGIA STENOPHYLLA Prain.

Lith: by K. D. Chandra.

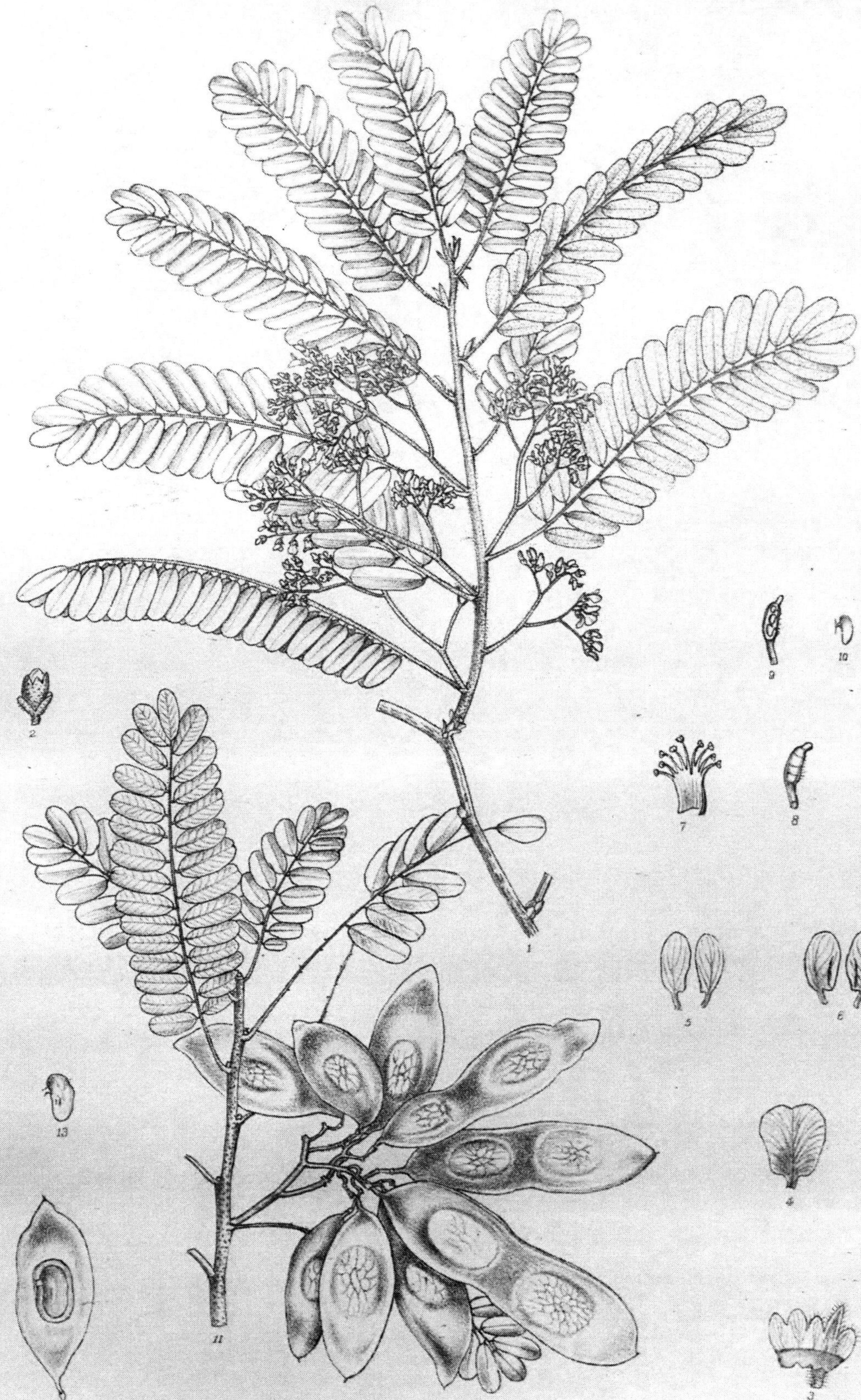

Drawn by K.P. Dass.　　DALBERGIA MIMOSOIDES Franch.　　Lith. by K.P. Dass.

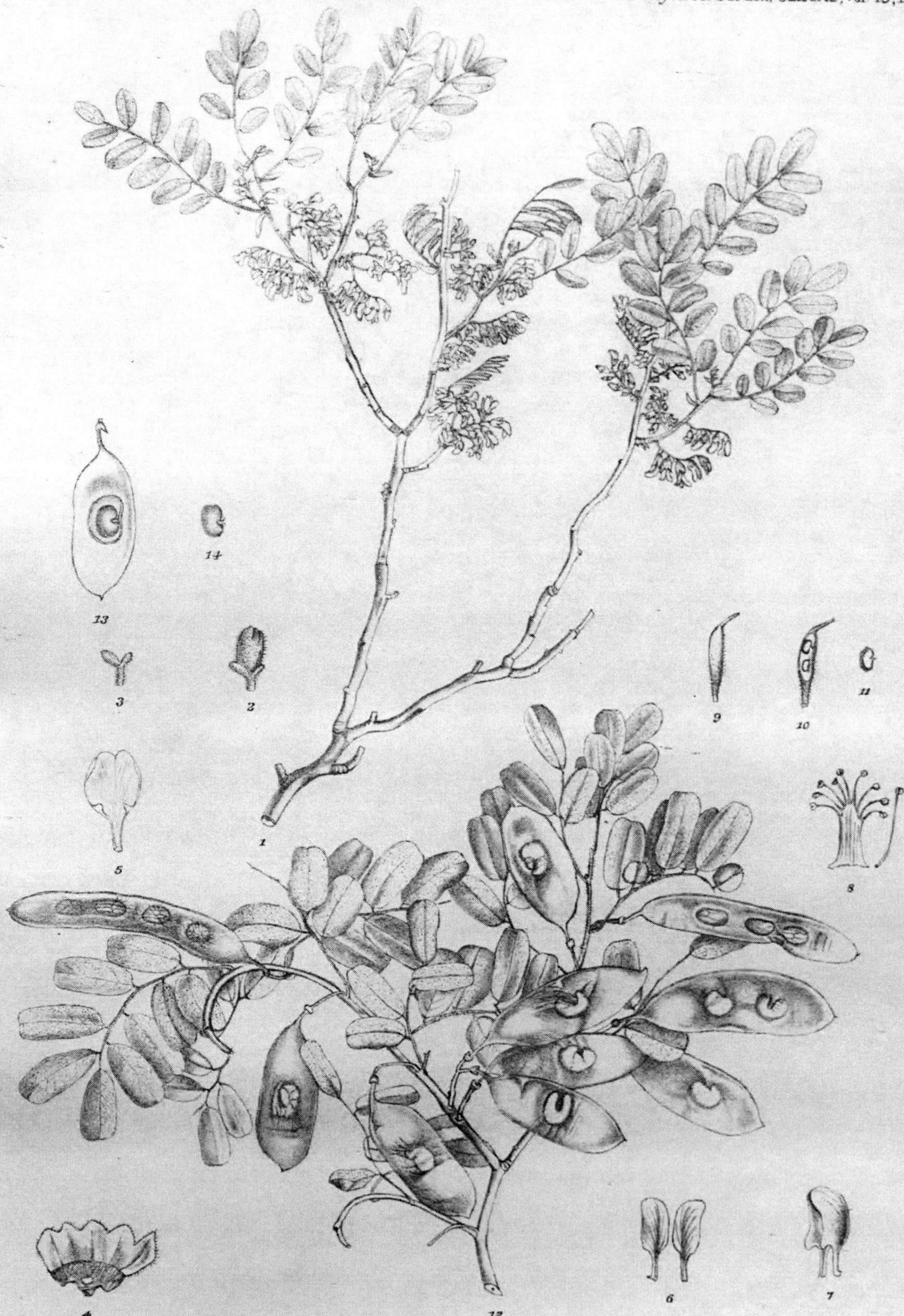

Drawn by K. P. Dass.

Lith. by Chitra Silpi Co.

DALBERGIA HANCEI Benth.

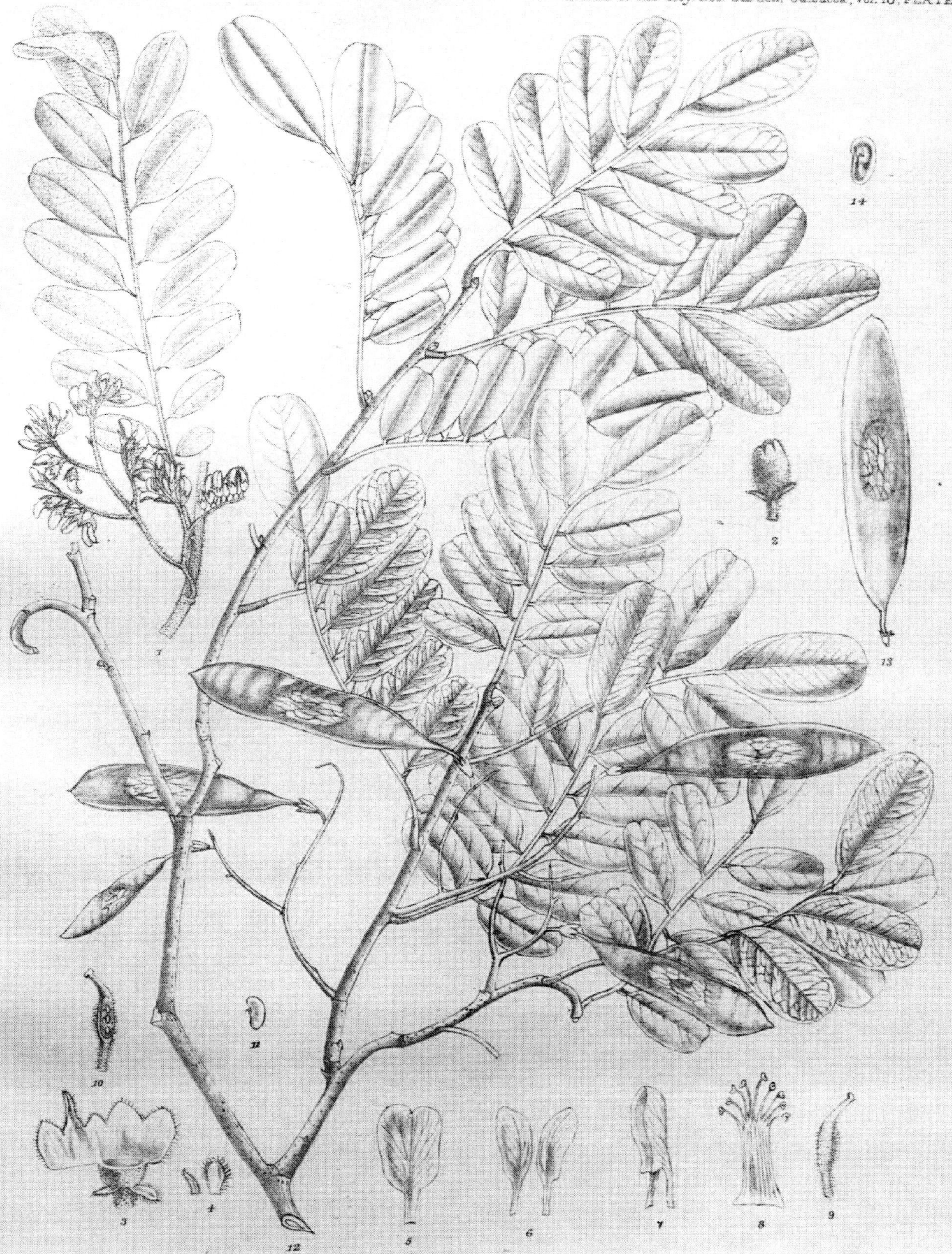

Drawn by A. D. Molla.

Lith: by Chitra Silpi Co.

DALBERGIA DYERIANA Prain.

Annals of the Roy. Bot. Garden, Calcutta, Vol 10, PLATE 28.

Drawn by K.P. Dass. DALBERGIA CONFERTIFLORA Benth. Lith: by K.D. Chandra.

Drawn by K.P. Dass. Lith: by K.P. Dass.

DALBERGIA YUNNANENSIS Franch.

Annals of the Roy. Bot. Garden, Calcutta, Vol. 10, PLATE 30.

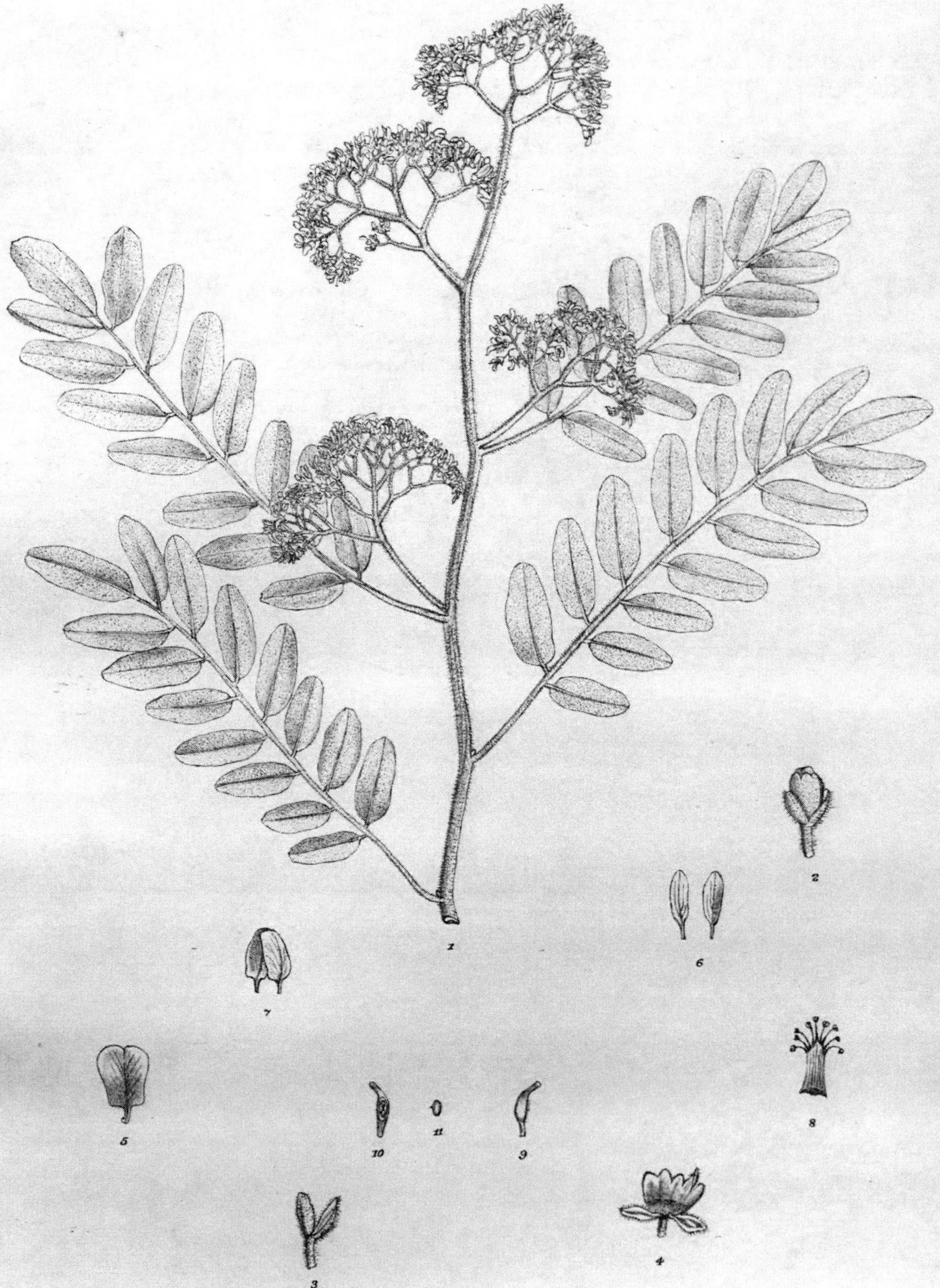

Drawn by K. P. Dass.

Lith: by Chitra Silpi Co.

DALBERGIA COLLETTII Prain.

Drawn by A. D. Molla.

Lith. by Chitra Silpi Co.

DALBERGIA FOLIACEA Wall.

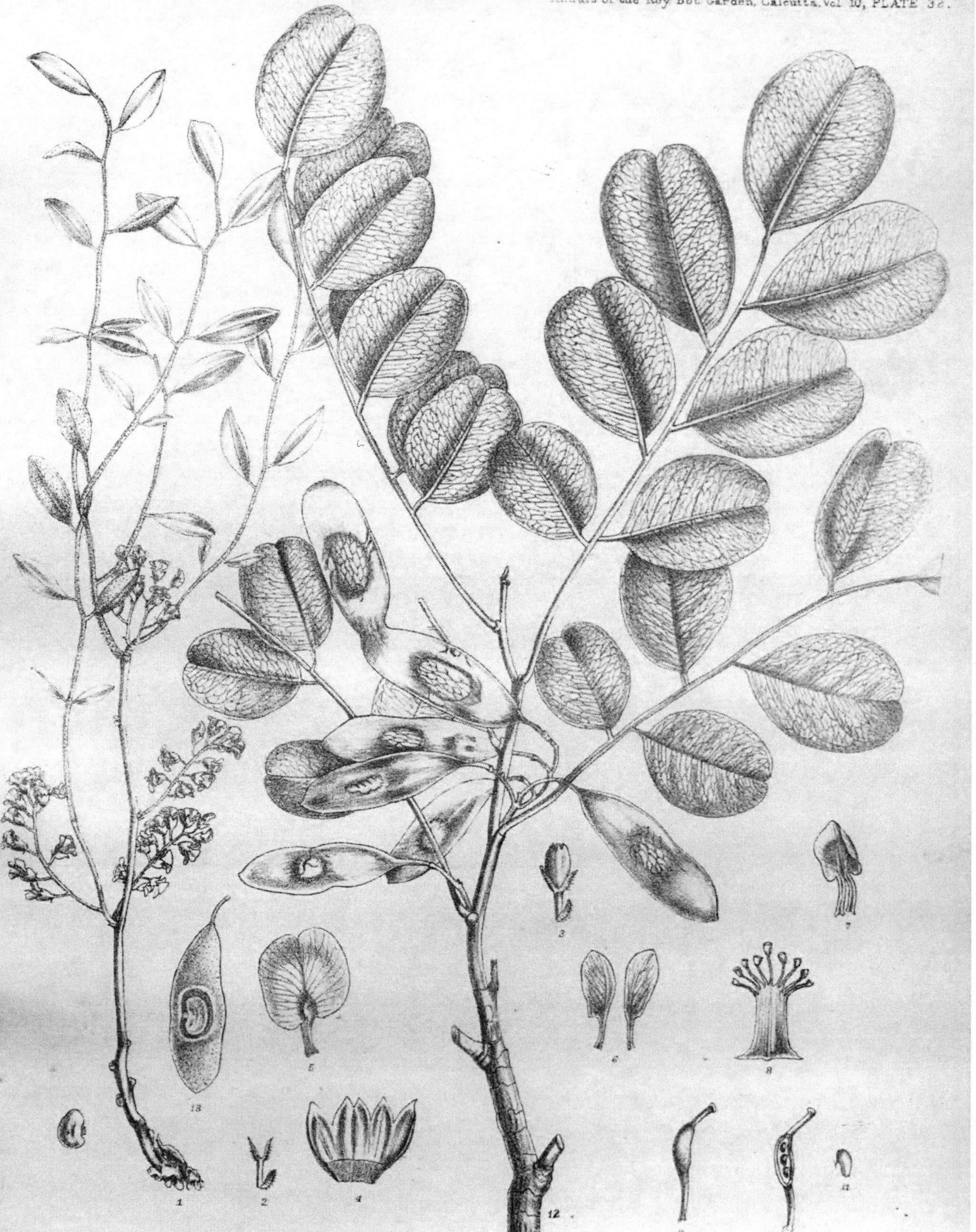

Drawn by K.P. Dass.

DALBERGIA CULTRATA Grah.

Lith. by A.C. Singha.

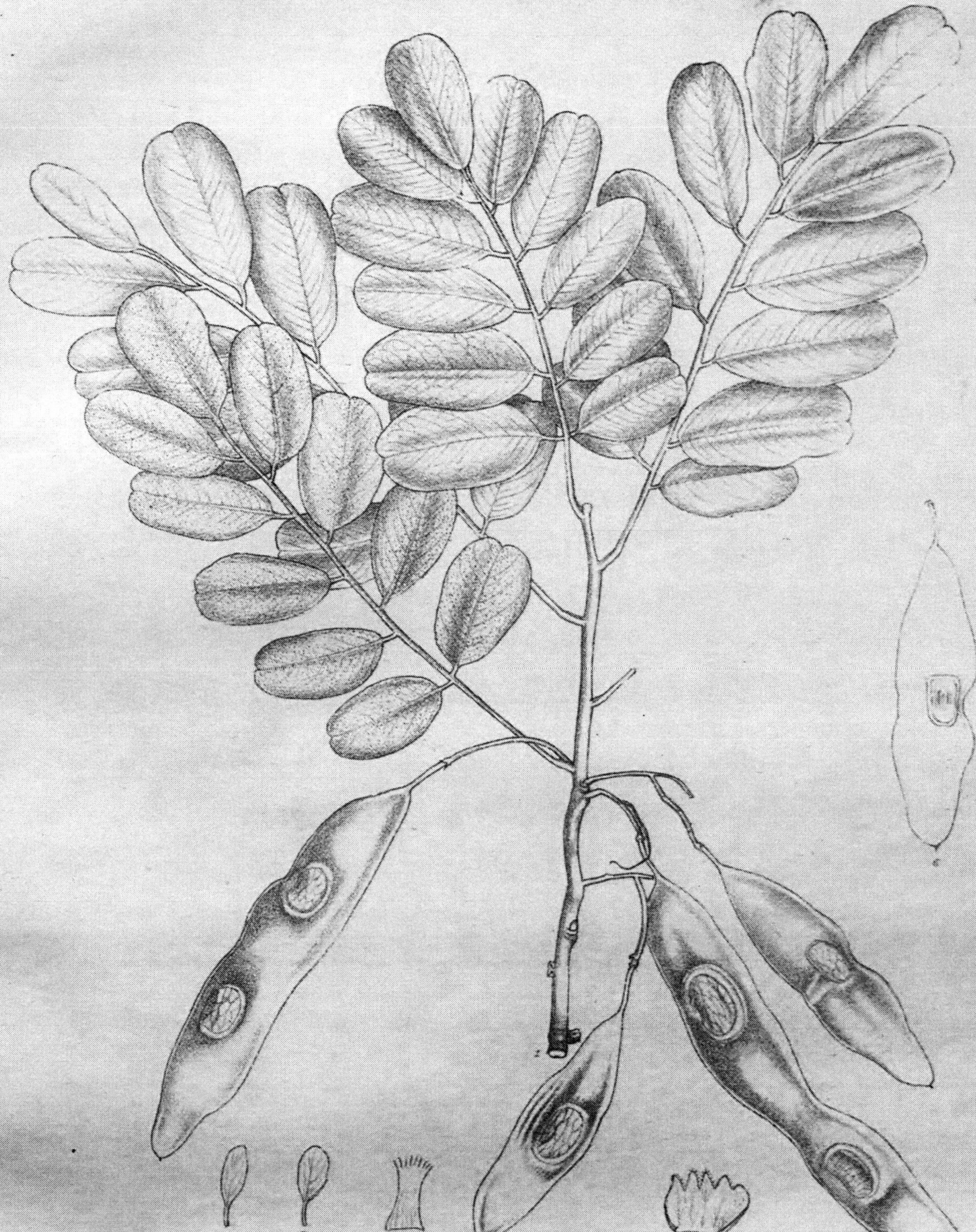

Drawn by K. P. Dass.

DALBERGIA FUSCA Pierre

Lith. by K. P. Dass.

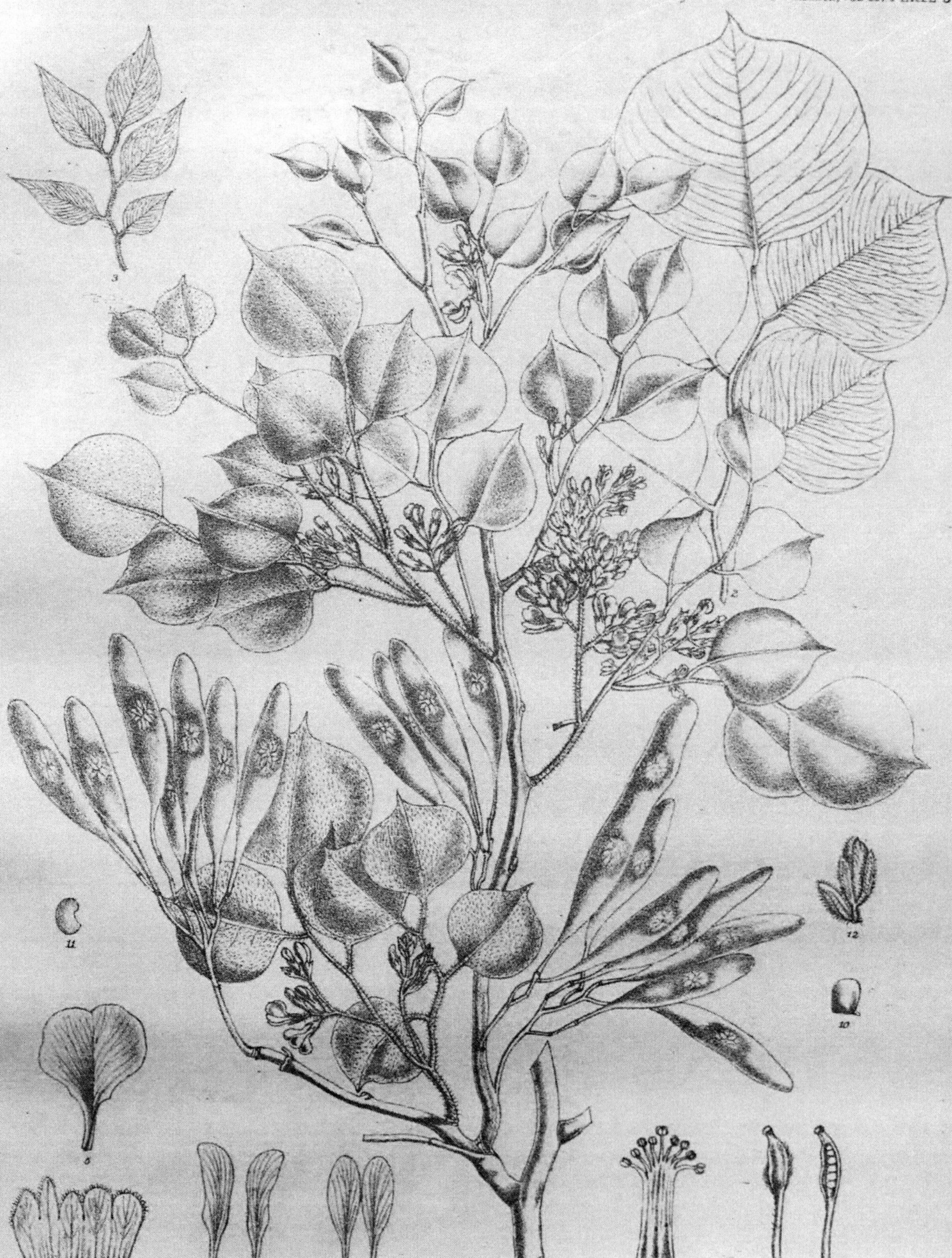

Drawn by K.P. Dass.

DALBERGIA SISSOO Roxb.

Lith. by A. C. Singha.

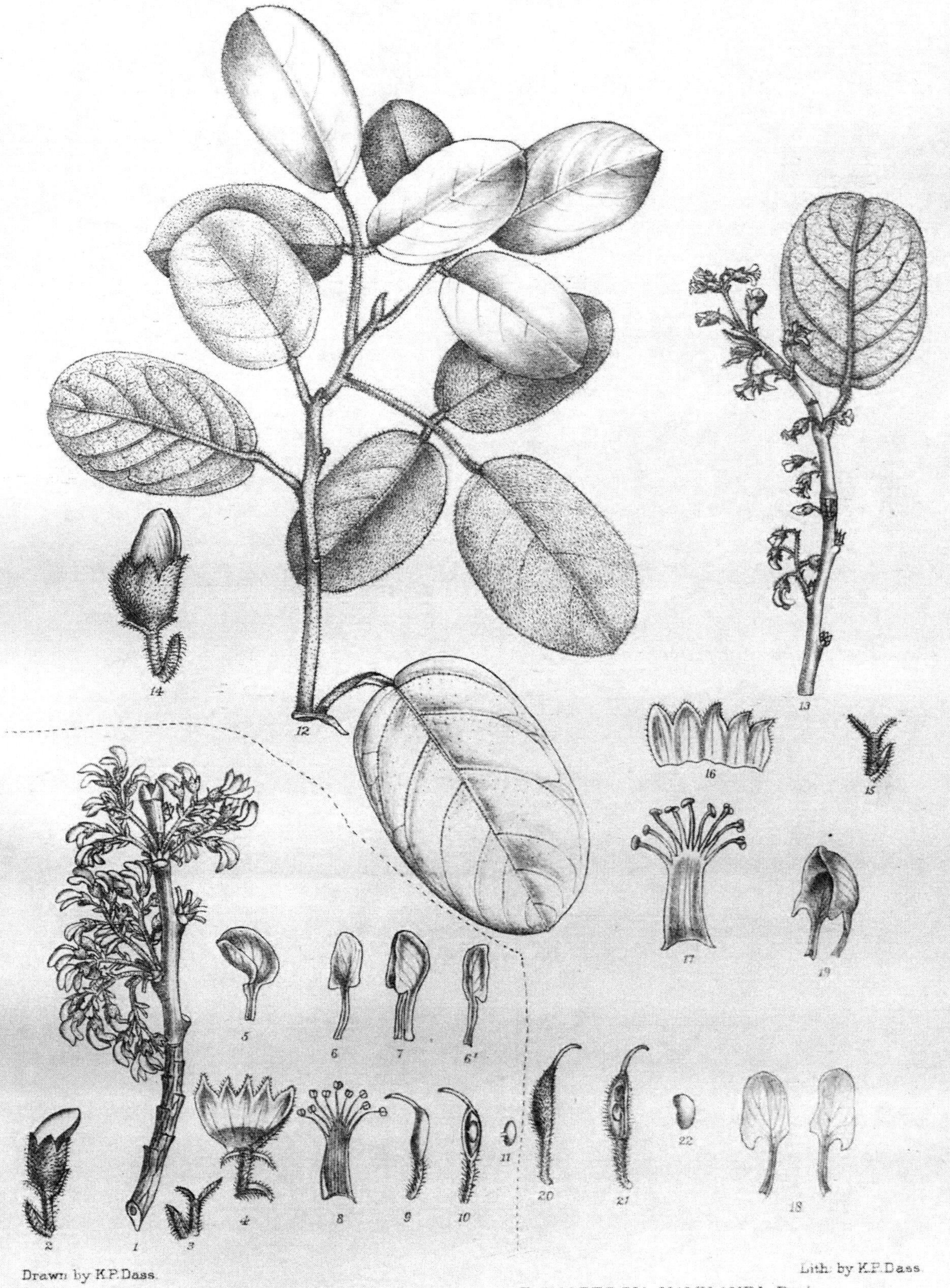

Drawn by K.P. Dass.

Lith: by K.P. Dass.

A. DALBERGIA HULLETTII Prain. B. DALBERGIA HAVILANDI Prain.

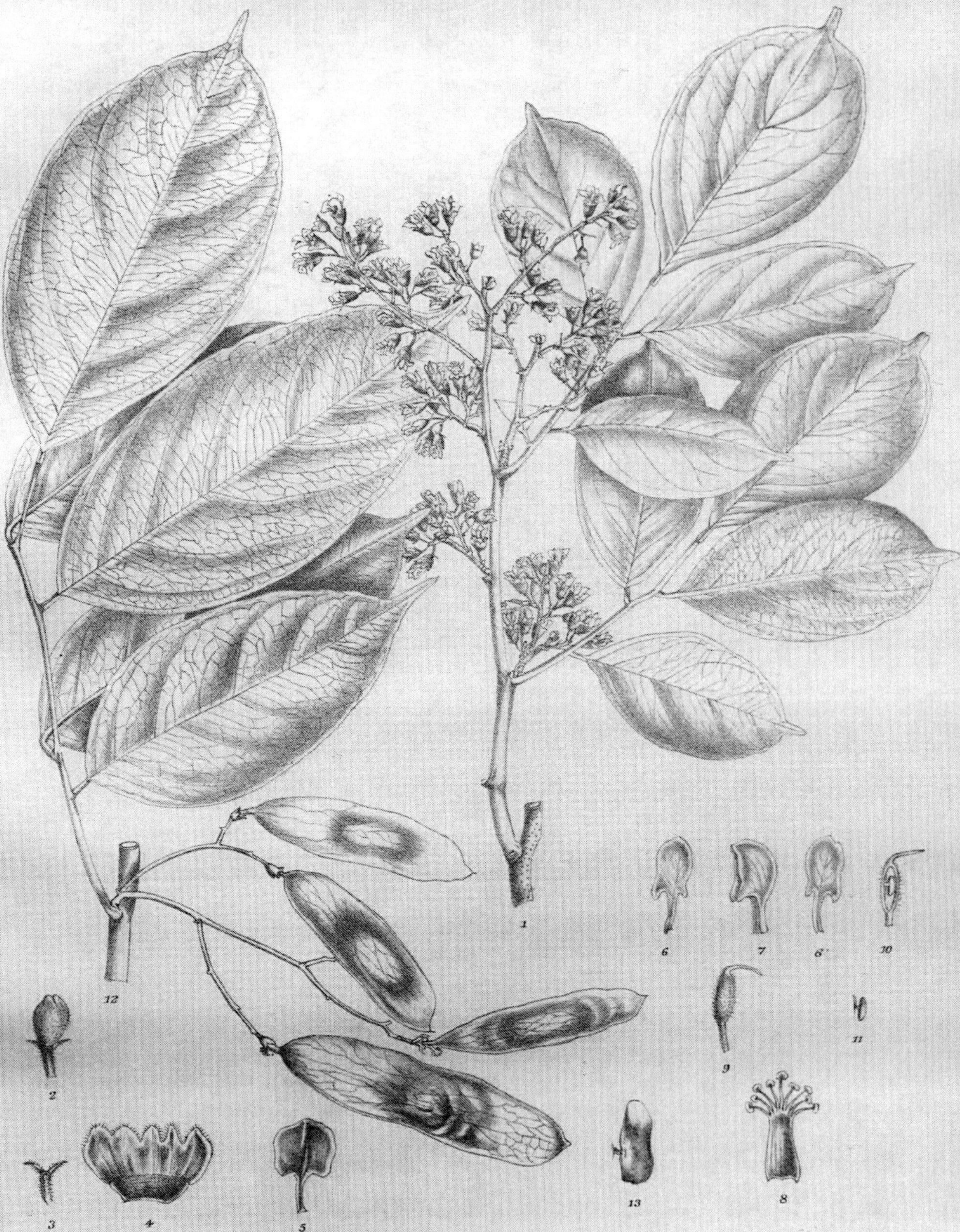

Drawn by K. P. Dass

Lith: by Chitra Silpi Co

DALBERGIA ROSTRATA Grah.

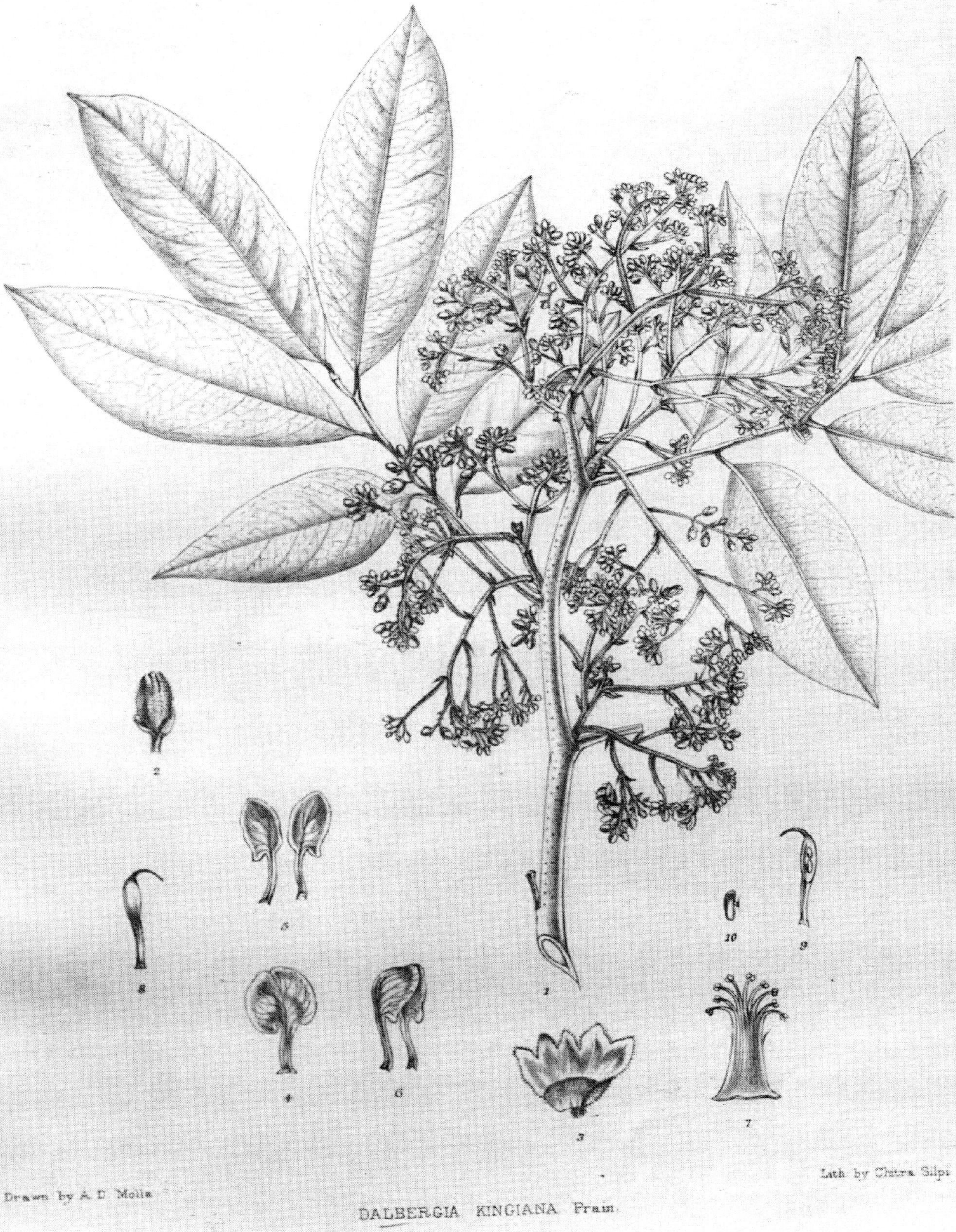

Drawn by A. D. Molla.

Lith. by Chitra Silpi Co.

DALBERGIA KINGIANA Prain.

Annals of the Roy Bot. Garden, Calcutta, Vol. 10, PLATE 38.

Drawn by K.P. Dass.

DALBERGIA HENRYANA Prain.

Lith: by A. N. Banerji.

Drawn by K. P. Dass. Lith. by A. C. Chowdhary.

DALBERGIA BENTHAMI Prain.

Drawn by A. L. Singh.

Lith. by S. C. Mondul.

DALBERGIA RUBIGINOSA Roxb.

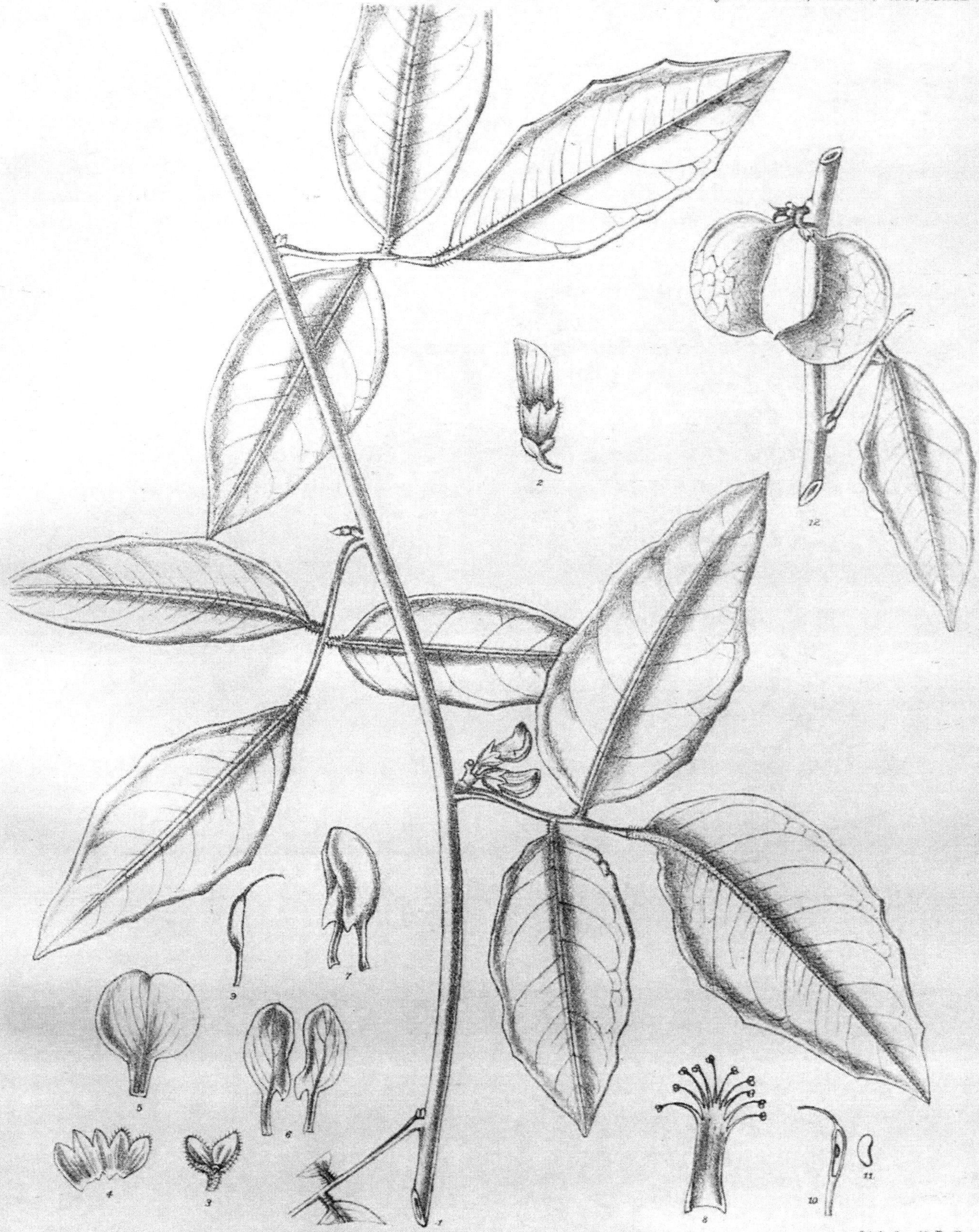

Drawn by A. L. Singh.

DALBERGIA MENOEIDES Prain.

Lith: by K. P. Dass.

Annals of the Roy. Bot. Garden, Calcutta, Vol. 10, PLATE 42

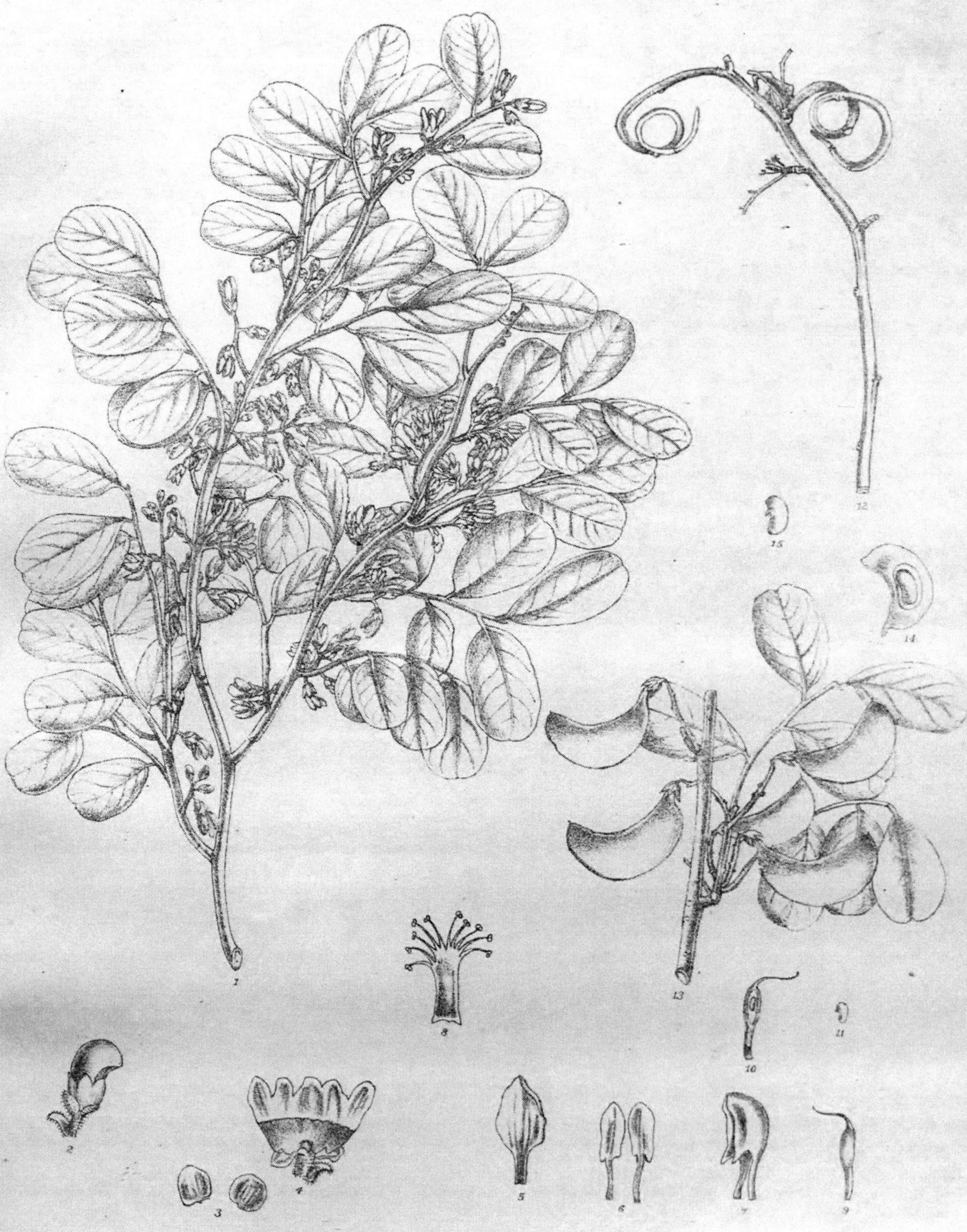

Drawn by D. N. Choudhury.

Lith. by K. P. Dass.

DALBERGIA TORTA Grah.

Drawn by A. D. Molla.

Lith: by A. C. Chowdhary.

DALBERGIA CONGESTA Grah.

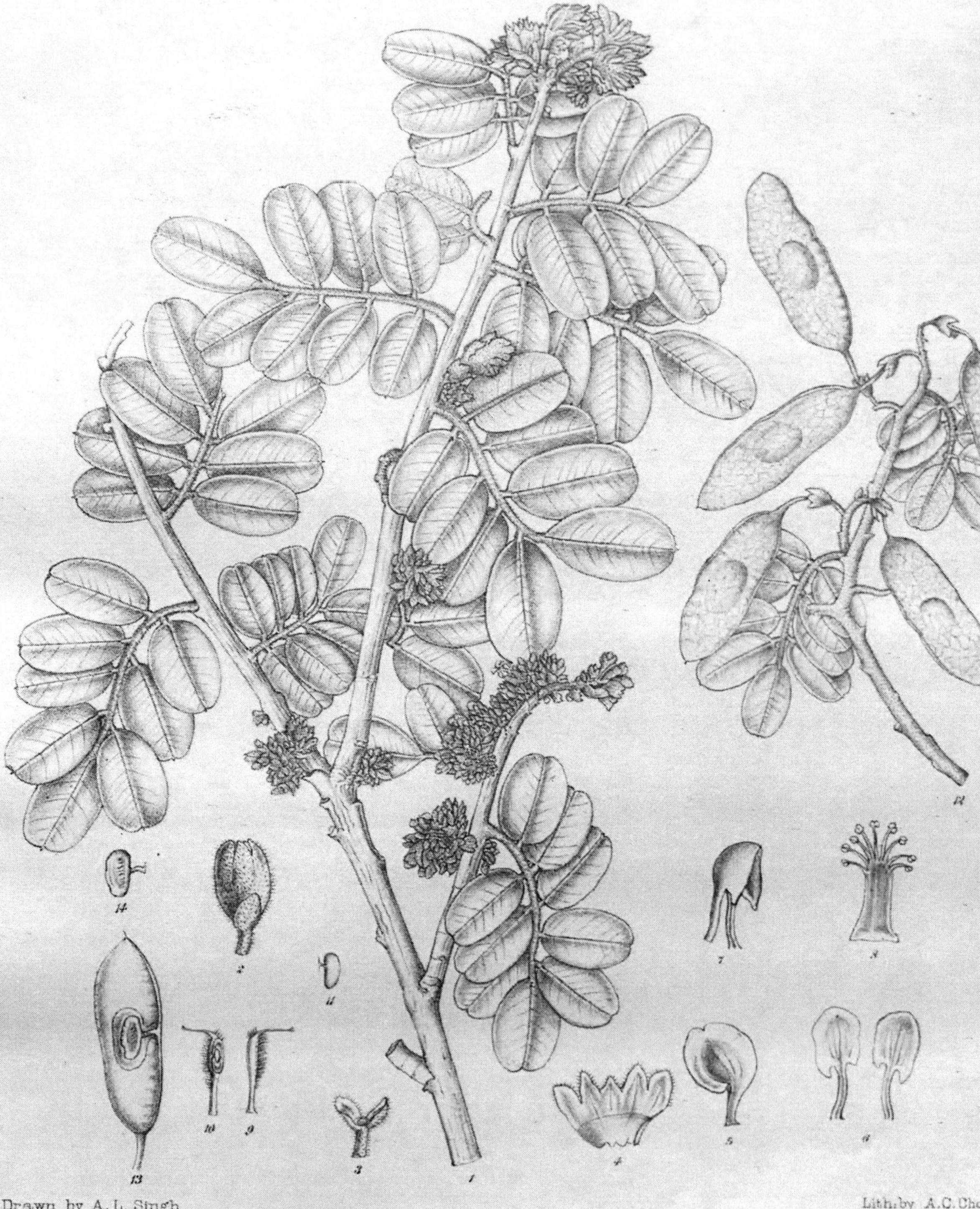

Drawn by A. L. Singh.

Lith. by A. C. Chowdhary.

DALBERGIA GARDNERIANA Benth.

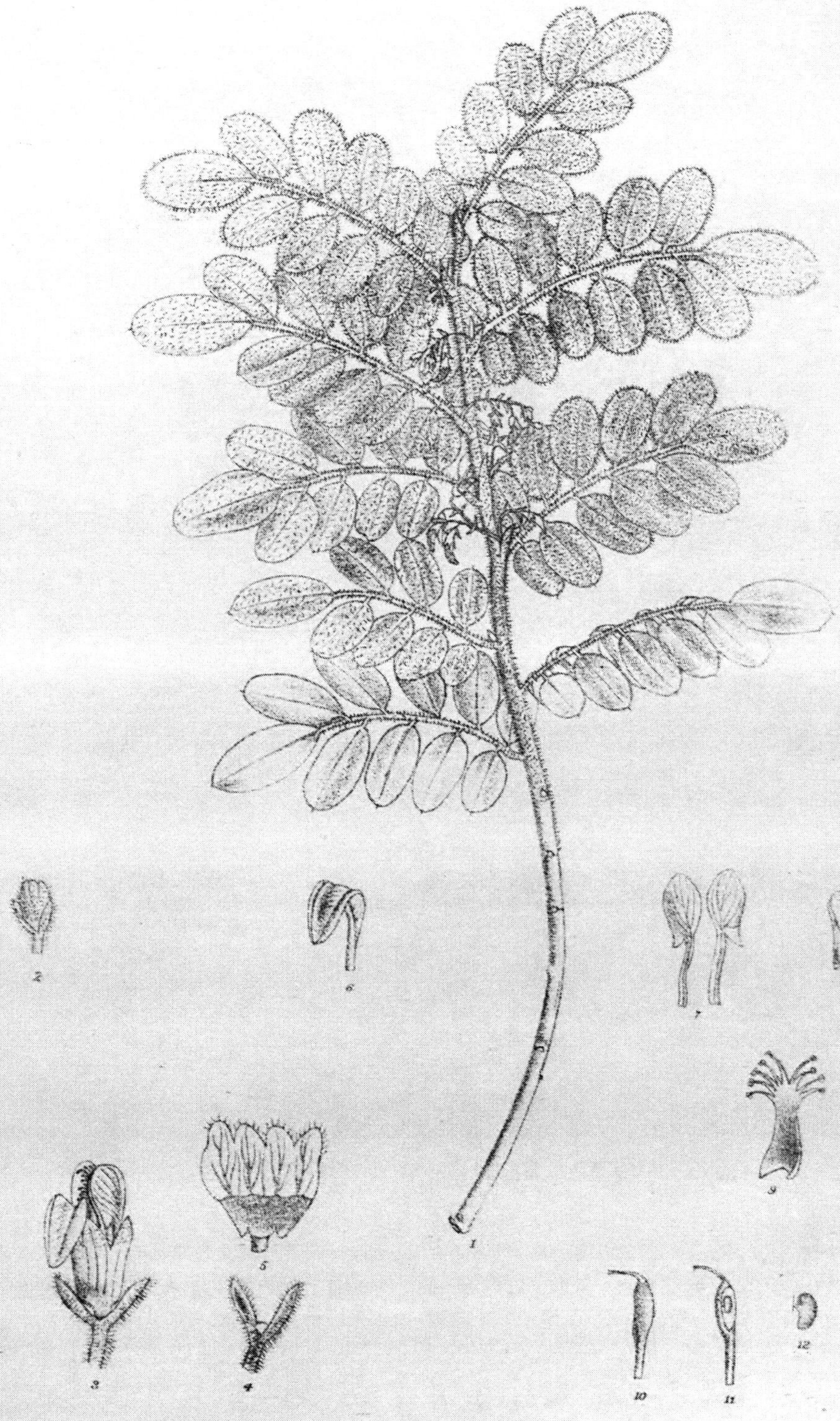

Drawn by K. P. Dass.

DALBERGIA HOSEANA Prain.

Lith. by A. K. Nath.

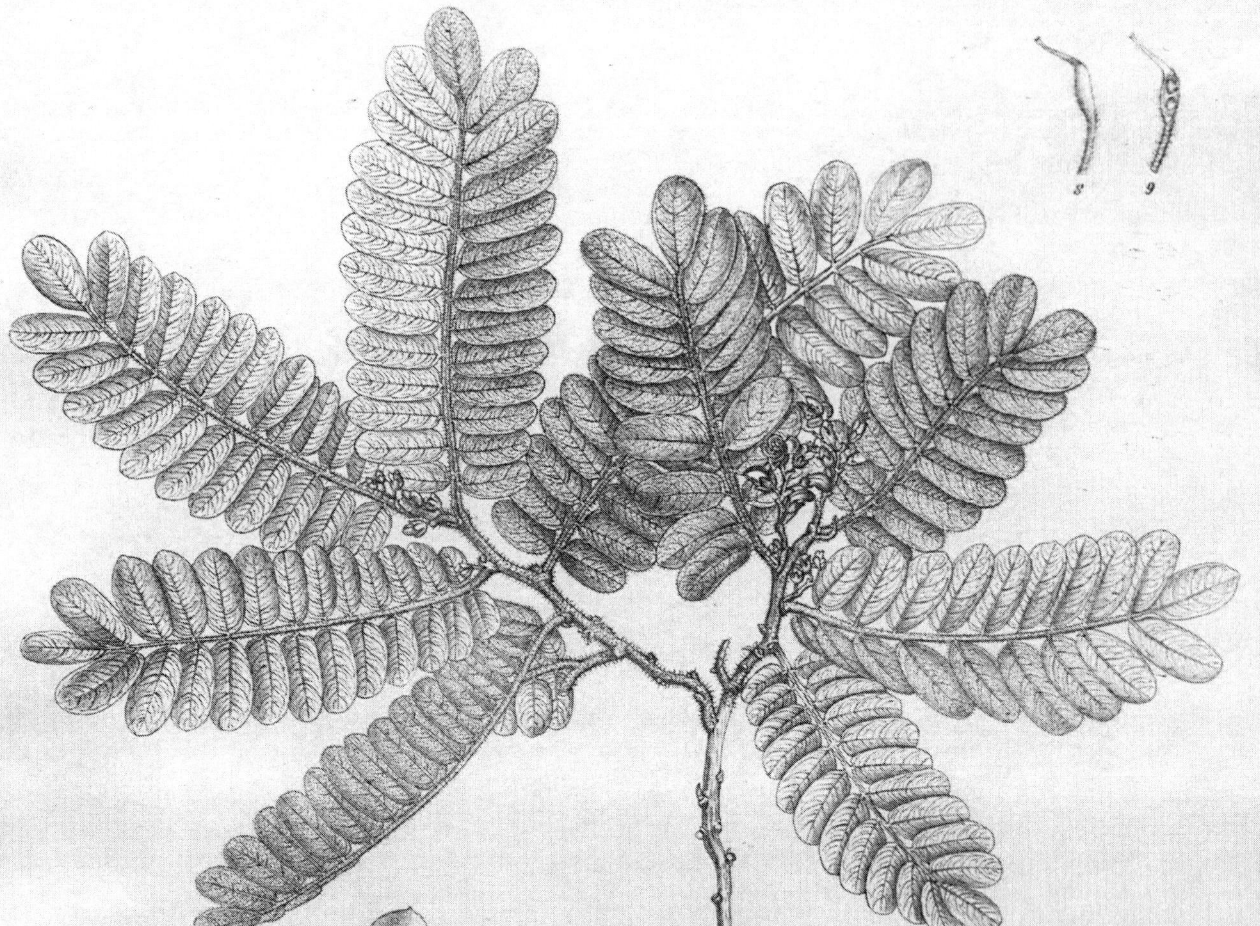

Drawn by K. P. Dass.

Lith: by S. C. Mondul.

DALBERGIA MALABARICA Prain.

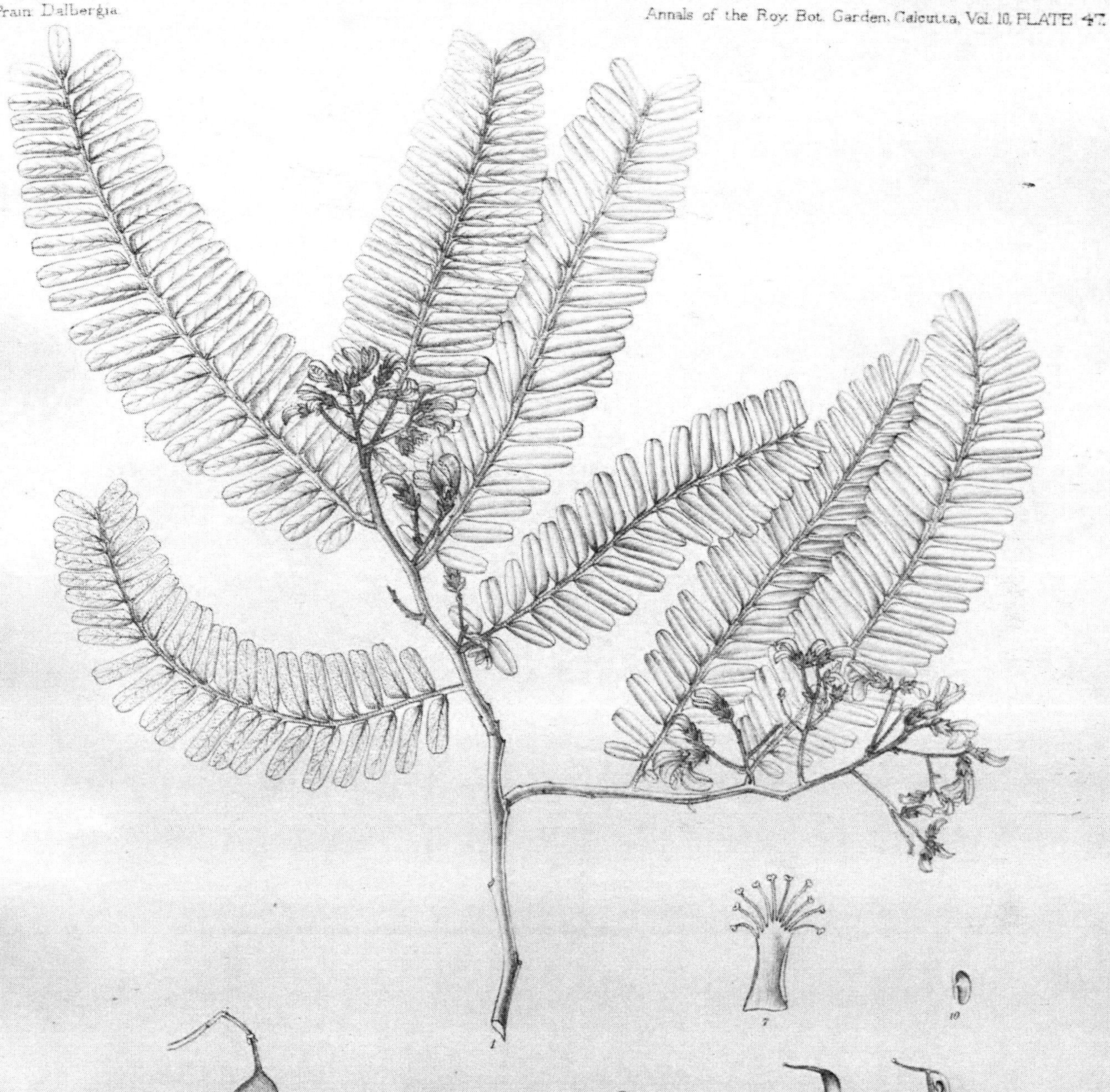

Drawn by D. N. Chaudhuri.

Lith. by K. D. Chandra.

DALBERGIA ACACIAEFOLIA Dalz.

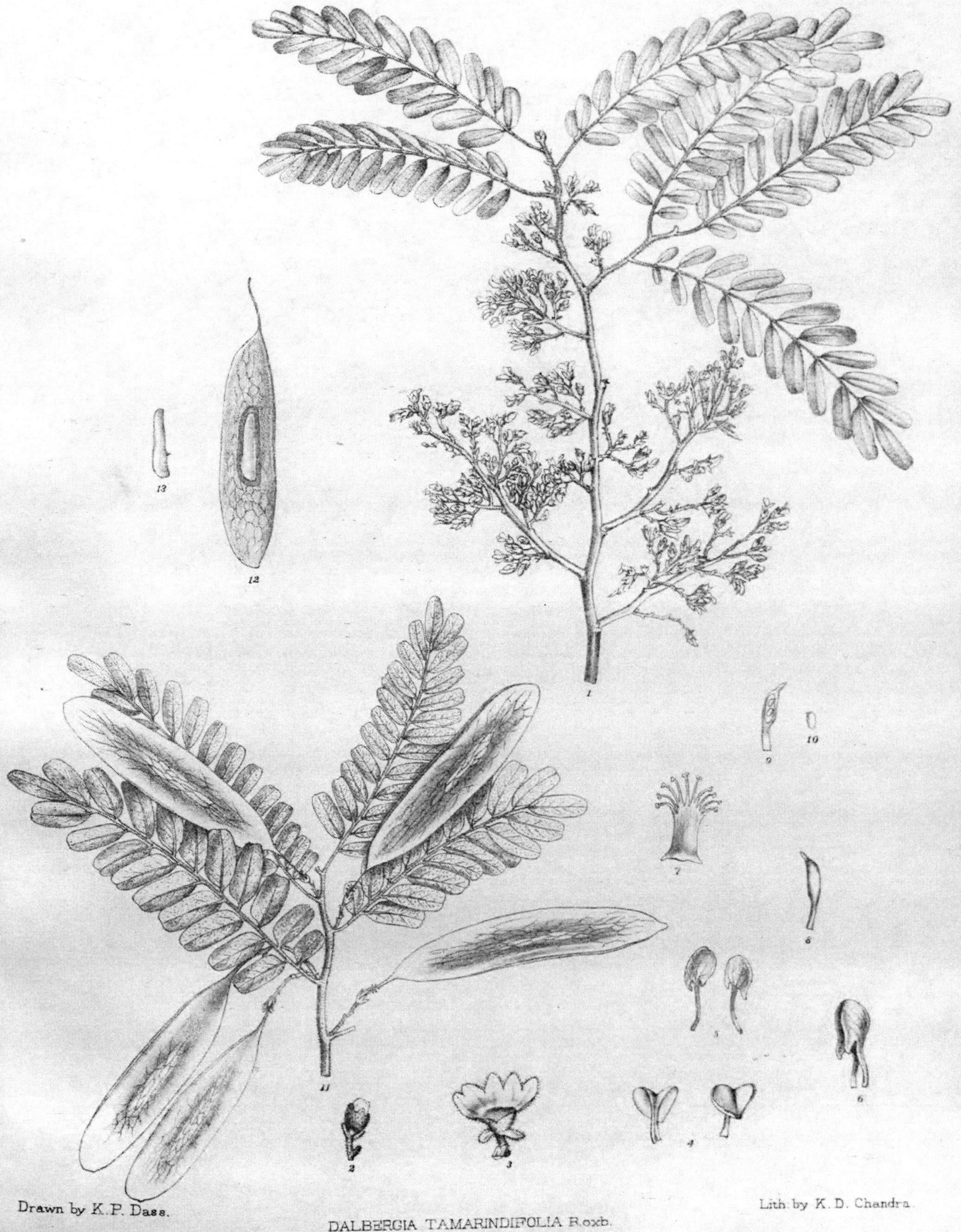

Drawn by K. P. Dass.

Lith: by K. D. Chandra.

DALBERGIA TAMARINDIFOLIA Roxb.

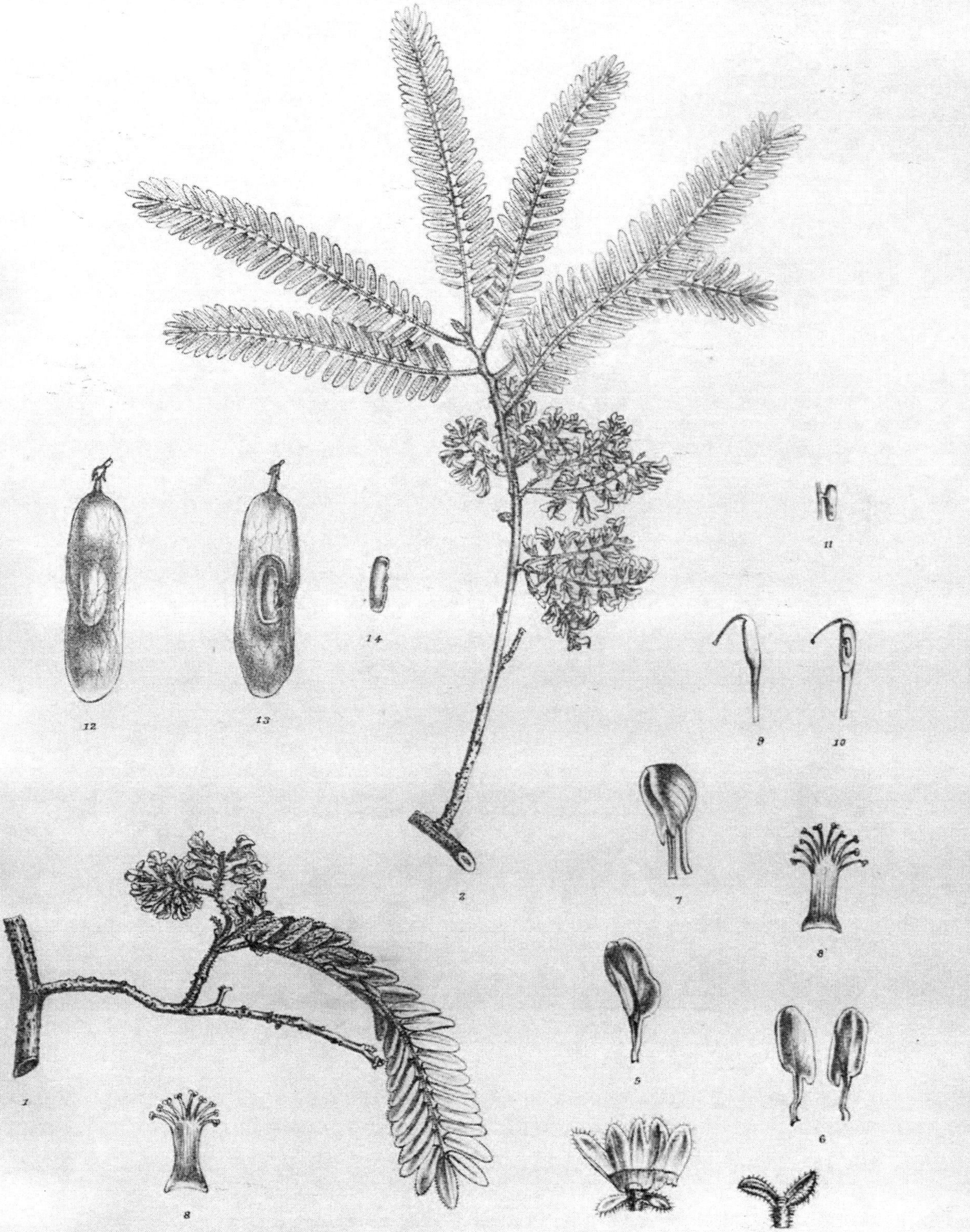

Drawn by K. P. Dass.

Lith: by Chitra Silpi Co.

DALBERGIA POLYPHYLLA Benth.

Drawn by A. D. Molla. Lith: by Chitra Silpi Co.

DALBERGIA JAHERII Buerck.

Annals of the Roy. Bot. Garden, Calcutta, Vol. 10. PLATE 81.

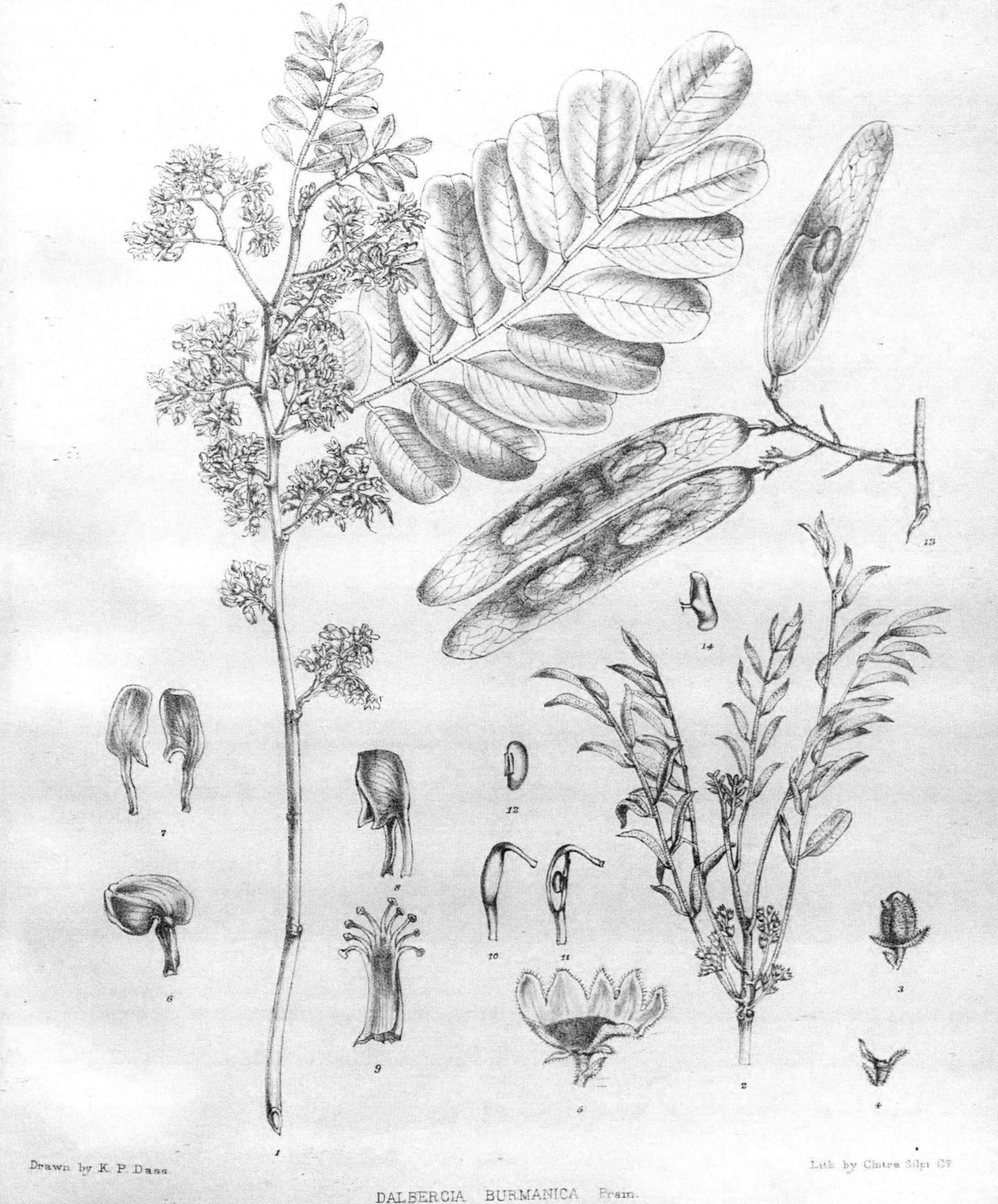

Drawn by K. P. Dass.

Lith. by Chitra Silpi Co.

DALBERGIA BURMANICA Prain.

Annals of the Roy. Bot. Garden, Calcutta. Vol. 10. PLATE 52.

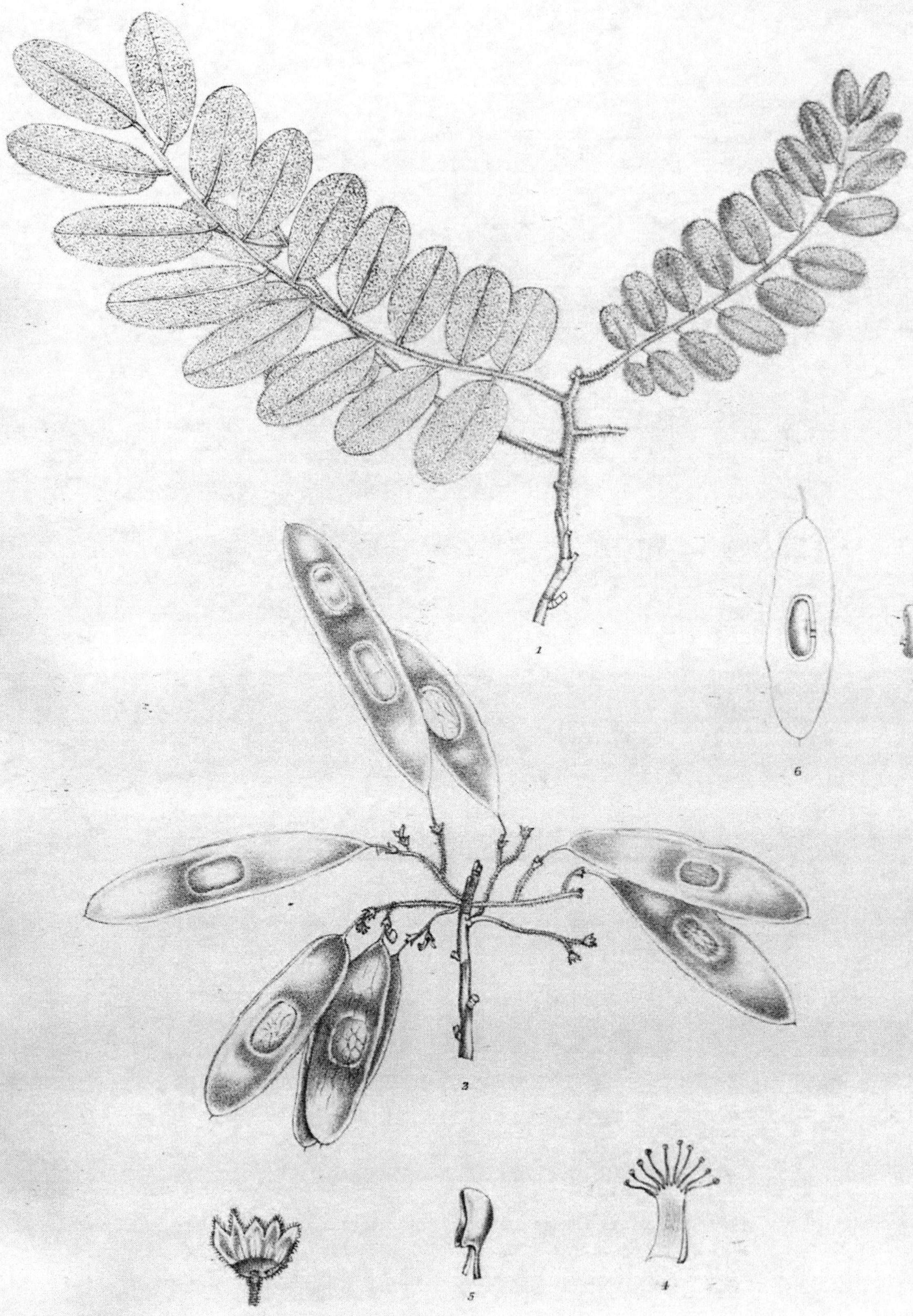

Drawn by K. P. Dass.

Lith. by Chitra Silpi Co.

DALBERGIA PIERREANA Prain.

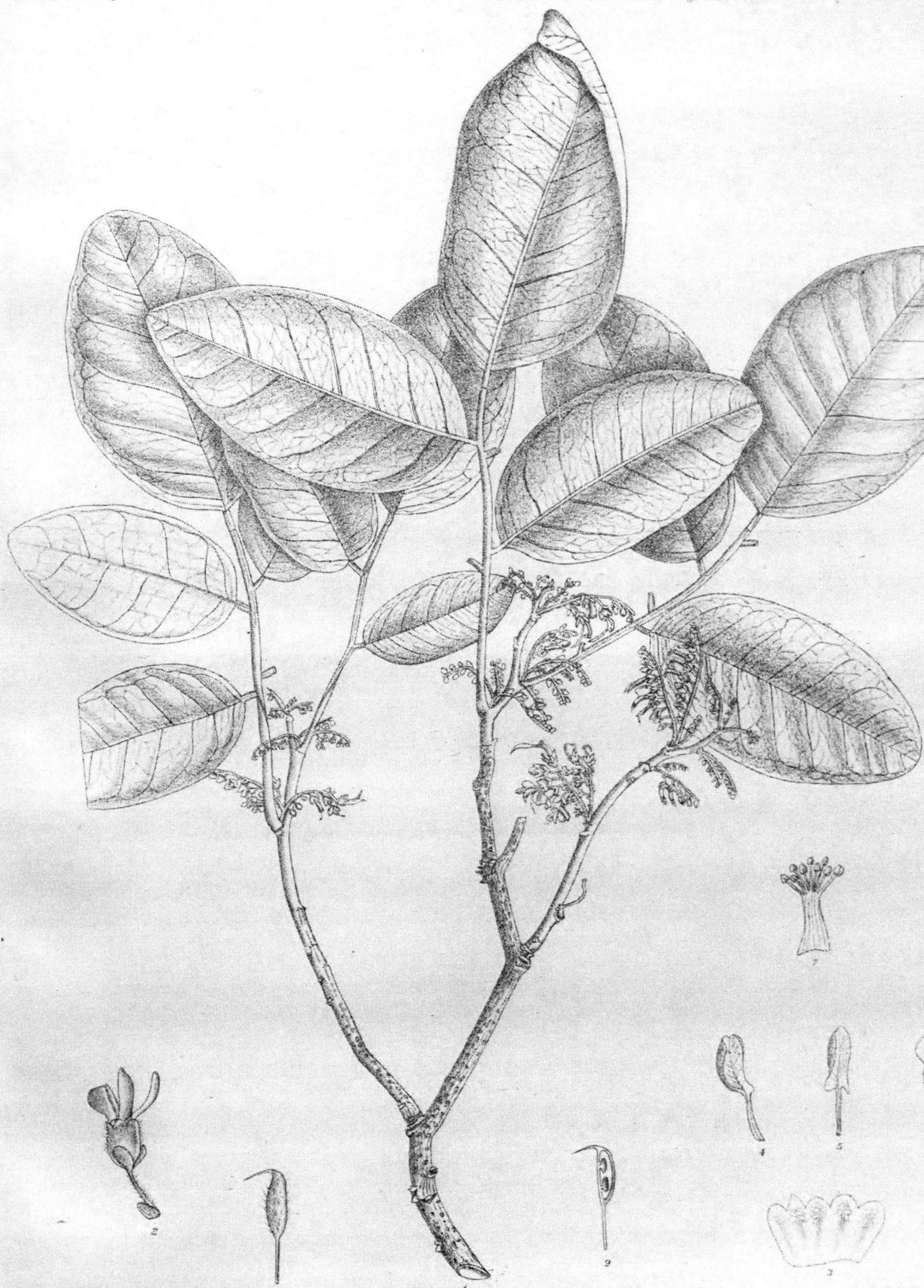

Drawn by K. P. Dass. Lith. by A. K. Nath.

DALBERGIA DENSA Benth.

Drawn by K. P. Dass.

DALBERGIA DENSA Benth. var. AUSTRALIS Prain.

Lith: by A. C. Singha.

Drawn by D. N. Choudhury.

DALBERGIA VELUTINA Benth.

Lith: by K.P. Dass.

Drawn by D. N. Choudhury.

DALBERGIA VELUTINA Benth. VAR MAINGAYI Prain.

Lith. by A. N. Banerji.

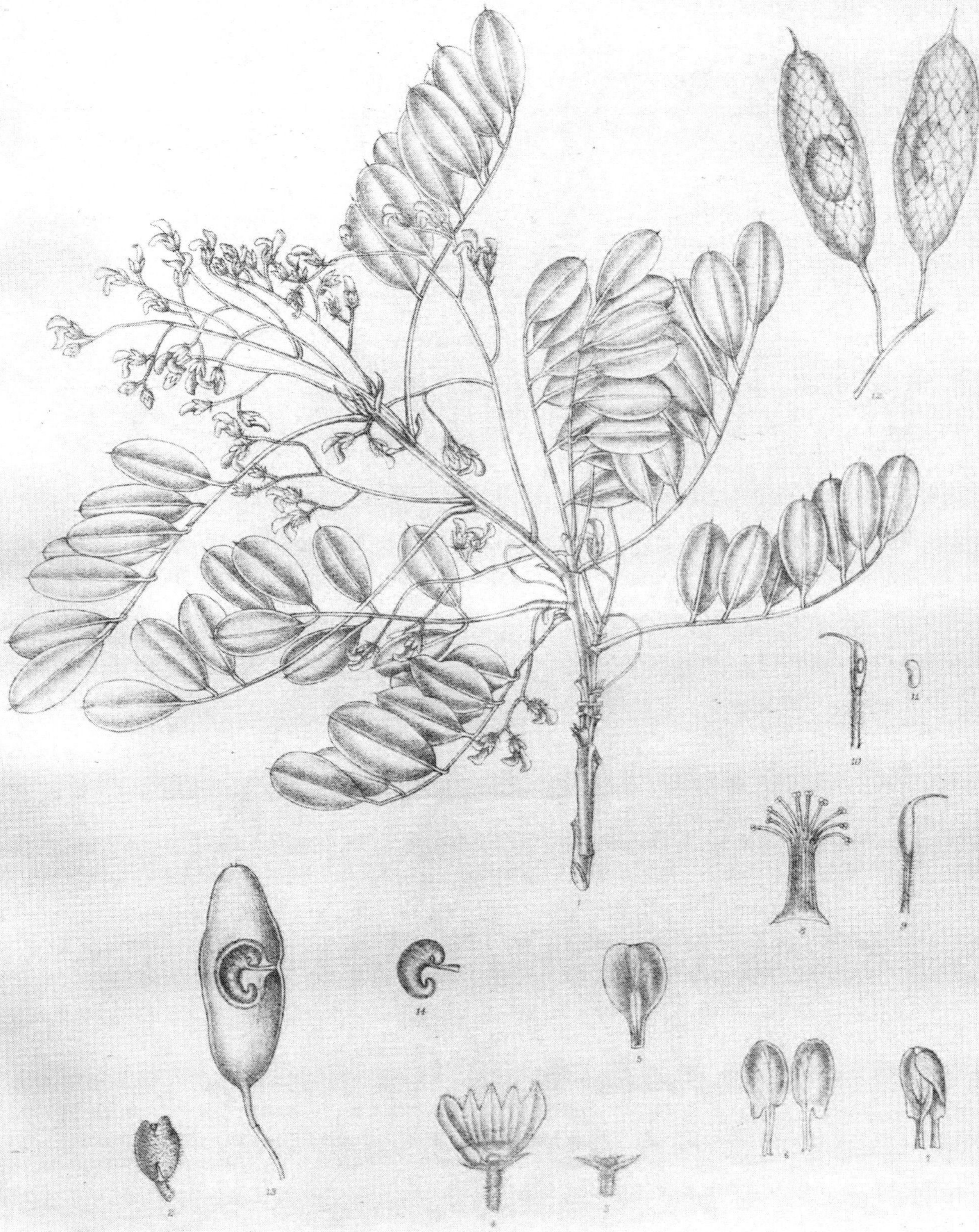

Drawn by A. L. Singh.

Lith. by A. C. Singha.

DALBERGIA BORNEENSIS Prain.

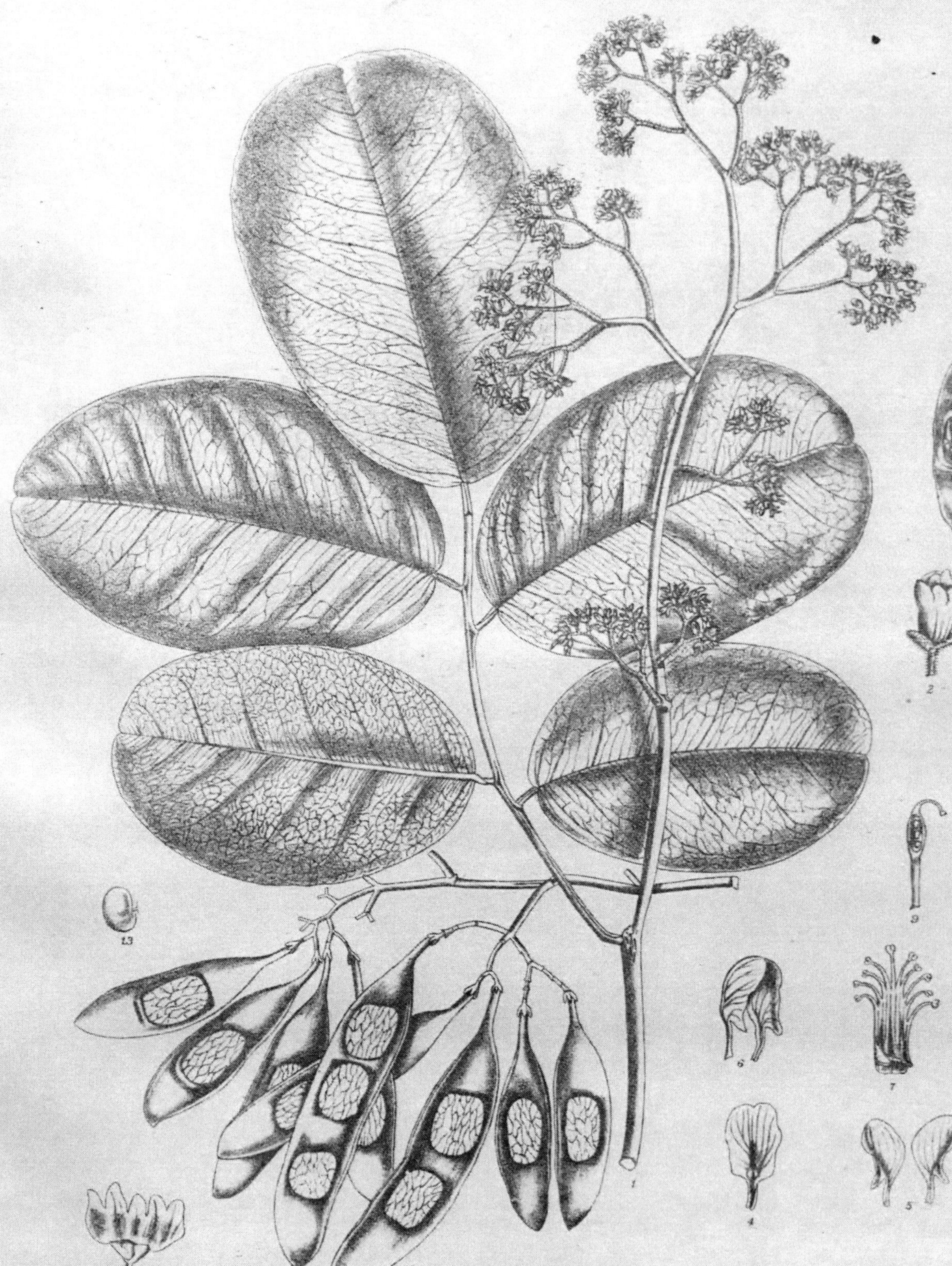

Drawn by K. P. Dass.

DALBERGIA OBTUSIFOLIA Prain.

Lith: by A. K. Nath.

Drawn by K. P. Dass.

Lith: by A. K. Nath.

DALBERGIA OVATA Grah.

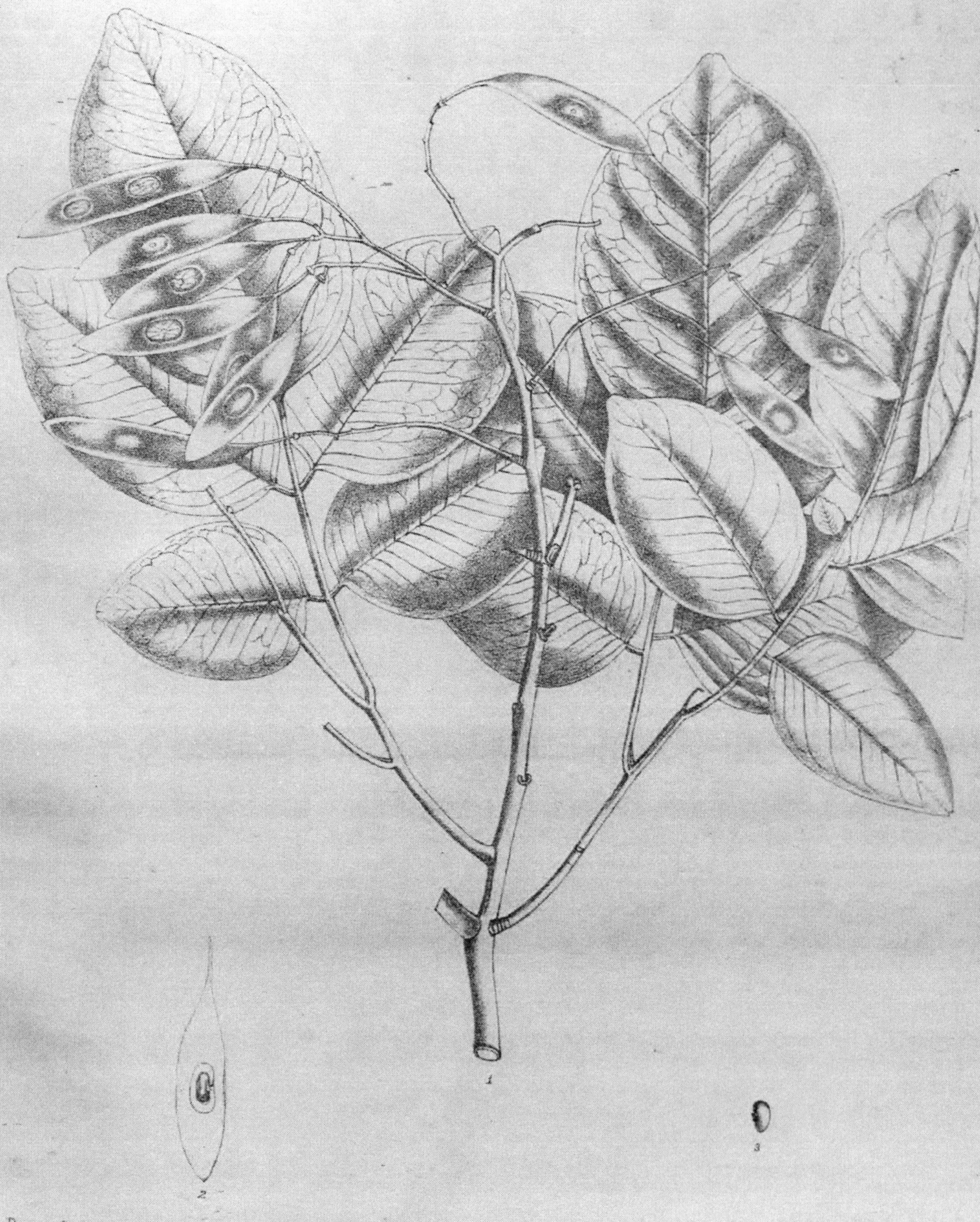

Drawn by K. P. Dass.

DALBERGIA CAMBODIANA Pierre.

Lith: by A. C. Singha.

Drawn by K. P. Dass.

Lith: by K. P. Dass.

DALBERGIA TONKINENSIS Prain.

Annals of the Roy. Bot. Garden, Calcutta, Vol. 10, PLATE 62.

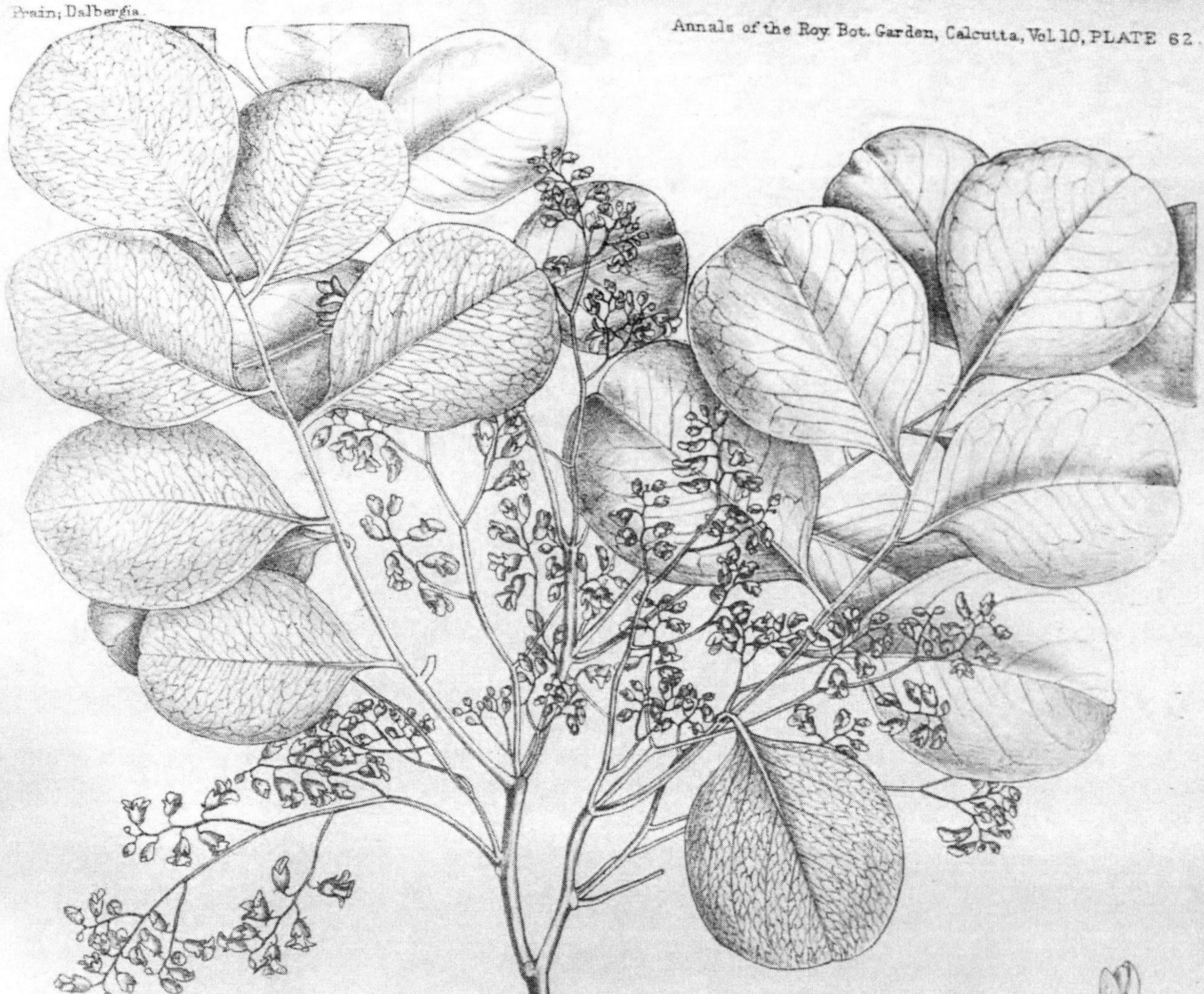

Drawn by K. P. Dass. Lith by K. P. Dass.

DALBERGIA LATIFOLIA Roxb.

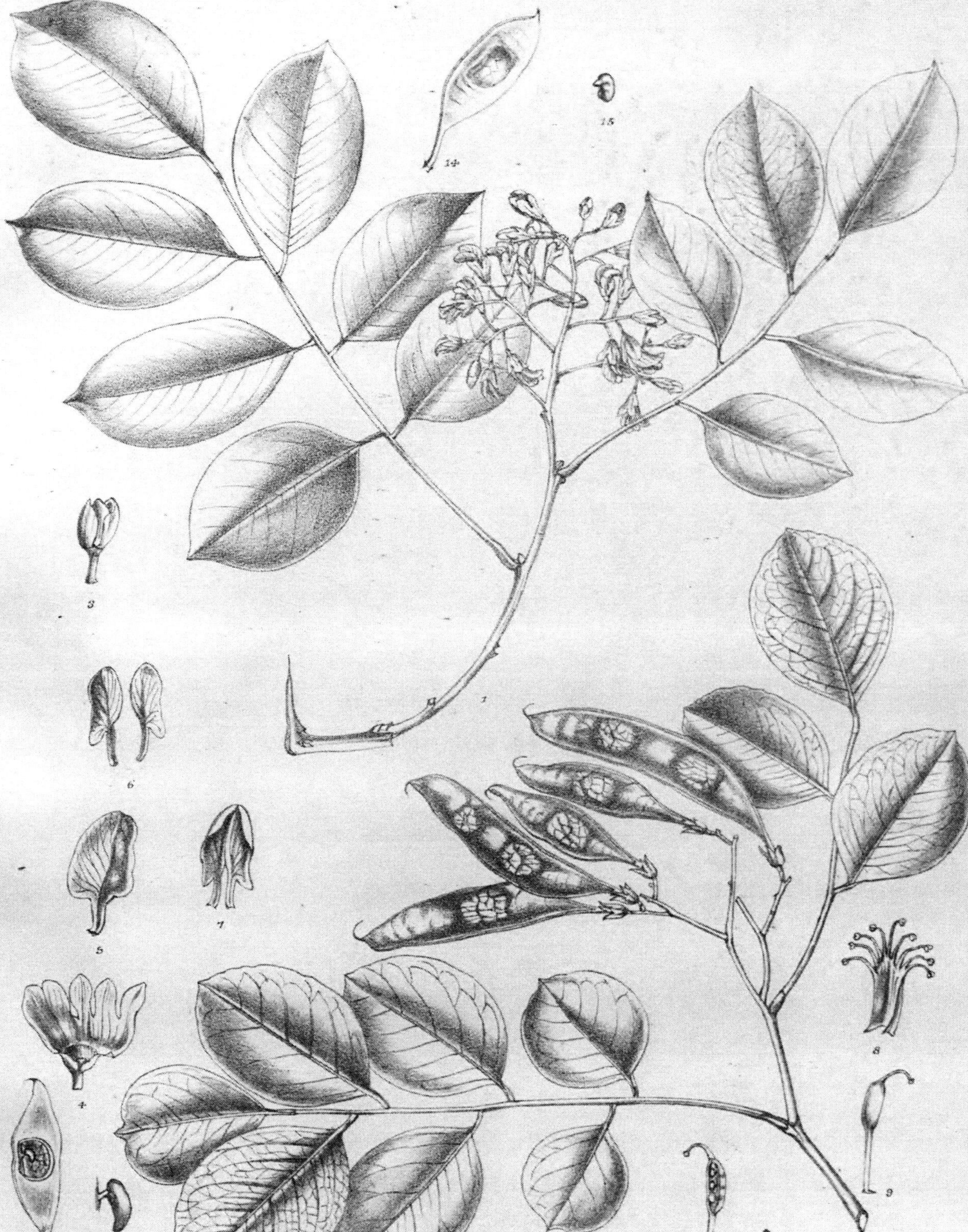

Drawn by K. P. Dass.

Lith: by Chitra Silpi Co

DALBERGIA SISSOIDES Grah.

Annals of the Roy. Bot. Garden, Calcutta, Vol 10, PLATE 64

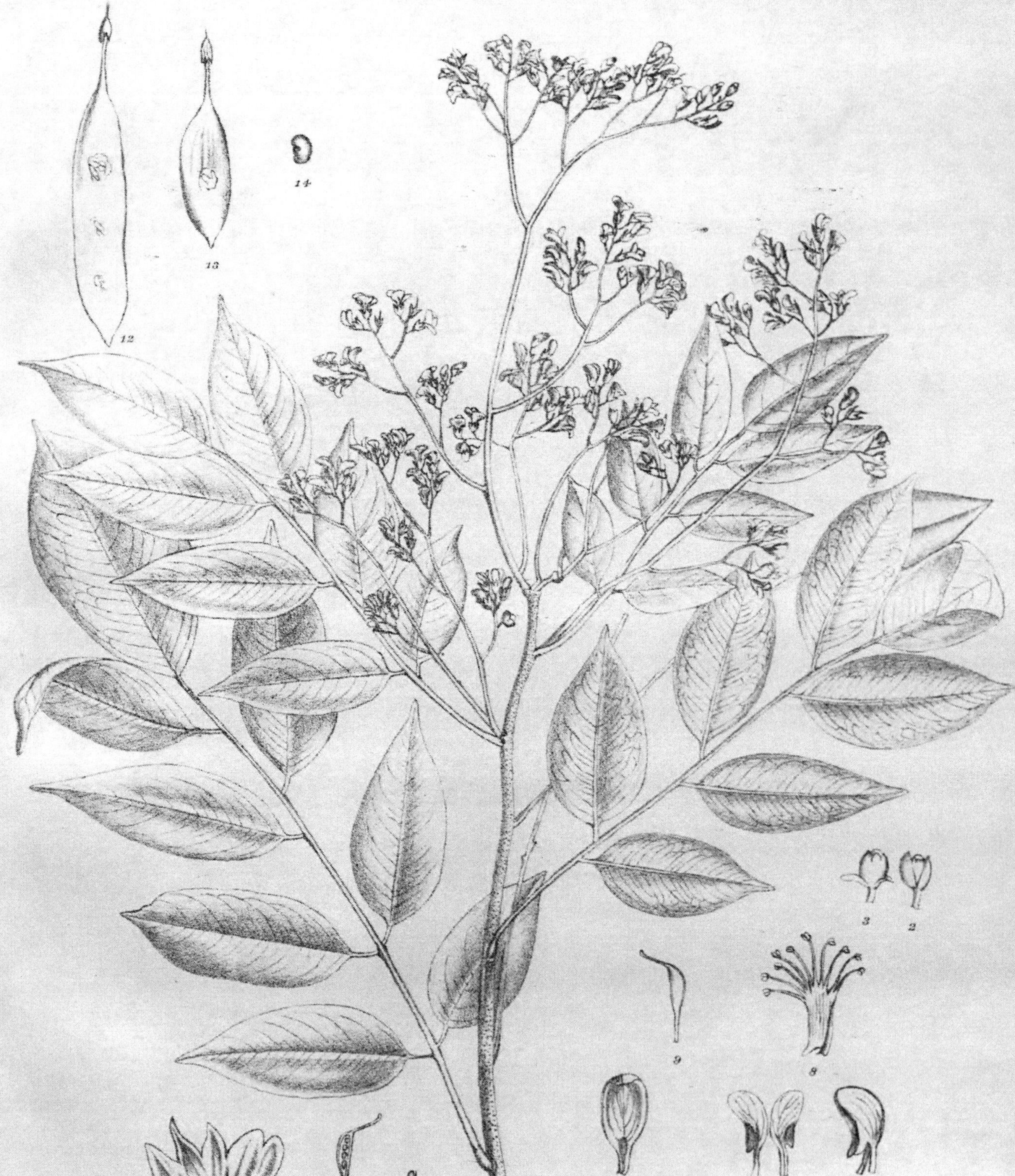

Drawn by K.P. Dass

Lith. by Chitra Silpi Co.

DALBERGIA COCHINCHINENSIS Pierre

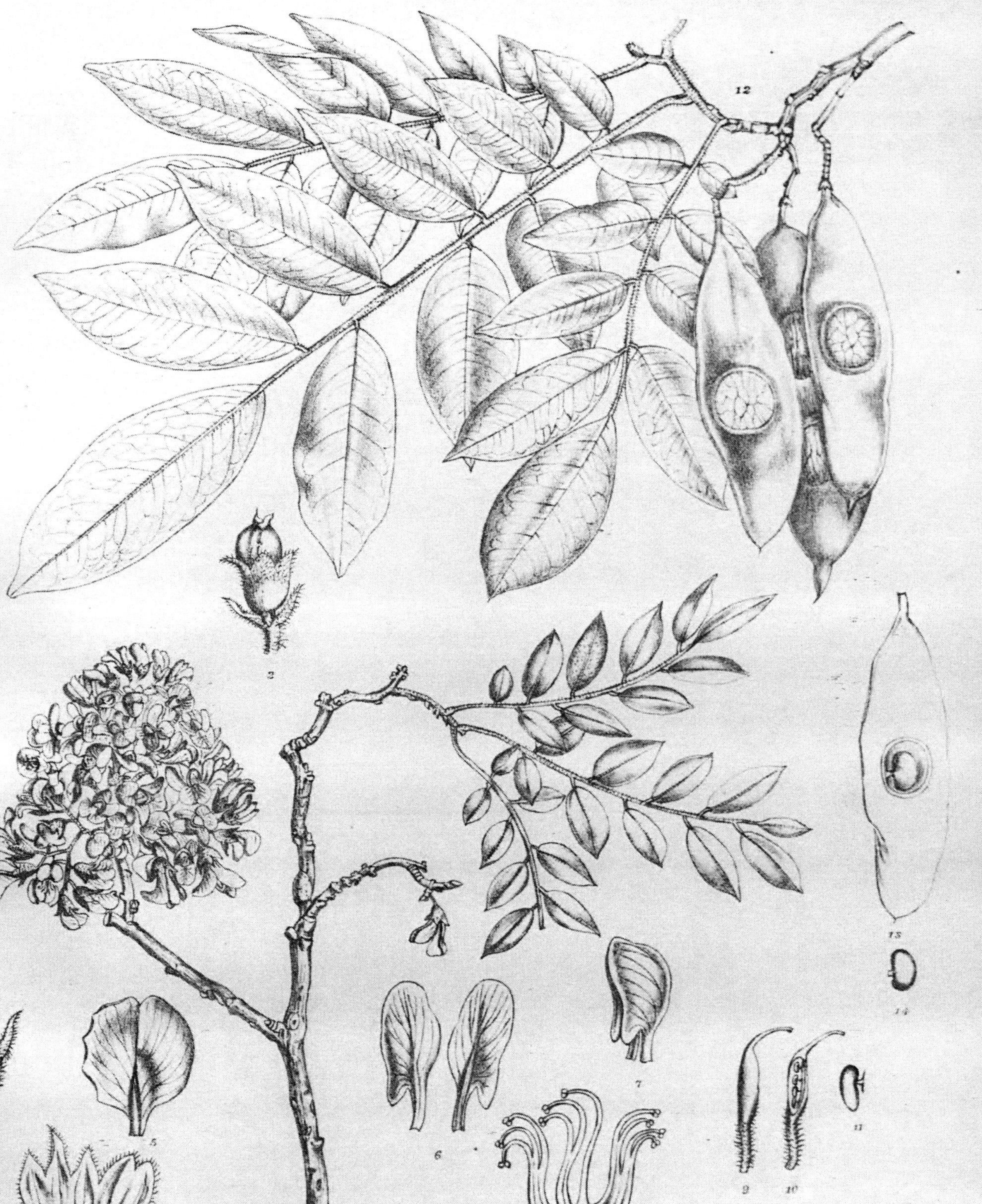

Drawn by K. P. Dass Lith. by Chitra Silpi Co.

DALBERGIA POLYADELPHA Prain.

Drawn by K. P. Dass.

Lith: by Chitra Silpi Co.

DALBERGIA SERICEA G. Don.

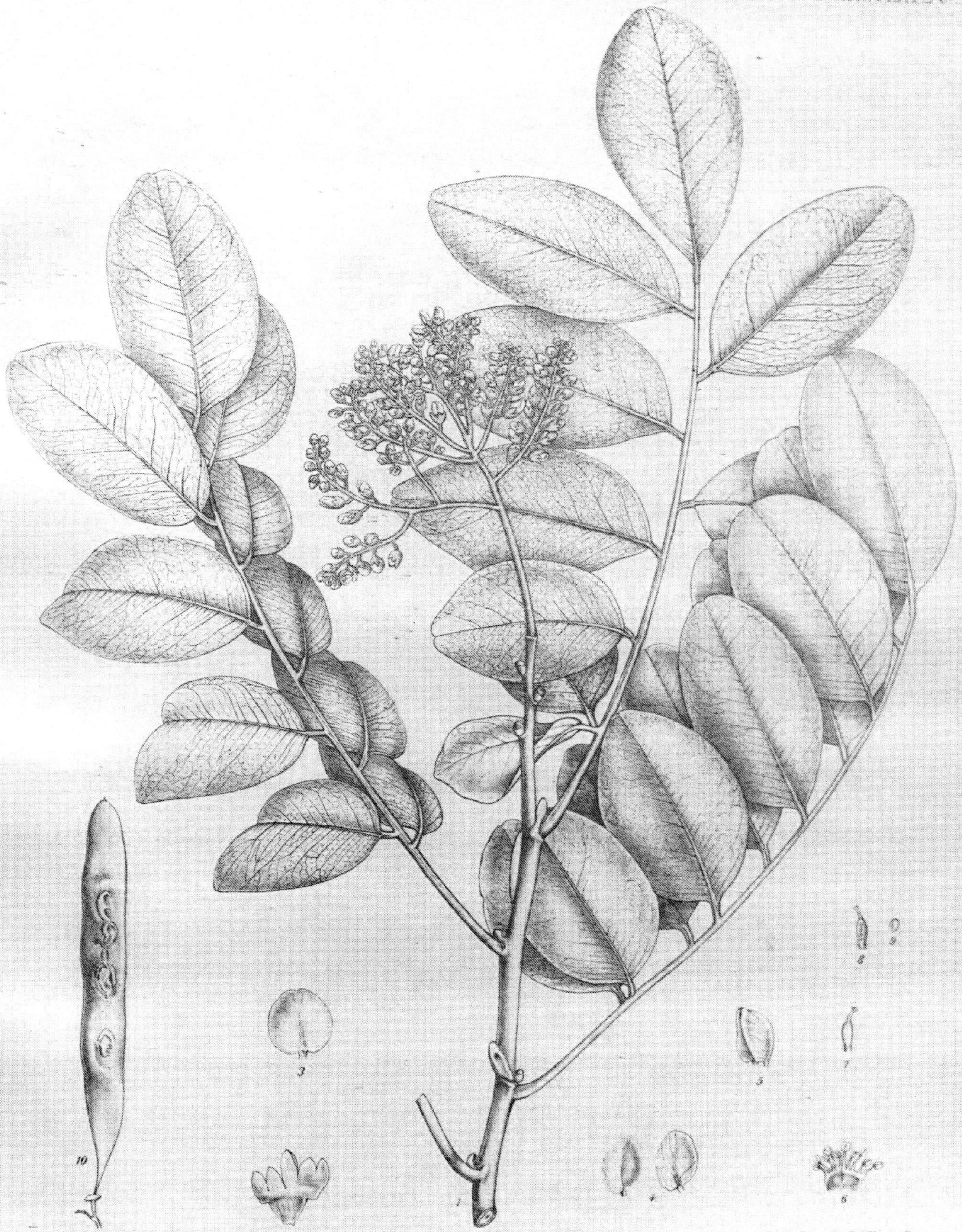

Drawn by K. P. Dass

Lith. by A. C. Chowdhary

DALBERGIA SACERDOTUM Prain.

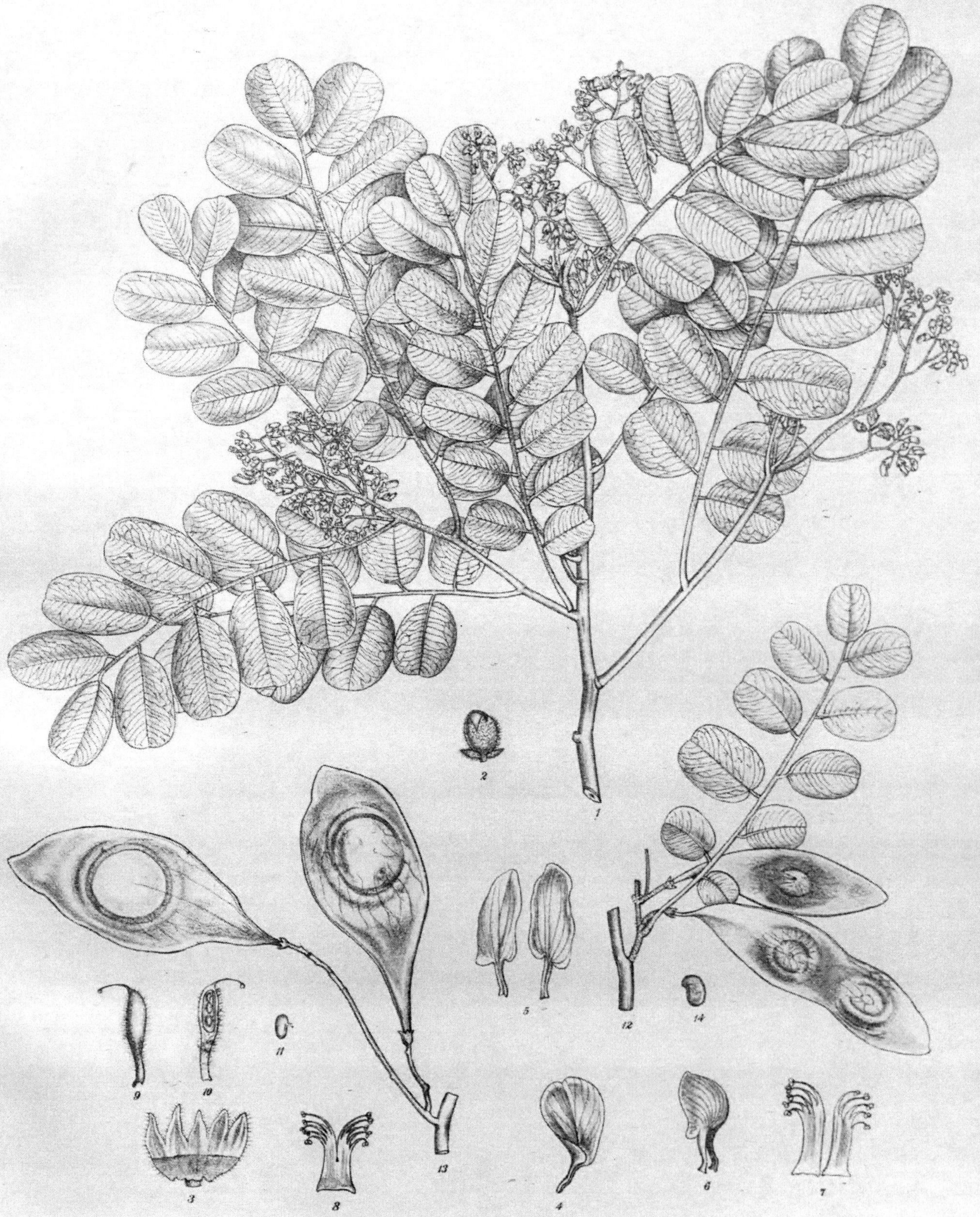

Drawn by K. P. Dass.

Lith. by A.C. Chowdhary.

DALBERGIA PANICULATA Roxb.

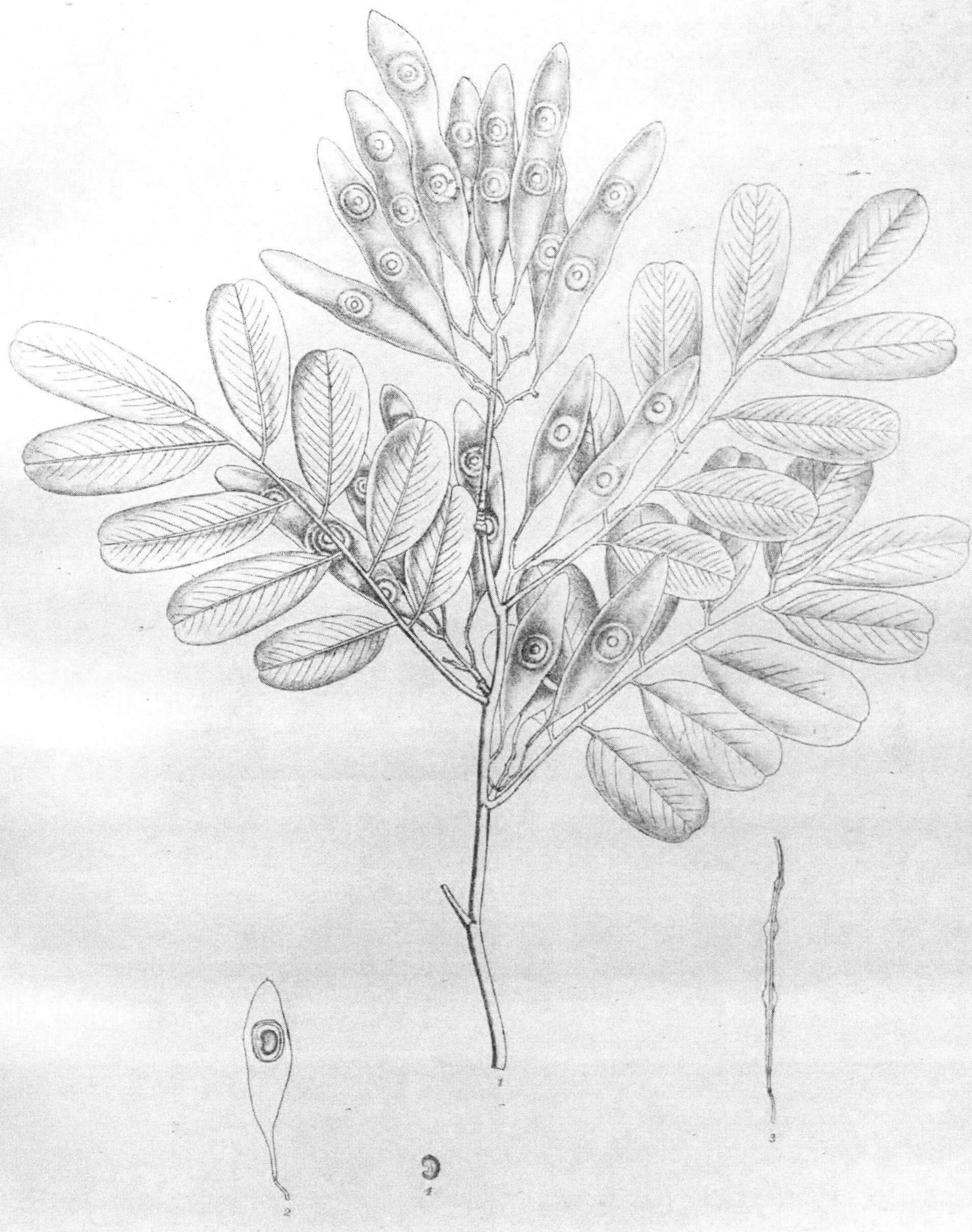

Drawn by K. P. Dass.

DALBERGIA PANICULATA Roxb. VAR. SAIGONENSIS.

Lith: by A.N. Banerji.

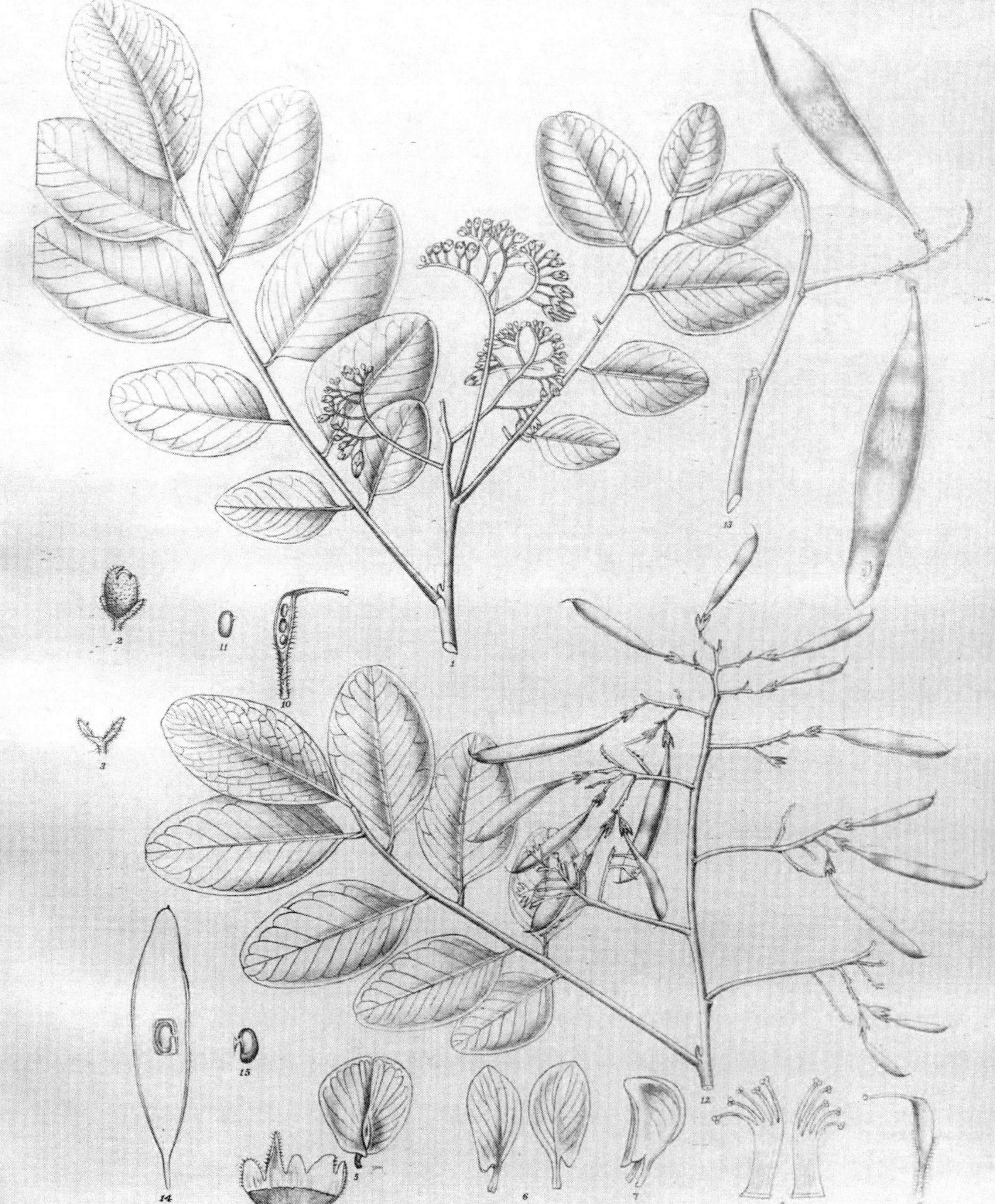

Drawn by A. D. Molla. Lith: by K. D. Chandra.

DALBERGIA HUPEANA Hance.

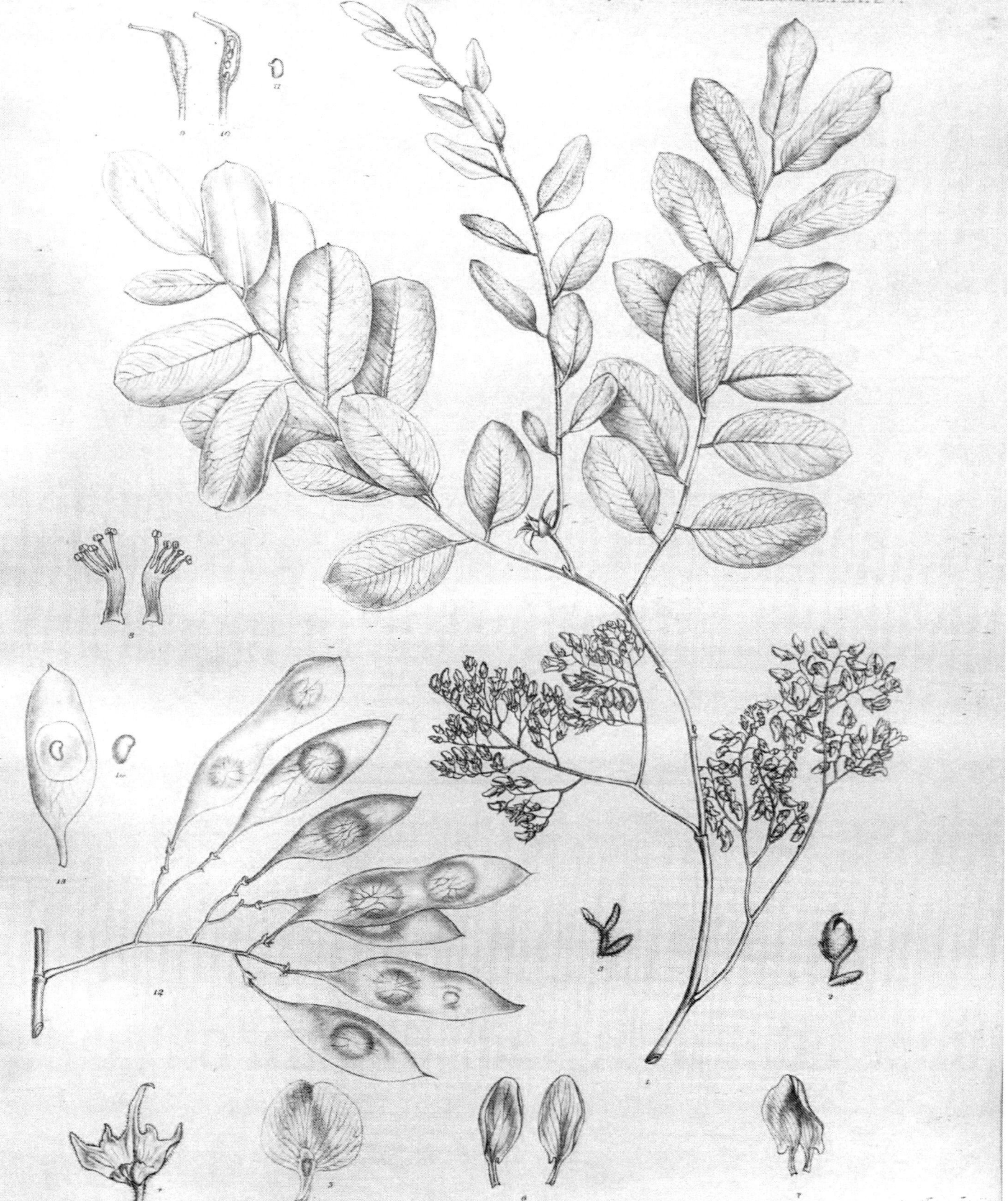

Drawn by K. P. Dass.

DALBERGIA ASSAMICA Benth.

Lith. by K. D. Chandra.

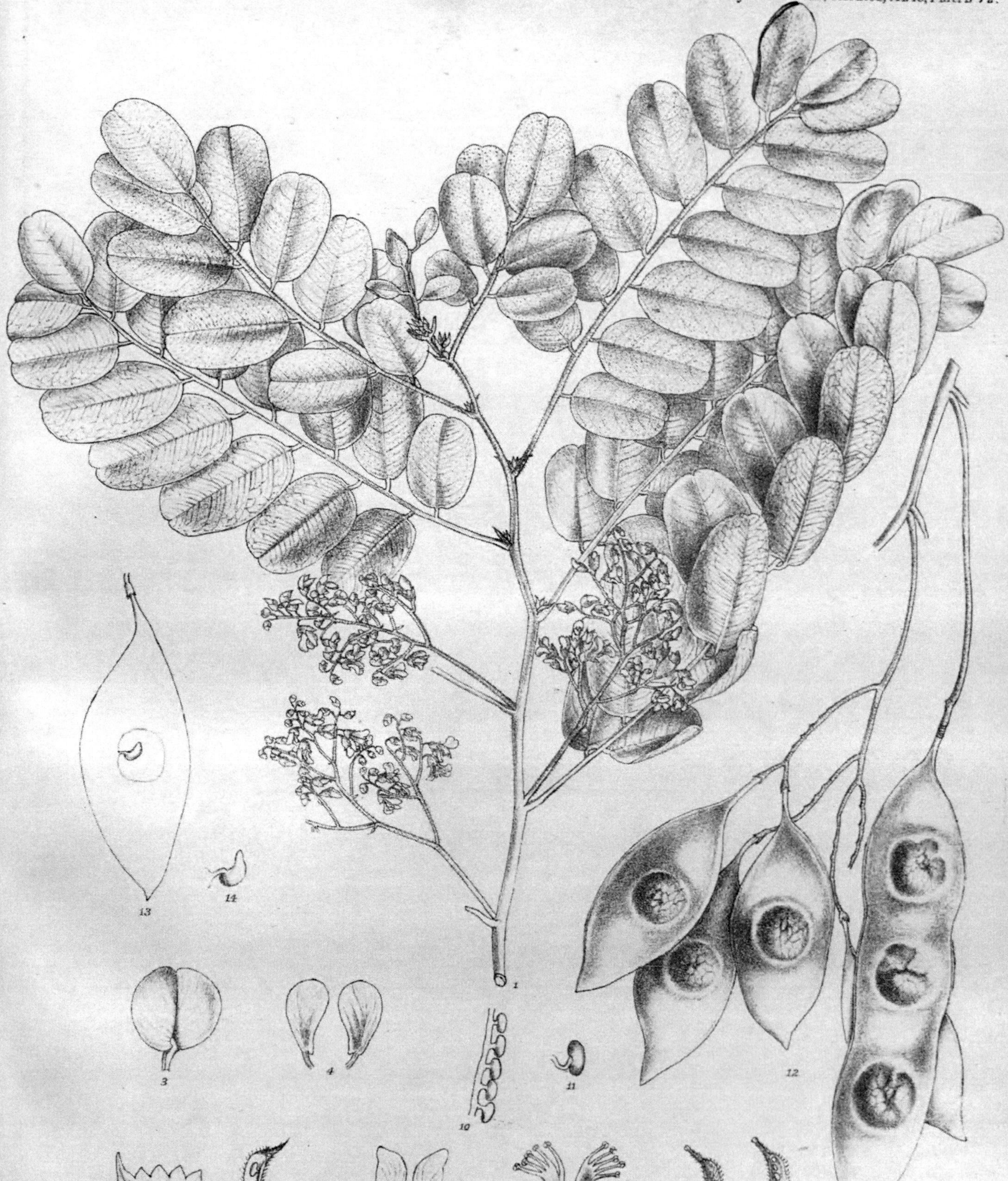

Drawn by K.P. Dass. Lith: by K.P. Dass.

DALBERGIA BALANSAE Prain.

Drawn by K.P. Dass.

Lith: by A.C. Singha.

DALBERGIA MINAHASSAE Koord.

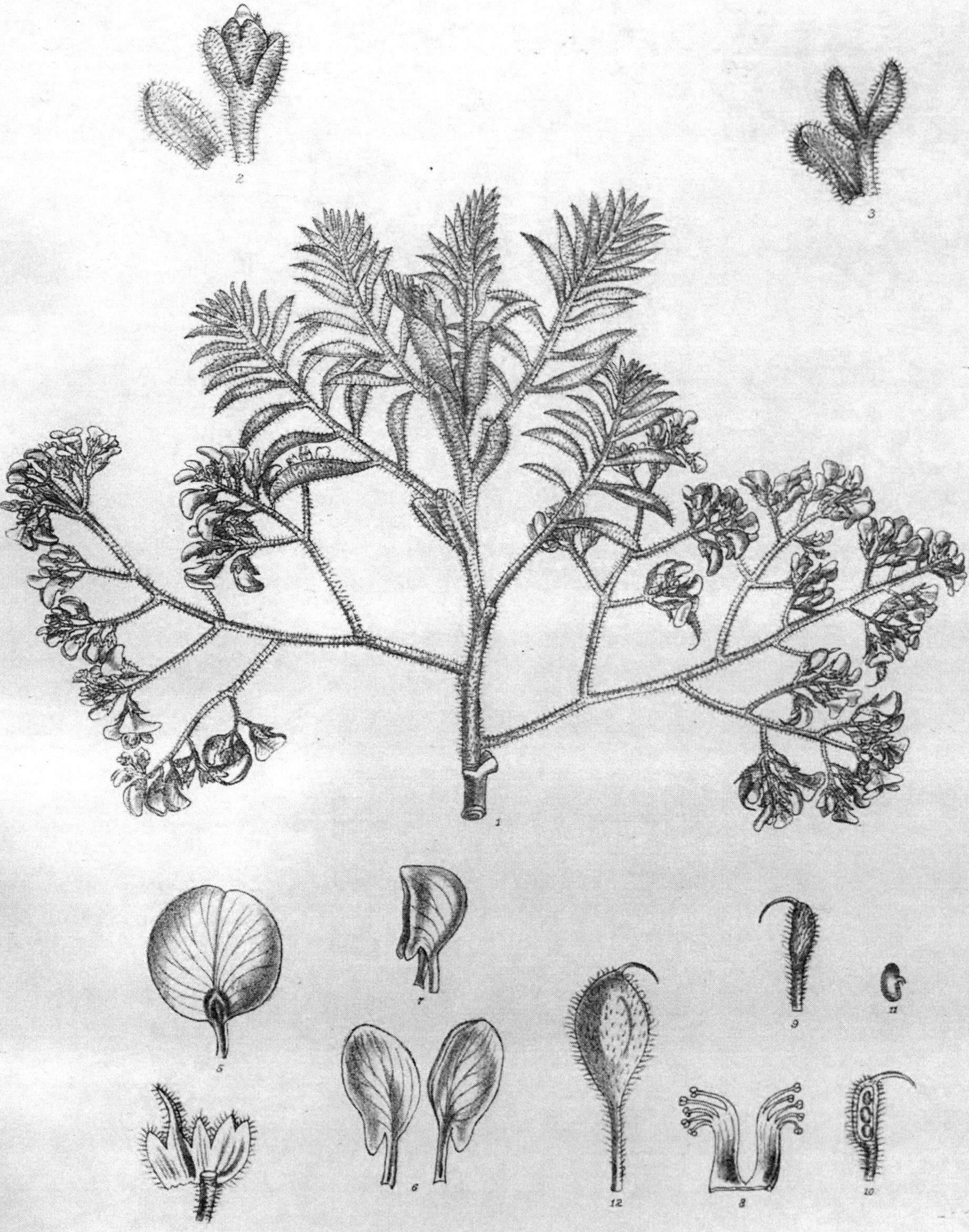

Drawn by K. P. Dass.

Lith. by A. C. Singha.

DALBERGIA SZEMAOENSIS Prain.

Annals of the Roy. Bot. Garden, Calcutta, Vol. 10, PLATE 75.

Drawn by K. P. Dass.

DALBERGIA OLIVERI Gamble.

Lith: by A. N. Banerji.

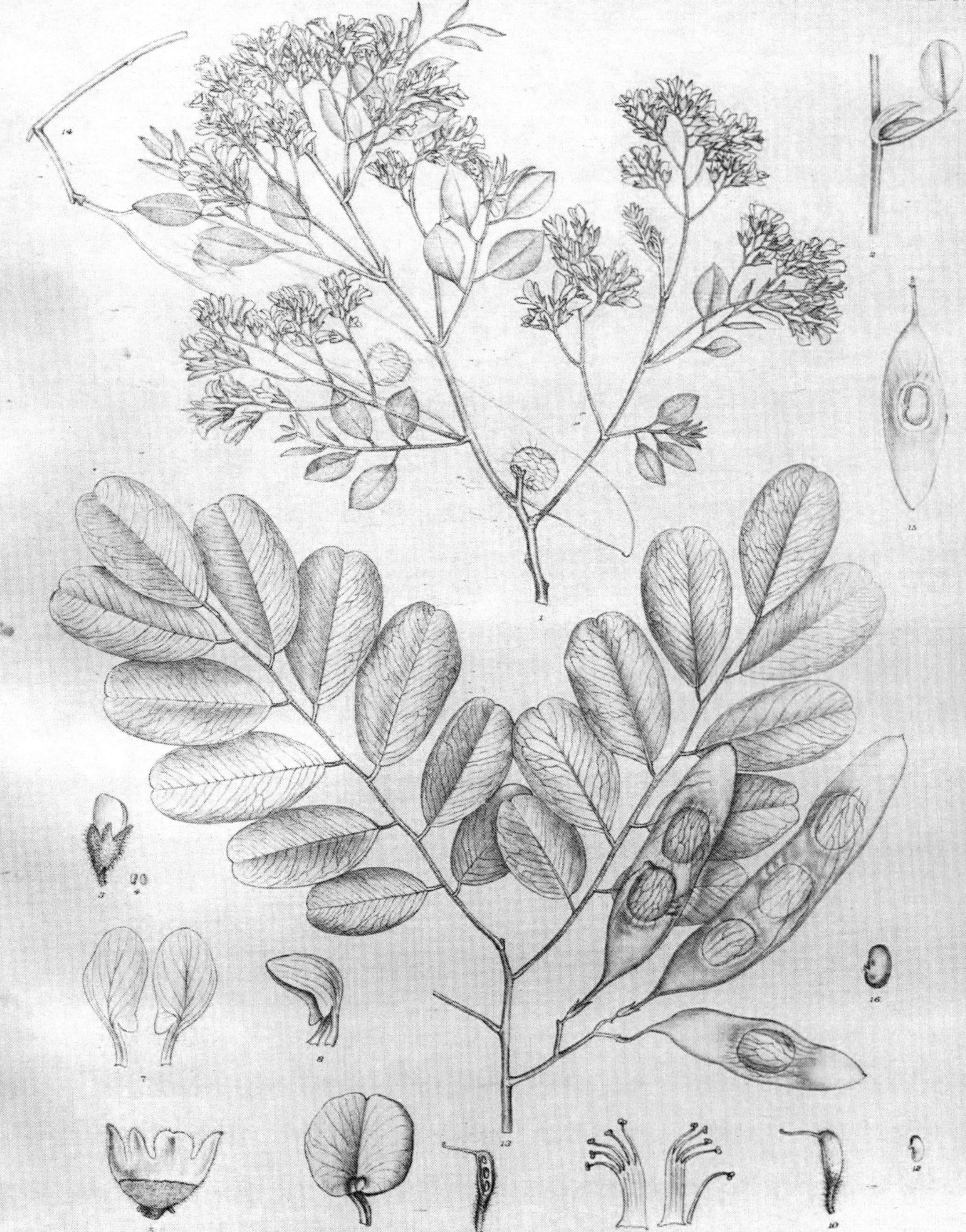

Drawn by K. P. Dass

DALBERGIA LANCEOLARIA Linn. f.

Lith by K. D. Chandra

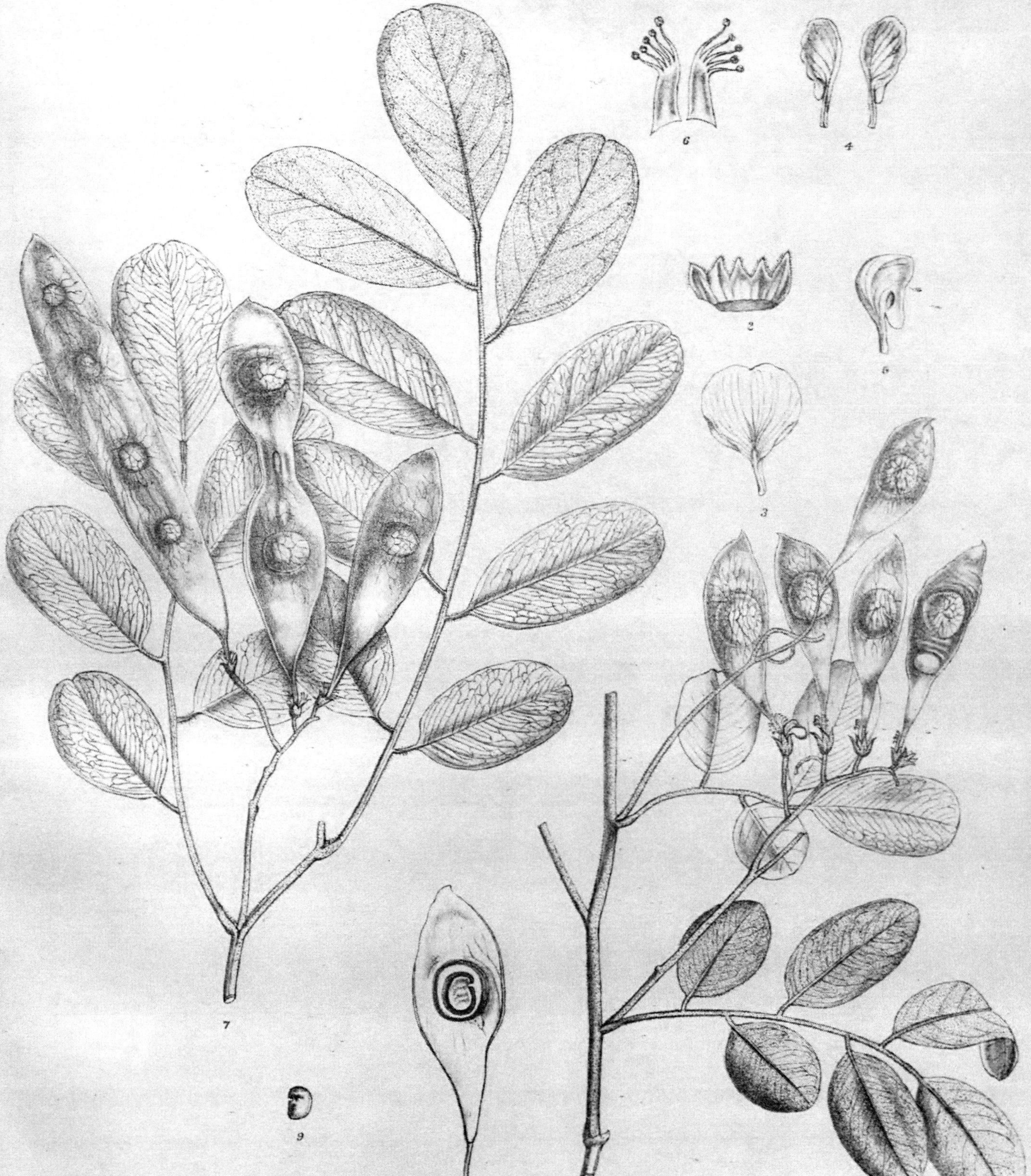

Drawn by K. P. Dass.

Lith: by Chitra Silpi Co.

DALBERGIA HEMSLEYI Prain.

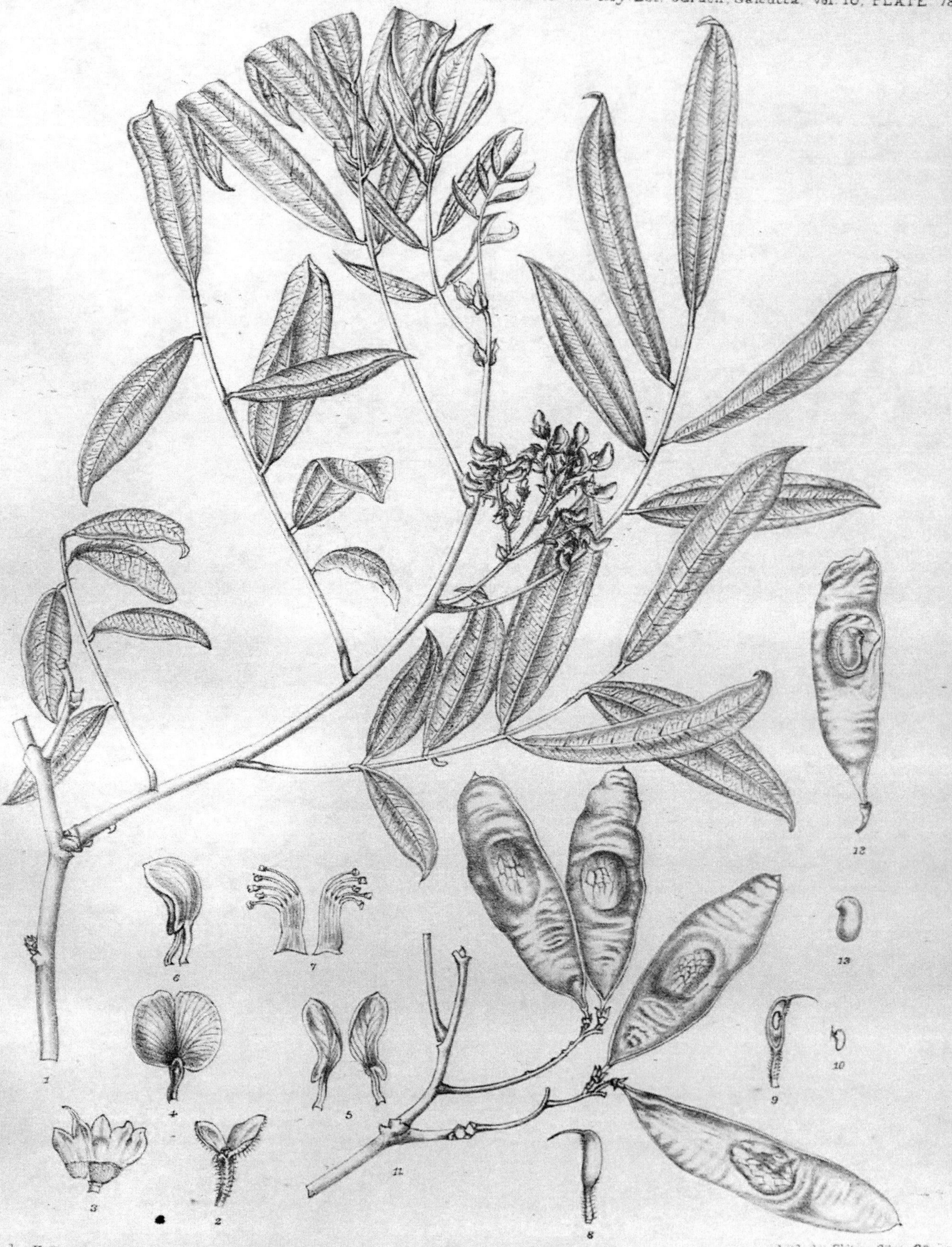

Drawn by K.P. Dass. Lith: by Chitra Silpi Co.

DALBERGIA WATTII Clarke.

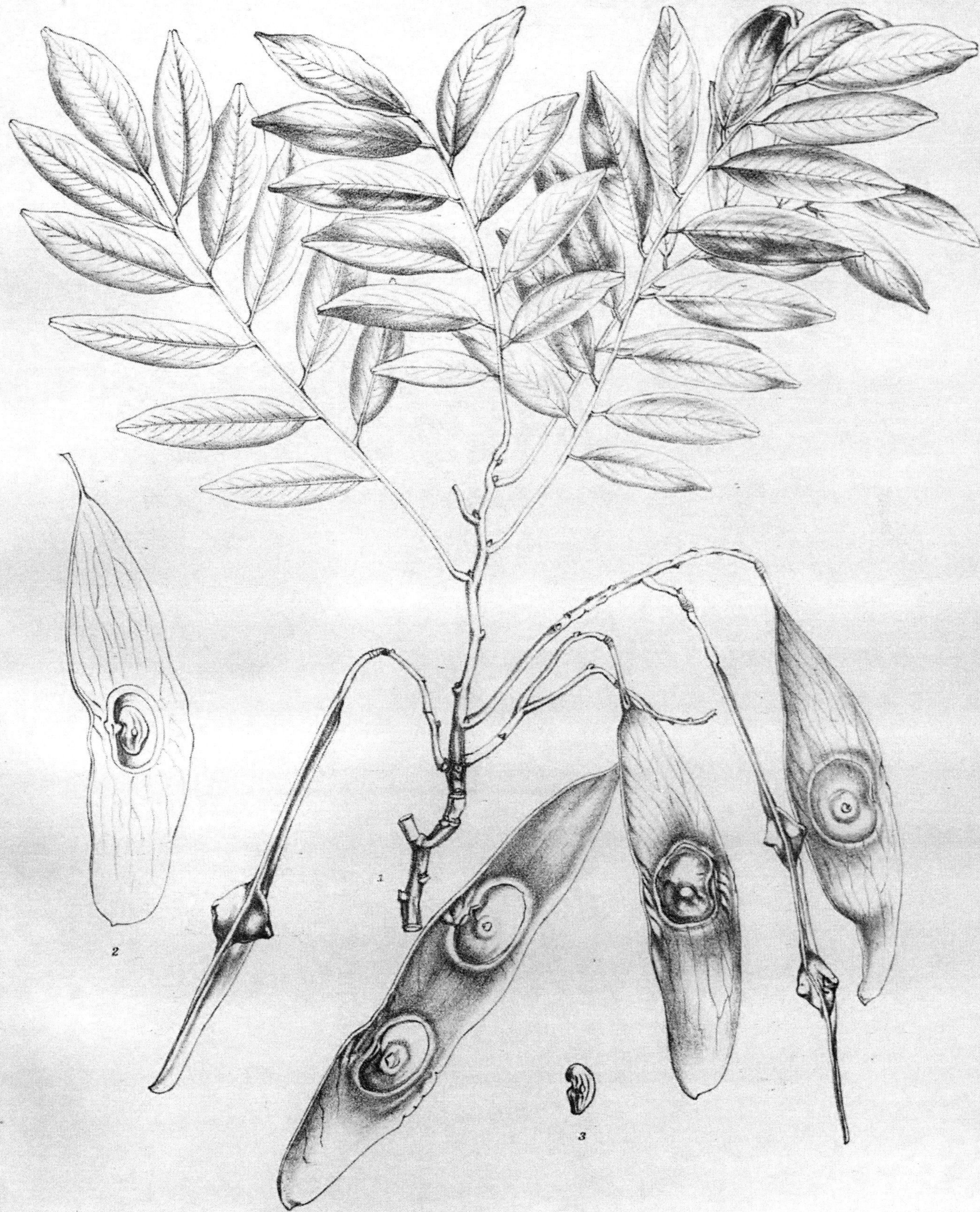

Drawn by K. P. Dass.

Lith: by Chitra Silpi Cº

DALBERGIA MAMMOSA Pierre.

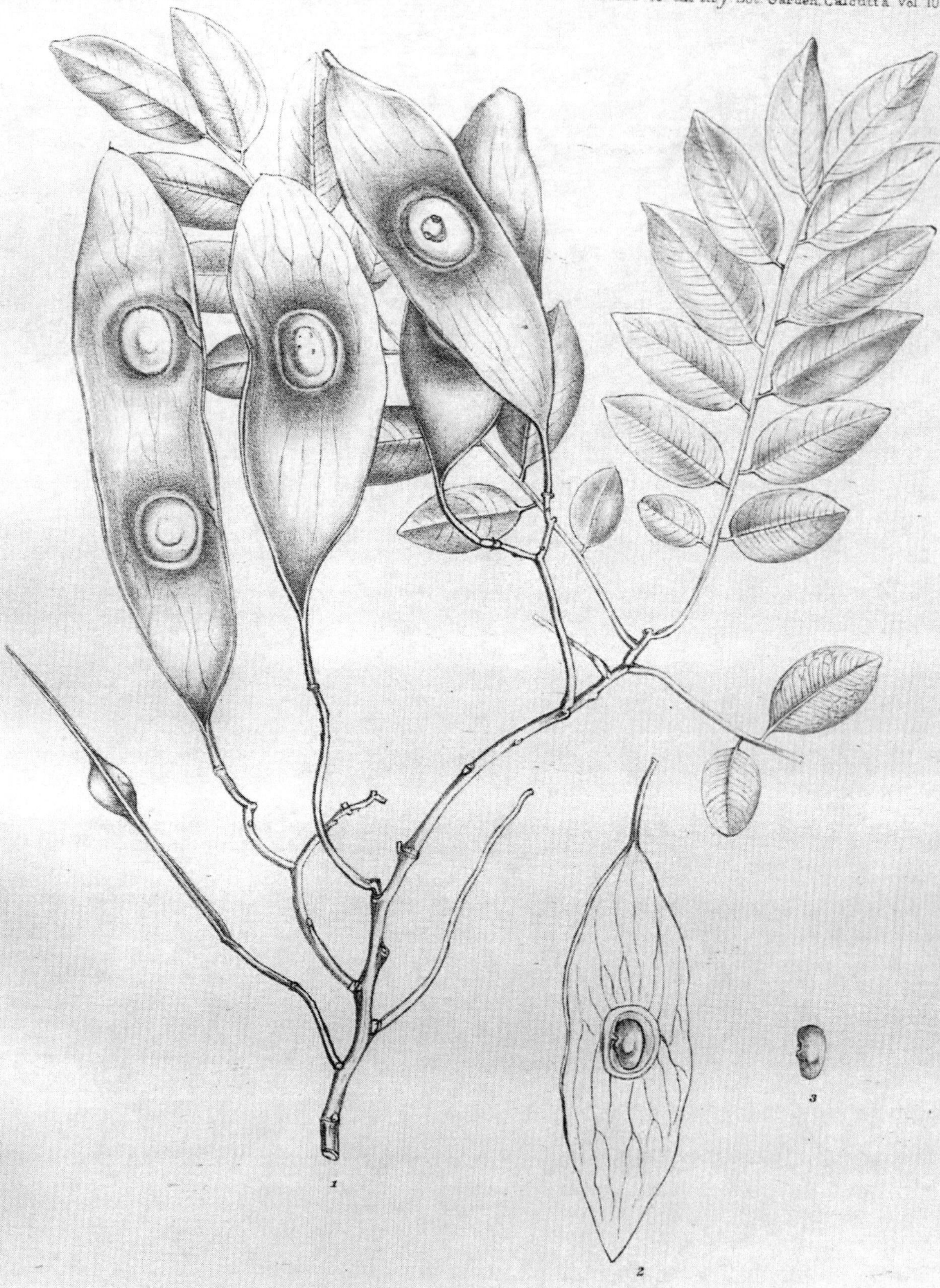

Drawn by K. P. Dass.

Lith: by Chitra Silpi C°

DALBERGIA BARIENSIS Pierre.

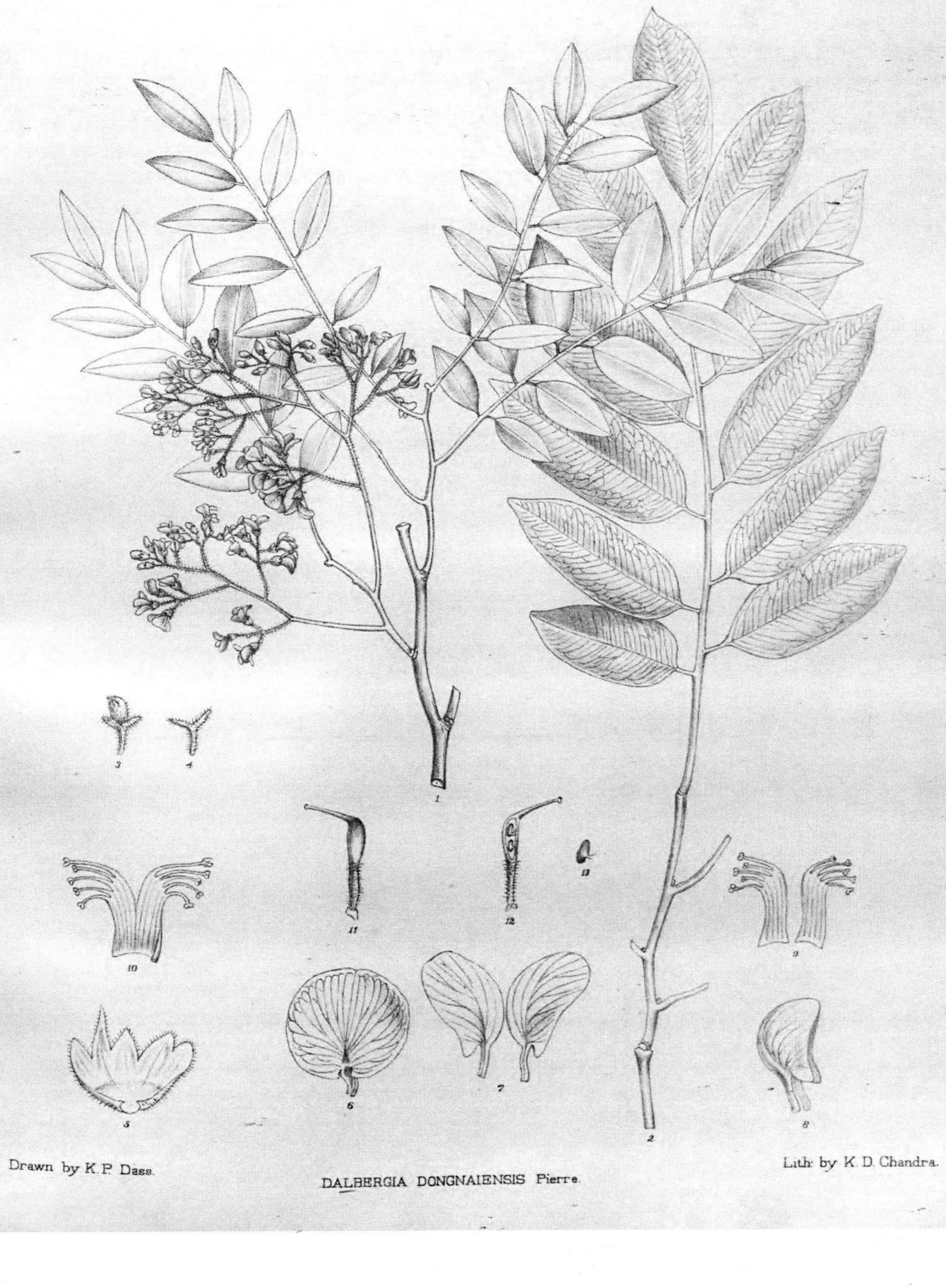

Drawn by K. P. Dass.

DALBERGIA DONGNAIENSIS Pierre.

Lith: by K. D. Chandra.

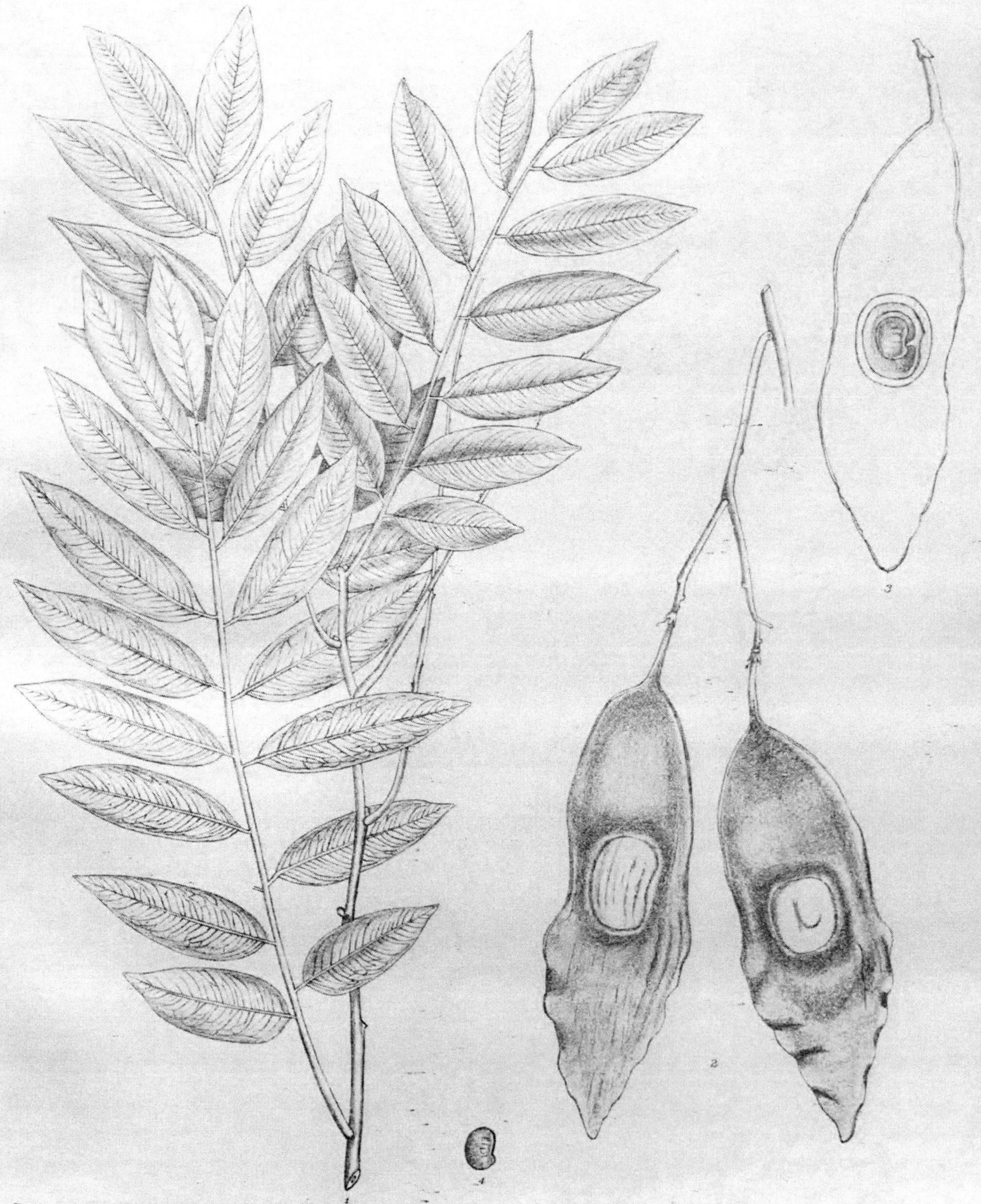

Drawn by K. P. Dass.

DALBERGIA DUPERREANA Pierre.

Lith: by A. K. Nath.

Drawn by K.P. Dass. Lith. by A.C. Chowdhary.

DALBERGIA KURZII Prain.

Drawn by A. L. Singh.

DALBERGIA CANA Grah.

Lith: by A. C. Singha.

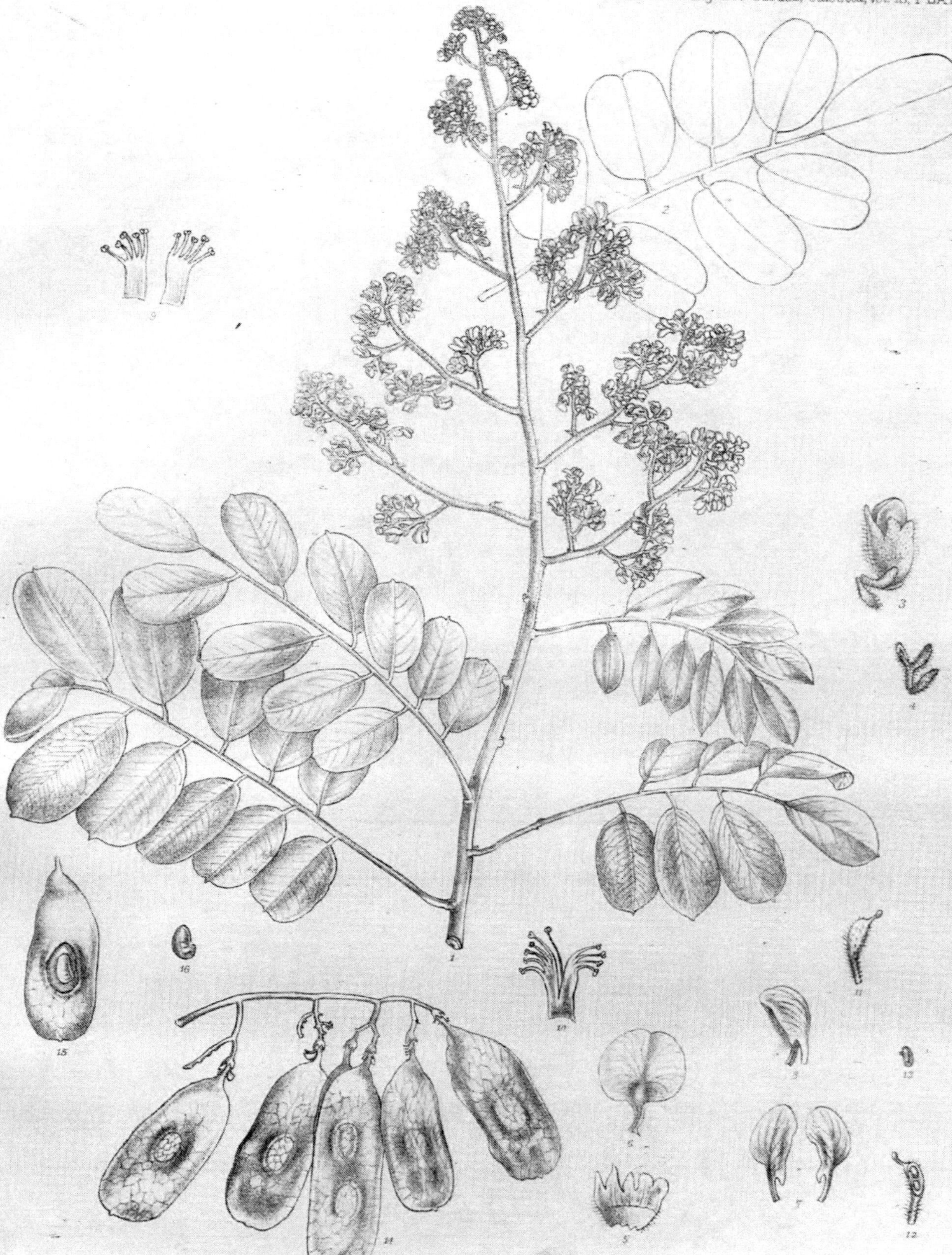

Drawn by K.P. Dass. Lith: by K.P. Dass.

DALBERGIA VOLUBILIS Roxb.

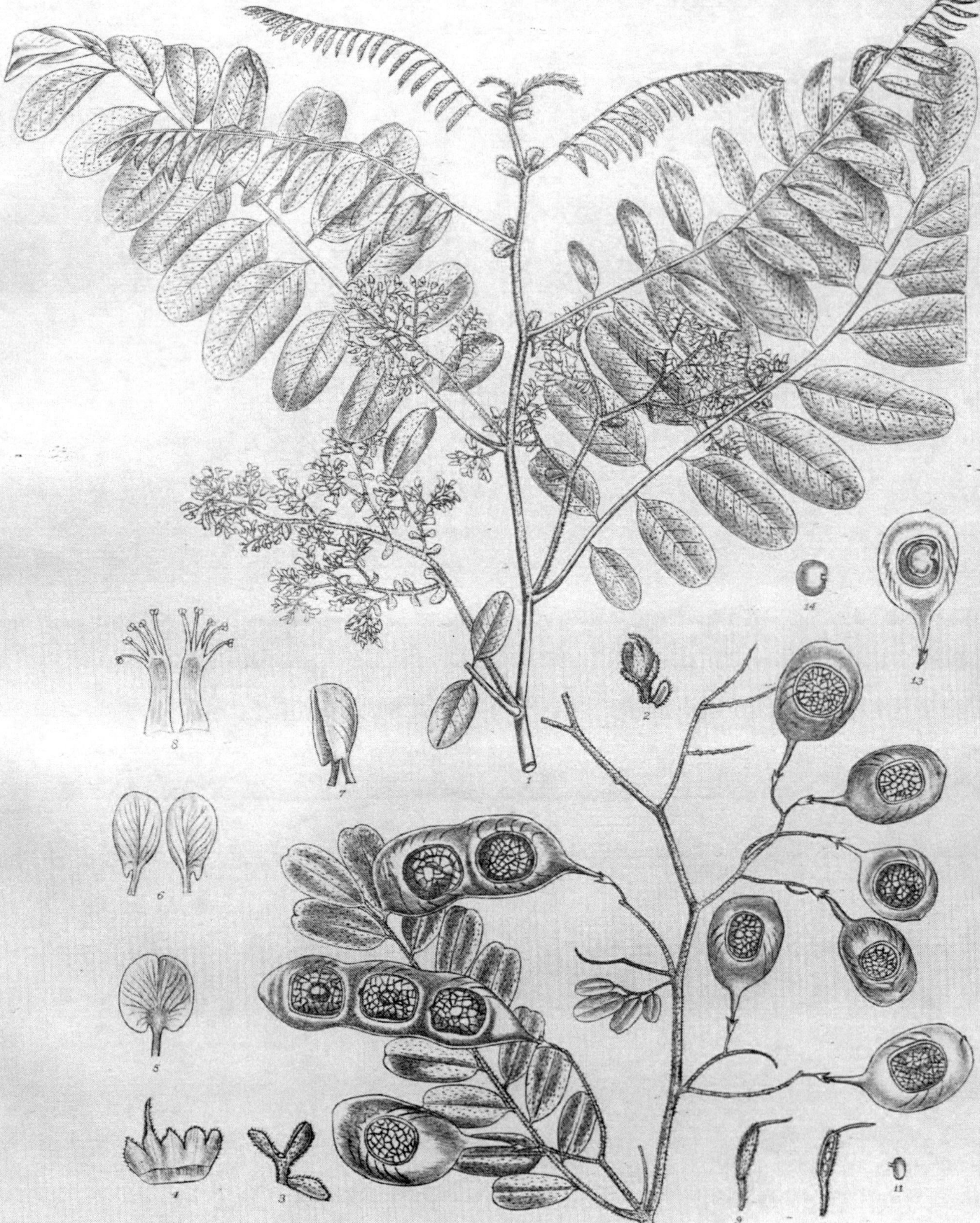

Drawn by K. P. Dass.

DALBERGIA FERRUGINEA Roxb.

Lith. by A. N. Banerji.

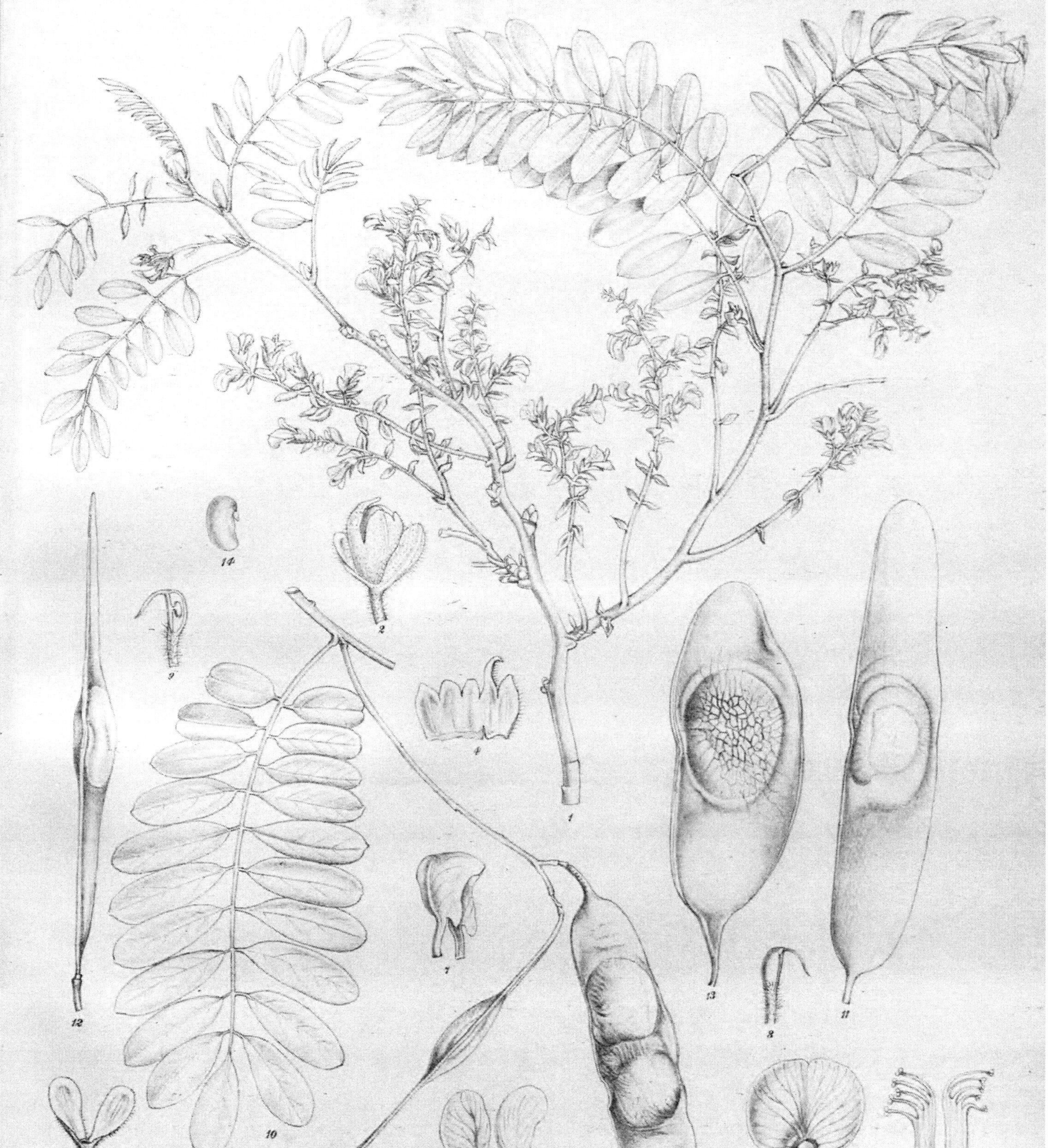

Drawn by K.P. Dass.

Lith. by A.C. Chowdhary.

DALBERGIA STIPULACEA Roxb.

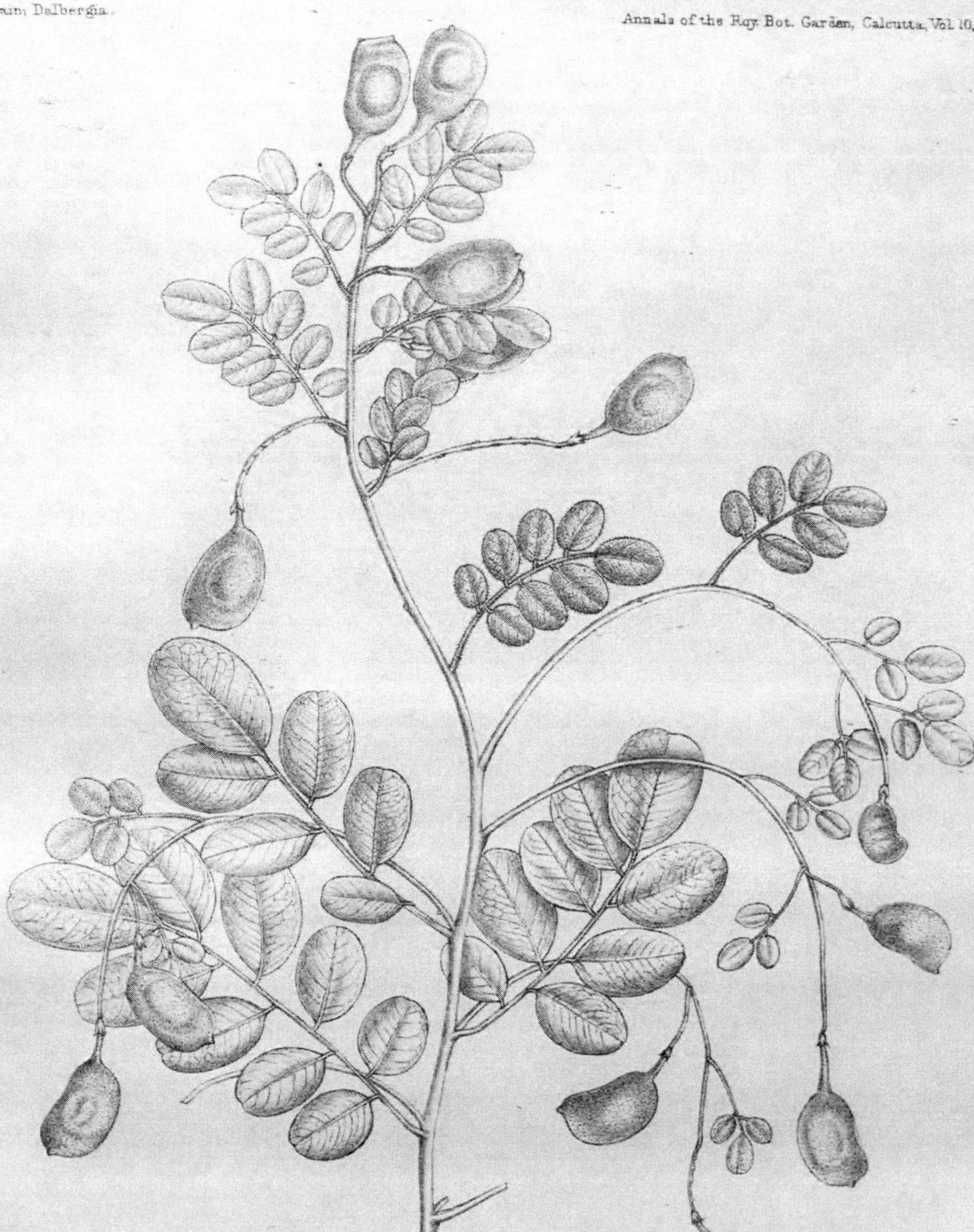

Drawn by K.P. Dass.

Lith. by A.C. Singha.

DALBERGIA GODEFROYI Prain.

Drawn by K. P. Dass.

Lith: by K. P. Dass.

DALBERGIA FALCATA Prain.

Annals of the Roy. Bot. Garden, Calcutta, Vol. 10. PLATE 90.

Drawn by K.P. Dass.

Lith by A.C. Singha.

DALBERGIA KUNSTLERI Prain.

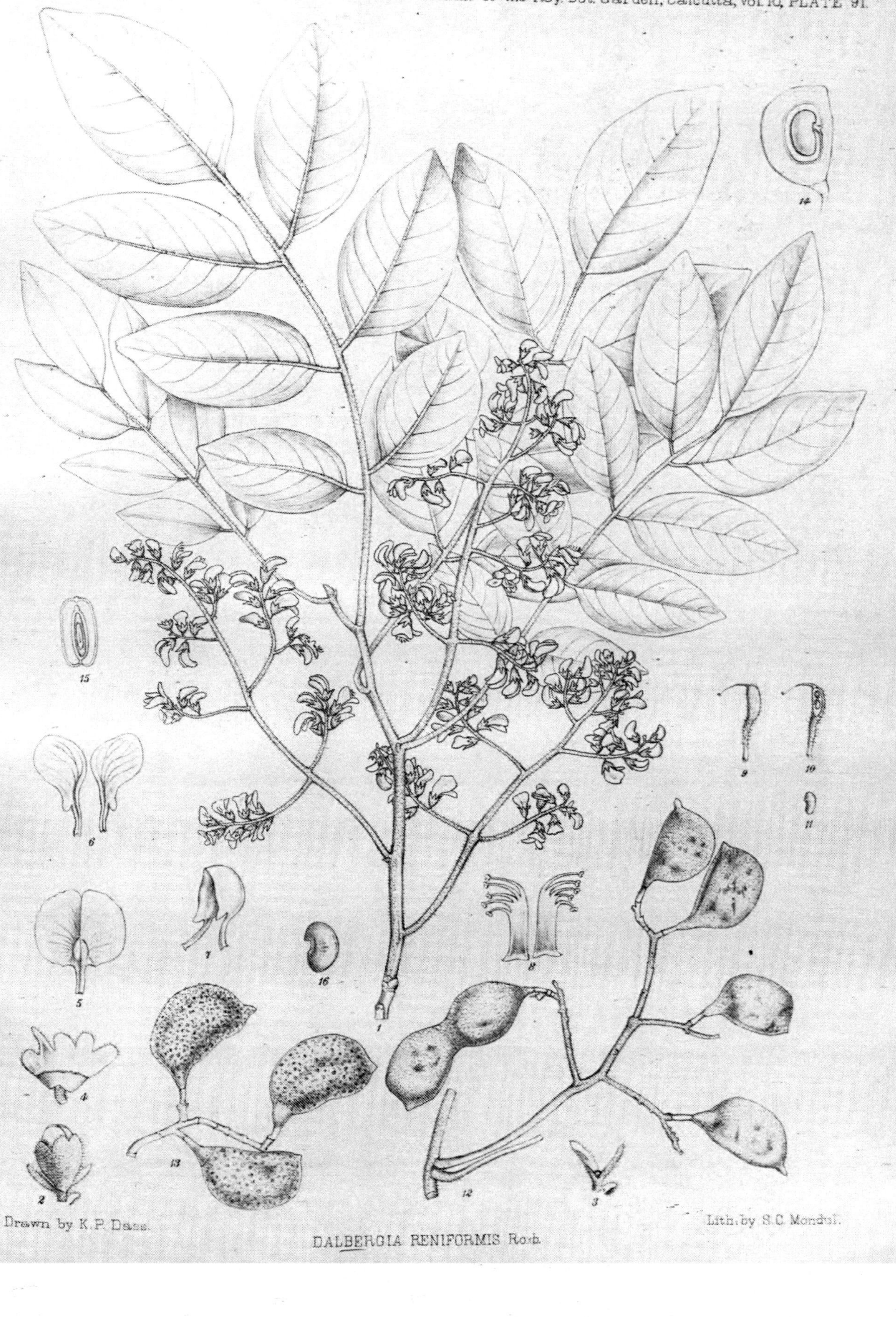

Drawn by K. P. Dass.

Lith: by S. C. Mondul.

DALBERGIA RENIFORMIS Roxb.

ANNALS

OF THE

ROYAL BOTANIC GARDEN, CALCUTTA.

Vol. X. Part II.

ANNALS

OF THE

ROYAL BOTANIC GARDEN, CALCUTTA.

Vol. X.

Part II.

THE ACONITES OF INDIA: A MONOGRAPH

By

OTTO STAPF, Ph.D., F.L.S.,

Principal Assistant, Royal Botanic Gardens, Kew.

CALCUTTA

Bengal Secretariat Press.

1905.

THE

ACONTIES OF INDIA:

A MONOGRAPH

By

OTTO STAPF, Ph.D., F.L.S.,

Principal Assistant, Royal Botanic Gardens, Kew.

WITH TWENTY-FIVE PLATES.

CALCUTTA

Bengal Secretariat Press

1905.

PREFACE.

RECENTLY Dr. (now Sir George) WATT, through his efforts to elucidate the questions concerning the poisonous and non-poisonous Aconites of India, has revived the interest in this economically important group of plants. Since then samples of Indian Aconites have reached Kew at various times from India, as well as from the Imperial Institute, London, where Prof. DUNSTAN has been carrying on investigations into the chemical properties of some of these plants.

As I was charged with the necessary comparisons and determinations, I had to make myself more particularly familiar with the genus Aconitum.

So far as the Indian species were concerned, many specimens had been added to the collections at Kew since the publication of part I of the first volume of the *Flora of British India* (1872), which contained Ranunculaceae.

Revising the whole of the old and new material, I soon became convinced that the old classification would have to be extended and essentially modified, particularly with respect to the two most important species . *Napellus* and *A. ferox*, as understood by the authors of the Ranunculaceae of India.

This appeared the more necessary, as the elaboration of the *ferox* group by Mr. P. J. BRÜHL, in the 5th Volume of the *Annals of the Botanic Garden of Calcutta* (1896), had proved the existence of a considerable number of new forms, but had also complicated matters by the adoption of a system of extreme synthesis.

At the same time, more than one-half of the new forms described by Brühl were not represented at Kew or could not be identified with certainty without seeing the original specimens.

To complete the revision which I had carried as far as the Kew material allowed, I asked for the use of the collections of Aconites at Calcutta and also of those at Saharanpur, where I expected to find some of Royle's types. Major PRAIN and Mr. DUTHIE responded with the greatest liberality to the official request which Sir W. THISELTON-DYER addressed to them on my behalf, and the collections were placed at my disposal.

With these collections at Kew and with those at the British Museum and Wallich's Aconites at the Linnean Society within easy reach, I had practically the whole existing herbarium material of Indian Aconites at hand. An opportunity more favourable than might ever occur again was thus given for a thorough monograph of this group, and I was directed by Sir W. THISELTON-DYER to work it out with a view to publication.

I have already acknowledged the great assistance I received from Major PRAIN and Mr. DUTHIE—without it it would have been impossible to accomplish the task satisfactorily; but I have also to thank Prof. BALFOUR for the loan of the Edinburgh collection, Prof. MARSHALL WARD for that of some of Royle's specimens in the herbarium at Cambridge, Mr. CASIMIR DE CANDOLLE for a beautiful photograph of the specimen from which Séringe described Wallich's *A. ferox*, and Prof. WARMING for sending me the Indian Aconites of the Copenhagen herbarium, among which were several sheets from Nepal, which Wallich had communicated to his friend Hornemann. Last, but not least, I feel deeply obliged to Miss SMITH for the great pains she has taken with the execution of the drawings, and to Major PRAIN for superintending the lithography.

As to the plan of my work, I thought it advisable to bring once more together all that can be said about the history of the more important among the Indian Aconites. Much of it has already been recorded by others, but the new facts that have come to light and new ways of seeing the old, have called for a fresh review of the whole.

The chemistry of the Indian Aconites has lately made some progress owing to Prof. DUNSTAN'S efforts. Much has still to be done, and I hope that the clearer insight we now have into the differentiation of this group of plants will prove a new stimulus in this direction.

Great importance attaches to the anatomy of the root tubers for the discrimination of the species, as such, and still more for that of the drugs as they are found in the bazars. I have introduced into my monograph as much of it as appeared necessary for diagnostic purposes and for field use, if I may say so. The finer details appeared to be out of place, and moreover they require further testing on still richer material. I have, however, added a short paragraph on the principal features of the structure of the Aconite roots, as I thought it might facilitate the use of the characters derived from it.

The Bibliography of the various references to the Indian Aconites and a list of the vernacular names applied to them have been added as appendices to the text.

OTTO STAPF.

HERBARIUM,
ROYAL BOTANIC GARDENS, KEW;
7th April 1904.

CONTENTS.

PART I.—INTRODUCTION.

PART II.—DESCRIPTIONS OF THE ACONITES OF INDIA.

APPENDICES.

LIST OF PLATES.

[Plates 92—116 to follow letterpress of part II.]

THE

ACONITES OF INDIA.

I.—INTRODUCTION.

§ 1. HISTORY OF THE INDIAN ACONITES.

I.—BISH (AND ATIS).

ROOT-TUBERS of Aconites have occupied an important place in the Indian Pharmacopœa from very remote times. Two distinct kinds or classes of Aconites may already be recognised in Susrutas' *Ayurvedas* (Latin Transl. by F. Hessler, 1844), namely, "Ativisha" and "Vatsanabha." The former is quoted by Susrutas over and over again as an ingredient of medicines, but it does not occur among the poisons. It is evidently *Aconitum heterophyllum*, to which the name *Ativisha* is still applied by modern Sanskritists (see Dutt, *Mat. Med. Hindus*, ed. 1900, p. 101). The same word is found practically unchanged and with the same meaning in Marathi and Guzerati; and more or less altered, but still recognisable, in such idioms as Dukni (*Atvika*), Cutchi (*Ativista*), Hindi (*Atis*), Bhoti (*Áis*), Telugu (*Ativasa*). Madden (in *Trans. Bot. Soc. Edinb.* v., 1858, p. 130) explains *Ativisha* as meaning "overcoming poison—antidote," adding in brackets "(erroneously rendered *summum venenum* by Wallich)." It is still regarded by the Hindus as an important medicine and antidote (Dutt, *l. c.*). Susrutas' *Ativisha* stands therefore for a non-poisonous Aconite. On the other hand, *Vatsanabha* is quoted by Susrutas (Hessler's Transl. ii., p. 216) as one of the 13 bulb poisons, and he mentioned (*l. c.*) 4 varieties of *Vatsanabha* among the 55 "stable"* poisons. Dutt (*l. c.*, p. 97) quotes *Vatsanabha* for "Aconitum ferox," which stands here in a broad sense for all or most of the poisonous Aconites of which the tubers reach the Indian market, and explains the same as indicating the resemblance of the roots to the navel of children, whilst Madden (*l. c.*, p. 128) renders *Vatsanabha* as "calf-destroyer." This name has also, in a more or less changed form, found its way into modern idioms, as Bengali (*Butsnab*), Bombay and Lahore bazaars (*Bachnab*), Hindi (*Bach nag*, see Madden, *l. c.*), Tamul (*Vasha-navi*), Telugu (*Vasa-nabhi*). Susrutas has also a *Sringivisha* among the 13 bulb poisons (*l. c.*, ii., p. 216), and he describes its action as causing "lassitudo membrorum aestus et abdominis intumescentia." The same name is quoted by Dymock (*Mat. Med. Western India*, 1883, p. 4) and by Dutt (*l. c.*, p. 97), as a vernacular equivalent of *Aconitum ferox* (*sens. lat.*), and it is quite probable that Susrutas' *Sringivisha* also stood for some poisonous Aconite root.

There is no evidence that the medical schools of Greece and Egypt had any knowledge of the Indian Aconites; but when, about the 8th century, the Arabs translated Susrutas, and became generally acquainted with the treasures of the medical sages of

* By "stable" poisons, vegetable and mineral poisons are meant.

ancient India, they incorporated the poisonous Indian Aconites into their Pharmacopœas under the generic name *Bish* (Sanskr. *Visha*), that is, poison, just as *Bish* (or *Bikh*) is used at present in India for the Aconite poison, as the poison κατ' ἐξοχήν. The first of the Arab writers to mention *Bish* is Hobaish of Bagdad (ninth century), who is quoted by Ebn Baithar (Transl. Sontheimer, i. p. 199) as stating that *Bish* is a plant growing in India. It appears again in Abu Mansur Muwaffak about 975 (*Lib. Fundam. Pharm.*, Lat. Transl. by Seligman, p. 47; Germ. transl. by Achundow, p. 168); and in Avicenna (980—1037; Lib. Canon. Lat. Transl., by Ger. Carmon. corr. Alp. Bellun. ii. cap. 499); but the use of the *nomen genericum* "bish" for the Indian drug could not fail to increase the confusion to be expected in a literature which was to a great extent based on uncritical compilation. No wonder that the comparison of the Arab pharmacopœas yields so little result concerning the origin and the nature of their "bish" beyond the broad fact that it consisted of the root of one of the poisonous Aconites of India. Still, there is perhaps, in the tangle of conflicting and absurd statements, a hint with respect to the particular part of India from which "bish" was then procured. Muwaffak enumerates "halahil" (Transl. Achundow, pp. 168, 169) as one of the kinds of *Bish*, adding that it grows by the side of *Valeriana Jatamansi*. It is the most deadly of all, and a dose smaller than a mustard-grain kills. It is like amber, or, as is stated a little farther on, quite black, shining and hard. Further, Ebn Baithar (Transl. Sontheimer, i. p. 199) quotes from Isa Ben Ali that there are three kinds of *Bish*, and that one resembles the horns which are found by the side of *Spica Nardus Indica*. Now there is no doubt about the *Valeriana Jatamansi* or its synonym, the *Nardus Spica Indica*, one of the few Indian drugs which reached the classic west long before the dawn of Arabian civilisation. It is *Nardostachys Jatamansi*, a native of the Alpine Himalaya from Tehri-Garhwal eastwards, the very region which, in our days, supplies the Indian bazaars with *Bikh*. Further, a portion of the modern drug has a fracture almost like amber, the result of roasting, whilst another, steeped in cow's urine, is black right through, hard and shining. Moreover, one of the common vernacular names of *A. ferox* (*sens. lat.*) in Hindi is *Singya* (*Singya Bish, Jur*), that is, horn (horn-poison), from the shape of the tubers. This description of the "halahil" *Bish*, as horns which are either amber-like or black, hard and shining, and its localisation in the Central Himalaya seems, indeed, to point strongly to its identity with *A. ferox* (*sens. lat.*). The strength of this evidence is scarcely weakened by the conflicting and confused descriptions of a *Bish from* Halahala by Ebn Samhun, a Spaniard who lived at some time between 998 and 1128, and of the *Halahala* plant mentioned by Dutt (*l. c.*, p. 98) as yielding one of the nine virulent poisons of the Sanskrit writers. Ebn Samhun (according to Ebn Baithar: Transl. Sontheimer, i. p. 199) says that "the 'bish' grows in the country of China in the neighhourhood of Sind, near a town called Halahal. Except in this place, it is found nowhere else. This plant raises a stem an ell high. The leaves resemble those of lettuce or cichory which are eaten. The plant is found near Halahal, in the neighbourhood of Sind. If dry it is one of the food-articles of the people of this country and does no harm: if one moves from Sind for one hundred paces and eats this plant, it kills him who eats of it on the spot." This sounds very like a confused echo from Greek, Arab, and Indian sources, whilst the description of the *Halahala* plant, quoted by Dutt as possessing bunches like grapes and leaves like those of the palm-tree, and its alleged distribution from the Himalaya to the Concan, excludes *Aconitum* altogether.

Whether the Indian *Bish* ever reached the drug-shops of Europe until quite recently is very doubtful. It is true that Mathaeus Sylvaticus of Salerno (about 1300) has "Bissum i. Napellus" and "Bix i. Napellus" in his *Liber Pandectorum*, but the paragraph is merely an abridged version of Avicenna's chapter on "Bis." Then it is lost sight of, and the herbalists of the 15th and the following centuries do not seem to have known it at all. Yet it was in the 16th century that the drug was rediscovered by two European travellers in the East, independently of each other. Christobal Acosta, who travelled in India about the middle of the 16th century and was much associated with the celebrated Garcia d'Orto, mentions the *Bish* root in his "Tractads" (*Tract. Drog. y Medic. Ind. Orient.*, 1578, p. 90) as an ingredient of certain pills prepared by the Brahman doctors with these words: "Y rayz de Bisa (que es una rays, que viene de las sierras de Bengala y Pattane)," the first direct reference to the Central Himalaya as the home of the *Bish* plant; but he does not seem to have seen the root itself, nor to have clearly connected it with *Napellus*, although in speaking of the poisons used by the doctors of the East, he mentions *Napellus* on p. 180: "Y tambien usan por veneno del Anapelo" (for "Anapelo" stands "Napello" in the Italian edition). There is, however, another reference to the same article in Acosta's *Tractads* on p. 179. Criticising Laguna's statement (in his *Commentary of Dioscorides*, libr. i. cap. vi) that there existed a suspicious kind of *Spica Nardi* in India, he says: "Y que la Spica Nardi es sospechosa en la India, porque della se haze une suerte da veneno mortifero llamado Piso; el qual no solamente bevido pero tambien aplicado a un hombre quando suda le mata. Por lo qual el uso del Nardo en aquellas partes es tenido por sospechoso . . . ni veneno que se llame Piso nunca el Doctor Orta con su diligencia lo pudo saber en la India, ni yo por aquellas partes, aunque lo pregunti a muchos." This deadly poison "Piso" is certainly nothing but "bis" or "bish" in disguise, and Laguna's strange association of it with the spikenard may perhaps be due to a misunderstanding of the statement of the Arab writers, already referred to, that the "bish" grows by the side of the spikenard. It is not to be wondered that Acosta and Orta failed to trace the poisonous Spica nardi, called "Piso." About the same time (1549 or 1550), the French traveller Belon visited the bazaars of Alexandria, and this is what he relates in his "Observations" (Lat. Transl. in Clus. *Hist. Exot. Plant.* p. 98): "Inter singularia quae nobis Florentinus Consul ostendit, cum aromata nos requirere animadvertisset, degustandam dedit radicem Arabibus Bisch nominatam: ea nobis tantum calorem in ore per integrum biduum excitavit, ut flagrare videretur . . . Exigua est, parvi napi instar (alii Napellum vocant) et adeo vulgaris Turcicis aromatariis ut nullus eorum venalem non habeat." This is unmistakably the "bish" of India. Belon's account seems, however, to have been overlooked entirely by later writers, and the only reference to Acosta's "bish" which I find is in Bauhinus' *Pinax Theatri* (1623), p. 259, under *Symphytum*: "VI. Symphyto viribus affinis: Bisa radix quæ ex Bengala et Patane montibus adfertur; Acosta cap. de Datura; sed quid?"

Whilst in the West, after the downfall of the Arab civilisation, the knowledge of the *Bish* of India was soon lost, conservatism and a pious regard for the authority of the Arab writers secured the drug a safe place in the Persian Pharmacopœas; but nothing was added that might have thrown further light on it. There is, however, a strange passage in the Latin version which a French Carmelite monk, Frater Angelus, gave of a Persian Pharmacopœa in 1681, recalling to some extent the fabulous account of Ebn Samhun's "halahil" *Bish*. He tells us (*l. c.*, pp. 358 and 359) in an annotation to *Bish* that the banyas or Indian traders living in the Kingdom of Ispahan use the root of the *Bish* or *Napellus*, or, as it is called in a prescription on p. 319, "Napelli Indici, aridi, innoxii, vel antithorae," with their desserts and spices, and that he himself tasted of it. The action of the drug is that of a tonic and digestive.

This *Bish*, he adds, is taken particularly by the Indians who hail from Tatta in Sind, then a flourishing commercial centre, and those people told him that the root was deadly if taken fresh and green, but was rendered inert and turned into a medicine by drying, whence he concluded it was a kind of *Antithora* and antidote to *Napellus*. The Tatta people, he continues, believe that a little animal, resembling a mouse, which nibbles at the roots of the *Napellus* and burrows assiduously around them, also is an eminent "alexitarium" (antidote). Angelus describes finally the root in these terms: "Radices porro Bisch omnino similes apparent ossiculis, seu vertebris mothuae piscis; levissimae sunt et candidae—foraminibus carie undique (ut ita dicam) fermentatae." This *Bish* of Frater Angelus was evidently not the true poisonous *Bish*; but can it have been the root-tubers of *Aconitum heterophyllum* or *A. palmatum*, which are white, smooth, and, as they are found in the bazaars, more or less of the shape of bones? They too are recognised as tonics. This closes the early history of "bish—" a quaint mixture of fiction and truth, lost at one end in the mist of the wisdom of ancient India, and dying out at the other in the barren traditions and reiterations of the Persian Pharmacopœas.

A new phase in the history of the Indian Aconites commenced when, in the beginning of the last century, the British East India Company came more intimately into contact with the tribes inhabiting that part of the Himalaya which had supplied India with *Bish* from the earliest times.

In 1802 and 1803 F. Hamilton passed fourteen months in Nepal—mostly in the neighbourhood of Kathmandu. During this time and during a subsequent stay of two years on the Nepal frontier he became impressed with the importance of this drug, as he says in his *Account of Nepal*, p. 99: "This dreadful root, of which large quantities are annually imported, is equally fatal when taken into the stomach and applied to wounds, and is in universal use throughout India for poisoning arrows, and, there is too much reason to suspect, for the worst purposes. Its importation would indeed seem to require the attention of the magistrate. The Gorkhalese pretend, that it is one of their principal securities against invasion from the low countries; and that they could so infect all the waters on the route by which an enemy was advancing as to occasion his certain destruction. . . . This poisonous species is called *Bish*, *Bikh*, and *Hodoya Bish* or *Bikh*, nor am I certain whether the *Mitha* ought to be referred to it or to the foregoing kind." Hamilton himself gathered information concerning the *Bikh* poison, and in 1810 he sent a native to the Alpine regions of the Himalaya mountains beyond the sources of the Kosi river. He was to collect specimens, fruits, and seeds of the Alpine plants, and his attention was particularly directed to procure the plant used in India for poisoning arrows (Brewst. *Edinb. Journ. Sc.* i., 1824, p. 249), which in this case meant the *Bikh* plant. The results of this investigation were published by Hamilton in his *Account of Nepal* in 1819, and reprinted, accompanied by technical descriptions of the herbarium specimens, in Brewster's *Edinb. Journ. Sc.* i. (1824), p. 249—251. Unfortunately Hamilton's man had been sent too early in the year, returning in July with specimens which were too young to allow of accurate determination; thus misleading Hamilton, who referred them to the genus *Caltha* as *C. Bisma*, *C. Nirbisia*, and *C. Codua*. A part of Hamilton's specimens was sent to the India House, and cannot be traced, while another was, with the bulk of his collections, incorporated in Wallich's herbarium, which already contained a number of Aconites from Nepal and the countries immediately to the west. Wallich attempted to reduce Hamilton's immature plants to certain of his species with what result may be seen from his catalogue under Nos. 4721 and 4723. Wallich's own specimens were collected in 1818, 1819, and 1821.

At the end of 1817, Wallich sent, with the sanction of the Hon. E. Gardner, Resident at Kathmandu, a Rajput of the name of Bharat Singha, who had been employed in a similar capacity by Dr. Hamilton, and a Portuguese, the son of an old servant of Dr. Roxburgh, to Nepal for the purpose of collecting roots, seeds, and specimens, and they returned in October 1818. There is no doubt that this is the expedition during which the first specimens of the supposed Nepal *Bikh* plant which Wallich sent to Europe was collected. They are (two sheets) at present in the herbarium of the British Museum, accompanied by a label in Wallich's handwriting, saying: "Aconitum atrox, Wall. Bicks. Bickma, Napalensibus." Independent of Wallich's collector, Gardner employed his own men in collecting plants for Wallich, and it must have been through this channel that the latter received the second set of samples of the same plant in 1819. This also is represented in the British Museum by a specimen with a label by Wallich: "Aconitum ferox, Wall. Radix venenata officinalis apud Napalensibus. E Napalia, 1819." Another went to A. P. De Candolle, and this was described by Séringe in his *Esquisse d'une Monographie du genre Aconitum* (read in February 1822 before the Société de Physique de Genève) under the name proposed by Wallich on the label accompanying the species, namely, *Aconitum ferox*. Finally, when Wallich was in Nepal in 1820 and 1821, he himself collected the same plant on Sheopore (Sivapore) Mountain, immediately to the north of Kathmandu. An excellent specimen of this is in Sir W. Hooker's collection now at Kew, labelled by Wallich "Aconitum ferox, Wall. Nepal," and dated by Sir W. Hooker "1821." I also refer to the same collection a number of specimens of *A. ferox* in the Copenhagen herbarium, which Prof. Hornemann received from his countryman Wallich independently and previous to the distribution set. All these Wallichian specimens agree absolutely with each other, and they leave no doubt as to the purely botanical question, which plant is to be understood under "Aconitum ferox Wall. ex Séringe"; but it was unfortunately not the species or rather one of the species which yield the common *Bikh* of the bazaars, although it belonged almost certainly to the class of the *Bikh* Aconites. I say unfortunately because under the circumstances the assumption that Wallich had actually discovered *the* plant producing the *Bikh* poison became soon the source of an almost interminable confusion. Wallich himself received an Aconite through a native collector from Gossainthan and another through Mr. Blinkworth from Kumaon, and, it seems, a drawing and notes concerning a further species from Dr. Govan in Sirmore,—all supposed to yield the *Bikh*. He was not unaware that they differed in certain respects, but, probably prepossessed by the idea that they all supplied the same article, he assumed that the plants he was dealing with were rather states of a very variable plant, dependent on differences of situation, than distinct species. Here is what he says in *Plantae Asiaticae Rariores* i., p. 35: "This plant varies considerably, according to the situation in which it is found. On Sheopore, at an elevation of about 10,000 feet (the only place where I have found it in Nepal Proper), it is a smaller, slenderer, and smoother plant with almost simple stem, narrow segments of the leaves, and thin racemes. As it approaches higher elevations, towards the snowy mountains, it attains a larger size and habit, and is covered with soft, greyish hairs, the divisions of the leaves become broader, the spikes larger, and the flowers more dense and numerous. These various appearances so gradually succeed each other that I am unable to discover any point on which to form a specific distinction; nor can I even sufficiently limit the varieties to render their enumeration a matter of utility."

Consequently when he published his work from which this passage is taken, he merged all these forms in his original *Aconitum ferox*, extending Séringe's description so as to cover them, yet retaining the old type for the plate illustrating the species; but even here, as a consequence of Wallich's overgeneralisation, an error seems to have slipped in, marring the otherwise faithful illustration; for I suspect that the root was added on, in good faith, from a bazaar specimen belonging to another species, very likely *A. Balfourii*, which is collected for trade. There is at least certainly no root with Wallich's specimens from which the drawing could have been made. In fact the specimen in Wallich's own herbarium at the Linnean Society in London from which the inflorescence and the infructescence was probably drawn has no tubers apart from a detached fragment of an old mother-tuber, and the attached tubers in the herbaria at Geneva, Kew,. and Copenhagen are quite different. The interest in the *Bikh* question aroused through Hamilton's and Wallich's efforts to trace the sources of the poison had meanwhile spread to the "North-Western" Himalaya. I have already mentioned Blinkworth, who collected in Kumaon, and Dr. Govan, who travelled in Sirmore and in what is now-a-days Tihri-Garhwal; but the botanical centre for this region was Saharanpur and the leading spirit Dr. Royle, whose botanical knowledge and familiarity with the "Materia Medica" would seem to have made him particularly fit for investigations of this kind. He collected root-specimens from the bazaars of Northern India, as far as Amritsar, herbarium specimens and notes on the article, and even succeeded in introducing an Aconite from Choor.* Yet, his account of the Bikh plant in his *Illustrations of the Botany of the Himalayan Mountains*, pp. 46—48, is somewhat disappointing. He accepted Wallich's theory of the variability of *A. ferox*, and also referred the *Bikh* or, as it was called, *Metha Tellia* of his district to the Nepalese *A. ferox*. This, however, belonged undoubtedly to another species which I have named *A. Falconeri*. The combined authorities of Wallich and Royle carried sufficient weight with them to secure the undisputed recognition of their theory that *A. ferox* was *the* source of *Bikh*, and it stood for a considerable time for any poisonous aconite found in India. Thus it came about, for instance, that the small Aconite roots which were brought in little wicker baskets from Assam to Calcutta, and which were possibly the tubers of *A. lethale*, were referred to *A. ferox* by O'Shaughnessey (*Beng. Pharmacop.* 1844, p. 190) as was also the *Mohra* of Madden (*Diary of an Excursion to the Shatool and Boorun Passes on the Himalaya* in *Journ. As. Soc. Bengal*, xv., 1846, p. 95), which was no doubt *A. deinorrhizum*.

When in 1848 and 1849 J. H. Hooker explored Sikkim, another part of the Himalaya, from which "bikh" had been obtained, was opened. So keen an observer could not overlook the considerable diversity which the genus Aconite displays in Sikkim, nor the importance attaching to the poisons derived from some of its species,

* A mountain reaching over 12,000 ft. in *Sirmor* (Simla Hill States).

and he at once (in *Journ. As. Soc. Bengal*, xviii., 1849, p. 738) pointed out that "probably *Bikh* is yielded by various Aconites," mentioning so far as Sikkim is concerned, particularly *A. palmatum* and an "undescribed congener." I explain under *A. palmatum* that the roots which J. D. Hooker had in view when speaking of this species were actually those of *A. spicatum*, the principal source of Nepal Aconite, and were erroneously connected with flowering specimens of *A. palmatum*. The "undescribed congener" was no doubt *A. luridum*, the name of which appears for the first time in Hooker's *Himalayan Journal* (1854), ii., p. 108, as that of a plant "whose root is *said* to be as virulent as *A. ferox* and *A. Napellus*." Hooker's rich Sikkim collections were not then critically worked out, but he and Thomson had already paid sufficient attention to the Himalayan Aconites to enable the author of the *Himalayan Journal* to add (*l. c.*) this footnote:—"The result of Dr. Thomson's and my examination of the Himalayan aconites (of which there are seven species) is that the one generally known as *A. ferox* and which supplies a great deal of the celebrated poison is the common *A. Napellus* of Europe." Thus another species which had not been mentioned before in connection with *Bikh* was introduced into the discussion of this poison. This view that *A. Napellus* was one of the sources of the celebrated *Bikh* poison was still more emphasized in the *Flora Indica* by Hooker and Thomson (1855) Introd. i., pp. 3 and 4; i., p. 58. Soon afterwards the import into England of Nepal Aconite for medical purposes began, leading almost immediately to the discovery of pseudaconitine, a new alkaloid of a somewhat different chemical and physiological character as compared with the active principle of the European *A. Napellus*, and to the discrimination of the English preparation as English Aconitine. This was, however, evidently more a coincidence than a consequence of Hooker and Thomson's statement referred to above, as Headland had already previously pointed out that "the native root (*i.e.*, the European *A. Napellus*) contains a much less and more variable quantity of the alkaloid than the Himalayan *Aconitum ferox*, so named on account of its highly poisonous properties," and that "it will be most economical to employ the Indian root;" (Headland in Royle *Manual Mat. Med. & Therap.*, 2nd ed., 1853, p. 289 and footnote). Still, ever since, *A. Napellus* has stood in nearly all the Indian Pharmacopœas and publications on economic products of India as one of the sources of *Bikh*, and repeated attempts have been made until quite lately to supplant the European product by preparations from Indian drugs supposed to be derived, in part at least, from a plant identical with the European *A. Napellus*. The views expressed by Hooker and Thomson in *Flora Indica* were repeated in Hooker f., *Flora of British India*, i. (1872), p. 27. They cannot be maintained any longer, as recent investigations into the chemistry of the Indian Aconites, and my own examination of a great mass of herbarium material, many times richer than that which was at the disposal of the authors of the *Flora Indica*, as well as histological studies concerning the root-tubers of the Indian Aconites, have convinced me that the European *Aconitum Napellus* does not occur in India, either in its typical form or in what we might be justified in calling varieties of it. I need not dwell here on the very extensive literature of the Indian Aconites which has since grown up. It consists to a great extent of repetitions, compilations, and suggestions often far from judicious. Abundant references to it will be found in the literature and synonymy of the species described in the special part.

In 1889 Watt gave an admirable and exhaustive summary of all that was, up to that date, known about the Indian Aconites. It is a faithful reflexion of the confusion in which he found the knowledge concerning this subject. He was, of course, perfectly aware of it, and he says in his *Dictionary of the Economic Products of India*, i., p. 85: "Of the other species (*i.e.*, the Indian Aconites with the exception of *A. heterophyllum*), some are poisonous, others not, and even some of the varieties of one species are poisonous, while other varieties are not. The poisonous forms have never been accurately identified, and the result is, that of a given weight of the root sold in our druggists' shops, a certain percentage frequently contains no aconitia whatever: indeed, an entire consignment may be perfectly inert," and on p. 86: "In the *Admiralty Manual of Scientific Inquiry* (and republished in *Hanbury's Science Papers*, 187) occurs the following significant interrogation, which, strange to say, remains unanswered: '*Aconite root* has been imported in considerable quantities from India. In what district is it collected, and from what species of *Aconitum*?' This admission of want of definite information regarding the source of Indian Aconite was made in 1871 by Professor Oliver and the late distinguished scholar and pharmacologist, Daniel Hanbury, and it has still to be answered before we can be said to possess any trustworthy data upon which to base a definite and accurate knowledge of what may be justly called India's most valuable indigenous drug." Impressed by the importance of the case, he suggested to the Government of India an organised enquiry into the matter. A few passages from this communication containing the essential points which would have to be determined are reprinted in the first volume of his *Dictionary* on pp. 85 and 86. They go to the root of the matter and show an admirable grasp of the essential; and so far as his recommendations have been acted upon, they have been of great help in elucidating some of the most obscure points. With a view to contributing himself to the solution of the problem, Watt has collected since 1893 personally, and with the assistance of several Forest officers and others, specimens of Indian Aconite. An almost complete set of his collections went to Calcutta, where Mr. Brühl of the Bengal Educational Service had already at an early date taken up the study of those Aconites which he considered most intimately connected which *A. ferox*, and of which a very large material had accumulated in the herbarium of the Botanic Gardens, mainly from King's Sikkim Collectors. The results of Brühl's studies appeared in Part II of the fifth volume of these Annals in 1896, forming part of a paper on rare Indian plants, which may be characterised as an example of extreme synthesis. The tendency to generalise and explain the diversities observable in a polymorphous group by the assumption of a high degree of plasticity and instability was carried so far that not only were six or seven species, as I understand them, merged in *A. ferox* proper, but also such marked types as *A. palmatum* and *A. moschatum* were reduced to sub-species of *A. ferox*. In general, where the species are so intricately related and so difficult to discriminate as is the case in *Aconitum*, an excess in the direction of synthesis becomes much more quickly fatal than an excess in the opposite direction. In dealing with practical questions it is often necessary to fix on small units of classification and to define them accurately, and it leads only to confusion if they are lost in a plethora of vaguely characterised "varieties" or in the complicated hierarchy of a speculative system of species, sub-species, varieties, sub-varieties, etc. Conflicts were therefore inevitable. They appeared in the results of the investigation which Dunstan undertook (see *Agric. Ledger*) into the chemical properties of certain Aconites which came under Brühl's *A. ferox*, in Goris' paper *De la structure des Aconites et de son utilisation pour la determination specifique des Aconites de l'Inde* (in the *Bulletin des Scienc. Pharmacol.*, 1901, No. 4), and more than anywhere else in Watt's sketch of *The Indian Aconites: their varieties, their distribution, and their uses* in the *Agricultural Ledger* (1902), No. 3, which was based chiefly on Brühl's work. Every one of the three authors felt obliged to make reservations or to doubt whether this or that form would not be better treated as an independent and distinct unit. Such was the condition of our knowledge of the poisonous Aconites of India when the circumstances which I have explained in the preface to this paper caused me to take up the study of the Indian Aconites on the broad basis of a monograph.

II.—BIKHMA.

The history of *Bikhma* is very short. It is, so far as I know, mentioned for the first time by Kirkpatrick (*Account of Nepal*, p. 182) who enumerates it among the medicines of Nepal. Judging from its intense bitterness, he took it to be a Gentian. Hamilton (*Account of Nepal*, p. 99) also mentions it as a strong bitter, very powerful in the cure of fevers. He obtained samples of it, which he named and described as *Caltha Bisma* (*Edinb. Journ. Sc.*, i., 1824, p. 251). This determination is very strange even if we take into consideration that he saw only young or abnormal flowers. Wallich, more fortunate in this case than with Hamilton's other two Calthas, reduced it rightly to his *Aconitum palmatum*, of which he himself had obtained complete specimens from Gossainthan. How after that doubts concerning the origin of the *Bikhma* should have arisen is difficult to understand. Through the erroneous combination of flowering specimens of *A. palmatum* with roots of *A. spicatum* in J. D. Hooker's collection, *Bikhma* acquired for a time the reputation of being poisonous; but Dymock (*Mat. Med. Western India*, 1883, p. 6) pointed out that it was one of the non-poisonous kinds of *Bish* or *Jadwar* of the Arabian and Persian Pharmacopœas. He also suggested (l. c., p., 7) that the bitter alkaloid of the *Bikhma* was "possibly identical with that contained in *Atees*," which has since been proved to be the case; but in spite of its containing Atisin, it never was so much appreciated as the root of *A. heterophyllum*.

III.—JADWAR.

In quoting from Frater Angelus' Persian Pharmacopœa, I referred to the strange story the Tatta people told him about the mice who live with impunity on the roots of the *Bish* plant. The tale is, however, much older. Hobaish has it already (Ebn Baithar, Transl. Sontheimer, i., p. 199), adding also the quails as immune devourers of the poisonous root. Muwaffak (Transl. Achudnow, p. 169) records it in connection with "Halahil," and Avicenna repeats it under the headings "Bish (de Napello)" and "Bish mus (de Napello Moysi)." He says (Lib. Canon. Lat. Transl. Ger. Carmon. corr. Alp. Bellun. II. cap. 499): "Theriaca vero eius est mus napelli, et ipse quidem est mus, qui eo nutritur. Semen vero ex eo cibantur et non moriuntur et ex omnibus confectionibus diamuschum magis et resistit"; and "Napellus Moysi buha quid est. Est herba nascens cum napello et cuicunque napellus appropinquat non crescit, vel non fructificat arbor eius, et est maior theriaca napello et in ipso sunt omnia iuvamenta quae sunt in napello ad albaras et ad lepram. Napellus vero Moysi est animal quod moratur in radice napelli, sicut mus. . . Est theriaca omni veneno et viperae." Further on (cap. 745) we read under the head *Jadwar* (or as it is rendered by the translator *Gieduar*, de Zedoaria): "Et melior quidem est illa (*i.e.*, Zedoaria) quae cum napello crescit et eius vicinitas debilitat plantam napelli. . .

Etiam sciverunt quod zedoaria resistit napello. . . Est theriaca venenosorum omnium, viperae et napelli et aliorum." It is evident that Avicenna's "melior Zedoaria" and his "Napellus Moysi buha" are one thing, whilst the inferior *Zedoaria* which he mentions in the same chapter (745) is *Zerumbeth*—he actually uses this word in giving the directions for the preparation of the theriacon—most likely *Curcuma rotunda.* The word *Zedoar*—the Greek form of *Zadwar* (Pers.) or *Jadwar* (Arab.) occurs, however, already with Actius (6th century) and Macer (9th or 10th cent.), who says of it: "Adprime sumptus Zedoar obstare venenis affirmunt" (Dymock, Warden, and Hooper, *Pharmacogr.* i., p. 20). Serapion (10th and 11th cent.) would also seem to have mixed it up with *Zerumbet,* but in cap. 172 he states according to Matthioli (*Comm. Dioscorides* Ed. Venet., 1565, p. 581):—"Zedoaria convehitur e Sinarum regione ultra extremas Indiae oras." However, Garcia d'Orto (*Arom. Hist.* Ed. Clus. in *Exot.*, p. 214) remarks:—"Serapionis autem legitimi codices non habent ad litam expositionem Zerumbet, id est, Zedoaria, sed ab interprete insertam verisimile est, qui differentiam inter Zedoaria et Zerumba ignorabat. Id ex sequentibus facile deprehenditur, cum ait, e Sinarum regione convehi. Certum enim est, Zedoariam non nasci apud Indos, sed e Sinarum regione advehi, raramque apud Indos inveniri. Zerumba vero abunde in India nascitur." Matthioli seems to have seen both drugs. The *Zerumbet* was then fairly well known, whilst he received specimens of the genuine *Zedoar* from a Belgian Gulielmus Qualcebenus:—"Medicus insignis et rei plantariae studiosus, qui . . . misit ad me Constantinopoli Antorae radices aliquot, quas mercatores a quibus emerat magno satis precio, zedoariam appellabant. Quae si non sunt, alterius quidem plantae radices esse non poterunt quam eius, de qua sub Napelli Moysi nomine meminit." (Matth., *Comm. Dioscorides,* p. 1097, see also Matth. *Epistol.* iii, pp. 102 and 105). The confusion of *Zedoar* and *Zerumbeth* must have begun very early; and as the genuine article hardly ever reached Europe, the name *Zedoar* seems to have fixed itself on its commoner substitute. That Matthioli compared the *Zedoar* he received from Constantinople with Anthora (*Aconitum Anthorae*) is not surprising, considering the great external resemblance of the *Zedoar* root and that of *Aconitum Anthorae;* and as to the alleged Chinese origin of the former, I need only refer to the fact that the most valuable kind of *Jadwar* is still known in India as *Jadwar-Khatai,* or "Chinese Jadwar." Garcia d'Orto (*l. c.*, p. 213) also distinguishes carefully between the true *Zedoar* and the one which they called *Zerumba* or *Zerumbet* at Goa, and he remarks:—"Quod nos hic Zedoariam appellamus, Avicennae lib. II, cap. 734, *Geiduar* dicitur, aliud nomen ignoro quia nascitur regionibus Sinensium provincae vicinis. Magno vero emitur Geiduar; nec facile invenias, nisi apud circumforaneos quosdam et circulatores, quos Indi *jogues,* Mauritani *calandares* appellant, hominum genus quod peregrinationibus et stipem emendicando vitam sustentat. Ab his enim et Reges et Magnates Geiduar emunt." Clusius (*Exot.*, p. 378) mentions, in a scholion to Garcia d'Orto's chapter on *Zedoaria,* that he received in 1605 from Pona of Verona two roots of "Gedwar veri," and figures one of them in three positions. But from the figures and his statement that the taste was hot and acrimonious I doubt that it was the genuine article.

Among the Persian Pharmacopœas the *Ulfas Udwiyeh* (about 1450; Trans. Gladwin) has *Jadwar* in three places, namely, No. 398: "Bar-Heo, also Neer Bissee. Zedoary v. Jedwar"; No. 668: "Judwar. Zedoary"; and No. 1352: "Mah-Fir-Feen. Zedoary, p. (Persian) Judwar." This is important because here for the first time *Jadwar* or *Zedoar* is clearly connected with *Nirbish;* but Royle (*Ill. Bot. Him.*, p. 50) states also that the Persian authors distinguished five kinds of *Judwar.* "The best, called *Khutai,* or

Chinese, procured from the mountains of that country. The two next kinds are the produce of the mountains of Tibet, of Nepal, of Morung, and Rungpore; the fourth kind is from the hills of the Dukhun, and the fifth, called *Antuleh*, is the produce of Andaloosee or Spain." Of these, the Morung, Rungpore, Dekkan, and Andalusian kinds may be dismissed, as they have certainly nothing to do with the Indian Aconites.

So much is then evident from these sources, that as early as the 10th or probably the 6th century the roots of an Aconite supposed to possess extraordinary powers as an antidote reached the Orient and India under the name of *Jadwar* or *Zedwar* (whence *Zedoar*), and that the home of this drug was China or Kathai, which of course need not have meant China proper, but merely Tibet.

When Hamilton in the beginning of the last century endeavoured to obtain the plant which yielded *Bikh*, he paid also some attention to the "Nirbishi or Nirbikhi," but met with the usual difficulties in procuring genuine specimens through natives, as he says in his Catalogue of the plants collected in Nepal, published by Madden, in *Trans. Bot. Soc. Edinb.* v., 1858, p. 127, under No. 1248: "Caltha? Nirbisia, Nirbishi vel Nirbikhi. Ham. Nepal, 99. . . . . . Montanorum unus hanc pro radice indica toxicaria ostendebat, alter autem sequentem (*Caltha? Codoa*) afferebat." Hamilton meant, as appears from p. 99 of his *Account of Nepal*, the plant which "has no deleterious qualities, but is used in medicine." The specimen, however, which is named "Caltha Nirbisia" in his herbarium (now incorporated in the Wallichian collection at the Linnean Society, London) has on the label the note, "Brought as the poison plant." It is a very young plant, no doubt an Aconite, but not determinable. I tasted a morsel of it; it was slightly and purely bitter, but did not cause the tingling sensation characteristic of the poisonous Aconites of the ferox-group. This was the basis of Don's genus *Nirbisia.* Royle was not more fortunate in his attempt to discover the source of the *Nirbisi* of the Indian bazaars. He had been told in Sirmore and Garhwal that *Delphinium pauciflorum* (= *D. denudatum*) was the plant which produced the *Nirbisi*; but on comparing it with the best kind of *Nirbisi* in the Indian bazaars which is brought down from Bissehur and Umritsar he "found it of a very different nature." The term *Nirbisi*, he adds (*Ill. Bot. Him.*, p. 50), implies that the drug is used as an antidote to poison, being composed of the privative preposition *nir* and *bis*, poison; and winds up the paragraph with this conclusion:—"It is therefore probable that the Nirbisi is the true *Zedoar* or *Geiduar* of Avicenna, whatever may be the plant which produces it." Since then Madden (*Trans. Bot. Soc. Edinb.* v., 1858, p. 129) has pointed out that he "found the beautiful *Delphinium kashmerianum* Royle......with cylindrical tuberous roots, absolutely identical in form with the ordinary Nirbisi," and he had no doubt that this was its true source. The root of *Delphinium kashmerainum*, however, can hardly be described as tuberous. It is long, slender, fusiform, more or less obliquely descending, and resembles rather that of an Aconite of the section *Lycoctonum*, on a somewhat reduced scale. If there exists in the bazaars of North-West India a drug of this shape under the name of *Nirbisi*, it may be the ordinary, but cannot be the genuine *Jadwar*. Having no doubt the latter in mind, Madden further on says: "The Tibetans told Major H. Strachey it came from the east." This agrees with a note by Strachey accompanying a sample of Jadwar obtained by him and preserved in the museum at Kew. It reads: "Nirbisi (Hind.) Bomar (Tib.) Jadwar (Pers.) from Khywong of Nianpyul (Nepal?) *vid* Gartok—Zedoary." Aitchison obtained evidently the same drug at Leh under the name *Jadwar-Khatai*, and he says (*Trade Prod. of Leh*, p. 101): "This root comes from Nepal to Lhasa, and thence *vid* Gartok to Leh.

From Leh nearly the whole of it is exported to Yarkand, a very little to Kashmir, and thence to India. It is highly valued as a talisman to carry continually about the person, and as an antidote to be taken in poisoning, or in certain fever illnesses, such as cholera. Owing to the above circumstances and the smallness of the supply, it is usually sold in its own weight of silver or gold. By the Yarkands it is called Farfi; by the Kashmiris Jadwar; by the Bhotes Bonga; and in the Panjab Nirbisi." I take this root to be the article to which the tales of the Arabs about the *Zedoar* and the *Bish mus* refer. A description of it will be found at the end of the special part: as to the species from which it is obtained, I can only point out that it resembles the roots of *A. heterophylloides* of Sikkim to a very high degree indeed. The vernacular name of the Nepalese settlers in Sikkim for this species is moreover *Nirbanshi*, which reads very like a corruption of *Nirbishi*.

It is quite intelligible that the origin of so valuable a drug should be kept secret, and that on the other hand substitutes should be sought which were more easily obtainable. Moodeen Sheriff (*Suppl. Pharm. Ind.*, p. 29) states that three varieties of *Jadwar* are generally used in medicine at present, adding that he believed them to be "the roots of some species of Aconite like *A. heterophyllum*, which is not poisonous," one of which he thinks is a kind of *Atis*, but I suspect that also the two others are not exactly the genuine article. Thus the mystery of the miraculous *Zedoar* is not yet quite unravelled, although it is certain that the plant is an *Aconitum*, closely allied to, if not identical with *A. heterophylloides*. Its home is probably Nepal, and possibly Sikkim, from whence it is exported to Tibet and by a very circuitous route to India, acquiring on its way the epitheton "Kathai"! Some of the poisonous and non-poisonous aconites of the Himalaya are so similar that even an otherwise well-trained eye might be deceived. Could it then be that the native collectors use as a guide the instinct of a mouse or some such rodent living about and feeding on the non-poisonous Aconite roots, but leaving alone the poisonous? And if so, would not their naïve imagination attribute to the plant, which is almost indistinguishable from its most deadly kindred and to the animal feeding upon it, miraculous powers such as were claimed for the *Zedoar* and the *Bish mus*? Is there not after all a grain of truth in the apparently absurd tale which has exposed the Oriental writers to the ridicule of the worthy herbalists of Europe?

§ 2. STRUCTURE OF THE ROOTS OF ACONITUM.

Three main types of root-structure may be distinguished in *Aconitum*. They are intimately connected with the duration and rejuvenation of the individual plants, and they afford at the same time the most salient feature by which to characterise the three principal sections of the genus.

1. **Annual roots.** There is only one species of annual duration known in the genus, viz., *A. gymnandrum*, a native of Eastern Central Asia from the frontiers of Sikkim to the mountains around Kuku Nor. The root is very slender, fusiform, usually vertically descending, of a type very common in annuals. This species, which is also very peculiar on account of the long slender claws of the sepals, constitutes the section *Gymnaconitum*.

2. **Perennial roots.** *A. laeve*, *A luridum*, and *A. moschatum* among the Indian species possess long, perennial, rhizome-like roots which pass at the upper end into a short

collar or much shortened axis which produces alternately cataphylls acting as bud-scales and foliage leaves, and when mature grows into a leaf- and flower-bearing stem. At the same time buds are formed in the axils of some of the basal leaves, the strongest of which secures or secure the rejuvenation of the individual after the dying down of the flower-bearing stem at the close of the season. If several buds develop and their bases persist, as is the case in robust individuals, a branched collar or '*caudex multiceps*' may be formed. If the root of a mature plant be examined, it will be found in cross-section to consist of cord-like strands which are embedded in dead suberised tissue and surrounded by a common bark (see PLATE 93) which is pierced by numerous root-fibres springing from the strands. These may be free, running parallel with each other for a considerable distance, or anastomose variously, or they may separate entirely and, becoming independent, give rise to new individuals. As the bark and the dead tissue surrounding the strands decay, these may be laid partly bare (see PLATE 92). The process by which the peculiar fission of the roots is finally brought about has been fully described by A. Meyer [in *Arch. d. Pharm.* vol. 219 (1881), pp. 184 & 185]. The species possessing perennial roots of this kind correspond to the section *Lycoctonum.* They also are distinguished by a peculiar habit by which they are generally easily recognised. Outside India a number of mostly very closely allied species with a similar root-structure occur over an area extending from the Pyrenees to Sachalin and Japan. Like the Indian species of this type, they are mostly confined to woods.

3. **Biennial roots.** The greatest number of species have, however, roots which are biennial and normally paired, and at the same time tuberous, one of each pair bearing, when mature, a stem producing leaves and flowers, the other crowned with a bud destined to grow out into a similar stem in the next season when that of the preceding year and also the root which supported it would be dead and withered. The tubers, and with them the individuals, are renewed from buds in the axils of the lowest leaves. Usually only one develops from each stem; hence the pairing. Under favourable conditions, however, two or even more may grow up, with the result that small clusters of tubers are formed. As the old and the new plant stand in the relation of mother and daughter, the old and new tubers have been called mother- and daughter-tubers, which must, of course, not be meant to imply that one root springs directly from the other. The bud which is going to produce the daughter-tuber is formed very early, but the growth of the bud proper is soon arrested and it remains in a dormant state for a whole year, whilst from its base an adventitious root springs which soon outgrows the bud by many times in volume and assumes the shape of a tuber, pushing aside what there may have been left of the petiole in the axil of which the bud originated. The connection of the daughter-tuber with the mother-plant is maintained by a usually very short neck through which the food material wanders from the stem into the new tuber to be there deposited mainly as reserve starch and alkaloids. It is therefore these daughter-tubers which are principally collected, and they should, of course, not be taken up before they have attained maturity.

The structure of these root-tubers exhibits a remarkable variety with respect to the disposition of the cambium and consequently of the secondary xylem- and phloem-strands. The importance of this condition from a purely scientific point of view as well as for the discrimination of the Aconite tubers as they come into the market has not escaped the attention of the students of anatomy and pharmacy. Irmisch who had as early as 1854 (*Zeitschr. f. d. gesammt. Naturwissensch.* iv., pp. 181—193, tab. 3, 4, 5) given a classic account of the development of *Aconitum Napellus* and *A. Lycoctonum*, explained in 1873 the structure of the tubers of *Aconitum Anthora*. A. Meyer followed eight years later with a most important paper on the anatomy and the development of *A. Napellus* and other species, among them *A. heterophyllum* and "*A. ferox*" (evidently my *A. spicatum*). He was, so far as I know, the first to try whether the anatomical differences of the root-tubers could be utilised for purposes of classification, though with a negative result so far as the "blue flowering" species were concerned. Since then the anatomy of the roots of various Aconites has been treated in a number of papers and text-books which I need not enumerate here, as they generally do not concern the Indian species. The systematists, however, took no notice of these researches, and it was not until 1901 that an attempt was made to supplement the definition of the more important Indian species of Aconites, so far entirely based on characters derived from the leaves, flowers and fruits, by the description of the anatomical structure of their roots, mainly with a view to utilise them for the determination of the tubers obtainable in the market. These investigations were carried out by A. Goris of Paris and published in the *Bulletin des Sciences Pharmacologiques*, 1901, pp. 102—122, with three plates and 34 figs. in the text. The following species—all belonging to the group of Aconites possessing paired biennial roots—were examined:—1. *A. Napellus* (= *A. chasmanthum*); 2. *A. palmatum*; 3. *A. heterophyllum*; 4. *A. ferox* var. *laciniatum* (= *A. laciniatum*); 5. *A. ferox* var. *spicatum* (= *A. spicatum*); 6. *A. ferox* var. *atrox* (= *A. deinorrhizum ?*); 7. *A. ferox* v. *polyschiza* (= *A. Balfourii*). Nos. 1, 4, & 5 were referred to the type *Napellus* ("cambium sinuous, star-shaped, always continuous"); 2 & 3 to the type *Anthora* ("cambium breaking up into 4 isolated strands"); and 6 & 7 to the type *Atrox* ("characterised by a normal central cylinder within which a phloem-xylem ring with inverted orientation is formed"). I have been able to extend the examination of the root-structure of the Indian Aconites considerably, and *A. Elwesii* and *A. lethale* are the only species of which I have not seen any tubers. Even with this extension, it seems to me that those three types may, with slight modifications, be retained, taking in between them all the species of the biennial-rooted Aconites of India so far as their tubers are known. However, before I show how the species which I describe in the special part under the section *Napellus* may be distributed over those three types, it will be necessary to say a few words on the general structure of the biennial root-tubers. I do not intend to describe here their development, but the condition in the mature tuber as it presents itself in transverse sections taken from the middle, or, at any rate, not too close to either end. This is necessary because the structure of the tubers undergoes some modifications as the ends are approached.

All the tubers are covered by a bark consisting of thin-walled periderma with or without sclerenchymatic elements in the inner zone and varying considerably in thickness according to the species, although always thin. The colour also varies in the dry, and probably to a lesser degree in the fresh species, from blackish through various shades of brown to almost whitish. Then the endodermis comes next, forming a continuous sheath round the central cylinder and consisting of a single layer of suberised cells of the kind generally characteristic of the endodermis of roots. The central cylinder, which is represented by the bulk of the tuber, consists mainly of parenchymatic tissue filled with starch, and, embedded in it, of the cambium, of sieve-tube strands, and of strands of the vasal elements of the xylem. This differentiation may already be observed with the naked eye or at any rate with a good pocket-lens. Sclerenchymatic cells may be added in certain species in the outer zones of the central cylinder, but they never become prominent with the exception of *A. ferox.* I have already pointed out that the modifications which allow us to distinguish several types in the structure of the root-tubers of *Aconitum* may be traced back to the disposition of the cambial tissue. The simplest case is represented by what Goris has called the *Napellus* type, to which the commonest kind of "bikh roots" sold in the Bengal bazaars and imported into Europe belongs, namely that which is derived from *A. spicatum.* Here, as in the European *A. Napellus,* the cambium appears in cross-section as a faint more or less sinuous ring. Without it we notice, scattered through the otherwise homogeneous tissue, minute dots which correspond to delicate strands composed essentially of sieve-tubes, whilst we find inside the cambium ring, and close to it, semilunar or horseshoe-shaped marks, or minute radially directed dashes and dots, the cross-sections of the vasal strands of the xylem. Where they are not very clear they can be made more conspicuous by the phloroglucin and chloric acid reaction to which they respond very readily, staining deep purple. The cambium line itself is so delicate that it would not be seen, except under a high power, but for the presence of zones of a more small-celled and compact tissue on both sides of it, and similar conditions contribute to the more prominent marking of the xylem strands, introducing a contrast of denser and looser parts into the otherwise uniform tissue. The whole of the central cylinder outside the cambium zone may practically be considered as consisting of secondary phloem in which the primary phloem is lost, whilst the tissue within the cambium and the xylem strands,—pith by origin and storage tissue by structure and function—conforms to the parenchyma of the secondary phloem. The same structure is repeated in the tubers of *A. soongaricum, chasmanthum, violaceum, Falconeri, spicatum, laciniatum, ferox, heterophylloides, leucanthum, dissectum,* and the "Jadwar" tubers, to whatever species they may belong. Further modifications are introduced into this type by the varying colour and the more or less "farinaceous" or horny or cartilaginous appearance which the tubers assume when dried—conditions difficult to trace as to their ultimate cause; by the more or less prominent development of the cambial zone and the xylem strands; and, in the case of *A. ferox,* by the formation of sclerenchymatic sheaths encasing the sieve-strands in the mother-tubers. These differences are mentioned in the descriptions of the species, and I need not dwell on them here, the less so, as they are perhaps not quite reliable, the number of observations from which they have been derived being in most cases very small. Besides, there are other characters, especially the differences in the taste of tubers, due to the presence of different alkaloids, that afford a better help for discrimination within this group.

The second type, of which I may quote *A. heterophyllum* as an example, exhibits an essentially different structure. We find, in place of one continuous cambium ring, several (up to six) small rings or irregular stars embedded in a uniform tissue, and generally arranged in a concentric ring. Sieve-strands occur not only outside this ring, but also within it, surrounding the little rings or stars; but they are usually so delicate that the compound microscope is required to see them. Inside the small cambium rings the lignified portions of the xylem may be observed as more or less V-shaped marks which almost meet in the centre. This structure also needs higher magnification to be seen well, and the phloroglucin and chloric acid reaction may be found very useful. The cambium zone itself is very delicate, and the star-, ring-, or dot-shaped markings indicating the isolated strands are chiefly determined by their xylem portions. We have then here almost the whole of the central cylinder consisting of secondary phloem plus an undefined and very small central pith, embedded in it a number of cambium cylinders, and inside them the xylem strands surrounding a very slender and much reduced column of secondary pith. Goris designated this type of root-structure as the *Anthora* type, as it comes very near to the structure of the tubers of *A. Anthora*. To it must be referred, among the Indian Aconites, *A. rotundifolium*, *heterophyllum*, *naviculare*, *palmatum* and probably also *A. Hookeri*. This type also shows modifications which may be used for the discrimination of the species. In *A. rotundifolium* and *A. naviculare*, the number of isolated strands is normally 4, and they are so small that they appear to the naked eye as mere dots. In *A. palmatum* they are, on the other hand, much larger and more irregular, and there is a tendency towards separating entirely by the formation of periderma between them—at least in the upper (acropetal) part of the tuber which becomes thus split or spuriously branched. In *A. Hookeri* there is only one very slender central strand present, the structure of which is that of the isolated strands of *A. heterophyllum*, and this species should therefore be referred to the *Anthora* type.

Goris' third type, which he called the *Atrox* type, is represented only by two species—*A. deinorrhizum* and *A. Balfourii*. As the name *A. atrox* cannot be maintained, I prefer to call it the *Deinorrhizum* type. There we have, as in the *Anthora* type, isolated cambium bands, embedded in secondary phloem which in the centre passes, as we may assume, into a column of pith, a part of the original fundamental issue. The cambium bands are, however, corresponding to the greater size of the tubes, much larger than in the *Anthora* type. They are approximately circular in cross-section or, more often, tangentially flattened and even horseshoe-shaped, and so arranged as to form a discontinuous ring. Moreover, they anastomose in places, as successive sections show. As the cambium produces at intervals along its entire length and on its inner side secondary xylem, the xylem strands are disposed centripetally on the peripheral side of the strands and centrifugally on the side nearer to the centre. The innermost part of the strands is occupied by a comparatively copious secondary pith. I must not omit to remark that the typical aspect of an Aconite tuber in cross-section may be modified if the section passes through a root-fibre trace or in the case of anomalies which occur, no doubt, in the Indian Aconites as they do in the European *A. Napellus*.

The mother-tubers differ from the daughter-tubers only in so far as the gradual exhaustion of the reserve material stored up in the parenchyma is accompanied by the collapse of the latter, both proceeding centripetally, with the consequence that the surface of the tuber becomes more and more shrivelled and wrinkled. As the old tubers dry up, the inner parenchyma often also tears up, forming cavities, particularly near the xylem strands, and in some cases I saw the greater part of the pith gone and replaced by a large cavity. The curious formation of sclerenchymatic sheaths around the sieve-strands in the tuber of *A. ferox* has already been mentioned.

If the species of the section *Lycoctonum* are typically woodland plants, those of the third principal group, which I comprise at present under the section *Napellus* (sens. lat.), are on the contrary found principally in open land in the Alpine zone above the forest region, and only few descend more or less into the subalpine woods.

The following is a synopsis of the Indian Aconites arranged according to the structure of their roots, so far as they are known; those marked with an asterisk (*) are known to be or suspected to be poisonous:—

I.—Gymnaconitum Type.

A. gymnandrum.

II.—Lycoctonum Type.

A. laeve;* A. luridum;* A. moschatum.*

III.—Napellus Type (sens. lat.).

1. **Napellus** Type (sens. str.).

   - A. soongaricum;*
   - A. chasmanthum;*
   - A. violaceum;
   - A. Falconeri;*
   - A. spicatum;*
   - A. laciniatum;*
   - A. ferox;
   - A. heterophylloides;
   - A. leucanthum;
   - A. dissectum;
   - A. (Jadwar).

2. **Anthora** Type.

   - A. rotundifolium;
   - A. heterophyllum;
   - A. naviculare;
   - A. palmatum;
   - A. Hookeri.

3. **Deinorrhizum** Type.

   - A. deinorrhizum;*
   - A. Balfourii.*

II.—DESCRIPTIONS OF THE ACONITES OF INDIA.

ACONITUM LINN.

CONSPECTUS.

SECTION I.—**LYCOCTONUM.**—*Root perennial, long, fusiform, usually breaking up at length into cord-like anastomosing or free strands; old plants often with several stems from the collar.*

- Upper sepal distinctly helmet-shaped, produced into a long deflexed or subhorizontal beak:—
  - Helmet high, linear-oblong or oblong in profile; nectaries extinguisher-shaped, hood oblique, much shorter than the claw . . . 1. *A. laeve.*
  - Helmet depressed, broad, hemi-elliptic in profile; nectaries hammer-shaped, hood as long as the claw . . . . 2. *A. luridum.*
- Upper sepal navicular, obliquely erect; nectaries extinguisher-shaped, hood erect, short, broad . . . . 3. *A. moschatum.*

SECTION II.—**NAPELLUS.**—*Roots biennial, paired, tuberous; each tuber producing normally one simple or (rarely) branched stem.*

- Stem erect, rarely ascending, never twining:—
  - Seed-angles winged, faces smooth or almost smooth (not transversely lamellate):—
    - All the leaves distinctly to very long petioled, cordate-orbicular or reniform in outline, deeply dissected:—
      - Cambium of tubers continuous, forming in cross-section a more or less sinuous ring; honey-gland of nectaries on the back of the hood:—
        - Tubers 2—3·5 cm. long, fracture (in the dry state) horny or cartilaginous, brown (at least the part outside the cambium); taste slightly bitter, followed by a tingling sensation; carpels glabrous or nearly so, never tomentose:—
          - Carpels 3, diverging after flowering . . . . 4. *A. soongaricum.*
          - Carpels 5, conniving . . . . 5. *A. chasmanthum.*
        - Tubers 0·5—2·5 cm. long, fracture (in the dry state) almost farinaceous, pure white; taste indifferent or slightly sweetish, not followed by any tingling sensation; carpels densely tomentose:—
          - Stem erect or shortly ascending, without a creeping hypogaeous part; nectary-hood erect, honey-gland subterminal . . . . 6. *A. violaceum.*
          - Stem ascending from a very slender, often creeping hypogaeous part; nectary-hood strongly curved and leaning forward, honey-gland basal . . . . 7. *A. Hookeri.*
      - Cambium of tubers discontinuous, forming usually 4 isolated strands; nectary-hood leaning forwards, honey-gland anticous . . . . 8. *A. rotundifolium.*
    - All the leaves with the exception of the lowest shortly petioled to subsessile, cordate-ovate, coarsely crenate . . . . . . 9. *A. heterophyllum.*
  - Seeds with hyaline wavy transverse lamellae:—
    - Sepals persistent round the mature follicles; stature dwarf . . . 10. *A. naviculare.*

Sepals early deciduous; stature not dwarf:—

Cambium of tubers discontinuous, forming in cross-section circular or tangentially flattened to horseshoe-shaped strands:—

Nectary-hood very slender with a minute lip; carpels quite glabrous; taste of tubers intensely and pure bitter, not followed by any tingling sensation . . . 11. *A. palmatum.*

Nectary-hood wide with a rather large lip; carpels hairy; taste of tubers rather indifferent, followed by a strong and persistent tingling sensation:—

Inflorescence and carpels greyish pubescent; leaves divided almost to the base, ultimate divisions narrow; carpels usually 3 . . . . 12. *A. deinorrhizum.*

Inflorescence and carpels spreadingly yellowish tomentose; leaves rather less divided than in the preceding species, ultimate divisions broad; carpels 5 . . . . 13. *A. Balfourii.*

Cambium continuous, forming in cross-section a more or less sinuous ring:—

Plants ½ m. to more than 1 m. high, with more or less robust or terete stems; tubers 2·25—20 cm. long, with a slightly bitter or indifferent taste, followed by a severe and tingling sensation:—

Secondary sieve-strands of mother-tubers not encased in sclerenchymatic sheaths; lip of nectary widened from the base upwards; leaf-segments not or slightly divaricate:—

Leaves divided to 6/7 in the inner, to 3/4 or less in the outer incisions, ultimate divisions rather broad; carpels 5; follicles 10—18 mm. long:—

Intermediate leaf-division rhomboid-cuneate, sparingly and coarsely inciso-crenate; nectary-hood much leaning forward, slightly widened at the top, scarcely gibbous; carpels glabrous or nearly so; follicles 14—18 mm. long . . . . 14. *A. Falconeri.*

Intermediate leaf-division mostly ovate in outline, copiously inciso-crenate or dentate; nectary-hood slightly leaning forward, distinctly gibbous at the top; carpels villous; follicles about 10 mm. long . . . . 15. *A. spicatum.*

Leaves divided almost to the very base, ultimate divisions narrow; carpels mostly 3; follicles 18—25 mm. long . . . . 16. *A. laciniatum.*

Secondary sieve-strands of mother-tubers encased in sclerenchymatic sheaths, forming persistent fibres; lip of nectary narrow; leaf-segments conspicuously divaricate . . . . 17. *A. ferox.*

Plants under 0·5 m. high, with slender, more or less angular stems; tubers 0·6—2·5 cm. long:—

Leaf-divisions ovate or ovate-lanceolate, acute, multicrenate. 18. *A. heterophylloides.*

Leaf-divisions (at least the intermediate) rhomboid, inciso-crenate or laciniate, laciniae mostly narrow, subobtuse. 19. *A. leucanthum.*

Stem very slender, twining:—
Flowers on recurved pedicels (up to 5 cm. long), nodding; helmet conic-ovate in profile . . . . 20. *A. Elwesii.*
Flowers on straight or almost straight pedicels (up to 7·5 cm. long); helmet depressed, semi-orbicular in profile . . . . . 21. *A. lethale.*

Position uncertain in the section; imperfectly known . . . . . . { 22. *A. nagarum.* 23. *A. dissectum.*

SECTION III.—**GYMNACONITUM.**—*Root fusiform, annual.*
Sepals long-clawed, covering the stamens imperfectly . . . . . 24 *A. gymnandrum.*

SECTION I.—LYCOCTONUM DC.

ROOT perennial, long, fusiform, usually breaking up at length into cord-like anastomosing or free strands; old plants often with several stems from the collar.

1. ACONITUM LAEVE Royle, Ill. Himal. (1834), pp. 45, 56.

A. Lycoctonum Hook. fil. & Thoms. Fl. Ind. i. p. 55; Hook. fil. Fl. Brit. Ind. i. p. 28; Atkins. Gaz. N.-W. Prov. (1882), p. 412; Watt Dict. Econ. Prod. India, i. p. 94, and in Agric. Ledger, 1902, No. 3, p. 89; Duthie in Rec. Bot. Surv. India, i. No. 3 (1894), p. 37, and No. 9 (1898), p. 143. Lawrence Valley of Kashmir, p. 85; not of Linnaeus.

A. vitifolium Royle Ms. (in Hb. Cambridge).

[TYPE SPECIMENS: A specimen at Kew, stated to be from Royle's herbarium, and marked (but not in Royle's writing!) "Aconitum Lycoctonum, A: (sic) laeve Royle, N.-W. India!" and another in the Saharanpur herbarium, collected by Royle (?) in 1825 on Mt. Choor, and named 'Aconitum palmatum' might pass as type specimens. Localities quoted by Royle, l. c., "Choor (!), Kunawur (!), Pir Panjal (!)."]

Root perennial, elongate, more or less cylindric, ultimately breaking up into separate or anastomosing strands. *Stem* erect, simple or branched, up to 6 ft. high with all the internodes elongate, hairy and slightly viscous in the upper, glabrous in the lower part, hairs short, spreading or curved and adpressed. *Leaves* few from the collar on very long (up to 30 cm.) petioles, usually withered at the time of flowering; 5 or more from the stem, distant, similar to the basal, but the upper gradually smaller, less divided and more hairy, passing into the floral leaves, with rapidly decreasing petioles; basal and lower blades glabrous, orbicular-cordate or reniform in outline with a deep (up to 10 cm.) narrow or wide sinus, up to 15 cm. high (from the sinus to the tip), up to 30 cm. across, 5—9-subpedati-partite to $\frac{5}{6}$ in the inner and to $\frac{3}{4}$ in the outer incisions, inner divisions obovate to obovate-oblong from a broad cuneate base, 3·5—7 cm. wide, 3-lobed, outer divisions trapezoid, 2-lobed, lobes acutely inciso-dentate. *Inflorescence* panicled, often over 50 cm. long, usually leafy, more or less hairy, hairs as on the stem but denser; floral leaves 5—3-partite, sparingly inciso-dentate; bracts lanceolate to linear-lanceolate or filiform, entire or the lowest dentate, usually exceeding the pedicels; bracteoles, if present, linear or filiform; pedicels erect or obliquely erect, the lower when mature often curved upwards and up to 3·5 cm. long. *Sepals* yellowish or white and tinged with purple or blue or wholly purplish, more or less pubescent or minutely hirsute, rarely almost glabrous; upper sepal helmet-shaped, linear-oblong or oblong, 12—16 mm. high, 3—5 mm. wide in the upper part, straight or sometimes slightly recurved at the top, usually abruptly widened in front towards the base into an obtuse or subacute beak, lateral margins slightly curved; lateral sepals rotundate-obovate, oblique, not clawed, 9—11 mm. long, 6—8 mm. broad; lower sepals deflexed, oblong or elliptic-oblong, subobtuse, 7—10 mm. long. *Nectaries* glabrous; claw erect, 8—10 mm. long; hood oblique, slender, conic, up to 5 mm. long

1 mm. wide, obtuse, tip straight and gibbous on the back or recurved (but not revolute), lip deflexed, oblong from a broad base, shortly 2-lobed. *Filaments* about 4 mm. long, glabrous, broadly winged up to the middle, wings suddenly contracted or produced into minute teeth. *Carpels* 3, contiguous and oblique in the flower, soon diverging, oblong, glabrous or covered with yellowish hairs, gradually passing into the style. *Follicles* divergent, obliquely oblong, straight or slightly curved on the back, 10—13 mm. long, glabrous or more or less yellowish-hirsute. *Seeds* elliptic-oblong, dorsally compressed, 2·5—3 mm. long, dark-brown, shining, finely transversely rugose (not hyaline-lamellate).

DISTRIBUTION: *Himalaya from Chitral to Kumaon, mostly in forests, locally abundant, from 5,000—12,000 ft.*

CHITRAL: Ziarat, 7,200—7,500 ft., *Harriss* 15830! 15831! (Hb. Calc. and Sah.); Ashreth Valley, 6,000 ft., *Gatacre* 17006! (Hb. Sah.).—HAZARA: Kagan Valley, *Inayat* 23295! (Hb. Kew); Daragan, *Duthie's Coll.* 21109! (Hb. Sah.).—BALTISTAN: Kamri Valley, Kalapani, 10,000—11,000 ft., *Duthie* 12550! (Hb. Sah.); Barjun and Zujmarg, *Falconer*! (Hb. Sah.); Gurais, *Falconer*! (Hb. Sah.), 7,000—8,000 ft., *Duthie* 12604! (Hb. Calc., Sah. and Edinb.); Tilail, Kargeh Valley, above Abdullan, 11,000—12,000 ft., *Duthie* 13925! (Hb. Kew and Sah.).—KASHMIR: Sind Valley, Baltal, below Zo-ji-la, 9,500—10,000 ft, *Thomson*! (Hb. Kew); Sonamarg, 8,000—9,000 ft., *Duthie* 13626! (Hb. Sah.); Liddar Valley, Kainmal, 10,000—11,000 ft., *Duthie* 13117! (Hb. Sah.); Badzulkod Nala, 12,000 ft., *Duthie*! (Hb. Sah.); Gulmarg, 7,000—10,000 ft., *Duthie* 11407! (Hb. Sah.), *Aitchison* 45! (Hb. Calc.), *Duthie's Coll.* (Hb. Sah.); between Hirpur and Pir Panjal, 7,000 ft., *Gammie*! (Hb. Sah.); Vernag, in shady forest, *Jacquemont* 845! (Hb. Kew); without precise locality, *Atkinson* in C. B. Clarke 24259 (Hb. Kew & Calc.).—CHAMBA: between Thanela and Chandra Junction, 5,000—6,000 ft., *Lace* 1380! (Hb. Sah., Calc. and Edinb.); without precise locality, 6,000 ft., *Thomson*! (Hb. Kew).—LAHUL; without precise locality, *Hay*! (Hb. Calc.).—BASHAHR: Nanab, *Drummond* 1208! (Hb. Sah.); between Zitua Kanda and Kut, 8,500 ft., *Lace* 916! (Hb. Kew, Calc., Sah. and Edinb.).—SIRMOR: Nagkanda, 8,000—9,000 ft., *Watt* 10022! (Hb. Calc. and Edinb.), *Browne* 7243! (Hb. Sah.), *Stoliczka*! (Hb. Calc.); Choor Mountain, *Royle*! (Hb. Sah.), *Drummond's Coll.* 1202! (Hb. Sah.), *Collett* 5456A! (Hb. Sah.); Suri (?), *Drummond's Coll.* 1207! (Hb. Sah.); Pattarnala, 9,000 ft., *Drummond's Coll.* 1206! (Hb. Sah.).—JAUNSAR: Mandali, 7,000 ft., *Rogers*! (Hb. Calc. and Sah.); Bamnai Gadh, below Mandali, 6,000—7,000 ft., *Duthie*! (Hb. Sah.).—TEHRI-GARHWAL: Jumna Valley in shady places and rich soil, *Jacquemont* 698! (Hb. Kew); in forest near Gokal, 7,000—8,000 ft., *Duthie* 14562! (Hb. Calc. and Sah.); Somderdunga Valley, *Anderson*! (Hb. Calc.); Kedarkanta, 7,000 ft., *Gollan* 1348! (Hb. Calc. and Sah.); without precise locality, *Falconer* 67! (Hb. Calc.).—DEHRA DUN: Mussoorie, *Falconer's Coll.*! (Hb. Sah.).—KUMAON: Madharee Pass, 8,000—9,500 ft., near water in woods, *Strachey and Winterbottom* 4! (Hb. Kew); Boora Pinnath, 8,000 ft., *Madden*! (Hb. Kew and Calc.)

VERNACULAR NAME: Unknown.

PROPERTIES AND USES: The root does not appear to be used medicinally, and its chemistry is unknown. Dr. Jowett's notes quoted by Dr. Watt in Agric. Ledger, 1902, No. 3, p. 89, refer to the chemistry of the European *A. Lycoctonum.*

Although the plants from which Royle actually drew up his description of *Aconitum laeve* seem to be lost, and the type specimens quoted above may only be considered as such by inference, there can be no doubt whatever about the plant which Royle had in view. Moreover, there is an excellent drawing in the collection at Kew, representing a young flowering specimen of the plant described here as *A. laeve*, and named in Royle's handwriting "*A. laeve* Royle, *v.* Ill. Ranunculaceæ" with the additional note "Peer Punjal." Royle was well aware of the close affinity of *A. laeve* and *A. septentrionale* Koelle (*i.e.*, the original *A. Lycoctonum* of Linnaeus), and considered them as representative species (*l. c.* 45). *A. laeve* is one of the rather numerous and ill-defined forms which make up the *A. Lycoctonum* of most authors, a "species collectiva" extending over nearly the whole of Europe and temperate Asia. It differs from the *A. Lycoctonum* of north and north-east Europe in the usually smaller yellowish or purplish flowers, in the straight and gibbous or recurved (not revolute) hood of the nectaries and their longer lip, in the more divergent follicles and the finer and more solid (not hyaline) transverse wrinkles of the seed. *A. laeve* varies considerably with respect to hairiness, the colour and size of the flowers, and the shape of the helmet. There is, however, only a vague indication of the geographical separation of some of those variations. Thus the specimens from Chitral, Hazara and Baltistan have hairy, those from Kashmir mostly glabrous, carpels, whilst further eastwards both forms seem to occur indiscriminately. In a similar way an imperfect differentiation into a small and a large-flowered race may be observed, the former being prevalent in the western parts of the area (Lahul and westwards), the other in the eastern.

PLATE 92. Aconitum laeve *Royle.*—1, Inflorescence, small-flowered form; 2, inflorescence, large-flowered form; 3, a basal leaf (petiole cut); 4, infructescence—*natural size*; 5, a flower in longitudinal section; 6, nectary, usual form; 7, nectary, extreme recurved form; 8, stamen; 9, gynœcium; 10, seed; 11, seed, transverse section—*all enlarged*; 12, root—*natural size.*

(1, 5, 6, 8, 9, from Kashmir, *C. B. Clarke* 24259; 2, from Garhwal, *Jacquemont* 698; 3, 4, 7, 10, 11, from Kashmir, Baltal, *Thomson*; 12, from Kedarkanta, *Gollan*, 1318.)

2. ACONITUM LURIDUM Hook. f. & Thoms. Fl. Ind. i. (1855), p. 55; Hook. fil. Him. Journ. ii. (1854), p. 108 (name only), and Fl. Brit. Ind. i. p. 28; Watt Dict. Econ. Prod. Ind. i. p. 94, and in Agric. Ledger, 1902, No. 3, p. 88; Brühl in Ann. Roy. Bot. Gard. Calcutta, v. ii. p. 112, plate 124.

[TYPE SPECIMENS: Collected by J. D. Hooker, on the Tankra Pass and Cho-la, Eastern Sikkim (Kew Herbarium)!]

Root perennial, descending, elongate, cylindric, ultimately breaking up into separate or anastomosing strands. *Stem* erect, from a simple or, in old specimens, 2- or several-headed collar which is covered with the brown, dilated bases of the old petioles, unbranched, up to 80 cm. high, softly hairy to tomentose or sometimes glabrate towards the base, hairs spreading, rarely curved and adpressed. *Leaves* few (up to 4) from the collar on very long (up to 30 cm.) petioles which are dilated at the base; 3—6, rarely more, from the stem, distant, similar to the basal, but gradually smaller with narrower divisions and the upper with rapidly decreasing petioles, basal and lower blades hairy on both sides (below chiefly on the nerves), orbicular-cordate or reniform in outline, with a narrow or more often wide sinus (1—2 cm. deep), 2·5—6·5 cm. from the sinus to the tip, 5—7, rarely 12 cm. across, 5-palmati-partite to $\frac{3}{4}$ (in the largest to $\frac{6}{7}$), inner divisions obovate-cuneate, 1·5—3 cm. wide, 3-lobed, outermost trapezoidal, 2-lobed, lobes sparingly and acutely inciso-dentate or apiculate-crenate. *Inflorescence* racemose, up to 40 cm. long, narrow, rather dense, rarely with a few additional branches from the base, with the same (if not denser) indumentum as the stem, lowest bracts 3-partite, the others lanceolate or the uppermost sublinear, exceeding the pedicels; pedicels erect, short to very short, except the very lowest which may be 2·5—3·5 cm. long; bracteoles, if present, small linear. *Sepals* lurid, reddish or brownish-red to purple without, yellowish within, hairy, upper sepal helmet-shaped, broad, hemi-elliptic in profile in the upper part, 5—7 mm. high, gradually descending into an obtuse beak of equal or more than equal length; lateral sepals somewhat obliquely obovate, scarcely clawed, 9—11 mm. long, 7—7·5 mm. broad; lower sepals deflexed, oblong, obtuse, 8—9 mm. long. *Nectaries* hammer-shaped, glabrous, claw erect, 4—5 mm. long; hood at a right angle to the claw, obliquely oblong, very obtuse; lip horizontal or slightly deflexed, shortly 2-lobed. *Filaments* 6—9 mm. long, glabrous, broadly winged up to or beyond the middle, wings abruptly contracted. *Carpels* 3, contiguous and very oblique to horizontal in the flower, obliquely oblong, densely hairy, rarely almost glabrous, shortly contracted into the somewhat shorter styles. *Follicles* erect, contiguous, oblong, subtruncate, 10—12 mm. long, glabrescent. *Seeds* triquetrous, oblong, up to 3 mm. long, blackish-brown; angles unequally winged, dorsal face transversely wrinkled, ventral faces smooth.

DISTRIBUTION: *Himalaya from Eastern Nepal to Chumbi, 12,000—14,000 ft.*

NEPAL: Neer Pokri, 13,000 ft., *Pantling*! (Hb. Calc.)—SIKKIM: Jongli Pokri, 13,000 ft., *Pantling*! (Hb. Calc.); between Jongri and Alukhtang, 13,000—15,000 ft., Gumba-than, *King's Coll.* 11,981! (Hb. Calc.); *Anderson*! (Hb. Calc.); Singalela Range, 12,000 ft., *C. G. Rogers* Reg. No. 14616 (Hb. Kew and Edinb.); Sandakphu, 12,000 ft., *Rogers*! (Hb. Calc.), *King's Coll.*! (Hb. Calc.); Phullut, *King's Coll.*! (Hb. Calc.), To-koo-la, *King's Coll.* (Hb. Calc.); Ze-lep-la, *King*! (Hb. Calc.); Tang-ka-la, N. of Ze-lep-la, *King's Coll.*! (Hb. Calc.); Cho-la, *J. D. Hooker*! (Hb. Kew); 14,000 ft, *Gammie*! (Hb. Calc.); Tankra, 14,000 ft., *J. D. Hooker*! (Hb. Kew); 12,500 ft., *Gammie*! (Hb. Calc.)—CHUMBI, Ta-key-kung, *King's Coll.*! (Hb. Calc.)

VERNACULAR NAMES: *Tchendook* (Bhot.) J. D. Hooker, on the label; *Soorja Banshi* (Darjeeling), Rogers, on the label; *Suya-banshi*, Watt in Agric. Ledg. *l. c.*

PROPERTIES AND USES: Sir J. D. Hooker states in his Himalayan Journals, *l. c.*, that the root of *A. luridum* "is said to be as virulent as *A. ferox* and *A. Napellus.*" Nothing more is known about it.

PLATE 93. Aconitum luridum *Hook. f. & Thoms.*—1, A flowering specimen; 2, a cauline leaf, larger size and more cut up than usual; 3, an infructescence—*natural size*; 4, a flower in longitudinal section; 5, stamens; 6, a seed, ventral face; 7, the same, dorsal view; 8, the same in cross-section; 9, a portion of the axis of the inflorescence; 10, transverse section of a root: *a*, decayed tissue *b*, strands into which the root breaks up ultimately—*all enlarged.*

(1 and 9, from Sandakphu, *Rogers*; 2, from Tankra, *Gammie*; 3, from Cho-la, *Gammie*; 4 and 5, from Tankra, *J. D. Hooker*; 6—8, from Cho-la, *J. D. Hooker*; 10, from Singalela, *Rogers* 14616.)

3. ACONITUM MOSCHATUM Stapf, sp. nov.

A. ferox var. *moschatum* Brühl ex Duthie in Rec. Bot. Surv. India, i. No. 3 (1894), p. 37; Brühl in Ann. Roy. Bot. Gard. Calcutta v., ii. p. 109, plate 111, figs. A, and 20, 26 (as subspecies); Watt in Agric. Ledger, 1902, No. 3, p. 93.

[TYPE SPECIMENS: See under 'distribution.']

Root perennial, descending, elongate, cylindric, ultimately breaking up into separate or anastomosing strands. *Stem* erect, from a simple or in old specimens several-headed collar which is covered with the brown, dilated bases of the old petioles, unbranched, up to 90 cm. high, glabrous below, more or less hairy above, hairs soft, spreading. *Leaves* few (up to 5) from the collar, on very long (up to 30 cm.) petioles, which are dilated at the base; 1—3 from the stem, very similar to the basal except for the much shorter petioles; blades somewhat thick, hairy on both sides or glabrate above, orbicular-cordate or subreniform in outline, with a usually rather wide sinus (2—3 cm. deep) up to 5 cm. high (from the sinus to the tip) up to 9 cm. across, 5-palmati- or subpedati-partite to $\frac{2}{3}$ in the inner and to $\frac{1}{2}$ in the outermost incisions, inner divisions broadly obovate from a cuneate base, 3-lobed, outermost rounded-trapezoidal unequally 2—4-lobed, lobes sparingly and coarsely inciso-crenate, crenae obtuse, apiculate. *Inflorescence* racemose, rarely with an additional branch from the base, up to 40 cm. long, very narrow, lax, with the same (but much denser) and more or less viscid indumentum as the stem; lowest bracts 3-partite, divisions sparingly inciso-dentate, or laciniate or entire; upper bracts lanceolate, entire, as long as or longer than the pedicels, bracteoles oblong-lanceolate, close to the flower; pedicels erect, lowest up to 2·5 cm. long, upper ones rapidly decreasing. *Sepals* lurid purple with long soft hairs; upper sepal navicular, scarcely beaked, 14—16 mm. high, 17—18 mm. from tip to base, 7 mm. wide at the middle (seen from the side), lateral margin very slightly curved; lateral sepals subobliquely obovate, very obtuse, obscurely clawed, 12—14 mm. long, up to 8 mm. broad; lower sepals deflexed, obovate-elliptic, subobtuse, 9—10 mm. long, up to 6 mm. broad. *Nectaries* glabrous; claws erect, 8—9 mm. long; hood in the continuation of the claw, shortly semi-elliptic, very obtuse, lip reflexed, short, entire or subemarginate. *Filaments* glabrous, 8 mm. long, winged to the middle, wings gradually attenuated. *Carpels* 3, contiguous, obliquely lanceolate-oblong passing into the slightly shorter style, loosely hairy. *Follicles* (not quite mature) oblong, contiguous except at the tips, obliquely truncate, 15 mm. long. *Seeds* obpyramidal, about 2—3 mm. long, with crisp hyaline transverse lamellae.

DISTRIBUTION: *Eastern Kashmir, between 12,000 and 14,000 ft.*

KASHMIR: Liddar Valley, Sausal Nala, 13,000—14,000 feet, on rocks, *Duthie* 14120! (Hb. Kew and Sah.); Musjid Valley, 12,000—13,000 feet on rocks, *Duthie* 13191! (Hb. Sah.)

VERNACULAR NAME: Unknown.

PROPERTIES AND USES: Unknown.

A. moschatum is a very distinct species. The structure and duration of the root are exactly as in the other species of the section *Lycoctonum* to which I refer it without hesitation, notwithstanding the shape of the helmet which is very unusual for this section.

PLATE 94. Aconitum moschatum *Stapf.*—1, An inflorescence; 2, lower part of a plant; 3, a collar and root; 4, an infructescence—*natural size*; 5, a portion of the axis of an inflorescence; 6, a flower, in longitudinal section; 7, a nectary; 8, a stamen; 9, a gynœcium; 10, a seed—*all enlarged.*

(1 from Kashmir, Musjid Valley, *Duthie* 13191; 2—10, from Kashmir, Liddar Valley, *Duthie* 14120.)

SECTION II.—NAPELLUS DC. (sensu latiore).

Roots biennial, paired, tuberous; each tuber producing normally one simple or (rarely) branched stem.

4. ACONITUM SOONGARICUM Stapf, sp. nov.

A. Napellus Kar. & Kir. in Bull. Soc. Nat. Mosc. 1841, p. 375, and *A. Napellus?* Kar. and Kir. l. c. xv. (1842), p. 139.

A. Napellus forma 3, Trautvetter in Bull. Soc. Nat. Mosc. xxxiii. (1860) ii. p. 86.

A. Napellus β. alpinum *lus.* soongaricum Regel in Pl. Radd. i. (1861), p 105.

A. Napellus δ. racemosum forma lobelianum Regel & Herder in Bull. Soc. Nat. Mosc. xxxvii. (1864), i. p. 404.

[TYPE SPECIMENS: See under 'distribution.']

Roots biennial, paired, tuberous; daughter-tuber conic, slender, 2—2·5 cm. long, 0·7 cm. thick, with very few root-fibres, brown externally, fracture horny, brown, taste faintly sweetish bitter, followed by a very slight tingling sensation, cambium continuous, forming a scarcely sinuous ring in cross-section; mother-tuber similar, more or less shrunk. *Innovation-bud* conic, about 5 mm. long; scales scarious, soon decaying after sprouting. *Stem* erect, simple, moderately robust, quite glabrous, rarely slightly pubescent in the upper part, up to 7 dm. high. *Leaves* scattered, lowest usually decayed at the time of flowering, intermediate remote, upper more approximate, glabrous; petioles more or less widened at the base, lower up to 12 cm. long, upper 1—2 cm. long; blades more or less cordate-orbicular or reniform in outline with a wide or narrow sinus, 2—3 cm. deep; 5—9 cm. from the sinus to the tip, 8—12 cm. across, 5-partite to the very base or in the outer incisions almost to the base, inner 3 divisions similar rhomboid in outline from a narrow cuneate base, 2·5—3·5. cm. wide, 3-lobed to or beyond the middle or pinnati-laciniate, lobes or laciniae broad-linear, subobtuse to shortly acute 1·5—3 cm. long, 3—5 mm. broad, entire or the larger with 1—2 coarse teeth or linear lobules, outer divisions 2-fid beyond the middle, inner segment 2—3-lobed, outer often entire, linear. *Inflorescence* an erect, dense or somewhat loose, terminal raceme 6—18 cm. long or with additional branches from the upper leaves, glabrous or sparingly and softly pubescent; lower bracts foliaceous, 3-partite with mostly entire long linear segments, considerably exceeding the pedicels, intermediate linear, entire, up to 2—5 cm. long, upper filiform, short; pedicels slender erect or often adpressed to the rhachis, lower 1·5—2·5 cm. long; bracteoles linear, above the middle of the pedicel, sometimes close to the flower. *Sepals* blue, pubescent, ciliate; uppermost helmet-shaped, helmet clawed, equally curved on the back and in front (seen in profile), descending into a long and slender beak, lateral margins deeply concave, 16—18 mm. high, 12—15 mm. from the tip to the base, 5—6 mm. wide at the top; lateral sepals oblique, obovate-orbicular, shortly clawed, 13—17 mm. long, not contiguous with the helmet; lower deflexed or sub-horizontal, elliptic to oblong, obtuse or subobtuse, 10—15 mm. long. *Nectaries* glabrous; claw erect, slender, up to 12 mm.

long, hood erect, 5 mm. long, top gibbous at the back, lip oblong-obovate, crenulate, as long as the hood. *Filaments* glabrous or sparingly hairy in the upper part, 7—8 mm. long, winged below, wings gradually or abruptly contracted. *Carpels* 3, lanceolate-oblong, gradually passing into the style, somewhat diverging, glabrous or almost so. *Mature follicles* and *seeds* unknown; young follicles distinctly diverging, inserted on the enlarging torus.

DISTRIBUTION: *Alpine region of the mountain ranges of Gilgit and Turkestan.*

GILGIT: Ghizur Valley, 10,000—11,000 ft., *Giles* A. 77! (Hb. Calc.)—TURKESTAN: Trans-Ili Alatau, N. of Issik-kul, Almaty Pass, *Semenow*! (Hb. Kew); Dschabyk, *Schrenk*, and without precise locality, *Schrenk*! (Hb. Kew); Alatau (Soongarian Alatau), at the sources of the Sarkhan River, *Karelin & Kiriloff* 1173! (Hb. Kew)!

VERNACULAR NAME: Unknown.

PROPERTIES AND USES: Unknown.

Of all the Indian species of *Aconitum* which I have seen, this comes nearest to the *A. Napellus* of Europe; and if that species is taken in a broad sense, *A. soongaricum* might perhaps be included in it as a variety, the principal differences being in the small size and shape of the tubers and the peculiar long-beaked helmet. The long, linear, usually entire laciniae of the leaves also are unusual in *A. Napellus*; still they occur occasionally. The fruits and seeds may possibly, when known, add other distinctive characters. Col. Tanner collected in 1880, in Gilgit, a specimen, now in the Saharanpur Herbarium, which represents most probably a luxuriant state of *A. soongaricum.* It consists only of a paniculate inflorescence with two leaves from the axils of which the lowest branches spring. These leaves are rather large, the intermediate division being 9 cm. long. The lowest pedicel of the terminal raceme is almost 9 cm. long, and like the others very slender; the flowers are distinctly larger than in Giles' plant, and the gaping of the upper sepals is particularly conspicuous. The whole inflorescence is sparingly and softly hairy, exactly like Schrenk's specimen.

PLATE 95. Aconitum soongaricum *Stapf.*—1, A flowering specimen (cut at x) with mother-tuber; 2, a pair of tubers (d, the daughter-tuber); 3, a flower—*all natural size*; 4, a flower in longitudinal section; 5 & 6, nectaries; 7, a stamen; 8, a pistil; 9, a cross-section through a daughter-tuber (s, spongy tissue of the bark)—*all enlarged.*

(Figures 1, 7 & 8 from Gilgit, *Giles*; 2, from the Almaty Pass, *Semenow*; 3 & 6, from Gilgit, *Tanner*; 4 & 5, from the Alatau range, *Karelin and Kiriloff.*)

5. ACONITUM CHASMANTHUM Stapf ex Holmes, Mus. Report Pharm. Soc. Great Brit. 1903, p. 2.

A. Napellus var. *spicatum* Duthie in Rec. Bot. Surv. Ind. i. No. 3, p. 37, in part.

A. Napellus Stewart, Punjab Pl. p. 2 in part; Dunstan in Agric. Ledger, 1897, No. 19, p. 5, not of Linnaeus.

A. Napellus var., Duthie in Rec. Bot. Surv. Ind. i. No. 9 (1898), p. 143, partly.

A. Napellus var. *hians* Goris in Bull. Sc. Pharmac. iii. (1901), p. 112. fig. 28.

A. hians Watt in Agric. Ledger, 1902, No. 3, p. 101, not of Reichenb.

A. dissectum Watt l. c., p. 100, in part, not of D. Don.

[TYPE SPECIMENS: See under 'distribution.']

Roots biennial, paired, tuberous; daughter-tuber conic to conic-cylindric from a broad base, 2·5—3·7 (rarely to 5) cm., 12—18 mm. thick, bearing more or less numerous root-fibres leaving behind the indurated bases when breaking off, bark brown to blackish-brown, smooth or wrinkled when dry, fracture cartilaginous, hard, white within the cambium ring, brownish without, taste slightly bitter, followed by a very persistent strong tingling sensation, cambium continuous, forming a wide central strand, sinuous in cross-section; mother-tuber shrunk, deeply grooved and wrinkled, black outside, brown right through. *Innovation-bud* conic, short from a very broad base. *Stem* erect, simple, inclusive of the inflorescence, 60—120 cm. high, rather stout, crispo-pubescent above, glabrous below, or almost glabrous all along. *Leaves* numerous, usually more distant in the lower part and crowded in the upper or more equally distributed, the lowest on petioles up to 7·5 cm. long, the upper shortly petioled or subsessile, passing into the floral leaves, quite glabrous, somewhat fleshy, lower and intermediate blades orbicular, reniform in outline, 4—6 cm. high, 5—9 cm. across, 3-palmati-partite almost to the very base, intermediate segment obovate-cuneate, long attenuated at the base, 3-lobed to the middle or beyond, lobes laciniate or the middle lobe pinnati-partite, ultimate laciniae linear, acute to very acute, lateral segments deeply 2-partite and laciniate with the inner division similar to the intermediate segment and the outer 2-lobed and smaller; uppermost blades similar to the preceding, but smaller, relatively longer and more sparingly divided. *Inflorescence* a long, narrow, stiff, dense or loose raceme, often over 30 cm. long, often leafy below and sometimes with slender, erect additional branches from the base, crispo-pubescent; rhachis stout; floral leaves like the preceding leaves, but still less divided or entire, passing into the linear to filiform bracts; bracteoles, if any, small; pedicels slender, the lowest at length 2·5—3·5 cm. long and adpressed to the rhachis when mature. *Sepals* blue or whitish and variegated with blue, crispo-pubescent or almost glabrous; uppermost helmet-shaped, helmet more or less depressed into a distinct and often long and slender beak, 15—20 mm. high, 12—18 mm. long from the tip to the base, 5—7 mm. wide (seen from the side), lateral margin conspicuously concave; lateral sepals not contiguous with the helmet except near the base, obliquely suborbicular or almost square, shortly or obscurely clawed, 12—15 mm. long and broad, lower sepals oblong, obtuse, 9—12 mm. long. *Nectaries* extinguisher-shaped, glabrous; claw 5—6 mm. long, leaning forward in the upper part; hood short, wide, very obtuse, top slightly gibbous on the back, honey-gland occupying the whole top or the gibbosity. *Filaments* glabrous or very sparingly hairy, winged, wings gradually or abruptly attenuated. *Carpels* 5, glabrous, rarely very sparingly hairy on the back, conniving, abruptly contracted into the short style, back convex. *Follicles* oblong, truncate, 10—16 mm. long, contiguous or with slightly divergent tips, glabrous. *Seeds* brown, obovoid to obpyramidal, 3·5 mm. long, unequally 3-winged, wings thin, faces smooth.

DISTRIBUTION: *Subalpine and Alpine zone of the Western Himalaya, from Chitral and Hazara to Kashmir, between 7,000 and 12,000 ft.*

CHITRAL: Mirga near Dir, 7,200 ft., *Gatacre* 17012! (Hb. Sah. and Calc.).—GILGIT: Shundur Pass and Shankar Gurch, 9,600 ft., *Giles* 637! (Hb. Kew); Kamri Valley, Rattu 9,000 ft., *Duthie* 12510! (Hb. Sah.) and near Kalapani, 10,000—11,000 ft. *Duthie* 12520! (Hb. Sah. and Edinb.).—KASHMIR: Gurais, 8,000 ft., *Falconer's Coll.* Kew Distr. 70! (Hb. Kew); *Clarke* 29477! (Hb. Kew); Gulmarg, among shrubs, 8,000 ft., *Aitchison* 7! (Hb. Kew); "Butta sums" and between "Derlah and Oriesertae," *Falconer's Coll.*! (Hb. Sah.)—HAZARA: Abbottabad, *Munro* 1901! (Hb.

Kew); Kagan Valley up to 12,200 ft., *Inayat* 19120! 19121! (Hb. Sah.) 23297! 23298! (Hb. Kew and Sah.); without precise locality, *Watt's Coll.* Reg. No. 10239! 14757! (Hb. Calc. and Edinb.)

VERNACULAR NAMES: *Mohri* (Jhelum Basin, Hazara), Stewart, *l. c.*; Watt, *l. c. Piún* (Jhelum Basin), Stewart, *l. c.*; *Ban-bal-nag* (Kashmir), Aitchison, on label.

PROPERTIES AND USES: The root contains, according to Prof. Dunstan (*l. c.*), aconitine, but in very small proportions. It seems that it is sometimes used in Northern India as a substitute for the imported tubers of the European *Aconitum Napellus* (Watt, *l. c.*).

A. chasmanthum differs from *A. Napellus*, Linn. in the smaller, shorter and comparatively thicker tubers; in the leaves, which are on the whole smaller, borne (the lower) on longer petioles and divided into narrower segments; in the long and very slender racemes; the slightly smaller, usually blue and white flowers; the rather depressed, widely gaping and rostrate helmet; in the conniving ovaries which are always 5 in each flower, and suddenly contracted into the style; in the position of the mature pedicels and fruits, which are tightly adpressed to the rhachis; and in the smaller lighter seeds, of which 650 go to a gramme, instead of 250 as in *A. Napellus*. Specimens of *A. chasmanthum*, which flowered at Kew this and last summer, by the side of plants of *A. Napellus*, showed the differences mentioned in a very marked way.

An alpine form with very small tubers and scarcely 20 cm. high is represented by a specimen collected by Inayat (23298 of Duthie's Distr.) at a locality called Chippran, in the Kagan Valley, Hazara. It resembles certain forms of *A. violaceum*, but may be recognised by the numerous cauline leaves and the glabrous carpels.

PLATE 96. Aconitum chasmanthum *Stapf.*—1, An inflorescence; 2, lower part of a specimen; 3, portion of an infructescence—*natural size*; 4, a flower in longitudinal section; 5, a nectary; 6, lip of a nectary, flattened out; 7, a stamen; 8, a gynœcium; 9, seeds; 10, transverse section of a seed; 11, a portion of a pedicel; 12, transverse section of a daughter-tuber—*all enlarged.*

(1 and 11, from Hazara, Kagan Valley, *Inayat*, 23297-a; 2, 9, and 10, from Hazara, *Watt's Coll.*, Reg. No. 14757; 3, from Hazara, Abbotabad, *Monro*; 4—8 and 12, from Kashmir, Gulmarg, *Aitchison* 7.)

6. ACONITUM VIOLACEUM Jacquem. Mss. in Herb. Kew.

A. multifidum Royle, Ill. Him. (1834), pp. 45, 56! (Hb. Cambridge), non Koch ex Reichb.

"*A. dissectum* (*Hamiltoni* or *speciosum*)" Madden in Journ. As. Soc. Beng., xv. (1846), p. 95, non D. Don.

A. Napellus Clegh. Rep. Forests Punjab and West Himal., p. 67; Stewart Punjab Pl., p. 2 (in part, according to Stewart's specimens); Gammie in Rec. Bot. Surv. Ind. i, No. 10, p. 192, non L.

A. Napellus var. *multifidum* and var. *rigidum* (in part) Hook. fil. and Thoms. Fl. Brit. Ind. i. p. 29; Atkins. Gaz. N.-W. Prov., p. 412; Watt Dict. Econ. Prod. India, i. p. 96; Duthie in Rec. Bot. Surv. Ind. i., No. 3, p. 37 (in part); Lawrence Valley of Kashmir, p. 85.

A. Napellus var. *dissectum* Duthie in Rec. Bot. Surv. Ind. i., No. 3, p. 37.

[TYPE SPECIMENS: Collected by Jacquemont, in Spiti (1962!) and Bashahr (1765!) Herb. Kew.]

Roots biennial, paired, tuberous; daughter-tuber ovoid to shortly fusiform, 0·75—1·8 cm. long, 4—6 mm. thick, bearing few fine root-fibres, breaking off easily, bark very thin, whitish to brown, smooth, fracture pure white, slightly sweetish, not followed by any tingling sensation, more or less farinaceous, cambium continuous, forming a central strand, circular or elliptic in cross-section; mother-tuber shrunk, grooved and wrinkled, brownish internally. *Innovation-bud* conical, up to 5 mm. long. *Stem* erect or ascending from a slender, short or long (up to 6 cm.) hypogæous base, simple or very rarely branched below, slender, crispo-pubescent to tomentose above, glabrous below, rarely quite glabrous, epigæous part (including the flowers) 10—30 cm. high. *Leaves* very few (1 or 2), if any, on the hypogæous stem, often much reduced or withered at the time of flowering, then 3—5 (rarely more) more or less crowded at the base of the epigaeous part of the stem, coëtaneous with the flowers, somewhat fleshy, glabrous or very sparingly pubescent, usually 1 or 2 higher up on the stem, often much reduced; all except the uppermost on long (3·5—12 cm.) slender petioles, widened at the base, lower blades orbicular-cordate or reniform in outline, with a wide or narrow sinus (1—2·5 cm. deep), 1·5—3 cm. high from the sinus to the top, 2·5—5 cm. across, 5-palmati- or subpedati-partite almost to the base, divisions very broad, obovate-cuneate, deeply 3- (or the outermost 2-) partite, secondary divisions laciniate, laciniae linear, acute or very acute, more or less divaricate, rarely shorter subacute and more approximate; upper cauline leaves similar to the preceding, but smaller to very small, shortly petioled or subsessile, more sparingly dissected. *Inflorescence* a short, lax or dense few-flowered raceme or corymb or reduced to a solitary flower, sometimes with additional 1—3-flowered branches springing from the cauline or basal leaves, and almost as long as the main-rhachis, greyish-pubescent to fulvo-tomentose, rarely quite glabrous, rhachis slender, sometimes very short; bracts like the uppermost leaves, or still more reduced; bracteoles, if any, linear to filiform, entire; pedicels slender, lower ones 1·5—5 cm. long, erect, indumentum more spreading and denser in the upper part. *Sepals* violet, blue or yellowish and variegated with blue, pubescent; uppermost helmet-shaped or almost navicular, obliquely erect, somewhat depressed, shortly rostrate, 14—20 mm. high, 18—24 mm. long from the tip to the base, 7—10 mm. wide (seen from the side) at or above the middle; lateral sepals contiguous with the uppermost, very oblique, broadly obovate, scarcely clawed, about 14—16 mm. long, 12—14 mm. broad, lower sepals deflexed, elliptic, obtuse or subacute, about 12 mm. long. *Nectaries* extinguisher-shaped, glabrous, claw erect, leaning forward in the upper part, 15—18 mm. long, hood more or less oblique, short, wide, very obtuse, gibbous on the back near the top; lip broad, truncate, crenulate, more or less recurved, honey-gland in the posticous gibbosity. *Filaments* finely and rigidly hairy in the upper part, winged below, wings gradually or abruptly attenuated or running out into minute teeth, 5—7 mm. long. *Carpels* 5, conniving, contiguous, oblong, somewhat abruptly or gradually contracted into the style, densely tomentose. *Follicles* oblong, truncate, erect, contiguous, 10—12 mm. long, densely hairy, *Seeds* 3-sided, obpyramidal or ellipsoid, 2·5—3 mm. long, angles winged, wings hollow, faces smooth.

DISTRIBUTION: *Alpine zone of the Himalaya from Gilgit to Kumaon, between 10,000 and 15,000 ft.*

GILGIT: Astor, *Falconer* Kew Distr. 71! partly (Hb. Kew).—BALTISTAN: Deosai plain, *Falconer* Kew Distr. 71! partly (Hb. Kew); "Tugchum to near Cootal," *Falconer*

Hb. Sah.); Marpu Nala 13,000—14,000 ft. *Duthie* 11818! (Hb. Sah.); on Pensi-La, 12,000—15,000 ft., *Stoliczka*! (Hb. Kew and Calc.).—KASHMIR: without precise locality, *Lance* 15! (Hb. Kew); *Thomson*! (Hb. Sah.) *Royle's Coll.*! (Hb. Cambr.); Burzil-La, 11,000—13,000 ft., *Duthie* 14026! 14,029! (Hb. Sah.); Margan Pass, 11,600 ft., *Atkinson* in Clarke Distr. 24162! (Hb. Calc.); from Gulmarg up to 14,000 ft., *Aitchison* 83! (Hb. Calc.); on the pass above Kilian, 13,000 ft., *Aitchison* 135! (Hb. Kew); above Pir Panjal, 9,000—10,000 ft., *Royle's Coll.*! (Hb. Cambr.); *Jacquemont* 1237! (Hb. Kew).—CHAMBA: Pangi Kilar, 10,000 ft., *Ellis* in Hb. Watt 2152! (Hb. Edinb.); Sanch Pass, 12,000—14,000 ft., *Ellis* 1677! (Hb. Kew and Calc.); *Ellis* 364! (Hb. Calc.), *Lace* 1210! (Hb. Sah.) Ravi Valley, Silrundi, 12,600 ft., *Watt's Coll.* 2052! (Hb. Edinb.); Kangra, *Watt's Coll.*, Reg. No. 8992! (Hb. Edinb.).—SPITI: without precise locality, at 12,000 ft., *Stewart*! (Hb. Kew); "Ghuyœmœul," *Jacquemont* 1962! (Hb. Kew.—BASHAHR: Shatal Pass, 11,000—14,000 ft., *Madden*! (Hb. Kew), Werung Pass, 13,200 ft., *Inglis* according to Royle; Kailas Range, 14,000 ft., *Lace*, 613! (Hb. Sah. and Edinb.); between Yurpo and Gontang-La, *Jacquemont* 1765! (Hb. Kew); "Chinese Tartary," *Munro* 288! (Hb. Kew).—TEHRI-GARHWAL: Kedarkanta, *Falconer*! (Hb. Sah.); 10,000—11,000 ft., *Duthie* 1035! (Hb. Sah.); Dudu glacier Moraine under Srikánta, 14,000—15,000 ft., *Duthie* 723b! (Hb. Sah.); Nila Valley, Ourie Gadh, 14,000—15,000 ft., *Duthie* 724! (Hb. Sah.); Gangotri, *Duthie's Coll.* 771! (Hb. Sah.).—BRITISH GARHWAL: Liti above Mana, 9,000—13,000 ft., *Edgworth* 47! (Hb. Kew).—KUMAON: above "Cheenee," *Vicary*! (Hb. Calc.), Barjikang, 13,500 ft., *Strachey & Winterbottom* 5! (Hb. Kew); Milam glacier, 12,500 ft., S. of Laptel, *Strachey & Winterbottom* 2! (Hb. Brit. Mus.); Laptel, 15,000 ft., *Strachey & Winterbottom* 2! (Hb. Kew); Darma, Nipchang, 13,000—14,000 ft., *Duthie* 2678! (Hb. Sah.); Byans, Kali Valley, Kutti Yangti, *Duthie* 24135! (Hb. Sah.); North Kumaon, 13,800 ft. *La Touche*! (Hb. Sah.)

VERNACULAR NAMES: *Tilia Kachang*, Sutlej Basin, Cleghorn, *l. c.*; Stewart, *l. c.*; Madden, *l. c.* (?); *Dudhia* (bazaar term for the root) Stewart, *l. c.*

PROPERTIES AND USES. Munro says on the label accompanying his specimen from the "Chinese Tartary" that the root is used medicinally "for good purposes," and the statement in Hook fil. and Thoms. Fl. Ind. i., p. 58, on the authority of Colonel Munro, "that the roots of the alpine form (of *A. Napellus*) are eaten by the hillmen of Kanawer as a pleasant tonic, under same name (Atees) as those of the next species" (*A. heterophyllum*) evidently also refers to *A. violaceum*, and possibly to *A. rotundifolium* which is found in the same area.

Var. ROBUSTUM Stapf.

A. Napellus var. *multifidum* Duthie in Rec. Bot. Surv. Ind. i., No. 3 (1894), p. 37.
A. Napellus var. *spicatum* Duthie, *l. c.* (in part).
A. Napellus var. *tauricum* Duthie, *l. c.*

Plant 30—50 (rarely 60 cm.) high; *daughter-tuber* 1·6—2·5 cm. long, 8—10 mm. thick. *Stem* erect, usually stiff and often rather stout. *Leaves* more scattered and often more numerous, blades larger, up to 8 cm. across, laciniæ usually longer and still narrower than in the type. *Inflorescence* an often many-flowered, rather dense and stiff raceme, up to 12 cm. long; rhachis sometimes stout; lower pedicels rarely over 2·5 cm. long.

DISTRIBUTION: *Alpine zone of the Western Himalaya, from 10,000—13,000 ft.*

GILGIT: Astor (Hasora), *Falconer* Kew Distr. 71! partly, (Hb. Kew).—BALTISTAN: Karpuchu Valley, 11,000—12,000 ft. *Duthie*! (Hb. Sah.); Shingo Valley, Goltari Nala, 11,000 ft., *Duthie* 11866! (Hb. Sah.); Chatpani Nala, near Dras, 13,000 ft., *Duthie* 13886! (Hb. Kew); Dras, 10,000—11,000 ft. *Thomson*! (Hb. Kew).—KASHMIR: Zoji-la, 10,000—11,000 ft., *Thomson*! (Hb. Kew); Sind Valley, above Gombour, *Jacquemont* 986! (Hb. Kew); Liddar Valley, Kolahoi, *Inayat* in Duthie's Distr. 25372! (Hb. Sah.); Zujmurgh, *Falconer* Kew Distr. 72! (Hb. Kew and Sah.)

The fact that the differences by which I am able to distinguish this variety from the typical form of *A. violaceum* are almost entirely dimensional suggests that it is merely an exceptionally robust state. This is the more probable, as the areas of the type and the variety overlap and intermediate forms occur which might be sorted with either. As there is, however, no evidence of a similar variation to the east of Kashmir and the extreme forms of what I call var. *robustum* differ so much in habit from Jacquemont's *A. violaceum*, I have considered it expedient for the time to separate them as a distinct variety.

PLATE 97. Aconitum violaceum *Jacquem.*—1, a typical (glabrous) specimen; 2, a high level specimen; 3, a leaf of a state of *var.* robustum with much dissected foliage; 4, a pair of tubers (large size) with the hypogæous portion of the stem; 5, an infructescence of *var.* robustum—*natural size*; 6, a flower in longitudinal section; 7, a nectary; 8, a filament; 9, a gynœcium; 10, a carpel; 11 and 12, seeds; 13, a portion of a pedicel (tomentose state); 14, transverse section of daughter-tuber—*all enlarged.*

(1 and 6—10, from Kashmir, Barzil Pass, *Duthie* 14029; 2, from Spiti, *Jacquemont* 1962; 3, from Kashmir, *Falconer*, Kew Distr. 72; 4, from Kumaon, Kali Valley, *Duthie* 24135; 5, from Baltistan, Chatpani Nala, *Duthie* 13886; 11—13, from Gilgit, Hazora, *Falconer* Kew Distr. 71; 14, from Chamba, Sanch Pass, *Watt* 1677.)

7. ACONITUM HOOKERI Stapf, sp. nov.

[TYPE SPECIMENS: See below under 'distribution.']

Roots biennial, paired, tuberous; daughter-tuber conic-oblong or ellipsoid or subcylindric, 0·5—2·5 cm. long, 3—5 mm. thick, bearing few very fine root fibres, breaking off easily, bark very thin, whitish to brown, smooth, fracture pure white, farinaceous, taste quite indifferent, cambium continuous forming a very slender central strand; mother-tuber more or less shrunk, deeply grooved and wrinkled, blackish, brownish internally. *Innovation-bud* slender, conic, up to 5 mm. long. *Stem* erect or ascending from a very slender, short or long (up to 10 cm.), often flexuous hypogæous base, simple or branched, crispo-pubescent above, glabrescent below, epigæous part (including the flowers) 5—20 cm. high. *Leaves* very few and scattered on the hypogæous stem, the following 2—3 (rarely more) crowded at the base of the epigæous part of the stem, coëtaneous with the flowers, like the rest somewhat fleshy, sparingly pubescent or glabrous, sometimes 1 or 2 higher up and much reduced, all except the uppermost on often long (up to 5 cm.) slender petioles widened at the base, frequently with a small tuft of minute petioled leaves (an arrested branchlet) in their axils; lower blades orbicular-cordate or reniform in outline, with a wide or narrow sinus (0·5—1·5 mm.

deep), 0·75—3·5 cm. high from the sinus to the top, 1·5—5 cm. across, 3—5-palmati-, or subpedati-partite almost to the base in the inner incisions, divisions obovate-cuneate (the middle one 0·4—1·75 cm. broad), 3- or (the outermost) 2-lobed to or beyond the middle, lobes entire or sparingly inciso-crenate, subacute, rarely obtuse; upper cauline leaves, if present, similar to the preceding, but smaller to very small, shortly petioled or almost sessile, more sparingly divided with narrower segments. *Inflorescence* a short, lax, few-flowered raceme or corymb or reduced to a solitary flower, crispo-pubescent; rhachis slender or sometimes thick and short; bracts like the uppermost leaves or still more reduced; bracteoles, if present, linear, entire, rarely 1—2-crenate, at or below the middle of the pedicel; pedicels slender or ultimately thickened, in the mature state up to 7·5 cm. long. *Sepals* deciduous, blue or deep purple, sparingly hairy, uppermost usually helmet-shaped, rarely navicular, helmet obliquely erect, somewhat depressed, more or less rostrate, 12—24 mm. high, 15—25 mm. long from the tip to the base 5—10 mm. wide (seen from the side) about the middle; lateral sepals contiguous with the helmet, oblique, orbicular-obovate, scarcely clawed, 12—18 mm. long, 12—16 mm. broad; lower sepals elliptic oblong, obtuse, 10—15 mm. long. *Nectaries* glabrous; claw erect, nearly straight, 14—22 mm. long; hood subhorizontal or deflexed, short, gibbous on the back at the base, wide and strongly convex in front, lip obovate, 2-lobed, deflexed or recurved; honey-gland in the posticous gibbosity. *Filaments* glabrous or hairy above the middle, winged below, wings gradually or abruptly attenuated above. *Carpels* 5, densely villous, contiguous, oblong, abruptly contracted into the style. *Follicles* oblong, truncate, erect, contiguous or nearly so, 8 mm. long, densely hairy. *Seeds* 3-sided, obpyramidal to almost ellipsoid, scarcely 2 mm. long, angles narrowly winged, wings hollow, faces smooth.

DISTRIBUTION: *Sikkim-Himalaya and adjoining Tibet, from 10,000—16,000 ft.*

SIKKIM: Pey-kiong-la, W. of Jongri, *Pantling*! (Hb. Calc.); between Jongri and Aloktong, 13,000—15,000 ft., *Anderson* 346! (Hb. Calc.); Mon Lepcha, 10,000—13,000 ft. *Anderson* 346 *bis*! (Hb. Calc.); Momay-Samdung, above 15,300—16,000 ft., *Hooker*! (Hb. Kew); *Gammie* 845! (Hb. Calc.); Donkia-la, *King's Coll.*! (Hb. Calc.) *Gammie* 824! (Hb. Calc.); Mapoku, 12,000 ft., *King's Coll.* (Hb. Calc.); Sanku (Tanku?), 14,000 ft., *Pantling*! (Hb. Calc.); without precise locality, *Elwes*! (Hb. Kew); *Blandford* in Clarke's Distr. 13594! (Hb. Kew); *Prain's Coll.* 408! (Hb. Calc.); Garareng pasture, *Prain's Coll.* 106! (Hb. Calc.); Giagong, *Prain's Coll.*! (Hb. Calc.); Niapokri, 12,000 ft., *Gammie*! (Hb. Calc.).—SOUTH TIBET: without precise locality, *King's Coll.*! (Hb. Calc.); Chumbi, Kung-met, *King's Coll.* 307! (Hb. Calc.)

VERNACULAR NAME: Unknown.

PROPERTIES AND USES: Unknown.

This species has a strong tendency to branch. The branches may grow out at once, or they remain arrested, producing a few minute, often long-stalked leaves forming small sessile tufts in the leaf axils. These arrested branches act probably as reserve shoots, and where they spring from the subterraneous part of the stem, they may develop adventitious roots very much like slender tubers.

The *A. Napellus* mentioned by Gammie as observed by him on Donkiah Pass up to 17,500 ft. and described as "reduced to a small plant with two or three leaves, bearing but one short-pedicelled flower," is no doubt this plant (Rec. Bot. Surv. Ind. i., No. 2, p. 17).

PLATE 98. Aconitum Hookeri *Stapf.*—1, A specimen with a stoloniferous base; 2, a specimen without stolons and less dissected leaves; 3, an infructescence—*natural size;*

4, a flower in longitudinal section; 5, a nectary; 6, stamens; 7, a gynœcium; 8, a carpel; 9, seed, front view; 10, seed, back view; 11, a cross-section of a seed; 12, a portion of a pedicel; 13, transverse section of a daughter-root—*all enlarged.*

(1 and 4—8, from Sikkim, Momay, *J. D. Hooker*; 2, 3, and 9—13, from Sikkim, Mapoku *King's collector.*)

8. ACONITUM ROTUNDIFOLIUM Kar. & Kir. in Bull. Soc. Imp. Nat. Mosc. xv (1842), 139; Led., Fl. Ross. i. p. 740; Trautv., Pl. Schrenk. in Bull. Soc. Nat. Mosc. xxxiii, ii. (1860), p. 86; Regel in Ann. Sc. Nat. Ser. iv, xvi. (1862), p. 153 and in Pl. Radd. i. p. 115, tab. III, fig. w, and in Gartenflora xxx. (1881), p. 357, tab. 1063, fig. 2; Regel & Herder, Enum. Pl. Semenow. (in Bull. Soc. Nat. Mosc. xxxvii, i. (1864), p. 404.

A. rotundifolium var. *elatior* Regel in Descr. Pl. Nov. Rar. Fedtschenko, p. 2.

A. Napellus var. *multifidum* Duthie in Rec. Bot. Surv. Ind. i. No. 3, p. 37.

A. thianschanicum Rupr. Sert. Thiansch. (1869) 38.

A. oliganthemum A. Kern. in Ber. Naturwiss. Ver. Innsbruck, i. (1870), p. 119.

A. Napellus var. *rotundifolium* Hook. fil. & Thoms. in Hook. fil. Fl. Brit. Ind. i. (1875), p. 29; Aitchison in Journ. Linn. Soc. xviii. (1881), p. 31; Watt Dict. Econ. Prod. Ind., i. p. 96; Duthie in Rec. Bot. Surv. Ind. i., No. 3 (1894), p. 37; Lawrence Valley of Kashmir, p. 85.

[TYPE SPECIMENS: Collected near the Sarthan River in the Alatau (Gov. Semirechinsk, Turkestan), by Karelin and Kiriloff, 1841 (Hb. Kew)!]

Roots biennial, paired, tuberous; daughter-tuber short- or long-conic or subcylindric, 1—2·5 cm. long, 6—8 mm. thick, bearing long fine root-fibres breaking off easily, bark very thin, whitish to brown, smooth, fracture pure white, farinaceous, taste slightly bitter, almost indifferent; cambium discontinuous, forming 4—5 isolated, very slender, cylindric strands arranged in a ring; mother-tuber more or less shrunk, wrinkled, dark brown to almost black, brownish internally. *Stem* erect or ascending from a short (1—5 cm.) hypogæous base, simple, 15—40 cm. high, terete, slender, crispo-pubescent in the upper part, glabrous below. *Leaves* mostly basal 4—5 (rarely 8), gathered in a loose rosette above the hypogæous part of the stem, coëtaneous with the flowers, somewhat fleshy, glabrous or scantily pubescent, on long (4—13 cm.) petioles which are dilated and more or less sheathing at the base; 1—2, rarely more, higher up on the stem on short or very short petioles; lower blades orbicular-cordate or almost reniform in outline, with a narrow sinus (0·7—2 cm. deep), 1—3·5 cm. high from the sinus to the top, 2—6 cm. across, 5—7-palmati-partite to $\frac{4}{5}$—$\frac{7}{8}$ in the inner, to $\frac{2}{3}$ or less in the outer incisions, divisions broadly obovate cuneate, 3- or (the outermost) 2-lobed to or beyond the middle, lobes narrow, sparingly crenate or inciso-crenate, crenae subobtuse, calloso-apiculate; cauline blades similar to the lower but smaller, less divided with narrower and longer lobes and more pubescent. *Inflorescence* a short (up to 8—9 cm.), few-flowered, usually loose raceme, or with a few slender, few-flowered additional branches from the uppermost often much reduced leaves, crispo-pubescent to tomentose; lowest bracts 5—3-partite with very narrow divisions, or like the upper entire, linear, as long as or longer than the pedicels, uppermost much reduced or suppressed; bracteoles, if present, minute; pedicels slender, lowest up to 2 cm. long, upper much shorter, erect in the mature state, more or less adpressed to the rhachis. *Sepals* pale or purplish blue, or white, or variegated with saturated veins, more or less pubescent. overlapping at the base only in the fully open flower; uppermost navicular, more or less beaked, obliquely erect, 12—20 mm. high, 15—25 mm. long (from the beak to the base), 4—7 mm. broad, obscurely clawed; lateral sepals oblique, broadly obovate or suborbicular, about 15 mm. long, 10—13 mm. broad; not or obscurely clawed, lower sepals deflexed, elliptic-oblong or elliptic, obtuse, about 8 mm. long. *Nectaries* glabrous, extinguisher-shaped; claw very slender, 12—15 mm. long, leaning forward in the upper part; hood horizontal, or more or less deflexed, saccate, very obtuse, top often widened and gibbous in front, lip 2 lobed, lobes often narrow and rather long. *Filaments* glabrous, very rarely with a few minute hairs, winged to the middle, wings gradually attenuate or running out into minute teeth. *Carpels* usually 5 (rarely 4 or 6), contiguous, oblong, abruptly contracted into the style, softly villous. *Follicles* contiguous or almost so, oblong, truncate at the top, 9—13 mm. long, softly hairy. *Seeds* brown, obpyramidal, 3-angled, obliquely truncate at the top, 2·5—3 mm. long, angles unequally winged, wings hollow, faces smooth.

DISTRIBUTION. *Alpine zone of Turkestan, the North-Western Himalaya, and the Safed Kuh on the Indo-Afghan frontier.*

TURKESTAN: Gov. Semirechinsk, Alatau, *Schrenk*! *Semenow*!; at the sources of the Sarchau River, *Karelin and Kiriloff* 1170! (Hb. Kew); Alaman Range, Almaty Pass in the Trans-Ili Alatau, *Semenow;* Thianshan, Turgen Pass, *Semenow;* in the neighbourhood of the Chatir Kul and the Arpa Valley, *Osten Sacken*! (Hb. Kew); Gov. Sir Daria, Alexandrovski Mountains, Karakia Pass, *A. Regel*! (Hb. Kew); Samarkand, Sarafschan, *O. Fedtschenko*.—HIMALAYA. NORTHERN PUNJAB: Hazara, Kagan, 12,500 ft., *Stewart*! —CHITRAL: Dorah Pass, 13,000 ft., in moist soil, *Giles* A. 209! (Hb. Kew); Pang-i-Sir, 10,000—12,000 ft., *Giles* 590! (Hb. Kew).—GILGIT: "Damot," 13,000 ft. *Tanner* 208 B! (Hb. Sah.); Gakuch, 12,000—13,000 ft., *Tanner* 208 A. (Hb. Sah.); Sai, 13,000 ft., *Tanner* 208! (Hb. Sah.); Niltar Valley, 10,000—11,000 ft, *Duthie* 12410! (Hb. Edinb., Sah. and Calc.); Astor Valley above Doian, 11,000—12,000 ft., *Duthie*! (Hb. Edinb., Calc. and Sah.); Ruckum Pass above Purpoo, 14,000 ft., *Winterbottom* 952! (Hb. Kew and Calc.).—BALTISTAN: Basha Valley and Nushik Pass, *Neve*! (Hb. Kew); Karakorum Range, Mango Brangsa, 12,700 ft., *Conway* 223! (Hb. Kew); at 14,000 ft., *Clarke* 30194! (Hb. Calc.), 30456! (Hb. Kew); Thale-la to Bagmaharal, *Schlagintweit*! (Hb. Brit. Mus.); Deosai plains and Skora La, *Falconer*! (Hb. Kew); "Naraize Kotul," *Falconer*! (Hb. Sah.); to the north-west of Pensi-la, 12,000—17,000 ft, *Stoliczka*! (Hb. Kew and Calc.).—CHAMBA: Sanch Pass, 14,000 ft., *Ellis* 1674! (Hb. Calc.); Pangi, Parmaur Valley, 13,000—14,000 ft., *Lace* 1666! (Hb. Edinb., Calc. and Sah.).—LAHUL: without precise locality, *Hay* (Hb. Calc.); at 13,000 ft., *Brandis* 3257 (Hb. Sah.); Kardong Mountains, 13,000—16,000 ft., *Jaeschke*! (Hb. Kew and Calc.).—SPITI: Chikkim Station, 13,500—15,500 ft., *Stoliczka*! (Hb. Kew and Calc.).—North BASHAHR: Yurpo Valley, between Yurpo and Gantang La, *Jacquemont* 1755! (Hb. Kew); Mangzang-zangh, 14,000 ft., *Lace* 553! (Hb. Edinb., Sah. and Calc.); between Hookio Ghat and Dubling, 13,000 ft., *Jacquemont* 1894! (Hb. Kew).—SAFID KUH: Kuram district; Shend-toi Valley, common in pastures, 10,000—11,000 ft. *Aitchison* 1001! (Hb. Kew, Calc. and Sah.)

VERNACULAR NAME: Unknown.

PROPERTIES AND USES: Unknown. See under *A. violaceum*.

There is a specimen at Kew collected by Krassnoff on the Sari Jassi River in the Thianshan, to the east of Issik-kul, which agrees in every respect very well with *A. rotundifolium*, except in the perfectly glabrous ovaries. It shares this peculiarity with *A. rotundifolium* var. *tanguticum* Maxim. (Flor. Tangut, p. 26), collected by Przewalski in Amdo and in the Burchan Budda Mountains in North Tibet. The specimens of this variety which I have seen differ, however, in the scapose stem, the very short and broad leaf-segments and the curiously truncate nectary. This plant—which I would rather treat as a distinct species (*Aconitum tanguticum*)—was also collected by Potanin in Szechuen, China.

PLATE 99. Aconitum rotundifolium *Kar. & Kir.*—1, A flowering specimen; 2, a pair of tubers of the same; 3, a leaf, form with more obtuse crenæ; 4, an infructescence—*natural size;* 5, a flower, longitudinal section; 6, a nectary; 7, stamens; 8, a gynœcium; 9, a seed; 10, a seed in longitudinal section; 11, a seed in transverse section; 12, portion of the axis of an inflorescence; 13, transverse section of a daughter-tuber —*all enlarged.*

(1, 2, 5, 12, and 13, from the Kurram Valley, *Aitchison* 1001; 3, 7, and 8, from Gilgit, Ruckum Pass, *Winterbottom* 952; 4, 9—11 from Turkestan, Karakia Pass, *Regel*; 6, from Turkestan, Sari Jassi, *Krassnoff*.)

9. ACONITUM HETEROPHYLLUM Wall. Cat. 4722 (name only); Royle Ill. Himal. (1834), p. 56, tab. 13. Hook. fil. & Thoms. Fl. Ind. Introd. p. 200, i. p. 58; Moodeen Sheriff Suppl. Pharmac. Ind. (1869), pp. 27, 28; Aitchison Trade Prod. Leh, p. 6; Hook. fil. Fl. Brit. Ind. i. p. 29, and in Bot. Mag. tab. 6092; Flück. & Hanb. Pharmacogr. p. 14; Bentl. & Trim. Med. Pl. No. 7 with plate; Atkins. Gaz. N.-W. Prov. p. 412; A. Meyer in Archiv. Pharm., Ser. iii, xviii & xix. (1881), pp. 175, 269—273; Dymock Mat. Med. W. Ind., p. 4; Duthie Rep. Bot. Gard. Sahar. & Muss. for 1886, p. 26, and in Rec. Bot. Surv. India, i. No. 3 (1894), p. 37 and No. 9 (1898), p. 143 (*cf.* form 2); Dymock, Warden & Hooper, Pharmacogr. Ind. p. 15; Watt Dict. Econ. Prod. India, i. p. 91 and in Agric. Ledger, 1902, No. 3, p. 92; Moodeen Sheriff Mat. Med. Madras, p. 4; Lawrence Valley of Kashmir, pp. 74 and 85; Dunstan & Jowett in Agric. Ledger, 1896, No. 32; Gammie in Rec. Bot. Surv. India, i. No. 10 (1898), p. 192; Köhler Mediz. Pfl. iii. No. 68; Dutt Mat. Med. Hind., ed. 1900, pp. 101 & 293; Goris in Bull. Sc. Pharmac. 1901, p. 114, fig. 30, pl. viii, figs. 19—21.

A. Atees Royle in Journ. As. Soc. Bengal, i. (1832), p. 459 (name only).

A. cordatum Royle Ill. Himal. (1834), p. 56.

A. ovatum Lindl. in Bot. Reg. xxvi. (1840), Misc. p. 53 (type specimen in Hb. Cambridge).

A. petiolare Royle Ms. (Hb. Cambridge).

[TYPE SPECIMENS: Wallich 4722 from Kumaon (A)! and Sirmor (B)! in Wallich's own herbarium at the Linnean Society, London, at Kew (A)! and Calcutta (A)!]

Roots biennial, paired, tuberous; daughter-tuber cylindric to cylindric-oblong or conic, 2—5 cm. long, 0·5—1·2 cm. thick (much smaller in weak or alpine specimens), bearing few root-fibres which break off easily, bark very thin, whitish or grey, smooth, fracture pure white, farinaceous, cambium discontinuous, forming (usually 4 or 5) isolated, slender, cylindric strands arranged in a ring; taste purely bitter; mother-tuber collapsed, deeply grooved and wrinkled, with conspicuous root-fibre scars. *Innovation-bud* of daughter-tuber conic, 3—8 mm. long. *Stem* erect, simple or branched, from 15—90 cm. (rarely to almost 2 m.) high, terete, glabrous below, finely crispo-pubescent in the upper part, lowest 2—4 (sometimes more) internodes short, the following 2—10 elongated. *Leaves* more or less heteromorphous, glabrous or the upper sparingly pubescent on the nerves below; lowest on long (up to 13 cm.) petioles, blade orbicular-cordate or ovate-cordate in outline with a usually narrow sinus (1—1·5 cm. deep), 2·5—3·5 cm. high from the sinus to the tip, 3—7 (rarely to 9) cm. across, usually 5-lobed to the middle, lobes crenate or inciso-crenate, crenæ rotundate, apiculate; intermediate leaves shortly petioled or sessile, ovate-cordate, often acuminate, 3·5—13 cm. long, 2·5—7·5 cm. broad, inciso-crenate or serrate or the lower ones obscurely lobed, serratures acute or apiculate; uppermost leaves similar to the preceding, amplexicaul. *Inflorescence* a slender raceme or a lax, leafy panicle, or in alpine specimens reduced to a few flowers, crispo-pubescent; floral leaves like the preceding infrafloral leaves, but smaller, passing upwards into the rapidly decreasing ovate or lanceolate, crenate or (the uppermost) entire bracts; bracteoles, if present, at or above the middle of the pedicel, elliptic or oblong, usually entire; pedicels erect, in the mature state often adpressed to the rhachis, lower up to 5 cm. long, upper much shorter. *Sepals* more or less blue or violet, rarely whitish, with dark conspicuous veins, finely pubescent or glabrous; upper sepal almost navicular, obliquely erect, shortly or obscurely beaked, 18—20 mm. high, and as long from tip to base, widest (8—9 mm.) above the middle, lateral margin sinuous; lateral sepals very oblique and broadly obovate with dark tips, 14—20 mm. long., 12—20 mm. broad, not clawed; lower sepals elliptic, obtuse or subacute, 8—10 mm. long. *Nectaries* glabrous, extinguisher-shaped; claw erect, 16—18 mm. long, hood short (up to 4 mm.) and very wide, more or less gibbous above, lip very short and broad, obtusely 2-lobed or entire. *Filaments* 6—8 mm. long, glabrous or sparingly hairy, winged beyond the middle, usually abruptly contracted, rarely produced into short teeth. *Carpels* 5, contiguous, elliptic-oblong, shortly contracted into the slightly shorter style, crispo-pubescent with adpressed hairs. *Follicles* contiguous, linear-oblong, straight, 16—18 mm. long, more or less glabrescent. *Seeds* obpyramidal, 3—4 mm. long, blackish-brown, angles acute or more or less winged, faces smooth.

DISTRIBUTION: *Common in the subalpine and alpine zone of the Himalaya, from the Indus to Kumaon, from 6,000 to 15,000 ft.*

GILGIT: Astor, *Falconer*! (Hb. Kew).—PUNJAB: Marri Distr., 10,000 ft., *Drummond* 2204 a! (Hb. Sah.) Marri, *Flemming*! (Hb. Edinb.).—KASHMIR: Pir Panjal, *Inayat* in Hb. Duthie 25374! (Hb. Kew), *Falconer*! (Hb. Sah.); Aliabad, 9,000 ft., *Gammie*! (Hb. Sah.); Hispar, 6,000 ft, *Gammie*! (Hb. Sah.); Gulmarg, 9,000—10,000 ft., *Stewart* 626! (Hb. Kew and Calc.); 8,000—9,000 ft., Hb. Duthie! (Hb. Sah.); between Gulmarg and Kilan, profusely among shrubs, *Aitchison* 8! (Hb. Kew); Liddar Valley, *Duthie* 13441! (Hb. Sah.) Aru, *Inayat* in Hb. Duthie 25375! (Hb. Sah.); Liddarwat, 9,000—10,000 ft., *Duthie* 13536! (Hb. Sah.); Chhut Panjal Nala, *Inayat* in Hb. Duthie 25373! (Hb. Kew); Zoji-la 10,000 ft., *Thomson*! (Hb. Kew); "Tanaghan," *Falconer*! distributed from Kew as part of No. 74 (Hb. Kew and Sah.), without precise locality, *Falconer* Kew Distr., 74! (partly-Hb. Kew and Calc.).—BALTISTAN: Gurais and between "Mukbana beelungsa" and Rantak Chu, *Falconer*! (Hb. Sah.); between Suru and Sanko, *Stoliczka*! (Hb. Calc.).—CHAMBA: Dalhousie, 8,000 ft., *Clarke* 22626! (Hb. Calc. and Sah.) and 23047! (Hb. Kew), *Drummond*

89 a! (Hb. Sah.); Kalatop forest, 8,000 ft. *Lace* 786! (Hb. Calc. and Edinb.) *Drummond* 89! (Hb. Sah.); between Dalhousie and Chamba, 6,000 ft., *Gammie* 18106! (Hb. Sah.), Baili, 7,000, *Watt's coll.* 2153! (Hb. Edinb.); Sauch Pass, 11,000 ft. *Lace* 1227! (Hb. Calc., Sah. and Edinb.); Pangi, head of Sanch Valley, 12,000—15,000 ft., *Harsukh* in Hb. Duthie 23395! (Hb. Kew), 13,000 ft., *Ellis* 1674! (Hb. Calc.), *Heyde*! (Hb. Calc.)—LAHUL: Bhagha Valley, in meadows, 9,000 ft., *Jaeschke* 212! (Hb. Calc.), without precise locality, *Jaeschke* 152! (Hb. Kew).—KULU: Sarahan, in Kangra, 8,000 ft., *Watt* 13605! (Hb. Edinb.).—SIRMOR: without precise locality, *Wallich* 4722 B. (Hb. Linn. Soc.); Simla, Baghi Forest, *Drummond* 1019! (Hb. Sah.); *Strong*! (Hb. Sah.); Muhassu, 7,000—10,000 ft. *Edgeworth* 46! (Hb. Kew), *Madden*! (Hb. Kew), *Lady Dalhousie*! (Hb. Kew), *Thomson*! (Hb. Kew and Calc.); *Brandis*! (Hb. Brandis); Mt. Hattu, *Drummond* 1018! (Hb. Sah.); Mt. Chor, *Royle*! (Hb. Sah. and coloured drawing from Royle's collection at Kew), *Drummond*, 1021! (Hb. Sah.); Jubal, 10,000 ft., *Collett* 5423 A! (Hb. Sah.); Fagu, *Thomson*! (Hb. Kew), 8,500 ft., *Collett* 5155! (Hb. Sah.), 8,700 ft., *Gamble*, 5505! 6581! (Hb. Sah.); Nagkanda, *Drummond* 1020! (Hb. Sah.); between Kotgarh and Koroo, *Vicary*! (Hb. Calc.).—BASHAHR, *Watt's Coll.* Reg. No. 6805 (Hb. Calc.)!—JAUNSAR: Deoban Range, 7,000—9,000 ft., *Hb. Drummond* 1033! (Hb. Sah.), *Keshava Nand* 103! (Hb. Edinb.)—.GARHWAL: without precise locality, *Falconer* Kew Distrib. 74! partly (Hb. Kew and Calc.); *Watt's coll.* Reg. No. 10118 (Hb. Edinb.); Kedarkanta! (Hb. Sah.) *Brandis*! (Hb. Brandis); *Duthie* (?)! (Hb. Sah.), Dudu Gach under Srikanta, 14,000—15,000 ft., *Duthie* 723! (Hb. Calc. and Sah.); high meadows under Srikanta, *Duthie* 3! (Hb. Edinb.), Chinpul, opposite Bandarpunch, 12,000—13,000 ft., *Duthie* 723 a! (Hb. Sah.); Derali in the Ganges Valley, 9,000—10,000 ft., *Duthie* 1349! (Hb. Sah.).—KUMAON: without precise locality, *Wallich* 4722A! (Hb. Linn. Soc., Kew and Calc.); *Reid* 5274a! (Hb. Sah.); *Davidson*! (Hb. Sah.); Milam Glacier, in open situations, 13,000 ft., *Strachey & Winterbottom* 1! (Hb. Kew); Surajkund, *Duthie* 24134! (Hb. Sah.)

VERNACULAR NAMES: *Atis or Atees* (Hind.), the usual name of the root, as sold in the bazaars, Royle, Dymock, Pharm. Ind., *ll. cc.*, etc.; *Ais* (Leh), Aitchison, Trade Prod. Leh, p. 6; *Ataicha, Ativiská* (Sanskr.), Dymock, Warden, Hooper & Pharmacogr. Ind. p. 15, Dutt, *l. c.*, Watt Agric. Ledg. *l. c.*; *Patis or Batis* (Punj.), Baden-Powell, Punjab Prod. p. 324; Stewart, Punjab Pl. p. 1; Aitchison, *l.c.* etc.; *Nar-Mada* (Kashmir), Lawrence, *l. c.* 74; *Manguálu* (Kashmir), Duthie in Rec. Bot. Surv. i. No. 3, p. 37; *Bonga** (Lahul) Aitchison, *l. c.*

PROPERTIES AND USES: "The root is extensively exported from the North-West Himalaya to the plains of India, and can be had practically in every drug-shop throughout the country . . . That it is a mild and pleasant tonic is universally accepted by Indian medical men" (Watt in Agric. Ledger, 1902, No. 3, pp. 92, 93). The active principle is *Atisine*, an alkaloid, non-poisonous in small doses and of a chemical structure very different from aconitine and pseudaconitine. An elaborate account of the chemistry of the root by Dr. Jowett may be found in the Agric. Ledger, 1896, No. 32.

The description of *A. heterophyllum*, as given above, makes allowance for a considerable amplitude of variation. There are, however, several forms represented in the collections at my disposal which

* This is, according to Aitchison (*l. c.* p. 31), also the Tibetan term in Ladakh for the root of an Aconite from Nepal.

do not come under it, and yet are so closely linked to *A. heterophyllum* that I do not consider it worth while devising names for them with the exception of one which stands out more clearly. This I describe as a distinct variety, whilst marking the others briefly as "forms" 1, 2, 3, 4, as they may when studied in the field well turn out to be mere individual variations.

FORM 1: *Inflorescence* loose, few-flowered; all the *bracts* inciso-dentate; *sepals* glabrous or subglabrous, violet-blue all over; *carpels* yellow-tomentose.—DISTRIBUTION: Kashmir; Toshumaidan, *Falconer*! (Hb. Sah.); on grassy slopes above Kilan Marg, profuse at 10,000 feet, *Aitchison* 9! (Hb. Kew). Garhwal (?), *Falconer* Kew distrib. 74! in part (Hb. Kew).—This form answers very well Royle's description of *A. cordatum*, Ill. Himal., p. 56, although the specimen marked "Aconitum cordatum" (not in Royle's handwriting) in Royle's Herbarium agrees not with it, but with "form 3."

FORM 2: *Upper leaves* softly hairy on both sides or glabrescent above; *inflorescence* many-flowered, stiff, like the sepals, velvety to tomentose; *bracts* rather large, entire; *carpels* tomentose.— (*A. heterophyllum* Duthie in Rec. Bot. Surv. India, i. No. 9 (1898), p. 143).—DISTRIBUTION: Chitral, Lowari Pass, at 9,000 ft., *Gatacre* 17010 in Duthie's Distr.! (Hb. Calc. and Sah.); Zarkhana Pass, 9,500 ft., *Gatacre* 17013 in Duthie's Distr.! (Hb. Sah.)

FORM 3: *Inflorescence* finely villous, many-flowered, stiff, almost 1 ft. long; *bracts* and *bracteoles* narrow, entire or sparingly inciso-dentate; *carpels* spreadingly tomentose.—DISTRIBUTION: Gilgit; Kala Pani, 10,600 ft., *Giles* 664! (Hb. Kew) and without precise locality, *Biddulph* 9! (Hb. Sah.).—Baltistan; Chatpani Nala, W. of Dras, 11,000—12,000 ft., *Duthie*! (Hb. Sah.); Kashmir; Sind Valley, Sonamarg, *Clarke* 27210! (Hb. Kew); Zoji-la, 11,000 ft., *Thomson*! (Hb. Kew); Liddar Valley, Naphran Nala, *Inayat* in Duthie's Distr. 25376! (Hb. Sah.)

FORM 4: *Inflorescence* and *bracts* as in the type, but the *sepals* more hairy, *carpels* densely and spreadingly tomentose.—DISTRIBUTION: Kumaon; Darma, near Shibu, 12,000—13,000 ft., *Duthie* 2679! (Hb. Sah.); Byans; Kutti Yangti Valley, 13,000—14,000 ft., *Duthie* 2680! (Hb. Sah.).—The Kutti Yangti specimen is the "*Aconitum heterophyllum, var. alba*," mentioned by Duthie in Rep. Bot. Gard. Sahar. and Muss. for 1885, p. 35.

VAR. BRACTEATUM Stapf.

Racemes or panicles lax; ***bracts*** persistent, inciso-dentate, narrowed into a broad, petiole; ***sepals*** quite blue; ***carpels*** quite glabrous.

DISTRIBUTION: Punjab, Black Mountain, Kahi Galli, 8,000—9,000 ft., *Duthie* 7427! (Hb. Kew, Calc., Sah. and Edinb.); Chittabat Plateau, *Gatacre* in Duthie's Distr. 7427! (Hb. Sah.); Hazara, Kagan, *Inayat* in Duthie's Distr. 23296! (Hb. Kew); Karkun 12,200 ft., *Inayat* in Duthie's Distr. 19125! (Hb. Sah.); Maluk, 12,000 ft., *Inayat* in Duthie's Distr. 19124! (Hb. Sah.); Siran Range, Musalla, *Inayat* in Duthie's Distr. 23296! (Hb. Sah.)

PLATE 100. Aconitum heterophyllum *Wall.* (figs. 1—12).—1, Inflorescence; 2, basal leaf, from a plant collected before flowering—*natural size*; 3, a flower in longitudinal section; 4, upper part of a nectary; 5, stamens; 6, gynœcium—*enlarged*; 7, an infructescence—*natural size*; 8 and 9, seeds; 10, portion of the axis of an inflorescence—*enlarged*; 11, a pair of tubers—*natural size*; 12, transverse section of a daughter-tuber—*enlarged*. A. heterophyllum VAR. bracteatum *Stapf*.—13, A complete specimen—*natural size*.

(1, 3—6, 10, Pir Panjal, *Inayat*, Hb. Duthie 25374; 2, Kashmir, *Falconer*; 7—9, N.-W. Himalaya, *Madden*; 11, between Dalhousie and Chamba, *Gammie* 18106; 12, Simla, *Col. Strong*; 13, Hazara, *Inayat* 23296.)

10. ACONITUM NAVICULARE Stapf, sp. nov.

***A. ferox* var. *navicularis* Brühl in Ann. Roy. Bot. Gard. Calcutta, v. (1896), ii, p. 111, plate 111, figs. 2 and 14.**

[TYPE SPECIMENS: See below under 'distribution.']

Roots biennial, paired, tuberous; daughter-tuber oblong-cylindric, up to 25 mm. long and 5—6 mm. thick, bearing few fine root-fibres, bark thin, whitish brown, smooth, fracture whitish, farinaceous, cambium discontinuous, forming 4 isolated, very slender strands, arranged in a ring, taste slightly bitter leaving no tingling sensation; mother-tuber more or less shrunk, brown, wrinkled with numerous filiform root-fibres. *Innovation-bud* conic-oblong, up to 6 mm. long, scales ovate to lanceolate-oblong with 1 or (the outer) 2 strong ribs, long-persistent round the base of the flowering stem, finally decaying with the exception of the ribs. *Stem* erect or ascending, from a slender, short (1—3 cm.) hypogæous base, simple, or branched from below, terete, slender, crispo- or reversedly pubescent or spreadingly hirtellous particularly in the upper part, ultimately glabrescent below, epigæous part 3—10 cm., rarely to 30 cm. long. *Leaves,* mostly basal, 5—6 or more, cöetaneous with the flowers, gathered in a dense or loose rosette, above the hypogæous part of the stem, on long (2·5—5, rarely to 10 cm.), slender petioles dilated at the base; blades slightly fleshy adpressedly pubescent, orbicular-cordate or orbicular-reniform in outline, with a wide or narrow sinus (3—8 mm. deep), 8—15 mm. high from the sinus to the top, 12—25 cm. across, 3—5-palmati-partite to $\frac{2}{3}$—$\frac{3}{4}$, rarely deeper, divisions subequal or equal, obovate, 2—3- lobed, lobes sparingly lobulate or crenate, lobules or crenae obtuse or apiculate, nerves inconspicuous; upper cauline leaves, if any, very few, on short or very short petioles, with blades similar to the lower, but much smaller and less divided, passing into the bracts. *Inflorescence* a short, loose, few-flowered raceme or corymb or reduced to a solitary flower, sometimes with one or few slender 1-flowered additional branches from the axils of basal leaves, spreadingly pubescent; pedicels slender, the lowest about as long as the primary axis, minutely 2-bracteolate; *sepals* reddish blue, paler when dry, with saturated veins, pubescent without, persistent, uppermost navicular, erostrate, obliquely erect, 16—20 mm. long (from the apex to the base), 6—8 mm. broad; lateral sepals oblique, orbicular-obovate, scarcely clawed, 16—18 mm. long, 14—16 mm. broad; lower sepals elliptic, obtuse, 8—12 mm. long. *Nectaries* glabrous, extinguisher-shaped; claw slightly curved about 12 mm. long; hood leaning forward or almost horizontal, short, wide, very obtuse, anteriorly gibbous; lip crenulate or shortly bilobed, broad, short. *Filaments* rigidly hairy above the middle, winged below, wings ending in teeth or suddenly contracted. *Carpels* 5, densely tomentose, conniving, oblong, abruptly contracted into the style. *Follicles* surrounded by the dry persistent sepals, oblong, almost straight along the back, truncate, 10—12 mm. long, hairy. *Seeds* brown, ovoid to obpyramidal, obliquely truncate at the top, not quite 2 mm. long, obscurely winged and transversely lamellate.

DISTRIBUTION: *High Alpine zone of North Sikkim and Chumbi.*

SIKKIM: Palung plains, 15,600 ft., *J. D. Hooker* ! (Hb. Kew and Calc.); from Tangu to Giagong, *Prain* ! (Hb. Calc.).—CHUMBI: Kung-met, *King's Coll.* 306! 307 (Hb. Kew and Calc.) and without precise locality, *King's Coll.* 317! (Hb. Calc.)

VERNACULAR NAME: Unknown.

PROPERTIES AND USES: Unknown.

Two of Prain's specimens collected at Tangu are much taller than the rest, and the tubers are 60 mm. long, but scarcely more than 8 mm. thick. The leaves are also larger (up to 3·5 cm. long) and more cut up. The flowers are, however, exactly as in typical *A. naviculare*.

PLATE 101. Aconitum naviculare *Stapf.*—1, A complete specimen, in flower; 2, a specimen in flower, without tubers; 3, a specimen in fruit—*natural size*; 4, a flower in longitudinal section; 5, a nectary; 6, stamens; 7, a gynœcium; 8, a mature fruit with the dried up persistent sepals; 9, a seed, back view; 10, longitudinal section of a seed; 11, a portion of a pedicel; 12, transverse section of a tuber—*all enlarged.*

(1 and 12, from Chumbi, Kung-met, *King's Coll.* 306; 2—11, from Sikkim, Palung plains, *J. D. Hooker.*)

11. ACONITUM PALMATUM D. Don Prod. Fl. Nep. (1825), 196. Royle Ill. Himal. pp. 47, 57; Hook. fil. Himal. Journ. i., p. 168; Hook. fil. & Thoms. Fl. Ind. i., p. 56; Fl. Brit. Ind. i., p. 28 (excl. syn.); Watt Dict. Econ. Prod. India, i., p. 98 and in Agric. Ledger, 1902, No. 3, p. 89; Dymock, Warden & Hooper, Pharmacogr. Ind., p. 18; Goris in Bull. Sc. Pharmacol. iii. (1901), p. 112 (excl. syn. *A. lethale*), fig. 29.

A. ferox subsp. *palmatum*, Brühl in Ann. Roy. Bot. Gard. Calc. v. ii, p. 111, plate 111, figs. 9—13, 24, 25, 31.

Aconitum sp. Dymock Mat. Med. W. India, 1st ed., p. 9; 2nd ed., p. 6.

Caltha Bisma Hamilt. in Edinb. Journ. Science (1824), p. 251.

Nirtisia Bisma G. Don Gen. Syst. i, p. 63.

[TYPE SPECIMENS: Wallich 4723A !, collected by E. Gardner's collectors on Gossaingthan, Nepal; in Wallich's own herbarium at the Linnean Society and at Kew and Calcutta.]

Roots biennial, paired, tuberous; daughter-tuber shortly conic to long-cylindric, often irregularly shaped, 4 to more than 10 cm. long, 0·75—3 cm. thick, simple or branched, sometimes flexuous or twisted, bearing root-fibres, some of which are threadlike from the base and break off easily, while others are much thickened at the base or thick-cylindric, light-brown, smooth, fracture more or less horny and brownish in the thickest part of full-grown samples, almost farinaceous and white towards the tips and in the root-branches, cambium discontinuous forming isolated strands of very varying shape and size, cylindric or tangentially flattened or crescent-shaped in cross-section, taste purely and persistently bitter; mother-tubers similar, but smaller, shrunk, usually more or less hollow and brown internally. *Innovation-bud* short, conic from a broad base. *Stem* erect sometimes slightly flexuous in the upper part, simple, or nearly so, inclusive of the inflorescence 2—4 feet high, stout, hollow, glabrous, shining. *Leaves* scattered, rather distant, up to 10, rarely more, the lowest usually withered at the time of flowering, quite glabrous, or the uppermost finely pubescent on the nerves below; petioles slender, 4—10 cm. long; blade orbicular-cordate to reniform with a very wide sinus (1—2 cm. deep), 6—10 cm. high from the sinus to the tip, 7—15 cm. across, 5- or (the uppermost) 3-palmati-partite to $\frac{2}{3}$ or $\frac{3}{4}$, rarely more (to $\frac{8}{9}$ in the inner incisions), divisions obovate-cuneate to broadly lanceolate-cuneate or the outermost trapezoid, 3-lobed to about the middle or the outermost 2-lobed, intermediate lobe often elongated like the others acutely inciso-dentate or apiculately crenate. *Inflorescence* a very loose, leafy panicle or raceme, 10—20 cm. long, glabrous, or pubescent in the upper part; rhachis rather slender; floral leaves like the preceding cauline leaves, passing into the ovate or deltoid, dentate, shortly petioled bracts; bracteoles similar to the bracts, but smaller, and sparingly dentate or entire, above the middle of the pedicels or even close to the flower; pedicels slender, curved, ascending, ultimately more erect, the lower up to 10 cm. long. *Sepals* blueish or variegated white and blue, glabrous at least outside; uppermost helmet-shaped, helmet obliquely semi-orbicular (from the side) or more depressed and gaping, very shortly or obscurely beaked, 20—24 mm. high, 18—24 mm. long from the tip to the base, 10—12 mm. wide (seen from the side) lateral margin very slightly concave or almost straight; lateral sepals contiguous with the helmet, obliquely orbicular-quadrate, not clawed, 18—20 mm. long; lower sepals obliquely oblong or elliptic, obtuse to acute, 12—15 mm. long. *Nectaries* glabrous, extinguisher-shaped; claw erect or the upper-end more or less leaning forward, 16—18 mm. long; hood subcylindric, 4—8 mm. long, oblique to almost horizontal, top gibbous posteriorly, honey-gland occupying the gibbosity or the whole top, lip extremely short, crenulate, very broad. *Filaments* glabrous, 8 mm. long, narrowly winged to or beyond the middle, wings gradually attenuated. *Carpels* 5, subcontiguous in the flower, but soon diverging, narrowly oblong, gradually passing into the shorter style, quite glabrous. *Follicles* subcontiguous or somewhat diverging in the upper part, oblong, obliquely truncate, 2·5—3 cm. long, 5—6 mm. broad, loosely reticulate. *Seeds* blackish, obovoid, about 3 mm. long, round in cross-section, obscurely winged along the rhaphe, transversely lamellate, lamellæ dark, undulate.

DISTRIBUTION: *Alpine Himalaya of Nepal, Sikkim, and the adjoining part of South Tibet, from 10,000—16,000 ft.*

NEPAL: Gossaingthan, *Wallich's Coll.*, Wallich 4723A! (Hb. Linn. Soc., Kew and Calc.); Headwaters of the Kosi river, *Hamilton's Coll.* 1810; (Hb. Linn. Soc.).—SIKKIM: Tonglo range, 10,000 ft., in *Rhododendron* bush, *Hooker*! (Hb. Kew and Calc.), *Thomson*! (Hb. Kew), *Kurz*! (Hb. Calc.), *Clarke* 27597! (Hb. Kew and Brandis); *Gamble* 764! 1605, C! (Hb. Calc.) *Watt's Coll.* 13939! (Hb. Kew, Calc. and Sab.); Sandakhund, *Rogers*! (Hb. Calc.), Phallut, 10,000 ft. *Thomson*! (Hb. Kew and Calc.); Phullalong, 11,000 ft., *Clarke* 13410! 13414! (Hb. Calc.); Natoung, 12,000 ft. *Pantling*! (Hb. Calc.); Yak-la, 16,000 ft. *Clarke* 9900! (Hb. Kew).—TIBET: Yatung, *Hobson*! (Hb. Kew); Goop near Phari, *King's Coll.*! (Hb. Calc.)

VERNACULAR NAMES: *Bikhma* (Hind.) Hamilton, Account of Nepal, p. 99; Dymock, *l. c.*; Pharmacogr. Ind. p. 18; Watt, *l. c.* *Wakhma* or *Vakhma* (Bombay), Dymock, *l.c.*, Pharmacogr. Ind. *l. c.*; Watt, *ll. cc.*

PROPERTIES AND USES: The statements as to the properties of the root of this species are contradictory. Hamilton remarks in his Account of Nepal, p. 99, that "the Bikhma used in medicine is a strong bitter, very powerful in the cure of fevers," and thus contrasts it with the bikh, "one of the most virulent poisons." Unfortunately no root-specimen of his "Bikhma" is preserved in his herbarium, which was subsequently incorporated in the Wallichian collections; but from the identity of the leaf-specimens of his "Caltha? Bikhma" (see below) with *A. palmatum*, which yields the *Bikhma* of the Indian bazaars as described by Dymock and others, it must be inferred that Hamilton's bitter, non-poisonous *Bikhma* actually is the root of *A. palmatum*. Moreover, Dymock, whose description of the drug *bikhma*, *bishma* or *wakhma* is unmistakable, says in his Mat. Med. W. Ind. 1st ed. pp. 9, 10, that the root "is intensely bitter like quinine," and he compares it for its "sensible properties" with *Atees*, suggesting (*l. c.* 2nd ed., p. 7) the identity of its bitter alkaloid with "that contained in *Atees*." This suggestion was afterwards confirmed by Y. Shimoyama [Pharm. Journ. and Trans. (1885) p. 86], who found in a sample of *wakhma*, communicated by Dymock, actually Atisine, adding that Dr. Kobert has proved that the alkaloid of Bikhma is "as little toxic as the ateesine from *A. heterophyllum*." King also states, according to Watt (Dict. Econ. Prod. India, i. p. 99), that "in Sikkim the natives consider the root of

A. palmatum as not poisonous." On the other hand, J. D. Hooker says positively, in the Himalayan Journal, i. p. 168, that *A. palmatum* yields one of the celebrated "Bikh poisons," and also on the label accompanying the specimen collected by him on Tonglo "one 'Bikh' poison; Gnuing-rip-gmok" (gniong being the Lepcha term for the Sikkim kinds of bikh, Him. Journ. *l. c.*); but from a sample in the Kew Museum of roots marked "Bikh poison, *Aconitum palmatum*" by J. D. Hooker, it is evident that he was misled as to the poisonous nature of *A. palmatum*, the roots mentioned being unmistakably those of *A. spicatum.* Speaking of *A. palmatum*, Royle remarks in Ill. Himal., p. 57: "This species, though not found by the author, no doubt exists in the same tract of country as the foregoing species (*i.e.*, *A. ferox*), as there is a drawing from Dr. Govan marked *A. hibiscifolium*, by Dr. Wallich, which is quite different from any of the foregoing, though a good deal resembling this species." There is, however, at Kew a fragment of a manuscript catalogue of plants of the North-Western Himalaya in Royle's handwriting and with notes by Falconer, and in this catalogue Royle indicates *A. palmatum* from "Choor, Uructa, Suen." Moreover, there is in the Saharanpur herbarium a specimen named *A. palmatum* by Royle himself, from the Chor Mountain, collected in 1825. This determination was subsequently changed correctly by Falconer into *A. laeve.* Later collectors also fell into the same error, as is evident from their specimens in the Saharanpur herbarium, and I have no doubt that also Madden's *A. palmatum*, stated by him (in *Journ. As. Soc. Bengal*, xv., 1846, p. 129) as growing "in the deepest recesses of the woods" of Mt. Hattu and (*l. c.* p. 130) in the Pindrow forest of Nagkanda, is really *A. laeve.** As to Govan's *A. hibiscifolium*, it is probably the plant to which he refers in Brewster's *Edinb. Journ. Science*, ii (1825), p. 282, in the following passage: "On the very summits of the Choor first appear the Juniper, Alpine Rhododendron, and the lofty Aconite, the well-known poisonous effects of which, when taken internally, seem to have given rise to a belief among the natives that it poisons the air in the vicinity." This I believe is neither *A. palmatum* nor *A. laeve.* Wallich quotes Govan's Sirmore plant under *A. ferox.*

PLATE 102. Aconitum palmatum *D. Don.*—1, An inflorescence; 2, a lower cauline leaf; 3, an infructescence; 4, a pair of tubers; 5, a particularly large tuber—*natural size*; 6, a flower, in longitudinal section; 7, a nectary; 8, a stamen; 9, a gynœcium; 10, a single carpel; 11, a seed, back view; 12, a seed, front view; 13, transverse section of a daughter-tuber—*all enlarged.*

(1 and 2, from Sikkim, Tonglo Range, *Rogers*; 3, 11, and 12, from Tonglo Range, *Clarke* 27597; 4 and 13, from Tonglo Range, *Watt's Coll.*, Reg. No. 13939; 5, from Sikkim, *Watt's Coll.*, No. 1484; 6—10, from the Sikkim-Tibetan frontier, Yatung, *Hobson.*)

12. ACONITUM DEINORRHIZUM Stapf, sp. nov.†

A. ferox Clegh. Rep. Forests Punjab and West Himal., p. 67; Stewart. Punjab Plants, p. 1 (in part), not of Wall. ex Séringe.

A. ferox vars. *laciniatum* and *atrox* Watt in Agric. Ledg. (1902) No. 3, p. 96 (Minniken's plant) and 97, in part.

A. atrox and *A. Brühlii* Goris in Bull. Sc. Pharm. iii. (1901), p. 122 (in part).

---

* This, Sir George Watt assures me, is actually the case.

† Name mentioned in Holmes, Museum Report, Pharm. Soc. Great Brit. f. 1895–1902, pp. 3, 38.

[TYPE SPECIMENS: See below under 'distribution.']

Roots biennial, tuberous, paired; daughter-tuber conical, rather elongated, up to 6·5 cm. long and at the upper end up to 18 mm. thick, with very few filiform root-fibres, brown externally, fracture scarcely farinaceous, whitish, taste indifferent followed by a strong tingling sensation, cambium discontinuous, broken up into strands arranged in a ring, the smaller circular in cross-section, the larger tangentially flattened; mother-tuber similar, more or less shrunk, wrinkled, with long filiform root-fibres. *Innovation-bud* a very low broad obtuse cone; scales very broad with a clasping base, decaying after sprouting. *Stem* several feet high, erect, straight, simple, terete, sparingly and finely crispo-pubescent in the upper part, otherwise glabrous, shining, or in young plants sparingly pubescent all along. *Leaves* up to 10 or 12, scattered, lower usually decayed at the time of flowering, the upper 6—8 rather distant, sparingly hairy when young, especially towards the margins and on the nerves below, soon glabrescent; petioles slender, mostly 5—7 cm. long, dilated at the base; blade reniform or ovate-reniform in outline, with a very wide sinus or an almost truncate base, 5-pedati-partite almost to the base (to $\frac{15}{16}$—$\frac{19}{20}$ in the inner, to $\frac{3}{4}$—$\frac{7}{8}$ in the outer incisions), inner divisions subequal or the intermediate distinctly longer, rhombic from a cuneate base, up to 8 cm. (or the intermediate to 10 cm. long), 5—6·5 cm. broad, 3-lobed to the middle, intermediate lobe much longer than the lateral, lobes deeply laciniate, laciniæ linear or broad-lanceolate, entire or sparingly inciso-dentate, shortly acute or subobtuse, outer divisions asymmetric, usually to or beyond the middle, otherwise similar to the inner, but smaller. *Inflorescence* straight, racemose, simple or sometime with an additional branchlet from near its base, 30—40 cm. long, narrow, not very dense, greyish crispo-pubescent; lowest bracts similar to the preceding leaves, or like the rest much reduced, coarsely and sparingly dentate, the uppermost very small; pedicels erect, slender, lower up to 6 5 cm. long, upper much shorter; bracteoles linear, up to 4 mm. long, or on the lower pedicels broader and sparingly dentate. *Sepals* blue, crispo-puberulous; uppermost helmet-shaped, helmet more or less oblique, depressed, 15—20 mm. high, 17—22 mm. from the tip to the base, about 7 mm. wide (in profile), slightly concave towards the base in front and produced into a short beak, shortly and broadly clawed; lateral oblique, suborbicular, scarcely unguiculate, ciliate, 14—18 mm. long; lower oblong, 10 mm. long, obtuse, deflexed. *Nectaries* hispidulous all over; claw almost straight, 12—13 mm. long; hood leaning forward, gibbous near the top on the back, 5 mm. long, lip short, broad, emarginate, reflexed. *Filaments* hairy in the upper part, 8—10 mm. long, winged beyond the middle, wings abruptly contracted. *Carpels* 3, oblong, conniving in the flower, then subdivaricate, adpressedly greyish-pubescent, contracted into the rather long style. *Follicles* unknown. *Seeds* obconic, 3 mm. long, terete with numerous small short transverse lamellae.

DISTRIBUTION: *Alpine Himalaya of Bashahr.*

BASHAHR: Jani Kanda, *Minniken*, *Watt's* Reg. No. 13999! (Hb. Kew); letter No. 1703 (Hb. Calc.)! Ind. Invoice No. 6806. Imp. Inst. No. 7149 (Imp. Inst.)!

VERNACULAR NAME: *Mohra*, Watt's Coll.; *Maura Bikh*, Cleghorn, *l. c.*; Stewart, *l. c.*

PROPERTIES AND USES: Watt quotes, in Agric. Ledg. *l. c.*, G. G. Minniken as saying "that in his part of the country (Bashahr) the poisonous aconites are collectively designated *Mohra*." The poisonous principle of this aconite is pseudaconitine. A sample of roots from Bashahr (Ind. Invoice, No. 6806, Imp. Inst. No. 7149), which I refer to *A. deinorrhizum*, yielded according to Prof. Dunstan (in Agric. Ledg. 1897, No. 19, p. 4) 0·40 p. c. of pseudaconitine.

The "Aconitum ferox" mentioned by Madden in his "Diary of an excursion to the Shatul and Boorun Passes" (in *Journ. As. Soc. Bengal*, xv., 1846, p. 95) is evidently *A. deinorrhizum*. He says of it: "The other species, *Aconitum ferox*, is called *Moura bikh* or simply "*Mora*" (from *mri*, to die) and is reckoned extremely poisonous. It only occurred in one spot, a mile or two above Kala Koondar, growing in an extensive patch, the stems from four to six feet high, with long dense racemes of splendid deep-blue flowers: the follicles three."

The *Mitha dúdya* of Aitchison (Trade Prod. Leh, p. 175), of which he says that it grows in the Kulu hills and "upon being boiled or steeped in hot water becomes black and then was called *mitha teliya* and as frequently *kala mohra*," is probably also this species, if not *A. Falconeri* var. *latilobum*.

PLATE 103. Aconitum deinorrhizum *Stapf*.—1, An inflorescence; 2 and 3, cauline leaves; 4, a pair of tubers—*natural size*; 5, a flower, in longitudinal section; 6, lip of a nectary; 7, a stamen; 8, a gynœcium; 9, a single carpel; 10 and 11, seeds; 12, transverse section of a seed; 13 and 14, transverse sections (halves) of a daughter-tuber—*all enlarged*.

(All from specimens from Jani Kanda, *Watt's Coll.*)

13. ACONITUM BALFOURII Stapf, sp. nov.*

A. ferox Wall. Pl. As. Rar. i. p. 35 (in part); Balf. in Edinb. New Phil. Journ. xlvii. (1849), p. 366, tab. v; Bentl. & Trim. Med. Pl. No. 5 with plate (in part); Hook. f. & Thoms. Fl. Ind. i. 56 (in part); Hook. f. Fl. Brit. Ind. i. 28 (in part); Atkins. Gaz. N.-W. Prov. p. 412, not of Wall. ex Séringe.

A. ferox var. *atrox* Brühl in Ann. Roy. Bot. Gard. Calc. v. part ii, p. 110 (in part ?); Watt in Agric. Ledger (1902), No. 3, p. 97 (in part).

A. ferox var. *polyschiza* Brühl ex Goris in Bull. Scienc. Pharm. iii. (1901), p. 118 (partly ?); Watt in Agric. Ledger (1902) No. 3, p. 98 (partly ?).

[TYPE SPECIMENS: See under 'distribution.']

Roots biennial, paired or ternate, tuberous; daughter-tubers sometimes paired or divided from the base, conic or elongate conico-cylindric, 3—7 cm. long, 1—2 cm. thick with few root-fibres, which are either slender-filiform or conspicuously thickened (up to 5 mm. diam.) at the base, externally greyish-brown, fracture white, almost horny, taste rather indifferent, followed by a tingling sensation, cambium discontinuous, broken up into strands arranged in a ring, the smaller circular in transverse section, the larger tangentially flattened to horseshoe-shaped; mother tubers with, often, numerous root-fibres much shrunk, grooved and wrinkled with conical stumps (root-fibre bases), collapsed. *Innovation bud* a much depressed, broad, obtuse cone or hemisphere, scales broad with a clasping base usually decaying after sprouting. *Stem* erect, several feet high, straight, robust, simple, terete, delicately pubescent in the upper part, otherwise usually quite glabrous. *Leaves* scattered, 6—10, the lowest

* Name mentioned in Holmes, Museum Report, Pharm. Soc. Great Brit. f. 1895—1902, pp. 2, 38.

decayed at the time of flowering, intermediate and upper leaves rather distant, pubescent when young, at length glabrous, with the exception of the nerves below, lower petioles up to 7·5 cm. long, intermediate and upper much shorter, somewhat dilated at the base, blades dark-green above, paler below, orbicular or ovate-cordate or subreniform, with a narrow or wide sinus, 1—2 cm. deep, 7—9 cm. from the sinus to the tip, 10—12 cm. across, 3-partite to $\frac{7}{8}$, intermediate division rhomboid-ovate from a broad cuneate base, 3-lobed to the middle, middle lobe much longer than the lateral, lateral divisions trapezoid, very unequally 2-lobed to the middle, all the lobes coarsely inciso-crenate or dentate, crenæ apiculate or acute. *Inflorescence* straight, racemose, narrow, up to 30 cm. long, many-flowered, rather dense, yellowish-tomentellous and slightly viscous; lowest bracts resembling the preceding leaves, following ovate or lanceolate, inciso-dentate or dentate, uppermost often entire; pedicels erect or the lower ascending, lowest up to 5 cm., upper 2·5 cm. long; bracteoles, if any, inciso-dentate or dentate, small. *Sepals* blue, pubescent; uppermost helmet-shaped, helmet oblique, sub-semi-orbicular in profile, slightly concave in front and shortly beaked, about 20 mm. high and 20 mm. from tip to base, 10—13 mm. wide, very shortly and broadly clawed, lateral sepals suboblique, orbicular or slightly broader than long, up to 16 mm. long, obscurely clawed; lower sepals elliptic or broad-oblong, obtuse, 12—14 mm. long. *Nectaries* glabrous, claw erect or slightly curved, 12-13 mm. long; hood leaning forward, rather wide, dorsally gibbous near the top, about 6 mm. long; lip short, broad, emarginate or crenulate. *Filaments* hispidulous in the upper part or almost glabrous, 6 mm. long, broadly winged to beyond the middle, wings gradually or abruptly running out. *Carpels* 5, oblong, yellowish-tomentose, conniving in the flower, then slightly divergent. *Follicles* oblong, slightly divergent above, otherwise contiguous, loosely hairy or glabrate, 12 mm. long, 4-5 mm. broad. *Seeds* obpyramidal, trigonous, 3—3·5 mm. long, dark-brown, broadly winged along the rhaphe, faces with narrow transverse lamellae giving out towards the back.

DISTRIBUTION: *Subalpine and Alpine Himalaya from British Garhwal to Nepal.*

BRITISH GARHWAL: Dudatoli, in forest 7,500 ft., *Ram Swarup*! (Hb. Kew) and without precise locality, 13,000—14,000 ft., *Duthie*! (Hb. Edinb).—KUMAON: Barjikang, in open situations, 13,500 ft., *Strachey and Winterbottom* 3! (Hb. Kew); Pindari, *Strachey and Winterbottom* 3! (Hb. Brit. Mus.); Milam, 13,000 ft., *Strachey and Winterbottom* 3! (Hb. Calc.); Pass above Ralam, 13,500 ft., *Strachey and Winterbottom* 3! (Hb. Calc.); Byans, Kali Valley, near Garbyang, 12,000 ft., *Duthie* 2682! (Hb. Sah.); Darma, near Shibu, 12,000—13,000 ft., *Duthie* 2691! (Hb. Sah.); without precise locality, *Blinkworth* in Hb. Wallich 4721, C! (Hb. Linn. Soc., London; Hb. Kew, exclusive of the inflorescence on the right; and Hb. Calc.); *Watt's Coll.* Reg. No. 8322! (Hb. Calc.)—NEPAL: Nampa Gadh, 12,000—13,000 ft., *Duthie* 5274! Gosain Than, *Wallich's Coll.* 4721 B! (Hb. Kew, Hb. Wallich at Linn. Soc., London; Calc.); without precise locality, *Scully* 220! (Hb. Calc.); *Watt's Coll.* No. 22! (Hb. Pharm. Soc., London).

VERNACULAR NAMES: *Gobriya*, Darma, Duthie on a label in the Calcutta Herbarium; *Gobari*, West Nepal, Duthie on a label in the Calcutta Herbarium; *Banwa*, British Garhwal, Duthie on a label in the Edinburgh Herbarium. See also Duthie, Rep. Bot. Gard. Saharanp. and Muss. (1885), p. 47.

PROPERTIES AND USES: "Gobriya" is quoted by Duthie, *l. c.* (see also Goris, *l. c.* and Watt, *l. c.*, p. 97), as the name of one of the nine poisonous Aconites of the Rálam

valley. A sample of tubers from Dudatoli was examined by Prof. Dunstan with the result that the daughter-tubers contained nearly 1 p. c., and the mother-tubers 0·5 p. c. of pseudaconitine.

The excellent figure of this Aconite which Prof. Balfour published as *A. ferox* in the Edinburgh New Philos. Journ. of 1849 was drawn from a specimen raised from seeds sent by the then Superintendent of Saharanpur, Dr. William Jameson. No specimen was, however, preserved and there is no record to show where the seeds had been gathered. Of the nine poisonous Aconites of the Rálam valley, mentioned by Duthie, *l. c.*, and by Watt, *l. c.*, under the names phatkia (phatikia, Watt*), bhanwa, kawriya, tiliya (dileya, Watt), dhaulia (dhaula Watt), dhumuriya, jhirina, gobriya, gobari (not in Duthie) and ratioa (not in Watt), I have only seen specimens of "gobriya," "gobari" and "bhanwa" (also "banwa"), the others not having been found in the collections at my disposal. There is, however, a sample of roots in the Calcutta herbarium, presented by Watt, which represents either the form "phatkia" (or "phutkia" or "fatkia") or that known as "gobaria." It was communicated to Watt by I. S. C. Davis of Almora and accompanied by two herbarium specimens which are not at hand. Brühl describes, in a manuscript note in the Calcutta herbarium, one (the phatkia plant) as having glabrous or sparingly hispid carpels and the other (the gobaria bikh) with hirsute carpels. As there is no vernacular name attached to the root sample, I cannot say to which of the two forms it belongs. The structure of the tuber is, however, exactly that of *A. Balfourii.* From Watt's note on *A. ferox* var. *polyschizum* I infer that the specimens came from Garbyang, and there is no doubt that Brühl's var. *polyschiza* of *A. ferox* belongs, at least in part, to *A. Balfourii.* How far this also is the case with the other Aconites mentioned by Duthie I do not know, but Watt and Brühl seem to consider them as local forms of "*A. ferox* var. *atrox*" which in this case probably means *A. Balfourii. A. ferox* var. *lancifida* Brühl, *l. c.* from the Rálam valley is probably one of them. I have not seen it. I may finally remark that Balfour noticed a difference between the plant figured by him as *A. ferox* and Wallich's, and he says: "The specimen does not agree completely, more specially as regards the form of the leaves, with the figure to Wallich's *Plantae Asiaticae Rariores.* The variation may depend on situation."

PLATE 104. Aconitum Balfourii *Stapf.*—1, An inflorescence; 2, an intermediate cauline leaf; 3, an infructescence; 4, a pair of tubers; 5, a large daughter-tuber; 6, a mother-tuber with the base of the stem—*natural size*; 7, a flower, longitudinal section; 8, a nectary; 9, lip of a nectary; 10, a stamen; 11, a gynœcium; 12, a single carpel; 13, a seed; 14, transverse section of a seed; 15, a portion of a pedicel; 16, transverse section of a daughter-tuber—*all enlarged*.

(1, from Darma, Shibu, *Duthie* 2682; 2, 4—6, and 16, from Garhwal, Dudatoli, *Ram Swarup*; 3, 13 and 14 from Kumaon, Barjikang, *Strachey and Winterbottom*; 7—12 and 15, from Kumaon, *Wallich* 4721 C.)

Var. RHOMBILOBUM Stapf.

***Blades* broadly cordate-ovate or subdeltoid in outline, 3-partite to $\frac{4}{5}$—$\frac{5}{6}$, 5—9 cm. from the sinus to the tip, 6·5—8·5 cm. across, intermediate division rhomboid from a broad cuneate base, 3—4 cm. wide, distinctly or obscurely 3-lobed with almost contiguous lobes, broadly apiculate-crenate, lateral divisions trapezoid, 3—4 cm. long, 2-lobed (at least in the lower leaves) to the middle, lobes contiguous or overlapping, crenate or inciso-crenate.**

DISTRIBUTION: *Alpine Himalaya of Kumaon.*

KUMAON: Byans, near Garbyang, 12,000 ft., *Duthie* 2682! (Hb. Calc.)

VERNACULAR NAME: Unknown.

PROPERTIES AND USES: Unknown.

---

* Watt's names were copied from the field-labels.

There is only the mother-tube of the specimen preserved. It is very slender, cylindric with a discontinuous cambium. The inflorescence agrees so perfectly with *A. Balfourii* that I prefer to treat it as a variety of it, notwithstanding the peculiar leaves the segments of which are unusually broad.

14. Aconitum Falconeri Stapf, sp. nov.*

A. ferox Royle Ill. Him. p. 47 (in part); Hook. f. & Thoms. Fl. Brit. Ind. i. p. 28 (in part).

A. ferox var. *atrox* Brühl in Ann. Roy. Bot. Gard. v. ii, p. 110 (in part), figs. 15 and (?) 23.

A. dissectum Royle, *l. c.* 56, not of D. Don, Tausch and Stein.

[Type specimens : See under 'distribution.']

Roots biennial, paired, tuberous ; daughter-tuber conic to cylindric from a broad, truncate base, up to 8 cm. long to 2 cm. thick, entire or divided, bearing more or less numerous filiform root-fibres, externally brown, fracture white, slightly farinaceous or horny, taste somewhat bitter, followed by a strong burning and tingling sensation, cambium continuous, forming in transverse section a slightly sinuous ring ; mother-tuber similar, much shrunk and wrinkled. *Innovation-bud* very short and broad, conic, bud-scales very short, broad and clasping, soon decaying after sprouting. *Stem* erect, simple, up to 1 m. high, moderately stout, finely pubescent or sub-glabrous in the upper part, quite glabrous below. *Leaves* scattered, 10 or more, if many, the upper sometimes rather crowded, the intermediate usually very distant, the lowest decayed at the time of flowering;† petioles slender, lowest up to 12 cm. long, upper much shorter, uppermost very short ; blades rather thin, very sparingly and finely pubescent or glabrous, with the exception of the nerves at the base below, lower and intermediate rotundate-cordate to reniform in outline, with a very wide and open sinus, 1—3 cm. deep, 6—10 cm. high from the sinus to the tip, 12—15 cm. across, 5—subpedati-partite to $\frac{6}{7}$ or more in the inner, to $\frac{3}{4}$ or more in the outer incisions, inner divisions rhomboid-cuneate, 3-lobed to the middle with the inner lobe elongated and pinnati-laciniate, outer divisions much smaller, trapezoid, 2-lobed, all the lobes and laciniae broadly inciso-dentate, teeth usually triangular ; upper blades very similar, but smaller and less deeply divided or 3-partite with the intermediate division much larger than the lateral. *Inflorescence* an erect, stiff, usually dense raceme, about 15—20 cm. long, rarely lax and with slender, few-flowered, ascending, additional branches from below, finely adpressedly pubescent or rarely with short spreading hairs ; axis rather slender ; lowest bracts 3-partite, upper ovate to deltoid, all acutely and coarsely dentate ; bracteoles usually present, resembling the upper bracts, but much smaller ; pedicels slender, erect, often almost adpressed to the axis, lowest up to 4 cm. long, the upper much shorter. *Sepals* blue with very dark tips (in the dry state), pubescent ; uppermost helmet-shaped, helmet obliquely semi-orbicular in profile, very shortly beaked, 16—22 mm. high, 18—22 mm. long from the tip to the base, 8-9 mm. wide ; lateral sepals oblique, sub-orbicular or obovate-orbicular, 14—18 mm. long lower sepals oblong-elliptic, obtuse, 8—10 mm. long. *Nectaries* extinguisher-shaped, claw erect, 13—15 mm. long, minutely hispid, hood leaning forwards or almost horizontal,

* Name mentioned in Holmes, Museum Report Pharm. Soc. Great Brit. for 1896—1902, p. 3.

† Consult general remarks in smaller type on next page.

slightly constricted or obscurely gibbous on the back close to the top, lip spathulate, broad, crenulate. *Carpels* 5, obliquely oblong, conniving in the flower, soon slightly divergent, gradually passing into the rather long style, quite glabrous and black when dry or sometimes more or less very minutely silky pubescent. *Follicles* erect and contiguous or slightly diverging upwards, oblong, rounded at the top, 14—18 mm. long, 4—5 mm. broad, glabrous, faintly reticulate. *Seeds* brown, obconic, 3—4 mm. long, winged (often broadly) along the rhaphe, with undulate, hyaline, rather wide and distant transverse lamellæ.

DISTRIBUTION: *Subalpine and Alpine zone of the Himalaya of Garhwal* (*See* also below).

TEHRI-GARHWAL: Kedarkanta, *Royle*! (Hb. Sah.); *Duthie's Coll.* (Hb. Sah.); *Falconer* Kew Distr. 69, partly! (Hb. Kew and Calc.); Jamnotri, near the hot springs, 11,000 ft., *Duthie*! (Hb. Sah.); Gulmar Pass, 12,000—13,000 ft., *Duthie* 725! (Hb. Sah. and Edinb.); "Mussooree," with no further indication (Hb. Sah.)!—BRITISH GARHWAL: without precise locality; *Falconer* Kew Distr. 68! (Hb. Kew); on Trisul near Bowani, *Falconer*! (Hb. Kew); Badrinath, *Falconer* Kew Distr. 69, partly! (Hb Kew.)

VERNACULAR NAMES: *Bis, Bikh, Meetha tellia*, Royle, in an incomplete manuscript catalogue (of Himalayan plants) at Kew.

PROPERTIES AND USES: Evidently poisonous.

VAR. LATILOBUM Stapf.

Roots up to 12 cm. long and 2·5 cm. thick, with few fibres. *Upper leaf-blades* 3-partite to $\frac{5}{6}$; up to 6·5 cm. high, 10 cm. across, divisions broadly deltoid or the outer trapezoid, up to 4·5 cm. broad, shortly 3- or (the outer) 2-lobed, lobes coarsely crenate or dentate. *Inflorescence* tomentose with spreading hairs. *Carpels* quite glabrous.

DISTRIBUTION: Bashahr; Nagli, *Watt's Coll.* Reg. No. 15039! (Hb. Calc.)

VERNACULAR NAME: *Kala mohra*, Bashahr, according to Watt's Collector.

PROPERTIES AND USES: This is evidently the plant to which Watt refers in the Agric. Ledger, 1903, No. 3, p. 96, when quoting G. G. Minniken, as saying that "it is called *Kala-mohra* in allusion to its being a more deadly poison than the *mohra.*"

Royle collected *A. Falconeri* on Kedarkanta. A specimen named in his handwriting "Aconitum virosum?—bis" and by Falconer "Aconitum ferox—virosum Don" is in the Saharanpur collection, and a beautiful coloured drawing from Royle's collection with the same names in Royle's own handwriting is at Kew. It corresponds to the "Aconitum ferox Wall.—virosum, Don" of Royle's manuscript catalogue (see p. 43) with the vernacular names "bis, bikh, meetha tellia," and the locality "Kedarkanta." Royle's specimen was numbered by Falconer $\frac{1}{75}$, and is absolutely identical with a specimen from Falconer's herbarium, at Kew, bearing the same number and the note „Aconitum ferox, Kedarkanta" in Falconer's handwriting. There is little doubt that *A. Falconeri* is the plant to which Royle's remarks on *A. ferox* and *Bikh* or *Meetha tellia* in his *Illustrations of the Botany of the Himalayas* refer, so far as they are based on his own observations.

Royle seems to have collected *A. Falconeri* a second time on the same mountain, but in a very young state, so that he did not recognise it, but took it for *A. dissectum* D. Don. He enumerates (in *Ill. Him.* p. 56) *A. dissectum* as found at Aarga'on, on the west side of Kedarkanta, adding that it was remarkable that it had never been found in flower. I have seen Royle's specimen of it in the Saharanpur herbarium. Although young and imperfect, there can be no doubt that it is not identical with D. Don's *A. dissectum* in Wallich's herbarium at the Linnean Society, London. On the other hand, it agrees perfectly with a number of other specimens collected, in a similar condition, on Kedarkanta and in other parts of Tehri-Garhwal, namely: Kedarkanta 10,000—11,000 ft., May, 1879, *Duthie* 1034! (Hb. Sah.); Chansil range, Chandar Tach, 11,000—12,000 ft., 27th May 1894, *Duthie* 14541; Garhwal, without precise locality, *King*, 1870, and "Mussooree Range," *King*, 1869. All these specimen with the exception of Royle's, have tubers which resemble externally those of *A. Falconeri*, and so far as I have been able to see from Duthie's two specimens also internally. This, and the distribution suggest that they are young states of *A. Falconeri*, a late flowering (end of August to October) species; but the comparison was rendered somewhat difficult by the circumstance that the young specimens had only the lower leaves well developed, whilst these had already disappeared through decaying from the flowering plants, and also by the fact that they did not seem so closely connected with the intermediate and upper leaves of the latter as one might expect. The young lower leaves point indeed rather to *A. deinorrhizum* than *A. Falconeri*, being more cut up with ultimate lobes or laciniæ longer and more linear than in the mature specimens of *A. Falconeri*. *A. deinorrhizum* is, however, excluded on account of the structure of the root, and on the whole I am inclined to connect, after all, the young state represented by *A. dissectum* Royle with *A. Falconeri*. No doubt, it will be easy to settle this question by observation in the field.

PLATE 105. Aconitum Falconeri *Stapf.*—A; Typical form: 1, an inflorescence; 2, a pair of tubers; 3, an infructescence,—*natural size*; 4, a flower in longitudinal section; 5, a nectary; 6, lip of a nectary; 7, stamens; 8, gynœcium; 9, a single carpel (8 and 9 represent the unusual slightly hairy state); 10, a seed; 11, a portion of a pedicel of a very hairy inflorescence; 12, transverse section of a daughter-tuber—*all enlarged*. B; VAR. latilobum *Stapf*—13, an intermediate cauline leaf; 14, a pair of tubers—*natural size*.

(1 and 4—9, from Tihri Garhwal, Kedarkanta, *Falconer*; 2, from Royle's specimen, named "A. palmatum"; 3 and 10, from Mussooree; 11, from Garhwal, Badrinath, *Falconer*; 13 and 14, from Bashahr, *Watt's Collector* 15039.)

15. ACONITUM SPICATUM Stapf, sp. nov.*

A. ferox Hook. f. & Thoms. Fl. Ind. i. p. 56 and Hook. f. Fl. Brit. Ind. i. p. 28 (partly, from the specimens at Kew), not of Wallich ex Séringe.

A. ferox vars. *spicata* (for the greatest part), *heterophylloides* (in part), *laxiflora* and *crassicaulis* Brühl in Ann. Roy. Bot. Gard. Calcutta, v, ii, p. 110, plate 111, figs. 6, 16, 21, 28, 29.

A. ferox var. *spicatum* Goris in Bull. Sc. Pharm. iii (1901), p. 117, fig. 32; Watt in Agr. Ledger (1902), Nos. 3, 94.

A. ferox var. *crassicaule* Watt, l. c. 96.

A. Napellus Gammie in Rec. Bot. Surv. Ind. i., No. 2, p. 19.

[TYPE SPECIMENS: See below under 'distribution.']

Roots biennial, paired, tuberous, daughter-tuber conic or conic-oblong, often rather elongated, 10—20 cm. long, 1·8—3 cm. thick, simple or sometimes deeply divided, with filiform root-fibres the bases of which are sometimes abruptly thickened and persist as conical or ovoid stumps, brown or blackish externally, fracture horny, yellowish or brown in the dry state, taste slightly sweetish-bitter, followed by a tingling sensation; cambium continuous, forming in cross-section a more or less sinuous ring; mother-tuber similar, shrunk and wrinkled. *Innovation-bud* a very broad, much depressed cone with broad clasping scales, decaying soon after sprouting. *Stem* erect, up to 1·5 m. high, straight or slightly flexuous above, simple terete or sometimes slightly angular, robust, sometimes as much as 3 cm. in diameter,

* Name mentioned in Holmes, Museum Report, Pharm. Soc. Great Brit. for 1895—1902, pp. 3, 38. I do not consider myself responsible for the statements attributed to me and made by Mr. Holmes on p. 38. They were published without my knowledge.

adpressedly greyish-pubescent with deflexed hairs, glabrescent or quite glabrous in the lower part, brown or almost black when dry. *Lowest* 5—8 *leaves* decayed at the time of flowering, their scars rather distant; intermediate and upper leaves as many as 12, approximate or congested, petioled; petioles 2·5—7·5 cm. long, dilated at the base; blades somewhat fleshy, more or less finely pubescent or at length glabrous above, orbicular cordate or reniform or broadly ovate (particularly the upper) with a usually shallow sinus, 3-partite to $\frac{4}{5}$—$\frac{6}{7}$ or the upper to $\frac{2}{3}$, intermediate division rhomboid or ovate from a linear cuneate base, sometimes acuminate, 5—10 cm. long, 3—7·5 cm. broad, lateral divisions separated by a narrow sinus from the intermediate, broad-trapezoid, 2·5—7·5 cm. long, very unequally 2—3-partite to $\frac{2}{3}$—$\frac{5}{6}$, all the divisions much inciso-dentate or laciniate with acute dentate laciniæ. *Inflorescence* stiff, racemose or often panicled, narrow, many flowered, dense, rarely loose and subflexuous, more or less tomentose with spreading or deflexed hairs; lower bracts like the preceding leaves, but smaller, more elongate and less dissected, longer than the pedicels intermediate and upper lanceolate or oblong, sparingly dentate or entire, often over 2 cm. long, pedicels erect, rather stout, lower over 2·5 cm. long, upper much shorter; bracteoles, if any, herbaceous, rather broad and dentate, or narrow and entire to very narrow. *Sepals* of a saturated blue, more rarely pale or purplish blue, more or less pubescent to almost tomentose; uppermost helmet-shaped, helmet erect or slightly oblique, depressed, semi-orbicular in profile, almost equally curved in front and on the back, 20—24 mm. high, 20—24 mm. from the tip to the base, 12—15 mm. wide, produced into a very short beak, claw very short and broad; lateral sepals oblique, suborbicular, 12—18 mm. long, obscurely clawed; lower horizontal or deflexed, oblong, obtuse, 8—12 mm. long. *Nectaries* glabrous or scantily hispidulous, claw slightly curved or straight, 10—12, rarely to 14 mm. long, hood much leaning forward or subhorizontal, dorsally gibbous or almost spurred on the top, 6—8 mm. long, lip usually short, broad, emarginate. *Filaments* glabrous or sparingly hispidulous in the upper part, 7—8 mm. long, winged to or beyond the middle, wings gradually running out or suddenly contracted into small teeth. *Carpels* 5, oblong or ovoid, contracted into the slightly shorter style, densely tomentose. *Follicles* 5, oblong, somewhat turgid, contiguous, about 10 mm. long, 4—4·5 mm. broad, hairy. *Seeds* obpyramidal, about 4 mm. long, winged along the rhaphe with undulate hyaline transverse lamellæ on the faces.

DISTRIBUTION: *Alpine zone of the Himalaya of Sikkim and Chumbi.*

SIKKIM: Tonglo, 10,000 ft., *King*, 28-10-1875! (Hb. Calc.); Sandampuk forest, *Prain's Coll.* 63! (Hb. Calc.); Sandaklam, *Rogers*! (Hb. Calc.); Singalela Range, Phullalong, 10,000 ft., *C. B. Clarke* 12693A! (Hb. Kew); 12693 B, D, and E! (Hb. Calc.); 13483 B! (Hb. Calc. and Edinb.); Bikhabanjan, 11,000 ft., *Rogers*, 21-9-1900! (Hb. Calc.); Samdong, *Prain's Coll.*! (Hb. Calc., a state with a lax panicle); Sandakphu, Subarkhan, 11,000 ft., *Rogers*, 20-9-1900! (Hb. Calc. and Sah.); 11,800 ft., *Watt's Coll.*, Reg. No. 11723, 16-9-1899! (Hb. Sah.); 12,000 ft., *Watt's Coll.* Reg. No. 11723, 20-10-1899! (Hb Kew and Sah.); 12,000 ft., *Gamble* 71 B and C! (Hb. Kew, Hb. Calc.); 71 H! (Hb. Kew); Phallut, 10,000—12,000 ft., *Thomson*, 5-10-1857! (Hb. Calc. and Kew); *Hooker* 114! (Hb. Kew); *C. B. Clarke* 25725! (Hb. Calc.); *Kurz*! (Hb. Calc.); 12,000 ft., 8-10-1875, *King's Coll.* 796! (Hb. Calc., a state with a lax panicle); *King's Coll.* 1888! (Hb. Calc.); Thunku, 12,000 ft., *King's Coll.*

1885! (Hb. Calc.); Thangu, *Prain*! (Hb. Calc.); without precise locality, but probably from the Singalela Range, *Watt's Coll.* letter No. 1484! (Hb. Calc.); and *Watt's Coll.* 7037! (Hb. Calc. and Edinb.); Lachung, 11,000—12,000 ft., *Hooker*, 29-8-1849! (Hb. Kew); 12,000 ft., *Gammie* 758! (Hb. Calc.).—TIBET: Chumbi; Yatung, *Hobson*! (Hb. Kew); Tsang; *King's Coll.* 1882! (Hb. Calc.)

VERNACULAR NAMES: *Bikh*, Rogers; *Kalo Bikhoma*, Watt's Collector in letter No. 1484, not elsewhere; *Dongho*, King; *Gniong Mot* and *Shodduk Mot*, J. D. Hooker on labels.

PROPERTIES AND USES: *A. spicatum* is the principal source of the "bikh" or "bish" of the Calcutta market. An account of the mode of collecting the root in Sikkim may be found in Kanny Lall Dey's "The Indigenous Drugs of India" (1896), where it is, however, introduced erroneously as *A. Napellus*. The poisonous principle is pseudaconitine. The existence of this principle in certain Indian Aconites was known, as early as 1857, to Schott, and its chemical properties were first examined by Hübschmann in 1868, who proposed the name pseudaconitine for it, but it is impossible to fix on the particular species which led Schott and Hübschmann to the discovery of the new alkaloid. In 1870, however, T. B. Groves read, at the meeting of the British Pharmaceutical Conference at Liverpool, a paper on "Nepal Aconite," which contains an account of his method of obtaining pseudaconitine from aconite roots alleged to have come from Nepal, and also a description and figure of those roots. Both agree completely with the tubers of *A. spicatum*. Whether Wright and Luff who subsequently worked out the constitution of pseudaconitine dealt with the same species, I have no means of knowing; but there is no doubt that the material on which Prof. Dunstan's and F. H. Carr's paper "On pseudaconitine" (Transact. Chem. Soc. 1897, reprinted in Agric. Ledger 1898, No. 3) and Prof. Dunstan's article "The constituents of some Indian Aconites" (in Agric. Ledger, 1897, No. 19), were based belonged, so far as it is stated to have come from Sikkim, mainly if not exclusively to A. *spicatum*. The amount of pseudaconitine found in the tubers of this species may, according to Prof. Dunstan, reach as much as 0·50 p. c.

This species is chiefly characterised by the robust growth, the large tubers, the dense tomentum of the inflorescence and the short turgid follicles. The tubers are among the largest in the genus, the stems often are as thick as a thumb at the base and may attain a height of more than 1·5 m. Some of these very robust specimens were described as var. *crassicaulis* whilst others with laxer panicles than usual formed the basis for another variety, namely *laxiflora*. Both forms have been collected in the same locality, for instance, at Sandakphu by Gamble, and near Lachung by J. D. Hooker, and they represent to me merely individual variations.

There are, in the museum at Kew, roots of an aconite from which the poison applied to their arrow barbs by the Akhas is made (Tezpur, Assam; Surg. R. Campbell). They are quite like those of *A. spicatum*.

PLATE 106. Aconitum spicatum *Stapf*.—1, Upper part of an inflorescence, large state (referred to var. *crassicaule* by Brühl); 2 and 3, intermediate cauline leaves; 4 and 5, pairs of tubers; 6, a divided daughter-tuber with the root-fibres rubbed off—*natural size*; 7, a section through a daughter-tuber—*enlarged*.

(1, from Lachung, *Gammie*; 2, from Phalut, *Kurz*; 3—5, from Sandakphu, *Watt's Coll.*; 6, from Sikkim, without precise locality, *Watt's Coll.* letter No. 1484; from Sandakphu, *Rogers*.)

PLATE 107. Aconitum spicatum *Stapf*.—1, An inflorescence, rather narrow state; 2, an infructescence—*natural size*; 3, a flower, in longitudinal section; 4, a helmet of a more oblique type; 5, nectary, usual glabrous form; 6, lip of the same; 7, hispidulous nectary; 8, lip of the same; 9, a stamen; 10, a gynœcium; 11, a single carpel; 12, a seed, front view; 13, a seed, back view; 14, cross-section of a seed; 15, a portion of a pedicel—*all enlarged.*

(1, 3, and 15, from Sandakphu, *Watt's Coll.*; 2, 12, 13, and 14, from Tonglo, *King*; 4, 7, and 8, from Lachung, *J. D. Hooker*; 5, 6, and 9—11, from Phalut, *T. Thomson.*)

16. ACONITUM LACINIATUM Stapf, sp. nov.*

A. ferox var. *laciniata* Brühl in Ann. Roy. Bot. Gard., Calcutta, v. ii. p. 111 (in part), plate 111, figs. 7, 8, 17, and 30; Watt in Agric. Ledger (1902), No. 3, pp. 96-97.

[TYPE SPECIMENS: See under 'distribution.']

Roots biennial, tuberous, paired; daughter-tuber conic-oblong, often rather drawn out into a slender point, 3·5—6 cm. long, about 1·5—2 cm. thick, simple or divided, with filiform root-fibres, which are generally not much thickened at the base, brown externally, fracture whitish, or pale brownish, almost horny, taste indifferent or very slightly bitter, followed by a tingling sensation; cambium continuous, forming a sinuous ring in cross section; mother-tuber similar, usually much shrunk and thinner. *Innovation-bud* an acute cone, up to 1 cm. high, outermost scale one very short, clasping, soon decaying after sprouting. *Stem* erect, stiff or flexuous, 6 to 9 dm. high, simple, terete, slender to rather robust, finely pubescent in the upper part with adpressed reversed hairs, otherwise glabrescent or quite glabrous and shining, drying usually chestnut brown. *Leaves* scattered; basal 5—6, rarely 8, decayed at the time of flowering, rather distant; intermediate and upper leaves up to 10, approximate or congested, petioled, petioles rather slender, 2·5—7·5 cm. long; blades somewhat fleshy, finely pubescent or almost glabrous, reniform, rarely cordate-orbicular in outline with a usually wide and shallow sinus, 4—7, rarely to 10 cm. from the sinus to the tip, 7—12 cm. across, 5-pedati-partite almost to the base in the inner, to $\frac{3}{4}$—$\frac{5}{8}$ in the outer incisions, inner divisions sub-equal, rhomboid from a narrow cuneate base, up to 5 cm. wide, 3-lobed to the middle, lobes narrow, inciso-dentate or laciniate, laciniae lanceolate or linear, acute or acuminate, outermost divisions asymmetric, mostly unequally 2-lobed, otherwise similar to the inner but smaller. *Inflorescence* racemose or usually loosely paniculate, few- to many-flowered, finely greyish pubescent with adpressed curved hairs; lower bracts similar to the preceding leaves, but smaller and less dissected, intermediate and upper lanceolate, sparingly laciniate or the uppermost entire and very narrow; pedicels ascending, slender, lowest 3·5—5 (rarely to 7·5) cm. long, upper much shorter; bracteoles herbaceous, resembling the upper bracts. *Sepals* saturated red-purple or dark red, finely pubescent; uppermost helmet-shaped, helmet erect or suberect, equally curved in front and on the back, or slightly concave in front, produced into a short lip or beak, about 20 mm. high and 20 mm. from the tip to the base, 9—13 mm. wide, claw broad, short; lateral sepals very oblique, suborbicular, ciliate, 14—16 mm. long, broadly and obscurely clawed; lower deflexed or subhorizontal, oblong, obtuse, 12—14 mm. long. *Nectaries* hispidulous, at least below; claw slightly curved, about 12 mm. long; hood suberect or slightly leaning forward, 6 mm. long, gibbous or almost spurred on the back close to the apex, lip short or elongate, rather broad, 2-lobed.

* Name mentioned in Holmes, Museum Report, Pharm. Soc. Great Brit. for 1895—1902, p. 3.

Filaments hispidulous in the upper part, 7 mm. long, winged up to or beyond the middle, wings gradually or abruptly running out. *Carpels* 3, rarely 4 or 5, conniving in the flower, oblong, attenuate into a slender, finely curved style, densely and adpressedly pubescent. *Follicles* at first divergent, then conniving, contiguous, linear-oblong, more or less convex on the back, 18—25 mm. long, 5—6 mm. wide, finely pubescent. *Seeds* obpyramidal, 3-gonous, 3 mm. long, brown, broadly winged along the rhaphe, with transverse, undulate, hyaline lamellae.

DISTRIBUTION: *Subalpine and Alpine Himalaya of Sikkim and adjoining Tibet.*

SIKKIM: Singalela Range, Phullalong, 10,000 ft., *Clarke* 12707! (Hb. Kew); Sandakphu, Subarkan, 11,000 ft., 20-9-1900 *Rogers*! (Hb. Calc.); Sandakphu, 12,000 ft., *Gamble* 8478A and 8479! (Hb. Kew); *King's Coll.* 1887 and 1888! (Hb. Calc.); *Rogers*, Reg. No. 11724 (Hb. Kew and Sah.); lett. No. 11779, Reg. No. 8484! (Hb. Pharm. Soc. London); To-ko-la, *King's Coll.*, 23-8-1877! (Hb. Calc.); *King's Coll.*, 25-8-1878! (Hb. Calc.); Yak-la Cho-la range, 14,000 ft, *Gammie*! (Hb. Calc.) Cho-la, *King's Coll.* No. 4483! (Hb. Calc.); Lachung, *Gammie*! (Hb. Calc.).—TIBET: (Chumbi?), without precise locality, *King's Coll.* 1882! (Hb. Calc.)

VERNACULAR NAME: *Kalo Bikhoma*, Rogers; Watt in Agric. Ledger (1902) No. 3, p. 96 (see also A. *spicatum*).

PROPERTIES AND USES: According to Rogers, it forms together with Bikh (*Aconitum spicatum*) the article known as "Nepal Aconite."

Although *A. spicatum* and *A. laciniatum* are easily distinguished by their foliage, flowers and fruit, it is very difficult to sort small-sized tubers of *A. spicatum* and large-sized of *A. laciniatum*.

PLATE 108. Aconitum laciniatum *Stapf*.—1, An inflorescence; 2, an intermediate cauline leaf; 3, part of an infructescence; 4, a pair of tubers (large size)—*natural size*; 5, a flower in longitudinal section; 6, a nectary; 7, lip of a nectary; 8, a stamen; 9, a gynœcium; 10, a single carpel; 11, a seed, side view; 12, a seed, front view; 13, section through a daughter-tuber—*all enlarged*.

(All from Sandakphu; 1 and 2, *Rogers*; 3, *King's Coll.* 1888; 4 and 6—13, *Watt's Coll.* Reg. No. 11724; 5, *Gamble*, 8478 A.)

17. ACONITUM FEROX Wall. ex Séringe, Mus. Helv. i. (1823) p. 160, tab. xv. figs. 43, 44; Wall. Cat. 4721A; Séringe in DC. Prodr. i. p. 64; Wall. Plant. As. Rar. i. p. 35, tab. 41 (partly); Hook. f. & Thoms. Fl. Ind. i. p. 56 and Fl. Brit. Ind. i. p. 28 (partly); Köhler Mediz. Pfl. iii. No. 68 (partly) with plate, not of others.

A. virosum D. Don Prodr. Fl. Nep. p. 196.

A. Napellus var. *rigidum* Hook. fil. & Thoms. Fl. Ind. i. p. 29 (in part).

A. dissectum Stein in Gartenflora, 1886, p. 226, fig. or p. 227 (copied from Wallich), not of D. Don, nor of Tausch.

[TYPE SPECIMEN: Specimen communicated by Wallich to A. P. DeCandolle as "Aconitum ferox Wall." in 1819, in the Herb. DeCandolle, Geneva. Of this I have seen an excellent photograph, which I owe to Mr. Casimir DeCandolle's kindness.

Roots biennial, paired, tuberous; daughter-tuber ovoid-oblong to ellipsoid, 2·5—4 cm. long, about 1—1·5 cm. thick, with few filiform root-fibres, dark-brown externally, fracture scarcely farinaceous, yellowish, taste rather indifferent, followed by a strong tingling sensation, cambium continuous, forming in cross-section a slightly sinuous ring; mother-tuber much shrunk and wrinkled with more numerous root-fibres, outer sieve-strands surrounded by a mantle of sclerenchymatic cells. *Innovation-bud* conic, 4—5 mm. long; scales ovate, prominently finely nerved, persistent. *Stem* erect, with or without a slender, hypogæous base (up to 3 cm. long) which emits numerous fine roots near the upper end, simple, erect, 40—90 cm. high, rather slender, covered with short spreading yellow hairs in the upper part, glabrous below, hollow. *Leaves* scattered, distant, excepting the lowest 2 or 3 which are usually decayed at the time of flowering, up to 7, glabrous or the uppermost very sparingly hairy; petioles slender, the lower up to 25 cm. long and much dilated at the base, uppermost very short; blade orbicular-cordate to reniform in outline with a rather wide sinus (up to 8 cm. deep), up to 11 cm. high from the sinus to the tip, up to 20 cm. across, 5-pedatipartite to the very base or almost so in the inner, and to $\frac{8}{9}$—$\frac{9}{10}$ in the outer incisions, divisions deltoid from a cuneate base or the outermost trapezoid, intermediate division 3-lobed to the middle, middle lobe elongate, pinnati-laciniate to inciso-dentate, ultimate segments or teeth acute or very acute, inner lateral divisions similar, but less symmetric, outermost 2 lobed or 2-partite, all laciniæ more or less linear-lanceolate and divaricate, the outermost often overlapping and thus closing the sinus; uppermost blades sessile or subsessile, much smaller and less dissected. *Inflorescence* a loose raceme, 10—25 cm. long, often with slender, erect, few-flowered additional branches from the leafy base; rhachis slender, densely yellow-pubescent to subtomentose; floral leaves like the preceding leaves, but much reduced, passing upwards into the trifid or entire and linear-lanceolate bracts; bracteoles at or below the middle, resembling reduced bracts, very often suppressed; pedicels slender, erect, the lowest at length up to 7 cm. long. *Sepals* blue, hairy; uppermost helmet-shaped, helmet semi-orbicular in profile, shortly beaked 20—24 mm. high, 17—20 mm. from the tip to the base, 7—9 mm. wide; lateral sepals, slightly contiguous with the helmet, oblique, orbicular-obovate, broadly clawed, 16 mm. long, 14 mm. broad; lower sepals deflexed, oblong, subacute, 10 mm. long. *Nectaries* glabrous; claw erect; hood oblique to subhorizontal, oblong, gibbous or the back from the middle upwards or near the top; lip deflexed, lanceolate, acute, entire. *Filaments* glabrous, about 7 mm. long, narrowly winged, wings gradually attenuate. *Carpels* 5, conniving and contiguous, tomentose, gradually passing into the style. *Follicles* oblong, obliquely subtruncate, 15—20 mm. long, 4—5 mm. broad, dorsally subconvex, loosely tomentose or at length almost glabrous, conspicuously reticulate. *Seeds* obovoid to obpyramidal, 2·6—3 mm. long, winged along the rhaphe, transversely lamellate on the faces, lamellæ undulate.

DISTRIBUTION: *Alpine Himalaya of Nepal.*

NEPAL: without precise locality, *Wallich*, 1818 sub "Aconitum atrox, Wall."! and 1819 sub "Aconitum ferox Wall."! (Hb. British Museum); *Wallich* 1819! (Herb. DeCandolle); *Wallich*, comm. by Wallich to W. Hooker in 1821! (Hb. Kew); *Wallich*, communicated by Wallich to Hornemann! (Hb. Copenhagen); *Wallich*, with the distribution label of Wallich's Catalogue 4721! (Hb. Linnean Society, London, with the pencil note "Sheopore 1821," and Hb. Kew). (4721, A of the Catalogue with the remark "Mont. altiss. Napaliæ, 1821," refers doubtless to this species).

VERNACULAR NAMES: *Bick, Bickma*, Wallich, MS. on the label accompanying the specimen sent to England in 1818 as "Aconitum atrox Wall."

PROPERTIES AND USES: As the specific names suggested by Wallich (*atrox* and *ferox*) imply, the plant has the reputation of being extremely poisonous. It is very probably the source or one of the sources of the "Bish, Bikh" or "Hodoya Bish" of Hamilton (Account of Nepal, p. 99), but it is not his *Caltha Codua*.

All the specimens quoted above agree absolutely with each other and also with the plant figured by Wallich in his *Plantae Asiaticae Rariores*, i. tab. 41 as *A. ferox*, with the exception of the tubers, and there can be no doubt as to what Wallich meant originally by his *A. ferox*. Later on, it is true, he confused other species with it, as his distribution set and the text in the work cited show. At that time, however, Séringe had already published a description of Wallich's *A. ferox* from one of the original specimens, and the name *A. ferox* will therefore have to be retained for the species represented by those originals. As to the tubers figured in Wallich's plate, they differ so much from the tubers I have seen still attached to Wallich's specimens in the Kew and Copenhagen collections and in the photograph of the type in DeCandolle's herbarium that I cannot help suspecting that the draughtsman added tubers of another Aconite, possibly of *A. Balfourii*, on to the stem of *A. ferox*. In any case, there is only a crushed fragment of a half-decayed mother-tuber of *A. ferox* in Wallich's own herbarium. I would only add that the cross-section of a tuber, shown in Wallich's plate, represents the cambium as a continuous sinuous ring, whilst the original drawing which is at Kew and from which the plate was made has in the place of the ring some faint patches which might just as well have been meant for isolated strands.

PLATE 109. Aconitum ferox *Wall.* ex *Séringe*.—1, An inflorescence; 2, a basal leaf; 3, an intermediate cauline leaf; 4, a pair of tubers with the hypogæous rooting part of the stem; 5, mother-tuber and old bud-scales removed; dt, daughter-tuber; ib, innovation bud of the same; s, hypogæous portion of the stem with rootlets and root-scars; 6, an infructescence—*natural size*; 7, a flower, in longitudinal section; 8, a nectary; 9, a stamen; 10, a gynœcium; 11, a single carpel; 12, a seed, back view; 13, a seed, front view; 14, a transverse section of a seed; 15, a portion of a pedicel; 16, a transverse section through a daughter-tuber, partly eaten by an insect—*all enlarged*.

(All from Wallich's original in W. Hooker's herbarium at Kew, excepting figs. 4 and 16 which were drawn from specimens in the Copenhagen Herbarium.)

18. ACONITUM HETEROPHYLLOIDES Stapf, sp. nov.

A. ferox var. *heterophylloides* Brühl in Ann. Roy. Bot. Gard. Calcutta, v, ii, p. 110 (in part), plate 111, fig. 18.

A ferox var. *leucanthum* Brühl, l. c. (in part).

[TYPE SPECIMENS: See below under 'distribution.']

Roots biennial, paired, tuberous; daughter-tuber ellipsoid or ovoid, bearing few filiform root-fibres, 1·25—2·5 cm. long, 9—14 mm. thick, externally blackish, internally brownish when dry, fracture almost horny, taste pure bitter, not followed by any tingling sensation, cambium very delicate, forming, in cross-section, a sinuous ring, which is sometimes interrupted in places; mother-tuber similar, but more or less shrunk and wrinkled. *Innovation-bud* conical, about 6 mm. high, acute, scales ovate, almost keeled, the outermost one very short and clasping, soon decaying after sprouting. *Stem* erect, often bent in a zigzag line, simple, conspicuously angular from long decurrent acute ridges continuing the petioles, rarely more than 30 cm. high, moderately stout, adpressedly pubescent from mostly deflexed hairs or glabrescent below. *Leaves* scattered 5—9, basal and lower leaves decayed at the time of flowering, intermediate 2·5—3·5 cm. distant, petioled; petioles

2·5—3·5 cm. long, the upper gradually shorter; blades finely pubescent, particularly on the nerves below, ovate to reniform in outline with a wide sinus, 0·5—2 cm. deep, 3·5—6 cm. from the sinus to the tip, 3—12 cm. across, 3-partite to $\frac{5}{6}$—$\frac{6}{7}$, or sometimes only to $\frac{2}{3}$, intermediate division elongate-rhomboid, mostly subacuminate, up to 3·5 cm. wide, lateral divisions trapezoid, 1·75—5 cm. long, very unequally 2-partite to $\frac{3}{4}$—$\frac{4}{5}$, all the divisions copiously inciso-dentate or laciniate in the lower part, laciniæ acutely (rarely obtusely) dentate; uppermost leaves very similar, but smaller and less divided with the intermediate division often much exceeding the lateral. *Inflorescence* racemose or panicled with additional branches from the upper leaves, few- to many-flowered, rather lax, pubescent; lower bracts like the preceding leaves, intermediate smaller, less dissected, as long as or longer than the pedicels, uppermost lanceolate, dentate; pedicels erect, lowest up to 3·5 cm. long., upper much shorter; bracteoles mostly linear close to the flowers, or scarcely any. *Sepals* blue or white and blue, pubescent; uppermost helmet-shaped, helmet more or less oblique in profile, scarcely depressed, wide, 16—24 mm. high, 15—22 mm. from the tip to the base, 8—12 mm. wide; slightly concave in front, shortly beaked, claw broad, short; lateral sepals oblique, broad-obovate, ciliate, up to 22 mm. long; lower horizontal or deflexed, oblong, obtuse, up to 16 mm. long. *Nectaries* hispidulous all over; claw slightly curved, up to 16 mm. long; hood almost erect, terminating in a short recurved spur, up to 8 mm. long, lip obovate to subspathulate, crenulate. *Filaments* hispidulous in the upper part, 8 mm. long, winged to or beyond the middle, wings suddenly or gradually running out. *Carpels* usually 5, sometimes 3, rarely 6 or 7, more or less diverging, oblong, contracted into the slender curved style, fulvo-pubescent, particularly on the back. *Follicles* 5 or 3, one or more of them frequently arrested, at first divergent, at length almost straight and contiguous with the exception of the top, linear-oblong, up to 20 mm long, 4 mm. broad, pubescent or glabrate. *Seeds* oblong-obpyramidal, 3 mm. long, winged along the rhaphe, with hyaline, undulate, transverse lamellæ, running out towards the back.

DISTRIBUTION: *Alpine Himalaya of South-Western Sikkim.*

SIKKIM: Singalela Range, 10,000 ft., *C. B. Clarke* 13507! (Hb. Brit. Mus. Calc. and Brandis); Sandakphu to Phalut, boundary road (34 miles), 11,000 ft., *Rogers*, 20-9-1900! (Hb. Calc.); Sandakphu to Subarkan, 11,000 ft., *Rogers*, 20-9-1900! (Hb. Calc.); Sandakhan, *Rogers*! (Hb. Calc.); Sandakphu, 12,000 ft., *Rogers*, 24-8 and 4-10-1899! 11998! (Hb. Calc.); Ling-too, 10,000 ft., *King's Coll.* 1882! (Hb. Calc.); "Sikkim," without precise locality, 10-1857, *T. Thomson*! (Hb. Calc.)

VERNACULAR NAME: *Nirbanshi*, Rogers.

PROPERTIES AND USES: Unknown (see the paragraph on Jadwar, p. 123).

A. heterophylloides is closely allied to *A. leucanthum*; the differences are mainly in the vegetative characters. *A. heterophylloides* is a more robust plant; its tubers attain a much greater size, the stem is stouter and stiffer and the leaves are larger. As to the differences derived from the flowers I might point out that they are generally more numerous in *A. heterophylloides*, that their helmet is less depressed and less oblique, and that the carpels are less pubescent.

PLATE 110. Aconitum heterophylloides *Stapf.*—1, An inflorescence; 2—5, cauline leaves; 6, an infructescence; 7, a pair of tubers—*natural size*; 8, a flower, in longitudinal section; 9, a stamen; 10, a gynœcium; 11, a seed, front view; 12, a seed, side view; 13, a cross-section through a daughter-tuber—*all enlarged.*

(1, 2, and 8—10, from Singalela, *Clarke*; 3, 4, 6, 7, and 11—13, from Sandakphu, *Rogers*; 5, from Ling-too, *King's Coll.*)

19. ACONITUM LEUCANTHUM Stapf, sp. nov.

A. ferox var. *leucanthum* Brühl in Ann. Roy. Bot. Gard. Calcutta, v, ii, p. 110 (in part).

A. ferox var. *cymbiformis* Brühl, l. c. p. 111, plate 111, fig. 3.

A. ferox var. *flavidiflora* Brühl, l. c. (in part?), plate 111, figs. 4, 5, 19, 22, 27.

[TYPE SPECIMENS: See under 'distribution.']

Roots biennial, paired, tuberous; daughter-tuber ellipsoid or oblong, 6—14 mm. long, 5—8 mm. thick, bearing few filiform root-fibres, externally dark brown, fracture white, farinaceous, taste somewhat bitter (pure), not followed by any tingling or burning sensation, cambium continuous, forming a slightly sinuous ring in cross-section, sometimes with a small inner cambium ring; mother-tuber similar, more or less shrunk at the time of flowering. *Innovation-bud* conical, about 5 mm. long, scales decaying after sprouting. *Stem* erect, up to 6 dm. high, simple or sparingly branched, often angular from raised lines decurrent from the leaf bases, adpressedly pubescent with mostly deflexed curved hairs. *Leaves* scattered, 4—7, lowest often decayed at the time of flowering or, if present, like those above them, remote, petioled; petioles slender, up to 20 cm. long, gradually decreasing upwards; blades sparsely pubescent particularly on the nerves below, cordate-ovate or rotundate in outline with a wide sinus, 1—2 cm. deep, 3—5 cm. from the sinus to the tip, rarely longer, 4—7 cm. across, rarely broader, 3-partite to $\frac{5}{6}$ or $\frac{6}{7}$, intermediate division rhomboid, 1·8—3 cm. broad, inciso-dentate or laciniate below, laciniæ 2-dentate near the apex, subacute or apiculate, lateral divisions trapezoid, unequally 2-partite to $\frac{2}{3}$ or $\frac{3}{4}$ otherwise like the intermediate; uppermost leaves smaller and less divided. *Inflorescence* terminal, racemose or subpaniculate, few-flowered, loose, pubescent; lower bracts like the preceding leaves, intermediate smaller, less divided, upper lanceolate or linear; pedicels erect, lowest up to 3 cm. long, the others much shorter; bracteoles often foliaceous on the lower pedicels, much reduced to filiform on the upper, near to the flower. *Sepals* whitish or suffused with blue, rarely quite blue, more or less pubescent; uppermost helmet-shaped, helmet very oblique in profile, broad, depressed, 15—20 mm. high, 18—23 mm. from the tip to the base, 10—13 mm. broad, slightly concave or very oblique in front, shortly beaked, claw broad, very short; lateral sepals oblique, suborbicular or obovate-orbicular, ciliate, 14—20 mm. long; lower horizontal or deflexed, oblong, obtuse, 12—16 mm. long. *Nectaries* hispidulous, claw curved, up to 12 mm. long; hood more or less leaning forward, 6 mm. long with a recurved obtuse spur. *Filaments* 8 mm. long, hispidulous in the upper part, winged to or beyond the middle, wings suddenly or gradually contracted. *Carpels* usually 5, sometimes 3, conniving, oblong-lanceolate, slightly hairy on the back or glabrous, drying black with a whitish bloom. *Follicles* 5 or 3, 1 or more often imperfect, erect, slightly divergent in the upper part, linear-oblong, up to 20 mm. long, scarcely 4 mm. wide, glabrous or nearly so. *Seeds* oblong-obpyramidal, 3 mm. long, winged along the rhaphe with undulate, transverse lamellæ, running out towards the back.

DISTRIBUTION: *Alpine Himalaya of Sikkim and adjoining Tibet.*

SIKKIM: Jongri, *King's Coll.*! (Hb. Calc.); *C. B. Clarke*! (Hb. Kew); Tenchang, 13,000 ft., *King's Coll.*! (Hb. Calc.); Jongli Pokri, 13,000 ft., *King's Coll.*! (Hb. Calc.); Megu pasture, *Prain's Coll.* 194! (Hb. Calc.); Tha-pah, 13,000 ft., *King's Coll.*! (Hb. Calc.); without precise locality, *King's Coll.* 1889! (Hb. Calc.).—TIBET: Chumbi, *King's Coll.*! (Hb. Calc.); Meerik-la, *King's Coll.* 636! (Hb. Calc.)

VERNACULAR NAME: Unknown.

PROPERTIES AND USES: Unknown.

PLATE 111. Aconitum leucanthum *Stapf.*—1, A specimen, cut above the lowest leaves; 2, an infructescence; 3, a pair of tubers—*natural size*; 4, a flower, in longitudinal section; 5, stamens; 6, a gynœcium; 7, a seed, back view; 8, the same, side view; 9, a portion of a pedicel; 10, a section through a daughter-tuber; 11, a section through an abnormal daughter-tuber, f: fissures, c: cavity, ic: inner cambium, nc: normal cambium—*all enlarged.*

(1 and 4—6, from Jongli Pokri, *King's Coll.*; 2, 7, 8, 9, and 10, from Sikkim, *King's Coll.* 1889; 3 and 11, from Jongri, *King's Coll.*)

20. ACONITUM ELWESII Stapf, sp. nov.

A. variegatum Hook. f., Himal. Journ. ii. p. 107; Hook. f. & Thoms. Fl. Ind. p. 56, not of Linn.

A. uncinatum (?) Hook. f., Flor. Brit. Ind. i. p. 28, not of Linn.

[TYPE SPECIMENS: See under 'distribution.']

Roots unknown. *Stem* scandent, branched, flexuous, slender, terete, crispo-pubescent from adpressed reversed hairs. *Basal leaves* unknown; intermediate and upper scattered, petioled; petioles flexuous, up to 3 cm. long; blades pubescent, ultimately glabrate, cordate-ovate or rotundate in outline, with a wide sinus, 0·5—1·5 cm. deep, up to more than 5 cm. long from the sinus to the tip, 4—6 cm. across, 3-partite to $\frac{7}{8}$—$\frac{9}{10}$, intermediate division rhomboid, acuminate, up to 2·5 cm. wide, lateral divisions trapezoid, up to 3·5 cm. long, unequally 2-lobed to the middle, all coarsely crenate, crenæ apiculate. *Inflorescence* axillary and terminal, racemose or subpaniculate, pendulous or nodding, few to many-flowered, loose, pubescent; lower and intermediate bracts representing reduced leaves, uppermost lanceolate or linear, entire, shorter than the pedicels; pedicels recurved, the lowest at length up to 5 cm. long; bracteoles linear or those of the lowest pedicels more or less dissected or lobed. *Flowers* erect (negatively geotropous). *Sepals* blue or violet, sparingly pubescent; uppermost helmet-shaped, helmet broadly semi-elliptic in profile or almost semi-orbicular, suboblique, 20—25 mm. high, 17—20 mm. from the tip to the base, 10—13 mm. broad, slightly concave or suddenly contracted in front, shortly beaked; lateral sepals sub-orbicular, suboblique, 14—16 mm. long, long-ciliate, not clawed; lower deflexed, oblong, obtuse, 10—13 mm. long. *Nectaries* glabrous; claw slightly curved, 12—15 mm. long; hood suberect, recurved, spurred, 5 mm. long, lip rather long, slightly 2-lobed. *Filaments* 6 mm. long, winged up to or beyond the middle, wings more or less abruptly contracted. *Carpels* 5, conniving, glabrous, obliquely oblong, passing into a slender style, at length up to 4 mm. long. *Follicles* (immature) 5, divergent, oblong, up to 12 mm. long, 3 mm. broad. *Seed* unknown.

DISTRIBUTION: *Alpine Himalaya of North-Eastern Sikkim.*

SIKKIM: Climbing in shrubs on moraines near Lachung, 9,000 ft., *J. D. Hooker*! (Hb. Kew); *Gammie*! (Hb. Calc.); between Lamteng and Samdong, *Prain*! (Hb. Calc.); Lachen, *Prain's Coll.* 317! (Hb. Calc.); *Younghusband*! (Hb. Calc.); without precise locality, *Elwes*! (Hb. Kew)

VERNACULAR NAME: "*Tukschak Gniong*," J. D. Hooker, on the label.

PROPERTIES AND USES: Sir Joseph Hooker remarks on the label attached to his Lachung specimen: "good Bikh," from which it may be inferred that the natives know it as a strong poison.

This species is perfectly distinct from the American *A. uncinatum* Linn. It belongs to a polymorphic group of scandent species ranging from Western China to Siberia and Japan, and approaches particularly *A. Hemsleyanum* Pritzel, of Central China, which differs in the glabrous stems and leaves, the broad depressed top of the nectary hood and the generally broader leaf-segments.

PLATE 112 A. Aconitum Elwesii *Stapf.*—1, A portion of a plant, with two pendulous inflorescences—*natural size*; 2, a flower, in longitudinal section; 3, a nectary; 4, stamens; 5, a gynœcium; a portion of a pedicel—*all enlarged.*

(All figures from a specimen from Lachung, *Gammie.*)

21. ACONITUM LETHALE Griffith, Not. iv., p. 732; Ic. Pl. Asiat. DCLX. fig. iii.
A. palmatum Hook. f., Flor. Brit. Ind. i. p. 28 (the Mishmi plant), not of Wall.

[TYPE SPECIMENS: Specimen raised by Griffith from tubers collected by him in the Mishmi Hills, at Kew.]

Roots (according to Griffith) fusiform, whitish or brown, bearing root-fibres. *Stem* scandent (?), branched, flexuous, slender, terete, glabrous or the uppermost part pubescent from minute adpressed reversed hairs. *Basal leaves* unknown; intermediate and upper leaves scattered, petioled; petioles slender up to 5 cm. long; blades shining, bright green above, pale below, glabrous or scantily pubescent on the nerves below, cordate-rotundate in outline with a wide sinus or reniform, 3-partite to $\frac{5}{6}$ (or the small leaves of the branches 5-lobed to the middle), intermediate divisions narrow, obovate-cuneate, almost 5 cm. long, up to 1·8 cm. broad, lateral divisions trapezoid, up to 3·5 cm. long, unequally divaricate-2-lobed to the middle, all coarsely dentate, teeth apiculate. *Inflorescence* loosely racemose (?), slightly pubescent; bracts foliaceous, 3-lobed, lobes sparingly dentate; pedicels slender, 3·5—7·5 cm. long; bracteoles foliaceous, 3-partite, divisions dentate, up to 12 mm. long, or more or less reduced, near the flower. *Sepals* blue (?), slightly pubescent; uppermost helmet-shaped, helmet semiorbicular-elliptic in profile, 18—20 mm. high, 18—20 mm. from the tip to the base, 12 mm. broad; lateral oblique, orbicular-obovate, shortly and broadly clawed, up to 16 mm. long, 10—12 mm. broad; lower deflexed, broad elliptic, subobtuse, up to 16 mm. long. *Nectaries* glabrous, claw erect, 12—14 mm. long; hood erect, oblong, very shortly spurred from the top, 6 mm. long, lip broad, 2-lobed. *Filaments* glabrous 8—9 mm. long, winged to or beyond the middle, wings gradually or suddenly contracted. *Carpels* 5, obliquely oblong, sparingly pubescent.

DISTRIBUTION: Higher parts of the Mishmi mountains, *Griffith*, Kew Distrib. 19! (Hb. Kew.)

VERNACULAR NAME: Unknown.

PROPERTIES AND USES: This is according to Griffith the source of the celebrated "Bhi" or "Bis" poison of the Mishmis.

Tubers of this species were collected by Griffith in the higher parts of the Mishmi mountains in 1836, and transferred to a garden at Sadiyah. From a specimen raised from those tubers Griffith described and figured his *A. lethale*. He states that he saw only one flower and this was deformed. There are, however, 4 excellently preserved flowers in the Kew Herbarium, presumably collected after he had written out his description. Unfortunately the flowers are detached, and it is consequently impossible to say with certainty what the inflorescence was.

The very slender, flexuous and probably scandent stems, the small leaves, the long and slender pedicels and the shape of the nectaries distinguish it sufficiently from *A. palmatum*, to which *A. lethale* has been reduced. Its affinity lies, among the Indian species, probably with *A. Elwesii* from which it differs in the cut of the leaves and the shape of the nectaries.

PLATE 112 B. Aconitum lethale *Griffith.*—1, A barren specimen, tips broken off; 2, a large-sized leaf: 3 and 4, detached flowers—*natural size*; 5, a flower in longitudinal section; 6, a nectary; 7, stamens; 8, a gynœcium; 9, a single carpel—*all enlarged.*

(All from Griffith's specimen at Kew.)

22. ACONITUM NAGARUM Stapf, sp. nov.

A. ferox C. B. Clarke in Journ. Linn. Soc. xxv. (1890) p. 3, non Wall. ex Séringe.

[TYPE SPECIMEN: See under 'distribution.']

Roots paired, biennial, tuberous; daughter-tuber unknown; mother-tuber much shrunk, slightly over 2 cm. long, broken up longitudinally in consequence of the more or less complete decay of the secondary phloem in which the vasal strands formed by the discontinuous (?) cambium are embedded, taste quite indifferent. *Innovation-bud* (see note below) conic, slender, over 1 cm. long. *Stem* erect, stout, almost 1 m. high, simple, terete, finely pubescent in the upper part with adpressed reversed hairs, otherwise glabrous. *Leaves* scattered; basal leaves approximate, the very lowest decayed at the time of flowering, upper few and very remote, lowest petioles up to 60 cm. long, widened, sulcate and amplexicaul at the base, upper much shorter; blades glabrous, rather firm, cordate-reniform in outline, with a wide sinus 5—8 cm. deep, 8—11 cm. from the sinus to the tip, 12—20 cm. across, 3-partite to the very base, intermediate division obovate-cuneate, 5—8 cm. broad, 3-lobed to the middle, intermediate lobe equally 3-, lateral unequally 2-lobuled, lobules acute, sharply 1—2-dentate, lateral divisions 8—12 cm. long, unequally 2-partite to $\frac{5}{6}$, lobes 3- or 2-lobuled, lobules sharply and very coarsely dentate, nerves very prominent below. *Inflorescence* a slender terminal raceme with an additional axillary raceme from the axil of the uppermost leaf, over 30 cm. long, greyish pubescent; axis short; lower and intermediate bracts foliaceous, 3-partite and inciso-dentate to ovate and entire, shorter than the pedicels; pedicels erect or sub-erect, lowest up to 2·5 cm. long; bracteoles none or very small on the lowest pedicels. *Sepals* blue (?), pubescent; uppermost helmet-shaped, helmet depressed, semi orbicular in profile, obliquely descending into an obscure beak, 20 mm. high, 17-18 mm. from the tip to the base, 7 mm. wide, claw rather distinct; lateral sub orbicular, sub-oblique, sometimes obscurely clawed, 14—15 mm. long; lower deflexed, elliptic, subacute, 8—10 mm. long. *Nectaries* glabrous, claw very slender, 17 mm. long; hood very narrow, 4 mm. long, tip widened and gibbous on the back, lip obcordate as long as the hood. *Filaments* glabrous, winged to the middle, wings abruptly or gradually contracted. *Carpels* 5, somewhat conniving, oblong, pubescent, gradually passing into the short style. *Follicles* contiguous below, very slightly divergent in the upper part, oblong, rotundate truncate, minutely pubescent, hairs adpressed. *Seeds* obpyramidal, brown, 3 mm. long, transversely lamellate.

DISTRIBUTION: *Higher mountains between the Brahmaputra and Chindwin rivers.*

NAGA HILLS: District Kohima; Japvo Mountains, 9,000 ft., *C. B. Clarke* 41332 A! (Hb. Kew); Siruifurar and Japvo Mountains, *Watt* 6467! (Hb. Kew.)

VERNACULAR NAME: Unknown.

PROPERTIES AND USES: Unknown.

I have no doubt that this is a species quite distinct from the Himalayan Aconites; but I am not sure where to place it, the material being in some respects too imperfect. There is only the mother-tuber, from which the flowering stem originated, with Clarke's specimen and no trace of a daughter-tuber although one should expect that it was completely developed at the time of collecting. The tuber is about 1 cm. thick near the base, where it gives off a few cylindric branches, 2-3 mm. thick. Just above this level the cambium seems to be continuous, but below, the tuber is broken up either into several branches or into strands which have become isolated by the decay of a portion of the parenchyma. Which is the case I cannot say, as the condition of the tuber is too bad. There are, however, in the Kew Herbarium three plants which represent young states of the same species all with the tubers still attached. They were collected in April by Watt (No. 6467) in practically the same locality. They are very young plants, having not more than 1 or 2 leaves developed. Their tubers are ovoid, 2-3 cm. long and 0·7 cm. in diameter, bearing numerous root-fibres, some of which are thickened at the base. Their cambium forms in cross-section a continuous sinuous ring, and the xylem strands are particularly well developed. The taste is slightly bitter, followed by a tingling sensation, which, however, is not intense. In one of the plants a bud was found in the axil of a decayed scale at the base of the stem; it was evidently an innovation-bud the roots of which had not yet formed.

PLATE 113. Aconitum Nagarum *Stapf.*—1, Lower part of the stem with one of the basal leaves; 2, a leaf from the middle of the stem; 3, an infructescence, with flowers at the top—*all natural size*; 4, a portion of the axis of the infructescence; 5, a flower, in longitudinal section; 6, a nectary; 7, stamens; 8, a fruit—*all enlarged.*

(All the figures from C. B. Clarke's specimen, No. 41332A.)

23. ACONITUM DISSECTUM D. Don, Prodr. Fl. Nepal., p. 197, not of Tausch, nor of Stein.

A. Napellus, 1, Hook. f. & Thoms. Fl. Ind. i. 57 (in part).

A. Napellus var. *rigidum* Hook. f. & Thoms. in Fl. Brit. India, i. 29 (in part).

[TYPE SPECIMEN: Collected by Wallich's Collector on Gossain Than, Nepal, August 1821, at present in Wallich's own herbarium, at the Linnean Society, London.]

Roots biennial, paired, tuberous; only daughter-tuber known in a very imperfect state; mother-tuber cylindric, almost 5 cm. long, 0·8 cm. thick, blackish, shrunk and wrinkled, with filiform root-fibres, cambium continuous, forming a sinuous ring in cross section. *Stem* erect, simple, up to 6 cm. high, terete, like almost the whole plant perfectly glabrous. *Leaves* scattered, the lowest early decaying, quite glabrous with the exception of some of the youngest which are sparingly pubescent; petioles widened at the base, lower up to 6 cm. long, uppermost 2—3 cm. long, slender; blades rotundate-reniform in outline, 3—5-partite to the base or nearly so, 4—5 cm. from the sinus to the tip, 6—8 cm. across divisions similar, but the outer smaller and more or less asymmetric, pinnatifid, laciniae linear, the lower divided again, subacute. *Inflorescences* terminal and from the axils of the upper leaves. *Sepals* glabrous in bud. *Carpels* 5, glabrous (at least when quite young).

DISTRIBUTION: *Alpine region of the inner Himalaya.*

NEPAL: Gossain Than, *Wallich's coll.*, Wallich Cat. 4724 (Hb. Wallich, Linn. Soc.)! without precise locality, *Scully*! (Hb. Calc.)

VERNAC. NAME: Unknown.

PROPERTIES AND USES: Unknown.

A specimen resembling D. Don's *A. dissectum* very closely in habit, and possessing leaves of exactly the same cut, was collected by Littledale in the Goring Valley, 90° 25′ : 30° 12′ at about 16,500 ft. (Hemsley in *Journ. Linn. Soc.* xxxv. 1902, p. 164); but the inflorescence inclusive of the flowers is greyish pubescent. Another specimen collected by Soulié at Ta-tsien-lu, Szechuan, (No. 622), is quite glabrous and also agrees, so far as it goes, with the Gossain Than plant. Both specimens are, however, not in very good condition, and have no roots. It will be necessary to have more complete material from Nepal before a satisfactory definition of Don's *A. dissectum* can be given.

PLATE 114A. Aconitum dissectum *Don.*—A specimen in Wallich's herbarium at the Linnean Society (cut at *)—*natural size.*

SECTION III.—GYMNACONITUM STAPF.

Root fusiform, annual.

24. ACONITUM GYMNANDRUM Maximowicz in Bull. Acad. Petersb. xxiii., (1877), 308 (Mel. Biol. ix. 711); Flor. Tangut., p. 26, t. vi. figs. 1—6; Brühl in Ann. Roy. Bot. Gard., Calcutta, v., ii., p. 113, t. 125; Diels in Futterer, Durch Asien: Beschreib. d. Pflanz., p. 9.

[TYPE SPECIMEN:—Collected by Przewalski in Kansu in 1872.]

Annual. Root slender, usually vertically descending, fusiform with numerous fine root-fibres, taste slightly bitter. *Stem* simple and erect, or branched from the base with usually ascending branches, from a few inches to 3 feet high, slender to robust, more or less hispid, hairs long, fine, spreading, few below, dense in the upper part. *Leaves* scattered, or in dwarf specimens gathered in a basal rosette, hispid like the stem, petioled; petioles slender, lowest up to 6 cm. long, upper much shorter, or all rather short, blades reniform, rotundate to ovate in outline, 1·5—5 cm. long, 2—6 cm. across, 3-partite to the base or ternate with distinct petiolules, divisions similar, but the lateral usually shorter and more or less asymmetric, more or less pinnatipartite, laciniae inciso-dentate, very variable in width. *Inflorescences* terminal, racemose or paniculate from additional lateral racemes, slender, narrow, loose or dense, hirsute. *Lower bracts* resembling the preceding leaves, upper much reduced, uppermost linear-lanceolate, subentire; pedicels erect, often adpressed to the rhachis, the lowest at length up to 6 cm. long, the intermediate and upper much shorter or all short, bracteoles lanceolate to linear, usually entire, close to the flower. *Sepals* violet to dark-blue, softly hispid with long white hairs; uppermost helmet-shaped, helmet almost navicular, much depressed, contracted into a long linear claw, slightly beaked, 17—28 mm. high (including the claw), 3—4 mm. wide at the top; lateral sepals abruptly contracted into a narrow linear claw, as long as or shorter than the rotundate limb, 15—17 mm. long, limb up to 8 mm. across; lower sepal similar but somewhat smaller and the limb more ovate or elliptic. *Nectaries* glabrous or very sparingly hairy; claw erect, up to 14 mm. long, hood large, slightly leaning forward or erect, top dorsally gibbous, lip very large rotundate, denticulate. *Filaments* hispidulous, winged up to or beyond the middle, wings gradually or abruptly contracted, long persistent. *Carpels* up to 12, parallel, oblong, abruptly contracted into the slender style, more or less villous or hirsute. *Follicles* oblong, rotundate, truncate, about 10 mm. long, 3 mm. broad, slightly divergent in the upper part, more or less glabrescent. *Seeds* obpyramidal, blackish, 2 mm. long, transversely minutely lamellate.

DISTRIBUTION: *Central Asia from the Sikkim frontier to Kansu and Szechuan.*

PHARI: Kang-ma, on the banks of the Penamong-chu, 60 miles to the north of Phari town, *King's coll.* 1878! (Hb. Calc.); Ting, *King's coll.* 1879! (Hb. Calc.); and without precise locality, *King's coll.* 1877! and 1882! (Hb. Calc.).—KIALIA (Eastern Tibet): Tongolo, *Soulié* 424! 665! (Hb. Kew).—SZECHUAN: Tachienlu, between 9,000 and 13,000 ft., *Pratt* 507! 496! (Hb. Kew and Calc.);—KANSU: near the convent Kadiger, *Potanin*! (Hb. Kew); mountains to the east and north of Kuku-nor, in alpine meadows, up to 11,000 ft., *Przewalski*, according to Maximowicz.

VERNACULAR NAME: Unknown.

PROPERTIES AND USES: Unknown.

PLATE 115. Aconitum gynmandrum *Maxim.*—1, An unbranched flowering specimen; 2, a branched specimen, partly in fruit—*natural size;* 3, a flower in longitudinal section; 4, a lateral sepal; 5, a nectary; 6, a stamen; 7, a gynœcium; 8 and 9, seeds; 10, a portion of a pedicel—*all enlarged.*

(All from specimens collected in Phari.)

DOUBTFUL SPECIES.

ACONITUM sp. (JADWAR-KATHAI).

Tubers conic from an almost truncate base; about 3 cm. long, 1·5 cm. in diameter, rarely more (up to 4·5 by 2 cm.), brown, moderately wrinkled, with few fibre-scars or sometimes with the stumps of thickened root-branches, fracture horny or cartilaginous, brown, taste very bitter (like quinine), not followed by any tingling sensation; cambium continuous, forming in transverse section a sinuous ring with conspicuous short radial lines within the cambium, corresponding to the xylem strands which project rather more towards the centre than in other species. *Innovation-bud* rubbed off, leaving a large almost orbicular scar in the middle of the truncate base.

DISTRIBUTION: *Inner Himalaya of Nepal.*

NEPAL: Khywong, trade samples, obtained by Capt. Strachey! (Mus. Kew).

VERNACULAR NAMES: Nirbisi (Hindi); Bomar (Botee); Jadwar (Pers.) according to Capt. Strachey.

PROPERTIES AND USES: See the paragraph on Jadwar on p. 124.

Very similar specimens are preserved in the museum of the Pharmaceutical Society, London, presented by Dymock and marked as "Judwar from Delhi, the only kind sold at Bombay." They are, however, smaller than Strachey's, and usually more abruptly contracted (hence turnip-shaped) about 2 cm. by 1·5 cm., and have a sweetish taste which is almost free from bitter. They answer fairly well to the description of Mooden Sheriff's (*Suppl. Pharmacop. Ind.*, p. 30) third variety of Jadwar which he considers to be Jadwar-Kathai.

ACONITUM? sp. (KODOYA BISH).

A. ferox Wall. Cat. 4721, D (in part); Plant. Asiat. Rar. i. p. 36 (in part).
Caltha Codua Ham. in Edinb. Journ. Sc. i, 1824, p. 251.
C.? Codoa Ham. ex Madden in Trans. Bot. Soc. Edinb. v, 1858, p. 127.

YOUNG SPECIMEN. *Root* tuberous (according to Hamilton). *Stem* erect, flexuous, 4 mm. thick, deeply grooved, very softly pubescent, almost silky in the upper part, lower internodes 9—10 cm. long. *Leaves* scattered; petioles rather slender, up to 14 cm. long, striate, widened at the base; blade rather thin, softly pubescent, at length glabrescent, peltate, almost orbicular in outline, unequally and deeply 7-partite, intermediate (upper) division longest, rhomboid from a cuneate base, 10 cm. long from the insertion of the petiole to the tip, 7 cm. wide, 3-lobed to the middle, lobes sparingly laciniate-dentate, teeth coarse, broad, apiculate, lateral divisions similar, but gradually smaller and less divided, the two basal up to 5 cm. long from the insertion of the petiole to the tips, sinus between them reaching to one-half of their length.

DISTRIBUTION: *Alpine region of the Himalaya of Nepal.*

NEPAL: snowy mountains at the sources of the Kosi River, *Hamilton's Coll.*! (Wallich's own herb., Linn. Soc. London).

VERNACULAR NAME: Kodoya Bish or Kodoya Bikh, *Hamilton.*

PROPERTIES AND USES: Hamilton says that he believes this to be the true "Toxicaria Indorum radix."

The peltate leaves, the strongly sulcate stems and the soft, almost silky tomentum of the youngest parts of the plant, have hardly a parallel in the genus *Aconitum*, but the general cut of the leaves is not unlike that of an *A. Balfourii* with the lower divisions of the blade fused up to the middle. I have tried various genera of Ranunculaceae and other orders, but without coming across a genus more fitting the Kodoya plant than *Aconitum*, except perhaps *Ranunculus*.

PLATE 116. Caltha? Codoa *Ham.*—1, The specimen in Wallich's herbarium at the Linnean Society—*natural size*; 2, a portion of the stem—*enlarged.*

ACONITUM sp. (NIRBISHI OF HAMILTON.)

Caltha Nirbisia Ham. in Edinb. Journ. Sc. i., 1824, p. 251.
C. Nirbisia Ham. ex Madden, Trans. Bot. Soc. Edinb. v, 1858, p. 127.
A. ferox Wall. Cat. 4721, D, (in part); Pl. As. Rar. i. p. 36 (in part).

Roots biennial, paired, tuberous; mother tuber (young) globose-ovoid, 1·5 cm. long, over 1 cm. across, with strong root-fibres, taste faintly bitter, not followed by any tingling sensation. *Scales of innovation-bud* broad, obtuse, thin. *Stem* (very young) very finely pubescent. *Leaves* scattered, lowest 2 or 3 close to the base, the following remote; petioles slender, up to 15 cm. long; blades finely pubescent when quite young, soon glabrescent, ovate or deltoid-orbicular-cordate in outline, with a sinus about 2 cm. deep, 3·5—4·5 cm. from the sinus to the top, 5—6 cm. across, 3-partite to near the base, intermediate division elongate-deltoid, 2—2·5 cm. wide, pinnati-laciniate in the lower, coarsely dentate in the upper part, laciniae entire or with 1 or 2 teeth, acute, lateral divisions trapezoid, unequally 2-lobed beyond the middle, lobes laciniate or coarsely dentate.

DISTRIBUTION: *Alpine region of the Himalaya of Nepal.*

NEPAL: sources of the Kosi river, *Hamilton's Coll.*! (Wallich's own) herb. Linn. Soc.)

VERNACULAR NAME: Nirbishi or Nirbikhi, (Nepal) *Hamilton.*

PROPERTIES AND USES: See the paragraph on Jadwar, p. 125.

The specimen is too young for identification, but I consider it closely allied to *A. heterophylloides* or *A. leucanthum* if it is not indentical with one of them.

PLATE 114B. Caltha? Nirbisia *Ham.*—1, The specimen in Wallich's Herbarium at the Linnean Society—*natural size*; 2, a portion of the stem—*enlarged.*

Other plants supposed to be Aconites and yielding *Bikh* are indicated in several papers and notes. Thus M. C. Cooke quotes [in *Pharm. Journ. and Trans.* iii. ser. III. (1870) 564] a Captain Lowther writing from Assam, in 1859, that the great Alpino region of the Digaru country abounds with the plant furnishing *Bish.* This is practically the same region as that in which Griffith found *A. lethale.* Gammie (*Rec. Bot. Surv. India*, i., No. 5, p. 74) states that roots of *Aconitum Napellus* and perhaps other species are used by the hill tribes (the Abors) to make their deadly arrow-poisons, and that the plants are said to grow only on the interior highlands, inhabited by the Tibetans. Finally, Pottinger, in Pottinger and Prain (*Rec. Bot. Surv. India*, i., No. 11, p. 223), relates that the Yawyins (in the extreme north-east of Burma) use metal-tipped arrows which, moreover, they poison. Apparently, to judge by the symptoms induced, an *Aconitum* is used for the purpose.

EXCLUDED SPECIES.

Aconitum salisburifolium Griff. Itin. Not. 306; collected in Kullu Mountains, Afghanistan. This is a species of *Delphinium.*

APPENDICES.

A.—Bibliography of the Indian Aconites.

Several papers, which are not specially referred to in the text of this memoir, have been included here. They have either a general bearing on certain questions connected with this paper or are hard on the border line of my subject. I have endeavoured to indicate the nature of the contents of the passages concerning Indian Aconites by adding after each title a few explanatory words in italics.

ABU MANSUR MOWAFIK: Liber Fundamentorum Pharmacologiæ (about 975 A.D.). Lat. donavit R. Seligmann. i. (1830); pp. 47-48: "*bisch—Napellus.*"

ABU MANSUR MUWAFFAK BIN ALI HARAWI: Die pharmakologischen Grundsätze (Liber Fundamentorum Pharmacologiæ). Übersetzt von Abdul-Chaling Achundow, aus Baku. Dorpat (1893); pp. 168-169: "Bisch, Aconitum."

ACOSTA, CHRISTOVAL: Tractado de las Drogas y medicinas de las Indias Orientales. (1578); p. 90: *Origin of the bisch root* (*rays de Bisa*); p. 179: *The poison "Piso;"* p. 180: *Use of Napellus poison.*

——————: Trattatto della historia, natura et virtu delle droghe che vengono portati dalle Indie orientali in Europa. Italian transl. printed by F. Ziletti, 1585: pp. 70, 136, 137: *as above.*

AITCHISON: On the Flora of Lahul, in Journal of the Linnean Society, x. (1869); p. 83: *Vernacular names of the tubers of Aconitum heterophyllum;* p. 90: *Enumeration of species of Aconitum.*

——————: Handbook of the Trade Products of Leh (1874); p. 6: *A'is* (*Aconitum heterophyllum*); p. 31: *Bonga;* pp. 100-102: *Jadwar Khatai;* p. 175: *Mitha dudya, Mitha teliya, Mohra, Kala Mohra.*

ANGELUS, Frater: – *see* Pharmacopœia Persica.

ATKINSON: Gazetteer of the North-West Provinces and Oude, x. (1882)—*see* Duthie, King, Watson.

AVICENNA: Liber canonis, a Gerardo carmonensi ex Arabico sermone in Latinum convers., postea ab A. Alpago Bellun. correct. factis etc. Venetiis (1555); Lib. II Tract. II. Lit. N, cap. 499: "*De Napello—Bis;*" Lit. Z, cap. 745: "*De zedoaria, Giedusr.*"

BADEN-POWELL: Handbook of the Economic Products of the Punjab, etc., i. (1868); p. 324: *Commercial Aconites of the Punjab, their vernaculars and properties.*

BALFOUR: Edinburgh New Philosophical Journal, xlvii. (1899); p. 366, with figure: *Description and figure of a plant, grown as A. ferox in the Edinburgh Horticultural Society's Garden* (A. Balfourii), *but not quite identical with Wallich's A. ferox.*

BAUHIN: Pinax Theatri botanici (1623); p. 259: *Bisa radix, its origin.*

BELLONIUS (BELON): Observationes, transl. by Clusius (in Exoticorum libri, 1605); lib. II, cap. 28. p. 98: *Bisch in Alexandria, its properties.*

BENTLEY & TRIMEN: Medicinal Plants, i. (1880); No. 5: *Aconitum ferox* (with good figure representing A. Balfourii, drawn from Strachey and Winterbottom's Kumaon specimen); No. 6: *Indian varieties of A. Napellus;* No. 7: *A. heterophyllum* (with good figure drawn from a specimen collected by Falconer in Garhwal).

BIRDWOOD: Catalogue of the Economic Products of the Presidency of Bombay (1862); pp. 1-2: *"Bikh" and its sources; Jadwar.*

BROUGHTON: Report on the tubers of Aconitum heterophyllum, or the native febrifuge "Atis," in Blue Book, East India (Cinchona Cultivation, 1877); pp. 133-134: *Atisine, its properties.*

BRÜHL: Some new or critical Ranunculaceæ from India and adjacent regions, in Annals of the Royal Botanic Garden, Calcutta, v. (1896); pp. 109-112; *Descriptions of A. ferox,* with plate 11?. *subsp.* i. *moschatum,* ii. *ferox proprium* (*with 11 varieties*), iii. *palmatum.—A. luridum,* with plate 124. —*A. gymnandrum,* with plate 125.

CLEGHORN: Report upon the Forests of the Punjab and the Western Himalaya (1864); pp. 66-98: *Atis as a tonic; p. 67: Tilia Kachang and Moura bikh, used for destroying wild animals.*

———: Notes on the Vegetation of the Sutlej Valley, in Journal of the Agricultural and Horticultural Society of India, xiii—i. (1865); p. 389: *As in the preceding paper.*

CLUSIUS: Exoticorum libri (1605); p. 378: Roots of "*Gedwar veri*" described and figured.

COLLETT: Flora Simlensis (1902); pp. 13, 14: *A. Lycoctonum, A. heterophyllum* (figured).

COOKE, M. C.: Oriental Aconite, in Pharmaceutical Journal and Transactions, 3rd ser., iii. (1873); p. 564: *Bish generally, summary; "Bish" abounding in the Digarroo Country; method of preparing the drug and poisoning the arrows; treatment of wounds.*

———: Mild Aconites, in Pharmaceutical Journal and Transactions, 3rd ser., iii. (1873); pp. 601-603: *Summary of knowledge of A. heterophyllum (Atis) and Jadvar.*

DON, D.: Prodromus Floræ Nepalensis (1825); pp. 196, 197. *Original descriptions of A. virosum, palmatum and dissectum.*

DON, G.: A general system of Gardening and Botany, i. (1831); p. 63. *Description of the genus Nirbisia* (*Caltha*, Hamilton).

DRURY: Useful plants of India, 2nd ed. (1873); pp. 11-12: *A. ferox;* p. 12: *A. heterophyllum.*

DUNSTAN: Report on the constituents of Aconitum heterophyllum, in Agricultural Ledger, 1896,—No. 32, pp. 311-315. *Therapeutic value of Atis. Its alkaloid "atisine."*

———: The constituents of some Indian Aconites, in Agricultural Ledger, 1897,—No. 19, pp. 373-377; *Quantity of pseudaconitine in five samples of roots of "A. ferox," mostly from Sikkim.—Very small quantities of aconitine in "A. Napellus"* (A. chasmanthum) *from Kaghan (Punjab).*

——— & CARR: Contributions to our knowledge of the Aconite alkaloids. On Pseudaconitine, in Agricultural Ledger, 1898, No. 3, pp. 163-173. [Reprinted from the Transactions of the Chemical Society, 1897.] *Properties of pseudaconitine; its salts and derivates.*

DUSQUENEL: De l'aconitine crystallisé, in Pharmaceutical Journal and Transactions, 3rd ser., ii.; p. 662: *A. ferox the most poisonous species of Aconitum, because it contains the largest proportion of aconitine.*

DUTHIE: Plants found in Kumaon, Garhwal and the adjoining parts of Tibet by Captain (now General) Strachey and Mr. Winterbottom, in Atkinson: Gazetteer of the North-Western Provinces and Oude, x. (1882); pp. 412, 413: *Enumeration of species of Aconitum;* p. 725: *Aconitum ferox, A. heterophyllum; vernaculars, distribution and uses.*

———: Report on the Botanical Gardens of Saharanpur and Mussoorie, 1885; p. 47: *"Aconitum ferox" and nine varieties in the Ralam Valley;*—1886; p. 26: *A. ferox and A. heterophyllum in Garhwal.*

———: Report on a botanical tour in Kashmir, in Records of the Botanical Survey of India, i. No. 3 (1894); p. 37: *Species of Aconitum observed.*

———: The botany of the Chitral Relief Expedition, 1895, in Records of the Botanical Survey of India, i. No. 9 (1898); p. 143: *Species of Aconitum collected.*

DUTT, UDOY CHAND: The Materia Medica of the Hindus. With a glossary of Indian plants by Sir GEORGE KING. Revised edition (1900); pp. 97-102: *"Aconitum ferox," Description of the nine virulent poisons of the Sanscrit writers, supposed to be mostly species of Aconite, e. g., Vatsanabha;* pp. 101-102: *A. heterophyllum.*

DYMOCK: Notes on Indian Drugs, in Pharmaceutical Journal and Transactions, 3rd ser., viii. (1877); p. 23: *Description of the tubers of Aconitum sp. known as Wakma or Bikma, supposed to be A. palmatum.*

———: The Vegetable Materia Medica of Western India, 1st ed. (1883); pp. 1-4: *Aconitum ferox;* pp. 4-6: *A. heterophyllum;* pp. 6-7: *Aconitum sp.* (*Bikhma*); pp. 7-8: *Delphinium denudatum as the source of Jadwar or Nirbishi.*—2nd ed. (1885); pp. 1-13.

———: WARDEN & HOOPER: Pharmacographia Indica (1889); pp. 4-11: *Aconitum ferox;* p. 11: *Aconitum Lycoctonum* (the whole paragraph refers really to the European "A. Lycoctonum" supposed by the author to be identical with the Indian *A. læve*); pp. 15-18: *Aconitum heterophyllum;* pp. 18-20: *Aconitum palmatum;* pp. 20-23: *Jadwar.*

EBN BAITHAR (died 1248, according to Meyer, Gesch. Bot. iii. 229): Grosse Zusammenstellung der Heil- und Nahrungsmittel. Übersetzt von J. V. Sontheimer (1840), i.; p. 199: "*Biech*" (compilation from Ebn Samhun, Hobaisch, Rhazes, Ebn Sinna); "*Bisch Musch Bischi, Napellus Moysis*" (from Ebn Sinna).

EBN SAMHUN (Ibn Samh'un, between 998 and 1128, according to Meyer, Gesch. Botanik, iii.; pp. 209, 210):—*see* Ebn Baithar.

EBN SINNA (Ibn Sinâ—Avicenna; Sep. 980—June 1037):—*see* Avicenna and Ebn Baithar.

FLÜCKIGER: Beitrag zur Kenntnis der Aconit.-Alkaloide, in Archiv der Pharmacie, 2nd. ser., cxli. (1870); pp. 198-213: *History of the aconitines; pseudaconitine and aconitine in several Indian aconites, known collectively as bikh.*

——— & HANBURY: Pharmacographia (1874); pp. 12-14: *Radix Aconiti Indici;* pp. 14-15: *Radix Aconiti heterophylli. Botanical origin, history, description, microscopic structure, chemical composition, uses, substitutes.*

GAMMIE: Report on a botanical tour in Sikkim, in Records of the Botanical Survey of India, i. No. 2 (1894); p. 19: *A. Napellus* (correct. A. spicatum) *at Sebu.*

———: Report on a botanical tour in the Lakhimpur district, Assam, in Records Botanical Survey of India, i. No. 5 (1894); pp. 74-75: *Roots of "Aconitum Napellus" used for poisoning arrows.*

———: A botanical tour in Chamba and Kangra, in Records of the Botanical Survey of India, i., No. 10 (1898); p. 192: *Species of Aconite observed.*

GARCIA AB HORTO: Aromatum et Simplicium .... apud Indos nascentium historia, lat. serm. contr. et illustr. a C. Clusio, in CLUSIUS, Exoticorum libri (1605); pp. 213-214: *Zedoary* (Avicenna's *Geiduar*) *grows in the provinces of China, not in India.*

GRIFFITH: Journal of a visit to the Mishmi hills in Assam, in Journal of the Asiatic Society of Bengal, vi. (1837); p. 335: "*Bee,*" *one of the staple articles of the Mishmis.*

———: Notulæ ad plantas Asiaticas, iv. (1854); pp. 732-733: *Description of A. lethale, the bis of the Mishmis.*

———: Icones plantarum Asiaticarum, iv. (1854); tab. DCLX. fig. iii: *Analyses of A. lethale.*

GORIS: De la structure des Aconits et de son utilisation pour la détermination specifique des Aconits de l' Inde, in Bulletin des Sciences pharmacologiques, iii. (1901); pp. 103-110: *anatomical types of the tubers of Aconitum;* p. 111: *A. Napellus var. hians of India;* pp. 112-114: *A. palmatum;* pp. 114-116: *A. heterophyllum;* pp. 116-120: *A. ferox var. laciniatum, spicatum, atrox, polyschiza;* p. 121: *origin of the commercial aconite tubers of India; A. ferox var. atrox a distinct species. Three plates and numerous good figures in the text, showing the roots and their anatomy.*

GOVAN: In Brewster's Edinburgh Journal of Science, ii. (1825); p. 282: "*Aconite on the summit of Choor Mountain.*"

GROVES: Nepaul Aconite, in Pharm. Journ. and Trans. i ser., iii. (1870); pp. 433-434: *Nepal Aconite with figure of root tuber as below.*

———: Nepaul Aconite, in Year-book of Pharmacy (1870), p. 447: *large importation of Indian aconite roots, represented as coming from Nepal; description of roots;* p. 448: *excellent figures of roots* (A. spicatum); p. 449; *it yields pseudaconitine.*

———: Further experiments on Nepaul Aconite and on the characteristics of the Aconitines, in Year-book of Pharmacy, 1873; pp. 500-510: *Identity of Nepaul Aconite and A. ferox still doubtful. The specific alkaloid of Nepaul aconite called Nepaline.*

HAMILTON: Account of the kingdom of Nepal (1819); pp. 98-100: *Information on Bish, Bishma, and Nirbishi, obtained in Nepal; botanical origin.*

———: An account of a genus including the Herba Toxicaria of the Himalaya Mountains, in Brewster's Edinburgh Journal of Science, i. (1824); pp. 249-251: *Expedition to the sources of the Kosi river in Nepal; Caltha Bisma, C. Nirbisia, C. Codua described.*

HANBURY: in Year-book of Pharmacy, 1874; p. 507: *Announcement of Broughton's discovery of atisine in A. heterophyllum.*

HARTWICH: Neuen Arzneidrogen aus dem Pflanzen-reiche (1897); p. 31: *A. heterophyllum and A. ferox.*

HENNING: in Journal of the Agricultural and Horticultural Society of India, ix. 1857, Proc.; p. 193, 263, 271: *Atis as a substitute of quinine.*

HOBAISCH (Hobaish Ben Alhasan Alasam, about the 9th century, according to Meyer, Gesch. Botanik, pp. 135-143): —*see* Ebn Baithar.

HONIGBERGER: Thirty years in the East (1852) ii.; p. 222: *Aconitum ferox and A. heterophyllum as medicine drugs;* pp. 372-373: *Vernacular names of Aconites.*

HOOKER, J. D.: Notes, chiefly botanical, made during an excursion from Darjiling to Tonglo, in Journal of the Asiatic Society of Bengal, xviii. (1849); p. 438: *Aconitum palmatum and other species as sources of Bikh.*

———: Himalayan Journal (1854), i.; p. 168: *Aconitum palmatum and other species of Aconitum as sources of Bikh;* ii.; p. 107: *Aconitum variegatum;* p. 108: *Aconitum luridum; Aconitum ferox identical with A. Napellus.*

———: Flora of British India, i. (1875); pp. 27-29: *Enumeration and description of species; poisonous and non-poisonous forms.*

———: Aconitum heterophyllum in Botanical Magazine, 3rd ser., xxx. (1874), tab. 6092.

——— & THOMSON: Flora Indica, i. (1855); pp. 3-4 of Introductory essay: *Bikh produced by Aconitum Napellus;* p. 54: *Variability of the Aconites;* pp. 55-58: *Description of species Bikh;* p. 58: *A. Napellus, its distribution and variability, non-poisonous varieties; A. heterophyllum as a tonic.*

HUSEMANN & HILGER: Die Pflanzenstoffe, i.; p. 655: *Physiological action of pseudaconitine, prepared from A. ferox.*

JONES: in note to ROXBURGH (*q. v.*); p. 333: *Nirbisi equivalent to the Arab appellation of Zedoary.*

JOWETT: On Atisine, the Alkaloid of Aconitum heterophyllum, in Agricultural Ledger, 1896, No. 32; pp. 315-338: *Source, preparation and properties of atisine.*

KANNY LALL DEY: The Indigenous drugs of India, ed. ii. (1896); pp. 337-340: *Collecting of Aconite roots in Sikkim.*

KARELIN & KIRILOW: Enumeratio plantarum in desertis Songariæ orientalis......anno 1841 collectarum, in Bulletin de la Societé Impériale des Naturalistes, xv. (1842); p. 139: *Original description of A. rotundifolium.*

KERNER, A.: Novæ plantarum species in Himalayæ montibus a cl. Jæschke collectæ, in Berichtedes Naturwissenschaflichen Vereins in Innsbruck, i. (1870); pp. 119-121 (pp. 23-25 of the reprint): *Description of A. oliganthemum* (=A. rotundifolium).

KING: List of the plants of Garhwal, Jaunsar Bawar and the Dehra-Dun, in Atkinson: Gazetteer of the North-Western Provinces and Oude, x. (1882); p. 304: *Enumeration of species of Aconitum.*

———: Glossary of Indian plants in Dutt: Materia Medica of the Hindus (1900): *Vernacular names (Sanskrit and Hindi) of aconites.*

KIRKPATRICK: An account of the kingdom of Nepaul (1811); p. 182: *Bikhma, a medicinal plant, a kind of Gentian.*

LAWRENCE: Valley of Kashmir (1895); p. 77: *Aconitum heterophyllum as a tonic;* p. 76: *A. Napellus as a poison;* p. 85.: *Enumeration of Kashmir species of Aconitum.*

LOWTHER: in Journal of the Agricultural and Horticultural Society of India, ix. (1857), Proceedings; pp. 154-155: *Atis as a tonic.*

MADDEN: Diary of an excursion to the Shatul and Boorun Passes over the Himalayas, in Journal of the Asiatic Society of Bengal, xv. (1846); pp. 82, 93: *Aconitum heterophyllum;* pp. 95, 115, 116: *Aconitum dissectum (i. e.,* A. violaceum) *in its natural stations;* p. 95: *A. ferox, moura bikh or mori (i. e.,* A. deinorrhizum), *habitat, derivation of the vernacular.*

———: The Turaee and Outer Mountains of Kumaon, in Journal of the Asiatic Society of Bengal, xvii. i. (1848); p. 364: *Derivation of utees, ativisha, and mour or mahoor;* p. 569: *meetha (A. ferox), a commercial article of Kali Kumaon.*

———: On some plants from the kingdom of Nepal, in Transactions of the Botanic Society of Edinburgh, v. (1858); pp. 127-130: *Hamilton's species of Caltha; Wallich's A. ferox as figured is A. dissectum, Don; vertical range of A. multifidum, A. palmatum, A. heterophyllum in the Himalaya; etymology of the vernaculars of aconites in India; Nirbishi, the root of Delphinium kashmirianum.*

MASTERS: Botanical observations in Upper Assam, in Journal of the Agricultural and Horticultural Society of India, Calcutta, iv. (1845); p. 200: *Mishmi bih, an ingredient of arrow poison.*

MATTHIOLI: Commentarii in libros Dioscoridis (1583), II. cap. 154, p. 532: *Zedoaria exported from "Sinarum regione ultra extremas Indiæ Oras," according to Serapion.*

————: Epistolarum medicinalium libri quinque (in Matthioli, Opera, Ed. 1598), lib. III.; p. 102 (letter from Qualcebenus, dated Aug. 1557): *Costliness of Indian Zedoary;* p. 105 (letter to Qualcebenus, dated Dec. 1557): *Doubts concerning the genuineness of the Indian Zedoary, mentioned by Qualcebenus.*

MAXIMOWICZ: Diagnoses plantarum novarum Asiaticarum, in Mélanges Biologiques, ix. (1877; reprinted from Bulletin de l'Académie Impériale des Sciences de St. Petersburg, ix. 1877); p. 711: *Original description of A. gymnandrum.*

MEYER, ARTHUR: Uber Aconitum Napellus und seine nächsten Verwandten, in Archiv der Pharmacie (1881); p. 175: *Tubers of A. heterophyllum and A. ferox;* pp. 176-177: *A. ferox, differences between the plants figured by Wallich and by Balfour;* p. 265: *anatomy of the tubers of A. ferox;* pp. 269-273: *anatomy of the tubers of A. heterophyllum; with figures.*

MOHAMMED ABDULLAH SHIRAZI (about 1450 A. D.): Ulfaz Udwiyeh, transl. by Fr. Gladwin, 1793; Nos. 37, 1026: *Bish;* Nos 398, 668, 1352: *Jadwar.*

MOHIDEEN SHERIFF, KHAN BAHADUR (formerly Moodeen Sheriff): Materia Medica of Madras (1891); pp. 1—4: *A. ferox;* pp. 4—5: *A. heterophyllum.*

MOODEEN SHERIFF: Supplement to the Pharmacopœia of India (1869); pp. 25-27: *A. ferox;* pp. 27-28: *A. heterophyllum;* pp. 29-32: *A. sp. (Jadwar)—Commercial varieties; vernacular synonymy.*

O'SHAUGHNESSY: The Bengal Dispensatory (1841); pp. 165-168: *Aconitum ferox,* Wall.; *A. heterophyllum,* Wall.

———— The Bengal Pharmacopœia (1844); p. 190: *Assam and Nepal varieties of A. ferox.*

PATROUILLARD, Des Aconits et l' Aconitine. Thèse presenté à l' école supérieure de Pharmacie (1872): *The Indian Aconites according to Wallich, Royle and Hooker fil.;* pp. 32-37: *Description of the "Bikh de Commerce."*

PEREIRA:—*see* WALLICH.

————: Elements of Materia Medica and Therapeutics, II. ii. (1853), p. 2177: *A. ferox, the bikh of Nepal, a violent poison; his experiments described in Wallich (q. v.), made with material 10 years old.*

PHARMACOPŒIA PERSICA: in Lat. conv. Fr. Angelus a Sancto Joseph Carm. disc. Thosolanus (1681); p. 317: *Bischi;* p. 319: *Innocuous Indian Aconite;* pp. 358-359: *translator's notes on a kind of Bish, used as a spice by the Indian traders.*

POTTINGER & PRAIN: A note on the botany of the Kachin Hills, north-east of Myitkyina, in Records of the Botanical Survey of India, i. No. 11 (1898); p. 223: *Aconite used by the Yawyins for poisoning arrows.*

REGEL: Aufzählung der von Radde in Baikalien . . . . gesammelten Pflanzen, in Bulletin de la Société Impériale des Naturalistes de Moscou, xxxiv. (1861), ii.; p. 105: *Description of A. Napellus β. alpinum, lusus f. soongaricum* (type of A. soongaricum).

RHAZES:—*see* Ebn Baithar.

ROXBURGH: Description of several of the Monandrous Plants of India, belonging to the natural order called Scitamineæ, in Asiatick Researches, xi. (1810); p. 332: *Jadwar referred to Curcuma Zedoaria.*

ROYLE: List of articles of Materia Medica, obtained in the bazars of the Western and Northern provinces of India, in Journal of the Asiatic Society of Bengal, i. (1832); p. 459: *Atis derived from Aconitum Atees* (=A. heterophyllum).

————: Illustrations of the botany of the Himalaya mountains, i. (1834); pp. 46-48: *Hamilton's varieties of bikh, their determination by Wallich; bikh and meetha tellia, derived from A. ferox; other vernaculars;* p. 48: *bikhma;* p. 49: *Hamilton's Caltha? Nirbisia and C? Codoa, young states of A. ferox;* pp. 49-50: *Nirbisi, source and derivation of name, probably the Zedoary of Avicenna;* p. 56: *original descriptions of A. multifidum, A. læve, A. cordatum and A. heterophyllum; A. dissectum;* p. 57: *A. ferox and A. palmatum;* plate 13: *good figure of A. heterophyllum.*

Royle: An essay on the Antiquity of Hindoo Medicine (1837); p. 93: *The ancients unacquainted with bish.*

Schneider: Über die Darstellung und Chemische Constitution des englischen und deutschen Aconites, in Archiv der Pharmacie, 3rd ser., xix. (1881); pp. 330, 331: *Description of commercial bikh, A. ferox; sun-dried and scalded tubers.*

Schroff: Haben die örtlichen Verhältnisse einen Einfluss auf die giftige oder nicht giftige Eigenschaft des Akonits?, in Zeitschrift des Allgemeinen Oesterreichischen Apotheker-Vereins, xiii. (1875); pp. 315, 333: *The poisonous or non-poisonous properties of the Aconites do not depend on local conditions, but are specific characters.*

Serapion (10th and 11th centuries):—*see* Matthioli.

Séringe: Esquisse d'une monographie du genre Aconitum; in Musée Helvetique d' Histoire-Naturelle i. (1823); p. 160, tab. 15, figs. 43, 44: *Original description of A. ferox, Wall.*

———: in A. P. De Candolle, Prodromus Systematis Naturalis, i. (1824); p. 64: *Description of Aconitum ferox.*

Shimoyama: in Pharmaceutical Journal and Transactions, 3rd ser., xvi. (1885); p. 86: *Non-poisonous Indian Aconite tubers called "Wakmah" contain atisine.*

Simpson: Native poisons of India, in Pharmaceutical Journal and Transactions, 3rd ser., ii. (1872); p. 606: *Bish (A. ferox, A. Napellus, A. palmatum, A. luridum) used very commonly for destroying wild animals; method; physiological action.*

Sprengel: Historia rei herbariae, i. (1808); p. 241: *The Arabs mistook possibly the Zedoary of India for the Aconitum of the ancients*; pp. 264-265: *Doubts as to the Arabs knowing Aconitum.*

Stein: Aconitum dissectum *Don*, in Gartenflora, xxxv. (1886); pp. 226-228: *The plant figured by Wallich as A. ferox reduced to A. dissectum, Don; Wallich's figure reproduced in part on p. 227.*

Stewart: Punjab Plants (1869); pp. 1, 2: *A. ferox, A. heterophyllum, A. Napellus; their distribution, vernaculars and properties.*

Susrutas: Ayurvedas. In Lat. serm. vert. F. Hessler (1844): *Ativesha quoted in numerous passages as an ingredient of medicines*; ii. p. 216: *Vatsanabha and Sringivisha quoted among the 13 "bulb-poisons" and the former among the 55 "Stable" poisons; Action of sringivisha.*

Taleef Shereef: Indian Materia Medica, transl. by Playfair (1833); p. 8: *Atees*; p. 33: *Batees, a synonym for atees*, p. 107: *Singia or Singia jur (Aconite), a deadly poison.*

Vogtherr: in Köhler's Medizinal Pflanzen, iii. (1898): *Aconitum ferox, with figure of A. ferox proper! (excepting root and capsule); A. heterophyllum.*

Wallich: Plantæ Asiaticæ Rariores, i. (1830); pp. 35-37: *A. ferox, sensu latione, with plate; Hamilton's species of Caltha identified with A. ferox; Colebrooke on the use of bikh; Choor Mountain Aconite grown at Saharanpur; Pereira's experiments on the physiological action of bikh; Govan on the belief that Aconite poisons the air; export of the root to the plains; vernaculars.*

Waring: Notes on some of the principal indigenous tonics of India, in Indian Annals of Medicine, Calcutta, x. (1858); p. 47 [reprint]: *A. heterophyllum is Atees, not Bhikma, which is poisonous.*

———: Pharmacopœia of India (1868); p. 3: *Bikh, derived from A. ferox, A. Napellus, A. palmatum and A. luridum; Description of the drug*; p. 4: *Atis from A. heterophyllum*; p. 433: *Varying amount of aconitine according to the season; etymology of bikh*; p. 434: *Amount of "Aconitia" varying according to the variety; medical properties of A. heterophyllum.*

Wasowicz: Aconitum heterophyllum Wall., in Pharmacognostisch-chemischer Beziehung in Archiv der Pharmacie, 3rd ser., xiv. (1879); pp. 193-225: *Description and figures of A. heterophyllum; tubers and their anatomy; preparation of Atisine.*

Watson, J. Forbes: Index to the native and scientific names of Indian Economic plants and products (1868): *Vernaculars.*

———: Plants of Kumaon in Atkinson: Gazetteer of the North-Western Provinces and Oude, x. (1882); p. 328: *Enumeration of species of Aconitum.*

WATT: Dictionary of the Economic Products of India, i. (1889); pp. 84-98: *A. ferox; A. heterophyllum; A. luridum; A. Lycoctonum; A. Napellus and varieties; A. palmatum. General history, habitat, botanic diagnosis, description of the drug, medical properties, chemical constituents, uses, vernaculars.*

——: The Indian Aconites, their varieties, their distributions and their uses, in Agricultural Ledger, 1902, No. 3; pp. 87-102: *A. luridum; A. Lycoctonum; A. Napellus vars. multifidum and rotundifolium; A. palmatum; A. uncinatum; A. heterophyllum; A. ferox vars. spicatum, laciniatum, crassicaule, atrox, polyschizum; A. Napellus; A. rigidum; A. dissectum; A. hians.*

WILCOX: Memoir of a survey of Assam and the neighbouring countries, in Asiatic Researches xviii. (1832); p. 456: *Two kinds of 'bis' among the products of the Dibong country.*

WRIGHT & LUFF: Third report on the chemistry of the Aconite alkaloids, in Pharmaceutical Journal and Transactions, 3rd ser., viii. (1877); pp. 167-170: *Constitution of pseudaconitine; pseudaconitine predominating in A. ferox over aconitine.*

B.—List of Vernacular names of the Indian Aconites.

This list is a compilation of the vernacular names of the Indian Aconites from the publications and collectors' notes which have been accessible to me. I am aware of its incompleteness. Still, I hope it may be of use for practical purposes and induce an expert linguist to revise and also reduce it. If the names which were introduced by Arab and Persian writers, as, for instance, *Khanek ul nimr*, *Agelghia*, *Mah-farfin*, etc., be cut out as foreign, it will probably be found that the remainder are traceable to a limited number of old names—mostly, if not exclusively, Sanskrit—from which the majority of the numerous vernaculars enumerated have been derived either by a natural process of evolution or by mere corruption. I also believe that such a critically revised list will show that the names had in most cases originally a sound basis, referring to roots of really distinct origin or to different methods of preparation. Working back in this direction, it might be possible to restore the vernacular nomenclature of the Indian Aconites to something like order.

Vernacular names.	Authorities.	Determinations.
Agelghees, *Agelghia*, *Ajelgeea* (Arab., Pers.)	Ulfaz Udwiyeh, transl. Gladwin: No. 37; Honigberger: Thirty-five years in the East, p. 373.	A poisonous species.
A'is (Bhoti)	Aitchison: Trade Prod. Leh, p. 6; Watt: Dict. Econom. Prod. India, i., p. 91.	*A. heterophyllum.*
Ataicha (Sanskr.)	Watt: l. c.; Kanny Lall Dey: Indig. Drugs India, p. 7.	*A. heterophyllum.*
Atarakha-ni-kali (Guz.) .	Dymock, Warden & Hooper: Pharmacogr. India, p. 15.	*A. heterophyllum.*
Atavish (Mar.)	Watt: l. c., p. 91	*A. heterophyllum.*
Atavishni-kali (Guz.) . .	Watt: l. c., p. 91..	*A. heterophyllum.*
Atees, *Atis* (Hind.) . . .	Taleef Schereef: Ind. Mat. Med., transl. Playfair, p. 8; Royle in Journ. As. Soc. Bengal, i. (1832), p. 459, etc.	Generally used for *A. heterophyllum.*
Atisingia, *atisyngya* (Hind.)	O'Shaughnessy: Beng. Dispens., p. 165; Honigberger: l. c.	A poisonous species, probably *A. spicatum.*
Ativadayam (Tam.) . . .	Drury: Useful Pl. India, p. 12; Mooden Sheriff: Suppl. Pharm. India, p. 27; Watt: l. c., p. 91; Dymock, Warden & Hooper: l. c.; Kanny Lall Dey: l. c.	*A. heterophyllum.*
Ativakh (Guz.)	Watt: l. c.	*A. heterophyllum.*
Ativasa, *ativassa* (Tel.) . .	Drury: l. c.; Birdwood: Cat. Econ. Pl. Bombay, p. 1.; Mooden Sheriff: l. c.; Watt: l. c., p. 91.; Dymock, Warden & Hooper: l. c.; Kanny Lall Dey: l. c.	*A. heterophyllum.*
Ativish, *Ativisha*, *Utivisha* (Sanskr.).	Madden in Journ. As. Soc. Beng. xvii. i, 364 and in Trans. Bot. Soc. Edinb. v. (1858), p. 130; Watt: l. c., p. 91; Dymock, Warden & Hooper: l. c; Dutt: Mat. Med. Hind.; p. 101.	*A. heterophyllum.*
Ativisha	Wallich: Pl. As. Rar. i.; p. 35	*A. ferox.*
Ativista (Cutch.)	Watt: l. c.	*A. heterophyllum.*
Atvika (Duk., Hind.) . .	Drury: l. c.; Mooden Sheriff: l. c.; Watt: l. c. . .	*A. heterophyllum.*
Bachhnag, *Bachnag*, *Bachnak*, *Bechnak* (Hind), *Buchnaga* (Cutch.), *Bachnab* (Bombay).	Madden in Trans. Bot. Soc. Edinb. v. (1858), p. 128 (derivation); Drury: l. c., p. 11; Mooden Sheriff: l. c., p. 25; Watt: l. c., p. 87; Dymock, Warden & Hooper: l. c., p. 1.	*A. spicatum* and other poisonous species.

Vernacular names.	Authorities.	Determinations.
Bachnab (Lahore) . . .	Watt: l. c., p. 88	*A. Balfourii?*
Ban-bal-nagh (Kashmir) . .	Aitchison, according to Watt: l. c., p. 95 . . .	*A. chasmanthum.*
Batis, Batees, Butees (Pers.)	Taleef Shereef: l. c., p. 33; Honigberger: l. c.; Baden-Powell: Econ. Prod. Punjab, i., p. 324; Aitchison: Trade Prod. Leh, p. 6.	*A. heterophyllum.*
Bachnag, Bachnak	*See* Bachhnag.	
Bar-Hee	Ulfaz Udwiyeh, transl. Gladwin: No. 398 . . .	Quoted as a synonym of *Jadwar*; see this.
Bechnak	Taleef Shereef: l. c., p. 33; *see* Bachhnag.	
Bee, Bih, Bhi, Bis (Mishmi)	Griffith: MS. on his label and in Journ. As. Soc. Bengal, vi. (1837), p. 331, and in Notul. iv., p. 733 (see also Madden: l. c., p. 130); Masters in Journ. Agr. & Hort. Soc. Calc., iv., p. 200.	*A. lethale.*
Bhanva (Ralam Valley, Kumaon).	Duthie in Report Bot. Gard. Saharanpur & Mussoorie, 1885, p. 47.	*A. Balfourii* or an allied species.
Bikh (Hind., Arab.), *Bish* (Hind., Pers.), *Bis* (Hind.).	......	From the earliest times indiscriminately used for the poisonous species of the *spicatum* and *Balfourii* group; in Sikkim applied particularly to *A. spicatum* (King and Rogers in notes on their labels).
Bikhma, Bishma, Bisma (Hind.).	Hamilton: Acc. Nepal, p. 99, and in Edinb. Journ. Sci. i. (1824), p. 251; Madden: l. c., pp. 127, 128, 130; Birdwood: l. c.; Dymock, Warden & Hooper: l. c., p. 18; Watt in Agric. Ledger, 1902, p. 90.	*A. palmatum.*
Bis, Bish	*See* Bikh.	
Bish-i-Kesem	Honigberger: l. c.	*A. violaceum* or *A. chasmanthum.*
Bish-nag, Bish-nak (Hind.) .	O'Shaugnessy: l. c.; Honigberger: l. c.; Baden-Powell: l. c.; Mooden Sheriff: l. c.; Watt: Dict. Econ. Prod. India, i., p. 87; Birdwood: l. c.; Kanny Lall Dey: l. c.	Evidently used in the same sense as *Bachhnag.*
Bonga (Bhoti)	Aitchison: Trade Prod. Leh, p. 101; Watt: l. c., p. 98.	Quoted as a synonym of *Jadwar Khatai*; see this.
Bonga (Lahul)	Aitchison in Journ. Linn. Soc. x. (1869), p. 83; Stewart: Punjab Pl. p. 1; Watt: l. c, p. 91.	*A. heterophyllum.*
Buchnaga (Cutch.) . . .	*See* Bachhnag.	
Bustnab-bish (Beng.) . . .	Drury: l. c.; Birdwood: l. c.	Evidently used in the sense of *Bachhnag.*
Chitijari (Jhelum) . . .	Stewart: l. c.; Watt: l. c., p. 91	*A. heterophyllum.*
Dagra, Dakra (Beng.) . .	O'Shaughnessy: l. c. and Beng. Pharm., p. 190; Waring: Pharmac. India, p. 433; Dymock: Mat. Med. West India, p. 4; Dutt: Mat. Med. Hind., p. 324.	*A. spicatum* and, possibly, allied species.
Dhaulia (Ralam Valley, Kumaon).	Duthie: l. c.	*A. Balfourii* or an allied species.

Vernacular names.	Authorities.	Determinations.
Dhumuriya (Ralam Valley, Kumaon).	Duthie: l. c.	*A. Balfourii* or an allied species.
Doodhiya moura (Bashahr)	Madden in Journ. As. Soc. Bengal xv. (1843), p. 95.	*A. deinorrhizum.*
Dudhia moura (Ravi district).	Stewart: l. c., p. 1	*A. deinorrhizum ?*
Dudhia bish (Kashmir and Punjab).	Watt: l. c., p. 95.	*A. deinorrhizum* or some allied species.
Dudhio vachhanag (Guz.)	Watt: l. c., p. 95	*A. deinorrhizum* or some allied species.
Erra-nabhi (Tel.)	Mohideen Sheriff: Mat. Med. Madras, p. 3	*A. spicatum ?* (black variety).
Furfi (Yarkand)	Aitchison, according to Watt: l. c., p. 98	Synonym for *Jadwar Khatai*; see this.
Gniong, gniong ning (Sikkim)	J. D. Hooker and King on their labels; Hooker fil. in Himal. Journ. i., p. 163.	A generic term for the poisonous aconites of Sikkim, but particularly for *A. spicatum.*
Gniong-rip-gmok (Sikkim)	Hooker fil. MS. on a label	*A. palmatum.*
Gobriya, gobaria (Ralam Valley, Kumaon).	Duthie: l. c.; Watt in. Agric. Ledg. 1902, p. 99	*A. Balfourii.*
Hodoya bish (Nepal)	Hamilton: Acc. Nepal, 99	A poisonous species of *Aconitum ?* (Caltha Codua *Ham.*).
Hong-i-safed (Kashmir)	Watt: l. c., p. 91	*A. heterophyllum.*
Jadwar, Jadvar (Arab., Hind.).		Used from immemorial times for one or several non-poisonous species of aconite (see p. 177 of this paper).
Jadwar Khatai	Mooden Sheriff: Suppl. Pharm. Ind., p. 30; Aitchison: Trade. Prod. Leh, 190.	*A. heterophylloides* or an allied species.
Jhirina (Ralam Valley, Kumaon).	Duthie: l. c.	*A. Balfourii* or an allied species.
Joker, Joker me-hin pat val (Kashmir).	Honigberger: l. c.	*A. violaceum* or *A. heterophyllum.*
Kala-bikhoma (Sikkim)	Rogers MS. on his labels; Watt in Agric. Ledger, 1902, p. 96.	*A. spicatum* and *A. laciniatum.*
Kala-bachhnag (Hind.)	Mooden Sheriff: l. c., p. 26; Mohideen Sheriff: Mat. Med. Madras, p. 2; Watt in Agric. Ledger, 1902, p. 96.	*A. spicatum* and possibly one or several other species; evidently the black kind, steeped in cow's urine.
Kala-mohra (Sutlej Distr.)	Baden-Powell: l. c.; Minnicken MS. on his label; Watt in Agric. Ledger, 1902, p. 96.	*A. deinorrhizum.*
Kat bish, Kath bish (Beng.)	Waring: l. c., p. 433; Watt: Dict. Econ. Prod. India, p. 87.	Probably *A. spicatum.*
Kawriya (Ralam Valley, Kumaon).	Duthie: l. c.	*A. Balfourii* or an allied species.
Khanek ul nimr (Arab.)	Honigberger: l. c.	*A. violaceum ?*
Kodoya bish	*See* Hodoya bish.	

Vernacular names.	Authorities.	Determinations.
Lal bach nag (Duk.) . . .	Mohideen Sheriff: l. c., p. 3	Probably *A. spicatum* (reddish kind).
Mahaushadham (Sanskr.) .	Madden in Trans. Bot. Soc. Edinb. v. (1858), p. 130.	*A. heterophyllum.*
Mafarfin, Mah-fir-feen, Mahparvin (Pers.).	Ulfaz Udwiyeh: l. c. No. 1352; Mooden Sheriff: l. c., p. 29; Dymock, Warden & Hooper: l. c., p. 20.	A synonym of *Jadwar;* see this.
Mahoor, Mahore, Maur, Maura bikh, Mora, Moura bikh, Muhura (Hind.; Sutlej district).	Drury: l. c., p. ; Madden: l. c., p. 128 and in Journ. As. Soc. Beng. xv. (1846), p. 95; Birdwood: l. c.; Baden-Powell: l. c.; Stewart: l. c.; Cleghorn in Journ. Agric. & Hort. Soc. India, xiii. (1865), p. 389.	*A. deinorrhizum;* possibly also *A. Falconeri* or *A. Balfourii.*
Meetha (mitha) *bish,—dodya* (doodya),—*teliya* (teelia, telya, tellia, tella),—*suhur* (zahr, zahar, zuher).	Govan, according to Wallich: Pl. As. Rar., i., p. 37; Honigberger: l. c.; O'Shaughnessy, Beng. Dispens., p. 165, and Beng. Pharm., p. 183; Birdwood: l. c.; Baden-Powell: l. c.; Waring: l. c.; Mooden Sheriff: l. c., p. 25; Aitchison: Trade Prod. Leh., p. 175; Watt in Dict. Econ. Prod. India, i., pp. 87, 95; Kanny Lall Dey: l. c., p. 8; Dutt: Mat. Med. Hindus, p. 97.	One or several poisonous species, probably mainly of the *deinorrhizum* or *Balfourii* group.
Mishri-bish	Baden-Powell: l. c.	Some poisonous species.
Mohand-i-guj-safed (Kashmir).	Aitchison, according to Watt: l. c., p. 91. . . .	*A. heterophyllum.*
Mohra (Sutlej district) . .	Minniken MS. on his labels	*A. deinorrhizum.*
Mohra (Tihri Garhwal) . .	Duthie MS. on his label	*A. Falconeri?*
Mohri (Jhelum)	Stewart: l. c.; Watt: l. c., p. 95 and in Agricult. Ledger, 1902, p. 101; Watt's collector MS. on his labels.	*A. chasmanthum.*
Mohundguji (Kashmir) . .	Lawrence: Valley of Kashmir, p. 76	*A. chasmanthum?*
Nabhi (Tel.)	Mooden Sheriff: l. c., p. 26; Watt: Dict. Econ. Prod. Ind., p. 87.	*A. spicatum* or an allied poisonous species.
Nar-mada, Nerr-Mada (Kashmir).	Honigberger: l. c.; Lawrence: Valley of Kashmir, p. 74.	*A. heterophyllum.*
Ning (Lepcha)	King on his label	*A. spicatum.*
Nir-banshi (Sikkim) . . .	Rogers on his label	*A. heterophylloides.*
Nirbisi (Hind.), *Neer Bissee, Nirbisha* (Sanskr.), *Nirbikhi.*	Ulfaz Udwiyeh: l. c. No. 398; Hamilton: Acc. Nepal, p. 99; Mooden Sheriff: l. c., p. 29.	A synonym of *Jadwar;* see this.
Navi (Tam.)	Mooden Sheriff: l. c., p. 26	*A. spicatum* or an allied species.
Patis, Patris, Putees (Bashahr).	Madden in Journ. As. Soc. Bengal, xv. (1846), p. 82, and in Trans. Bot. Soc. Edinb., v. (1858), p. 130; Baden-Powell: l. c.; Stewart: l. c.; Aitchison: Trade Prod. Leh., p. 6; Watt: l. c., p. 91.	*A. heterophyllum.*
Phatkia, phutkia, futkia (Ralam Valley, Kumaon).	Duthie: l. c.; Watt in Agricult. Ledg. 1902, p. 99.	*A. Balfourii.*
Piun (Jhelum)	Stewart: l. c.	*A. violaceum?*
Prativisha (Sanskr.) . . .	Madden in Trans. Bot. Soc. Edinb. v. (1858), p. 130.	*A. heterophyllum.*
Ratwa (Ralam Valley, Kumaon).	Duthie: l. c.	*A. Balfourii* or an allied species.

Vernacular names.	Authorities.	Determinations.
Safed (*sufid*) *bachnag* . . .	Mohideen Sheriff: Mat. Med. Madr., p. 2; Watt in Agricult. Ledg. 1902, p. 98.	*A. Balfourii*, *A. deinorrhizum* or an allied species.
Sen-nabhi (Tam.) . . .	Mohideen Sheriff: l. c, p. 3	*A. spicatum* or an allied variety, the black kind.
Selo-bikhoma (Sikkim) . .	Rogers on his labels; Watt in Agric. Ledg. 1902, p. 90.	*A. palmatum.*
Shimai-ativadayam (Tam.), *Sima-ati-vasa* (Tel.).	Mohideen Sheriff: l. c., p. 4	*A. heterophyllum.*
Shinga-diovachnág (Guz.) .	Dymock, Warden & Hooper: l. c.	A poisonous Aconite, possibly *A. spicatum.*
Singya (Hind.) *Singia*, *singiya*, *singyi*,—*jar* (jur), —*khar*,—*bis*,—*bish*.	Taleef Shereef: l. c. p. 107; O'Shaughnessy: Beng. Pharm., p. 190; Baden-Powell: l. c.; Mooden Sheriff: l. c., p. 25; Watt: l. c., p. 87.	*A. spicatum* and possibly allied species.
Soorja (suya),—*Banshi* (Sikkim).	Rogers MS. on his labels; Watt: Agric. Ledg. 1902, p. 89.	*A. luridum.*
Sringi bish (Sanskr.) . .	Dymock: Mat. Med. West. India, p. 4. Dutt: Mat. Hind., pp. 96, 324.	*A. spicatum* or an allied species.
Sukhi-kari (Jhelum) . . .	Stewart: l. c.; Watt. Dict. Econ Prod India, i., p. 91, and in Agric. Ledg. 1902, p. 90.	*A. heterophyllum.*
Teliya (tilia)—*bis* (Hind.), —*bachnag*; *Tiliya* (Ralam in Kumaon).	Mooden Sheriff: l. c., p. 25: Duthie: l. c.; Watt: Dict. Econ. Prod. India, i., p. 87.	*A. Balfourii* or an allied species.
Tilia-kachang (Kachung) .	Madden in Journ. As. Soc. Bengal, xv. (1846), p. 95; Cleghorn: Forests Punjab and West Himal., p. 67; Stewart: l. c.; Watt: l. c, p. 95.	*A. violaceum.*
Tukschak gniong (Lepcha) .	J. D. Hooker MS. on his label	*A. Elwesii.*
Upavisha (Sanskr.) . . .	Madden in Trans. Bot. Soc. Edinb. v. (1858), p. 130.	*A. heterophyllum.*
Vachanabhi (Cing.), *Vachnag*, *Vachla-nag* (Guz.), *Vasanabhi* (Tel., Can.), *Vashanavi* (Tam.), *Valsa nabhi* (Malyal).	Drury: l. c, p. 11; Mooden Sheriff: l. c., p. 26; Watt: l. c., p. 87, 95; Mohideen Sheriff: l. c., p. 1; Kanny Lall Dey: l. c., p. 7.	*A. spicatum* and probably also other poisonous species.
Vajje-turki (Pers., Duk.) *Vuggi turki* (Pers.).	Mooden Sheriff: l. c., p. 27; Kanny Lall Dey: l. c., p. 7.	*A. heterophyllum.*
Vakhma (Bombay) . . .	Dymock, Warden & Hooper: l. c., p. 18; Watt in Agric. Ledg. 1902, p. 90.	*A. palmatum.*
Vatsanabha (Sanskr.). . .	Madden in Trans. Bot. Soc. Edinb. v. (1858), p. 128; Watt: Dict. Econ. Prod. India, i, p. 87, and in Agric. Ledg. 1902, p. 97; Dutt: Mat. Med., p. 97.	*A. spicatum* and other poisonous species.
Vish, *Visha* (Sanskr.) . .	Wallich: Plant. As. Rar., i., p. 35; Watt: l. c., p. 87; Dutt, l. c., p. 97.	*A. ferox.*
Wakhma	*See* Vakhma.	
Zadvar, *Zadwar*, *Zhadwar* (Pers.).	*See* Jadvar.	

B. S. Press—2163J—276—13-2-1906—W. M. D'C & other.

INDEX.

A SKETCH OF THE LIFE

OF

Francis Hamilton (once Buchanan),

SOMETIME

SUPERINTENDENT OF THE HONOURABLE COMPANY'S BOTANIC GARDEN, CALCUTTA.

Calcutta:

BENGAL SECRETARIAT PRESS.

1905.

A SKETCH OF THE LIFE

OF

Francis Hamilton (once Buchanan),

SOME TIME

SUPERINTENDENT OF THE HONOURABLE COMPANY'S BOTANIC GARDEN AT CALCUTTA.

1. INTRODUCTORY.

In these Annals Sir George King has already published *A short account of Colonel Kyd, the founder of the Royal Botanic Garden, Calcutta*[1] to whose care this institution was committed from its origin in 1786 till his death in 1793. This was followed by *A Brief Memoir of William Roxburgh, Author of the Flora Indica*[2] who succeeded Lieutenant-Colonel Kyd and was Superintendent till 1814. In continuation of the series of sketches thus initiated the writer proposes to give here an outline of the career of Dr. Francis Buchanan (subsequently Hamilton) who was Superintendent of this garden, as successor to Dr. Roxburgh, for a brief period in 1814-15.

Notices of Buchanan Hamilton, of various degrees of merit, are to be found in Chambers' *Biographies of Eminent Scotsmen*, in the *Dictionary of National Biography*, in Higginbotham's *Men India has known*, in Anderson's *Scottish Nation*, in Britten and Boulger's *Biographical Index*, and in the *Calcutta Review* for July 1894. The basis of most of these articles has, however, been an incidental account, by Buchanan himself, in the *Transactions of the Royal Society of Edinburgh*,[3] of his service in India; the Indian portion of Buchanan's career is therefore easily followed.

As regards, however, Buchanan's career before entering the service of the East India Company and as regards his life after retiring from India, the majority of his biographers have apparently found it difficult to obtain facts and have been content at times to substitute surmises, without always clearly indicating the statements that are merely surmises.

In the Library of the Royal Botanic Garden at Calcutta are preserved many letters, written during his Indian career by Buchanan to his friend and predecessor

---

[1] Annals of the Royal Botanic Garden, Calcutta, vol. iv.
[2] Ditto ditto vol. v.
[3] Vol. x., p. 171, (read June 18, 1821).

Roxburgh.[1] These deal mainly with botanical subjects and therefore rarely admit of being suitably reproduced in their entirety. They do, however, in many cases throw light on his Indian career, as passages extracted from them will show. In the same collection are also preserved a number of letters written by Buchanan (now Hamilton) to his friend and successor Wallich; these are invaluable as a record of Hamilton's life after he retired.

In his endeavour to obtain further information regarding points that in previous notices seemed doubtful or inexact the writer has received much assistance from many friends, to whom his warm thanks are due for their kind interest in the subject. For information regarding Buchanan's family history and the history of the house of Buchanan since 1682, he is indebted to J. Hamilton Buchanan, Esq., of Leny and Spittal, and to A. C. Cameron, Esq., LL.D., of Edinburgh; for facts and dates relating to Buchanan's education and to his connection with the Indian Medical Service he has to thank Lieutenant-Colonel D. G. Crawford, I.M.S.; for an examination of Naval and other Records with the object of throwing light on Buchanan's career before he entered the Company's service he is indebted to J. F. Duthie, Esq., and through him to Lord Walter Kerr, J. Britten, Esq., and B. Daydon Jackson, Esq.; for an opportunity of consulting an extremely interesting series of letters regarding his father written by Buchanan's son and successor, the late J. B. Hamilton, Esq., of Leny, Spittal and Bardowie, he has to thank Sir George King and through him H. Beveridge, Esq.

To the kindness of Mr. Hamilton Buchanan of Leny the writer is further indebted for the use of two letters from Lord Wellesley and of two other very interesting documents; a sketch of the life of his grandfather Francis Hamilton (formerly Buchanan) by his own father, the late Mr. Buchanan Hamilton of Leny who was Dr. Buchanan's son and heir; and a copy of the 'Retour' in the claim successfully advanced by the subject of our sketch, towards the close of his life, to represent the house of Buchanan and to be therefore chief of the name.

2. EARLY LIFE AND FAMILY HISTORY.

Francis Buchanan was born at the Branziet, in the county of Stirling, a dower house on his mother's estate of Bardowie, on 15th February 1762. He was the fourth son of Thomas Buchanan, of the house of Buchanan of Spittal, by his second wife, Elizabeth Hamilton, daughter and eventually heiress of John Hamilton of Bardowie.

---

[1] These letters are 149 in number and may be classified as follows:—

Relative to the Burmese mission	... ...	1
Ditto	his life in Luckipur (Puttahaut)	19
Ditto	the Chittagong survey	1
Ditto	the Mysore survey	19
Ditto	the Nepal mission	96
Ditto	his life at Baruipur	2
Ditto	the Bengal survey	11
	Total ...	149

There were other 21 letters written from Nepal that were stolen or otherwise lost in transit.

Thomas Buchanan, the father of the subject of this sketch, was a younger son of John Buchanan of Spittal, a small property in the county of Dumbarton[1] consisting of a few farms and possessing now no mansion house.[2] As a younger son Thomas Buchanan had to adopt a profession and he is described variously as a physician[3] and as an officer in the Dutch service;[4] he is, moreover, usually spoken of as Thomas Buchanan of Spittal. The statements regarding his occupation, which are not necessarily incompatible, the writer has not succeeded in verifying; his territorial designation, though correct, requires some explanation.

In an entry in the *Service of Heirs in Scotland,* dated 12th January, 1759, Thomas Buchanan is erroneously described as the son of Robert Buchanan of Spittal.[5] Robert Buchanan was the elder brother, not the father of Thomas Buchanan. Robert inherited Spittal from his father, John Buchanan, about 1730. The estate being encumbered was disposed of by Robert Bunchanan to a younger brother, Peter Buchanan, in 1735. Peter in turn sold it, in or about the year 1755, to his brother Thomas Buchanan. By an entail, dated 10th December 1786, the succession to, as apart from possession of, Spittal was vested in Thomas Buchanan, who had already been in possession for over 30 years, and his heirs. As both Robert and Peter Buchanan[6] died without issue, Thomas Buchanan thus, about 1755, acquired by purchase a property that he or his successors must ultimately have obtained by inheritance.[7]

Thomas Buchanan married, as his first wife, Katherine Buchanan, daughter of Henry Buchanan of Leny, in Perthshire, the head of a house that has been intimately associated with the parent house of Buchanan of Buchanan throughout their joint history. Allan Buchanan, second son of Sir Maurice Buchanan, whose charter of confirmation in the lands of Buchanan was granted by David II., married the daughter and heiress of the last male representative of the house of Leny of Leny, and founded the house of Buchanan of Leny. The last male representative of this first line of Buchanan of Leny was John Buchanan, great-grandson of Allan Buchanan, whose daughter and heiress, Janet Buchanan, married John Buchanan, eldest son of Walter Buchanan of Buchanan, whose charter of confirmation was granted by Robert II. This John Buchanan, who predeceased his father, left three sons: (1) Sir Alexander Buchanan, a notable soldier, who was killed, leaving no heir, at the battle of Verneuil on 17th August 1421; (2) Sir Walter Buchanan, who married a daughter of Murdoch, Duke of

---

[1] Burke: Landed Gentry for 1900—*article* Buchanan-Hamilton of Spittal, Leny and Bardowie.

[2] Though comparatively unimportant in a material sense this small estate has been of much historical and genealogical consequence to the branch of the house of Buchanan to whom it belongs; it was in virtue of his ability to demonstrate that he was the representative of his ancestor Walter Buchanan, younger of Buchanan and first of Spittal, that Dr. Francis Hamilton established his claim to represent also the house of Buchanan of Buchanan and to be chief of the name.

[3] Chambers: *Biographies of Eminent Scotsmen.* Higginbotham: *Men India has known.*

[4] Anderson: *Scottish Nation.*

[5] This entry refers, it may be remarked, to his second wife, Elizabeth Hamilton, not to himself, a fact that probably explains the error.

The widow of Peter Buchanan of Spittal, whose name was Agnes Hamilton, was still living on 15th January 1809.

In connection with this it is interesting to find that although, on the death of his own elder brother Colonel John Hamilton, Dr. Francis Buchanan acquired possession of the property of Spittal in 1818, he considered it necessary, as a preliminary to the establishment of his larger claim to represent his ancestor Walter Buchanan, first of Spittal, to serve himself heir, on 18th September 1826, to his father's elder brother, and his own uncle, Robert Buchanan of Spittal.

Albany by his wife Isobel, Countess of Lennox in her own right, and inherited the Buchanan estates from his grandfather; and (3) John Buchanan, who inherited his mother's estate of Leny and so began the second line of Buchanan of Leny. Sir Walter's son, Patrick Buchanan of Buchanan, whose charter of confirmation in the Buchanan estates is dated 1460, became owner of some portion of Strathyre in 1455, and in that year was a party, along with his cousin, Andrew Buchanan of Leny, to a mutual entail of their respective estates in favour of each other and of their lineal descendants, passing over their brothers on either side. For the next two centuries the writer can trace no matrimonial alliances between the houses of Buchanan of Buchanan and Buchanan of Leny, but the penultimate Buchanan of Buchanan, Sir George Buchanan, who died in 1651, had by his second wife a daughter, Janet Buchanan, who married Henry Buchanan of Leny.

Henry Buchanan of Leny is stated to have died in 1723.[1] By his first wife he had six children: (1) John Buchanan, who died unmarried; (2) Colin Buchanan, who also died unmarried—he was served heir, on 23rd January, 1728, to his father Henry Buchanan of Leny, and to his brother, John Buchanan of Leny; (3) James Buchanan, who died without leaving descendants; (4) Robert Buchanan, who also died without leaving descendants—he was served heir to his brother Colin Buchanan of Leny on 14th September, 1734; (5) Elizabeth Buchanan, wife of Francis Buchanan of Arnpryor,[2] who succeeded to the estate of Leny on 22nd March 1740, but died leaving no issue; (6) Magaret Buchanan, who succeeded her sister Elizabeth in the estate of Leny and died unmarried.

By his second wife, Henry Buchanan of Leny had two sons, Henry Buchanan and John Buchanan[3] both of whom died without issue; and three daughters, (1) Lilias Buchanan, died without heir; (2) Jean Buchanan, who appears to have married but to have left no issue; (3) Katherine Buchanan, the lady who, as already stated, was the first wife of Thomas Buchanan. There were no children by this marriage, but, on the death of his wife's half-sister, Margaret Buchanan of Leny, Thomas Buchanan inherited the estate of Leny, and was thus the founder of the existing line of Buchanan of Leny.

---

[1] *Scottish Nation*, i., 463. This is possibly a printer's mistake for 1728.

[2] Francis Buchanan of Arnpryor, the husband of Elizabeth Buchanan of Leny, was the representative of a family founded by John Buchanan, younger son of Walter Buchanan of Buchanan, and grandson of the Patrick Buchanan of Buchanan who, in 1455, was a party to the joint-entail of the estates of Strathyre and Leny. This John Buchanan, to whom the estate of Arnpryor, formerly owned by one of the Menzies, had been left by testament, was the well known 'King of Kippen,' the friend of James V. His descendant, Francis Buchanan, husband of Elizabeth Buchanan of Leny, accepted a commission as Major in the Duke of Perth's rebel cavalry and was beheaded at Carlisle in 1746. As relics of this gentleman there still are preserved at Leny one of the gloves worn by him at his execution and part of his commission signed by Prince Charles' Secretary. The house of Buchanan of Arnpryor is now believed to be extinct. The name Francis is not one that was in use in the family of Buchanan of Spittal and it is just possible, though there is no direct proof of the fact, that the name borne by the subject of our sketch was bestowed in commemoration of his unfortunate kinsman. It may be remarked here that the subject of our sketch was not the first of his name to enter the Indian Medical Service; a Francis Buchanan, M.D., was appointed Assistant Surgeon on 1st July, 1758, and resigned the service on 16th July, 1769.

[3] The fact that there was a John in Henry Buchanan's second family proves that the eldest son of the first family, who also was John Buchanan, must have predeceased his father; and as the *Index to Service of Heirs in Scotland* shows that Henry's second son, Colin, succeeded to the estate of Leny in 1728, it is clear that he must have succeeded his father immediately and that, although he was at the same time served heir to his elder brother John, this brother never was in possession of Leny. This being the case, the date of the death of Henry Buchanan should be 1728 and not, as has elsewhere been stated, 1723.

Elizabeth Hamilton, the second wife of Thomas Buchanan, and mother of Francis Buchanan was, in 1757, about two years after her marriage, served heir-portioner to the estates of her two brothers, John Hamilton and Robert Hamilton, and in 1759, along with her sister Mary, served heir-portioner to the estate of her father, John Hamilton of Bardowie. Subsequently she became the sole possessor of the Bardowie property[1] and an entail was executed in terms of which such of her descendants as might avail themselves of the succession to her estate were obliged to assume her own name of Hamilton.

The family of Thomas Buchanan and Elizabeth, his second wife, included five sons, Henry, John, Robert, FRANCIS, and Peter, with two daughters, Elizabeth and Marion. Henry Buchanan, born in 1756, predeceased both his parents.[2] John Buchanan, the second son, born in 1758, became a soldier and saw a good deal of service abroad. He married Margaret, daughter of Sir Hew Crawford of Jordanhall, and on the death of his mother succeeded to her estate of Bardowie and, in accordance with the terms of her entail, assumed the name of Hamilton. When his father Thomas Buchanan died in 1790, Colonel John Hamilton succeeded to the paternal estates of Spittal and Leny but continued to make Bardowie his residence. He died on the continent, whither he had gone for the benefit of his health, in 1818, and left no issue. Robert Buchanan, the third son, born in 1760, who predeceased his brother, Colonel John Hamilton, married and had a son, Robert Hamilton Buchanan, who entered the service of the East India Company and also died, as a Captain in the 24th Regiment of Native Infantry, leaving no legitimate descendants, before his uncle, Colonel John Hamilton. Francis Buchanan, the fourth son and the subject of this sketch, born, as already stated, in 1762, survived and succeeded his brother, John Hamilton, in all three estates of Bardowie, Spittal and Leny. Peter Buchanan, the youngest son, born in 1767, died unmarried. The two sisters Elizabeth and Marion were both married but have now no living descendants.

Francis Buchanan received part of his early education in Glasgow. The schools that he attended are not recorded but he entered the University of Glasgow at the early age characteristic of the period. The Professors at Glasgow then were William Richardson,—Humanity; John Young,—Greek; James Williamson,—Mathematics; John Anderson,—Natural Philosophy; James Clow,—Mental Philosophy; Thomes Reid,—Moral Philosophy. As his subsequent career and writings show, Buchanan in Glasgow acquired a scholarly knowledge of the classical languages and a thorough training in physics and philosophy. Of these teachers, probably the now venerable Reid, who himself

---

[1] In a letter dated Leny, 16th October, 1821, Dr. Francis Hamilton, referring to Sir Robert Colquhoun, Bart., then serving in India, writes:—"I am happy that Sir Robert Colquhoun is a botanist or, at least, an amateur. His sister is married to a relation of mine and her son, unless I marry, will succeed me in my maternal inheritance of Bardowie." There were thus, when the entail referred to was executed, residuary rights of succession beyond the immediate descendants of Elizabeth Hamilton. The entail she executed was removed some years ago and in consequence of this, although Dr. Francis Hamilton's son continued, till his death in 1903, to be known as J. Buchanan Hamilton, his grandson, who is now proprietor of Spittal and Leny and chief of the name of Buchanan, has been able to revert to the original family name. More recently the estate of Bardowie, as Mr. Hamilton Buchanan informs the writer, has been disposed of.

[2] Henry Buchanan would appear to have died young; this may explain how it happens that previous notices of the life of Francis (Buchanan) Hamilton speak of him, erroneously, as having been the third son of Thomas Buchanan of Spittal.

used the Baconian method in his lectures with such effect, had the greatest real influence on Buchanan's career, if one may judge by Buchanan's skilful and often masterly use of the inductive process with regard to those matters as to which he had only native reports and opinions to guide him. From Glasgow Buchanan obtained the degree of M.A., when he was 17 years of age, in 1779.

Being, like his father, a younger son, it was necessary for Buchanan to adopt a profession. He accordingly decided to follow that of his father and, after graduating at Glasgow, he proceeded to Edinburgh where he studied medicine. John Hope,[1] pupil of Jussieu, and friend of Linnaeus, had been teacher of Botany for eighteen years when Buchanan's studies began, while John Walker[2] had entered on his duties as teacher of Natural History during Buchanan's final year at Glasgow. The influence of the teaching in these two classes on Buchanan's mind and future career was evidently great. The Professor of Materia Medica at Edinburgh then was Francis Home,[3] who possibly did not so greatly influence Buchanan, but he evidently benefited by the inspiring influence of Alexander Monro *secundus*,[4] who was then the Professor of Anatomy. A fellow-student and college friend of Buchanan while at Edinburgh was James Edward (afterwards Sir J. E.) Smith, the purchaser of the herbarium of Linnaeus and founder of the Linnean Society of London, and from Smith we learn that, after the often temporary enthusiasm for natural history which accompanies attendance on the scientific classes of a medical curriculum might have worn off, Buchanan during the intervals between the sessions of the University was still a keen collector.[5] Buchanan obtained the degree of M.D. from the University of Edinburgh in 1783, when he was in his 22nd year.

The year following graduation appears to have been spent at home and we learn incidentally from Sir J. E. Smith that he was still collecting, and that Smith and he were attempting conjointly to identify his specimens.[6] His attention at this time was apparently given largely to mosses.[7] It is clear from the references that provide us with this information that Buchanan, though already a keen collector, was a collector of an unselfish type, forming no permanent herbarium for himself but making over his specimens to friends, just as he did in later years.

Early in 1785 Buchanan embarked on the first of his Eastern voyages[8]—we find from one of his subsequently published papers that on the last day of July 1785 he was in the Arabian Sea on a vessel bound for Bombay from Johanna in the Comoros The paper in which this fact is recorded,[9] and a later reference to the conditions of the cotton export trade in Bombay, contained in a letter dated

---

[1] Dr. John Hope, Professor of Medicine and Botany in the University of Edinburgh, 1761—1786.

[2] Dr. John Walker, Professor of Natural History, 1779—1804.

[3] Dr. Francis Home, Professor of Materia Medica, University of Edinburgh, 1768—1798.

[4] Alexander Monro *secundus, patris eminentis filius eminentior*, Professor of Anatomy, University of Edinburgh, 1754—1798.

[5] His name is associated with the first record of a British Moss, collected at Leny, his father's home, in 1782, the year before he obtained his medical degree. *English Botany*, xxiii., t. 1590: 1806.

[6] *English Botany*, t. 2004: 1809; another first record of a British moss.

[7] This branch of Botany is one that Buchanan evidently did not continue to cultivate in later life, for one of his letters, given in a subsequent chapter, laments his ignorance of the group and is interesting as showing that the example and influence of Hooker and Greville almost tempted him to renew his acquaintance with these fascinating plants.

[8] It is not clear in what capacity Buchanan's voyage was made; the point is dealt with more fully below.

[9] *Edinburgh Philosophical Journal*, vol. v.; 1821.

1st November, 1828, which is given further on, show that Buchanan thus early in his career already possessed all the faculty for careful observation that was to be so distinguishing a feature of his later life. It is not therefore surprising to find that, just before he started on another voyage, Buchanan joined, as one of its original associates, on March 18, 1788, the Linnean Society founded in London by his friend, Dr. (afterwards Sir) J. E. Smith.

During Buchanan's second voyage his vessel, evidently outward bound, was, on May 24th, 1788, somewhere in the latitude of Walfisch Bay. The 8th of January, 1789, found him in the Sea of Celebes about midway between the Philippines and the Moluccas and on the 12th of April, 1789, his vessel, obviously homeward bound, was somewhere in the Southern Atlantic.[1] There is an indication, in two contemporary records, that Buchanan may have made a third Eastern voyage, for he is spoken of, in works[2] published in 1791, as being then in the East Indies. Nothing definite has been traced with regard to Buchanan's life between 1791, assuming that he was again on a voyage in that year, and 1794 when he accepted a commission from the Honourable East India Company.

Most previous notices of Buchanan's career state that after graduating in medicine in 1783 he entered the Royal Navy as an Assistant Surgeon, but that he soon had to resign this service owing to the delicate state of his health, and on this account spent a considerable number of years at home before proceeding to India in 1794. This belief has almost crystallized into a family tradition and in a letter from his son, written in 1894, that gentleman, who was a small boy at the time of his father's death, refers to his dim recollection of a wound, which Buchanan was believed to have received in a naval engagement in the West Indies, that gave trouble to the end of Buchanan's life.

It has to be remarked, however, in the first place, that the grade of Assistant Surgeon did not exist in the Navy between 1783 and 1794, and further, that a thorough search of our naval records for the period 1783—1794, kindly undertaken on behalf of this memoir by Lord Walter Kerr, fails to show that Buchanan ever did serve in the Navy. That Buchanan's health was, during some part of the 1783—1794 period, in an indifferent state may, the writer believes, be accepted, for it is extremely unlikely that a family tradition of this kind should be without foundation. But it is clear that the period of ill-health was at any rate shorter than has been supposed, and that there was certainly no enforced residence at home at Leny between 1783 and 1789, possibly none till after 1791. The prolonged ill-health recorded by previous biographers is thus reduced at most to the four years 1790—1794, and is quite likely to have lasted only for two years from 1792—1794.

[1] *Edinburgh Philosophical Journal*, vol. v.; 1821.

[2] *Statistical Account of Scotland; Callander:* also *Transactions of the Linnean Society of London*, vol. i.; 1791. The Rev. Dr. Robertson, author of this account of Callander, mentions Dr. Francis Buchanan as "the most learned person who is known to have belonged to this parish" and speaks of him as "at present in the East Indies." The manuscript of this account of Callander was placed in the hands of the Editor of the *Statistical Account* in 1791, but it is of course not impossible that it was written, at least in part, two or three years before 1791, and the passage quoted may therefore very well refer to the voyage of 1788-89. This, however, can hardly be the case with the list of members given in the first volume of the Linnean Society's *Transactions*, where Buchanan's address, *for the year* 1791, is given as the "East Indies."

There is no reference, so far as the writer can ascertain, in any of Buchanan's own papers, to a third Eastern voyage or to his movements at all, between 1789 and 1794 when he first took service in India.

As Buchanan did certainly make two and possibly made three voyages to India and the East before he joined the Indian Medical Service, and as it has been shewn to be improbable that he ever served in the Navy, we may almost with safety conclude that, like many other adventurous young physicians of his day—his future friend and predecessor in the Botanic Garden at Calcutta, Dr. Roxburgh, may be quoted as a known example—Buchanan served during this period as Surgeon's mate, and in due course as Surgeon, on an East Indiaman. The intervals between one voyage and another would naturally be considerable, since the sailings of the East Indiamen were seasonal. These intervals most probably were largely spent at his father's house, at Leny. If so, these considerable and repeated periods of residence at home might easily, especially if his health were, as is possible, indifferent at the time, be confused by neighbours with a continuous and prolonged period of illness and inactivity.

Buchanan made no contributions to scientific literature between 1783 and 1794 and the only published observations relating to this period appeared in 1821 in the *Edinburgh Journal of Science*, five years after he retired. But a perusal of Buchanan's papers on the language, religion and literature of Burma, published in the *Asiatick Researches* in 1798-99 affords indications that the years which intervened between his graduation at Edinburgh and his receiving a commission from the Honourable East India Company must have been marked by wide reading and extended observation of men and things.

3. SERVICE IN INDIA, 1794—1805.

SURVEYS OF AVA, CHITTAGONG, MYSORE AND NEPAL.

Dr. Francis Buchanan entered the service of the Honourable East India Company as an Assistant Surgeon on the Bengal Establishment on 26th September, 1794. Soon after his appointment he was attached to the embassy which was deputed under Captain Michael Symes to the Court of Ava. This embassy left Calcutta on 21st February, 1795 and, on its way to Rangoon, the vessel in which the embassy sailed called at Port Cornwallis in North Andaman.[1] Buchanan was thus given an opportunity of seeing something of the Andamans and of seeing and learning a good deal about Pegu and Ava before the embassy returned to Calcutta on 22nd December, 1795.

From the account of this embassy published by Symes (now a Major), in 1800,[2] we learn how valuable as a colleague and how delightful as a companion Buchanan

[1] This was the second site occupied by Government as a settlement in the Andamans. The site originally occupied was that which is now the head-quarters of the Andaman Commission; it was occupied by Lieutenant Blair during the cold weather of 1789-90 under orders issued by Government in September 1789. To the harbour thus occupied Blair gave the name of Port Cornwallis. In November 1792 orders were issued for the removal of the settlement to another and more spacious harbour in North Andaman; to this new settlement, which was the one visited by Symes and Buchanan, the original name of Port Cornwallis was again applied. In 1796 orders were issued for the removal of the whole establishment to Penang. The present establishment in the Andamans dates from 1858 and, owing to the transfer of its original name "Port Cornwallis" to the harbour in North Andaman, for which that name is still used, the third settlement, which occupies the site of the first settlement of 1789, has, to prevent confusion, been renamed Port Blair in commemoration of the original founder.

[2] Symes: *An Account of an Embassy to the Kingdom of Ava*; 1 vol. 4to. London, 1800.

must have been, and we further gather both from Symes and from various papers published by Buchanan himself while in India and after he had retired,[1] that he made the most of the opportunities afforded by this journey not only in the matter of direct observation but in the way of acquiring information by questioning the more intelligent inhabitants of the country with whom he came in contact. Though only one passage is given by Symes in Buchanan's own words[2] we are told that a good deal of the geographical as distinguished from the political fruit of this mission was the outcome of Buchanan's assiduity. There are also, in Symes' narrative, incidental references to Buchanan's work as a botanical collector,[3] and a number of the more interesting species of plants obtained during the journey, of which drawings had been made on the spot, were selected for publication and described, so Symes says, by Sir Joseph Banks, as a portion of Symes' work.[4] His correspondence with Roxburgh began during this journey though only one of the letters in Roxburgh's collection, dated Rangoon, 21st May, 1795, belongs to this period. It is too technical for reproduction in full but the closing passage:—

"any of the seeds you think worth the planting in your garden I beg you may use; the others, if any opportunity offers, be so obliging as to send to Smith in my name,"

is interesting owing to its reference to his friend the founder of the Linnean Society.

On his return from Burma, Buchanan was posted to Luckipoor (Lakshmipur) the head-quarters of the present district of Noakhali in South-Eastern Bengal. His actual residence was at Puttahaut six miles north of Luckipoor and, except for occasional visits to Commillah, Chittagong and Calcutta, he was here during the latter half of 1796, the whole of 1797, and a considerable part of 1798. He was, as we learn from his letters, in constant correspondence with Roxburgh,[5] who took a great interest in Buchanan's welfare and career, and did much to push his fortunes at the outset of his Indian service.

Shortly after settling at Puttahaut he applied unsuccessfully to be allowed to return to Pegu. Besides travelling in the district and crossing the Megna to make occasional botanical excursions in the Eastern Sundribuns we find that he busied himself with the arrangement of his Burmese notes and papers. Thus, in a letter dated Puttahaut August 13th, 1796, he says:—

"I have finished my account of the Pegu plants some time ago and would have sent it up but am in daily expectation of bringing it up myself. It has turned out much longer than I

---

[1] *Asiatick Researches*, vols. v. & vi.; *Edinb. Phil. Journ.*, vols. ii., iii., iv., v., vi., vii., ix., x.; *Edinb. Journ. Sci.* i.

[2] A note on the rivers of Burma; Symes: *Embassy*, p. 241.

[3] *E. g.*, Symes: *Embassy*, p. 437, where reference is made to Buchanan's search for the Launzan tree, which was also the subject of a short paper (*Asiatick Researches*, vol. v.) by Buchanan himself, and which now perpetuates his memory by having been made the type of the genus *Buchanania*.

[4] Symes: *Embassy*, p. 473. Descriptions of rare and curious plants, selected by the President of the Royal Society. We know, however, from Buchanan's letters to Roxburgh, and from his own published papers, that he prepared a full account of the collection made in Burma and that what Symes says Banks did was really entirely Buchanan's work.

[5] The following 19 letters to Roxburgh belong to this period: 1796; August 13th, November 17th, December 14th: 1797; 12th February, 11th March, 11th April, 10th May, 25th June, 6th July, 10th July, 19th July, 26th July, 2nd August, 17th August, 20th August, 4th September, one without date received by Roxburgh on 3rd October, 30th November: 1798; 7th January.

expected; 168 folio pages. Since it was finished I have been busy in arranging my geographical papers."

In the same letters he gives an indication of his zoological studies:—

"I believe I have discovered a new genus of animals. It is very near the Limax but differs in several particulars. It is impossible to preserve the animal in spirits so as to show its limbs, but I have got very good drawings."

In the next letter of the collection, dated Puttahaut November 17th, 1796, he says:—

"I should very willingly have described the new animal here, but Mr. Fleming when I offered it thought that it would not answer, and I am affraid Smith would not take it kind should I withdraw it from him."[1]

He had joined the Asiatic Society at Calcutta on August 6th, 1796, and in his letters there are several allusions to the fact, only one of which, given in a letter dated Pullahaut 11th April, 1797, need be here given; the interest of the extract lies particularly in the concluding sentence, which seems to indicate that Roxburgh's *Flora Indica*, which was not published in its entirety till 1832, was already, in manuscript, at the disposal of his friends. Roxburgh, as previous letters of the series show, had arranged to visit Chittagong, passing by Luckipoor and being Buchanan's guest on the way. The proposed excursion had to be abandoned, owing to the breakdown of Roxburgh's health which necessitated his making a voyage to the Cape of Good Hope.

"Two days ago I received yours and am sorry that you have given up your intention of coming this way, especially as it proceeds from so bad a cause. I am much obliged to you for undertaking to make up my engagements to the Society; be so obliging as to let me know the amount and I shall procure an order on Calcutta as soon as possible. I am also greatly obliged to you for securing the number of your Flora Indica."

From a letter dated 10th May 1797 we learn that Roxburgh had endeavoured to obtain for Buchanan a place on an expedition then being organised to proceed to Manilla. Nothing came of this, but a subsequent recommendation of Roxburgh's that Buchanan should be posted to the 24-Pergunnahs: so as to bring him within reach of the books to be had in the libraries of Calcutta, was successful, as was another recommendation of Roxburgh's, submitted to the Board of Trade at Calcutta, that Buchanan's services should be utilized in making an economic survey of Chittagong. During the rainy season of 1797 Buchanan was still engaged in arranging his Burmese papers, for in a letter dated 19th July 1797 he says:—

"I have now nearly finished my account of the Burmese religion and should be glad to show it to Sir John Shore, whose opinion relative to the publication of a part or of the whole I should like to have. * * * I do not think that it would answer for a separate publication, but although rather long it might do for the Asiatick Researches."

He reverts to this subject in several subsequent letters; in one received by Roxburgh on 3rd October 1797 he says:—

"I intend setting out for your house on the twentieth of October. * * * By the time I have come I hope Sir John and perhaps Mr. Fleming may have looked them over and we shall then be able to determine what ought to be done with them. If the contents are thought

[1] This, and another Zoological paper belonging to the same period, appeared in *Trans. Linn. Soc.*, vol. v.

interesting enough for publication, I can get Shoolbred or perhaps Bruce to look over them with me and to correct the language. Both of them write with a considerable degree of elegance."[1]

The temporary cessation of Buchanan's correspondence with Roxburgh, for there is no letter after 7th January 1798 till 16th October 1798, was due to Roxburgh's absence from India. The letter of 16th October, which was addressed to Roxburgh at the Cape, is given below:—

"Your application to the Board of Trade for my going to Chitagong was successful and I had a charming botanical excursion for near 3 months; the latter part of it, however, was much interrupted by the rains which set in remarkably early and are not yet over. I found many places with a most excellent soil in Chittagong, but have my fears that the climate will not be sufficiently mild for the spice plants. I however sent in a report to you, communicating it to Fleming and mentioning that I would communicate my journal[2] which contains the remarks I made on the soil, produce, culture, and people of the country through which I passed, and that I would also communicate my specimens of dried plants which are pretty numerous. I have sent a good many seeds and growing plants to the garden and have laid things in such a train that I expect many more. In what condition the seeds and plants have arrived I cannot say, as I have not yet been able to go down to the garden. Among my specimens are four species of Gurgeon or wood oil trees; a tree which yields a very acrid varnish which I suppose is the same with that of the Burmas and Chinese; another the bark of which united with indigo is said to form a black dye. I saw not the fructification of either, but suspect the first to be a species of Semecarpus and the latter to be a Ricinus. I sent growing plants of both. What will be the result of my report I cannot say, as Fleming does not intend giving it in till Smith goes away to the eastward which he will do in a few days. He says that I will have some difficulty in getting expenses paid owing to my being so late of making a charge.

* * * * * * * * * *

According to your recommendation I was appointed to Barripur on the 15th May * * * * * * * I could not leave with propriety before the first of this month. I was thus for a long time kept in a disagreeable situation and run great risks of having my interests materially injured, yet as very frequently happens in our profession I did not even receive thanks from those I had so materially served. Fleming has been very angry with me for staying so long, but I know that if I had come away * * * would have raised such a clamour about inhumanity that I should probably [have] been looked upon by every civil servant as a monster.

Fleming at one time I am told had strong intentions of going home, but as he is now as much in favour as ever I hope he will not think of it. I dined yesterday with Boswell, who is very well and in good spirits, and I am happy to hear from him that you are so much pleased with the Cape."

From the beginning of October 1798 till the commencement of 1800 Buchanan was stationed at Baruipur in the 24-Pergunnahs, not far from Calcutta, and while here he had occasion to make several voyages in the Western Sundribuns. Not having Roxburgh to correspond with, he appears to have given less attention than usual to botany, for he collected no specimens; any drawings or descriptions that he made were sent to his friend Smith. His zoological studies were, however, steadily pursued, more particularly his investigation of the Gangetic fishes. This subject had already engaged his attention while at Puttahaut, for in a letter from there to Roxburgh, dated 30th November 1797, he says:—

"I have given my old painter a gold mohur a month and have him employed on fishes. I am attempting to make him do the outlines with some degree of accuracy; when he succeeds in that I shall begin to colour."

[1] This paper, and another on the languages spoken in Burma, were published in *Asiatick Researches*, vols. v. and vi.

[2] This journal was never published, but a good deal of the information it contained appeared subsequently in three papers on the frontier between Bengal and Ava, in the *Edinburgh Journal of Science*, vols. ii., iii. and iv.

Again, in a letter, dated 7th February 1798, just before Roxburgh sailed, he remarks:—

"If you do not take Blocke and Forster's Termini Ichthyologici with you, I should esteem it as a great favour to have the use of them till your return."

At Baruipur, therefore, the fishes received his chief attention and it was here that he really laid the foundation of his great knowledge of the Gangetic species, embodied in one of his most finished publications.[1] Roxburgh returned to India in October 1799 and their correspondence was immediately renewed. Before, however, Roxburgh had returned, Buchanan was offered an opportunity of visiting Nepal, and that he was able to set out on this journey we learn from a letter dated Gorasan, 12th February 1800.

"We have been waiting at this place, which is the village nearest to Nepal, for 14 days. The chief minist r arrived two days ago at the village next to us on the frontier of his country. There has been as yet no interview nor do I know when we shall advance, but it is expected to be in the course of a few days. I am very well pleased at the delay, as I shall have a greater chance of finding the forest trees in flower the later we are.

* * * * * * * * *

Captain Craufard who commands the escort * * has commenced the study of Botany with eagerness. He has rather forgotten his Latin and wishes to have the families of plants and vegetables of the Litchfield Society. * * * *.

The Nepal journey had, however, for the moment to be deferred, and Buchanan had once more to thank Roxburgh for an opportunity of distinguishing himself. While on his way back from the Cape in 1799 Roxburgh landed at Madras and had the privilege of an interview with Lord Clive, then Governor of Fort St. George. In the course of their conversation Lord Clive mentioned to Roxburgh his desire to investigate the newly acquired territories in his Presidency, and asked Roxburgh whether he could recommend a suitable officer for the work. On his return to Calcutta Roxburgh wrote, in October 1799, to Lord Clive as follows:—

"When in Madras I took the liberty of mentioning to your Lordship that I thought Dr. Francis Buchanan of the Bengal Medical Establishment a very proper person to be employed in your newly acquired territories above the Ghauts. He is the best botanist I know of in India and in every other respect the best qualified to furnish you with an account of the Vegetable Productions of these countries. He is also a good Zoologist; in short every way well qualified for the research. I have had a good deal of conversation with him on the subject and find him willing to be employed by your Lordship in the above manner. Could Mr. Heyne accompany him as Mineralogist and Chemist, I have no doubt but their joint endeavours would soon furnish a more complete account of the natural History, state of Agriculture, etc., of these provinces than we at present have of any of the British Possessions in Asia. Should your Lordship wish to employ this gentleman it will, I imagine, be necessary to apply to this Government for him."

When Lord Clive's suggestion reached Calcutta the Marquis of Wellesley took it up warmly and adopted it as his own. He appears to have been greatly impressed by the perusal of Buchanan's Chittagong Journal and decided to adopt Roxburgh's opinion that Buchanan was the officer to whom the duty could best be entrusted. Buchanan was therefore recalled from the Nepal frontier, and instructions, dated 24th February 1800, were issued to him to visit and report on the territories of the Rajah of Mysore, and on the country acquired by the Company after their war with the Sultan as well as on that part of Malabar previously occupied by the Marquis Cornwallis.

---

[1] *Account of the Fishes found in the river Ganges and its branches.* 2 vols. Text, 1 vol. 8vo. Plates 1 vol. Royal 8vo. Edinburgh, 1822.

The chief object of this enquiry was to be the agriculture of the country, including a report on all esculent vegetables; cattle; farms. Next, the natural resources of the country, such as cotton, pepper, sandalwood, cardamoms were to be investigated; as were mines, quarries, minerals, and mineral springs; also manufactures and manufacturers. An account was to be drawn up of the climate and seasons and, as far as possible, of the forests; finally, he was to report on the condition and character of the people. His instructions included an order to transmit seeds and living plants to the Botanic Garden at Calcutta, with observations as to their nature and their culture.

Soon after receiving these comprehensive instructions Buchanan sailed for Madras, leaving that place on 23rd April 1800 to carry them out. He travelled through Arcot, Mysore, Coimbatore, then crossed the Anamalai Hills to Malabar, and returned to Madras on the completion of his survey on 6th July 1801. His itinerary is given in his published journal, so that little additional information is to be obtained from the letters addressed to Roxburgh[1] during the journey. The following, however, dated Seringapatam, 20th May 1800, from the glimpse it affords us of Colonel Wellesley, who was in time to become Duke of Wellington, is sufficiently interesting for reproduction on that ground alone:—

"I expected to have been able on my journey to this place to have procured many seeds to have sent you, but hitherto it has not been a favourable season, and I have got absolutely nothing. Almost every plant that I have got has been already described by you,[2] and of the few that appear to be new I have not been able to get the seeds. The whole country above the ghauts through which I have passed is very naked, and at this season is entirely burnt up for want of water. Besides, I had no authority to call upon any of the natives for information and assistance and, without that, it is impossible to procure the most trifling thing. I arrived here on the night of the 17th and have been very well received by Colonel Close, who seems disposed to give me every assistance, and has procured me an interview with Purneah the Rajah's Dewan. He is very profuse in his promises but, from the little I can see, I imagine that privately he will throw every delay in my way that he can.

I live with Colonel Close in the Lal Baug, one of the late Sultan's garden houses. The garden is laid out in the French taste, but suffered much from Lord Cornwallis's army and has been much neglected ever since, for our army made it an hospital and, many Christians having been buried in the grounds, gave Tippco a disgust to them. The soil is very good and admirably well watered by canals from the river. For my own part I think it a much preferable place to Bangalore for a botanica establishment, but I find Dr. Heyne is of a contrary opinion. The European vegetables thrive at all seasons of the year. Coffee and mulberry trees thrive much better than any I have seen in Bengal. One great advantage of this place is its vicinity to the Coorg Mountains and Western Ghauts where I am told there is a wonderful variety in the vegetable productions. Besides, its being the seat of Government, useful things that may be introduced will be much more likely to spread than if they are cultivated at a remote place such as Bangalore.

I shall probably remain here for some time and then proceed through the eastern parts of the Rajah's dominions to Coimbatore. I must leave the north-western parts, the most favourable for botanical pursuits, till the last, as at present they are in very unsettled state. Colonel Wellesley marched to-day with the 73rd Regiment to join a considerable force that is going to make a settlement.

---

[1] There are again 19 letters in this series:—Seringapatam, 20th May 1800; Sera, 1st August 1800; Seringapatam, 4th September 1800; Polinura, 16th November 1800; Palighautchery, 2nd December 1800; Paryanuri, 6th December 1800; a letter without place or date, replying to one from Roxburgh dated 26th September 1800, but by its context intermediate between the last and the next; Calicut, 27th December 1800; Tellicherry, 9th January 1801; Buntwal, 31st January 1801; Coondapoor, 14th February 1801; Nugger, 24th March and 27th March 1801; Chitteldroog, 15th April and 16th April 1801; Seringapatam, 30th May and 1st June 1801; Madras, 7th July 1801.

[2] This statement is a further indication that Buchanan possessed a manuscript copy of Roxburgh's *Flora Indica*.

This place is very fortunate in two such men as Colonels Wellesley and Close. Every person is pleased with them and they are both men of great abilities and perfectly men of business. There can be no doubt of their producing a wonderful alteration in a few years. Tippoo's Government since Lord Cornwallis's war has been dictated entirely by caprice and bigotry and together with depredations of hostile armies, especially the Marratahs, has reduced the country to a very wretched state. Nothing can be barer than this place. On my last day's march of 15 miles, I hardly saw a bush large enough to make a broom. I have therefore little employment for my painter. On the road I got hardly anything completed by him. A most beautiful Stapelia, very different from your adscendens, is the most valuable of his performances."

Another letter of the series, dated Buntwal, 31st January 1801, is interesting, as the subjoined extracts show, because it gives the first indication of the interest which Buchanan subsequently took in the *Hortus Malabaricus*, to the preparation of a much-needed commentary on which he devoted about five years of his life after retirement, only in order that two-thirds of the work should be buried in the archives of a Botanical Society. It is almost equally interesting because of the light it throws on Hamilton's views regarding a subject which was only dealt with by him once again and then in what apparently is the last paper he ever wrote :—

"I got yours of the 4th and 5th instant two days ago and am obliged to you for the great trouble you have had in making the extracts from the *Hortus Malabaricus.* I am sorry that the nature of my visit to Malabar will afford very little prospect of illustrating the work of Von Rheede. It was performed in the middle of winter, when you know how very few plants are in fructification, and I found no native who could or rather who would inform me of the names of plants. The obstinacy of the people of Malabar is astonishing and every man you meet suspects you have an evil design in every question you ask. Without therefore making some stay in the province and breeding up a man or two to collect plants and procure their names nothing [more] can be done than to collect specimens and describe such plants as you find in a proper state.

. . . .

I am informed that a nephew of mine, Robert Hamilton Buchanan, came out in the *Milcil Castle*—Captain Lamb. I do not know in what capacity, but I think it probable in the service, Civil or Military, for the Bengal establishment. I hope you will have the goodness to inquire after him and to show him any attention in your power.

I have no specimens of stones with me, but when I arrive Mr. Fichtel will be extremely welcome to such as I can spare. I must confess myself a great sceptic with regard to the theories formed concerning the present appearance of fossils. My opinion is that we should believe them to have existed from the beginning just as we find them unless the contrary can be demonstrated. In the few cases even when this can be done the agency by which the changes have been produced seems to me very seldom to be demonstrable."

. . . .

Buchanan's practice throughout this survey was to make a stated daily march and in the morning before leaving camp to gather round him the leading people of the neighbourhood, whom he questioned on the various points enumerated in his instructions. During his march and at the places where he halted his own observations were carefully noted, and extensive botanical and geolgical collections and notes were made. The journal of this survey was remitted to the Court of Directors and by their orders was published in three quarto volumes[1] exactly as it stood and not, as it should have been, and as Buchanan had wished it to be, in a digested form. Luckily, he was able to provide for it a well-ordered index.

The Nepal journey was after all only deferred by reason of the Mysore Survey, for Buchanan had hardly returned to Calcutta after the completion of the Mysore journey when he was appointed to accompany the embassy that had been despatched under Captain Knox to the Court of Nepal. Leaving Calcutta during the cold weather of 1801-02, Buchanan proceeded by river to Patna and marched from there by easy stages and with numerous halts through Saran and Tirhoot, collecting and making notes of the vegetation of the country by the way.

In a letter dated 28th January 1802 from Dacca, a small village on the Nepal frontier, which was the last halting place in the Company's territories, where the mission waited till Captain Knox should be joined by some notables from Khatmandu, he asks Roxburgh to send him up a native collector to join the mission. Roxburgh found, as was natural, that none of his Bengali collectors would face the risk of a visit to Nepal and suggested the deputation of his son William, who had lately been appointed Assistant Superintendent of the Botanic Garden, and who was a great personal friend of Buchanan's. Replying from Bassaria on March 2nd, 1802, Buchanan shows how much this arrangement would have pleased him both on personal grounds and because the botanical work of the mission would thus have been greatly benefited. But he feared that for once Roxburgh's influence would not be able to overcome the difficulties that stood in the way. Buchanan's anticipations were correct; young Roxburgh was not allowed to join the mission.

"I shall be very happy if you succeed in sending William, but I am afraid you will not meet with success in the application to Government for the purpose. I spoke to Captain Knox on the subject, who informed me that very serious objections have been made by the Nepal Government to the number of Europeans now in company with him, although they are only the usual number attached to the number of troops composing the escort.

* * * * * * * * * * *

I have taken a particular account of the cultivation in Bettiah, which will be sent down by and by to Government. No buckwheat is raised there. The Canabis sativus grows there spontaneously.

I am much obliged to you for the genus named after me. Lucirero's having given a name to the Roxburghia will not at all deprive you of that fine genus, but should it so happen, there are plenty of your own discoveries to which your name may be given. I had a letter from Smith the other day; he desires to be kindly remembered to you. * * * I had sent him and Sir Joseph four species of Gurgeon under the title of Hopea, which name he seems inclined to adopt.

* * * * * * * * * * *

We have made our entry into the dominions of Nepal and were received near the frontier by many of the principal men of the country with the greatest civility and attention. We have halted after advancing about two miles and political arrangements have occasioned a long delay, but it is expected that every thing will be adjusted and that then we shall proceed towards the capital."

---

[1] *A journey from Madras, through the countries of Mysore, Canara, and Malabar, performed under the orders of the Most Noble the Marquis of Wellesley, for the express purpose of investigating the state of Agriculture, Arts and Commerce, the Religion, Manners and Customs, the National and Civil History and Antiquities in the Dominions of the Rajah of Mysore and the countries acquired by the Honourable East India Company in the late and former wars from Tippoo Sultan*, 3 vols., 4to, London, 1807.

However on March 11th Buchanan wrote again from Bassaria acknowledging a communication from Roxburgh himself 'and a letter from William,' and continues:—

"It is said that we are to advance to-morrow, but we have been so long waiting that I am quite doubtful. A short time must determine, as the pestilential season is fast approaching."

Buchanan's next letter to Roxburgh, dated Norcotera, March 26th, 1802, says:—

"Since I wrote you last we have had a retrograde motion and are now again in the Company's territory, but we expect to move on again to-morrow morning, and in five days march to reach the top of the hills."

Writing from Chitlong on April 11th, 1802, he says:—

"I have now got above the ghauts and find myself in Europe both respecting the climate and vegetable productions. I wish the people also were like those of Europe."

Four days later Buchanan writes from Tancote, April 15th, 1802:—

"We arrived here yesterday and are in sight of Catamandu in a bare ugly valley resembling many of those in Scotland before the introduction of fences and other improvements."

Ten days later he writes from Khatmandu, 25th April, 1802:—

"I have much professional duty, the country being most unhealthy and wish for nothing more than to be out of it again as soon as possible."

He spent, however, the next fourteen months in Nepal, in the neighbourhood of Khatmandu, bringing together a large botanical collection and making numerous drawings and descriptions. During his sojourn in Nepal, Buchanan was accompanied by a very intelligent Brahmin from Calcutta, Babu Ramajai Bhattacharji,[1] whom he employed in obtaining information of the most varied description, so far as this could be prudently done without causing alarm to the jealous Government of Nepal or giving offence to the Resident, under whose authority Buchanan was acting.

The instructions which Buchanan received before setting out for Nepal would appear to have been much like those issued to him before his visit to Mysore. At all events the information he obtained and recorded was of the same general character.[2]

During his stay in Nepal Buchanan was in constant correspondence with Roxburgh. We know that he despatched, between the date of his leaving Patna in 1802 on his way to Nepal and the date of his return to Patna in 1803, 117 notes or letters and that there are 96 of these present among the Roxburghian letters. The bulk of the communications are however, for obvious reasons, very brief[3] and are entirely confined to botanical subjects. When a complete round of the seasons had enabled him to

---

[1] Babu Ramajai Bhattacharji, of whom Buchanan writes, long after his retirement, in very affectionate terms, accompanied Dr. Buchanan during his subsequent Survey of Bengal and was evidently at all times one of the most trustworthy and respected of his lieutenants.

[2] This information, with information subsequently gained during 1810, when Buchanan lived on the Purnea-Nepal frontier, and during 1813-14, when he was in Gorakhpur, was published in his *Account of the Kingdom of Nepal* in 1819.

[3] The letters sent by the members of the Mission were doubtless often opened and perused by agents of the Nepalese Government before, perhaps even after, they reached the Company's territory, and many of them, as Buchanan explains in one of his letters, never reached their destinations at all. We see that of the 117 sent off to Roxburgh, as many as 21 disappeared on the way. For this reason Buchanan hardly wrote to any one except Roxburgh while he was in Nepal, and deliberately made his letters brief and, except as regards botanical subjects colourless.

exhaust the botanical interests of the valley of Nepal he began to realise that the life at Khatmandu was tiresome and once again expressed a wish to be back in Bengal. Thus, on 18th December 1802, he says:—

"I would write you news occasionally were it proper in a person attached to a political expedition. I am heartily tired of my situation, but hear nothing of my removal"

Roxburgh evidently recognised that this was natural and that Buchanan's talents would be more usefully employed elsewhere. We accordingly find that once more he had interested himself on Buchanan's behalf, for in a letter, dated 22nd February 1803, Buchanan says:—

"I received yesterday yours of the 5th of February. I am much obliged to you for having mentioned my wish to return to M. Malcolm. I wonder it had not been done before from another quarter. The people with you are so dilatory that I suspect the season will be past before my recall comes. However, there is no occasion to trouble his Lordship further on the subject."

The news of his wished for recall reached him on 1st March but before his successor could reach Khatmandu the whole mission was recalled. It left Khatmandu on 18th March and reached Segouli on 28th March 1803. Here Buchanan was relieved and pushed on to Patna, where he arrived on April 4th.

On his return to Calcutta Buchanan took up his old appointment at Baruipur, in the 24-Pergunnahs, as we learn from letters dated from that place in August. One of these, dated 16th August 1803, is so interesting in many ways that it is here given in full:—

"I have been so busy for some time past that I have not stirred one day from home since I left Calcutta a few days after I saw you last. I think my hurry will be over in a few months and among the first visits I pay [one] will certainly be at the Botanic Garden. The Buchanania growing in the Sundurbuns with a dichotomous panicle is called Amor by the natives. The fruit is three-lobed, three-celled and of a coriaceous substance not opening or dividing into valves. Each cell has a large seed covered by a kind of aril much resembling mace. If the plant which has been sent to you as the Pursar is a Buchanania there has been a mistake, for the Pursar is of two kinds—the one the Carapa moluccensis of Lamark and the other a new species.[1] Wildenow calls Lamark's species the Xylocarpus Granatum, which is a stupid name I have got a half of the Encyclopedie Methodique which is a noble work—by far the most satisfactory thing I have ever seen except Jussieu's Genera."

The Marquis of Wellesley, then Governor-General, had formed a menagerie at Barrackpur, for the purpose of bringing together examples of as many species of animals as possible, as part of his comprehensive scheme for investigating the natural history of India. During the cold weather of 1803-04, Lord Wellesley attached Buchanan to his staff as Surgeon to the Governor-General, and confided the management of this menagerie to his care. Buchanan's time was therefore now mainly devoted to zoological studies and was largely spent in identifying and making drawings and descriptions of the animals in the Barrackpur collection.

None of the results of his observations during the two years thus employed appear to have been published, but at least copies of some, if not all, of his descriptions

[1] That there are two very distinct *Carapas* in the Sundribuns is a fact which the writer has found botanists who have not visited the region, for some reason, unwilling to admit. It is interesting to know that a century ago Buchanan was perfectly well aware of their existence.

and drawings belonging to this period are carefully preserved in the library of the Asiatic Society of Bengal.

In the end of 1805, when Lord Wellesley retired, Buchanan accompanied him to England. His habit of observing natural phenomena, we learn incidentally, was exercised as usual during this voyage.[1] During his stay in England Buchanan was able to prepare the excellent index which accompanies his work on Mysore, with the object of enabling readers to understand the Indian terms employed in the journal and in order to compensate, to some extent, for the absence of method in the arrangement of the work.

During this visit Buchanan renewed his old intimate intercourse with Smith. One result of this renewal of their companionship was that Buchanan gave Smith all his Nepal specimens, a gift that was subsequently to be far from beneficial to Buchanan. Smith refers to the transaction as follows[2]:—

"My excellent friend and fellow-student Dr. Francis Buchanan having most generously put me in possession of all his drawings of Indian plants, together with his manuscripts and an herbarium of about 1,500 species collected in his journey to Nepal, I hasten to communicate some of these rarities to the public."

Another result was that Smith took up some of the Perthshire specimens collected by Buchanan in their student days, and described them. Regarding one of these Scottish plants Smith writes[3]:—

"These specimens were collected by Dr. Francis Buchanan in 1782 at Leny near Sterling, his native place. The glen of Leny has recently been celebrated in the beautiful poetry of Mr. Walter Scott, and from these romantic and sequestered scenes a long residence in various parts of India has neither perverted the taste nor weaned the heart of our friend."

During this visit to England Buchanan joined, on 1st May 1806, the Royal Society of London.

It appears that Buchanan's official Nepal journal, and many of the drawings executed at Barrackpur, reached the Court of Directors during the course of this visit to England. The Court were so impressed by the excellence of Buchanan's work in Ava, Chittagong, Mysore, Nepal, and at Barrackpur that they nominated him successor to Roxburgh as Superintendent of the Calcutta Botanic Garden when Roxburgh should retire, and decided that in the interval his peculiar ability as a statistical surveyor should be utilized in making a survey of the territories forming the Presidency of Fort William.

4. SERVICE IN INDIA, 1806–1815.

Survey of Bengal.

Towards the end of 1806 Buchanan sailed again for India, reaching Calcutta early in 1807. The instructions from the Court of Directors with reference to his future employment were issued on 7th January 1807. The Court in their despatch observe:—

"We are of opinion that a statistical survey of the country under the immediate authority of your presidency would be attended with much utility; we therefore recommend proper steps to be taken for carrying the same into execution."

[1] *Edinb. Philosoph. Journ.*, vol. v, 1821.
[2] *Exotic Botany*, ii., p. 73, t. 97 : 1805.
[3] *English Botany*, xxiii., t. 1570 : 1806.

In this despatch the Court nominated Buchanan, on the ground that he had been deputed by Lord Wellesley to carry out the survey of Mysore and had afterwards been given the management of the menagerie which Lord Wellesley had formed at Barrackpur, as the Surveyor to be employed.

In accordance with this recommendation Lord Minto, then Governor-General, appointed Buchanan to the post of Surveyor. Buchanan, who had in the meantime been promoted to the rank of Surgeon (on 20th June 1807), made preparations to begin work, so that when the Government at Calcutta issued final orders on 11th September 1807, he was in a position at once to carry them out. The survey was directed to be commenced in the district of Rangpur and to be continued thence westward, district by district, throughout the Gangetic plain to the north of the Ganges, till the western limits of the Company's territories were reached. This done, the districts to the south of the Ganges were to be taken up, one by one, in reverse order, and when they had been completely surveyed, Dacca and the districts along the Company's Eastern frontier were to be dealt with. At the same time Buchanan's enquiries were to be extended to adjacent countries and to minor states with which the Government at Calcutta had no regular intercourse, though as regards all such foreign territories the information was to be obtained either by cross-examining natives of such countries or states as might be temporarily sojourning within the Company's territories, or from the reports of subjects of the Honourable Company who had travelled or resided across the Company's borders; Buchanan himself was expressly prohibited from quitting the Company's possessions.

For each district Buchanan was instructed to prepare a full topographical account. The climate and meteorology, the history and antiquities of the area were to be described. The number and condition of the inhabitants were to be reported on; their food, their habits, their diseases, the state of education among them and the resources of their poor were to be dealt with. The nature and state of their religion, the number and character of their various tribes and sects; the resources and the influence of their chiefs and their priests; the feeling of these temporal and spiritual leaders towards the Company's Government were all to be assessed. The natural productions of each district, animal, vegetable and mineral; the fisheries, forests, mines and quarries were to be enumerated and discussed. Agriculture in the widest sense, including the nature and quality of the crops grown and the stock reared; the character and conditions of the tilth, as regards methods, implements, manures, means of irrigation and the like; the size of farms and the bearing of this on the condition of the farm labourers; the state of landed property and the systems of tenure prevailing, so far as these affected agriculture, were all to be considered. The progress made by the inhabitants in the fine arts, the common arts and manufactures; the architecture, sculpture, and paintings; the processes and the machinery employed; the quantity of goods manufactured and the amount of raw material and capital available were all to be estimated. Finally, an account was to be given of the character, the channels and the extent of their commerce.

A more comprehensive programme than this was probably never entrusted to a single officer in or out of India, and it is equally probable that no officer better qualified than Francis Buchanan to undertake the task ever lived. For this, it must be recollected, was a *real* survey, undertaken on the spot by a competent observer, not an assessment, by an officer at the head-quarters of a Government, of reports submitted by district officials, but derived, when their source is finally reached, from the often hardly responsible statements of the village watchman.

Buchanan was liberally supplied with everything that was required for the successful accomplishment of his gigantic task, save one. He entered the service of the Company after his thirty-second birthday, and had already completed 11 years of service when the huge survey began. It is therefore no matter for surprise, though it certainly is for regret, that the survey was never completed.

Buchanan's time was wholly occupied in the work for eight years, from the rainy season of 1807 till the hot weather of 1814, and the marvel, when the sustained high quality of his work is considered, is that during so short a period he accomplished so much as he did.[1]

The itinerary outlined in the original instructions was not precisely followed. The survey commenced towards the close of the rainy season of 1807, not with Rangpur, but with the district of Dinajpur, and the examination of this district having been finished early in 1808, Buchanan began the survey of the north-eastern portion of Rangpur, which district then included a considerable part of what is now Lower Assam. By the commencement of the rainy season of 1808 he had reached Goalpara, where he had his head-quarters till the advent of the ensuing cold weather. He then continued his investigation of Rangpur till the onset of the rains of 1809. During the 1809 monsoon his head-quarters were in a house close to the town of Rangpur; this he left, as the end of the rains approached, for Purnea, the district investigated during the cold weather of 1809—10. The rains of 1810 were passed in temporary head-quarters at Nathpur, near the Nepalese frontier, and during his stay here Buchanan made carefully organised efforts to obtain information as regards Nepal supplementary to that acquired by him in 1802—03. When the cold weather of 1810—11 began, Buchanan took up the survey of the adjacent district of Bhagalpur which lies partly to the north, partly to the south of the Ganges. Having finished his work for the season in the southern part of the district, Buchanan fixed his head-quarters for the monsoon of 1811 at Monghyr. When the rains were over he undertook the survey of the two districts of Gaya and Patna, which lie to the south of the Ganges, finishing up his work for the season at Patna which became his head-quarters during the rains of 1812. The seasons of residence at Monghyr and Patna were utilized, among other things, in studying, with the assistance of a Hindu Physician, both in the field and in the bazar, the characters and identities of the various officinal plants of South Behar.[2] Quitting Patna on the advent of the cold weather, Buchanan devoted the dry season of 1812–13 to the survey of Shahabad, the next district to the west, still south of the Ganges. When the rains of 1813 set in Buchanan embarked on a journey up the Ganges to Allahabad and thence up the Jumna to Agra. During this journey he was able to visit and obtain information regarding the Diamond mine at Panna. Leaving Agra before the close of the rains he dropped down-stream to the mouth of the Gogra, sailing up that river as far as Gorakhpur, which district he investigated during the cold and hot seasons of 1813–14.

---

[1] The subsequent treatment of the information he accumulated and the fate of the records he left have been the subject of a good deal of controversy. This controversy will be dealt with further on; for the moment it is sufficient to trace the progress of the survey and Buchanan's movements in connection with it.

[2] This particular work was undertaken on behalf of Ainslie, who was at the time engaged in preparing his well-known *Materia Medica*.

Advantage was taken of his being again near the frontier of Nepal to acquire further information regarding that country. When the rains of 1814 commenced he went up the Ganges by boat to Fatehgarh, where his head-quarters were till the cold weather of 1814 set in. While stationed at Fatehgarh he was able to obtain information regarding the Corundum quarry at Singraula.

From Buchanan's letters to Roxburgh during this period[1] we learn that except when at Goalpara in Lower Assam he was in a country far from inviting botanically. As usual these letters refer mainly to despatches of roots or seeds for the Botanic Garden and are not of very general interest. Writing from Nathpur on 1st August 1810 he refers to Roxburgh's well-known paper on the *Scitamineae* as follows:—

"I am very much obliged to you for your paper on the Scitamineae which was very much wanted and throws great light on the subject. I have just now, in treating on the gardens of this district, had occasion to mention some of the Scitamineae and am happy to have some well-known name to which I can refer though I shall be obliged to differ from you respecting some of the synonames, especially those of Rumph."

From one of his letters to Roxburgh from Monghyr in 1811 we learn that his health was beginning to suffer from the survey work, and in a letter from Patna, dated 10th June 1812, we find that he had made up his mind to visit Europe:—

"I take this opportunity of a boat going with my annual report to send you such seeds as I have been able to collect here. The country is so much cultivated that it is not a good field for a botanist. I am a good deal surprised to find the Cerbera Thevetia with a fine yellow flower, which I think you must have introduced from America, with numerous Sangskrit names and in common use as a medicine. The same also is the case with a red or scarlet flowered sage which I believe you also introduced from America. I send you a small specimen that you may judge of its identity with your plant. I hope you will have the goodness to let me know when and from whence you procured the two plants.

Unless some very unforeseen accident happens, it is my intention, about this time next year, to bend my way towards Calcutta in order to embark for Europe and I hope that I shall then have the pleasure of finding you stout and hearty."

The unforeseen did happen and, as we have seen, Buchanan, instead of coming to Calcutta in 1813 in order to go to Europe on furlough, spent the dry season of 1813–14 in surveying Gorakhpur. The prolonged labour of the survey had, however, unmistakeably told on Buchanan's health, and in place of undertaking the survey of another district in the cold weather of 1814, Buchanan returned by river from Fatehgarh to Calcutta in order to prepare for his return to Europe, not now merely on furlough, but with the intention of retiring.

However, even if Buchanan had been able to carry out his original plan, he would not have been in time to see his friend Roxburgh again. During the cold weather of 1812–13 Roxburgh's health gave way, and at the commencement of the hot season he left Calcutta for the Cape, making over charge of the Garden to Mr. H. T. Colebrooke,[2] an accomplished botanist and a warm personal friend. Roxburgh's voyage extended, however, beyond the Cape to St. Helena, where he arrived on

[1] Only 11 letters for the whole period are preserved in the Roxburgh collection, viz., from Dinajpur, 1; from Goalpara, 4; from Kaliyachak and Nathpur in Purnea, 3; from Monghyr, 2; and from Patna, 1.

[2] Henry Thomas Colebrooke, who, among the many men of outstanding ability whose services it was the good fortune of the Honourable Company to command at the end of the 18th and the opening of the 19th centuries, was by no means the least remarkable, though mainly famous as a scholar, historian and antiquarian, was a true

7th June, 1813, so ill that he had to be left in the island as the only hope of saving his life. Towards the end of February 1814 Roxburgh was able to go on to England, apparently still hoping to regain health and to return to the Botanic Garden.

At the time of Roxburgh's departure the health of Colebrooke's wife was a cause of great anxiety to her friends, and the correspondence between Roxburgh and Colebrooke at this period indicates that both he and Roxburgh hoped that, under the circumstances, the comparative exemption from social duties that a life at the Botanic Garden ensures would 'increase her health and comfort.' Apparently there was at first a marked improvement, but from a sudden illness, which she had no strength to shake off, the unfortunate lady died in October 1814. The blow was so keenly felt by Colebrooke that he decided to leave India, where he had served since 1783, at once, and on 3rd November 1814, he requested Government, as it was his intention shortly to proceed to England, to be relieved from the charge of the Honourable Company's Botanic Garden. Replying to this request on 5th November 1814, Government informed Colebrooke that Dr. Buchanan of the Medical Service on the Bengal establishment had been directed to receive charge of the Garden. A letter of the same date,[1] addressed to Buchanan, who had just arrived from Fatehgarh, informed him that:—

"His Excellency the Vice-President in Council has been pleased to appoint you to take charge of the Honourable Company's Botanical Garden until further orders and to succeed to the situation of Superintendent of the Garden in the event of Dr. Roxburgh proceeding to England from St. Helena."

---

member of the Asiatic Society and a worthy companion of Jones, its founder, for his interests included 'whatever is performed by man or produced by nature.' It appears strange that Colebrooke's biographers, including his son, are unaware of the fact that Colebrooke's last duties in India, from March 1813 till November 1814, included those of Superintendent of the Botanic Garden.

[1] The precise expressions of this letter of 5th November 1814 are important in connection with misunderstandings that have arisen, and that are reflected in various notices of the lives of Buchanan and of Roxburgh, with regard to the connection of the former with this garden.

In more than one account of Buchanan's life it is said that he was appointed successor to Roxburgh by the Court of Directors in 1807. Buchanan himself states, in a paper read in 1821, that the Court of Directors had appointed him to be Roxburgh's successor, but he does not say when the Court did this. The terms of the letter quoted in the text show that the statement is literally accurate, even if the date 1807 be wrong; and though the writer has failed to confirm the date there is every reason to believe that it also is correct. The Government of Fort William were not empowered to make a permanent appointment—when, in 1816, they proceeded to do so, the Court of Directors ordered the Government of Bengal to revoke their appointment forthwith and to instal another officer nominated by the Court. The terms of Buchanan's letter of appointment therefore may be accepted as confirming the statement that Buchanan had at some previous date been appointed successor to Roxburgh. By a lapse of memory, however, which is unusual in him, Buchanan says he took over charge of the Garden at Calcutta on Roxburgh's death. In the *Calcutta Review* for July 1894 Beveridge detects this obvious error only to fall into another, because Beveridge says that 'Roxburgh left India for ever in 1803.' The source of Beveridge's belief the writer has failed to trace; he can only suppose that in some notice of Roxburgh which he has not seen, the printer is accountable for the date 1803, by a mistake that had escaped the proof-reader, instead of 1813, the actual year in which Roxburgh left never to return. As a matter of fact Roxburgh died in Edinburgh on 18th February 1815, so that though Roxburgh was dead five days before Buchanan left Calcutta, he was still alive when Buchanan succeeded him.

One point that does not seem clear, in connection with the whole incident of Buchanan's superintendentship, has hitherto escaped notice. When Roxburgh left Calcutta, Government were aware of his intention to return whether he had on this particular voyage to go beyond St. Helena or not; and even from St. Helena Roxburgh had signified his intention of returning to the Botanic Garden. This letter of 5th November 1814 indicates that Government were not yet made aware officially from London that Roxburgh had been obliged to proceed to England from St. Helena, though they probably were aware unofficially, since Roxburgh had intimated the fact in a letter to Colebrooke from St. Helena, dated 21st February 1814. They had, however, evidently made up their minds to dispense with Roxburgh's services whether he recovered his health or not, since by their order of 5th November 1814 they definitely deprived him of the post he had filled so worthily and so long.

As the state of Roxburgh's health did compel him to proceed to England from St. Helena, Dr. Buchanan therefore actually succeeded to the situation of Superintendent of this Garden.

Buchanan's tenure of office here was brief. His health, as he himself has explained, had been impaired by his long continued exertions in connection with the survey. He therefore carried out his intention of proceeding to England; and in a letter from Government, dated 10th February 1815, Dr. Nathaniel Wallich, who in 1817 was confirmed by the Court of Directors as Superintendent, was informed that Dr. Buchanan, 'the Superintendent of the Botanical Garden,'[1] had intimated his intention of proceeding to England in the Honourable Company's ship *Marchioness of Ely*, and was directed to receive charge of the Garden from Dr. Buchanan until further orders.[2]

When applying for permission to return to Europe Buchanan at the same time asked for official sanction to take with him the whole of his collections for presentation to the Court of Directors. He desired, in fact, to deal with the collections made during his Bengal Survey precisely as the collections made during his Burmese and Chittagong journeys had been dealt with. The only difference was that on this occasion he desired to take them home himself. The Honourable the Vice-President in Council granted the permission asked for and everything had been packed in readiness to be put on board when on 5th January 1815 His Excellency the Earl of Moira, afterwards Marquis of Hastings, who had called for the papers connected with Buchanan's application, made a note regarding the proposal which resulted in the issue of the following letter to Buchanan from the Secretary to Government, dated 31st Jannuary 1815:—

"The Governor-General having communicated his opinion to the Honourable the Vice-President in Council that the drawings of plants and animals which you have lately intimated your intention of taking to England for the purpose of presenting them to the Honourable the Court of Directors are already the property of the Honourable Company, the survey on which you have been employed since your return from England to India having been undertaken by their directions and at their expense, and delineations of the animal and vegetable productions of the country being particularly necessary as references to the reports on the several districts received from you, I am directed to desire that you will transmit the drawings in question to me for the purpose of being disposed of as Government may direct."

---

[1] From the use in this letter of the designation "Superintendent of the Botanic Garden" it is probable that during the interval between 5th November 1814 and 10th February 1815 *official* intimation had reached Calcutta that Dr. Roxburgh had gone beyond St. Helena and that Dr. Buchanan had in consequence definitely succeeded him. As explained in the text Roxburgh had himself intimated the fact privately to Colebrooke.

[2] Permission to return to Europe was accorded to Buchanan towards the end of December, as we learn from a note by Sir George Nugent, Bart., addressed to His Excellency the Vice-President of Council, dated 23rd December 1814, in which Sir George signifies his intention of directing Mr. Assistant Surgeon Wallich, who was under orders to proceed to Nepal for the purpose of joining the army, to remain at head-quarters in order to take temporary charge of the Botanic Garden on Dr. Buchanan's departure. Wallich relieved Buchanan on 24th February 1815. On 11th December 1815, Wallich was directed to make over charge to Dr. James Hare, who on that date was appointed Superintendent by the Government at Calcutta. Hare did not relieve Wallich till 20th April 1816. He was himself soon replaced by Dr. Thomas Casey, who on 7th December 1816 was appointed Superintendent in place of Hare Wallich was reinstated, by an order from the Court of Directors in London, on 1st August 1817.

On 18th February 1815 Hamilton replied as follows:—

"I have been honoured with your letter of the 31st ultimo withdrawing the permission of the Honourable the Vice-President in Council for sending to the Honourable Court of Directors such drawings of natural productions as have been made at the public expense and desiring me to deliver them to you, which I have accordingly done by the bearer. I hope you will have the goodness to return a receipt annexed to the accompanying list. I request that you will be pleased to represent to the Honourable the Vice-President in Council that upon examination it will, I am persuaded, be found that the drawings in question are little, if at all, calculated to explain the reports which I have delivered to Government, all of which were accompanied by such of the drawings made at the public expense as appeared to me likely to elucidate the subject. Have the goodness also to represent that my object in requesting that I might be permitted to present the drawings to the Court of Directors did not originate in a view of claiming the merit of making a present to the Company of its own property, but arose from a conviction that their being deposited in the collection at the India house was the most probable means of rendering them useful to science. I am persuaded that they will be found of little use to natural history unless they were accompanied by the descriptions which it was my intention to have prepared; but accompanied by these and open to the inspection of naturalists with the liberality shown at the Honourable Company's collections they no doubt would contribute to render the Natural History of India more complete. While, however, I am deprived of that access to the drawings and of the means of elucidating my descriptions by their use, which I would have enjoyed had they been deposited in the Honourable Company's collection, I shall probably be altogether deterred from wasting my little remaining time on the labour of descriptions, always imperfect without the elucidation of engravings."

Two days later, in a letter to Government, dated 20th February 1815, with which he forwarded his Statistical Report on the district of Gorakhpur, Buchanan said:—

"I now return by the bearer the papers and drawings which were collected at the menagerie, and which I obtained from your office by order of Lord Minto, as an assistance in my investigation of the Natural History of India. I hope you will be pleased to acknowledge their receipt."

Buchanan made over charge of the garden to Wallich on 23rd February 1815, and embarked that evening carrying with him, as we gather from his later writings, no very pleasant memory of this incident marking his last days in India.[1]

As mementos of his Superintendentship two of Buchanan's official letters are given here in full. They are selected because they refer to matters that are of as much interest to-day as they were when the letters were written.

The first letter, dated 16th December 1814, deals with *Boehmeria nivea*—China grass, Ramia or Rhea, names that are now familiar but that were all quite unknown in India ninety years ago. Evidently, however, the article itself, and the difficulties connected with it, were very well understood even then.

"I have this day sent to the sub-export Warehouse-keeper two bales of Caloee hemp packed in gunny and marked "Caloee for the H. C. of D." containing 185 lbs. each and request that the necessary orders may be given for their being sent by one of the ships of the present season.

I beg leave to mention that the Caloee plant is by no means a new species of *Urtica* as Dr. Roxburgh supposed. It is the *Urtica nivea* of Willdenow, and the *Ranesum majus* of Rumphius' *Flora Amboinensis*, volume 5th, table 79, figure 1st. The plant, under the name of Kankora, has from

[1] In *Trans. Roy. Soc. Edinb.* x. 186 (1821) Buchanan refers to the incident as an ill-judged act of authority unworthy of the character of the Marquis of Hastings.

time immemorial been cultivated in the Dinajpur and Ronggopur districts of Bengal, and its fibres are used for a few purposes that require great strength with little thickness, but the expense of cleaning the fibrous part has always prevented it from coming into general use, so that the fishermen of the above-mentioned districts, even for their nets, use the *Crotolaria juncea* or Sun. As Dr. Roxburgh has in vain made every exertion to discover means for reducing the trouble of cleaning the fibres of this plant, I consider as groundless the expectation of its turning out of general use, and unless I receive further instructions to the purpose, shall direct the cultivation and cleaning of the plant to be abandoned as an unnecessary expense."

The next letter, dated 22nd February 1815, on the subject of the Rules for the Regulation of the Botanic Garden, is the last official communication from Buchanan before he left India.

"On taking charge of this Garden it was my wish to afford every accommodation to those whose curiosity might induce them to visit the place. For this purpose I directed that no gentleman nor lady, who chose to come, might be interrupted, in full confidence that such persons would avoid doing any voluntary injury. In order to prevent such injuries as might arise from inadvertency, I directed a book to be shown to each party, in which it was requested that no person should pluck either flowers or fruit. If they wanted either, application should be made to the nurseryman, who was directed to furnish all persons that applied with whatever could be spared without injury. These measures, I am sorry to say, have not answered my expectations. On one occasion I observed some ladies who ran upon the borders and broke various plants for their flowers, and I am informed that another, notwithstanding the remonstrances of the gardener, tore up a plant, of which only one individual existed in the garden, and had been reared with great difficulty.

It would give me great uneasiness that on account of the misconduct of a few individuals many respectable persons should be deprived of an innocent and perhaps instructive recreation, and I beg leave to suggest that the inconsiderate may be deterred from injuring the garden by an order published by Government directing the Superintendent to report the names of any persons, who in future visits to the garden may assume unbecoming liberties; the publication of such persons' names with an order for any party, in which they may be, to be prevented from visiting the garden, or even a private reprimand, would probably deter the most thoughtless from doing any considerable injury."

On the way to England the *Marchioness of Ely* made a sufficiently long stay at Galle to enable Buchanan to make a cursory examination of the vegetation there, and to provide him with material for a subsequent note on the Vanderon monkey.

Except for the account of the Mysore journey, which was issued without reference to the author and without the editorial attention he had himself wished to give it, very little of Buchanan's work was published during his service under the East India Company. Articles contributed by him during this period to scientific and literary periodicals include only one short botanical paper and two literary papers relative to his Burmese journey[1] and two short zoological papers written during his service in Lower Bengal between 1796—99.[2] A brief geographical note by Buchanan is incorporated in the account of the embassy to Ava, and at the end of that work there are some descriptions of Burmese plants with which Buchanan's name is usually associated, but for which, if we are to credit Symes, he was only partly responsible.[3] All these

[1] *Asiatick Researches*, vols. v., 1798, and vi., 1799.

[2] *Trans. Linn. Soc.* v. (1800).

[3] Symes: *An Account of an Embassy to the Kingdom of Ava*, pp. 211. 473. London, 1800.

notes and papers were written, it may be remarked, before 1800, and except for the journal of his Mysore journey, the publication of which did not primarily rest with himself, nothing that he wrote was given to the public, after 1800, until he had retired from India and could devote himself to the arrangement of the voluminous memoranda collected by him between 1795 and 1814.

Buchanan's formal retirement took place, after he had reached Europe, on 14th August 1816, with which date his direct connection with India and his lien on the Superintendentship of the Botanic Garden at Calcutta ceased.

5. LIFE AFTER RETIREMENT.

In an interesting article on the Buchanan Records in the *Calcutta Review* for 1894 Buchanan's life after retirement is briefly summarised.[1] He survived his return to Scotland for many years and resided during most of the time at Leny near Callander. He married late in life, had children, and occupied himself in gardening; he published, in 1819, a book of which only 50 copies were printed, consisting of tables of Hindu dynasties extracted from the Puranas, &c., by his pandit. This sketch, though not inaccurate, is hardly adequate as an account of Buchanan's life during the fourteen years which he devoted to rendering accessible to the world, so far as he could, the results of observations made during the previous thirty years.

Buchanan reached England about August 1815. He was apparently at first well received at the East India House, though he seems subsequently to have been indifferently treated. Soon after his arrival he received the greeting from Lord Wellesley contained in the following letter, dated East Cliff Lodge, Friday, September 8th, 1815, in which the feelings entertained for Buchanan by his former chief are shown :—

> "I sincerely congratulate you on your safe return to Europe, and I trust that your native air and a season of repose from labour will soon recover your strength.
>
> It would have afforded me great pleasure to have seen you and to have learnt from so good an authority what is really the present condition of India; a subject in which I feel a warm interest. Whenever you may be at liberty, I shall be happy to see you; if I should be at this place, I can always give you a room and your society would be particularly acceptable to me.
>
> If I can render you any service, I shall be happy to receive your commands; being always, dear Sir, with the most sincere wishes for your prosperity and welfare, and with the greatest respect for your talents, attainments, and integrity, your faithful and obliged servant."

Buchanan's early tastes appear to have been for a country life and his long experience of Indian camps must have aggravated his natural dislike for the cramped conditions of existence in a city. He therefore left London for Scotland with the intention of settling somewhere near Callander and Leny where he appears to have thought of building a house. While passing through London he appears to have

[1] *Calcutta Review*, July 1894. In this part of a careful article Mr. Beveridge thinks that Buchanan might have done more than he did to induce the Court of Directors to make the valuable results of his last survey work available. Beveridge's reference to a letter from Buchanan, dated 8th February 1820, 'in a feeble hand-writing' conveys the impression that after his retirement Buchanan was 'used up' by his Indian service, occupying his waning intelligence with trivialities like garden shrubs and genealogical trees. Instead, however, of discussing what Buchanan might have done, it may be well to form some estimate of what he actually did after his retirement.

arranged for a change of his status in the Linnean Society, of which he was elected a Fellow early in 1816.[1]

As events turned out, it was not necessary to build a house. Buchanan's elder brother Robert, who was, however, younger than Colonel John Hamilton, had died before Buchanan returned. Robert's only son, Robert Hamilton Buchanan, who, as we have seen, joined the service of the East India Company in 1801, was, when Buchanan left India, a Captain in the 24th Regiment of Native Infantry. This officer, Colonel Hamilton having no children, was therefore next-of-kin to his uncle and heir-presumptive to his estates. Early in 1816, however, Captain Hamilton Buchanan died, and Francis Buchanan became his brother's heir.[2] It has been recorded that, when this happened, Buchanan at once redeemed the encumbrances on the family estates.[3]

When Colonel Hamilton succeeded to his mother's property he made Bardowie his home and continued to occupy the Bardowie mansion after his subsequent succession to his father's estates. The mansion at Leny was therefore at his disposal and he was able to offer it, as a residence, to his brother Francis when the latter became his heir-apparent. At Leny therefore Buchanan set up an establishment, and in spite of being in indifferent health he began at once, with characteristic energy, to arrange for publication some of the papers in which were recorded the results of many years of observation. This task, with gardening and forestry to which he was devoted, and with his duties as a county magistrate, filled his time. Though we know of occasional visits to Edinburgh and of at least one visit to London, we find that these journeys were made mainly, if not entirely, subsidiary to what was now the work of his life.

On January 27th, 1817, we find that Buchanan was elected a Fellow of the Royal Society of Edinburgh. About the same time he became a member of the two Societies of Antiquaries of London and Edinburgh.

When Buchanan left India in the end of February 1815 Dr. Nathaniel Wallich was placed in charge of the Botanic Garden at Calcutta. Circumstances prevented the confirmation of Wallich as permanent Superintendent when Buchanan's actual retirement from the Company's service took place. With the object of overcoming the difficulties that had been raised Wallich naturally invoked the assistance of friends and among others wrote to his predecessor Buchanan. Buchanan's reply, which is given below, forms part

---

[1] As already explained Buchanan had been, since 1788, one of the original Associates of the Linnean Society. He attended one meeting, that of 21st January 1806, when in England on furlough. His name was proposed as a Fellow on 6th February 1816; he was elected on April 2nd of that year. He does not appear to have attended a meeting of the Society during his visit to London in the winter of 1819-20, the only subsequent visit to London of which the writer can find any record, so that he never was formally admitted.

[2] The following notes relative to Captain R. H. Buchanan's service in India have been kindly communicated to the writer by N. L. Hallward, Esq., in charge of the Record Department of the Government of India:—

Buchanan, Robert Hamilton; Lieutenant, April 10th, 1801; Adjutant and Quartermaster, February 5th, 1810; Captain-Lieutenant, March 3rd, 1813 (Senior Captain-Lieutenant according to the Register of 1814); Captain (Regimental Rank), December 16th, 1814. Died, at Ghazipore, as Captain, 24th Regiment, N. I., May 10th, 1816.

[3] Chambers: *Biographies of Eminent Scotsmen*. The sum expended by Buchanan in effecting this is given at £15,000 sterling.

of a correspondence with Wallich[1] which continued unbroken till a few months before Buchanan's death. This letter is dated Callander, 4th February 1817.

"I was some time ago favoured with yours of the 2nd of January 1816. I would have answered it immediately had I not intended going to London where I might have had an opportunity of forwarding your views. I have however now given up all intention of ever visiting England and have taken up my abode in the Highlands of Scotland in the vicinity of this where I shall occupy my father's house which my elder brother has given me. I am within an easy day's journey of Edinburgh from whence vessels sail almost every day for Denmark, so that I shall be scarcely out of your way when you return to your native country, and I therefore hope for and expect a visit. In the meantime my situation is so remote from people of influence * * * * * that I can do you no good in that quarter. The Court of Directors has indeed received my collection with such contempt and arrogance that I would neither ask nor receive any favour * * * * * * * * * . My collection would have been received with the utmost thankfulness by the most learned bodies here and might have gratified several of the most distinguished. Do not therefore throw any of your pearls before swine but collect largely and keep your collection for the learned of your own country, who I have no doubt will be thankful.

I am highly pleased with the engravings and descriptions of the Asclepiades which you sent. The workmanship does great credit to the natives and the whole is highly scientific. If you can go on with your Hortus Bengalensis you will ensure your reputation as a Botanist and above all will please our friend Browne. The expense in this country would be altogether intolerable nor is there at present any encouragement for works on natural history so that the first volume of Browne's Prodromus Florae Novae Hollandiae, a most scientific work, finding no sale whatever, he has stopt short.

I am just now engaged in preparing for the press an account of Nepal, Asam and the Gangetic fishes. I remain with great esteem and regard, yours very truly."

Colonel Hamilton, who had gone abroad for the winter of 1817-18, died on January 10th, 1818. Buchanan consequently succeeded to the estates of Spittal, Leny and Bardowie,[2] and in terms of the entail regulating the succession to Bardowie, assumed the name of Hamilton, as we learn from another letter to Wallich, dated 'Leney,' 27th April, 1818.

"I have very lately received your valuable despatch of seeds, which I immediately sent to Mr. Macnabb, who has charge of the Botanical Garden, Edinburgh. He received it with great thankfullness; and as he sends very curious plants which are more suited for this climate and which I am attempting to naturalise in my hills and woods, you will much oblige me by sending him once or twice a year a dispatch of seeds directed for Mr. William Macnabb, Edinburgh, care of John Hanneman, Esq., No. 5 Meard Street, Dean Street, Soho, London, for which you will find it much easier to procure a conveyance than if the parcels were directed for Mr. Macnabb, Botanical Garden, Edinburgh, or to me at Leney, near Callander, N. Britain.

Inclosed I send you a list of those seeds which Macnabb is most desirous of procuring; but whatever else you send will be very agreeable.

I was very happy to see from your signing the list of plants that you have been confirmed as Superintendent, in which situation I am sure you will be both happy and contribute much to advance science. I should, however, have great satisfaction in hearing from you often.

---

[1] Only those letters of the collections are printed here which throw light on the work on which Buchanan was for the time being engaged; they enable us to give almost as complete an account of Buchanan's life in Scotland as we have been able to give of his life in India.

[2] He was served heir on 3rd November 1818. The entries (there are two) are as follows :—"Francis Buchanan (or Hamilton), Doctor of Medicine, to his brother, John Buchanan or Hamilton, Bardowie, who died 10th January, 1818. Heir of Taillie and provision special in the lands of Kilmatrog, the Tiends of Formiston, Quilts, Treen, Little Leny, etc., Perthshire. 3rd November, 1818;" and again :—"Francis Hamilton (or Buchanan), Doctor of Medicine, to his brother, John Hamilton of Bardowie, who died 10th January, 1818. Heir of Line Special in the lands of Burdston and Bothkennar, Stirlingshire. Dated 3rd November, 1818."

By my elder brother's death I have succeeded to his landed property, and have been under the necessity of relinquishing the name of Buchanan, and adopting my mother's name of Hamilton. I have not yet commenced arranging my botanical papers, that science being at present rather unfashionable in this country. I have prepared for the press an account of Nepal which will appear in November; an account of the Gangetic fishes which will appear in January; and an account of Asam; and I am now busy in preparing genealogical tables of the Kings and Princes of India. I find considerable difficulties in residing so far from London where my collections are deposited; but the management of my lands and the healthiness of a country life render, in my opinion, the situation where I now am more desirable. Nothing indeed I detest more than the life led in overgrown Capitals such as London. I was very unwell for some time after my arrival but my health is now completely restored. Please remember me to all old friends that may be talking of me, especially Sir John Royds, Dr. Russell and Mr. Leny, and believe me to be most truly yours."

In 1819, the year which saw the appearance of three of Hamilton's published works,[1] he paid, in spring, as we find from the following letter, one of his visits to Edinburgh; the letter is dated Edinburgh, 12th March 1819:—

"A short time ago I had the pleasure of receiving yours of the 9th October 1817, and it was fortunate that you sent a copy of that of the 25th of July as the original did not reach me.[2] The success you have had especially in procuring plants from the northern mountains gives me the greatest pleasure. I have shown your letters to two of the most eminent cultivators in this country—Mr. Macnabb, who has charge of the Royal Garden here, and Mr. Shankly, of the house of Dicksons & Co., who has a most astonishing collection—I think more curious than the late Lee of Hammersmith near London. Both are eager to participate in the spoils of Nepal, and I am anxious to assist them because they would give me a share of every hardy plant they could rear, and my favourite object at present is to naturalize as many hardy exotics as I can in my woods and mountains at Leny. I hope therefore that you will have the goodness to send seeds of every kind to Mr. Macnabb, who has given me the accompanying letter to commence a direct correspondence with you. He will be an excellent correspondent for the garden as being both able and willing to send you plants from all the warmer parts of America and the West Indies. He is a most skillful cultivator and has many of our Indian plants in a very thriving state.

Mr. Shankly being a dealer of course wishes chiefly for ornamental plants with which Nepal abounds. All those from Gosaingsthan I am sure would thrive here and even the greater part of those from the hills surrounding Kathmandu will, I am persuaded, bear our winters as many of the plants of Japan, Spain and the Cape of Good Hope do. The grand Rhododendron in particular ought to be tried. Mr. Shankly is anxious especially for all new species of Rhododendron, Viburnum, Androsace, Lonicera, Gentiana, Hydrangea, Clematis, Gaultheria, Andromeda, Fritillaria, Caryophyllaceæ, Primula, Lysimachia and Orchidiæ, but there are many others equally interesting, especially all trees from the higher parts of the mountains.

The seeds sent to him should be addressed to Messrs. Dicksons & Co., Seedsmen, Edinburgh, care of Messrs. Menier, Nash and Edmonds, Seedsmen, Strand, London.

In this country there is at present little turn for Botany as a science, but there is a great demand for exotic shrubs, trees and ornamental herbs, with which most country gentlemen have their seats adorned to a much greater extent than was done formerly.

Owing to my living so far from London I find the utmost difficulty in having access to my collection which I consider as in a great measure lost. I hope you will take greater care of yours and never part with it.

---

[1] The *Account of Nepal*, the *Genealogies of the Hindus* and the *Genealogical Tables* that are associated with the second work.

[2] *Note by Dr. Wallich:* "It was sent by the missing *Atlas* in 1817."

If ever you come to this part of the world it will give me great satisfaction to know Mrs. Wallich to whom in the meantime I beg to offer my best respects and you will much oblige me by remembering me to Colonel Mackenzie, Dr. Russell and Mrs. Robertson as well as to any old friend that you may meet. If you have any opportunity of seeing my old servant Ramajayi Batacharji it would give me much satisfaction to hear how my old people are. I am much pleased with your account of Bharat Singha. Yours most truly."

Towards the end of 1819 or the commencement of 1820 Hamilton visited London. This visit had two interesting sequels. Colebrooke, from whom he took over charge of the Botanic Garden in 1814, obtained sanction from the Court of Directors to publish the antiquarian portions of Hamilton's Bengal Survey journals in the *Transactions* of the newly founded Royal Asiatic Society, which owed its origin to Colebrooke's enthusiasm and of which Hamilton became a member. At the same time Hamilton himself obtained from the East India House the botanical collections deposited there. in 1815. With his usual energy Hamilton began to name and arrange them for issue. In connection with this he took up commentaries on the *Hortus Malabaricus* and the *Herbarium Amboinense*, tasks that occupied much of his spare time for the next five years.

The letter in which this visit to London is alluded to is dated Leny, near Callander, N. B., 8th July 1820. The passage omitted deals with matters regarding the estate of his late nephew, Captain R. H. Buchanan, who had died in India, and does not concern our narrative.

"I had the pleasure of receiving your very obliging letter of 6th December, 1819, some time ago, but deferred answering it until I received the seeds which have arrived safe. I have sown part of these from Gosaingsthan and sent part to Macnabb and part to Shankly. I have also sown part of the rice and sent part to Macnabb. The remainder with all other seeds I sent to the Botanical Garden at Glasgow where there has been lately appointed a professor likely to be somewhat distinguished. Mr. Hooker, this person, is, I believe a correspondent of yours. Should you be able to procure any more seeds from the higher Alps, especially of trees, I shall be much obliged to you for them. I have no hot house and it is hardy plants therefore alone that I can cultivate and an addition to our hardy trees is very desirable, the number of those which bear this climate well being rather confined.

I went lately to London and have got my dried specimens and descriptions, in arranging which for the Company's collection and for publication in such journals as may accept them I am now very busily engaged.

The paper which Mr. MacCulloch took charge of for me has not yet arrived and poor Dr. Wright is dead. When I was in London poor Sir Joseph Banks was quite gone, evidently fast hastening to dissolution. His loss will be severely felt, nor do I see any likelihood of any fit person succeeding to his situation at the head of the Royal Society. Brown refused the Botanical Chair at Edinburgh worth £1,200 a year, so that I suppose he has good prospects in London, I suppose however not equal to what he refused, but he seems to have been unwilling to part with Sir Joseph's library and collection.

• • • • • • • • • •

I beg to be remembered to all old friends, especially to Colonel Mackenzie, Mr. and Mrs. Robertson and the Russells and please present my best respects to your Lady. I remain, dear Wallich, yours faithfully.

Fleming, whom I saw in London, is very poorly. Shoolbred I have not seen for a long time. I hear that he is at Bath."

In 1821 the Marquis of Wellesley, when appointed Lord Lieutenant of Ireland, invited Hamilton to join his staff. However, Hamilton's love for a country life and, though he does not say so, his desire to complete the arrangement of his papers and notes for publication while he had strength and health to do so, led him to decline this kindly invitation. From the letter given below which is dated Leny, 16th October 1821, we gather moreover that, though now in his 59th year, the idea of marriage had suggested itself to him. Shortly after this he married a lady named Brooke, by whom he had two children:—(1) Katherine, who died unmarried in 1839, and (2) John, who ultimately succeeded to the family estates and died in 1903.[1]

"I have had the pleasure of receiving yours of the 23rd March and rejoice at your good luck in having had access to the treasures of Nepal. A great part of what I have done there has been in a sort lost as having been given to Sir J. E. Smith who is rather indolent and not likely to publish any considerable part of what he has. A Mr. Don, however, who lives with Mr. Lambert, to whom I gave duplicates of the collection presented to Sir J. E. Smith, is engaged in publishing an account of them together with those which you have sent, and I believe has both abilities and industry to produce a very valuable work. Whether or not Sir J. E. Smith will allow him the use of my drawings and written descriptions I have not learned. Your offer of joining me in a work on Nepal is very flattering, but I have no intention of taking upon myself such a labour; indeed I have not a single note respecting any of the plants I brought with me from Nepal—Smith has the whole. I believe I shall confine myself to publishing commentaries on the *Hortus Malabaricus* and *Flora Amboinensis*, having a good many materials for the purpose. You have my notes on the latter and I should be happy [to] have from you any new information on the subject and any corrections that may occur to you from further investigation, which in my publications shall be duly acknowledged.

My advice to you as an old man of a good deal of experience both in India and Europe is, along with your search after science, to collect money as fast as possible and, whenever you have a competence, to return to your native country. Already your collection far exceeds what you will be able to arrange and publish. From all that I can learn Copenhagen is vastly superior to London for publishing works on natural history. The expense is much more moderate and works of real science are more saleable. Nothing will pass in London without a degree of splendour which puts the work far beyond the reach of the man of science. Such, to see works of science, must now have recourse to public libraries which contain the splendid works published in the great capitals. Brown's work on the plants of N. Holland, one of the most scientific that has of late appeared, would not sell in London and he was so mortified that I believe he will publish no more of his Prospectus.

I am vastly obliged to you for offering to add to my collection, but I have none. I have given away the whole. You will, however, do me a favour in sending me seeds of anything that you think will bear the open air in Scotland, where I hope to see you on your way to Copenhagen. Between Edinburgh and this your capital is as easy a trip as from Edinburgh to London, and from Edinburgh to my house is an easy day's work, two-thirds of the way by water.

I have sent extracts from your letter to Brewster for the Philosophical Journal and shall send the descriptions of your two new Genera to Brown for the Linnean Transactions by the first

[1] Most of the accounts of Hamilton's life give this lady's name as Miss Brook; the late J. Buchanan Hamilton, Esq., of Leny, however, gives his mother's name as Anne Brooke. An entry in Burke's *Landed Gentry*, for 1900, seems to imply that Hamilton's daughter Katherine was senior to her brother, and it is definitely stated in another passage that the late J. B. Hamilton, Esq., of Leny, was born on February 14th, 1822. As Hamilton himself explains that he was not yet married on 16th October 1821, some error has found its way into Burke's usually accurate pages.

opportunity. I am happy that Sir Robert Colquhoun is a botanist, or at least an amateur. His sister is married to a relation of, mine, and her son, unless I marry, will succeed me in my maternal inheritance of Bardowie, from whence I take my present title in this Aristocratic land.

I have not yet seen Professor Hooker, but shall probably be in Glasgow in February next. Last year when there he had gone on a visit to his relations in England. I do not know what map you mean when you ask whether his has priority. I have written to Mrs. Roxburgh what you mention. I remain, my dear Wallich, yours truly.

I have seen the first volume of the Flora Indica, with which I am pleased. The greatest defect will be found in the specific characters which appear to me often inaccurate. I suspect indeed that our friend Roxburgh sometimes mistook his own plant and took his specific characters from a different one from what he had described. His names also are often grievously barbarous, owing chiefly to his ignorance of the Latin language, and his synonyms very incorrect as he generally quoted merely from the figure, although this I find is a common error among botanists who had plenty of learning to understand the descriptions, which was not his case. The work will however be highly useful and I hope you will make large additions to it; and also amendments."

In 1822 the account of the Gangetic fishes, perhaps the ablest and most finished of all Hamilton's works, was published, and for the next five years the *Hortus Malabaricus* and *Herbarium Amboinense*, more particularly the former, occupied much of his time, as may be gathered from the letter that follows,[1] written from Edinburgh, 10th February 1826:—

"About three weeks ago I had the pleasure of receiving your valuable present of the second volume of the Flora Indica. I had been long in vain searching for it, as it will be of great use in my future commentaries. I have now nearly finished the tenth volume of the *Hortus Malabaricus* and will have completed the whole in the course of the year, when I shall resume the *Herbarium Amboinense* of which I have as yet only explained the two first books. I live entirely in the country and enjoy excellent health. A little business has brought me to this city, but I never visit it except in cases of necessity. The new botanical garden here is on a grand scale, and Dr. Graham, the Professor of Botany, who has charge of it, is becoming a goood botanist, but I do not learn that he is about to publish anything. Dr. Hooker at Glasgow I see frequently as I have a property in that vicinity. He is more active than Graham, but I have some doubt whether or not he will be able to go on with his intended translation of Decandolle's System, a very valuable work, but that would require very numerous corrections. Brown, I understand, has become a very lazy and Smith is nearly *ab agendo*. Don, I believe, is at present the most active botanist about London, but has not yet acquired sufficient experience to render him at all correct. His Prodromus Floræ Nepalensis abounds in errors.

Greville's work on the Cryptogamia of Scotland, going on here, is a most beautiful and correct work, fully equal in merit to Hooker's Exotic Flora, which is saying a great deal for it. Whether any of them pay the expense I cannot say. These two botanists are great friends and their Muscologia, about to be published, promises to be a very valuable production and may tempt me to commence the study of these plants with which this country so much abounds, but of which I am entirely ignorant. I remain with great regard, yours faithfully."

In 1826 Hamilton was made a Deputy Lieutenant of the county of Perth, having been already on the Commission of the Peace for a number of years. In this year he satisfied himself that he was the male representative of the house of Buchanan and

[1] Various letters written between 1821 and 1826 which belong to this series are omitted because they deal only with private matters and throw no additi nal light on Hamilton's life.

took steps to have his conviction legally admitted. The first measure was to have himself recognised as the heir and representative of his uncle, Robert Buchanan of Spittal, and as thus the male representative and head of the house of Spittal.[1] This point established, he presented his *Claim of Dr. Francis Hamilton Buchanan of Spittal to be considered chief of the name as male representative of the family of Buchanan of Buchanan.*

To explain this claim it is necessary to advert once more to the history of the Buchanan family. When Sir George Buchanan of Buchanan died in 1651, he was succeeded by his only son, John Buchanan of Buchanan, who died without issue in 1682. The Buchanan estates, being much encumbered, were sold by his creditors after he died. Buchanan itself was purchased by the head of the house of Graham, and is now the seat of the Dukes of Montrose.

On the extinction of the main line the headship of the house of Buchanan devolved on the house of Buchanan of Auchmar, the youngest of its cadet branches. When the house of Auchmar in turn died out in 1816, the headship devolved on the next youngest cadet branch, that of Spittal.

The house of Buchanan of Auchmar was founded by William Buchanan, son of Patrick Buchanan, younger of Buchanan, by his second wife, a daughter of the Earl of Argyle. Patrick Buchanan was killed at Flodden in 1513, and his son George, elder half-brother of William Buchanan of Auchmar, succeeding his grandfather, was, as we learn from contemporary records, head of the house of Buchanan before 11th July 1526, and was still in this position on 26th January 1594.

George Buchanan's uncle Walter Buchanan, younger brother of the Patrick Buchanan who was killed at Flodden, had a son, also named Walter Buchanan, to whom in 15:9 he conveyed the lands of Spittal. Dr. Francis Hamilton's claim to be the lineal descendant of this Walter Buchanan, first of Spittal, was brought to a successful issue in 1828, and the entry on the subject in the *Index to Service of Heirs in Scotland*, which is dated July 9th, 1828, is as follows:—"Dr. Francis Hamilton (Buchanan), M.D., to his Great, Great, Great, Great, Great, Great, Great, Grandfather Walter Buchanan of Spittal—Heir male in general."

This finding established, as a corollary, the fact that Dr. Francis Hamilton was, as he believed himself to be, the representative of the Buchanans of Buchanan and therefore the chief of the name. To the kindness of Hamilton's grandson, the present head of the house of Buchanan, the writer is indebted for a copy of the interesting 'Retour,' given below, of the 'inquisition' that was held with reference to Hamilton's 'claim.' This document establishes Hamilton's claim to be heir male in general of his *proavus tritavi*, that is, of the great-grandfather of his great-grandfather's great grandfather.

---

[1] *Index to Service of Heirs in Scotland.* Entry dated 13th September 1826; "Dr. Francis Hamilton (Buchanan) of Leny and Bardowie, to his uncle Robert Buchanan of Spittal." As Hamilton, like his brother before him, and like their father, at all events subsequent to 1756, was already proprietor of Spittal, it is clear that this 'Service' was intended merely to establish Hamilton's right to represent the house of Buchanan of Spittal, as being the representative of his uncle Robert Buchanan, his father's oldest brother, who while he lived was the head of the house of Spittal.

Beveridge, in the article in the *Calcutta Review* for July 1894 already referred to, hazards the suggestion that Hamilton's work on the Genealogies of the Princes of India may have led him to think of his own family. There is nothing in Hamilton's correspondence to favour the suggestion.

"This Inquisition was made in the Court of the Sheriffdom of Edinburgh before an honourable man George Tait, Esquire, Sheriff Substitute of the said Sheriffdom, on the 9th day of the month of July in the year of the Lord 1828, by these generous worthy men and faithful to their country underwritten, viz:—John Grahame Dalyell, Esquire, Advocate, Chancellor, James Balfour, Esquire, Writer to the Royal Signet, David Wardlaw, Esquire, Writer in Edinburgh, George Gorse Scott, Esquire, of Suiton, James Gibson Thomson, James Buchanan, Esquires, Merchants in Edinburgh, George Buchanan, Esquire, Civil Engineer of the same place, Joseph Gordon, William Gardiner, James Burnett, George Dalziell, Augustus Maitland, James Cunningham, James Thomson Gibson Craig, and David Cathcart, Esquires, Writers to the Signet: who being sworn say, their great oath intervening, that the late Walter Buchanan, some time of Spittal, who lived in the year of the Lord 1519, son of Walter Buchanan of Buchanan and Spittal, great grandfather of the great grandfather's great grandfather of Francis, lately designed Francis Buchanan, of Leny, M.D., now designed Francis Hamilton of Bardowie, according to the conditions of Taillie and Settlements of the Estate of Bardowie which he holds under the same, the bearer of the presents, died at faith and peace of our Sovereign Lord the King. And that the said now designed Francis Hamilton of Bardowie is the only surviving son of Thomas Buchanan, sometime of Spittal, and brother's only surviving son of his brother Robert Buchanan of Spittal, and as such served and retoured next and lawful heir male in general to the said Robert Buchanan his paternal uncle, who was the son of John Buchanan, who was the son of Edward Buchanan, who was the son of James Buchanan, who was the son of Edward Buchanan, who was the son of Walter Buchanan, who was the son of Robert Buchanan, who was the son of Edward Buchanan, who was the son of the first-named Walter Buchanan of Spittal, who lived in the year 1519: therefore he is the nearest blood relation and lawful heir male of the said Walter Buchanan of Spittal, great grandfather of his great grandfather's great grandfather, who lived in the year 1519, and who is of lawful age. In Witness of which thing the seals of the greater part of those who were present at the said Inquisition together with the King's brief enclosed therein and the seal of the office of the Sheriff of the said Sheriffdom are appended to the presents, together with the manual subscription of James Wilson, clerk to the Sheriff of the said Sheriffdom and clerk in the premises in the place, day of the month, and year respectively before specified (thus it is subscribed) Ja. Wilson, clk.

This is a true copy of the principal Retour upon the premises in the Chancery of our Sovereign Lord the King remaining, extracted, copied and collated by me John Dundas, substitute of James Dundas, Depute of the most honorable James St. Clair Erskine, Earl of Rosslyn, Director of said Chancery, under this my subscription John Dundas Subt."

The last letter of the collection from which those in this chapter are taken, dated Leny, 1st November 1828, is the longest and in one respect the most important of all, for it conveys to Wallich authority, so far as Hamilton was concerned, to make use of Hamilton's botanical collections in connection with the Wallichian distribution. It was written just after Wallich had reached Europe with the large collections made in Nepal, Penang, Burma, Assam and elsewhere, which he spent the next few years in distributing to the great European Herbaria. Whether it bears the interpretation that Wallich put upon it, and entitled Wallich to include the Hamilton plants with his own collection in the actual distribution seems doubtful.

"I am happy to learn that you have fairly settled. Mrs. H. and family are well and join in best regards to Mrs. W. with whom we should be happy to be better acquainted. Before I heard from you I had received notice of the safe arrival of the commentary on the Hortus Malabaricus.

You are perfectly welcome to use all my collections so far as depends upon me, but I have given the whole away. Those at the India House you may, I have no doubt, have free access to on showing this to my good friend Mr. Wilkins who will oblige me much by giving you every assistance in his power to facilitate your works.

The plants I collected in Ava and Chittagong were sent to Sir Joseph Banks with descriptions and some drawings and to these you can have access through Mr. Brown, to whom I beg to be remembered.

Those which I collected at Mysore and Nepal were given to Sir James Smith with descriptions and drawings. How you are to procure these unless they are purchased by the Linnean Society I know not.

I know nothing of the Varnish tree if it be different from the Holigarna as you seem to think. By far the finest varnish work made in Ava is done at a town according to my orthography called Gnaun-u, a large town a little above Paukgan what you call Paghammew. I did not see the process but understood that the ware made even at Gnaun-u is reckoned inferior to that made in Siam. The basis used in both countries is ratan basket work which is covered with the gum and then painted or guilded.

I have considerable doubt of the cotton of Ava, at least of that produced near the Ayrawadi, which alone I know, being superior to that of Hindustan. I indeed admit that it may be rather better than what is reared in the hilly countries surrounding Gangetic India and extending from Rajmahal to Bombay where no doubt most of the Indian cotton is reared, but what grows on the plains especially to the north-west of Dacca is vastly superior and I beg to call your attention to the report which I have made on the cultivation of that kind in my report on the Agriculture of the Dinajpur district, which you can readily procure at the India house. A small portion of the country favourable for the fine cotton extends into the south-east corner of the district and is distinguished by being sufficiently high to escape inundation and by having a considerable portion of strong clay in its composition. The hill cotton however constitutes more than nine-tenths of the produce of India and you will find reports on its management in the agriculture of Bhagalpur. Its great inferiority to the American cotton seems to me owing in a considerable measure to two circumstances: first, the want of proper machines for cleaning it and removing the seed as you justly state: secondly, the injury it receives in transportation in bales very badly secured from rain both in the carriage by land and by water; the Pateli boats especially in which it is conveyed being to the last degree miserable. Nor are those by which the cotton is brought from Surat to Bombay much better, while the manner in which the bales are exposed on Bombay green before they are shipped is truly deplorable. Were these two defects in management remedied the quality even of the hill cotton would be greatly improved and I have no doubt that the fine cotton produced near Dacca is one cause of the superiority of the manufacture, nor do I think that any American cotton is so fine, but then there can be no doubt that the American kinds have a longer filament and on that account are more fitted for European machinery. I think however that if the good Dacca cotton were sent home, which I do not suppose has ever been done, that our people would contrive to spin it and find it superior to any other; and the first experiments to be tried on the subject should I think be directed to that quarter. Although I am inclined to think that there is really only one species of cotton plant, this is to be taken in the sense used by the botanists of the true Linnean school; and by no means supersedes the necessity of choice in selecting seed of a good kind for cultivation. A Crab apple and a Newington Pepin belong to the same species, but you may work to eternity with the seed of a Crab without producing one eatable apple, much less a Pepin. I therefore think that the introduction of the best seed from America of the long stapled cotton would be of the utmost importance especially to try its cultivation on the sea coast in places similar to where it grows in America.

Cotton is not so universally cultivated in India as you seem to think. The quantity reared in the south is very trifling: the great supply there comes from the Marhatta territory in the line east from Bombay as I have mentioned before: and except in the land N.-W. from Dacca the quantity raised on the Gangetic plains is inconsiderable. The banks of the Ayrawadi is another great field, and supplies a great quantity to China. The capability, however, of producing this crop, were there any sufficient demand for it, is enormous, and probably no parts are better fitted for it than the coast and islands along the coast of Tavoy or Tenasserim.

I have already mentioned the two kinds of soil on which I have seen cotton reared: the clay level land N.-W. from Dacca, and the dry soil of the hills surrounding Gangetic India and the Ayrawadi. The produce of the former is by far the finest, but still that of the hills might be vastly more valuable were pains bestowed on bringing it to market. I think however that seed of the long stapled kinds from America should be tried in both situations, and perhaps a careful person should visit the best parts of America and examine their processes and the situations chosen for cultivation and then be sent to India to select proper places and instruct the people in a proper management. I sincerely hope that the people who have sent their cursed spinning and weaving machinery to India may suffer the penalty due to so nefarious an innovation. Were they successful they would reduce the poor people there to the same deplorable state that the labouring classes here have been brought to, that is wallowing one day in the most gross dissipation, and next day starving for want of employment. It is however to be hoped that the want of fuel and of perennial streams will prove a bar to their endeavour, and I hope to see the importers return beggars.

I shall be very happy to assist you so far as I am able with the native names of plants. The best authenticated names that I have are given in the catalogue which accompanies the specimens sent to the India house. The Hindwi and Bengalese names of these were taken down by a native on the spot in their own characters, and afterwards written in English according to the plan given by Mr. Wilkins. In the account of the plants of Ava sent to Sir Joseph Banks you will also find the names written in the Burma characters by a native. The Sanscrit and Hindwi synonyms of the materia medica, which with the assistance of a learned Hindu at Mungger I made there, would afford a great many accurate names, but this collection was sent to the India house for the use of Mr. Ainslie. Whether or not he has it I know not. If you can lay your hands on it the names in the catalogue above mentioned will in general point out the plant meant The names of plants collected in Mysore and Nepal were taken entirely by the ear, an intelligent Brahman pronouncing the words, but much less reliance can be placed on these than on such as were written in a native character. All of the names are however liable to numerous mistakes, among the chief of which is that a native seldom hesitates in giving some name or other to every plant which you meet, although it is probable that with a great many he is quite unacquainted.

Should you see Mr. Tucker please present him with my best respects. He is a person for whom I have a great regard both on account of his talent and heart. I remain, dear Wallich, yours sincerely."

There is no sign in this letter of any impairment of Hamilton's physical powers; its directness and lucidity show that his intellectual powers were as keen as ever. Nor is there any suggestion either in the tone of the letter or in its allusions that it was to be the last. This, however, it unfortunately proved to be. Dr. Francis Hamilton died at Leny, in the 68th year of his age, on June 15th, 1829.

6. JOURNALS AND COLLECTIONS.

As early as 1782, while still a student of medicine at Edinburgh, Buchanan was a collector, at all events of mosses, and was endeavouring, along with his friend Smith, to whom he gave all his specimens, to identify his species, but there is no indication that he kept any journal at this time. On the other hand there is no indication that during the period of his eastern voyages any collections were made, though from his subsequently published papers it would seem that the habit of keeping a journal had already begun in 1785.

With the commencement of his Indian service in 1793 opportunities for collecting presented themselves, and he appears both to have made collections and kept journals during the whole of his Indian career, though, just as in his student days, he made no permanent personal collection, preferring to give away the whole to his friends. Further he appears to have been somewhat chary of collecting duplicates and to have been inclined to rely on good drawings accompanied by field descriptions as equivalent to actual specimens.

Dealing first with Hamilton's journals we find now no trace of any that may have been kept between 1785 and 1791 and only surmise their existence from the occurrence of two papers, published in the *Edinburgh Philosophical Journal* for 1821.

The journal kept while he was attached to the Embassy to Ava, under Symes, in 1795, was never published in full. Two copies of it were made and retained in Calcutta; one of these was placed in the Home office, the other in the office of the Surveyor-General. Both copies had disappeared before 1857;[1] whether the original which was sent to the Court of Directors be in the India Office Library now, is unknown. Much of the information contained in this journal has, however, been made available. The philological, ethnological and historical portions were published in two papers in the *Asiatick Researches* for 1798 and 1799. The geographical portion was communicated to the Surveyor-General and was used by Dalrymple along with the results of the surveys executed by Hamilton's colleague Lieutenant Wood of the Bengal Engineers, in preparing a map to accompany Symes' account of he embassy.[2] A short geographical passage from the journal is given by Symes[3] but the bulk of the geographical material was extracted and arranged by Buchanan himself in 1796–97; it was not, however, published till 1820—24, in the form of a series of thirteen papers, descriptive of maps he had obtained from natives of Burma. This series of papers appeared in the *Edinburgh Philosophical Journal* and the *Edinburgh Journal of Science*.

The journal kept during the survey of Chittagong in 1798, which was undertaken at Roxburgh's instance by order of the Board of Trade at Calcutta, seems to have disappeared. It was submitted to Fleming, who acted as Superintendent of the Botanic Garden during Roxburgh's absence on leave in 1798–99, and by Fleming was forwarded to Government. The historical, ethnological and geographical information it contained was published in a series of three papers in the *Edinburgh Journal of Science* during 1825–26.

The journal kept during the journey in Mysore in 1800–01 was transmitted to the Court of Directors, by whom it was ordered to be published. This journal therefore has to be dealt with in the next chapter.

The whereabouts of the journal made during the journey to, and residence in, Nepal during 1802–03 are not known. The information it contained, along with information subsequently acquired on the Nepal-Purnea frontier in 1810 and on the Nepal-Gorakhpur frontier in 1813–14 and embodied in Buchanan's journals for these two years, formed the basis of the descriptive account of the Kingdom of Nepal

---

[1] Yule: *Narrative of the Mission to the Court of Ava in* 1855, p. 263.

[2] Symes: *Embassy*, Preface: Hamilton, *Edinb. Philosoph. Journ.* ii. 90.

[3] Symes: *Embassy*, p. 241.

which appeared in 1819 and which will be dealt with in the chapter relating to publications.

No journal appears to have been kept while Buchanan was a member of the Governor-General's staff during 1803–05 or during his visit to Europe in 1806; at any rate none can now be found.

The great Survey of Bengal during 1807–14 was duly recorded in a journal of the utmost value, which has never been completely published or properly edited. So much of it has, however, from time to time appeared that though the whole will be dealt with from another point of view in the chapter on Buchanan's publications, it may be convenient to enumerate the minor parts that have been issued and state when these appeared.

From the 1807, or Dinajpur portion, a brief extract on hunting was issued in 1829 by the editor of *Gleanings in Science*. From the 1808, or Goalpara portion, Buchanan himself extracted much of the historical, ethnological and scientific matter to form an account of Assam that appeared in 1820 in the *Annals of Oriental Literature*; from the 1809, or Rangpur portion, Jenkins in 1838 extracted and edited, for the *Journal of the Asiatic Society of Bengal*, a history of Cooch Behar. The transfrontier researches included in the 1810, or Purnea portion of the journal, were incorporated in the account of Nepal by Buchanan himself. A portion of the 1811, or Bhagalpur portion of the journal, relating to the minerals of the Rajmahal hills, was extracted and published in *Gleanings in Science* in 1831, while most of the archæological results of the Surveys of 1811–13, in Bhagalpur, Patna, Gaya and Shahabad, were edited by Colebrooke as a series of four papers published in the *Transactions of the Royal Asiatic Society* in 1826 and 1830. From the journal for the rainy season of 1813, Buchanan himself published in the *Edinburgh Philosophical Journal* in 1819 the passages relating to the Diamond mine at Panna. Of the 1813—14, or Gorakhpur portion, all the transfrontier information was incorporated in the account of Nepal, and from the journal for 1814, or Fatehgar portion, Buchanan printed in the *Edinburgh Philosophical Journal* in 1820 an account of the Corundum quarry of Singraula. The India office copy of the Bengal Survey Journal was placed without reserve at the disposal of Walter Hamilton, and much of the topographical and statistical information it contains is to be found in Hamilton's Hindostan,[1] published in London in 1820.

An abortive attempt to publish the whole journal in India, undertaken at Calcutta in 1831, will be dealt with in the next chapter; as will the ineffective endeavour to compress and issue it as a complete work in 1838. The omission of many of the scientific references from this 1838 edition has, however, rendered it necessary for all of the matter relating to fishes and fisheries to be issued as a separate work, which forms a considerable portion of the concluding volume of the *Statistical Account of Bengal* edited by Hunter in 1877. The same cause induced Beveridge to publish, in the *Calcutta Review* for 1894, a series of interesting archæological and historical passages that are neither dealt with in the papers edited, by Colebrooke between 1826 and 1830 nor included in the work published in 1838.

A puzzling feature about this Bengal journal is that we have three distinct accounts of its extent and condition, and that these three accounts are not in entire

[1] W. Hamilton: *A geographical, statistical and historical description of Hindostan and the adjacent countries.* London, 2 vols. 4to. 1820.

accord. As all three are accounts by people who actually have handled the journal, and whose accounts are entitled to equal respect and attention, it is necessary to record them here.

When Hamilton left India in 1815 the journal and its accompanying drawings remained behind in order that the whole might be copied. As we have seen, the last portion of the journal, dealing with Gorakhpur, was handed over to Government only three days before Buchanan sailed. From the preface to the account of Dinajpur, issued in Calcutta in 1833, we learn, from the actual editor of the Calcutta copy of the journal, who had the Indian set of manuscripts before him that—

"The original records, occupying twenty-five folio volumes in manuscript, were transmitted by the Indian Government to the Honourable Court of Directors; a copy of the whole having been previously made and deposited in the office of the Chief Secretary at Calcutta. Duplicates of the drawings and maps were unfortunately not preserved with the rest, probably from the difficulty at that time of getting them executed in India.[1]"

In the introductory note to his edition of Buchanan's *Fish and Fisheries of Bengal*,[2] Dr. Francis Day explains how he obtained access to the manuscript of Dr. Francis Buchanan, so long withheld from the general reader, and goes on to say:—

"His exhaustive work fills twenty-one large volumes of manuscript, besides seven more of tables of statistics, all of which have now been re-transferred from the India House to Hindustan and are at present in the charge of W. W. Hunter, Esq., LL.D., the Director-General of Statistics, who is engaged in utilising the materials they contain.

Irrespective of the twenty-eight volumes alluded to, there are others in the charge of the Asiatic Society of Bengal, but I shall only remark upon two, wherein are one hundred and forty-nine original coloured delineations of fish and forty-five copies. These drawings were made use of for the purpose of illustrating the observations in the Statistical Accounts.[3]"

This interesting passage shows us that possibly the copy kept in Calcutta in 1816 was not arranged exactly as was the original one sent home to the Court of Directors. It further shows that in 1877 Sir W. W. Hunter either was unaware of the existence, or had been unable to ascertain the whereabouts, of this Indian copy of the journal.

Beveridge in the *Calcutta Review* for July 1894 gives an account which has the appearance of having been written with no knowledge of Day's one, and therefore possesses the value of being quite independent. In this notice Beveridge, criticising the statements made in the preface to the *Account of Dinajpur*, issued in 1833, writes:—

"In fact there are twenty-six folios in the India Office; that is, there are twenty-two volumes of manuscript in one press,[4] including a thin volume of statistics relating to Dinajpur and in

---

[1] As we shall see presently, there was no difficulty about this, and the reason for the despatch of the drawings without copies having been taken must have been altogether different.

[2] *Statistical Account of Bengal*, xx. 1877.

[3] It will be shown presently that Dr. Day has here confused two more or less distinct things—the set of drawings intended to illustrate the journal, and the set of drawings meant to illustrate the detailed accounts of the natural productions of the districts surveyed, which Buchanan hoped to publish, and to some extent did succeed in publishing, as ancillary to the actual statistical journal. The main point is that the original journal, arranged as Day describes, was for some time retransferred to India.

[4] The Scottish vernacular term for a book-case or cupboard.

another there are four handsomely bound volumes of drawings, etc. The first of these contains the costumes of Bihar; the second, figures and architecture; the third, maps and plans; and the fourth, inscriptions."

From this we see that the twenty-one large volumes of manuscript which Sir W. W. Hunter brought to India have been safely replaced in the India Office. But of the seven statistical volumes that were lent to Hunter, Beveridge was only shown one; possibly the others are present in another book-case. It is clear from this, too, that Hunter did not bring the four volumes of drawings illustrative of Buchanan's text temporarily back to India.

Turning now to Buchanan's collections of natural history specimens, drawings and descriptions, as apart from his journals, we find no proof that prior to 1785 he did more than collect mosses. The specimens were given to his friend and fellow-student Smith, in whose collection they were between 1806—09, as references in *English Botany* show, and these specimens may be in Smith's collection still.

We have no evidence that collections were made between 1785 and 1793. Drawings, however, accompany one of Buchanan's published papers—that dealing with water-spouts—taken from notes of this period.

During the Ava journey of 1795 extensive botanical collections were made, with a good many drawings and notes. All these were sent to the Court of Directors in London, Buchanan, however, keeping partly coloured copies of most of the drawings and a copy of the notes. With the assistance of his notes and drawings he prepared an account of the plants of Ava, which was finished by the middle of August 1796. The Court of Directors made over the collection to Sir Joseph Banks, then President of the Royal Society, to whom, as his letters explain, Buchanan also subsequently gave the manuscript account of the plants of Ava alluded to above. Banks, we know, selected—Symes says also described—a number of these Ava plants and drawings for publication in Symes' account of his embassy. The specimens were incorporated in Banks' herbarium, so that all of them should now be in the British Museum (Natural History) collection.

Buchanan's period of residence at Puttahaut (Luckipur) was largely occupied in zoological research. He kept on his old artist to make drawings, chiefly of fishes. In some instances he was evidently unable to preserve his zoological specimens and had to be satisfied with drawings, but it appears that of some, if not all, the fishes, specimens were preserved in spirits.

The botanical collection made during the visit to Chittagong in 1798 was sent to the Court of Directors and the specimens, as in the case of the Ava ones, were by them made over to Sir Joseph Banks. These specimens should therefore also be, with the other Banksian collections, in the British (Natural History) Museum.

Owing to Roxburgh's absence from India, the stay at Baruipur and the journeys in the Sundribuns during 1798 and 1799 were not utilized in making a botanical collection, but drawings and descriptions were obtained as usual. These were sent to Buchanan's friend Smith, in whose collection they ought still to be. The lull in his botanical activity was compensated for by increased devotion to the collecting, drawing and describing of fishes.

During the Mysore journey considerable mineralogical and geological collections were made. The bulk of these were presented to Lord Wellesley, who subsequently placed them in the Library of the Company in Leadenhall Street, but some were apparently given to Mr. Fichtel, a mutual acquaintance of Roxburgh and Buchanan. There is no indication that Buchanan made any zoological collection at this time, but a very considerable herbarium was formed and many drawings and descriptions were prepared. This particular collection was greatly damaged owing to the carelessness of the parties entrusted with its conveyance from the vessel, in which it had come from Madras, to Calcutta. Such as it was, however, it was given, along with the drawings, to Smith. How, exactly, it happened that the Court of Directors consented to its being given to Smith and not to Banks the writer has been unable to discover. It was, as we learn from the preface to the Mysore journal, Buchanan's intention to have published some, if not all, of these drawings in a botanical appendix to the journal. The publishers were, however, unable to incur the cost of the plates and only one of the drawings, with its corresponding description, was ever published.[1]

A large herbarium was accumulated during the journey to and residence in Nepal; numerous drawings and many descriptions were also made. The whole collection was made over to Smith who explains that Buchanan gave him 1,500 specimens with all his drawings and all his descriptions.[2] The drawings, according to Britten and Boulger,[3] were 400 in number. Of this fine collection Smith published only 12 species, with Buchanan's drawings, in *Exotic Botany*, and some others, without drawings, in Rees' *Cyclopædia*. A duplicate set of the specimens of this collection, as complete as Buchanan could make it, was given to another botanical friend, Lambert. This set was put to greater use than Smith put the original set, because it formed, along with Wallich's earlier, or 1819, Nepalese collections, the basis of D. Don's *Prodromus Floræ Nepalensis*. From Buchanan's letters we gather that he had hoped that Don might be able to consult the fuller original set of specimens and the drawings and descriptions he had given to Smith, but from Don's preface we learn that in preparing the *Prodromus* he was entirely restricted to the use of the less perfect Lambertian collection. This doubtless to some extent explains the fact that, as Buchanan tells us, Don's work abounds with errors. The fine original collection given to Smith should still be in Smith's herbarium; if not there, the authorities in charge of the Linnean Society's collection should be able to say where it now is. The fate of the duplicate collection which formed part of Lambert's collection is one of the minor tragedies with which the history of botany is replete. The fact of its having formed the basis of the *Prodromus Floræ Nepalensis* converted its specimens into types of the species that Don had described and thus rendered it priceless. Yet, when the Lambert collection was dispersed, and the bulk of Lambert's plants were purchased by Decaisne and other botanists in charge of the large national collections in Europe, the packages of Nepalese plants provoked no competition and bundle after bundle fell to Mr. Pamplin for quite trifling sums. Even for Mr. Pamplin the adventure proved unfortunate, for there is no record of his ever having been able to resell them, and they appear now to be irretrievably lost. At all events the writer, who has been endeavouring for

[1] *Exotic Botany* ii. t. 119, 1805, where Smith published Buchanan's figure and edited Buchanan's description of, and his notes regarding *Utricularia reticulata*.

[2] *Exotic Botany* ii, p. 73. The gift of this collection to Smith had consequences, which Buchanan appears not to have foreseen.

[3] *Biographical Index of British and Irish Botanists*, p. 76.

12 years to ascertain the whereabouts of this invaluable collection, can find no trace of it.[1]

There is no record of any natural history specimens having been preserved while Buchanan was in charge of the menagerie at Barrackpur in 1803-05, but many drawings and descriptions were prepared. These were lent to Buchanan, by order of Lord Minto, when he began the survey of Bengal in 1807, and were duly returned by him to Government, on 20th February 1815, when handing in the manuscript of his report regarding Gorakhpur, the last of the districts that he had surveyed. The manuscripts and the drawings are now in the library of the Asiatic Society of Bengal where they appear to have been deposited in or about 1839. Their history has, since 25th February 1815, become blended with that of the collections, drawings and descriptions relative to the great survey of Bengal.

From Buchanan's letters to Roxburgh we know that except during his stay at Goalpara in 1808, and except for what he was able to obtain by means of native collectors despatched across the Nepalese frontier in 1810 and again in 1813-14, he did not find it possible to make large botanical collections. Still the total number of specimens obtained during the seven years of survey was very respectable, because the manuscript catalogue of the collection, that he succeeded in making in 1822, reaches 2599 numbers. We know, too, that he made drawings and descriptions, and from the evidence of the native artists whom he employed, which was submitted to Government, in connection with an order received from the Court of Directors early in 1816, we learn that the preparation of these was undertaken with Buchanan's usual method and forethought. The artists he employed, who had previously been in the employment of Roxburgh, and had in fact been provided by him, assured Dr. Hare, who superseded Wallich as Superintendent of the Botanic Garden in April 1816, that they were directed to make drawings only of such plants as had not already been figured by Roxburgh. It is equally certain that his drawings and descriptions of animals were similarly restricted to species not previously dealt with by himself at Barrackpur; to ensure this being so, he borrowed these Barrackpur drawings. The drawings and descriptions of fishes were similarly altogether supplementary to those made by himself when stationed at Puttahaut and Baruipur; these latter drawings were of course his own private property and remained in his own custody during the survey; after he reached Europe, they were utilised subsequently in illustrating his account of the Gangetic fishes. Whatever the details as regards these survey period drawings may have been, we know that after asking for and obtaining permission to take all these collections with their drawings and descriptions home to the Court of Directors, Buchanan was

---

[1] For the benefit of workers who, like himself, may have occasion at times to deal with the species first described by D. Don in the *Prodromus* it may be here mentioned that even as regards Wallich's specimens there is a way out of the difficulty created by the loss of Lambert's Nepal collection. Sets corresponding to the lost one which Wallich gave to Lambert were given to Mr. A. P. DeCandolle and to Professor Hornemann so that a journey to Geneva or Copenhagen should afford an opportunity of consulting actual duplicates of Wallich's missing plants. The reason for the neglect of this particular collection was largely personal dislike for Don. The excuse was that Wallich had in the meantime distributed the great E. I. C. Herbarium which included in it all Wallich's Nepal plants. This was doubtless true. But the difficulty is that Wallich and the friends who assisted him in distributing his magnificent collection between 1828—32 omitted to go back on what had already been done, and the treatment accorded to the Nepalese portion of this distribution is often somewhat different from that of Wallich himself in 1819 and his little reference to what Don did or said between 1822 and 1825.

deprived of the drawings relating to natural history a few days before he sailed. He was not, as the letter of 31st January 1815 shows, asked to give up anything except those drawings that dealt with animal and vegetable productions, and there is no indication that he did give up anything else. At all events his drawings of Indian scenery, some of them of a quite spirited character, are still in safe keeping at Leny. That Buchanan felt the deprivation we gather from his letter to Government, dated 18th February 1815, on the occasion of his making over the collection to Government; and from a subsequent public reference to the subject, made in 1821, which from its bearing on an incident that has given rise to some controversy, deserves to be quoted in full:—[1]

> "While preparing for the journey I was deprived by the Marquis of Hastings of all the botanical drawings which had been made under my inspection during my last stay in India; otherwise they would have been deposited, with my other collections, in the library at the India House. By this ill-judged act of authority, unworthy of this nobleman's character, the drawings will probably be totally lost to the public. To me as an individual they were of no value, as I preserve no collection, and as I have no occasion to convert them into money."

How far Buchanan's criticism of the action of the Marquis of Hastings is justified has been much disputed, some agreeing with Buchanan, indeed going far beyond what Buchanan has stated, since they accuse His Excellency of having deprived Buchanan of what was his private property. This latter accusation is perfectly groundless and is as unjust to Buchanan as it is to Lord Hastings.

When, morever, this exercise of his authority is considered, it is necessary to recollect that the Marquis of Hastings was far from being indifferent to scientific studies and pursuits: he had, on the contrary, much sympathy with, and took great interest in, matters pertaining to science generally, as we learn from a contemporary allusion in a letter to Roxburgh from Jannet, then in charge of the Jardin de Reduit, dated October 20th, 1813:—

> "A la requisition du Noble Lord Moira qui a visité ce Jardin en savant botaniste, etc."

and as we know from the fact that the Marquis (then Earl of Moira) accepted the post of President as well as Patron of the Asiatic Society at Calcutta in 1815 and again in 1822.

M'Clelland, who champions Buchanan's cause so warmly that he allows himself to alter what Buchanan actually said,[2] nevertheless admits that—

> "In deciding that Buchanan's papers should be retained in India, it may be presumed that the object was that they should here be rendered more useful to the country than they could be in England. It could scarcely have occurred to the Marquis of Hastings that these works would be consigned to oblivion and the author in consequence superseded by his successors."

It is not necessary to do more than to remark that in the official correspondence the question of Buchanan's papers did not arise; the subject of discussion was such of his drawings as pertained to natural history generally and were moreover already the property of Government. Day, who deals soberly with what M'Clelland treats

---

[1] *Trans. Roy. Soc. Edinb.* x. 186.

[2] *Asiatic Researches* xix, 219; foot note.

rather warmly, has gone carefully into the subject and explains[1] that the drawings were kept in India

"to illustrate Dr. Buchanan's statistical reports on several of the districts and it was proposed to take copies of the originals which were subsequently to be transmitted to England."

This, though given as one reason in the Governor-General's note, was not the only reason for retaining the drawings. It so happens, too, that it was the reason given by his Lordship which was least sustainable. The drawings required to *illustrate* the statistical reports were all already carefully arranged by Buchanan in their proper places and all duly referred to in the body of his reports. As we know, they accompanied from the first, and still accompany, his reports and journal. The natural history drawings which were the subject of Lord Hastings' note were meant by Buchanan to illustrate the descriptions that he hoped to base, after his retirement, on his notes and specimens. They had no immediate reference to, or bearing upon, his reports or his journal as such.

Beveridge, in his account of the Buchanan Records in the *Calcutta Review* for June 1894, thinks that if the Marquis of Hastings' action was dictated by a desire to keep the drawings in India and for the benefit of the Botanic Garden, he was right in preventing their removal to England. We know, however, that the official order was to transmit them to the Secretariat and that this order was complied with. The question of benefiting this Garden, or any other public institution in India, is not touched upon in the actual correspondence.

The author of the article on Buchanan's life in the *Scottish Nation*, more correct in this, as he is in most matters, than the majority of those who have dealt with the subject, has alone divined, or had access to, the *ostensible* official reason; the deprivation is said by him to have been 'probably on account of his (Buchanan) having been officially employed to prepare them' (the drawings).

This was, as we have seen, the reason given to Buchanan himself. But it was not the only reason, and to settle once for all the vague surmises to which the incident has given origin to it is only fair both to the memory of the Marquis of Hastings and of Dr. Buchanan to state, in the Marquis of Hastings' own words, why he decided to deprive Buchanan of these drawings. His Excellency's note, dated 5th January 1815, is as follows:—

"By a letter from Dr. Buchanan received here it appears that he proposes to carry to Europe all the drawings of animals and plants collected by him during the tour which he was employed to make in this country. Dr. Buchanan states that it is his object to request the Court of Directors to accept this collection as a present from him. Now, I apprehend that these drawings are already the property of the Hon'ble Court, the service for which Dr. Buchanan was employed and paid having specifically been the furnishing Government with a knowledge of the animal and vegetable productions of this country, delineations are essentially included in this service, and I am particularly informed that the descriptions given by Dr. Buchanan on his written account of specimens examined by him are so vague and indistinct as to be absolutely useless without the aid of the drawings to which they refer. I therefore beg leave to suggest the propriety of requiring from Dr. Buchanan the drawings in question. From the condition in which his observations have been left the present transmission of them to the Court of Directors could serve no end. They must be

[1] *Proc. As. Soc. Beng.* for 1871, p. 197.

methodized here on the spot by persons sufficiently conversant with this country to avoid error in fashioning them into form. This you will perceive to be an additional reason for retaining here the drawings illustrative of the several subjects."

In this note it will be observed that His Excellency anticipates the confusion of ideas in the statement made by Dr. Day. Two very distinct things,—the passing observations, mainly of an economic character, with which Buchanan's reports and journals are replete, and the formal descriptions, of a purely scientific nature, which were to be drawn up after Buchanan's retirement, of the natural objects whereof his collections were composed—are assumed to be identical. The confusion of these two things on the part of the Marquis of Hastings is quite excusable because his sympathy with science, though great, was after all only that of the cultured and intelligent amateur, not that of the expert worker. His Excellency is by no means the first who has taken an economic reference for a scientific contribution.

To this error, in any case natural, His Excellency was further predisposed by the particular information that Buchanan's scientific descriptions were 'so vague and indistinct as to be absolutely useless without the aid of the drawings to which they refer.' A man of the Marquis of Hastings' abilities and judgment cannot be accused of accepting lightly an opinion of this kind regarding one whose work he had not seen, and whose reputation in the scientific world stood so high as did Buchanan's. His particular informant was clearly therefore some scientific man of assured position, whose opinion was entitled to the greatest consideration. Whether the opinion of Buchanan's work thus expressed be accurate or not, it is not necessary to discuss here, but the fact that the Marquis of Hastings had good reason to trust its accuracy must be admitted by us, as doubless it would have been by Buchanan himself, to justify his action as Governor-General. What, however, does interest us is to ascertain the source of the particular information which biassed a Governor-General of such high character as the Marquis of Hastings against a public servant so faithful and so eminent as Buchanan.

In seeking a solution to the problem we have to reflect on the whereabouts of all Buchanan's descriptions and drawings at the time His Excellency's note of 5th January 1815 was written. These were (1) the Ava drawings and descriptions, with Sir Joseph Banks; (2) the Chittagong ones, also with Banks; (3) the Sundribun ones, with Sir J. E. Smith; (4) the Mysore ones, with Smith; (5) the Nepal ones, also with Smith; (6) the Barrackpur ones, all with Buchanan, to whom they had been lent by order of Lord Minto, and by whom they were not returned till 20th February, six weeks after the note was written; (7) the Bengal Survey drawings, which were also with Buchanan and for which no descriptions had been prepared. With the departure of Roxburgh in 1813 and of Colebrooke in 1814 no one was left in India capable of expressing an opinion on Buchanan's work at all. But, apart from this, no one in India on 5th January 1815 had access to any of Buchanan's drawings or descriptions except Buchanan himself. Clearly therefore the particular information so damaging to Buchanan's reputation could not have been derived from any one in India, but must have been imparted to the Marquis of Hastings before he left England.

Now in England there were two men, and two only, who possessed both drawings and descriptions prepared by Buchanan. These were Buchanan's lifelong friend and fellow-student Smith, who was the recipient of the Nepal treasures, and Banks, to whom the Court of Directors had given Buchanan's Ava and Chittagong specimens, descriptions and drawings, but who had not received a share of the Nepal collections. What, however, His Excellency lays stress on is the vagueness, indistinctness and absolute uselessness, without the aid of drawings, of Buchanan's descriptions. The only descriptions, without the aid of drawings, *arranged for publication* by Buchanan prior to 1815 were those drawn up by him in 1796 for his account of the plants of Ava, the manuscript of which, as Buchanan himself tells us, was forwarded to Banks.

When Buchanan reached London in 1815 he presented all his collections to the Court of Directors, who sent the following despatch, dated December 15th, 1815, on the subject to the Government at Calcutta:—

"Dr. Francis Buchanan, of the Bengal Medical Establishment, who is lately arrived in this country, having made us an offer of his collections in natural history, coins and Hindu manuscripts, which he brought home with him on the *Marchioness of Ely*, we have accepted of the same and directed that the several articles of which they are comprised should be deposited in the Company's library.

At the same time that Dr. Buchanan made us this offer he represented that during the progress of his survey of the territories under your Presidency, which we are informed has now been brought to a conclusion, he made a considerable collection of prepared plants and minerals and that he had employed the painters attached to the survey, when not required in making drawings illustrative of that work, in delineating plants and minerals, also that it was his intention to have presented the whole of these specimens and drawings to us if your Government, after having directed them to be forwarded to this country freight free, had not thought fit to detain them in India as appendages to the reports which he had made of his survey.

As the proceedings of your Government of January and February last (the date of the correspondence submitted by Dr. Buchanan) are not yet arrived, we are unable to form any opinion on the circumstances under which these articles were detained by you; but as it is desirable that the whole of the materials illustrative of the natural history of India which have been accumulated by Dr. Buchanan should be deposited in the Company's library, we direct the immediate transmission to us of the drawings and collections in question, copies of such of the drawings being retained in India as may be deemed indispensably necessary for the illustration of Dr. Buchanan's reports."

The striking feature of this despatch is the inaccuracy with which it is drafted. The statement that Buchanan had made drawings of 'plants and minerals' is an obvious *lapsus calami* for 'plants and animals,' but the statement that the Government at Calcutta detained any 'specimens' or 'collections' is a more serious error. The despatch admits that Buchanan had laid the correspondence before them, and the writer of the despatch was therefore well aware that only certain specified drawings had been retained; it further admits that Buchanan had brought home and given to the Court all his natural history collections. Yet the despatch accuses the Government at Calcutta of retaining, and asks that Government to send home, not only the drawings of which Buchanan had, as the letters show, been deprived, but part of the collections which the despatch itself announces that the Court had already received.

From what actually happened to the drawings we know that they were not kept, as Day supposed, to illustrate Buchanan's reports, and it is not quite a fair interpretation of the facts of the case to say, as Beveridge suggests, that they were retained for the benefit of the Botanic Garden. Buchanan embarked, as we have seen, on February 23rd, 1815, and two days later Wallich, who relieved Buchanan, was requested to call at the Secretariat and take away Buchanan's drawings. The following letter, dated 25th February 1815, was subsequently sent to him:—

"I am directed by the Honourable the Vice-President in Council to transmit to you the accompanying drawings of natural productions, &c., collected by Dr. Buchanan during the period he has been employed on a Statistical Survey of districts in the Lower Provinces, also drawings of the animals, birds, etc., in the menagerie at Barrackpore with the descriptions of them, and to desire that you will take charge of these drawings until further orders."

In the margin of this letter is the following pencil note by the Secretary to Government :—

"My dear Sir, This is the letter which I mentioned to you when you took away the drawings, that I would send you."

The acknowledgment of their receipt by Wallich, dated 26th February 1814, is as follows :—

"I beg leave to acknowledge the receipt of your letter of the 21st instant together with the accompanying descriptions and seven hundred and forty-five drawings of Dr. Buchanan, which the Hon'ble the Vice-President has pleased to commit to my charge, viz.,—

One hundred and forty-four drawings of fishes.
Two hundred and thirty-one ditto of birds.
Twenty drawings of other animals.
Twenty-seven unfinished drawings.
One hundred and thirty-eight drawings of plants.
One hundred and forty-seven drawing of birds of the Barrackpore Menagerie.
Thirty-eight drawings of other animals."

The most interesting feature of these letters is the fact that not only were the botanical drawings of which Buchanan was deprived sent to the Garden, but the zoological ones as well. Moreover, not only were the zoological drawings of the Bengal Survey sent, but those made at the menagerie at Barrackpore.[1] The whole occurrence shows that no attempt was made to utilise the drawings in the manner recommended by His Excellency, and that, although the duty of acting as their custodian was certainly imposed on the Superintendent of this Garden, there was no intention of making them permanently over to this institution.

Further orders were not long delayed. On receipt of the despatch of 15th December 1815, an order, dated 22nd June 1816, was sent to Hare, who had superseded Wallich as Superintendent, along with all the correspondence in the case, calling for a report from him on the subject and directing him—

"to send the drawings in question to the public department for transmission to the Honourable Court of Directors, after having had copies made of such as may be useful for botanical purposes."

In submitting the report asked for, Hare suggested the advisability of his being permitted to copy the zoological as well as the botanical drawings before returning them to the Secretariat for transmission to England. The reply to this suggestion, which is dated July 17th, 1816, says that—

"His Lordship in Council entirely approves of your retaining copies accordingly, and requests on their completion that you will cause the originals to be carefully packed up for transmission to the Honourable Court of Directors by the first fleet of the season."

From this point much obscurity exists as regards the fate of the drawings. The natural history collections which they illustrated went home with Buchanan in the "Marchioness of Ely" and the mistake in the despatch of December 15, 1815, which said that certain collections had been retained in Calcutta, was no doubt pointed out. The note of 5th January 1815 by the Marquis of Hastings, which Buchanan had

[1] There is no indication in Wallich's or in Buchanan's letters that Wallich ever told Buchanan that the drawings were sent to the Botanic Garden, where the bulk of them were useless, the day after he had gone. Probably he did not desire to wound the feelings of his friend.

not seen and which was not therefore among the correspondence handed by Buchanan to the Court when he arrived in England, appears to have also reached the Court of Directors and to have led to enquiries on their part from the authority who had so depreciated Buchanan's work to Lord Hastings. The result was a change of the attitude of the Court towards Buchanan and his collections which, as Buchanan explains in a letter of February 1817, they treated with 'arrogance and contempt,' an attitude which they for a time unfortunately adopted towards his journals and reports as well.

The Court in 1820 so far unbent as to permit Buchanan to take away his botanical specimens and arrange them "for the Company's collection and for publication in such journals as may accept them." About the same time, as we have seen, the Court allowed Colebrooke to extract and edit certain portions of Buchanan's reports. The interesting point is that when Buchanan (now Hamilton) obtained his botanical collections, the corresponding drawings had not reached England, so that the order of the Government of Bengal, dated July 17th, 1816, was not yet fulfilled in June 1821.

Why the order was not carried out the writer cannot ascertain. There is no record that the drawings were transmitted to Government by the Superintendents of this Garden between 1816 and 1821. At the same time it is difficult to understand how orders so definite as those quoted above could have remained unfulfilled without reminders from the Government at Calcutta, or the Court of Directors, or both.

The next reference to the Buchanan drawings that the writer is able to find is the indignant one by M'Clelland of 1836.[1] From the somewhat vigorous manner in which M'Clelland writes, we gather that M'Clelland believed the drawings which Wallich, Superintendent of this Garden, had placed at his disposal in 1833 were the original zoological drawings of which Buchanan had been deprived in 1815. Nor is there anything in Day's careful notice[2] to indicate that he had a different belief. As we see, however, from the letter of 25th February 1815 the drawings made over to M'Clelland included not only the drawings of which Buchanan had been deprived in 1815, but the drawings that were made at the menagerie, and if the orders of July 17th, 1816, was really carried out, the drawings, at any rate of the 1807–14 survey period, could only be copies. If there be any originals, these originals should belong only to the menagerie collections of 1803–05.

The much discussed collection is in the Library of the Asiatic Society at Calcutta at this moment. It consists of zoological drawings only, in four volumes, of which three are respectably and one, marked vol. IV, is shabbily bound. The first contains mammals for the most part, and they appear to the writer to be chiefly copies of other drawings made at Barrackpore and sent to the India House. The second and third are mainly devoted to birds, but though often endorsed by Buchanan they are not drawings of his own supervising but drawings by a Mr. Gibbons; as the endorsements show, they are, moreover, in many cases, only copies.[3] The fourth volume is chiefly devoted to fishes, and is the

---

[1] *Asiatic Researches*, xix., 213. M'Clelland, while criticising severely the action of the Marquis of Hastings, practically repeats the accusation in the case of the descriptions of the Gangetic fishes that the particular informant of the Marquis of Hastings made as regards the descriptions of the plants of Ava.

[2] *Proc. As. Soc. Beng.* for 1871, p. 195.

[3] Some of these endorsements may be quoted :—

Drawings delivered at the India House, 1806. Drawings left at India House, 1806. Drawings of Mr. Gibbons left with Dr. Fleming. Among the drawings of Mr. Gibbons left with Mr. Fleming, sent home, 1808. Drawings by Mr. Gibbons left at India House, 1809. Done after my return to Bengal. Drawings made after my return to Bengal. They are arranged without much order whether as to systematic or chronological sequence.

one which has received most attention from M'Clelland and Day; the latter says that in two volumes there are 149 original coloured delineations of fish and 45 copies. The writer's opinion is that the majority, though not all of the 149, are replicas made under Buchanan's supervision of drawings that in due course found their way to the India House and are the same in the main as a set described by Günther in the *Zoological Record* for 1869[1] as preserved in the British (Natural History) Museum. The obvious copies are possibly the copies that Hare was directed to make in 1816. Whether the drawings from which these copies were made, which are the ones that were ordered to be sent home, did or did not go home after 1820 perhaps might be ascertained at the India Office. As far as the botanical drawings are concerned, we know that though they did not go home in time to be of use for Buchanan in 1820–22, or if they did go home before 1820 they were not given to him then, they certainly ultimately went home, for there is no botanical drawing made by Buchanan in the Botanical Garden now, and the collection there has not even Hare's copies of any of Hamilton's original drawings of plants.

Buchanan's bulky archæological collections went apparently to the Asiatic Society's museum at Calcutta. Beveridge in the *Calcutta Review* from July 1894 has cleared up satisfactorily the story of the disinterment of two statues now in the Indian Museum, and there is a letter from Buchanan, in Wallich's correspondence, recording the gift to the Asiatic Society of four carved stones. One, containing numerous figures of Buddha, was found in the ruins of Rajagriha, the city of Javersanda in Behar; the other three were found near the Kavatiya river in the southern part of Dinajpur.

The manuscripts that are associated in the Asiatic Society's collection with the four volumes of zoological drawings are in two folio volumes, one of which is endorsed by Wallich:—

"Dr. Buchanan's Zoological MSS. deposited in the Botanic Garden in 1815."

The descriptions and notes are mostly but not always in Buchanan's handwriting; they appear with few exceptions to be rough drafts from which finished accounts might afterwards have been prepared. A few are copies of finished descriptions in another handwriting. Some but not all are dated. Of the dated ones, some are from Barrackpore, 1804, others are of later dates up to and including Gorakhpur, 1814.

The existence now of zoological specimens connected with much of Buchanan's work in India appears to be doubtful. Günther states that the types of the fishes to which his drawings refer have been lost.[2] But Day appears to question this,[3] and refers to a passage in a British Museum Catalogue[4] which suggests that at least some of these types may be in the Natural History Museum. The question is one on which the writer can form no opinion.

---

[1] Günther speaks of some of Buchanan's (then Hamilton's) figures being copies of figures by Hardwicke. It was of course Buchanan's figures that were copied by Hardwicke. M'Clelland says, General Hardwicke did this without acknowledgment; but as a matter of fact he did this with the consent of Buchanan, according at least to Richardson; Day thinks with only Wallich's consent. But Hardwicke and Buchanan were intimate friends, and Richardson is probably quite accurate.

[2] *Zoological Record* for 1869, p. 127.

[3] *Proc. As. Soc. Beng.* for 1871, p. 197.

[4] *Catalogue of the Fishes of the British Museum* iii. p. iv. (1861).

The botanical specimens of the 1807—14 period, as we have seen, were taken home and given to the Court of Directors in 1815. They were handed to Buchanan (now Hamilton) in 1820 for arrangement. A duplicate set of the specimens and a copy of the manuscript catalogue were given to the University of Edinburgh.[1] The original set, and the original MSS. of the catalogue, were sent back to London in 1822. When Wallich reached London with the great East India Company's herbarium he had a copy of Buchanan's manuscript catalogue prepared for his use; this copy is now in the Calcutta Herbarium. The corresponding specimens were incorporated among and distributed with the Wallichian plants between 1828 and 1832. A complete set of the plants is therefore present in the Wallichian type herbarium, at the rooms of the Linnean Society. Other herbaria, recipients of Wallichian duplicate sets, have many of Buchanan's plants, but not one of these subsidiary sets is so complete, so far as Buchanan's numbers and specimens go, as the original type Wallichian collection.

In 1808, while stationed at Goalpara, Buchanan brought together a collection of timber specimens for transmission to the Honourable Company's Master Builder at Kidderpore. The history of the catalogue which accompanied these wood specimens belongs to the chapter which follows.

The collections of seeds, roots, or living plants sent to the Botanic Garden at Calcutta during Buchanan's various journeys were extensive. From Ava, as his letters show, more than twenty species were thus contributed; from the Gangetic delta during 1796—98 more than one hundred; from Mysore about two hundred; from Nepal about one thousand.[2] From Assam in 1808 a considerable number of species were thus sent, but from all the other districts surveyed between 1807—14 he sent comparatively few. The reasons for this are obvious; the flora of the districts surveyed, except Lower Assam, is not very rich; Roxburgh and Carey, too, had, between them, already pretty fully explored the greater part of the Lower Provinces and, if not Assam proper, at least a good part of Sylhet. The number of those species that eventually survived and proved to be new accessions to the Botanic Garden collection may be traced from Roxburgh's *Hortus Bengalensis* and *Flora Indica*. From Ava and the Andamans one each are recorded; from the Gangetic Delta in 1796—98 about 20; from Chittagong in 1798 the same; from Mysore and Malabar about 40; from Nepal 70; from the Gangetic Plain during 1807—14 about 20.

7. PUBLISHED WORKS AND PAPERS.

In dealing generally with Hamilton's publications it will be found simpler to neglect the sequence of their appearance and to follow rather the sequence of their inception. This makes it impossible to separate the few that were published while he was still in India from the bulk of his papers, which appeared after his retirement, and in some cases were edited by others after his death. The list which closes this chapter,

[1] Madden: Elucidation of some plants mentioned in Dr. Francis Hamilton's account of the Kingdom of Nepal. *Trans. Bot. Soc. Edinb.* v. 116. As Madden points out, the Edinburgh collection is very incomplete so far as Nepal plants are concerned. This is because the Edinburgh collection includes only the plants collected in Nepal by Buchanan's native collectors in 1810 and again in 1813-14, but contains none of the specimens of the main Nepalese collection given to Smith and Lambert. Madden appears to have considered the Edinburgh copy of the catalogue the original one, which is not the case.

[2] There were 117 different despatches of seeds, rhizomes, bulbs, etc., rarely of fewer than six species, often of more than ten.

however, gives a chronological view of the whole[1] so that the method here adopted, while it lends itself to more satisfactory treatment from the biographical side, can cause no practical inconvenience. Had Hamilton's range of interests been less wide, the papers might have been arranged either by subject or by place of publication, but the advantages gained by such a treatment are more than counterbalanced by the drawbacks incidental to any system of artificial classification.

None of Hamilton's observations during his student days, if the subject matter of his graduation thesis be excluded, have been recorded by himself. There are, however, references to some by his friend and fellow student Smith.[2] A short paper published by Hamilton in 1821[3] records observations made during the Eastern voyage of 1785, and another paper which appeared in the same year[4] records observations on water-spouts made during the similar voyage of 1788–89 and includes a reference to observations made in 1805. This latter paper is one of considerable importance and has been the subject of more than one critical reference.

Hamilton's papers relative to the Ava journey are rather numerous. The earliest of these, an account of the Launzan tree,[5] the search for which is incidentally alluded to by Symes,[6] gives a full description of what Hamilton deemed a new genus, though he did not venture to give it a name till botanists in Europe should 'have ascertained whether or not it be reducible to any known genus of plants.' The original paper was published in 1798 and, when copies of the description reached Europe, Sprengel, reviewing the contribution, endorsed the author's opinion and very appropriately named the genus *Buchanania* in honour of the discoverer.[7] A curious dubiety subsequently arose with reference to the genus that should perpetuate Hamilton's memory among botanists. We find that in a letter dated Puttahaut November 17th, 1796, Hamilton (then Buchanan) had already expressed a wish to have a genus named after him:—

> "As I make little doubt but that the palm will prove a new genus should you be inclined to honour me with the name of a plant I would prefer this, as I have discovered it with some labour and danger."

The palm in question appears to have been the species now known as *Pinanga gracilis*, so that Hamilton's view as to its natural rank was sounder than that of Roxburgh, who was contented to treat it as an *Areca*, and was therefore unable to associate it with one of its earliest discoverers. Later on Roxburgh, as we learn from Hamilton's letters, did give the name *Buchanania* to one of Hamilton's discoveries, the tree known to the Sundribun wood-cutters as Amúr. To this tree, however, Roxburgh in his published works gave the name *Andersonia*, doubtless because he had discovered in the meantime that Sprengel had employed the name *Buchanania* for the Launzan tree. What is odd with regard to this is that, though Roxburgh obviously followed Sprengel in this use of the name *Buchanania*, the editor of Roxburgh's works attributed the name to Roxburgh,

---

[1] In the list in question the writer has recorded all the writings that can be traced by him. It is more exhaustive than any previous list and probably is practically complete, though it is not impossible that some of Hamilton's minor notes may even yet have escaped him. The Royal Society's *Catalogue of Scientific Papers*, usually a safe guide in matters of this kind, is, in the case of Hamilton's contributions, somewhat inadequate.

[2] Smith and Sowerby: *English Botany*: see t. 1590 (1806) and t. 2004 (1809).

[3] Account of an extraordinary appearance of the sea, observed 31st July 1785, in a voyage from Johanna to Bombay, long. 61° 25′ E., lat. 6° 32′ N.: *Edinb. Phil. Journ.* v.

[4] Account of water-spouts observed at sea on voyages to and from India: *Edinb. Phil. Journ.* v.

[5] Description of the tree, called by the Burmas Launzan: *Asiatick Researches* v.

[6] Symes: *Embassy*, ed. 1. p. 437.

[7] Sprengel in Schrader's *Journal*: 1800.

an error[1] that has been followed in most works on Indian Botany. Smith in 1806 proposed the recognition of a second *Buchanania* in Hamilton's genus *Sussodia*;[2] finding, however, between the time that the plate was prepared and the text was printed, that Sprengel had already established a genus *Buchanania*, Smith in the text replaced Hamilton's name *Sussodia* by the name *Colebrookea*. Hamilton in 1796 wrote, as we have seen, a detailed account of the vegetation of Burma which he sent to Banks, to whom the Court of Directors had given all the specimens and drawings obtained during the Embassy. Part of this paper, with the corresponding drawings, Banks selected for publication as an integral portion of the work of Symes[3] in 1800. In the title to this paper and in the prefatory note, for which Banks is responsible, we find no acknowledgment that Hamilton was the author either of the names or the descriptions. The note is as follows:—

"The plants of which the following descriptions and figures are given, have been selected by the President of the Royal Society as the most rare and curious among a copious and valuable collection made by Dr. Buchanan, who transmitted to the Court of Directors an *Hortus Siccus* in excellent preservation, together with delineations of each plant, executed on the spot."

Symes in his preface further categorically states that Banks provided the descriptions. Roxburgh, who knew of Hamilton's manuscript—as a matter of fact extracts from it exist in the Roxburghian correspondence in the library of the Calcutta Botanic Garden—was aware, at first hand, of the true facts of the case, and in the *Flora Indica* consistently attributes the species first published in Symes' work to Hamilton (Buchanan), and not to Banks.[4] In this Roxburgh has been generally followed by subsequent writers; but as Hamilton has nowhere himself claimed the authorship of these species, and as the statement of Symes is precise, the citation usually adopted is technically erroneous.[5]

Two important papers regarding the Burma journey were written while Hamilton was stationed at Puttahaut in 1796, and published in the *Asiatick Researches* in 1798 and 1799.[6] They deal with the languages, the religion and the literature of Burma; they are of much intrinsic interest and bear moreover the marks of previous extensive and critical study. In the paper on the religion and literature of Burma there is a curious and important error, the origin of which is explained by Colebrooke,[7] where Hamilton states that there is a reference to Buddha in the Vedas.

The geographical results of Hamilton's researches in Burma, which were, at the time that they appeared, of very great importance, were mostly published, after Hamilton's

---

[1] This is not the only error that has escaped the editor of Roxburgh's *Flora Indica;* the conversion by the printer of Launzan into Larmzon in Roxburgh's citation, has escaped the notice of the proof-reader and may explain the omission of Hamilton's name for the tree, and of his interesting economic information regarding it, not only from the pages of Kurz's *Forest Flora of Burma* but from those of Sir G. Watt's *Dictionary of the Economic Products of India.*

[2] *Exotic Botany.* ii. t. 115.

[3] Descriptions of Rare and Curious plants selected by the President of the Royal Society; in Symes: *Embassy* ed i. p. 473.

[4] Roxburgh: *Flora Indica.* iii. 142; iii 696.

[5] Here, as sometimes in other matters, law and equity are at variance. As the best means of reconciling the two the writer would suggest that, now that the whole facts of the case are known, the species described in Symes' *Embassy* be cited as of Buchanan and Banks conjointly: *e.g. Heritiera Fomes* Buch. & Banks in Symes: Embassy ed. i.

[6] A Comparative Vocabulary of some of the Languages spoken in the Burma Empire: *Asiatick Researches,* v.; On the Religion and Literature of the Burmas: *Asiatick Researches,* vi.

[7] Life of H. T. Colebrooke, by his son Sir T. E. Colebrooke, p. 261.

retirement, in the *Edinburgh Philosophical Journal* and the *Edinburgh Journal of Science*, in a series of papers explanatory of maps in which he had taught travelled Burmese to record the information they possessed.[1] By this means Hamilton filled the complete blanks that had previously existed in the charts of Indo-China, and fixed even remote places like Bhamo and Mogoung with fair accuracy. The last paper of this series, that dealing with Pegu, which was not necessary for geographical purposes, was interesting in another way; it provided a standard whereby the accuracy of the information contained in the other maps might be estimated. The painstaking work of Hamilton in this geographical study has stood the severe test of subsequent exploration and survey work in a wonderful manner, the only cardinal error into which he fell was the fashionable geographical belief of the time that the waters of the Sanpo reached the sea by way of the Irrawaday. Besides these papers on maps there is a short note on the rivers of Burma, contributed by Hamilton, which is incorporated in Symes' work.[2]

While stationed at Puttahaut in 1796, Hamilton contributed a zoological paper to the Linnean Society which was published in the Society's *Transactions* in 1800.[3] This paper, as we find from his letters, was at first not considered suitable for the *Asiatick Researches*, but when subsequently it was asked for, Hamilton could not give it to the Asiatic Society as he had already promised it to Smith. Another zoological paper, written in 1798, was published in the same periodical.[4] Hamilton did not write any other papers during his Indian Service; his copious notes on fishes, collected while he was stationed at Puttahaut and at Baruipur, were incorporated in his *Account of the Gangetic Fishes*, the publication of which will be referred to further on. The ethnological, geographical and historical portions of his Chittagong journal of 1798 formed the basis of a series of papers published in the *Edinburgh Journal of Science* in 1825 and 1826.[5] The first of the papers of this series, which deals mainly with Tippera, is still our chief authority for that territory; the

---

[1] Account of a map of the countries subject to the King of Ava, drawn by a slave of the King's eldest son: *Edinb. Phil. Journ.* ii. 1820.

Account of a map of the route between Tartary and Amarapura: *Edinb. Phil. Journ.* iii. 1820.

Account of a map of the country north from Ava: *Edinb. Phil. Journ.* iv. 1821.

Account of a map, constructed by a native of Taunu, of the country south from Ava: *Edinb. Phil. Journ.* v. 1821.

Account of a map of the country between the Erawadi and the Khiæn duæn rivers: *Edinb. Phil. Journ.* vi. 1822.

Account of a map, by a slave to the heir-apparent of Ava: *Edinb. Phil. Journ.* vi. 1822.

An account of a map of the Tarout Shan Territory: *Edinb. Phil. Journ.* vii. 1822.

Account of a map of the vicinity of Paukgan or Pagan: *Edinb. Phil. Journ.* vii. 1822.

Account of a map drawn by a native of Dawæ or Tavay: *Edinb. Phil. Journ.* ix. 1823.

Account of two maps of Yænmæ or Yangoma: *Edinb. Phil. Journ.* x. 1824.

An account of the map of Koshanpri: *Edinb. Phil. Journ.* x. 1824.

Account of a map of Upper Laos or the territory of the Lowa Shan: *Edinb. Journ. Sci.* i. 1824.

Account of a map of the kingdom of Pegu: *Edinb. Journ. Sci.* i. 1824.

[2] Symes: *Embassy,* Ed. i. p. 241.

[3] An account of the Onchidium, a new genus of the class of Vermes, found in Bengal: *Trans. Linn. Soc. Lond.* v.

[4] Description of the Vespertilio plicatus: *Trans. Linn. Soc. Lond.* v.

[5] An account of the Frontier between part of Bengal and the Kingdom of Ava; *Edinb. Journ. Sci.* ii. 1826.

An account of the Frontier between Ava and the part of Bengal adjacent to the Karnaphuli river: *Edinb. Journ. Sci.* iii. 1325.

An account of the Frontier between the southern part of Bengal and the Kingdom of Ava: *Edinb. Journ. Sci.* iii. 1825; iv. 1826.

second, which deals with northern Chittagong or the Saksah country, and the third, which treats of Southern Chittagong or the country of the Jumia Maghs, well repay perusal if only because they show how little Hamilton has left for subsequent writers to add.

The Mysore journey of 1800–01, as described in Hamilton's original journal, was published in 1807 at the instance of the Honourable Court of Directors, in three quarto volumes, under one of the exhaustive and unquotable titles fashionable at the time.[1]

As issued the work consists of Hamilton's journal, precisely as it was written, without any attempt at co-ordinating and codifying the enormous mass of varied and valuable information it contains, and particularly without that patient and critical estimation of the information derived from native sources, that makes Hamilton's papers based on his Ava and his Chittagong journals so extremely valuable. It is moreover destitute of the scientific appendices that Hamilton was anxious to add to it.[2]

Its weak points did not escape the reviewers at the time that it appeared, and more recently Sir Alexander Arbuthnot, with whom Mr. Beveridge agrees, has expressed the perfectly just opinion that the work would have been far more useful if the journal had been recast and condensed. There is nothing original in this view, however, seeing that it was Hamilton's own. In the preface that he was luckily able to supply to the work, which was in the press when he reached England on leave in 1805, he explains that it had been his desire to abridge the journal and re-arrange its matter before publication. However, the printing had already commenced before he arrived in London, and his stay in England was likely to be too short to admit of his undertaking the necessary alterations. He did, however, supply an index of a most satisfactory character, which at least renders the work easily consultable, and adds very greatly to its value. The first reviewer of the work[3] sums up the discussion as follows:—

"Those who will take the trouble to peruse Dr. Buchanan's book will certainly obtain a far more accurate notion of the actual condition and appearance of India and of its existing arts, usages and manners, than could be derived from all the books relating to it in existence, but they will frequently be misled as to its religion, literature and antiquities, and must submit to more labour than readers are usually disposed for, in collecting and placing together the scattered and disjointed fragments of information of which the volumes are composed."

From the manner in which the information was obtained, which has been already explained, it will be seen that Hamilton was under the necessity not only of recording all that he saw, but all that he was told. The passage quoted therefore comes simply to this, that on everything which Hamilton records as having been seen by

[1] *A journey from Madras, through the countries of Mysore, Canara and Malabar, performed under the orders of the Most Noble the Marquis of Wellesley, for the express purpose of investigating the state of Agriculture, Arts, and Commerce; the Religion, Manners and Customs, the Natural and Civil History and Antiquities in the dominion of the Rajah of Mysore, and countries acquired by the Honourable East India Company in the late and former wars, from Tippoo Sultan.* 3 vols. 4to. London, 1807.

[2] One of the botanical drawings made during this journey was published in *Exotic Botany* in 1805.—*Utricularia reticulata*: Exotic Botany, ii. p. 119, t. 119.

[3] *Edinburgh Review*; October 1808.

himself implicit reliance may be placed, while, as regards what he was told, it is advisable to keep the open mind that Hamilton himself kept. The summary was therefore fair and just, and fully anticipates the views expressed later by Arbuthnot and Beveridge, though it after all only confirms what Roxburgh predicted when he recommended Hamilton to Lord Clive as the most suitable officer to conduct this survey.

Shortly after the work appeared, an extract from it was republished by Tilloch in the *Philosophical Magazine*,[1] and twenty years later another series of extracts were collated by a contributor to *Gleanings in Science*.[2] A second edition of the work in two octavo volumes was published in Madras in 1870; this is perhaps the best evidence of the importance of the information in the journal and of its value, in spite of its author not having been given an opportunity of revising and, in the true sense, editing it.

The subject of Nepal, a region as to which Hamilton had acquired much information during his residence at Khatmandu in 1802–03, was taken up immediately he retired. The early information had been greatly supplemented in 1810 when Hamilton resided at Nathpur on the Nepal–Purneah frontier, and still further added to while he was engaged in surveying Gorakhpur during 1813–14. The result of his labour was the publication in Edinburgh in 1819 of an account of Nepal[3] which still remains one of the principal sources of information regarding that country. In preparing this work Hamilton was able to give all that attention to arrangement of matter and revision of statement which was denied him in the work on Mysore. The result is a condensation of the corresponding information into something like one-third of the space. Thirty years later a *Blackwood* reviewer,[4] dealing with various works on Nepal that had been published since Hamilton's work and that of Kirkpatrick, of 1811,[5] had appeared, remarks that all these works were—

> "very largely indebted to the Doctor and the Colonel, although their authors very rarely remember to acknowledge their obligations."

The work is a mine of information from which much of what has since been written regarding Nepal has been extracted.

In the account of Nepal Hamilton makes reference to a considerable number of plants, and in Rees' *Encyclopædia*[6] and in *Exotic Botany* some of his descriptions and notes have been reproduced.[7] In the case of *Exotic Botany* these descriptions are accompanied by copies of the corresponding drawings. Don in his *Prodromus*, although he was perfectly well aware that the names and descriptions were those of Hamilton,

---

[1] Account of the manufactures carried on at Bangalore and the processes employed by the natives in dyeing Silk and Cotton: *Phil. Mag.* xxx. 1808.

[2] Machines for Irrigation: *Gleanings in Science* i. 1829.

[3] *An account of the Kingdom of Nepal and of the territories annexed to this dominion by the house of Gorkha.* 1 vol., 4to. Edinburgh, 1819.

[4] *Blackwood's Magazine*; July 1852.

[5] Kirkpatrick: *An account of the Kingdom of Nepaul, being the substance of observations made during a Mission to that country in the year* 1793. London; 1 vol., 4to: 1811.

[6] Rees: *Enclopædia*. Cfr. art. *Paris polyphylla*.
Exotic Botany, ii. tt. 97—101; t. 107; t. 108; tt 113—117.

for some unaccountable reason cites Smith as the authority for them.[1] The practice, for which there was little excuse, seeing that Don not only had Hamilton's names before him, but that Hamilton had in 1819 incidentally pointed out the true state of affairs in an interesting contribution to the *Edinburgh Philosophical Journal*,[2] has been almost universally followed. It is one of the oddities of modern citation that a different treatment should be accorded to the Hamilton plants described in Symes' *Embassy* and in Smith's *Exotic Botany* respectively. We know that in both cases the relationship of Hamilton to the actual publication was identical. Yet in the case of the Ava plants, though Symes tells us explicitly that Banks wrote the descriptions, we attribute the publication to Hamilton; in the case of the Nepal ones, though Hamilton expressly states that the names were his, we attribute the publication to Smith.[3]

The only other paper relative to Nepal that Hamilton issued was a brief account of the Nepalese aconites, which he was induced by Mr. (afterwards Sir) W. J. Hooker to publish in the *Edinburgh Journal of Science* for 1824.[4] This, as it happens, is one of the most interesting of Hamilton's short papers; at the same time it is one of the least satisfactory. He was greatly interested in the question of the identity of the source of this arrow poison, but could get no satisfactory information during 1802–03. When at Nathpur in 1810 he organised a search for the plant or plants by means of native collectors, but unfortunately the men returned too early in the year, and some of the specimens he obtained are still indeterminable.[5] A short field note sent by Hamilton from Nepal is given in full by Roxburgh in the *Flora Indica*. The note refers to *Hovenia dulcis*[6] and, in the first edition of Roxburgh's work, the veteran Carey makes an interesting comment on the vernacular name obtained by Hamilton, which illustrates the risk of taking down names by the ear only, a practice that, as we learn from his letters, Hamilton always avoided where he could do so: the comment further gives Carey's shrewd estimate of vernacular names generally.

We find from Hamilton's letters that Wallich suggested collaboration with him in a new work on the botany of Nepal, but that Hamilton did not accept the invitation. We learn, too, from the same source, that though Don gives Hamilton's name equal

---

[1] Don quotes Hamilton's names or synonyms for all other species, but for those given in *Exotic Botany* he has quoted Smith as the author, in spite of what Hamilton himself has told us; though, even with regard to these species, his citation of Hamilton's name *Sussodia oppositifolia*, which Smith changed first to *Buchanania oppositifolia* and then to *Colebrookea oppositifolia*, shows that Smith was not even responsible for the suggestion that the plant dealt with was a new genus, and that, moreover, Don was aware of the fact.

[2] Notice of the Progress of Botanical Science in Bengal, being the substance of a letter from Dr. Wallich, Superintendent of the Botanical Garden near Calcutta to Francis Hamilton, F.R.S. & F.A.S., L.S.: *Edin. Phil. Journ.* i. 1819. This paper is usually attributed to Wallich! The authors who do this, however, are not quite just to Wallich—the age of self-advertisement had hardly begun in 1819.

[3] The simplest way out of the difficulty is to recognise frankly the connection of both author and editor with these species and to cite them accordingly. Neither Banks nor Smith themselves assert their own authorship, and now that the facts are known, it is advisable to cite the names or synonyms as being of joint authorship, *e.g.*, *Epidendrum praecox* Buch. & Smith.

[4] An account of a genus including the Herba Toxicaria of the Himalayan Mountains, or the plant with which the natives poison their arrows: *Edinb. Journ. Sci.* i. 1824.

[5] Stapf: Monograph of the Aconites of India: in the present volume of the *Annals of the Royal Botanic Garden Calcutta*.

[6] Roxburgh: *Flora Indica*, ed. Carey & Wallich, ii. 416: 1824.

prominence with his own on the title page of the *Prodromus Floræ Nepalensis*,[1] published in 1825, Hamilton in no way directly assisted Don in preparing this work. His later Nepal collections Hamilton named and catalogued for the Honourable East India Company in 1822, but none of the material thus dealt with, and none of the information contained in that catalogue, was utilized by Don.

A very careful review of the plants alluded to by Hamilton in his *Account of Nepal* by Lieutenant-Colonel Madden, based on a study of the text itself, on a comparison of the plants of Hamilton's later collections, and on an examination of the manuscript catalogue given to the University of Edinburgh in 1822, was published in the *Transactions of the Botanical Society of Edinburgh* in 1858.[2]

The majority of Hamilton's other publications deal with the period of his great survey of Bengal between 1807—1814; those that are of a more general character, such as his commentaries on Rheede and Rumphius, his works on the genealogies of the Hindus, and his account of the Gangetic fishes, if not entirely or even mainly concerned with the survey, at any rate include observations made during its progress. The main results of the survey were not published during Hamilton's lifetime, so that for the moment their consideration must be deferred, or only incidentally alluded to, as the scientific contributions relative to the different stages of the survey are dealt with.

During Hamilton's lifetime nothing was published with regard to the work of 1807 in Dinajpur and the northern part of Rangpur. But in 1829 a brief note regarding methods of capturing wild animals in Dinajpur was edited in *Gleanings in Science* by Captain Herbert,[3] and in 1833 an account of Cooch Behar was edited in the *Journal of the Asiatic Society* by Major Jenkins.[4] The full text of Hamilton's account of Dinajpur was issued at Calcutta in 1833 under circumstances presently to be described.

The work of 1808 in Rangpur, which then included a good deal of what is now Lower Assam, afforded material for a geographical, topographcial and ethnological account of Assam published in the *Annals of Oriental Literature* in 1820.[5] This paper is of the style of the accounts of Tippera and Chittagong already referred to, but its existence does not appear to be alluded to in any of the accounts of Assam published since it was issued.

Several short botanical papers were published by Hamilton relative to the Assam or Rangpur part of the survey. One of these, which appeared in the *Journal of Science* in 1825, deals with the genus now known as *Chloranthus*;[6] another, published in the same periodical in 1827, discusses a species of *Garcinia*.[7] A third paper, read

---

[1] *Prodromus Floræ Nepalensis, sive Enumeratio Vegetabilium, quæ in itinere per Nepaliam proprie dictam et regiones conterminas ann.* 1802—1803, *detexit atque legit* D. D. Franciscus Hamilton (*olim* Buchanan) M.D. Societ. Reg. et Linnæan. Londin. Soc. *Accedunt plantæ a* D. Wallich *nuperius missæ. Secundum methodi naturalis normam disposuit atque descripsit* David Don. London; 1 vol 8vo: 1825.

[2] Madden: Elucidation of some plants mentioned in Dr. Francis Hamilton's Account of the Kingdom of Nepal: *Trans. Bot. Soc. Edinb.* v. 116.

[3] Manner of Hunting in District Dinajpur: *Gleanings in Science* i. 374.

[4] History of Cooch Behar, being an extract of a passage from Dr. Buchanan's account of Rangpur (Rangapura) revised and communicated by Major F. Jenkins: *Journ. As. Soc. Beng.* vii. 1.

[5] An account of Asam, with some notices concerning the neighbouring territories. *Ann. Orient. Lit.* 244. 1820.

[6] Account of a plant allied to the genus Piper: *Edinb. Journ. Sci.* ii, 1825.

[7] Description of a plant of the order Guttiferæ, which Dr. Roxburgh called Garcinia pedunculata: *Edinb. Journ. Sci.* viii. 1827.

before the Royal Society of Edinburgh in 1828, on the structure of various *Cucurbitaceous* fruits,[1] we know from an allusion in a letter written to Roxburgh from Goalpara on 13th June 1808, to belong also to this period. Besides these a useful list of timber trees of the Goalpara district, prepared in 1808, was published by M'Cosh in 1837.[2] This list was originally drawn up as an accompaniment to the collection of 90 Assam timbers prepared at Goalpara for the information of the Honourable Company's Master Builder in Calcutta. When in 1828 Wallich took home his large collection, it was arranged that he himself, with the aid of botanical friends, should undertake the distribution of all herbarium specimens. The timber specimens, however, with the sanction of the Court of Directors, were made over to the Society of Arts for arrangement and distribution.

The collection formed the subject of a paper by Aikin, Secretary to the Society, in their *Transactions* for 1831.[3] Aikin, who had access to Hamilton's original list of Assam timbers, decided, for the sake of its vernacular names and its notices regarding the various species, to incorporate it in his general list, indicating, however, in every case the source of his information. M'Cosh, having been deputed in 1837 to prepare a topographical account of Assam, extracted from Aikin's list all the entries that Aikin had obtained from Hamilton's catalogue, and issued them as being a fair statement of the 'timbers of Assam.'

Nothing regarding the survey of Purnea in 1810, beyond what is included in the account of Nepal, was published prior to the posthumous issue of his journal.

Part of the archæological results of the surveys of Bhagalpur, Patna, Gaya and Shahabad is dealt with in a series of interesting and valuable papers extracted from the India Office copy of the reports and journals, and edited by Colebrooke between 1826 and 1830.[4] A paper dealing with the mineralogy of the Rajmahal hills was extracted by Captain Herbert from the Calcutta copy of the journal in 1831.[5] The results of Hamilton's enquiries into the indigenous drugs of South Behar generally, are incorporated in Ainslie's *Materia Medica*.[6]

A paper describing a journey to the diamond field in the Panna State, made during the rainy season of 1813 in connection with Hamilton's survey work, was published in the *Edinburgh Philosophical Journal* in 1819.[7] In the same journal

---

[1] Observations on the structure of the fruit in the natural order Cucurbitaceæ: *Trans. Roy. Soc. Edinb.* xi. 1831.

[2] Catalogue of woods peculiar to Goalpara: M'Cosh: *Topography of Assam.* 1 vol, 8vo. Calcutta 1837. The list of timbers occurs at p. 36.

[3] Aikin: *List of Indian woods collected by N. Wallich,* M.D., F.R.S., *Corresponding Member of the Royal Institute of France and of the Academy of Sciences at Berlin, &c., and of the Society of Arts of London; Superintendent of the Botanic Garden at Calcutta.* Trans. Soc. Arts Manuf. and Comm. xlviii. 439. The list, which subsequently was issued as a separate pamphlet, is by some misapprehension ascribed by Pritzel to Wallich; no doubt the greater portion, but as the text shows, by no means all of the entries were made by Wallich.

[4] Inscriptions upon rocks in South Behar, described by Dr. Buchanan Hamilton and explained by H. T. Colebrooke: *Trans. Roy. As. Soc.* i. 1826; Descriptions of Temples of the Jains in South Behar and Bhagalpur: *Trans. Roy. As. Soc.* i. 1826; On the Sravacs. or Jains: *Trans. Roy. As. Soc.* i. 1826; Description of the Ruins of Buddha Gaya by Dr. Francis Buchanan Hamilton, M.R.A.S., extracted from his report of a survey of South Behar: *Trans. Roy. As. Soc.* ii. 1830.

[5] On the minerals of the Rajmahal cluster of hills: *Glean. in Sci.* iii. 1831.

[6] Ainslie: Materia Medica. 2 vols. 8vo. London: 1826.

[7] Description of the Diamond mine at Panna: *Edinb. Phil. Journ.* i. 1819.

Hamilton published in 1820 an epitomé of the information derived by him from various sources regarding the corundum quarry of Singraula.[1]

Two brief botanical papers, both of some economic importance, and both referring mainly, if not wholly, to Bengal were published in the *Edinburgh Journal of Science* in 1824 and 1827. The particular year in which the notes were originally made cannot be traced from the existing papers and correspondence. The first deals with a plant used in many parts of India in refining sugar;[2] it has, however, considerable scientific as well as economic interest, and shows that Hamilton had come to very sound conclusions as to the relative position of the genera in the natural family *Hydrocharideæ*, a family that, when he wrote, was imperfectly understood. The second, mainly an economic paper, deals with two vegetables in fairly common use in Bengal.[3] These exhaust the list of papers, based on or extracted from the reports and journals of the Bengal survey of 1807–14, that were published prior to Montgomery Martin's attempt to issue these documents as a whole in 1838.

Hamilton's brief visit to Galle on his way home in 1815 provided material for a short zoological note published in the *Edinburgh Journal of Science* in 1827.[4]

At the time that Hamilton was engaged in preparing his accounts of Nepal and of Assam, which were the two first subjects taken up by him on his return to Scotland, he arranged for publication tables of the genealogies of Hindu dynasties and other remarkable personalities, extracted from the Puranas and other sacred writings by his Pandit. These were published in 1819.[5] Only 50 copies were printed, one of these is in the library of the Asiatic Society of Bengal.

As soon as these works were completed Hamilton arranged for publication the most sustained and notable of his zoological works, the account of the Gangetic fishes.[6] In this treatise Hamilton has embodied the observations of nearly 20 years. His attention was first given to Indian fishes in 1796; his studies were carried on with hardly a break till the end of 1799; they were renewed while he had charge of the menagerie at Barrackpur during 1804-05, and were continued while he was engaged in the Bengal Survey of 1807–14. The numerous drawings made at Puttahaut and at Baruipur were his own property and there is reason to believe that copies of the Barrackpur drawings were also at his disposal. Those made between 1807–14 were, under circumstances already dealt with, taken from him, so that the volume of plates accompanying the text is less complete than it otherwise might have been.

M'Clelland says that Hamilton's specific descriptions are so obscure as to render the task of identifying individual species most difficult and uncertain, and implies that

---

[1] Account of the mine or quarry of Corundum in Singraula: *Edinb. Phil. Journ.* ii. 1820.

[2] An account of the Jangi, or Vallisneria alternifolia of Dr. Roxburgh, the plant used in India in refining sugar: *Edinb. Journ. Sci.* i. 1824.

[3] Description of a plant (Beta bengalensis) used in Bengal as a common green vegetable (Olus) and of another nearly allied to it: *Edinb. Journ. Sci.* vii. 1827.

[4] Notice respecting the Vanderon Monkey, or the Guenon a face pourpre of Buffon: *Edinb. Journ. Sci.* vii. 1827.

[5] *Genealogical Tables of the Deities, Princes, Heroes and Remarkable Personages of the Hindus, extracted from the sacred writings of that people. With an Introduction and Index.* Edinburgh: 1 vol. fol. 1819. *Genealogies of the Hindus, extracted from their sacred writings.* Edinburgh: 1 vol. 8vo. 1819.

[6] *An Account of the fishes found in the River Ganges and its branches.* Edinburgh: 1 vol. 4to. With a volume of plates; 1 vol. Royal 4to. 1822.

Cuvier found the same difficulty in dealing with those fishes not illustrated by drawings. But, in a letter written by the late Mr. J. B. Hamilton of Leny, Hamilton's son and successor,[1] there is a reference to an interview with Dr. Günther who, speaking of this work on the fishes of the Ganges, informed Mr. Hamilton that—

> "he always kept it on his table for reference, as he had implicit reliance on it as an authority, for it was the work of one who recorded in absolute truthfulness the results of his own observation and nothing more or else."

While this work was passing through the press Hamilton, as we have seen, was engaged in preparing the catalogue of his 1807—14 botanical collection, which unfortunately was never published, though the preliminary sketch, intended evidently as an introduction to a series of botanical papers corresponding to the geographical series which he did succeed in completing, was read before the Royal Society of Edinburgh on 18th June 1821. In this paper he incidentally summarises his own Indian journeys, and gives a valuable general sketch of the physical, botanical, historical and political geography of India.[2] The geographical treatment was intended to provide a key to the localities he might subsequently cite, and the references to his own journeys were made in explanation of the circumstances under which the different collections were procured, and of the places in which they might be consulted. The necessity for such a key arose from his determination to employ their ancient Sanskrit names for the provinces he had explored. This determination was due to his considering the method at once more scientific and more useful, because probably more permanent, than any other. There is much to be said in favour of his design though it has not been adopted by subsequent Indian botanists. As Hamilton very justly says, the Sanskrit names of localities continue, after the lapse of ages—

> "to be known to all Hindus of learning, while each new invasion or revolution sinks into immediate oblivion the unknown appellations imposed by modern rulers, whether Muhammadans or Christians."

The settled system of Government that has prevailed since Hamilton wrote has made the system adopted by him less immediately necessary, but we can only congratulate ourselves that Hamilton should have formed the resolution he did, since it has been the means of giving us, in the excellent map of 'India according to the ancient divisions used in the Sanskrita language' the first western attempt to illustrate cartographically the old Hindu geography, and has moreover given us an attempt so satisfactory that it has not since required any serious modification.

The impossibility of getting access to the collections of specimens and drawings that the Court of Directors had given to Banks or that he himself had given to Smith, and the absence of the corresponding drawings from the later botanical collections the use of which was permitted by the Court, diverted Hamilton from his original design and led him to devote his energies instead to the preparation of commentaries on the works of Rheede[3] and Rumphius.[4] He seems to have begun the two commentaries

---

[1] Letter dated Leny, March 24, 1894, addressed to H. Beveridge, Esq., Eastbourne.

[2] Some notices concerning the plants of various parts of India, and concerning the Sanscrita names of those Regions: *Trans. Roy. Soc. Edinb.* x. 171: 1826.

[3] Rheede: *Hortus Indicus Malabaricus.* 12 vols. fol. Amsterdam: 1678—1703.

[4] Rumphius: *Herbarium Amboinense.* 6 vols. fol. Amsterdam: 1750.

simultaneously about 1821, but about 1825 he laid aside Rumphius after having dealt with the two first books and concentrated his attention on Rheede. With the latter his progress became more rapid, for he had finished the tenth volume early in 1826, and sent the manuscript of the last part of the work to the Linnean Society of London in 1828.

It was perhaps unfortunate that a writer of Hamilton's calibre should have devoted himself to so thankless a task as he set before himself. Yet his object in taking it up is very evident. We are apt now-a-days to forget the extent to which the figures of Rheede and Rumphius form the basis of species and even genera recognised by Linnæus, Lamarck and other less influential exponents of the binominal method of nomenclature. The conflicting views held regarding the plants figured in these two works, and the often extraordinary identifications of the plates of the two authors, suggested in the seclusion of European herbaria by the botanists of the latter half of the eighteenth century, were only too distracting to the ordinary field worker in India and Malaya; and the serious attempt made by Hamilton to satisfactorily elucidate these two books, then considered and treated as fundamental, strikes us now as a singularly public-spirited act. He certainly brought to the task the three essential qualities of ripe scholarship, cultivated observation, and wide personal knowledge; all that was lacking for the successful accomplishment of his design was sympathy on the part of those whom he desired to benefit.

To the *Hortus Malabaricus* Hamilton devoted about six years of his valuable life.[1] The discussion of the first book was published in 1822 by the Linnæan Society; that of second appeared in 1825; that of the third in 1827; that of the fourth was not published till 1837.

The delay in publishing the fourth part till ten years after the manuscript reached the Society appears to have been due to the same cause that led to the disappearance of Lambert's Hamiltonian specimens. The distribution of the great Wallichian Herbarium in 1828 led to the idea that Rheede and Rumphius were now of minor importance. A year later Dillwyn, who had for some years been endeavouring to ascertain the names of the plants figured by Rheede, and for this purpose had consulted the libraries and collections in London, printed privately a review of the references to Rheede's work.[2] This public-spirited action, instead of stirring the Linnæan Society's council to a sense of their duty to their Indian and Malayan fellow workers, had the unlooked for result of putting an end altogether to the publication of Hamilton's work. Dillwyn, as he tells us, had access to Hamilton's unpublished manuscripts, and it seems to have been supposed that Dillwyn's references made further publication of Hamilton's work unnecessary. However, Dillwyn's list, excellent as it is, does not pretend to be much more than an improved Dennstedt,[3] and the decision to suppress the greater part of Hamilton's *Commentary*, though doubtless it seemed wise and necessary to the council of the Linnæan Society at the time, has been a source of keen regret to botanists in India ever since.

---

[1] A commentary on the Hortus Malabaricus: I. *Trans. Linn. Soc.* xiii: II. *Trans. Linn. Soc.* xiv: III. *Trans. Linn. Soc.* xv: IV. *Trans. Linn. Soc.* xvii.

[2] *A review of the references to the Hortus Malabaricus of Henry van Rheede van Draakenstein.* 1 vol. 8vo. Swansea 1839: *not published.* The preface is dated Dec. 25, 1838.

[3] Dennstedt: *Schluessel zum Hortus Indicus Malabaricus.* 1 vol. 4to. Weimer: 1818.

The corresponding commentary on Rumphius was published by the Wernerian Society of Edinburgh.[1] The first part appeared in 1824: the second, which we know was completed before February 1826, was published sometime between 1826 and 1831. There is nothing to show that more of the work was ever written; probably it was not. The original rough comments, as Hamilton explains in one of his letters, are written on the backs of the plates of the copy of Rumphius which belongs to the Calcutta Garden Library; on the Calcutta copy of Rheede he has written no notes.

Hamilton's claim to represent the house of Buchanan of Buchanan was publicly presented and tried in 1826–28 and may therefore be included among his publications.[2] The only other paper for which he is believed to have been responsible during his lifetime, is one that was actually published after his death in the *Edinburgh New Philosophical Journal.*[3]

In 1831 an attempt was made in Calcutta to publish in their entirety Hamilton's reports regarding the Bengal Survey. Captain Herbert, editor of *Gleanings in Science*, being anxious to increase the local as opposed to the general interest of his excellent journal, asked for permission to publish Hamilton's manuscript. The plan suggested was to print a certain number of pages, not fewer than eight at one time, with a separate pagination, along with each number of the *Gleanings*. Government readily granted the request and the manuscript of the 1807 or Dinajpur report was made over to Herbert by Mr. Swinton, then Chief Secretary, for the purpose. When the publication of *Gleanings in Science* ceased and the newly founded *Journal of the Asiatic Society of Bengal*, under the editorship of James Prinsep, took its place, Prinsep continued Herbert's idea and completed the issue of the Dinajpur journal. The separate portions were provided with a title page, etc., and became available as a complete work in 1833.[4]

In this edition of the Hamilton manuscript nothing was omitted, even the references to drawings were left as they stood, although the drawings themselves had been sent home to the Court of Directors without copies having been kept. The hope of the editors, Herbert and Prinsep, was that even if the Court were unable to publish the original manuscript, they might publish the drawings.

The determination how far it was advisable to continue the publication of the accounts of the other districts surveyed, was made dependent on the amount of immediate interest which the Dinajpur one might command. The Anglo-Indian community in 1833 was much like the same community in 1904; no more of the work appeared.

In 1838 the records left by Hamilton were at last made available in a connected form. Permission was given by the Honourable Court of Directors to a Mr. Robert

---

[1] Commentary on the Herbarium Amboinense: *Mem. Wern. Soc. Edinb.* v. (part 1) and vi (part 2). From the manner in which the reference to part 1 is given (read 14th June 1823, etc.) it appears as if the paper may have been read by instalments.

[2] *Claim of Dr. Francis Hamilton Buchanan of Spittal to be considered the chief of the name as male representative of the family of Buchanan of Buchanan.* 1 vol. Edinburgh: 1826.

[3] A Uniformity of Climate prevailed over the earth prior to the time of the Deluge?: *Edinb. New Phil. Journ.* viii. 1830.

[4] *A Geographical, Statistical and Historical Description of the District, or Zila, of Dinajpur in the Province, or Soubah, of Bengal.* 1 vol. 8vo. Calcutta: 1833.

Montgomery Martin to 'collate' from the original documents at the East India house a work on Eastern India, which is found when critically examined to consist of Hamilton's reports of the Bengal Survey with those parts left out which the collater did not understand or which did not interest him.[1] Day found the allusions to Fish and Fisheries, one of Hamilton's favourite subjects, so casual in Martin's edition that they were useless both from the scientific and the economic point of view. With exemplary piety he printed *verbatim*, with an introduction and explanatory notes of his own, Hamilton's original account of the Bengal fisheries.[2] The same is equally true of the allusions to plants and vegetation; unfortunately no one has had the time to do for these what Day has done for the fishes. Beveridge on the other hand finds that Martin has left out much less that is of value in the historical or antiquarian chapters,[3] though he has been able to contribute a series of most interesting passages omitted by Martin.[4] Martin's edition of the work is marred by an unsuitable introduction and a somewhat tedious dedication; the title-page[5] is distinguished by the absence of the author's name and the substitution of Martin's own. This substitution has given rise to many severe remarks, but the writer agrees with Beveridge in believing that the procedure was a simple act of folly, and that Martin had no intention either of passing off the work as his own or of depriving Hamilton of the merit of having written it. If, however, we can with Beveridge acquit Martin of anything more serious than stupidity as regards his title-page, we must admit that Martin had extremely rudimentary ideas of the duties of an editor, and that his work in this direction is as primitive and unsatisfactory as Hunter alleges it to be. This, however, is only a misfortune and, as Beveridge says, 'one is disposed to feel grateful to Mr. Martin for having done something.' In one respect, however, Martin's conduct was truly criminal; he provided no index for the work.

The following list exhibits in chronological sequence the various publications referred to in the foregoing paragraphs:—

1. De Febribus intermittentibus medendis. 1 vol. Edinburgh: 1783. Graduation Thesis; M.D.

2. Description of the tree, called by the Burmas Launzan. *Asiatick Researches* v. 123: 1798.

3. A comparative Vocabulary of some of the Languages spoken in the Burma Empire. *Asiatick Researches* v. 219: 1798.

---

[1] Hunter: *Imperial Gazetteer of India*, vi. p. 205, footnote.

[2] Fish and Fisheries of Bengal; edited, with an introduction and notes, by Surgeon-Major Francis Day, Inspector-General of Fisheries in India: *A Statistical Account of Bengal.* xx. 1877.

[3] Beveridge: *Calcutta Review* for July 1894.

[4] Beveridge: *loc. cit.* The passages include the following: *Discovery of two statues in the Ganges near Patna: the Panchpahari at Patna: the worship of Buddha,* as a Hindu goddess, *at Patna; Notes on temples at Patna and Goya: a short account of an old fort called Lakragar: the Pal Rajahs: Notes on the ruins of Tāngra: Origin of the caste of the Sarvariyas: the Kosi.*

[5] *The History, Antiquities, Topography, and Statistics of Eastern India, comprising the districts of Behar, Shahabad, Bhagalpoor, Goruckpoor, Dinagepoor, Puraniya, Rungpoor and Assam; in relation to their Geology, Mineralogy, Botany, Agriculture, Commerce, Manufactures, Fine Arts, Population, Religion, Education, Statistics, etc., surveyed under the orders of the Supreme Government, and collated from the original documents at the East India House with the permission of the Honourable Court of Directors,* by Montgomery Martin. 3 vols. 8vo. London: 1838.

4. On the Religion and Literature of the Burmas. *Asiatick Researches* vi. 163: 1799.

5. [Note on the Rivers of Burma.] Symes: *An Account of an Embassy to the Kingdom of Ava*, 241: 1800.

6. Descriptions of Rare and Curious Plants selected by the President of the Royal Society. Symes: *An Account of an Embassy to the Kingdom of Ava*, 473: 1800.—The drawings were by Buchanan, the actual descriptions are said by Symes to be the work of Banks.

7. An Account of the Onchidium, a new genus of the class of Vermes, found in Bengal. Read 5th June, 1798. *Transactions of the Linnean Society* v. 132: 1800.

8. Description of the Vespertilio plicatus. Read November 5, 1799. *Transactions of the Linnean Society* v. 261: 1800.

9. Utricularia reticulata [edited by J. E. Smith in] *Exotic Botany* ii. p. 119; t. 119: 1805.

10. [Figures and Descriptions of Nepal Plants, edited by J. E. Smith in] *Exotic Botany* ii. p. 73, tt. 97—101; p. 95, tt. 107, 108; p. 107, tt. 113—117: 1805.—The species figured are:—97. *Epidendrum præcox;* 98. *Epidendrum humile;* 99. *Orchis pectinata;* 100. *Orchis gigantea;* 101. *Begonia picta;* 107. *Hedychium coronarium;* 108. *Roscoea purpurea;* 113. *Androsace rotundifolia;* 114. *Primula denticulata;* 115. *Colebrookia oppositifolia* (*Buchanania oppositifolia* on plate, and *Sussodia oppositifolia* in Hamilton's manuscript); 116. *Leucosceptrum canum;* 117. *Globba racemosa.*

11. A journey from Madras, through the countries of Mysore, Canara and Malabar, performed under the orders of the Most Noble the Marquis of Wellesley, for the express purpose of investigating the state of Agriculture, Arts and Commerce, the Religion, Manners and Customs, the Natural and Civil History, and Antiquities in the Dominions of the Rajah of Mysore, and the countries acquired by the Honourable East India Company in the late and former wars, from Tippoo Sultan. 3 vols. 4to. London: 1807. [*Edinburgh Review,* October 1808.]

Account of the Manufactures carried on at Bangalore and the Processes employed by the Natives in dyeing Silk and Cotton. *Philosophical Magazine* xxx. 259 and 322: 1808. [Reprinted by A. Tilloch from the above.]

Machines for Irrigation. *Gleanings in Science* i. 278: 1829 [Reprinted by Captain Herbert from the above.]

Second edition. 2 vols. 8vo. Madras: 1870.

12. An Account of the Kingdom of Nepal and of the Territories annexed to this Dominion by the House of Gorkha. 1 vol. 4to. Edinburgh: 1819. [*Blackwood's Magazine,* July 1852.]

Prodromus Floræ Nepalensis, sive Enumeratio Vegetabilium, quæ in itinera per Nepaliam proprie dictam et regiones conterminas, ann. 1802—1803, detexit atque legit D. D. Franciscus Hamilton (olim Buchanan) M. D. Societ. Reg. et Linnæan. Londin. Soc. Accedunt plantæ a D. Wallich nuperius missae. Secundum methodi naturalis normam disposuit atque descripsit David Don. 1 vol. sm. 8vo. London: 1825.

Elucidation of some plants mentioned in Dr. Francis Hamilton's Account of the kingdom of Nepal. By Lieutenant-Colonel Madden. *Trans. Bot. Soc. Edin.* v. 116: 1858.

13. Notice of the Progress of Botanical Science in Bengal, being the substance of a letter from Dr. Wallich, Superintendent of the Botanical Garden near Calcutta, to Francis Hamilton, M.D., F.R.S., & F.A.S., L. & E. *Edinburgh Philosophical Journal* i. 376: 1819.—This paper is accredited, in the Royal Society's catalogue, to Wallich. It is, as a matter of fact, a review of a letter from Wallich, with comments by Hamilton.

14. Genealogies of the Hindus extracted from their sacred writings. 8vo. Edinburgh: 1819.

15. Genealogical Tables of the Deities, Princes, Heroes and Remarkable Personages of the Hindus, extracted from the sacred writings of that people. With an Introduction and Index. Fol. Edinburgh: 1819.

16. Description of the Diamond Mine at Panna. *Edinburgh Philosophical Journal* i. 49: 1819.

17. Account of the Mine or Quarry of Corundum in Singraula. *Edinburgh Philosophical Journal* ii. 305: 1820.

18. An Account of Asam with some notices concerning the neighbouring territories. *Annals of Oriental Literature* 244. 1820.

19. Account of a Map of the Countries subject to the King of Ava, drawn by a slave of the King's eldest son. *Edinburgh Philosophical Journal* ii. 89 and 262: 1820.

20. Account of a Map of the Route between Tartary and Amarapura. *Edinburgh Philosophical Journal* iii. 32: 1820.

21. Account of a Map of the Country north from Ava. *Edinburgh Philosophical Journal* iv. 76: 1871.

22. Account of a Map, constructed by a native of Taunu, of the Country south from Ava. *Edinburgh Philosophical Journal* v. 75: 1821.

23. Account of Water-spouts observed at Sea on Voyages to and from India. *Edinburgh Philosophical Journal* v. 275: 1821. [*Annal. de Chimie* xix. 70: 1821. Gilbert: *Annal.* lxx. 104: 1822.]

24. Account of an extraordinary appearance of the Sea observed 31st July 1785, in a voyage from Johanna to Bombay, long. 61° 25′ E., lat. 6° 32′ N. *Edinburgh Philosophical Journal* v. 303: 1821.

25. An Account of the Fishes found in the River Ganges and its branches. 4to. With a volume of plates, Royal 4to. 2 vols. Edinburgh: 1822.

26. Account of a map of the country between the Erawadi and the Khiænduæn rivers. *Edinburgh Philosophical Journal* vi. 107: 1822.

27. Account of a map, by a slave to the Heir Apparent of Ava. *Edinburgh Philosophical Journal* vi. 270: 1822.

28. An account of the map of the Tarout Shan Territory. *Edinburgh Philosophical Journal* vii. 71: 1822.

29. Account of a map of the vicinity of Paukgan or Pagan. *Edinburgh Philosophical Journal* vii. 230: 1822.

30. A Commentary on the Hortus Malabaricus, I. *Linn. Soc. Trans.* xiii. 474: 1822. II. *Linn. Soc. Trans.* xiv. 171: 1825. III. *Linn. Soc. Trans.* xv. 78: 1827. IV. *Linn. Soc. Trans.* xvii. 147: 1837. [Oken; *Isis* xxi. col. 180: 1827: Dillwyn: *A review of the References to the Hortus Malabaricus of Henry van Rheede von Draakenstein.* 1 vol. 8vo.

Swansea: 1839—not published.]—This work was finished in 1821; we learn from Dillwyn, who has made full use of Hamilton's text, that the remainder of the unpublished MSS. was, when he wrote, in the library of the Linnean Society of London.

31. Account of a map drawn by a native of Dawæ or Tavay. *Edinburgh Philosophical Journal* ix. 228: 1823.

32. Commentary on the Herbarium Amboinense, I. *Memoirs of the Wernerian Society of Edinburgh* v. 307: 1823-4. II. *Memoirs of the Wernerian Society of Edinburgh* vi. 268: 1826—31.—Whether this work was ever completed is doubtful; the Wernerian Society, which afterwards became absorbed in the Edinburgh Botanical Society, published the commentaries on the two first books. If more was written, this must have been after the completion of the *Hortus Malabaricus*, and the whereabouts of the MSS. is unknown.

33. Account of two maps of Zænmæ or Yangoma. *Edinburgh Philosophical Journal* x. 59: 1824.

34. An account of the map of Koshanpri. *Edinburgh Philosophical Journal* x. 247: 1824.

35. An account of the Janji, or Vallisneria alternifolia of Dr. Roxburgh, the plant used in India in refining sugar. *Edinburgh Journal of Science* i. 34: 1824.

36. Account of a map of Upper Laos, or the Territory of the Lowa Shan. *Edinburgh Journal of Science* i. 71: 1824.

37. An Account of a genus including the Herba Toxicaria of the Himalayan Mountains, or the plant with which the natives poison their arrows. *Edinburgh Journal of Science* i. 249: 1824. [Madden: *Trans. Bot. Soc. Edinb.* v. 1858; Stapf: *Ann. Roy. Bot. Gard. Calcutta* x. part 2. 1904.]

38. Account of a map of the Kingdom of Pegu. *Edinburgh Journal of Science* i. 267: 1824.

39. Observations on Mun Kokhosee [Munko-Khoshee] (dated Katumanda, 10th and 14th November 1802). *Roxburgh, Flora Indica,* ed. Carey and Wallich ii. 415: 1824; *Roxburgh, Flora Indica,* ed. Carey i. 631: 1832. [Carey in *Roxburgh,* ed. 1824 *l. c.*]

40. Account of a plant allied to the genus Piper. *Edinburgh Journal of Science* ii. 9: 1825.

41. An account of the Frontier between Part of Bengal and the Kingdom of Ava. *Edinburgh Journal of Science* ii. 49: 1825.

42. An account of the Frontier between Ava and the Part of Bengal adjacent to the Karnaphuli River. *Edinburgh Journal of Science* iii. 32: 1825.

43. An account of the Frontier between the Southern part of Bengal and the Kingdom of Ava. *Edinburgh Journal of Science* iii. 201: 1825; iv. 22: 1826.

44. Some notices concerning the Plants of various parts of India, and concerning the Sanscrita names of those Regions (read June 18, 1821). *Trans. Roy. Soc. Edin.* x. 171: 1826. [*Flora* ix. 689: 1826; Froriep: *Notizen* xi. col. 97: 1825; *Calcutta Review;* for July 1894.]—This paper forms the basis of most of the notices of Buchanan's Indian career.

45. Inscription upon rocks in South Bihar, described by Dr. Buchanan-Hamilton, and explained by H. P. Colebrooke, Director (read December 4, 1821). *Trans. Roy.*

As. Soc. i. 201: 1826.—[Beveridge in *Calcutta Review*, July 1894.] Extracted by Colebrooke from the original Buchanan manuscript in London.

46. Descriptions of Temples of the Jainas in South Bihar and Bhagalpur. *Trans. Roy. As. Soc.* i. 523: 1826.—Edited by H. T. Colebrooke, from the original Buchanan manuscript in London.

47. On the Sravacs or Jains. *Trans. Roy. As. Soc.* i. 531: 1826. Edited by H. T. Colebrooke, from the original Buchanan manuscript in London.

48. Claim of Dr. Francis Hamilton Buchanan of Spittal to be considered the chief of the name as male Representative of the family of Buchanan of Buchanan. 1 vol. Edinburgh: 1826.

49. Description of a plant of the order Guttiferæ, which Dr. Roxburgh called Garcinia pedunculata. *Edinburgh Journal of Science*, vii. 45: 1827.

50. Notice respecting the Vanderon Monkey, or the 'Guenon a face pourpre' of Buffon. *Edinburgh Journal of Science* vii. 60: 1827.

51. Description of a plant (Beta bengalensis) used in Bengal as a common green vegetable (Olus) and of another nearly allied to it. *Edinburgh Journal of Science* vii. 244: 1827.

52. Description of the ruins of Buddha Gaya, by Dr. Francis Buchanan Hamilton, M.R.A.S., extracted from his report of a survey of South Bihar (read May 5, 1827). *Trans. Roy. As. Soc.* ii. 40: 1830.—Extracted and edited by H. T. Colebrooke, from the original Buchanan manuscript in London.

53. Manner of Hunting in District Dainajpur. *Gleanings in Science* i. 374: 1829.—Extracted by the editor of *Gleanings in Science* from the Calcutta copy of the Buchanan manuscript.

54. A Uniformity of Climate prevailed over the Earth prior to the time of the Deluge? *Edinb. New. Phil. Journ.* viii. 366: 1830.—This article is incorrectly cited as to title in the *Roy. Soc. Cat. of Sc. Papers.* The authorship is not formally claimed; no name is given in the list of contents or with the title of the paper; the signature is simply H——N.

55. Observations on the structure of the fruit in the order Cucurbitaceæ (read 4th February 1828). *Trans. Roy. Soc. Edinb.* xi. 229: 1831.

56. On the Minerals of the Rajmahal cluster of hills. *Gleanings in Science* iii. 1: 1831.—Extracted by the editor of *Gleanings in Science* from the Calcutta copy of the Buchanan manuscript.

57. A Geographical, Statistical and Historical Description of the District, or Zila, of Dinajpur in the Province, or Soubah, of Bengal. 1 vol. 8vo. Calcutta: 1833.—Printed and issued with the monthly numbers of *Gleanings in Science* and afterwards of the *Journal of the Asiatic Society*, the former under the editorship of Herbert and the latter under that of J. Prinsep.

58. Catalogue of Woods peculiar to Goalpara. M'Cosh: *Topography of Assam*, p. 36: 1837.—This list of 90 timbers was drawn up by Hamilton when stationed at Goalpara in 1808, and was sent, along with the corresponding timber-specimens, to Mr. James Kyd, the Honourable Company's Master-Builder at Calcutta. When Wallich's Herbarium was taken home in 1828, the timber specimens were, with the permission of the Court of Directors, transferred to the Society of Arts for arrangement and examination. They formed the subject of a paper by Aikin, the Secretary to the Society, entitled *List of Indian Woods collected by* N. Wallich, M.D., F.R.S., *Corresponding Member of the Royal Institute of France*

and of the Academy of Sciences at Berlin, etc., and of the Society of Arts of London; Superintendent of the Botanic Garden at Calcutta; Trans. Soc. Arts Manuf. and Comm. xlviii. 439 : 1831. Aikin, for the sake of the vernacular names and the notices regarding the species, incorporated Hamilton's catalogue in his list, in all cases indicating the source of his information by adding—*Ham.* M'Cosh, who was directed to prepare a topographical account of Assam, in 1837 extracted from Aikin's *List* (which Pritzel ascribes to Wallich) all the entries that Aikin indicates as derived from Hamilton's Catalogue, and issued them as being 'a fair statement of the Timbers of Assam.'

59. History of Cooch Behar, being an extract of a passage from Dr. Buchanan's account of Rangpur (Rangapura) revised and communicated by Major F. Jenkins. *Journ. As. Soc. Beng.* vii. 1 : 1838.—Extracted by Major Jenkins from the Calcutta copy of the Buchanan manuscript.

60. The History, Antiquities, Topography and Statistics of Eastern India, comprising the districts of Behar, Shahabad, Bhagalpoor, Goruckpoor, Dinagepoor, Puraniya, Rungpoor, and Assam; in relation to their Geology, Mineralogy, Botany, Agriculture, Commerce, Manufactures, Fine Arts, Population, Religion, Education, Statistics, etc., surveyed under the orders of the Supreme Government, and collated from the original documents at the East India House with the permission of the Honourable Court of Directors, by Montgomery Martin. 3 vols. 8vo. London: 1838.—The 'original documents' in question are Buchanan's manuscript journals. The 'collation' referred to consists of the omission of passages in which Martin was not interested, or which he did not appreciate. [*Quarterly Review*, No. cxxvi., vol. 63; *Calcutta Review*, July 1894.]

61. The Fish and Fisheries of Bengal [edited, with an introduction and notes, by Surgeon-Major Francis Day, Inspector-General of Fisheries in India; from the India Office copy of the Buchanan Records in.] *A Statistical Account of Bengal*, xx. 5: 1877.

62. [Passages from the Manuscript Record of the Survey of Bengal by Dr. Francis Buchanan, afterwards Hamilton, omitted from the edition by Montgomery Martin.] *Calcutta Review.* July: 1894.—Extracted by H. Beveridge from the original Buchanan manuscript in London.

The passages are as follows:—i. Discovery of two statues in the Ganges near Patna; ii. The Panchpahari at Patna; iii. The worship of Buddha, *as a Hindu Goddess*, at Patna; iv. Notes on temples at Patna and Gaya; v. Notes on Inscriptions in the district of Shahabad; vi. A short Account of an old Fort called Lakragar; vii. The Pal Rajahs; viii. Note on the Ruins of Tāngra; ix. Origin of the Caste of the Sarvariyas; x. The Kosi.

8. CONCLUSION.

There unfortunately appears to be no extant portrait of Francis Hamilton,[1] and the only clues to his personal appearance are some stray allusions in his own letters and the necessarily vague reminscences of his son and successor, the late J. B. Hamilton, Esq., who was quite a child when his father died. In a letter dated March 1894, Mr. Hamilton writes:—

"My personal recollection of him is that he was a tall man with a very ruddy complexion and very white hair."

[1] At Leny there are portraits of Hamilton's mother a very handsome lady with a strong intellectual face, and of his brothers, Colonel John Hamilton and Robert Buchanan, Esq., but none of himself.

ERRATUM SLIP.

Sketch of the Life of Francis Hamilton (once Buchanan).

Page lxix, lines 5 to 8 from top should read as follows:—

"There is no indication that Roxburgh recommended Hamilton's selection as Surgeon and Naturalist to accompany the Ava Mission; the actual appointment was probably secured for him through the influence and interest of Sir James Murray."

B. S. Press—74496—386—8-7.1905—W. M. D'C.

From Hamilton's letters we gather that between the ages of 35 and 40 he was inclined to become stout. Whether this tendency was temporary or remained permanent is not recorded.

Hamilton's capacity as a public servant may be deduced from the estimate which Roxburgh, an excellent judge of character, had formed. Roxburgh recommended Hamilton's selection as surgeon and naturalist to accompany the Ava mission; there is no indication that the actual appointment was probably secured for him through the influence and interest of Sir James Murray. But we know that Hamilton was the subject of remarks in letters that passed between Roxburgh and Banks, Smith, and other scientific friends in Britain, and it is not improbable that Smith, perhaps also some of Roxburgh's Edinburgh acquaintances, may have provided Hamilton with letters of introduction and recommendation to Roxburgh when he entered the Company's service in 1794. However this may be, it is clear that Hamilton had made Roxburgh's acquaintance before he left for Burma, and that a warm friendship sprang up between the two men during Hamilton's period of residence at Puttahaut after his return from Ava. We know, too, that Roxburgh showed his practical interest by endeavouring to obtain a place for Hamilton in a projected Philippine expedition in 1797, when the latter had explained that his position at Puttahaut was uncomfortable. In this application Roxburgh was not successful, but he did succeed in having Hamilton deputed for special service to investigate Chittagong and in obtaining his transfer from Noakhali to the 24-Pergunnahs. We find also that Hamilton was primarily indebted to Roxburgh for the opportunity of carrying out the Mysore Survey, an undertaking which, among other things, brought him the personal acquaintance of the Marquis of Wellesley. Again, it was to Roxburgh that Hamilton was indebted for his recall from the Nepal mission when it was obvious that he could do no more useful work there. This recall gave Hamilton the opportunity of joining the staff of the Governor-General; here his previous acquaintance with Lord Wellesley ripened into a mutual friendship which endured for the rest of Hamilton's life.

The feelings entertained by Lord Wellesley towards Hamilton are shown in many ways; perhaps the strongest evidence of the Governor-General's regard is to be seen in the fact that among Hamilton's papers, in the possession of his family, are drafts of memorials or reports in which he had been requested to submit his opinions, among other matters, as to the conduct of contemplated compaigns, as to the annexation of territories, and even as to the colonisation of New Zealand! But we see the same regard displayed in the letter of welcome addressed to Hamilton on his return to England in 1815, and in the fact that Lord Wellesley subsequently invited Hamilton to join his staff in Ireland. There is, however, further evidence of the feelings with which the Marquis of Wellesley regarded Hamilton, in his Lordship's reply to the request of the latter for permission to dedicate his *Account of the Kingdom of Nepal* to his former chief. The letter, which is dated Richmond, December 27, 1817, is given below:—

"I have been wandering so much for several months past that I have not been able to return so early an acknowledgment of your obliging letter as was demanded by its tenor and by my sincere and warm sentiments of respect and gratitude towards you.

I accept the honour which you propose to confer upon me, with a deep sense of its value. No part of my Government affords me more matter of satisfactory reflection than the opportunities of which I availed myself to render your talents and knowledge useful to the world. In discharging this duty, the intimate acquaintance and friendship which was established between us enabled me to appreciate the integrity, independence, and frankness of your character, and the manly spirit of truth and honor which animated your intercourse with all persons in power.

These advantages furnish me with the certain means, not only of anticipating the high success which must attend your work, but of estimating the benefit which must accrue to my reputation from your public declaration of our mutual esteem.

Be assured that I take a strong interest in your happiness and welfare, and rejoice in the ease and comfort of your situation.

If you should approach London, I hope to see you at this place, where you will always find the most friendly reception from, dear Sir, your most faithful and obliged servant."

It is often said that the Court of Directors suppressed Hamilton's journals and reports relating to the survey of Bengal. It certainly is unfortunate, as the editorial preface to the attempt to publish them from the Calcutta copy in 1833 says—

"that those valuable documents were not given to the public when stamped with the interest of originality and immediate applicability to the actual circumstances of the districts, and when they would have proved of great utility to the public officers of Government."[1]

This one immediately admits, and one is constrained further to regret that the public interest in the reports proved to be so slight that it was not considered advisable by the Government of Bengal and the Calcutta Editors to continue the series beyond the first, or Dinajpur, report.

The Court of Directors perhaps only anticipated what the Calcutta editors themselves experienced; at any rate the accusation that the reports were suppressed either because they were deemed of no value or because they contained matter which it would be dangerous to publish,[2] may be dismissed at once. The only danger that could conceivably arise must have been with regard to transfrontier information; yet the bulk of this Hamilton was, as a matter of fact, allowed to publish in his accounts of Nepal and Assam. That the Court did not depreciate the value of the documents is clear; even at the time when Hamilton complains of the arrogance and contempt shown towards his collections there is no suggestion that this feeling was exhibited towards his reports. On the contrary we find that the Court gave full permission to Walter Hamilton to consult the whole, and to incorporate as much of the topographical and statistical information that they contained as was necessary for his purpose in his work on Hindustan;[3] this information is there always fully acknowledged. We find too that the Court gave full permission to Colebrooke to publish any extracts he might care to edit for the Royal Asiatic Society's *Transactions*. That anything sinister, or indeed that anything careless, underlay the long suppression of these manuscripts is therefore not only unproven but improbable. In all likelihood the question was mainly a financial one, and while one may regret the circumstance, there is little doubt that the Court deemed it impossible at the time to vote the funds required to meet their publication. It will be noticed that when in 1820 Hamilton was

---

[1] Account of Dinajpur, Editorial preface.

[2] Higginbotham; *Men India has known*, p. 41.

[3] Walter Hamilton: *A Geographical, Statistical and Historical description of Hindustan and the adjacent countries. In two volumes.* 2 vols., 4to. London: 1820. In his *East India Gazetteer* published in 1815 this author cites freely Hamilton's Mysore journal.

given his collections for arrangement and publication, there was no suggestion that the Court should assist in publishing Hamilton's results; these were to appear in the form of papers 'in such journals as might accept them,' a circumstance that is in keeping with the suggestion made regarding the manuscripts.

It has also been suggested that it is singular that Hamilton did not make more persistent efforts to have his reports made use of.[1] Before, however, forming an opinion on this aspect of the question it is necessary to recall what Hamilton actually did. We have already seen what his publications were; it may throw light on this suggestion that the fault was Hamilton's own, if we examine the principle that underlay his action.

Considering the extent and the methodical nature of his observations Hamilton had published remarkably little before he retired. When he reached England he therefore had much material that called for publication. Some of this material, for example his Hindu genealogies, we know was prepared for issue while he was in India, and practically all that had to be done was to find a publisher and send the manuscript to the press. Other portions, such as the accounts of Nepal and Assam, must also have been nearly ready for publication before he left India, for they were issued soon after Hamilton's return to England. Still other parts appear to have only existed in the form of notes or journals which required to be revised, collated with subsequent notes, and edited.

The publication of his *Account of Nepal* in 1819 exhausted the general information he could give with reference to his fourth survey, just as the appearance of the Mysore journal in 1807 exhausted the general information he could give regarding his third survey. But when in 1819 he had completed the issue of the works mostly written and arranged in India, and could turn his attention to his other notes and journals, there still remained to be dealt with not only the results of the final or Bengal survey but those of the Chittagong survey and much of those of the Ava survey. It was only natural that he should attempt to clear off the Ava and Chittagong materials before he dealt with the Bengal ones; and as regards the Bengal results, which, in accordance with the instructions under which he had acted, included information obtained regarding countries beyond the Company's frontiers, it was not only natural but proper that he should try to clear off the outlying transfrontier notes before attempting to edit the Bengal results. Accordingly we find that he dealt with the transfrontier results of the Rangpur survey in a separate work on Assam; incorporated the transfrontier results of the Purnea and Gorakhpur surveys in his work on Nepal; made his observations in, or information obtained from the Panna State and from Singraula the subject of separate papers; dealt exhaustively with the geographical results of his Ava journey and codified the results of his Chittagong deputation; finally, cleared off such notes as he deemed worthy of publication from the journals kept or observations recorded during his voyages of 1785-91, of 1805-6, and of 1815.

As regards the whole of the surveys and travels prior to the Bengal series, he was greatly handicapped by the absence of his botanical collections, which had found their way into the herbaria either of Banks or of Smith, and had thus become practically inaccessible to him. He had as a matter of fact prepared a systematic account of the vegetation of Burma which he gave to Banks, but which Banks

---

[1] Beveridge: *Calcutta Review* for July 1894.

suppressed; and had at least contemplated the preparation of a similar account of the vegetation of Mysore, which the publishers of the Mysore journal were unable to accept on the score of its expense. Whether he ever intended to do the same by Nepal is not clear, at all events he was relieved of this task owing to Don having undertaken it. But it is clear that Hamilton was fully alive to the fact that economic references to natural products are very unsatisfactory if they are not accompanied by a full systematic and scientific account of the species that yield them, and it is evident that he was determined to provide the necessary scientific foundation for the numerous economic references to the animals and plants that are mentioned in the Bengal survey reports.

To meet the necessity he therefore published his account of the Gangetic fishes, which is the scientific basis of his remarks on the fishes and fisheries of Bengal, long afterwards edited by Day; and he prepared the still unpublished catalogue of plants, which is the scientific basis of his references to the vegetation of the various districts of Bengal that have never yet been adequately edited. That he never published the plant catalogue, or dealt systematically with any zoological family save the fishes, was owing to the retention in India of the drawings which related to natural history made under his supervision during the Bengal survey.

Another circumstance which delayed any attempt by Hamilton himself to deal with the body of his Bengal Reports was his having devoted his energies to the much-needed critical examinations of the works of Rheede and Rumphius, of which the first though completed was never published in full, while the second was possibly only partially completed at the time of his death.

On the whole perhaps it was unfortunate that Hamilton devoted his attention to the *Hortus Malabaricus* and the *Herbarium Amboinense* so seriously as he did. Had he given the six or eight years he bestowed on this task to the careful editing of his Bengal journals, which, even in the mutilated condition in which Martin has supplied them, form one of the finest works of the kind that was ever written, we should have been in possession of a masterpiece of Indian statistical and topographical literature. But this cannot now be helped and, however much we may regret that Hamilton's botanical energies were diverted into the channel which they took, we cannot complain that the non-utilisation of his Bengal reports was due to any lack of energy on his part. Probably no one has ever given the whole of his life after retirement more persistently and single heartedly, and with less consideration for money or reputation, to the task of making his observations available to the public than Hamilton did. The pity of the situation, as regards Hamilton's great commentaries, does not lie so much in their preparation as their fate. The *Herbarium Amboinense* we in India miss least, because in the first place Hamilton's identifications are still available in the Calcutta copy of Rumphius, and because, since then, Hasskarl has provided an excellent key to the work.[1] But the *Hortus Malabaricus* commentary, of which only one-third has been printed, is a continual regret to the Indian botanist, for the keys of Dillwyn and Dennstedt, though painstaking and useful, are not the works of men who had the great advantage of an Indian experience.

The mistake that Hamilton made, though it is one that was perfectly natural, was that he should have sent the Malabar manuscript to London and the Amboyna one to

[1] Hasskarl: *Neuer Schluessel zu Rumph's Herbarium Amboniense.* 1 vol. 4to. Cleve: 1864.

Edinburgh. Had some happy accident led him to reverse their destinations the results would probably have been very different. The study of botany had, as we learn from Hamilton's letters and as we know from other sources, became very unfashionable at the time that he prepared these two works. In England Banks was no longer able, and Smith no longer willing, to stem the tide of philistinism that had set in. Brown had attempted to face the situation but the treatment which the botanical world accorded to his *Prodromus Floræ Novæ Hollandiæ* had so mortified him that he refused to go on with the work. This being the case with the giants who were on the spot, there is little room for surprise that the Linnean Society's council should have been induced to relegate Hamilton's manuscript to a cupboard. In Scotland, as we know, the successful termination of the Napoleonic wars was marked by the same exacerbation of indifference to science in high places. There, however, a few vigorous intellects refused to be disheartened by the conditions that prevailed, and the philistinism so rampant at the time, if it went naked, could hardly, in the presence of men like Brewster, W. J. Hooker, Greville and a few others, walk wholly unashamed. Had Hamilton's manuscript of the *Hortus Malabaricus* commentary been given to an Edinburgh journal it is highly probable that we should now be in possession of the whole, and even the Linnean Society of London might have given us the two books of the *Herbarium Amboinense* for which we are indebted to the Wernerian Society of Edinburgh.

In estimating Hamilton's place as an observer one has to take into consideration the many-sided nature of his interests. The earliest estimate of his powers that we possess is one by the Rev. Dr. Robertson, minister of Callander.[1] "In classical and medical knowledge," says this authority, writing in 1791, "he has few equals, and he is well acquainted with the whole system of nature." Beveridge, it is true, will have it that "Buchanan was not a scholar," but it is necessary in dealing with matters of the kind to define one's terms, and the statement that the author of the 'Map of India according to the ancient divisions used in the Sanskrits language,' and of the commentaries on the works of Rheede and Rumphius, was not a scholar, is one that the writer at any rate, cannot for a moment admit.

That Hamilton was keenly interested in linguistic studies we know not only from the paper on the subject of the Burmese languages in the *Asiatick Researches*, but from an interesting reference in the life of Colebrooke.[2] It appears that 'in furtherance of the views developed by Sir James Mackintosh' Colebrooke attempted to compile practically useful vocabularies of all the languages spoken in India. In order to obtain the necessary data Colebrooke issued to officers who were considered competent, blank forms to be filled up with vocabularies of provincial languages. Almost the only answer he received was from Hamilton.

Hamilton's interest in the literature, religion and history of the peoples of India was equally real and equally lasting. It is first shown in one of his early papers on Burma, but we find from the papers extracted from his journals and edited by Colebrooke between 1826 and 1830 that it was as keen and direct as ever towards the close of his Indian service, and the publication of his genealogical tables of the Hindu dynasties shows that it continued after his retirement.

---

[1] Statistical Account of Scotland: Callander 1791.

[2] Life of H. T. Colebrooke, by his son Sir T. E. Colebrooke, p. 228.

If Hamilton can be said to have been more eminent and to have done more to advance human knowledge in one branch of science than in another, that science was geography. One has only to allude to his excellent work in Ava, Chittagong, Assam and Nepal as evidence of this; the combined and uniformly appreciative testimony of geographers so eminent as John Crawford, Carl Ritter, Henry Yule and John Anderson renders supererogatory anything that might be said here.

M'Clelland says that Hamilton was professedly a botanist,[1] a statement which may be true; but if this was the case he certainly did not neglect zoology, and there is nothing in his writings to show that he was more interested in, or gave greater attention to, the one science than to the other. The practical testimony of Drs. Day and Günther as to the quality of Hamilton's zoological observations renders any allusion by the writer to his merits as a zoologist unnecessary.

As regards Hamilton's place among the botanists of India at the close of 18th and the commencement of the 19th century, it is needless to do more than quote the opinion of his ablest contemporary. In a letter to Banks, dated 13th July 1797, Roxburgh says :—

"I have mentioned Dr. Buchanan in the accompanying memorandum. He is a worthy valuable man and no doubt the best botanist in India."

Looking back, as we now can, with all the advantage that a true perspective affords, and with the further advantage of being able to judge by results, we cannot entirely endorse Roxburgh's view. In spite of his limitations Roxburgh himself, though not a scholar and though, as his works show, obviously a less critical observer than Hamilton was, has proved himself the greater and more useful constructive worker of the two. But, while this is the case, there is no doubt that, after Roxburgh, Hamilton was the best botanist in India of his day, and we can readily concede that as a botanical critic he was certainly Roxburgh's superior.

Hamilton's knowledge of mineralogy and geology was well abreast of the time in which he lived, as allusions in his letters and as his various papers dealing with these subjects show. He appears, indeed, to have given the same attention to these matters that he gave to zoology and botany.

The change of name from Buchanan to Hamilton has led to some rather oddly illogical results. Cuvier suggested that as Hamilton was best known to naturalists by his earlier name he ought always to be cited as "Hamilton Buchanan" in systematic references. M'Clelland has gone further and has said that Cuvier's suggestion should be adopted because most of Hamilton's publications appeared under the name Buchanan. It is not at all clear that Cuvier was correct in what he said; it is not known, and it is hardly to be supposed, that Hamilton had an extensive personal acquaintance with European workers while he served in the East, and before he changed his name. In any case M'Clelland's remark has been made without due consideration for facts; Hamilton only published two brief zoological papers and one brief botanical one under the name Buchanan, and only one of the journals in which economic, as opposed to scientific, references to natural products appear, was published before Hamilton had to assume his later name.

---

[1] *Asiatic Researches* xix. 2?3.

Don, who published many of the Nepal species of plants during Hamilton's lifetime, always cites him, correctly, as Hamilton. Since then the erroneous and unnecessary practice adopted by zoologists has been followed by botanists who, however, usually cite Hamilton as "Buchanan Hamilton." Why, in deciding to deliberately and conventionally err, the botanist should reverse the error of the zoologist, is not at all clear. The one convention is as needless as the other and both should be dropped.

Hamilton's shrewd sense is shown again and again in his letters, and is perhaps nowhere seen to more advantage than in his early appreciation of the outstanding ability of Sir William Hooker, and in his remarks on other contemporary workers. It is perhaps least pleasantly seen in his estimate of Roxburgh, though even in this instance it was not unjust; as it was only made in a letter to Wallich, the one other person who was as greatly indebted to Roxburgh as Hamilton himself had been for opportunities, at the commencement of his service, which led to his ultimately rendering himself distinguished, there was no danger of its being misinterpreted.

Montgomery Martin, in introducing the first volume of Hamilton's Bengal reports to the public, promised to prepare a memoir of Hamilton's life. But at the close of the third and last volume Martin explains that he had failed to find material for the purpose.

It is hard to realize that Martin could find nothing, within ten years of Hamilton's death, to aid him in enabling us to form some conception of Hamilton's interesting personality. What was difficult in 1838 is naturally still more difficult now, and we must therefore unfortunately content ourselves with a review of what Hamilton did as some substitute for a picture of what Hamilton was. The writer, however, cannot help feeling selfishly grateful to Martin, since Martin's failure has afforded him this opportunity of performing, as best he might, a pious duty to the memory of his predecessor Francis Hamilton, once Buchanan.

D. PRAIN.

ROYAL BOTANIC GARDEN, CALCUTTA;
October 30, 1904.

B. S. Press—2166J—276—27-2-1905—E. J. H. & others.

M. Smith del.
A. K. Nath lith.

ACONITUM LAEVE Royle.

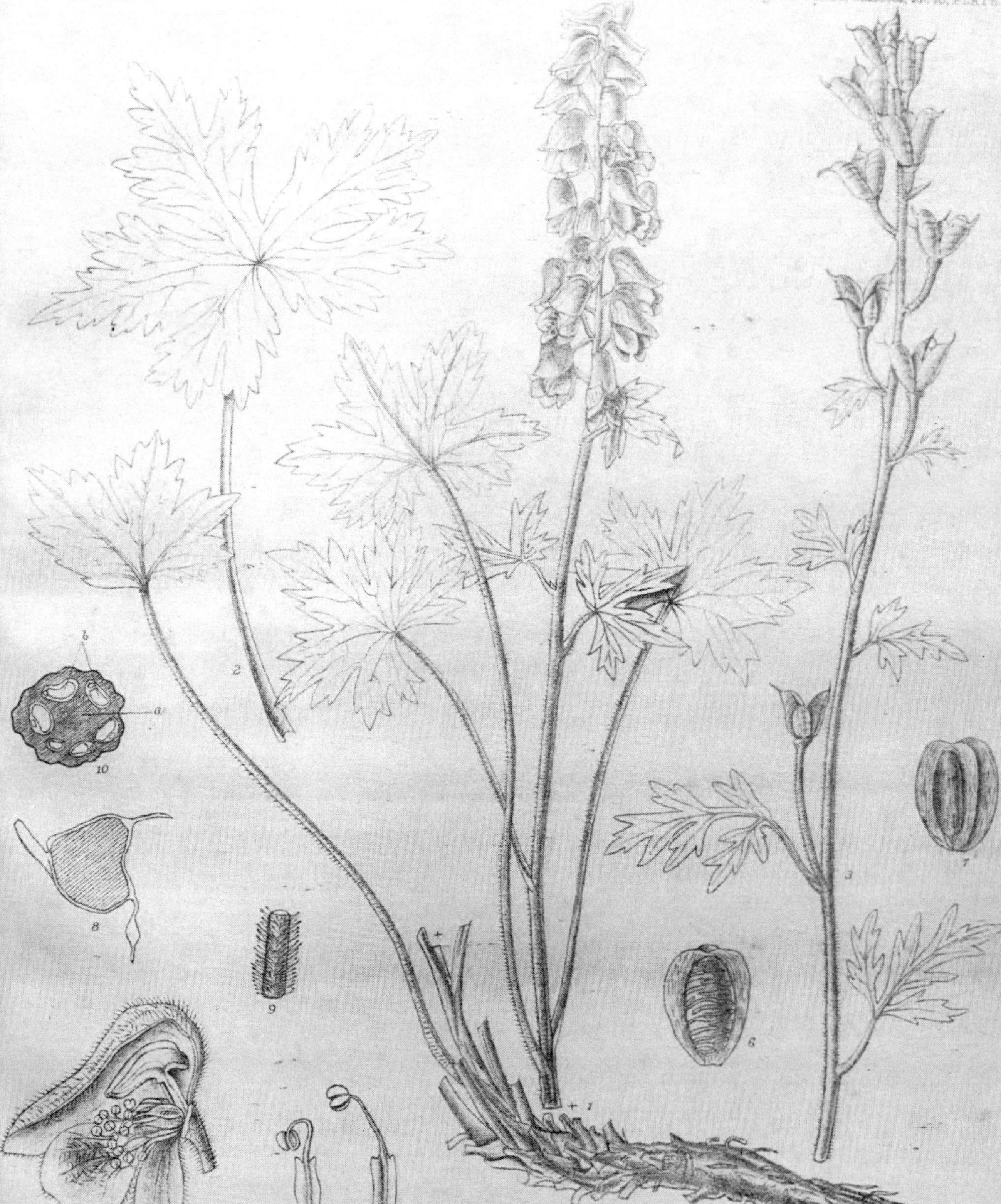

M. Smith delt.

ACONITUM LURIDUM Hook. f. & Thoms.

A. K. Nath lith.

M. Smith delt.

A.C. Singha lith.

ACONITUM MOSCHATUM Stapf.

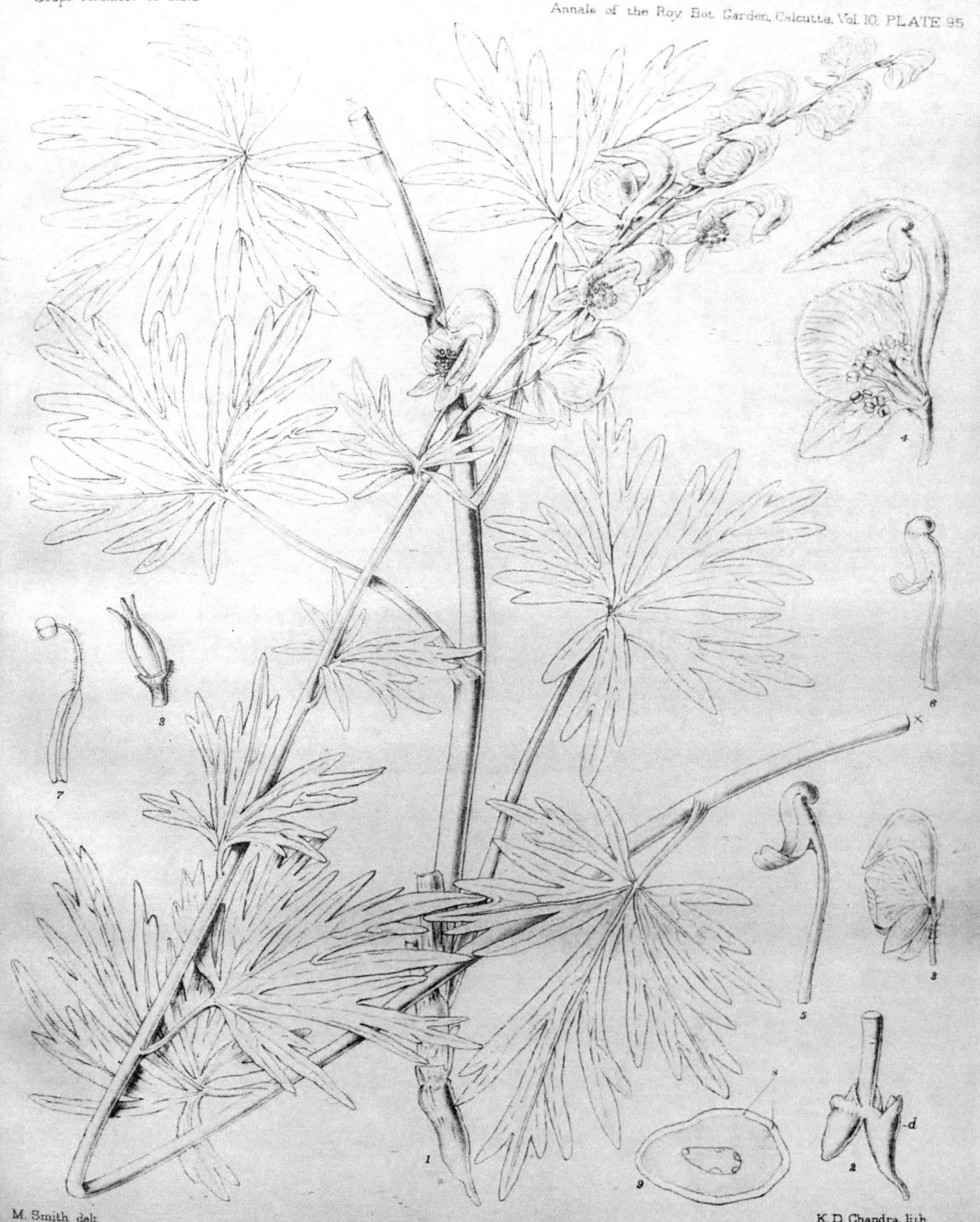

M. Smith delt.

K.D. Chandra. lith.

ACONITUM SOONGARICUM Stapf.

M. Smith delt. A.C. Singha lith.

ACONITUM CHASMANTHUM Stapf.

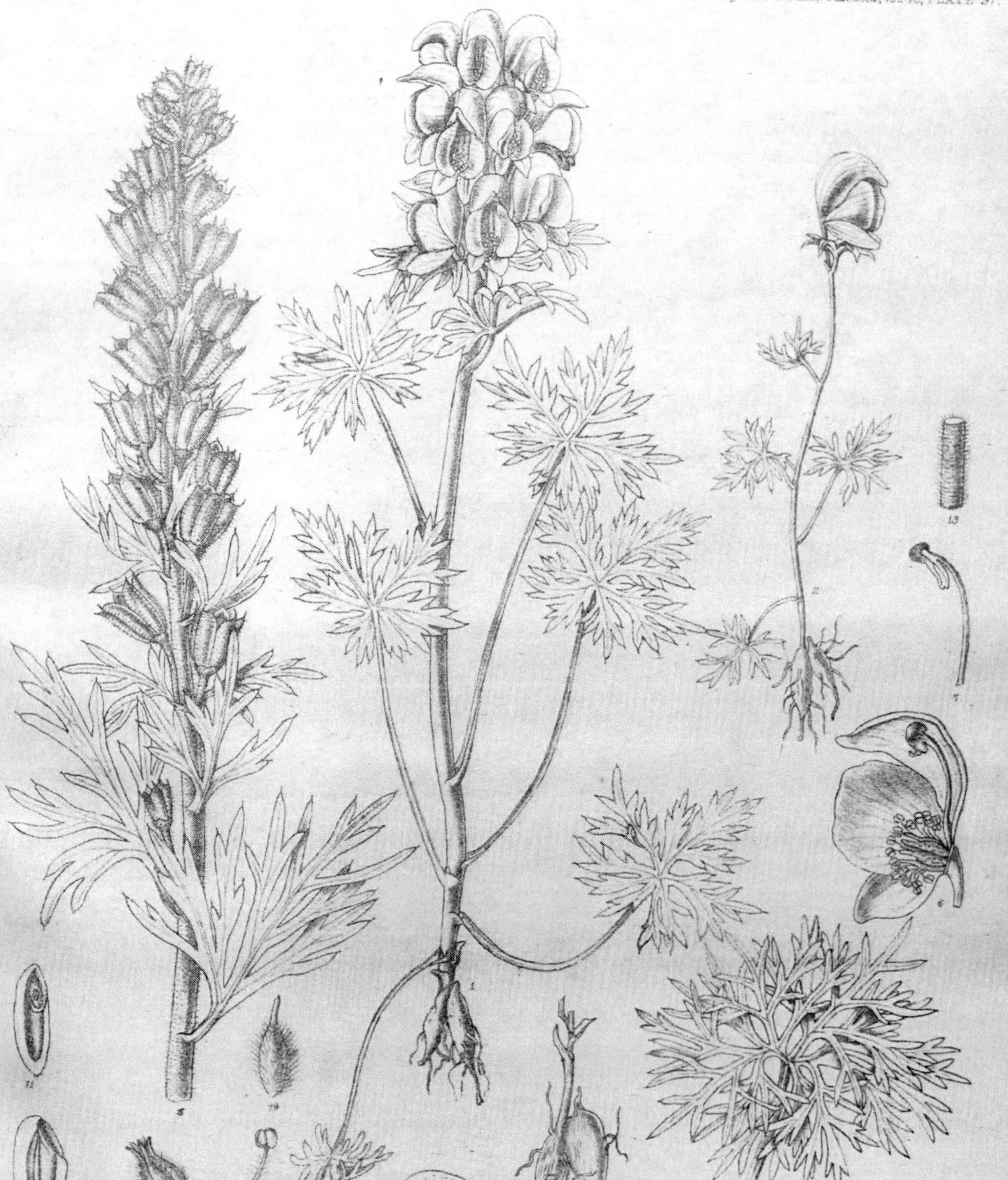

M. Smith delt. K.P. Dass lith.

ACONITUM VIOLACEUM Jacquem.

M. Smith dels. A. C. Singha lith.

ACONITUM HOOKERI Stapf.

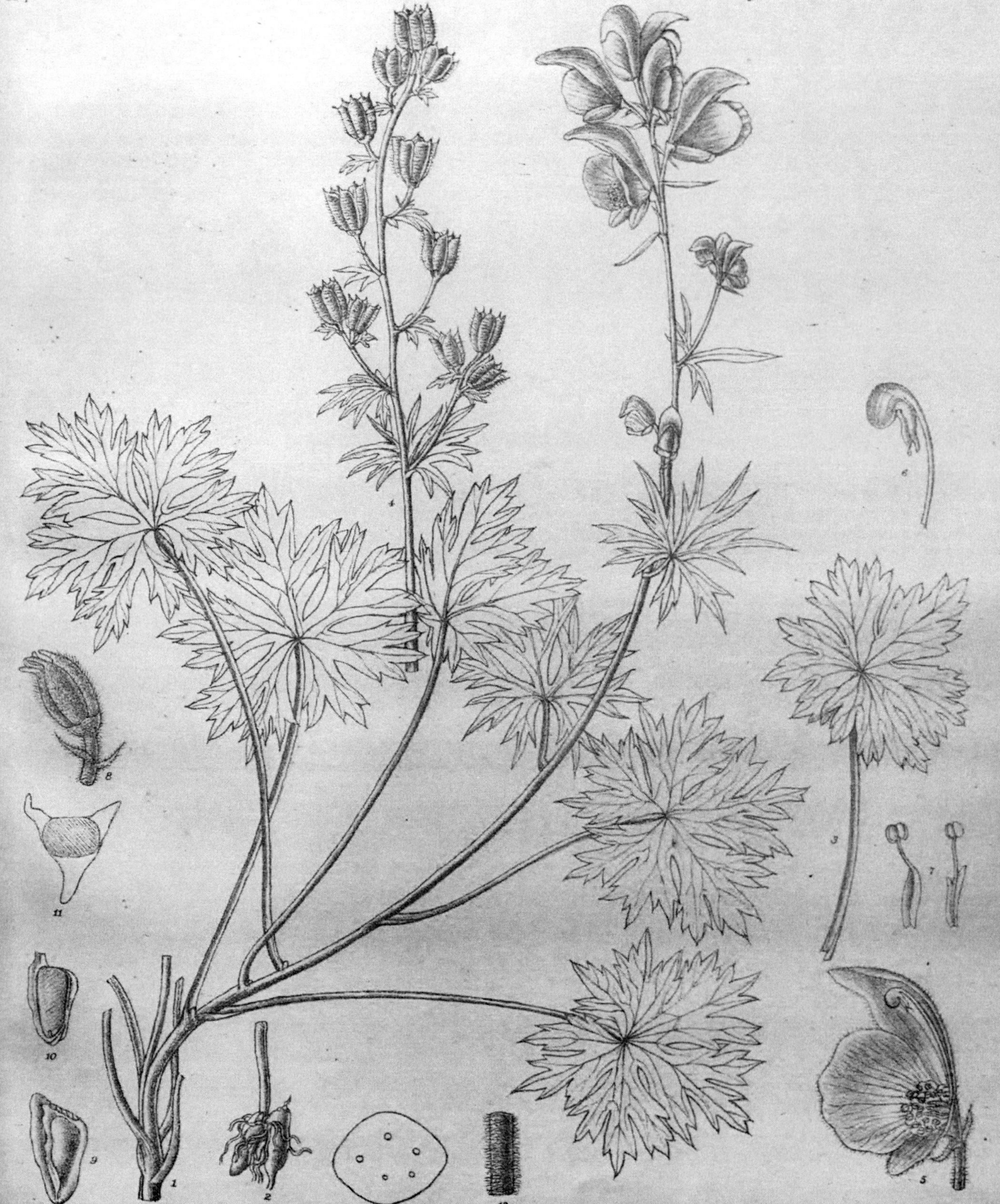

M. Smith delt. A. C. Singha lith.

ACONITUM ROTUNDIFOLIUM Kar. & Kir.

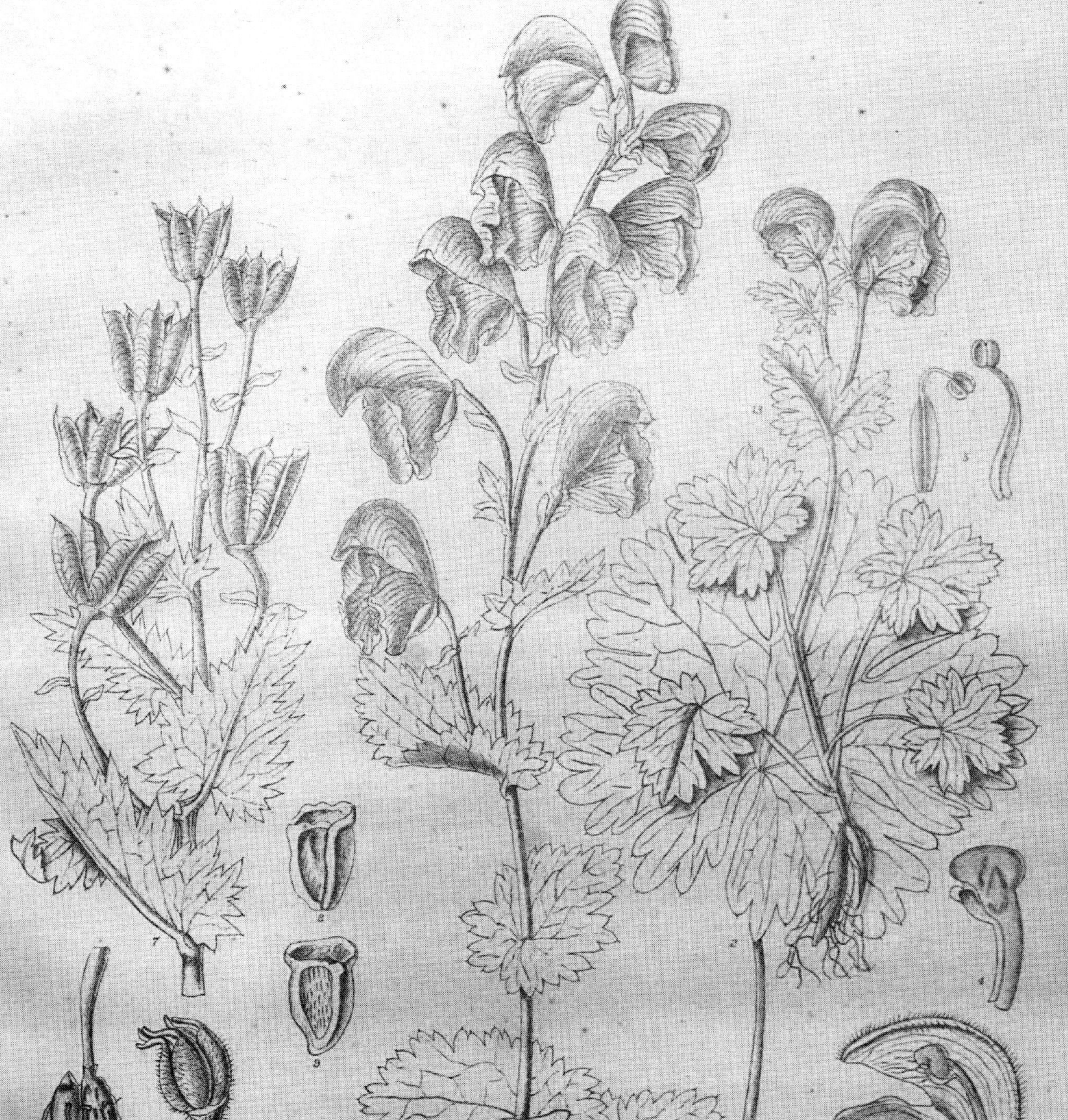

M. Smith delt. A. K. Nath lith.

ACONITUM HETEROPHYLLUM Wall.
Figs.1-12, Type: Fig.13, VAR. BRACTEATUM Stapf.

M. Smith delt.

A. C. Singha lith.

ACONITUM DEINORRHIZUM Stapf.

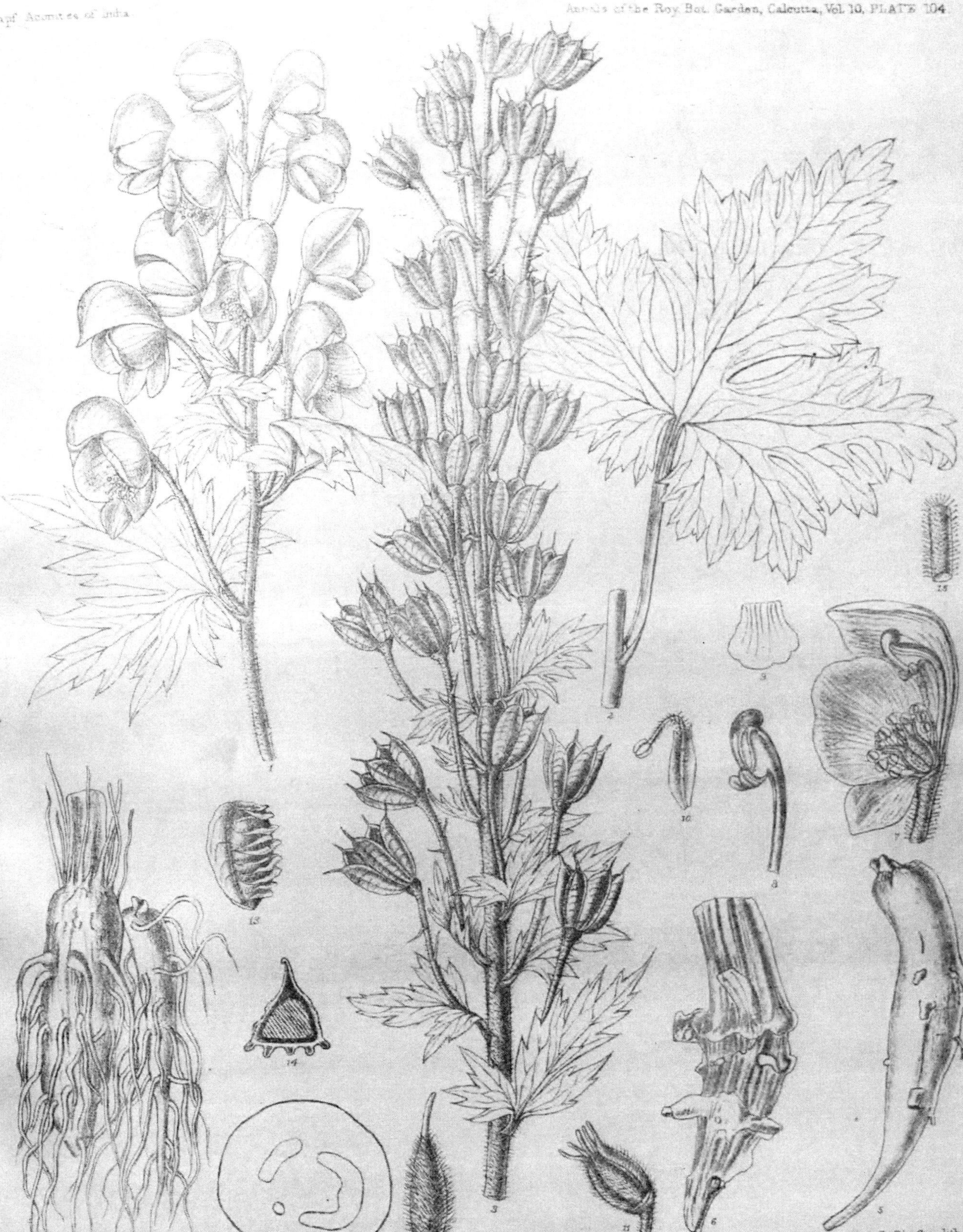

M. Smith del^t. A.C. Singha lith.

ACONITUM BALFOURII Stapf.

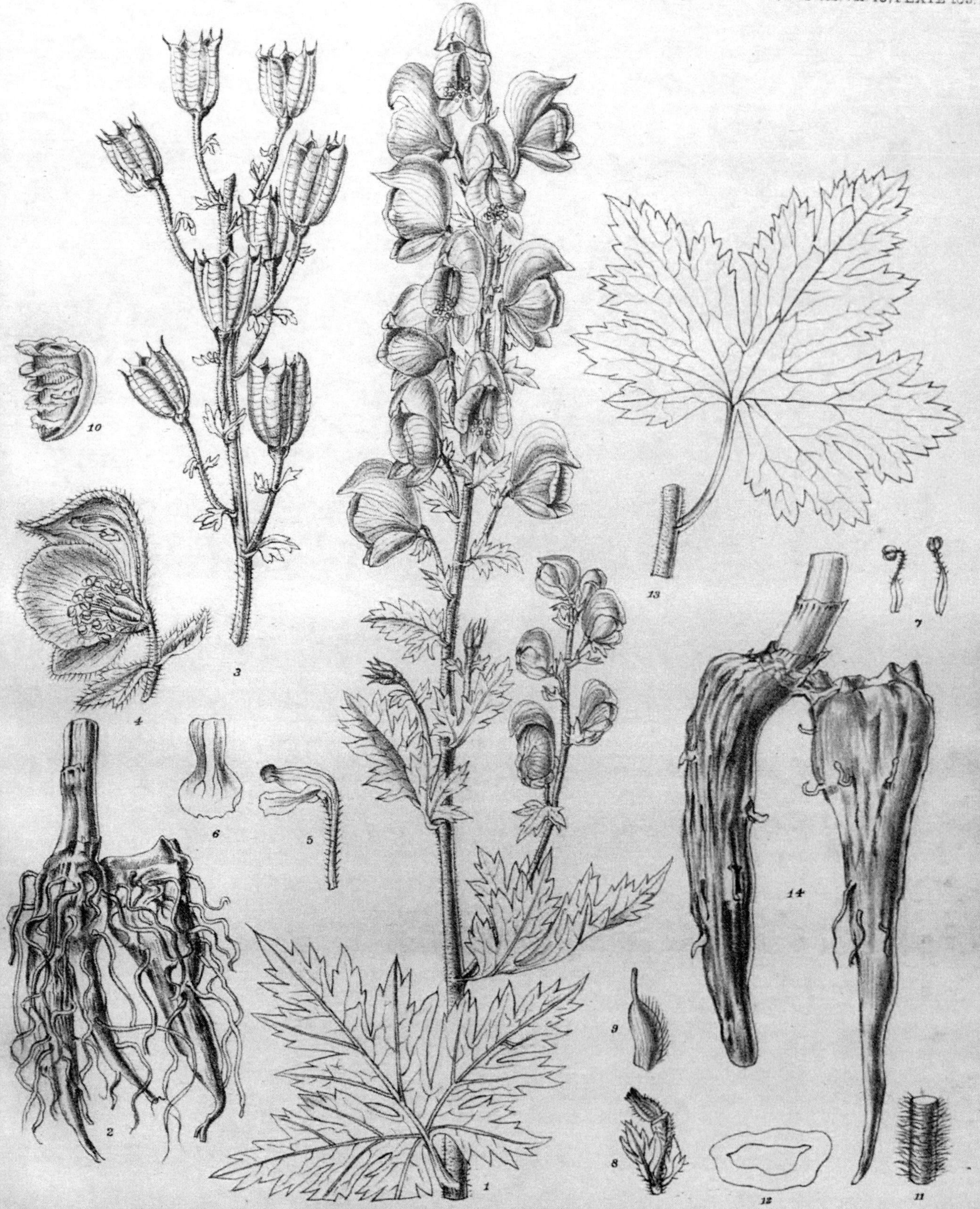

M. Smith delt.

Lith: by Chitra Silpi Co.

ACONITUM FALCONERI Stapf.

Figs. 1-12, TYPE : Figs. 13, 14, var. LATILOBUM Stapf.

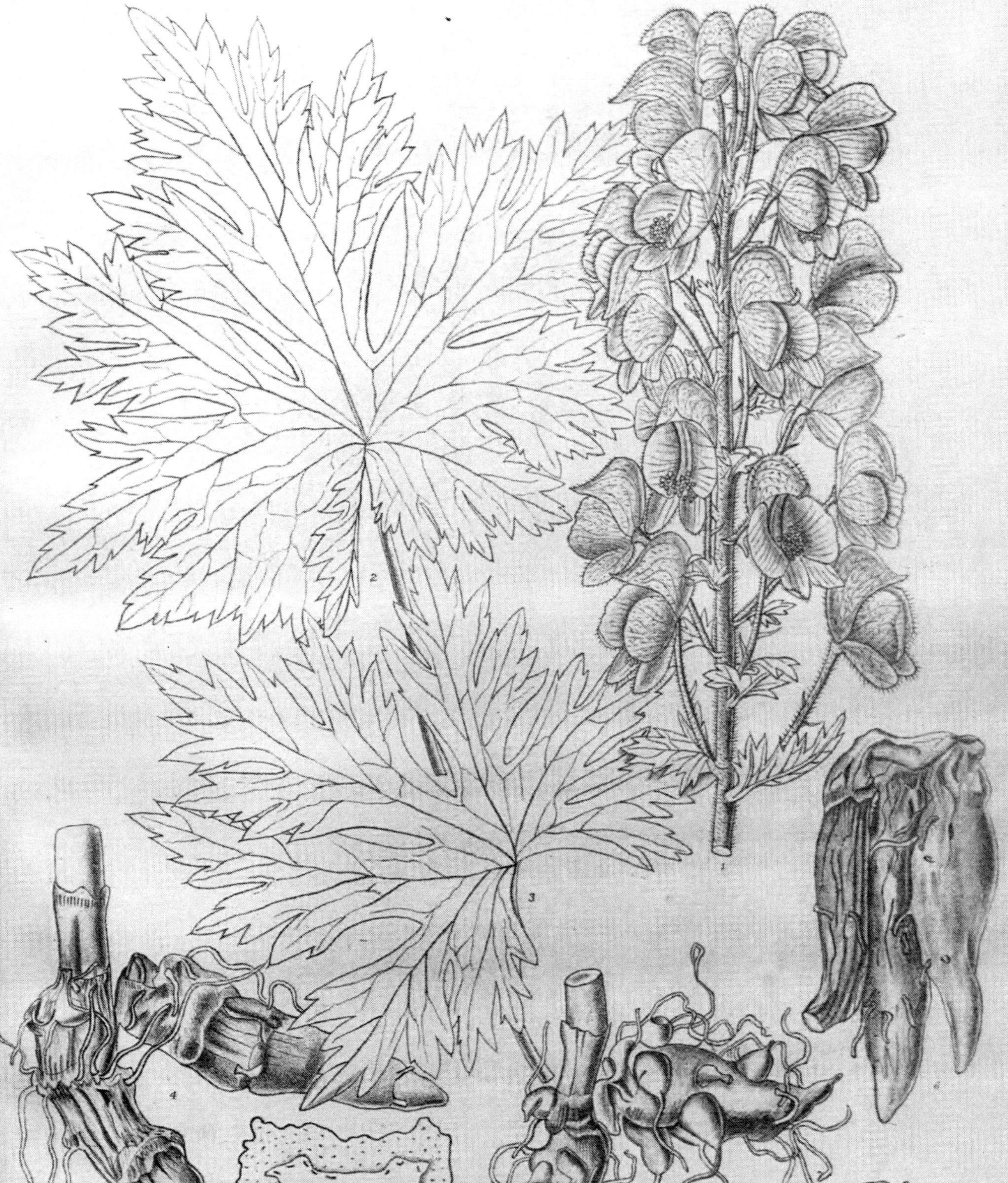

M. Smith delt. A. K. Nath lith.

ACONITUM SPICATUM Stapf.

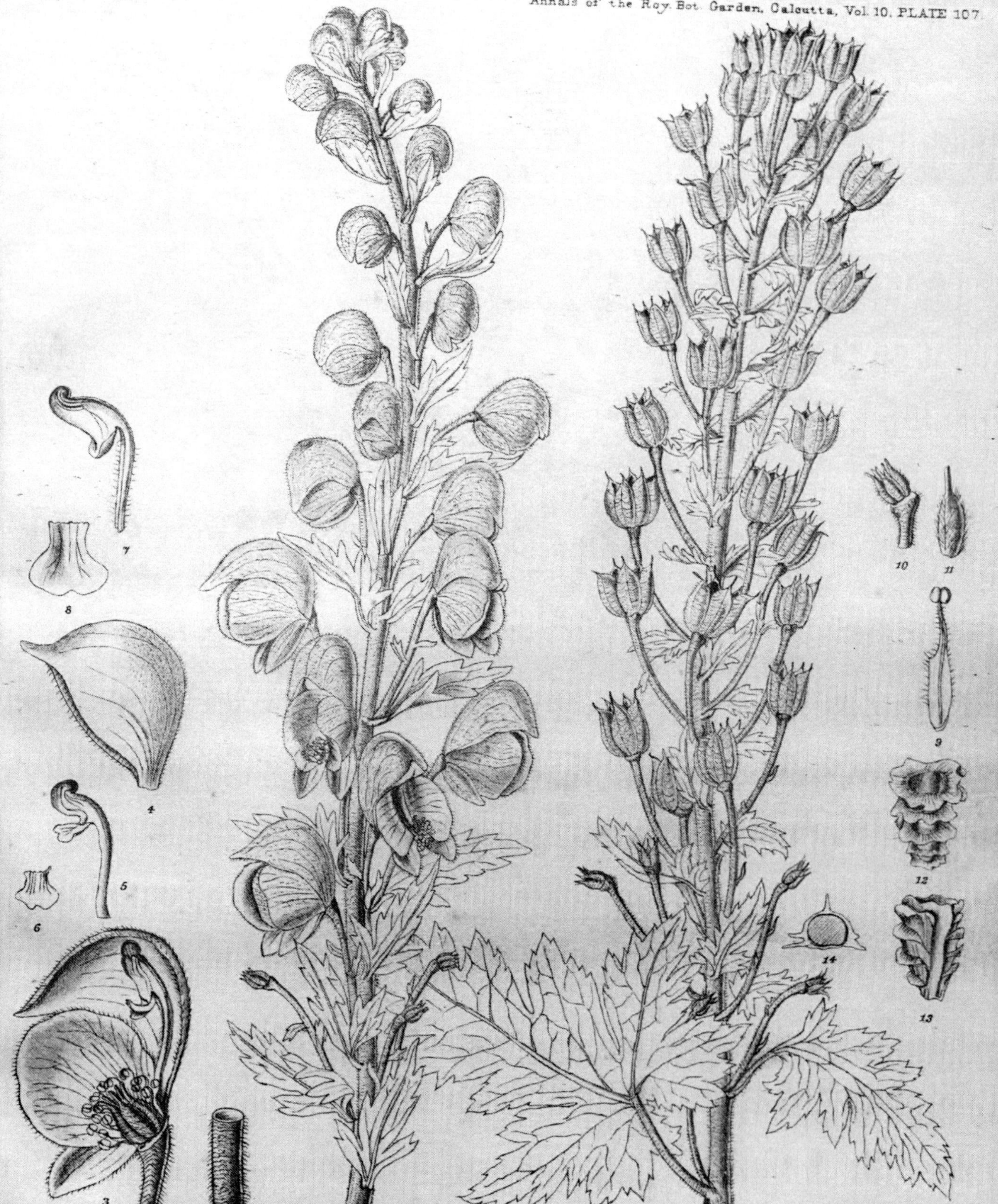

M. Smith del[t]. Lith: by Chitra Silpi C[o]

ACONITUM SPICATUM Stapf.

M. Smith delt.		Lith: by Chitra Silpi Co.

ACONITUM LACINIATUM Stapf.

M. Smith delt.

ACONITUM FEROX Wall.

K. D. Chandra. Lith.

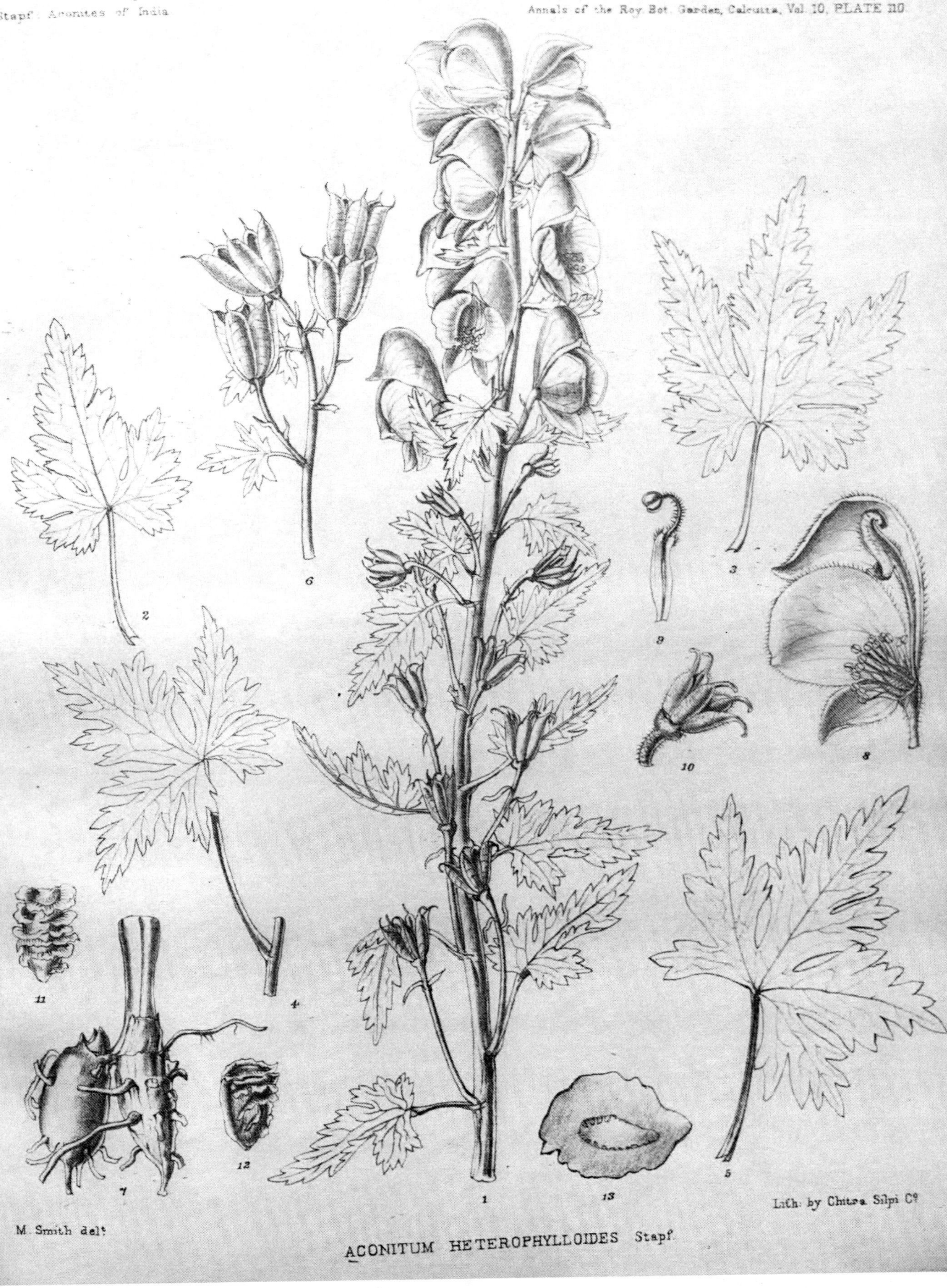

ACONITUM HETEROPHYLLOIDES Stapf.

Annals of the Roy. Bot. Garden, Calcutta, Vol. 10, PLATE III.

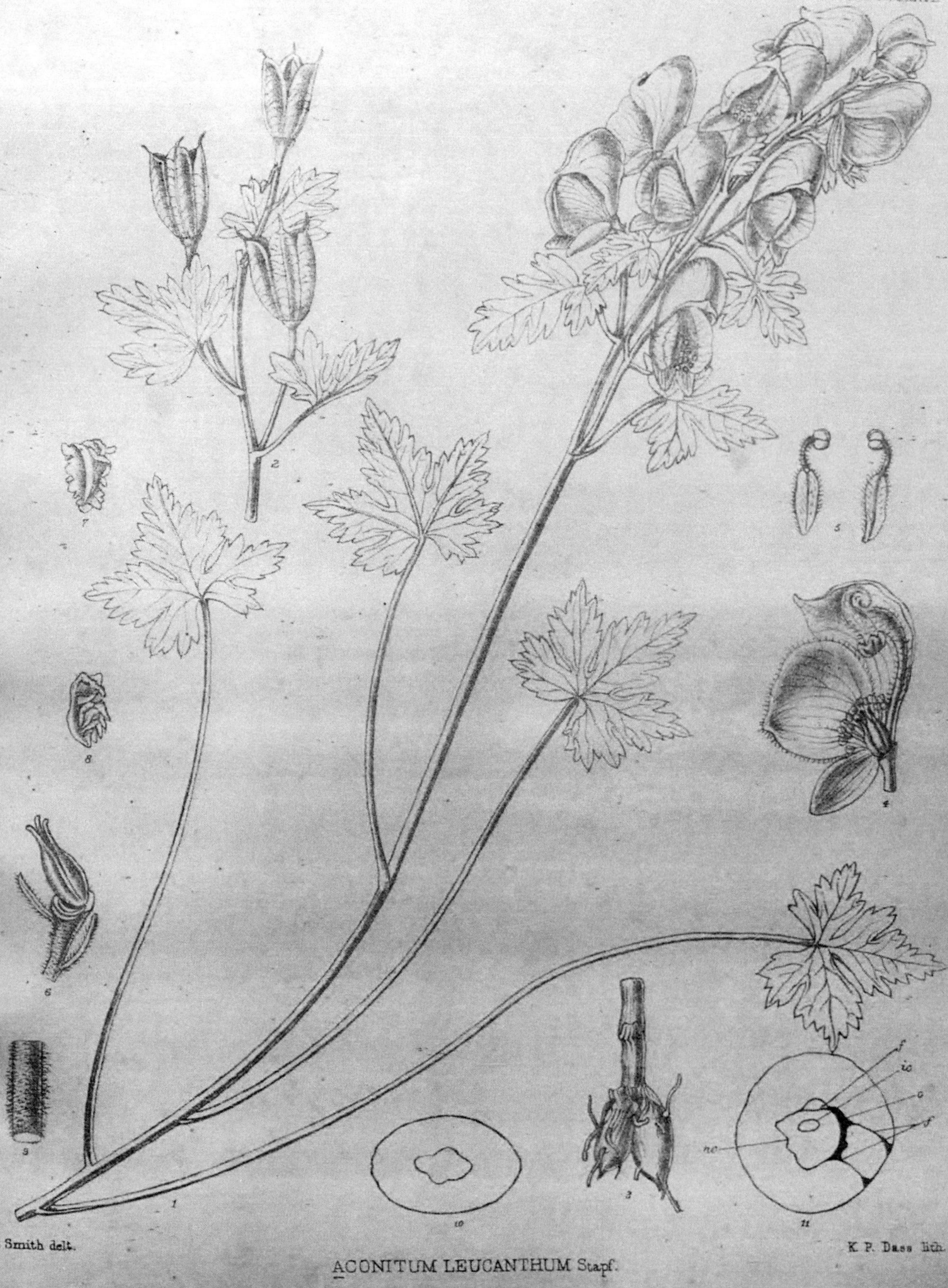

M. Smith delt. K. P. Dass lith.

ACONITUM LEUCANTHUM Stapf.

M. Smith delt.

K. P. Dass lith.

A. ACONITUM ELWESII Stapf. B. A. LETHALE Griff.

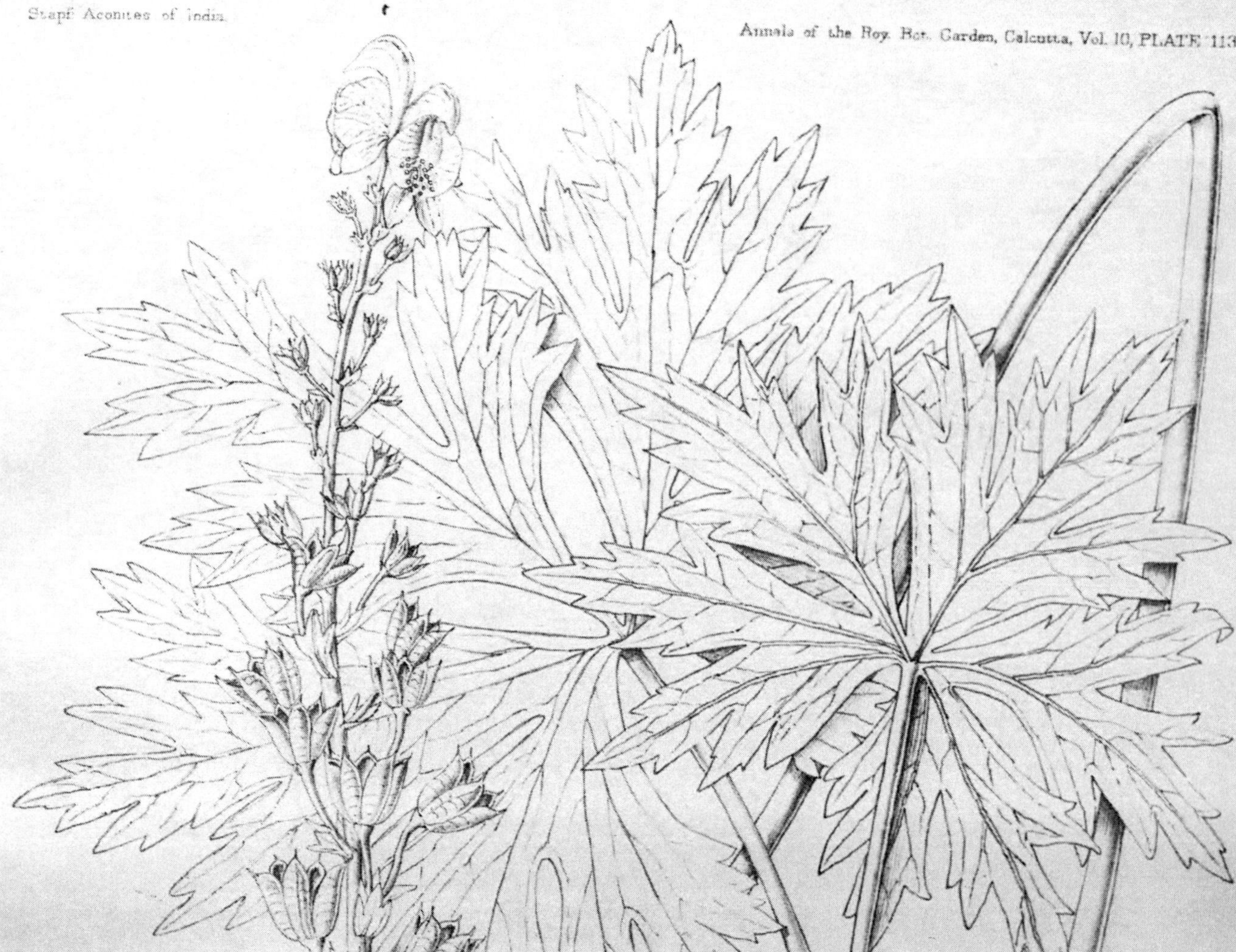

M. Smith delt.

ACONITUM NAGARUM Stapf.

K.D. Chandra Lith.

M. Smith delt.

K.D. Chandra Lith.

A. ACONITUM DISSECTUM D. Don. B. CALTHA NIRBISIA Ham.

Annals of the Roy. Bot. Garden, Calcutta Vol. 10, PLATE 115.

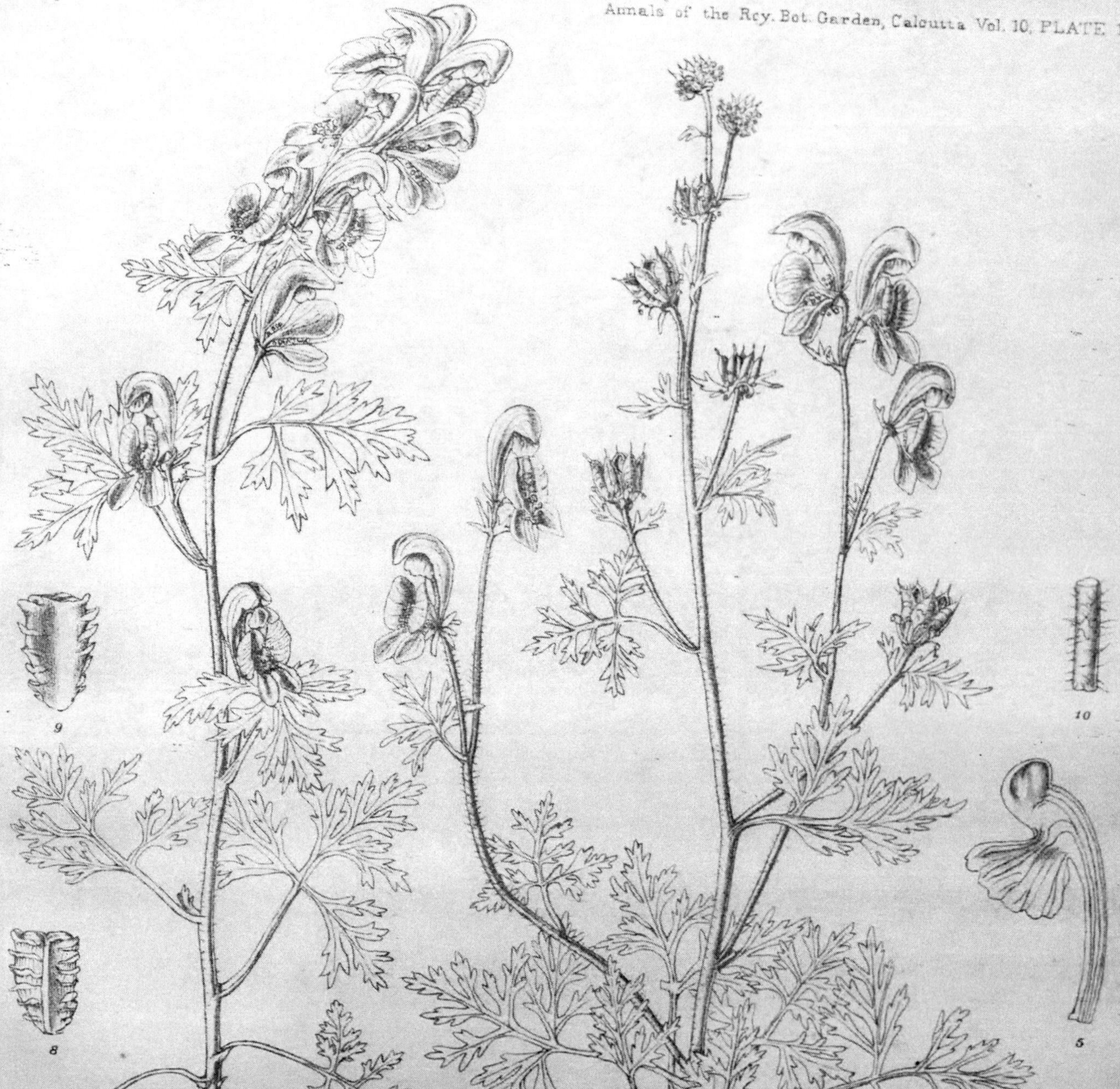

M. Smith delt. Lith: by Chitra Silpi Co.

ACONITUM GYMNANDRUM Maxim.

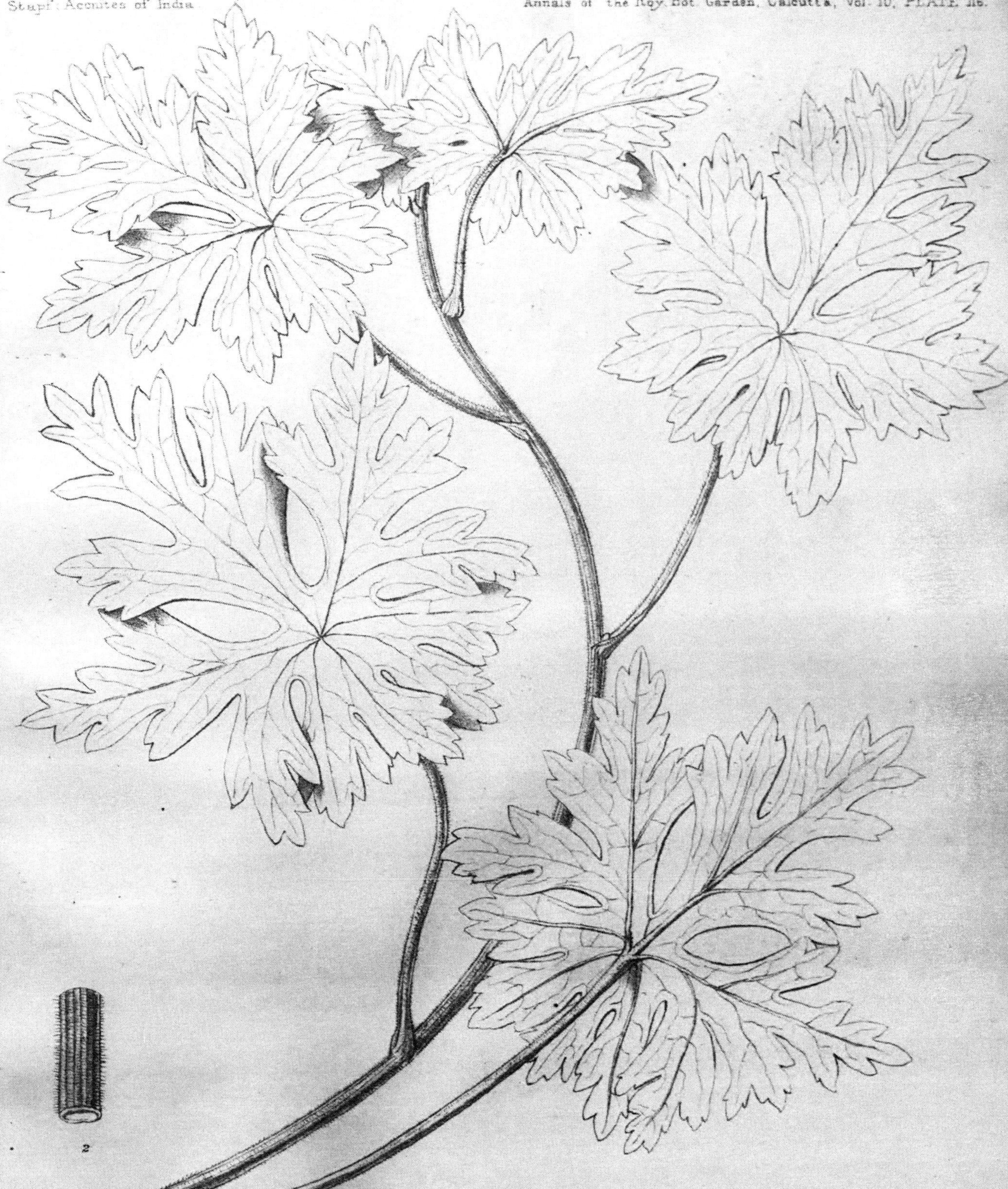

M. Smith. delt.

CALTHA ? CODOA Ham.

Lith: by Chitra Silpi Co.